L. GOODWIN

Promise
and
Power

Also by Deborah Shapley

THE SEVENTH CONTINENT:
Antarctica in a Resource Age

LOST AT THE FRONTIER:
U.S. Science and Technology Policy Adrift
(with Rustum Roy)

Promise and Power

The Life and Times of Robert McNamara

by Deborah Shapley

LITTLE, BROWN AND COMPANY
BOSTON   TORONTO   LONDON

To the millions who, like me, were born
as World War II ended and the cold war began,
and whose lives were changed by this one life.

First Edition

Library of Congress Cataloging-in-Publication Data

Shapley, Deborah
        Promise and power : the life and times of Robert McNamara / by
    Deborah Shapley. — 1st ed.
            p.   cm.
        Includes bibliographical references and index.
        ISBN 0-316-78280-7
        1. McNamara, Robert S., 1916–   .   2. Cabinet officers — United
    States — Biography.   I. Title.
    E840.8.M46S47   1992
    973.92'092 — dc20
    [B]   92-15614

10 9   8   7   6   5   4   3   2   1

HC

*Published simultaneously in Canada
by Little, Brown & Company (Canada) Limited*

Printed in the United States of America

Contents

Prologue vii

I **Coming to Power** 1

1 The Helper of the Largest Number 3
2 The Student of Control 20
3 The Legend of Control 39
4 Organization Man and Mole 58

II **The Promise** 75

5 Sons of the Morning 77
6 Power in the Pentagon 95
7 Cold Warrior Stepping Up 112
8 Statistician Against Communism 135

III **The Uses of Power** 163

9 Battling Chaos 165
10 Untying the Knot 187
11 Controller of Technology 202
12 Dawn and Darkness 224
13 Crisis Manager Challenged 247

IV   The Test   267

14   Test of a New Leader   269
15   The Choice of War   289
16   Intervention and Promise   319
17   Two Enormous Miscalculations   349
18   Utopia Postponed   378
19   Hawk and Dove   407
20   The Modern Public Servant   438

V   The World   461

21   "McNamara Yanqui"   463
22   The Promise of Development   498
23   Management Is the Gate   527
24   The World Takes Its Price   555

Epilogue   An American Journey   583

Acknowledgments   616
Notes   618
Bibliography   683
Index   704

Illustrations follow page 366

Prologue

I T WAS NOON, February 29, 1968. Robert Strange McNamara, secretary of defense of the United States of America and commander of 4.3 million men under arms, was stuck in an elevator.[1] Thirteen people were jammed inside, including President Lyndon Baines Johnson. The elevator had stalled unaccountably in the heart of the Pentagon, the nexus of U.S. forces in the continental United States and overseas, and the intercontinental nuclear strike forces. On the lawn outside the Pentagon, an estimated one thousand federal employees and Army, Air Force, and Marine guards, along with the press, were waiting, wondering at the delay of a farewell ceremony that was supposed to run like clockwork.

Inside the elevator, Master Sergeant Clifford Potter struggled with the controls. It lurched upward, stopped between floors, and then shot up again and halted midway between the third and fourth floors. Its occupants could hear running footsteps in the halls outside.

Presidential aide Lawrence Levinson, trapped inside, thought of the assassination of John Fitzgerald Kennedy in Dallas some four years before. Since then, America had become ever more violent: Fifty thousand antiwar protesters marched on the Pentagon vowing to shut it down; Detroit burned; Stokely Carmichael broadcast from Cuba calling for the overthrow of the government. Could a coup begin here, inside the Pentagon? he wondered. Levinson saw the calm on the president's face even as he was squeezed by his Secret Service guard barking on his radio. McNamara snapped orders, to no avail.

Exactly thirteen minutes after the elevator stopped, they succeeded in pushing the doors open from inside. Presidential photographer Okie Okamoto was the first out. He turned in time to photograph Johnson climbing out. Then McNamara scrambled up onto the hallway floor, his signature wire-rimmed glasses straight across the nose, his dark hair still slickly in place. He brushed the crease of his trousers and started racing down two flights of escalators with the others practically at a run behind him. Outside, the crowd finally saw the presidential party coming through the great columns of the high Grecian portico and down the steps toward the reviewing stand. It was drizzling. As though a jammed elevator were not enough to mar McNamara's farewell ceremony, now they would have to stick it out under giant black umbrellas, a Munich-like pageant of surrender to the rain.[2]

Few public officials tried as hard as Robert McNamara to manage the giant organizations entrusted to them. No other civilian has ever tried to shape America's defenses in such detail — the policies, the weapons, the nuclear forces and strategy — as McNamara. He did not stop there; during more than seven years as secretary of defense, he worked to transform the cold war into détente. He leapt in to control the little, distant war in Vietnam; even as he escalated it into a much bigger war, he tried to control the troop levels and the bombing, acting more forcefully than any other civilian in the chain of command in history.

Few Americans of the twentieth century have been so admired — and so despised. When the 1960s opened, McNamara was an outstanding executive, praised for his brilliance, efficiency, and responsibility. He had instantly given up one of the highest salaries in the world as president of the Ford Motor Company for twenty-five thousand dollars a year as a Cabinet officer. He had gone beyond the letter of the law by putting his fortune in blind trust to avoid even the appearance of any conflict of interest.

But the adulation that greeted him at the beginning of the decade had changed to disillusion by its end. Public anger was focused on government generally. Four years after John Kennedy sought a Pax Americana in which the United States would safeguard emerging nations against communism, his successor had bogged America down in a rice-paddy war ten thousand miles away, and civil strife at home.

South Vietnam, where Kennedy and Johnson tried to pursue the national mission, had turned into a disaster for the Democrats. For two generations they had been the party of just wars, wars to end wars, and, above all, successful wars. Now the party had delegitimized itself as the bearer of this global role, due to the misjudgments and subterfuges of two presidents and their circle of famous advisers.

It is fair to say that by February 1968 the country was suffering a kind of nervous breakdown. Crazy things were happening, things that had been unimaginable only a short time before. Through January, American Marines were besieged at Khe Sanh and at risk of decisive defeat. Then North Korea's puny government thumbed its nose at the mighty United States by seizing the Navy's spy ship *Pueblo* before Washington could lift a finger. On January 30–31, despite months of assurances from U.S. generals that the shooting war was going well, the Communists staged a massive Tet offensive all over South Vietnam. The press described it as the worst setback to the U.S.–South Vietnamese side since the war began. (These events portended America's vulnerability to Third World tyrants, which would be driven home again with the Arab oil embargoes of the 1970s, the seizure of U.S. diplomats in Tehran by Iranian students in 1979, and Saddam Hussein's 1990 invasion of Kuwait, which sent America into yet another limited war.)

Historic civil rights laws and the Great Society, both meant to rectify a century of oppression of black Americans, had unleashed deep frustration and rage; riots worsened each summer; white National Guardsmen and federal troops fired on black crowds. The antiwar movement was gaining and rained a steady fusillade of accusations against the administration for waging an immoral war, including the charge of genocide.

Aide Levinson had grounds to fear that the jammed elevator was the start of a coup: A decade that had opened with Kennedy's calls for a government of reason and consensus had become dark and divisive. Commanding it all, and largely the cause of it in the public imagination, was Robert McNamara. When John Kennedy had raised hopes for a rational world, the spectacled, soberly dressed McNamara, widely credited with shaping the success of Ford, presented himself as the embodiment of rational policy-making. McNamara's rule would be based on analysis and logic, not politics or emotion, he said.

Nobody else used numbers the way McNamara did. They symbolized his supposedly detached, objective approach to policy. He embodied the school of statistics-based management, which originated early in the century to run mass-product enterprises like General Motors and which was used to run many U.S. industries in their heyday. He stood for quantification and technology when the American romance with both was at its height.

When Kennedy faced Nikita Khrushchev over Berlin and then Cuba — and, in the Cuban crisis, veered toward nuclear war — McNamara was known for his calm self-control, even when the president came close to having to push the nuclear button. Two and a half years later, as Johnson assured the public that Vietnam would be a small war, that by sending only seventy-five thousand troops the United States was not going to war, McNamara echoed his line. But when suspicious reporters and congressmen began to probe behind Johnson's many lies, the trail led to McNamara, too. Meanwhile, word spread among his bureaucratic foes and the press that the man was not what he pretended to be, that the real McNamara was unfair, manipulative, and dishonest.

On this February day, Robert McNamara seemed ill at ease, barely in control of himself. As the farewell ceremony came to an end, he stood at attention, alone on the lawn for a final salute: hatless, coatless, feet moving restlessly as though he hated being there. When the group turned to go back indoors, he gave his deputy Paul Nitze a rough shove in the back to hurry him up.

Back in his office that afternoon, McNamara kept up the appearance of working away, right to the last minute. He seemed wooden. Those in the press and civil service who admired him paid their respects to a performance some considered great and all considered tragic.

His visitors noticed that McNamara looked as awful as he had for the past year. The face was no longer full but gaunt. The collar of the eternally clean white shirt hung loose around his neck. His eyes had a trancelike glaze.

After finishing work, McNamara rode down in the elevator to the garage, where his driver, Mr. West, would carry him away from the Pentagon for the last time. He left, keeping himself hidden, as before, while more and more people drifted into his office in a gathering that turned into "a wake."[3]

The man himself is an enigma. Many colleagues insist the real McNamara is decent, idealistic, and smart. "He's a rather simple man, underneath," says William P. Bundy. But others say McNamara simply cannot tell the truth. By the mid-1960s, especially in the State Department, the press, and some quarters of the military, the warning was: Don't believe a word McNamara says.

Some, including his old friends from his native California and the two presidents he served, found him insightful and modulated, with a shrewd grasp of men and ideas. But the "simple" truths and "absolute" facts he presented to congressional committees often called his candor into question. "I never knew if Bob really believed all those simplifications he put forward," says Stanley Please, a colleague from the World Bank.

In the early days, to see him and John Kennedy walking briskly away from the presidential helicopter, both blown by the wind of the slowing blades, was to notice how alike they were and how different. They were both young, trim, and brisk. Kennedy's profile was strong, his sandy hair blew, one button of the jacket closed; McNamara, next to him, in his neat dark suit, slicked-down hair, and wire-rimmed glasses, the perfect aide-de-camp. After Kennedy was killed, McNamara was a loyal legatee, taking Jackie to lunch in Georgetown and, five years later, helping arrange Bobby's burial; the year after that, he rushed to Ted's side after Chappaquiddick.

Yet when Johnson made McNamara "executive vice president of the United States"[4] and put his own labyrinthine stamp on the presidency, McNamara followed his lead dutifully. The two spent much time in the Oval Office, Johnson in shirtsleeves, gesturing with his long arms. His endless talk was a stream of orders, homily, personal barbs, "showing a little garter," as he would say. Johnson could be ruthless; McNamara showed he could be ruthless, too.

To millions of Americans in the 1960s who witnessed scenes from Vietnam beamed into their living rooms, the close-up sight of McNamara in front of a map, waving his pointer, rattling off the numbers of targets attacked, sortie rates, enemy infiltration and body counts, was disturbing.[5]

Television conveyed something about him that print could not: the forced hardness of voice, the studied coldness, the arrogance with which certain questions were dismissed. Viewers sensed that one of the most powerful men in the world, a man who sought ever more roles and responsibilities, perhaps should not have so much power.

Then it became known, first in whispers, that McNamara had doubts about the war he was running. The strain that became more visible in his face, in his manner, now seemed to come from conflict within himself. He was of the war, identified with it, running it all day and into the night. But he saw it wasn't working; he warned reporters that the bombing was futile and privately told the president to push harder for talks with Hanoi. Many people concluded, watching the pallid, nervous figure he was in his last year, that this confident American, who had had the world in his grasp, who used to know all the answers and absolute truths, was having regrets. Bob McNamara seemed to be turning inward.

In 1971, when the Pentagon Papers, based on McNamara's top-secret office files, were revealed to the world, the public and those still fighting in Vietnam learned how soon he had had doubts about the war; he had held on to his office and urged them to fight on, for more than two years, even though he saw the chance of military failure looming. When this was disclosed, doubts about McNamara in many military quarters turned to hatred, for McNamara seemed to have sent soldiers to fight for a cause he no longer believed in. Later, at a 1984 trial at which he said he believed at the time that the war was "unwinnable militarily" as early as "1965 or 1966," some in uniform came to despise him even more.

There are many who believe to this day that had McNamara gone public with his knowledge of the long odds of victory in Vietnam, either while he held office or afterward, the nation would have been spared its ordeal. If any of these charges are true — and they depend critically on what McNamara believed and when he believed it — the man carries a large load, indeed.

The man bearing these burdens had an unusual marriage, to say the least. He met Margaret Craig when they were both undergraduates at Berkeley in the 1930s. Margy, as she was called, was tiny, wide-faced, persistent, laughing, brave. She was as informal as Bob was stiff. She stayed plainspoken even as he became more public and adopted a language of impersonality and numbers. Some women around Washington were envious that a man they found brilliant and attractive should depend so utterly on simple Margy. They complained she wasn't that bright, when you came down to it.

But she had many strengths, and she knew her husband better than anyone, although she never explained him to the outside world. "Margy was probably the only human being who understood Bob McNamara and she's dead," says a long-term aide.[6] Her death from cancer in 1981 was the central trauma in McNamara's life, even greater than Vietnam. It set him adrift, friends say. That there were other dimensions to the straight-arrow boy from Berkeley who was devoted to his youthful-sweetheart wife was shown when, soon after her death, he began seeing Joan Braden, a prominent Washington figure. They have been close friends and traveling companions for more than a decade, while Braden remains married and living with her husband, Tom.

Friends often characterized Bob and Margy as "two halves of one person." They meant it as a compliment to the marriage. But the remark suggested they sensed Bob lacked part of himself: He could not spread affection to others, even his children, without an effort.

The man ill at ease with his farewells at the Pentagon was also uncomfortable with his only son. There were two older daughters; "Little" Margaret, the eldest, was the child most like her mother. Kathleen resembled her father in ability and temperament. As often happens when two personalities in a family are alike, they seemed destined not to get along. Craig defied his father over Vietnam, among other things.

Bob's diffidence toward Craig started long before Vietnam, long before the antiwar movement swept the boy up in its emotionally charged embrace. Craig inherited his mother's humanity along with her wide cheekbones. He grew up in their big white Italian-style house, in a household centered on his dad, hoping that the man who dashed in and out, and who was so smart and famous, would notice him.

He didn't, so Margy compensated. She coached Craig on his reading; she worried when he went to a psychiatrist. But all her worry could not stop the boy from running through the streets with antiwar demonstrators, smashing windows. He ran as far as South America and then to Easter Island, putting a continent and one fourth of the Pacific between him and Washington.

The first time I saw McNamara I saw not a face but a tan oval across the desk, lit in the dim office by a single overhead light. After a moment I realized that he was hunched over and peering at a paper on the desk and that I was looking at the bare top of his head, which was no longer covered with the dark thick hair shown in old photographs.[7]

The desk was enormous and covered in black leather, with a border of carved wood. He had used it as president of the World Bank;

it was big enough, certainly, to be the launchpad for running the world. A faded globe, one he had evidently used for a long time, was next to him.

Hearing my footfall on the carpet, he stirred and rose. He greeted me as if we had seen each other just yesterday, then waved me to a barrel-backed chair beside the desk and sat down again, in one agile movement. The paper he was reading was my letter, telling him I planned to write a book about him, with or without his cooperation, and asking for six interviews. He had placed the letter before him at precise right angles to the edge of the desk.

He composed himself to speak. I had expected to debate the question of cooperation, but he had made up his mind and came straight to the point. He announced he would grant the six interviews. With a guardedness I would hear many times, he added that he was unsure if his participation would be "productive" for him or for me. He required one condition, that he be able to review his quotes from our sessions before I used them in the book. He liked to be precise, he said.

McNamara was a reclusive figure, known for giving carefully selected interviews. Since I had expected little or no cooperation, I agreed. It occurred to me that this gave me access to the "off-the-record" McNamara, who might be more revealing than the public man talking stiffly into a tape recorder. During the years it took to complete the project, our six interviews stretched to more than twenty. And in these discussions, off the record, he delved more and more into the one topic he has not discussed in public since that last day in the rain: his role in and feelings about the war in Vietnam.

In subsequent meetings after that first, I tried to explore the enigma. Much of the time McNamara seemed uncomfortable talking about any aspect of the past. Simple questions, such as What lessons did you learn in World War II?, got no reply. Too general, apparently. Subjective questions, such as What was your father like?, got nowhere. McNamara is not self-revealing — at least he does not reveal himself on purpose. I discovered that many of his friends find him this way, too.

For some, the only point about McNamara is his supposed bad character, evident in a series of deceits that have defined his life and career. Others describe him as a true scout, eager to take up the challenges of the world and fight the good fight admirably.

Views are equally polarized on his supposed genius as a manager. At the time they happened, his makeovers of Ford, the Defense

Department, and the World Bank won public acclaim. But there are many who have argued since that McNamara "ruined" the auto industry, the U.S. military, and even the Bank.

To me, the charges that the "real" Robert McNamara is a pure manipulator and that his attempts to appear virtuous, like his dedication to fighting poverty at the World Bank, are insincere seem incompatible with the facts: He helped remake Ford into a successful company after the war; he reformed the defense budget and ran defense policy in two administrations in positive ways that endure; he was critical in unhooking the military, the public, and America's allies from plans to use nuclear weapons in war and in changing NATO doctrine. And at the World Bank, by vigorous executive action, he helped redirect the Green Revolution to feed millions of people in Asia, Latin America, and Africa who otherwise would have gone hungry or worse. Many men who have done less have been treated kindly by history.

At a time when the U.S. auto industry and armed forces are in transition, if not a downright crisis, the legacy of McNamara's management deserves study. Americans today also face Africa's long depression and the deepening problems in the poorest parts of the Third World. So his thirteen years at the Bank trying to actively manage foreign aid to help the poor are relevant today.

"Bob is so American," says a high-ranking Pakistani at the World Bank. "He really believes that if he is not taking two steps forward he is falling behind."[8] If, as Walter Lippmann wrote, leaders should be judged by what they leave behind,[9] then McNamara's impact on the American Century must be judged, not only on Ford, the Pentagon, and Vietnam, but also on his attempt at the World Bank and after to define post-Vietnam American liberalism, with all its lights and shadows.

Neither did the theory that the real McNamara is the man of total sincerity and balance seem the whole story, although in the course of many sessions I saw this side of him, too. Arthur M. Schlesinger, Jr., once referred in his diary to McNamara's "inextinguishable decency."[10] But if this is the real man, why, in each of his three careers, has he from the start left a trail of bitter enemies, enraged not by his values but by his conduct?

It was hard to get him to look back, but I soon found one way. The man loves combat. Give him documents, raise the charges against him, and he springs to life, reliving old disputes, often with a detailed and accurate memory. One side, which is neither a liar nor a scout, loves confrontation; this must be part of his story, too.

Then there is the reflective McNamara. Not the man who says that black is white and white is black, that he thought the war he led was militarily unwinnable, or that he never considered initiating the use of nuclear weapons despite frequent public statements that he would. The sobered McNamara seemed to me deeply troubled by his errors on Vietnam and regretful on other scores as well.

I also heard him lie, to cut off a line of questioning or for some other quick advantage. Some of the stories he told on himself also revealed he lied on occasion. It seemed to be a reflex, a habit he has used to grab and hold on to power. It revealed a different side of him from historian McNamara, who at other times pored over documents with precise care and frequent self-criticism.

I concluded during our alternately tense and friendly sessions that the "real" Robert McNamara is — awkwardly enough — both a man of a ruthless will to win and the thoughtful analyst. Simpler explanations do not suffice. In the end, I could not avoid the fact that he is both manipulator and scout, a devious tactician and a man of sincere and noble goals. This twinning of opposites has shaped his life, his story as a manager, Vietnam; it has, one way or another, affected all of our lives.

McNamara released most of the quotes I asked for, with some negotiation but few exceptions overall. He did not approve — or see — the contents of this book before it was published, nor did he control what I put in, except for the quotes from our meetings. He maintained his stance of not speaking publicly on Vietnam; but he did release quotes from two oral histories, in which he discussed the subject, for quotation in this book. I also quote here what he said on Vietnam in the CBS-Westmoreland lawsuit; McNamara then clarified his statements from the oral histories and lawsuit by releasing portions of his background interviews with me on the subject.

These statements on Vietnam go well beyond mere clarifications, however; in this book, he now explains haltingly, for the first time, why he urged the United States to enter the conflict, where he thinks he and the government erred, the nature of his supposed "disillusion" with the shooting war, and why, in his opinion, he spoke validly and optimistically when he urged American soldiers to fight on.

So this book is a biography, not the memoir he says he will never write. It does not focus on one part of character but tries to present the whole, insofar as anyone outside McNamara, Margy, or their children has seen the whole man.

His story starts between the two world wars, nearly eight years before Henry Luce, in a *Life* editorial in February 1941, gave the American Century its name.[11] It opens in the hills of northern California, where two boys in early morning mists are getting off to school.[12]

When the boys were very small, Woodrow Wilson had entered the war to end all wars, and won. Now, in 1933, storm clouds were rising in Europe, although they seemed faraway problems, for the British and French to solve. America had troubles enough of its own, with the stock market crash of 1929, with banks and companies failing, with good men out of work. Even these crises seemed remote to the boys, reared in the isolation of the valleys. The region was just entering the twentieth century; the farmlands were starting to yield wealth to organized human effort.

The boys are sitting in a Ford Roadster that rolls silently down a steep hill. They coast and avoid turning on the engine until they reach the bottom. They are always short of cash, and by coasting down hills as often as possible, they can save on gasoline and put away some change.

I
COMING TO POWER

1

The Helper of the Largest Number

I F THEY FOLLOWED THE ROADS that wound east through the hills, the two boys could see the great, rolling valley that seemed to stretch on forever into a limitless void of sky and space. Most days, however, the boys drove the direct route north, through low-lying streets draped in sheets of ghostlike fog. They would drive in semidarkness and avoid using the headlamps to conserve the battery.[1]

Driving home on afternoons when there was no fog, they could detour through the hills and catch a glimpse of the Moraga Valley, riotous in rich greens and yellows that hinted at the wealth of the farms that were spreading there. It was an inspiring view even in the fall of 1933, when the Depression had forced many of the little one-story businesses along the road to board up and close. The boys would see bands of men loitering near open drugstores and filling stations, beginning their long day of looking, endlessly looking, for work.

Even before the Great Depression, Bob McNamara had known the importance of saving money. He was more fortunate than some; his father still had a job, whereas some people's fathers were desperate, even committing suicide. But his father's pay had been lowered, and the family became more and more frugal as conditions grew worse. When Bob and his friend Vernon Goodin were accepted at Berkeley for the fall of 1933, there had been no discussion. They would live at their homes in Oakland and make the lengthy drive every morning to the campus and back every night; the cost of dormitory living would be extravagant compared with that of maintaining Bob's used 1931 Roadster.

In 1933, gasoline cost eighteen cents a gallon, making the price of a week's fuel for the commute about a dollar. As they rolled down the hill each morning, Bob steered while the car accelerated silently, like a sled over ice. At the last possible moment, as they hurtled straight for the hairpin turn at the bottom, he turned on the engine, making the Roadster start with a jolt just as he spun it around the curve. Saving a few cents in fuel hardly made them rich, but it helped one of them afford a date. Or it allowed them to make another long, spectacular drive, to a large dairy farm to the east, to buy a treat of fresh ice cream.

The McNamaras and the Goodins and other couples who bought homes in the 1920s in Oakland, which was then a modest crossroads town across the bay from San Francisco, were among the city of promise's first suburbanites.[2] The parents were the children of migrants, foreign and American, who had crowded the Golden City itself by the time of the 1849 gold rush and the discovery of the fabulous silver Comstock Lode in the late 1850s. Like thousands of other midwesterners, Gideon Strange was lured by the boom. He moved from Missouri in the 1870s to Yuba City, about forty-five miles north of Sacramento.

Strange was a French name — in French *étrange* means foreign or unusual — and the Stranges came from French and English stock. They were Southern Methodists and somewhat prosperous: Gideon Strange's in-laws had a house in Yuba City that was large and surrounded by porches. Gideon had five children, a son followed by four daughters.

The Stranges settled in Yuba City at the time the first families of San Francisco were building their gaudy mansions on Nob Hill. They were purposeful people, determined to achieve education and the professions, even for the girls. Shelby, the son, went to Stanford University and became a pharmacist; then he obtained an M.D. and built a good practice in San Francisco. Of the daughters, the eldest, Bess, was very intelligent and mathematical. She went to Stanford, too, and graduated in the university's second graduating class, along with future U.S. president Herbert Hoover. Educated women did not enter the professions; Bess went into the school system and eventually became the mathematics head of the San Francisco schools.

While Gideon Strange's older children were entering the Bay Area's sparse professional classes, thousands more immigrants — Italians, Irish, Germans, even Japanese — were flocking to San Francisco, many directly from their countries of origin and many after first trying life in the East. They were known as urban homesteaders because they hoped to carve new and better lives from the city's sudden industrial and financial importance, an alternative to the sweatshops of the East and the poverty of their native lands. An Irishman in San Francisco expected to face less prejudice and would not be held back, as in the East.

Exactly that dream of open horizons drew an Irish family named McNamara. They had emigrated from County Cork after the Great Famine to Stoughton, Massachusetts, where their second son, Robert James, was born in 1863. They then traveled west by ship and mule, the latter bearing them across the Isthmus of Panama in 1865.

So while John F. Kennedy's forebears were gaining a grip on Boston politics back east, the McNamaras were struggling to build a new life on the far side of the continent. Like the arriving Italians, Germans, and other immigrant groups, they manned San Francisco's new industries. They practiced Catholicism, and they hoped the eldest son, named Timothy, would go to college, and were disappointed when he didn't. Their daughters married securely: One, named Anne, married Ray Ward; when Anne later died, Ward married her sister. Ward prospered working for Dole Pineapple and lived in Hawaii.

But education and the professions remained an unfulfilled hope, and Timothy's failure to advance further made a deep impression on his brother Robert James, who never was able to attend high school. "My father had no education beyond the eighth grade," said McNamara.[3]

Instead Robert James worked all his life to support parents and siblings. Like other Irish Catholic sons, he refrained from marriage until these obligations were largely met. Only by his midforties was he secure enough to consider marrying: He had a steady record with a wholesale shoe concern called Williams Marvin Company, later renamed Buckingham and Hecht.

Robert James is remembered as a man of "imposing personal presence."[4] Even the earliest photographs show an impeccable figure in waistcoat, coat, tie, shined shoes, sometimes spats. The face is round yet severe and shielded by round-rimmed glasses and a hat. No one

who describes him mentions humor, and, for all his faith in education, no one recalls him reading a book.

Robert James was nearly fifty when he caught the eye of the
youngest and liveliest of Gideon Strange's girls. Claranell was in her
late twenties and still unmarried. She was apparently interested
enough in the prospect to consider the suit of a practicing Catholic.
More than twenty years apart in age, Claranell and Robert James
married in San Francisco's St. Mary's Cathedral on June 30, 1914,
and moved into an apartment at 804 Balboa Street.

Robert James would not leave his faith to marry, and Claranell
refused to convert from Presbyterianism. Accordingly, their daughter says, the ceremony was held on "the other side of the altar."
Claranell also extracted an agreement from her intended that their
children would be raised as Protestants. In their world, religion was
as much a matter of social class as of faith. Catholics who married
Protestants improved their social position. Claranell was determined
not to lower her own; she was assuring — even before her vows —
that her progeny would be free of what she no doubt feared as the
mystical and lower-class taint of Catholicism.

No one says that romance, let alone passion, played a part in the
union. Robert James's habits of rigid self-discipline and routine were
long established. Paramount among his concerns was the ability to
provide financially for a family and maintain its respectability. He
rose to be the shoe company's western regional manager and was
accorded the privilege of business trips.[5]

Whatever her feelings about her new husband, once Claranell gave
birth to a baby son at Mount Zion Hospital, at 5:45 on the morning
of June 9, 1916, she focused dotingly on the child. Although he was
named Robert for his father, the Strange clan was commemorated by
his middle name. Claranell kept careful records of her boy in a pre-
printed Baby Book, lovingly setting down each development in
weight, growth, new teeth, with unusual attention to statistics. She
noted the date of each photo, along with the exact address where it
was taken, and the names of all the aunts, uncles, grandmothers, and
assorted friends present.

> First Word — Mamma December 1 — 1916. Am very sorry I cannot
> write "Daddy" in that space. It is certainly no fault of your mother's
> that it is not there, as I have said "Da-da-da" to you constantly since
> birth, but, "what's the use?" He is saying mamma very plainly now.

First Tooth — January 11 — 1917 — The two lowers popped through today. . . .

February 23 — 1917 — Two uppers are showing this morning, a birthday gift to mother.

March 9 — 1917 — Another lower is through.

April 9 — 1917 — The third upper is in today.

May 1 — 1917 — The fourth lower is in, making seven teeth a week before he's eleven months.

The photos record gifts: a little red chair (speaking for Bobby, Claranell writes: "I think it fine. My first chair"); a large soldier doll Tom, almost as big as its owner ("his first 'chum' "). In December 1916 his father gave him his first shoes, from his employer ("tan with white buttons and brown silk tassels — how fond he is of them. . . . The tassels stayed on about five minutes").

By January 7, 1917, "Bobby is crossing corners in his pen now. — [I]t looks as though he will walk early." In April, his son not yet a year old, Robert James presented some hard-soled shoes of black patent leather.

He is walking around in his pen all the time now — just won't sit down, and is very much insulted if anyone holds him. . . .

April 6th — Bobby is going all over the house holding to the wall.

April 19th — Today Aunty Mayme and I took him to Boch's to have his hair trimmed and he ran all over the store while we waited for the barber.[6]

The boy got sick with bronchitis, which caused the family to move in 1923 out of San Francisco, from the various rental addresses. They moved to San Rafael, a town well north of the city and a long commute for Robert James. Claranell and Robert James "thought the climate would be better" for Bob, says Peg, his younger sister.

They moved again, now clear across the bay to Oakland. They bought a home. It was a smallish, low-roofed stucco house, with a porch, at 1036 Annerly Road, little different from dozens of others a developer had built up and down the gentle hills. The McNamaras chose it because Oakland's port assured ferry service to San Francisco, and because Grandma McNamara lived nearby.

But the real reason they chose 1036 Annerly Road had less to do with a particular porch or lawn than with the address. The McNamaras' side of Annerly Road was within Oakland city limits; the other side was in the fancier, adjoining town of Piedmont. Piedmont had steeper hills, spectacular views of the bay, and large, expensive homes built by the nouveaux riches. And, even though Bob was only seven at the time of the move to Oakland, his parents knew the rules of the local school system. Near Annerly Road was Westlake Junior High, a good school. More important, the town of Piedmont allowed families who lived on *either* side of Annerly Road to send their children to Piedmont High School, a lavishly appointed public high school, more like an exclusive private school, which had the sons and daughters of the wealthy citizens of Piedmont as its students. If they lived on Annerly Road, then Bobby could go to Piedmont.[7]

Peg, born in 1919, recalls that their mother continually took them to lessons, especially on Saturdays, in San Francisco, because Robert James habitually went to work on Saturdays. The Baby Book records her enrolling Bobby at St. John's Presbyterian Church, on First Avenue, for Sunday school by age four ("a very good class").

"My brother was incredible from the start," Peg says. The boy was not particularly athletic but competed furiously at every activity. (Childhood illness could account for the concerted effort McNamara made as a youth and an adult at physical fitness, through crew, skiing, and climbing. In his sixties he shunned the elevator and galloped each morning up eleven flights to the president's office at the World Bank.) When there were no lessons, he played in the neighborhood with newly arriving Germans, Italians, and Asians. ("Hell, the first girl I ever danced with was Japanese.") His pal was Vernon Goodin, who lived around the corner; they fought furiously and intricately in their boyish wars in the changing light of the Oakland hills until called in for supper.

Claranell became an expert housekeeper and first-rate cook. She made a habit of shopping for bargains and preferred to travel across town rather than pay what she thought was too much.

Peg recalls that Claranell seated her and Bob at the dining room table and read aloud from *David Copperfield,* for their enlightenment.

Clearly, Claranell's intensive training of the children, particularly her son, came from frustrated ambition. The pride of the Stranges made her determined to assure her children a higher rung on the social and economic ladder.

Peg remembers that their mother told them she would have gone to Stanford, just like brother Shelby and sister Bess, except that she got amnesia.

Her son waves the story away. "Oh well," he later said, his voice trailing off. "Mother used to say these things." He did not elaborate, evidently unwilling to delve further into the complexities of the woman who reared him.

Clearly she thought her son extraordinary — everything her values told her a son should be. The effect on young McNamara was powerful. At an early age he sensed his superiority and his specialness in the household. The logic of Claranell's upbringing was that he had to go further than they had or could; he was supposed to reach some distant horizon of ambition that they could not circumscribe or define. He says, "My parents were determined that I should go to college, even though they did not know what college was like."

At Westlake Junior High, Bob was a good student, though not the formidable performer he was later. His social studies teacher, Marie Carriker, described him as "a student of perfection," quiet, sitting in the last row and making "beautiful books." His teachers gave a sharper impression of Claranell, who would appear at school and question them about his grades: "It was a good idea to have answers," one of them says.[8]

McNamara does not talk about himself easily or especially candidly. But he did confirm, late one afternoon, that "the pressure on me was unbelievable. If I got an A minus, the question was 'Why didn't you get an A?' It was like growing up in a Jewish home."

He told a story about going to first grade in a "shack house" school back in San Francisco: "My first-grade teacher gave the first grade an examination at the end of every month and reseated the class based on the results of the examination. The class was seated in vertical rows, and she put the person with the highest grade in the first seat in the left-hand row. And I worked like heck to be in that seat every month.

"My principal competition were Chinese, Japanese, and Jewish classmates who worked to beat me five days a week. And then on the sixth day, while I went out and played with my playmates, they went to their ethnic schools and learned their languages, learned their history, and learned to take pride in their culture, and came back on Monday determined to beat that Irishman. Which, I am happy to say, they rarely did."

Memories of pressure from both his parents, and others' observations, suggest McNamara was raised according to the then-common belief that boys should be trained to be free of emotion or affect.

McNamara remembers pressure, while Peg, only three years younger, a cute child with long red curls, remembers her home fondly: Robert James listening to the radio, Mother's many friends, the excellently prepared meals. Besides little Peg, another female presence was that of unmarried Mary May Strange, called Aunt Mayme, who lived with the family much of the time and supported herself as a milliner. She decorated the Christmas tree, played games with the children, and was a lot of fun. The gaiety Peg recalls and the pressure Bob recalls are telling: It was common in aspiring households of that time for daughters to be taken less seriously while parents poured energy and ambition into their sons.

Besides the preoccupation with Bob and his success, the family's other major trait was a concern about money. McNamara claims — with evident sincerity — that they lived "under severe financial constraints." Until Bob bought the Roadster, they owned no car. One summer he was unable to go to a camp he wanted to attend because they could not spare the thirteen-dollar-a-week fee.

The photographs suggest otherwise. Claranell was sick when Peg was born; they show a nurse in a starched dress strolling with the new baby. Robert James arranged for the family to spend summers first at Phillips, California, then Tahoe. McNamara's love of the mountains may come from these summers.

This was surely not "absolute poverty" — the term he later made famous on six continents, as he discoursed with evident emotion and directed the World Bank to uplift eight hundred million people from that condition. His family provided for him yet was habitually, obsessively frugal. They saved from a sense of living on the edge, and saved money was a form of power, because it created opportunities otherwise denied: For young Bob McNamara, money saved was a means to exercise ambition.

He followed their program, entering Piedmont High, where he and Vernon made friends with the sons and daughters of Piedmont. Quickly they moved into the high-achieving set. Bob attained the rank of Eagle Scout and made the high school honors society. He dated an energetic, smart girl named Annalee Whittmore. By the end of high school, he had a long list of achievements in the school yearbook to show for his time and energy.

The man who would make over three massive institutions and shape America's role in the American Century and, it is charged, its decline, began as a product of the emerging middle class. He was a blend of immigrant and American midwestern roots, inculcated with the drive to succeed in a melting pot. He was not without a certain protectiveness toward women but was schooled in an image of manhood in which a lack of emotion was admired and coldness was desirable.

A revealing statement he made was that "in my family, there was no expectation of communication between the generations." The tensions in the household shaped conflicts in his nature: The Protestantism and rationalism of Claranell contrasted with the remoteness and faint mysticism of Robert James. In the family there were optimism and faith that the boy's abilities would allow him to build a better future. His upbringing also had a moral cast, an emphasis on service and using money for higher goals. So Claranell and Robert James provided not only the biological product of a boy with a slight frame, poor eyesight, and frantic energy, but also his uneasy mix of moral purpose and raw ambition.

The Bob McNamara who as an adult would emerge as so extraordinary and contradictory a person, given the averageness and anonymity of his forebears, seems an aberration. Marion Goodin, who married Bob's friend Vernon, says: "How you get Bob McNamara out of that pair of people, I don't know. Maybe it was just an aberrant gene, like Peg's red hair."

In one sense, McNamara emerged from typical American circumstances at the start of the American Century. But in another sense, given the limitations of his home in answering the underlying demands of his exceptional personality, he sprang from nowhere.

Bob and Vernon's drive north through the foggy hills took them to the teeming, sophisticated campus of the University of California at Berkeley starting in the fall of 1933. The town itself was like others that ringed the bay, having a few straight streets lined with storefronts and coffee shops leading to winding roads along which were small homes that clung to the hillsides. But the campus dominated the place: It was large, sprinkled with oversize neoclassical buildings and crowded with a student body of twenty-five thousand, half of them undergraduates.

Cal, as Berkeley was known, was an exciting place in the thirties. Its president, Robert Gordon Sproul, was known throughout the state. He lured prominent scientists and scholars from better-known universities in the East, with the aim of building the West's first, and at the time only, great research university. Robert Oppenheimer, the outstanding physicist and future developer of the atomic bomb, had been lured there. Ernest O. Lawrence at Berkeley was building the world's first cyclotron. Anyone approaching Sather Gate, the main entrance off Bancroft Street, was usually accosted by some of Cal's politically active students, waving leaflets or making speeches.[9]

Faculty and students had been galvanized by the immediate crisis of the Depression and the more distant rise of fascism in Europe, which threatened the agreements of Versailles. In the fall of 1932, Franklin D. Roosevelt was elected, and his Hundred Days started the next year. The philosophy and programs of the New Deal conflicted with the conservative California legislature, which, among other things, paid Sproul's salary. Bob and Vernon, as they crossed campus or went to classes, could not avoid the activism and controversies — an ironic foreshadowing of Berkeley in the 1960s, when students would protest "McNamara's war" and all he stood for.

The university also sported an outstanding football team and crew. Fresh from the isolation of Oakland, Bob McNamara at age seventeen found a new world of unlimited choice. If there was ever a place to invent himself, it was here.

He was pledged by Phi Gamma Delta fraternity and named chairman of the first big social event of the freshman year, the Mardi Gras dance. He joined freshman crew, thereby discovering a new form of exhausting physical activity, "pushing himself to the limit," as a friend says.[10] He continued to date Annalee Whittmore, his crush from Piedmont High days, who was now at Stanford. When he visited her he would drive with Vernon on the long road south around the foot of the bay to avoid paying a twenty-five-cent bridge toll. Annalee, forewarned, would scrounge up a date for Vernon. "They were always broke," she says.[11]

His early choices were less than successful. Phi Gamma Delta was a beer-drinking group McNamara didn't care for much, although sister Peg remembers Claranell joining its mothers' committee. Recalls a classmate, "He was never much of a frat man; at least his heart wasn't in it." Bob McNamara, the 150-pound crewman, did not show intercollegiate potential; he became crew manager instead.

His most important revelation came sophomore year, when he happened to take a particular mix of courses he still remembers vividly: Lowenberg on philosophy, Adams on ethics, and a course on logic.

"All S is P but not all P is S" is how he summarizes the impression this last course made on him, citing this basic statement from set theory and logic.[12]

The basic of logic in mathematics struck a resonant chord in McNamara's mind. He was already accustomed through his high school math courses to think in quantitative terms. The use of quantitative techniques to argue problems, to apply logic to larger issues of philosophy and politics, even questions of daily life, was emotionally congenial, since he had been raised by people steeped in popular notions of the virtues of rationalism. He told me that he began, at that point in his life, to talk and think in numbers; it was a consciously adopted style. Perhaps it was a way of distinguishing himself from his ordinary roots. At the least, it was an identity.

Popular literature and radio in the twenties and thirties glorified physics and mathematics as keys to human progress. Albert Einstein, the greatest savant of the time, preached rationalism among men and nations, and was mobbed when he arrived in New York and feted at the Mount Wilson Observatory, near Pasadena. The glorification of science qua progress had a heyday in the twenties; when the 1929 crash and Depression spread their terrifying grip, many intellectuals and leaders looked to science as a beacon. Similarly, many fields aspired to the lofty condition of being scientific by adopting mathematical techniques: The failures of government were to be cured by the science of public administration; the study of government would henceforth be political science; social problems stood a better chance of solution if they were treated as social science. Even the sprawling giant of American manufacturing could yield greater productivity and wealth using science: Since the turn of the century the more progressive companies had adopted F. W. Taylor's system of "scientific management" of production.

Although McNamara took an elective in astronomy, science as an investigation of the unknown held less appeal for him than applied mathematics. He also learned to write, perhaps as an outgrowth of

his interest in logic. His graduate school papers are models of organized argument and precise, impersonal language.

Physics, math, and engineering were possible majors, but he chose
economics. The field was popular at the time, since it, too, pretended
to analyze the location, growth, and transfer of resources with scientific precision. Thousands of students flocked to economics in the
1930s; it claimed to be able to reveal the causes of the economic
debacle that had hurt the country, blighted many of their own families, and, not irrelevantly, could leave them with empty pockets and
uncertain job prospects at graduation time.

This choice worked. McNamara's freshman grades had been mid-
dling, for him: A's in math and philosophy, a C and a B in English,
and a C in advanced French — the latter revealing a lifelong tin ear
for languages. But sophomore year he earned eleven A's and one B,
a performance for which he was elected to Phi Beta Kappa that June,
he says. His grade point average remained very high through his
senior year.[13]

Academic success made him stand out in a class three thousand
strong. Sophomore year he was invited to sit on the prestigious Student Affairs Committee. Accepting, he wrote to J. Arthur Harris,
president of the Associated University Students of California, "I
wish to express my appreciation of the honor. . . . I shall endeavor to
perform my duties conscientiously and wisely."[14]

Success bred ambition, in a pattern to become familiar. Cal had the
usual range of so-called secret societies, of which the most select was
the elite senior group called the Order of the Golden Bear, which
admitted only thirty male members. President Sproul encouraged
these societies as "a profitable investment . . . from which [students]
must expect their dividends of personal happiness and public leadership in later life."[15]

More to the point, men who were Golden Bears got to know
Sproul personally. Recommendations from him in one's senior year
were an important help in landing a job or getting into the graduate
school of one's choice. While many other Berkeley students argued
about the Spanish civil war or the Townsend Plan for California,
while students physically attacked some visiting Japanese naval officers because of Japan's growing aggression against China, and while
the local Communist cell was highly active, the student government–
Golden Bear members were straight men, concerned with their
records and careers, and Sproul's vision of public service.[16]

As a sophomore, McNamara was invited into Triune, the sophomore society that was the first rung on the ladder of the most select student societies. His real interest in campus politics was helped the day he made two new friends, Walter "Wally" Haas and Willard Goodwin. Goodwin was from Los Angeles. Like McNamara, he had grown up in modest circumstances and worked conscientiously for grades and his Eagle Scout rank. Haas came from San Francisco, from a wealthy Jewish family that owned the Levi Strauss Company. Another Triune member was Stanley Johnson. The female members included a beauty named Hattie Booth, and Margaret Craig, whom Vernon took out.[17]

They had much in common as the straights on a campus so teeming with activism; they were hardworking students, and Willard, like McNamara, was very high in his class. All, except Wally, had little to fall back on and needed jobs and good careers; all had some sense of social service. Two years and many intrigues later, after Vernon was elected class president one year and Willard another, they were all meeting around a table, all elected to the Order of the Golden Bear. Their leader, with the august title of warden, was Bob McNamara.

He had invented another role for himself, that of intermediary between Sproul and the dissident elements on campus. Sproul and Provost Monroe Deutsch used the Golden Bears as a forum to advise them on how they should respond to campus protests and demands made on the administration. At one meeting one of the Bears, who belonged to the campus Communist cell, stood up to denounce Sproul; in those times, students did not insult the president to his face.

The following year, after McNamara had left the university, he heard that Sproul had decided to stop going to the meetings, so raucous had they become. In a letter, McNamara shows something of his need for attention from a well-respected figure in authority: Sproul's kindly regard was perhaps compensation for the remoteness of his own father. He called the matter "close to my heart."

> I quite understand that our position will not allow you to be left open to such remarks. . . . I would like you to know how much the members of my class appreciated your attendance and participation in the meetings . . . and how greatly I hope that you will consider all possible alternatives before permanently deciding to give up activity in the Order.[18]

His eagerness to be noticed — approvingly — by men in authority cropped up in other places. Vernon Goodin remembers that Malcolm Davisson, his economics professor, invited the two boys to his house, a singular honor. McNamara also had an early chance to impress Deutsch, the provost, when during his freshman year he received an invitation to tea with him and Mrs. Deutsch.

"I was always taught to be prompt," he told me, reflecting the stern training of home. So he had stepped up to the Deutsches' door promptly at four o'clock and entered, to find himself the first and only guest. Then others began to arrive, and he saw the Deutsches shaking hands with each new arrival, saying their names and nodding and smiling.

Freshman McNamara concluded this was what people did at teas. He stood next to them, making a receiving line of three, and started shaking hands and saying his name to each person who came. Whether the mathematician in him computed what would happen when all the other guests had added themselves to the line is unclear. He laughed as he told this story on himself years later.

McNamara could be intensely self-conscious. His friends arranged for him to take Marion Sproul, the daughter of the president, to a dance. Her recollection of him is that he seemed "stiff." How did they get on? "We both survived," she says. "He never asked me out again."

Meanwhile, he commuted home in his Ford Roadster, back to Annerly Road and Claranell's obsession with the house, the schedules, the money, back to his father, whom a friend remembers sitting silently in a chair in the parlor, being "very austere" and "terribly polite" and taking little interest in his son's friends who came through.[19]

It would have been only natural for father and son to experience tension, given Bob's growing sophistication and confidence, which would have showed up the old man's narrowness. The fast-moving campus star would have noticed the gulf between them: His mission — and theirs, too — was that he outgrow them and leave them, educationally, socially, financially. That time was drawing near.

Willard Goodwin, who visited the household at Annerly Road during this period, remembers Robert James as "an indrawn, withdrawn, in-turning person." He says he thought the son showed "great respect" for his father but that this was mixed with a strong sense of "knowing full well that the old man wasn't always right but you better not question it."[20]

"Stories of an abnormal childhood because there was a generation gap between our father and ourselves are untrue," Peg McNamara Slaymaker says.[21] But the later record of McNamara's utter obedience, his self-chosen role as a servant of individual men in authority — Henry Ford II, John Kennedy, and Lyndon Johnson — suggest a special requirement for obedience to his ignorant father, whom "you better not question," even as the boy outgrew him.

By the fall of his senior year, in 1936, McNamara was a known figure on campus. He would recall that as head of the student judicial committee he disciplined a member of the football team — a star player — for cheating at his studies. The football coach later crossed the yard to compliment McNamara on the courageous decision.

He had made friends with the sons and daughters of some prominent families. He had found a circle of friends and, with his friends, managed to get to know both the university's distinguished president and its provost.

More important, he had discovered an internal identity, bolstered by his special talent for numbers and logic. To a young man growing up in a working-class household, this was not just any talent. His facility matched the forward direction of the age, possibly yielding him special insights in the new gospel of rationalism that some Cal faculty preached.

His grades gave him confidence; he was one of the highest-ranking in the class. And having come this far, he wanted the next rung: a Rhodes scholarship to Oxford University, in England, one of the nation's most prestigious awards.

He and Willard Goodwin were both interviewed for the honor, but a third man, Bruce Weber, was chosen. McNamara's missing the Rhodes was obviously a deep blow — all his professional life he would pride himself on hiring Rhodes scholars, and he would mention that friends or protégés had been Rhodes scholars, always as a compliment and certification of their abilities.

Failing to win the Rhodes caused him to agree to enroll at the Harvard Business School, where he had applied. Wally Haas had been accepted, too, so they would go together. Although graduate study in economics or law might have been alternatives, the business school filled his need for a sure route to a high-paying job. There were not many business schools in the country then, and Harvard's was known as the best. Having lost out on the status and certification of the Rhodes, he would have the status of Harvard instead.

Meanwhile, McNamara had found out he could be physically daring when Goodwin introduced him to mountain climbing. They took long drives to climb mountains in the High Sierras; they skiied, another outlet for his energy.

That summer, McNamara got his first look at Asia. He and Willard had a long summer ahead before they were to go east in the fall. McNamara had gone to sea before, at age seventeen working on a ship that went through the Panama Canal to New York and back. During college he had worked on ships, once planning to get hired during the big 1934 San Francisco dockworkers' strike, until Robert James stopped him from crossing the picket line. But in 1937, there was nothing to prevent him and Willard from gaily going down to the hiring hall to see what they could get. Says Goodwin, "We wanted to do something exciting so we decided to go to sea . . . we had to join the union, which we did. . . . We were assigned to one ship which we didn't like which never got out of port. Then we went back to the hiring hall. We hoped to go around the world . . . but we got signed on . . . [by] the old Dollar Line, on the *President Hoover,* which was the biggest passenger ship in the Pacific at that time."

They berthed in the forecastle with thirteen other sailors. Goodwin remembers that "one of the showers had a red cross on it. And I said: Well, that's obvious. Everyone here has venereal disease, so this is the one we should use so we won't get venereal disease. It happened to be just the opposite. . . . One day I was stepping out of the shower with the red cross on it and one of the guys said: Gee, did you get the clap in Tokyo?"

McNamara got acquainted with the chief mate on one leg of the voyage. "The man took a real liking to him," says Goodwin. "He used to let him steer the boat." The long nights at sea also provoked long conversations. Goodwin remembers telling McNamara that he wanted to go into medicine to help people; his friend commented that, for himself, he would never want to be a doctor because you could help only one person at a time. "I want to help the largest number of people," McNamara said.

Their biggest adventure came as the ship hove near Shanghai during the days the Japanese attacked that city. The bombing of Shanghai made headlines around the world: It was plain evidence of

Japanese aggression toward China, which the United States was officially bound to protect. Japanese military moves had been reported regularly in the West Coast press. A theme of McNamara's political education, then, had been the weakness of China against another, militant and organized Asian power.

Now they saw it firsthand. As the *President Hoover* waited at anchor for the tide to change, an aircraft they thought was Japanese began attacking the ship itself, apparently by accident. The bomb's explosion wounded several and tore up the deck and lifeboats. McNamara was so excited taking pictures of the action on deck that he had to be pulled below for his own safety.[22] Ever after, he would keep on his desk a fragment of the bombshell that he had picked up, a memento of boyhood adventure, Asian aggression, or both.

2

The Student of Control

NOW BOB TRAVELED OVERLAND by train clear across the country to the East for the first time. The train took him through the majestic Rockies and across the amber Great Plains, through the great industrial centers of Chicago and Pittsburgh. Willard was traveling separately to Baltimore and Johns Hopkins University. Bob, meanwhile, branched north to Boston. He found the Graduate School of Business Administration to be a cluster of new, brick Georgian-style buildings on the Boston side of the Charles River, looking across it at the spires of Harvard College and built on a site that, since the Civil War, had been called Soldiers' Field.

McNamara asked to room alone,[1] a curious choice, since he and Wally Haas, the two Cal men, might be expected to band together. He unpacked in a single room in Gallatin Hall, plunged into his courses, and wrote home.

"The policy of this school seems to be one of piling more work on the students than they can possibly do," he wrote to Cal president Sproul. "I heartily approve of the general atmosphere, which the Dean expressed very well when he said 'It is no sin to make a profit.' "

The budding capitalist was more idealistic in another letter penned at the same time in his pointy left-hand script, to Provost Deutsch: "Although the work here has proved very interesting, I sometimes think the faculty places too much emphasis on the chase for the almighty dollar." He tried awkwardly to reconcile the conflict he already sensed between his economic mission of uplifting himself from the straits of Annerly Road and higher social and ethical aims, writing, "However, perhaps this is necessary for the achievement of their aim of instilling in us a conception of the means by which the ethical and moral standards of business may be raised."[2]

Furious effort paid off. McNamara's first-term grades were the highest in the class. He showed a trait that marked him later: a knack for jumping cold into a new mental challenge and grasping it fully, with speed and confidence. He computed well and fast. His papers showed the effects of his study of logic at Berkeley. In the small group discussions of case problems — the core of the curriculum — he honed an instinct for combative argument. Wally said later, "It was terribly tempting for the rest of us to sit back and let Bob do the work."[3]

What McNamara discovered in the next two years was not only that he could place in the competition for high class rank, teacher referrals, and a good job at graduation. He had come east needing something deeper, a mission. And he found it: a field of specialization he would make his own and use to change three institutions and, arguably, the United States.

Even the name of this new field suited McNamara's emerging personality. At different times and in different applications, it has been termed *financial control, management control, statistical control,* or *control accounting.* In all variants, the word that had the most meaning for the stiff, cautious McNamara was *control.*

All first-year students took accounting and business statistics, but because of this new method these were not as humdrum as their names implied. The major revolution of control accounting was unfolding in America's most progressive companies by 1937; the whiff of grapeshot gusted across Soldiers' Field.[4]

The revolution had started back in 1902, when a crisis of succession in the du Pont family's gunpowder business caused three young cousins — Alfred, Coleman, and Pierre — to win control of the core company and its affiliates and create a new entity, the E. I. du Pont de Nemours Powder Company.[5] The new company effectively controlled the entire gunpowder industry in the United States and used 5 percent of the world's nitrate supply. Like International Harvester, General Electric, National Biscuit, American Tobacco, Pittsburgh Plate Glass, and U.S. Steel, Du Pont was suddenly a mammoth organization spanning widely different activities. It was "vertical" in that it took raw materials, such as nitrates from mines in Chile, through manufacture and marketing worldwide. The cousins innovated their own distribution system and an international sales operation. Their management job became more complex later, when the company's explosives research spawned the discovery of how to make plastics, which generated wholly new product lines for a different group of consumers. The cousins could not run all this, let alone assure profits, if they stuck to the management patterns of nineteenth-century industrialists, who were usually owner-entrepreneurs running their own, one-product manufacturing operations, such as textile mills. The new Du Pont company, like the other new conglomerates, faced serious problems of integration.

The cousins' concern was how to exert central control over divergent, massive operations that had to be run in the field; the central office could not run them all, much less run them effectively while managing companywide affairs. So, in a remarkable burst of creativity in two short years, the cousins invented a solution that was destined to become "standard procedure for twentieth century industrial enterprises," according to management authority A. D. Chandler. Old accrual accounting was replaced with a new way of assigning costs that took account of the varied activities involved in making the product: the capital invested in plants, raw materials, foremen, administration, the distribution network, and others. Income from the sales of a given product line could be set against these costs, giving a new measure of earnings. By 1904, Pierre du Pont, the new company's treasurer, could produce monthly figures on costs, income, and rate of return for total capital investment for each of its thirteen products.

The du Ponts had created the new, vertical conglomerate in the hope that greater profits could be realized by having production, distribution, and sales under one roof. The cousins were therefore interested in efficiency. When an unknown assistant handed Coleman a brilliant report on efficiency, he was noticed and soon transferred to work for Pierre in his new, enlarged finance department.

The assistant was F. Donaldson Brown, an electrical-parts salesman who soon showed a real genius for accounting, in which he was self-taught. It was Brown who largely finished developing the cousins' financial control system. One of their inventions was the Chart Room, where the cost and income data for each division were posted; the Chart Room was meant to promote honesty and cooperation among the divisions, as well as to spur friendly competition.

Brown's most important invention was a rate-of-return formula that encompassed all the complex operations of a modern corporation and that would be adopted throughout U.S. industry, and is used today. Now that he had the means to compare rates of return for different kinds of operations, and for one operation over time, Brown conceived the idea of *throughput*. Throughput means that financial returns will increase when production volume rises for a given investment and time. Throughput offered a way to measure the performance of managers in the new conglomerates: They sought to operate each segment of their business as efficiently as possible over the short, medium, and long term to obtain the most throughput.

With these common yardsticks the du Ponts or their counterparts at GE or International Harvester, meeting with division heads in an overall executive committee, could make rational allocation of funds — for plant, materials, or workers and the like — among the divisions. Company chiefs could measure the performance of the divisions and their heads. A key aspect of the new system was the ability to project costs and incomes forward, agree on forecasts for three, six, or twelve months in the future, and measure performance against the forecast. Thus, financial data became a tool for centralized control of many kinds of operations and the men who ran them.

So in the Du Pont system, numbers became the common language linking far-flung, varied operations and the company chief. The results, in terms of sales, profits, and expansion, were spectacular.

An impressive application of the new control accounting followed. The cousins had invested Du Pont heavily in General Motors. GM had come into being in an orgy of acquisitions by its erratic, imperial founder, Will C. Durant between 1908 and 1911. Snapped up were Buick, Cadillac, Champion Spark Plug, and Louis Chevrolet's company, as well as others, which failed and are now forgotten. Durant started to founder trying to manage this empire. When the company nearly failed in 1920, the du Ponts stepped in to save their investment.

Pierre du Pont worked closely with Alfred P. Sloan, Jr., a former roller-bearing manufacturer and Durant protégé. He also brought in Brown and other Du Pont financial wizards. They built a control system to link what Sloan called the "formless aggregate" with headquarters. General Motors not only survived; profits soared as the new system allowed Sloan to take advantage of the moving assembly line, which Henry Ford invented in 1913, and the enormous mass demand for cars that followed World War I. General Motors not only overtook Ford's regnant Tin Lizzie; it offered an unprecedented variety of models and evolved the annual model change. Thus the modern U.S. auto industry was born.

Forty years later, in the late 1970s, running companies "by the numbers" would become a dirty word. Brown's focus on obtaining maximum throughput — as opposed to looking closely at the quality of products being built — bore some blame for the American manufacturing decline. But in the late 1930s, financial control was a modern, progressive technique.

For not only did the system of control make General Motors prosper in the boom years of the 1920s. It also allowed Sloan to have timely warning of slumping sales as the car market was hit by the Depression. Despite the fact that the company's gigantic operation shrank at one point to 60 percent of its pre-Depression level, it both survived and turned a profit every year of the 1930s.

To arriving business school students in the fall of 1937, when 25 percent of the work force was unemployed, the tools invented and refined by the du Pont cousins and Sloan must have come as a great revelation — not as a miracle or a lucky shot, but as the inexorable, logical result of rational management.[6] The system of control was taught primarily by Ross Graham Walker, who showed how it could help companies to stay afloat in bad times and workers to keep their jobs. Society, students could conclude, benefited from the system.

McNamara's quick mind absorbed this situation. As he practiced the math of financial control in his classes at Soldiers' Field, he might have found a resolution of his economic mission (the "chase for the almighty dollar") and raising "the ethical and moral standards of business." Fifty years later he would tell me fervently, banging his left hand on a table, that one of the main principles of his life was: "There needs to be *no conflict* between the goals of a large institution and those of society."

McNamara seemed conscious that his special affinity for logic and statistics made him remarkably gifted in the field of control. In the larger sense, *control* reflected what he was doing with his life, in getting out of Annerly Road, getting a college degree, getting control of his time and social life by rooming alone, control of "more work" than students "can possibly do" by careful, tidy preparation.

The accounting teachers quickly marked him as faculty material. Although he was again successful in being noticed by his teachers, other students could be put off by his growing self-consciousness and isolation.

"Bob did not tolerate fools lightly," recalls one classmate.[7] And another says of him in this period: "He was the most aloof man I ever met."[8]

In the fall of McNamara's second and final year, he heard from Annerly Road that his father, Robert James, had died.[9] He made the long train trip to California, spent a solemn Thanksgiving at home around a spartan table, and rode back again, having agreed with Claranell that he would return in June. Exams were imminent.

He flubbed his orals. Edmund P. Learned, a marketing professor who had followed this student closely, was one of the three men who gave the exam and knew McNamara was likely to get a "high distinction," which would help win a faculty appointment. After the orals, Learned asked the other two examiners to allow for grief and give the boy the high mark anyway, but one man refused. So McNamara won only a "high pass."

Also depressing was the return to Oakland that summer. McNamara was now the breadwinner. He got a job with the accounting firm of Price Waterhouse and began commuting to San Francisco every day in his father's pattern.

The job was evidently an unhappy experience. He later explained the problem as a disagreement in principle between the Harvard view of accounting and Price Waterhouse's. The more likely cause was that he hated having a junior job and doing drudge work. He remembered that one adding-machine tape he ran was forty feet long. This was not what accounting should be, he thought.

It was not what Bob McNamara should be, either. There are signs he was not only unhappy with the job but also with the confinement at home.

He accidentally ran into Margy Craig, Vernon's onetime girlfriend. He called Vernon and asked if he could take her out. Sure, said his old friend. I'm still in law school and in no position to get serious about a girl. After a date or two, McNamara found himself in love.

Margy was tiny, weighing perhaps a hundred pounds. Her clear blue eyes, set in a wide, angular face, had a way of looking at a person with a bright gaze that seemed approving. She was from Seattle but had moved with her family as a child to Alameda, another town on the eastern fringe of the bay, south of Oakland. She knew Bob through Vernon and the Golden Bear group at Berkeley. She had worked at the campus Y on community projects, as Bob had.

She was not stunning like Hattie Booth, or a superachiever like Annalee Whittmore. She was definitely not of the smart Piedmont High set. But "we all liked her," Willard Goodwin says. Her nature was to accept life and enjoy it directly. McNamara first noticed her at a college party, when one of the boys hoisted her, laughing and kicking, onto his shoulders.

Margy took a job after college as a physical education teacher; she would teach or tutor, one way or another, all her life. It took patience and persistence, qualities that she said came from her Scottish side and that would influence her life and McNamara's.

As a girl she learned to love the outdoors by going fishing with her grandfather. McNamara loved the outdoors, too; they went on picnics. Bob often brought along a can of kippers, so her name for him became Kip.[10]

Meanwhile, McNamara was bent on escaping Annerly Road and his job. An offer came from Dean Wallace Donham at Harvard to be a junior instructor in accounting. He went to Boston to discuss the matter. While in Baltimore to see Willard at Johns Hopkins, he realized he could not move back east without Margy. Typically in a rush, he called from a pay phone to propose.

She accepted and began wedding arrangements. So little did these children of the new world and new century care about roots or tradition that she wrote to him to ask what his middle name was. He cabled back one word: "Strange."

There followed a plain wedding in an Episcopal church in Alameda in August 1940, and a simple reception at the dock from which they were leaving on a honeymoon. On the eve of war, they had scant taste for frills. Besides, this group of friends needed no props to have a good time. Their friends all knew each other: the Berkeley group, the Piedmont High crowd, the Craigs, some of the Stranges, Claranell, Mayme, and Peg.

From dockside Margy and Bob were waved off on their journey through the Panama Canal, then up the East Coast to Boston and his new job at Harvard — another careful allocation of funds. The route was a fitting symbol: McNamara was retracing the trip his father had taken in 1865 to the city of promise and, as a college graduate and about-to-be Harvard teacher, he was fulfilling his father's quest for a better future.

Outwardly, the new Mr. and Mrs. McNamara were little different from thousands of couples who hurried to marry in the shadow of war. But they would be typical for just a moment, before their unique personalities shaped a future that no one at the dockside send-off could have foreseen.

A story McNamara tells on himself shows how eager he was to find favor with the business school faculty.

That fall, Franklin Roosevelt was running for a third term, against Republican Wendell Willkie. A straw poll was taken by the school's faculty.[11] They were men with strong pro-business attitudes and ties to the industrialists and bankers who funded the school and hired its graduates, and who believed that FDR was a traitor to his class and the free-market system. (The bitterness about Roosevelt in Republican circles in 1940 resembled the bitterness about McNamara in liberal circles later.) It was no surprise that the straw poll overwhelmingly favored Willkie.

The real news was that three faculty men had voted *for* Roosevelt. Dining hall gossip immediately centered on who they were. One was known as distinctly odd; another was one of the few Jews on the junior staff, Eugene M. Zuckert. Says Zuckert, "We never could find out who the third one was. I always suspected it was McNamara but he would never admit it."

He concealed his vote in 1940, but to me, more than half a century later, McNamara confessed that he had voted for FDR. He showed no discomfort about having hidden the fact, only pain that one senior faculty man might think he was dumb for the way he voted. "I remember what I was eating, even. It was half of number sixteen, since the menu items were listed by number and instructors like me were too poor to afford a complete item. So I was eating half of number sixteen, which was bacon and eggs. And I felt like sinking in my chair when one of the senior professors said that he considered the vote an intelligence test and he considered that there were three dummies in the school."

The incident of the straw vote seems minor, yet it reveals much about the twenty-four-year-old McNamara. Had he only wanted to please the senior faculty, he could have simply voted for Willkie. But he voted for FDR out of conscience, then lacked the courage to reveal his preference publicly. He resolved the tension between morality and ambition in favor of the latter.

Indeed, McNamara's support for FDR was long-lived. FDR supported labor against business. Robert James had sympathized with labor to the point of refusing to let his son cross a picket line to be hired as a seaman. To me, McNamara once said of FDR, "He changed the way men think." He said "think" with such force that I sensed changing the way men think was a very great achievement in his mind, perhaps McNamara's own goal later in life.

A year and a half of teaching followed the return to Boston and Soldiers' Field. Bob and Margy lived in a walk-up apartment near Harvard Square. She introduced a sorority sister to one of Bob's friends, Charles Anderson. Soon the newlywed Andersons lived next door to the newlywed McNamaras, who in October 1941 added a baby, Little Margy, to their household. The family lived on McNamara's $1,800 yearly salary as an instructor; if he got tenure, he would make $4,000 per year. Charles Anderson recalls, "If we really wanted to live it up, we bought a bottle of sherry."

McNamara worked at being onstage as a public personality. He was systematic even about how to amuse. There is a story that someone found in his desk drawer a chart, laid out along two axes — a format that thousands of subordinates, later, would recognize. Along one axis was noted the date, and along the other was the "joke"; the squares on the grid were filled in to show the students' "response."

His own memory of teaching stresses that his students were "very intelligent." Curiously, his teaching technique used emotional conflict. He recalls: "I will create a tense situation at times just to dramatize a point. . . . You really have to move people to want to understand more than they did when they came into the room. Sometimes — I won't call it tricks — I focus on what will interest them: strained relations between two people, or some slight exaggeration of a point, or framing it in an emotional way. As a teaching device [it] is useful."

France and Britain were at war with Germany. Pearl Harbor had been attacked by Japan. The best and brightest college graduates were getting commissions and going off to fight. The Harvard Business School seemed likely to become a backwater, since only "dregs" would apply, or it could become a haven for draft dodgers. A fellow instructor, Myles Mace, recalls that he and McNamara were restless at the thought of spending the war teaching dregs in a lame-duck school.

Their call was not long coming. One morning in the spring of 1942, McNamara was summoned to the office of Dean Donham along with some other junior faculty, including Mace. The commanding general of the Army Air Forces, H. H. Arnold, wanted them to contribute to the war effort by teaching statistical control to newly minted officers then training in Miami. They needed the course to start June 1. It was now May.

"Many of us had low draft numbers and we were likely to be called. We didn't relish going in as privates. And the school idea offered us a chance to use our professional training . . . and get into the action. By noon we were enthusiasts for the idea," says Mace. They hopped a train for Washington.[12]

It was probably the next day that the "stiff" and "aloof" McNamara met a young man, three years older than he, who was the original Whiz Kid. Charles Bates Thornton, nicknamed Tex for his home state, was one of the brasher young moths who flitted to Washington at the start of the war. Later he would be the leading figure in the rise and fall of another conglomerate, Litton Industries. Meanwhile, his impact on McNamara would be enormous.

Thornton operated out of a tiny office near those of General Arnold and Robert A. Lovett, assistant secretary of war for air, a distinguished banker and confidant of the president. Thornton's phone rang constantly, and there seemed to be generals on the other end of the line, although his captain's stripes were fresh on his sleeve. He had been working at the Housing Authority when his knack for statistics and his verbal flair drew Lovett's notice. Lovett hired him as an aide, landing him right in the thick of things.

Thornton was magnetic, no doubt about it. He had wavy, perfectly combed hair, a strong jaw; he smoked cigarettes in a long holder, which he brandished about in clear imitation of Roosevelt. To Professor Edmund Learned, McNamara, Mace, and the others, Thornton outlined the task before them. Mace recalls that Thornton could be hypnotic when he painted "verbal pictures" of a challenge.[13]

He explained the problem to the Harvard delegation. At the time of Pearl Harbor, General Arnold had perhaps fifty airplanes; he even knew each one by name. The United States did not have an "air force," really, only a relic of the glory days of the flying aces of the

Great War. Now the war was going to be global; the president was ordering new aircraft by the thousand.

There was no overall system for tracking planes, engines, crews, spare parts, and other inventory needed to keep the air war going. Arnold and Lovett had no way to manage the projected air force or allocate resources among theaters. Learned and another faculty member had had talks with Washington about a role for the business school and proposed that financial control could be adopted to provide the answer. Thornton agreed: A system of statistical control — tracking objects, resources, and people instead of money — could enable Arnold and Lovett, like the chiefs in a large corporation with many divisions and different kinds of operations, to manage the air war.

The assignment was huge, bigger than anything the Harvard instructors had imagined. McNamara and some others spent the next weeks racing around bases, gathering data to create forms and a reporting system for Statistical Control, as the operation was henceforth called. McNamara helped draw up forms on aircraft, inventory, parts, military and training specialties, and the like: properly formatted forms with x and y axes, to be filled out by Army Air Forces units worldwide and then sent to Washington. Besides the regular casualty system, Statistical Control had its own casualty report to analyze patterns of death and injury — a precursor of the Vietnam body counts.[14]

The Harvard teachers then joined others back at Soldiers' Field to teach the first class of 150 military men from Miami, many of whom knew the Army better than their instructors. They taught by "the seat of our pants," says Mace.

As the men were trained, they were sent to set up Statistical Control Units at U.S. bases where the Army Air Forces were receiving and testing aircraft, training pilots and crews, and assembling matériel.[15] Then a first overseas Stat Control unit was started, with the AAF command in Australia. But by late 1942, the new teaching had become routine. McNamara and Mace were restless again, impatient for commissions and action.

Thornton told them that commissions weren't being given out anymore in the Zone of the Interior, as the continental United States was called. They had three choices: to stay civilians at Harvard and risk being drafted as privates; to go to Officer Candidate School and be commissioned as second lieutenants (junior to many of the men they had just taught); or to go overseas, leaving their families, and try to get higher commissions there.

Overseas it would be. Thornton arranged for them to be assigned as consultants to the nascent Eighth Air Force in Great Britain and paid the then-princely sum of twenty-five dollars a day ("More money than we had ever seen before," says Mace) plus an eight-dollar-a-day allowance for expenses. They flew first-class in a Pan Am clipper that rumbled over the ocean and landed to refuel in Bermuda, the Azores, and Lisbon — there, for nearly nothing, they got a big dinner at a hotel. Finally they landed in Ireland, out of range of the Luftwaffe, and reported to Bushy Park, outside London, head-quarters of the Eighth. They billeted with an English family in Ted-dington. They never forgot the freezing house and cold beds, or the German air force rumbling every night above the houses, whose curtains were drawn tight.

They wanted to be instant majors, these Harvard junior teachers. Mace recalls that they stopped in the men's room on their way to the key interview, with Ira C. Eaker, commanding general of the Eighth Air Force, about their commissions. McNamara's absurdly boyish face was a clear disadvantage. Mace combed what few gray hairs he had into prominence to try to impress the general with his maturity. Although the ploy to appear older failed, on March 12, 1943, they were commissioned temporary captains in the U.S. Army. Then they went to a warehouse and ran up and down racks of clothes to find uniforms that showed their new rank.

The two professors turned captains worked seven days a week. Mace ate breakfast, but McNamara left their billet beforehand to start work at seven or seven-thirty each morning. It was not a comfortable life, but McNamara didn't need comforts: Absorbing his enormous energy in work was a form of comfort. Margy wrote to Learned, "They think the English heating and food situation would be about the same even when the war isn't on."[16]

McNamara showed an enormous appetite for administration, for getting things done — not traits of every college teacher. His excited urgency, his confidence, and his sense of his superior intelligence bred arrogance.

A key fact about Thornton's Statistical Control operation was that he did not have legal authority to require commanders overseas to comply with the system. In addition, the new Stat Control officers were junior in rank and military experience to the veterans in top posts overseas. For the system to work, Stat Control officers had to convince their commanding officers that their carbon-copy forms and Teletype records, their analyses of data from the scene, could be critically useful. As explained by an Army description of the Harvard Stat Control school, certain qualities would make a man an impressive briefer: "Neatness, imagination in development and presentation, understanding of the man who would pass judgment on the completed report, these factors were constant in the teaching of the entire program." Bad qualities, on the other hand, were "impetuosity, failure to delegate authority, lack of persuasiveness, violation of the chain of command, and failure to achieve coordination." In sum,

> the School was interested in turning out officers who were able to defend their ideas and to get along with their superiors and colleagues in whatever unit they were assigned. . . . It was fully understood that an officer, however able, who failed in this aspect was of little use to the army.[17]

Now, McNamara and Mace were very "able" — which was why Thornton sent them to the all-important theater in England, where preparations were under way for an air campaign against Germany. But having taught diplomacy to several hundred Stat Control students, these teachers lacked it themselves. They met with strong resistance around the Eighth Air Force.

Mace recalls visiting an engine-assembly unit and trying to spot the inefficiencies. He and McNamara were hindered by the fact that "neither of us were mechanics." They had to work a long time to get good data on engine assembly and repair. On a different occasion, they ordered another officer to work late, as they were doing. The man balked, and the next day his commanding officer told McNamara and Mace in no uncertain terms that he was the one giving orders, not they. McNamara wrote to Margy that their work was "uphill" because they had "no authority to back them."

Then Dusty Porterfield arrived. Porterfield was an early Stat Control–school graduate who had started the first overseas Stat Control Unit, in Australia. Porterfield began bossing the two teachers around, and McNamara fought him openly. "We don't take orders from you," he snarled.

The problems were severe enough to warrant a visit from Thornton, who was en route to North Africa to straighten out Jimmy Doolittle, the fabled World War I ace, who was resisting the blandishments of Stat Control. Mace later claimed Thornton's visit to England was unneeded, but certainly Professor Learned was worried. He knew his two fledglings and their faults — and counseled patience.

> [W]inning your way slowly and with difficulty, as you have undoubtedly had to, will really strengthen your stature in the organization. . . .
>
> I feel from word I have had . . . that you have been working too hard and I think you should make some definite plans to relax before you collapse. If you become too tired, your relationships with other men will become strained and in a military organization, you cannot afford to snap at superiors, no matter how sincere your objectives are nor how distressing they may be. Where you are dealing with complete strangers, they are unable to make such allowances.[18]

Besides arrogance and impatience, McNamara also showed his drive for order and results. Harvard dean Donald David noticed his administrative talent back when McNamara had been going to Washington to design the reporting system. "He came back with the situation all tied up in a neat package: there were no loose ends."[19]

Eventually the problems in England were worked out, and General Eaker approved of McNamara's and Mace's performance. Learned had massive praise for their work. One Stat Control job followed another; each time, McNamara took over a Statistical Control Unit in the field, helped adapt procedures to the new situation, and produced analyses and reports for his local commander and Thornton back in Washington.

In the fall of 1943 he was assigned to Salina, Kansas,[20] the headquarters of the B-29 Superfortresses, which, since coming off the production line in 1942, had shown many mechanical problems. McNamara returned from England by way of New York, and he, Margy, and their little girl made the drive to Kansas. In April 1944, just as he was promoted to major, he left to accompany some of the B-29s to India; several had crashed on their transglobal flights. His detail to Asia made him miss the birth of his second child, Kathleen, in July of that year. Meanwhile, he was assigned to Kharagpur, a British-built base ninety miles west of Calcutta with huts and thatched-straw roofs. Years later, he could recall vividly how his feet had itched with prickly heat in the constant tropical rains.[21]

As Stat Control officer for the Twentieth Bomber Command, McNamara spent the next six months analyzing and reporting on one of the most wasteful, dangerous, and ill-conceived air operations of the war: the airlift from northeastern India over the Himalayas, known as the Hump, into Kunming, China, to supply the Twentieth with B-29s, crews, fuel, and supplies, and also to supply Chiang Kai-shek's Chinese Nationalists and General Claire Chennault's Eighteenth Air Force.[22] Through the back door of the Chinese interior, air attacks would be made on Japan.

The Hump route had been conceived far away, when Chiang's people were lobbying Roosevelt for support against the Japanese. To supply the Nationalists overland, the Allies would go through impossible terrain and jungle, and would be blocked in any event by Japanese positions in Myitkyina, in northern Burma. An airlift would be more efficient, although the high command did not notice, at first, that the air route they adopted crossed 15,000-foot mountains. This meant pilots would fly at between 17,000 and 20,000 feet in freezing cold. Their slow transport planes lacked aids to navigation or arms, and the men aboard needed oxygen for the altitude. Those planes that did not get lost or meet natural obstacles were harassed by Japanese fighters; if a plane went down, the jungle terrain and few roads made getting its crew out impossible. And those who succeeded in landing their cargo knew much of it went to graft among Chiang's men. The cost of fuel alone was incredible: For every gallon that arrived over the Hump in Chungking, twenty-eight were used to get it there.

The Hump assignment suited McNamara, who computed tonnages delivered and lost, fuel consumption, pilot loss and recovery. All the elements of the operation could be quantified and analyzed to create efficiencies and reduce the terrible loss of men and planes.

It seems likely that the waste of the Hump operation galvanized McNamara. His work in India earned him a promotion to lieutenant colonel after only six months as a major, and a Legion of Merit award. Learned later said that his reports from the China-Burma-India theater were the best he had ever seen.

No one on the scene could miss how ineffectual the operation was at hurting the Japanese war effort. No one could fail to notice that it was draining precious aircraft from more vital theaters, in Europe and the Pacific. The high command considered ending the Hump flights but continued them for a time for political reasons, to avoid undercutting Chiang. The route did become safer during 1944, due to the fall of the Japanese at Myitkyina. Now that the planes could fly over northern Burma without harassment, they flew lower and more efficiently: Tonnages increased from 18,000 in June to 35,000 in October. The Hump was effectively flattened before the airlift was finally stopped.

Six months of studying and helping run the Hump operation provided a searing lesson in the wastage of war and doubtless influenced McNamara when he ran his own air war in the same part of the world, twenty-one years later.

Late in 1944, McNamara was sent to the Pacific, where he watched AAF general Curtis E. LeMay mastermind the raids on Tokyo and the bombing of Japan.[23] After a stint in the Pentagon, McNamara transferred to Wright Field, in Ohio, headquarters of the now-mechanized statistical control of aircraft worldwide.

At the height of the air war, in 1944, Thornton had produced an analysis with a surprising but statistically convincing conclusion: Arnold and Lovett should start phasing out aircraft production because the curve of demand for new planes would fall off at a predictable date. McNamara went to Wright to manage the phasedown so as to avoid wasteful overproduction — another precursor of his management of Vietnam. He and Margy and their two daughters put up in a two-room apartment in Dayton, sharing it with a fellow officer named Cling and his wife and their two babies — four small children and two couples in two rooms — as the distant war drew to a close.

Besides the big lessons Thornton, McNamara, and the other Stat Control leaders took away from their wartime experience about America's obligations to protect the weaker nations in Europe and the rest of the world from tyranny, they learned much about the practice of control. After the war Professors Learned, Ross Walker, and others at Harvard put the statistics and accounting courses under the new heading of control and taught the technique to a generation of students.

"Much of the success of the system," said the Army report on the Harvard Stat Control school, "has been due to the Harvard method which stresses 'the meaning of figures' — the power to analyze something for oneself."[24]

The "meaning of figures" and the power to analyze data for oneself gave these Stat Control officers the talent of seeing interpretations in the data not obvious to the untrained eye. The ability to format findings and present them impressively to a commanding officer ("the man who would pass judgment," in the words of the

Army report) went beyond salesmanship. It meant using the statistics to tell leaders what should be done, how to improve operations, how to win.

Statistical information was power. After Thornton got his reporting system running, once he had the Teletype data and carbon copies flowing in and mechanical equipment (big computers, using vacuum tubes, in the basement of the Pentagon and at Wright Field), he began producing analyses and reports to help Lovett and Arnold set war policy.[25]

Analysis of the combat experience of the B-24s and the B-17s showed the B-17 was better; so production of B-24s was curtailed. When the B-17s in England were scheduled to be moved to the Pacific, Stat Control analysis convinced Arnold's air staff that if B-29s were sent instead, there would be a 70 percent saving in lives, airplanes, gasoline, and ground personnel for the same tonnage of bombs dropped. The deployment plan was changed, and the B-29s were sent against Japan.[26]

Information also could help the fighting man and save lives. One project McNamara may have worked on — the records and his memory are not clear — concerned the chances of pilot survival in the air bombardment of Germany. Many men who flew were convinced that by the end of their standard tour of twenty-five missions they were sure to have been killed, because the death rate was 4 percent on any one raid. More careful computation of the odds showed that not 100 percent but only 36 percent of crews were lost in the course of twenty-five raids and that, when capture and return were taken into account, 80 percent were likely to return alive.

Alfred Sloan and the du Pont cousins' control system envisaged data flowing to the central managers: They made the decisions because only they had the necessary information. The key distinction was between "staff" men, who made policy, and "line" men, who carried out operations. In Stat Control, Thornton's men were, in effect, both of the staff and the line. They helped their local commanders and so were part of the line organization; yet they were emissaries of Arnold and Lovett in Washington, with power that derived from higher authority and the ability to report bad or inefficient performance in the devastating language of numbers.

In the Pacific, McNamara found that General LeMay was fudging figures, according to another source.[27] McNamara reported LeMay's action to Thornton, who had LeMay called on the carpet. Thornton was by then a colonel, and LeMay was a general and a hero at his peak of military fame. Yet afterward, LeMay stopped fudging.

In this capacity, the Stat Control men were like inspector generals. Before them higher-ranking officers trembled. They were brash; they told people off. Thornton believed in throwing the rules out the window to get something he wanted done. The power of information, the importance of data, the need for control and analysis, were lessons many, including McNamara, took back to their civilian lives. In this new guise *control,* often under the name *management control,* influenced a generation of American managers in the years after the war.

Shortly after the McNamaras reached Wright Field, Bob, in generally weakened physical condition, became sick with malaria. He had a polio attack in July 1945, bad enough for him to be admitted to the AAF regional hospital at the base. The base supported an enormous Stat Control operation central to the wind-down of the war. Thornton sent Charles Bosworth, another Stat Control officer, to take it over.

Bosworth found the hospital, room, and bed. But instead of the paralyzed figure he expected, he found Lieutenant Colonel McNamara bolt upright, penning orders, examining papers. Bosworth knew he was not getting this plum assignment after all. He could never displace McNamara, who was busy defying the chart on the bed, which said he had one of the scourges of the age.

Something worse had happened. A week after he was hospitalized, Margy had been riding the bus in town and felt nauseated. She got off, went to a shop, found a paper bag, and threw up in it. Worsening rapidly, she got to a hospital. She was tested and found to have had a massive polio attack. Her lower body was paralyzed, as was most of her right side.[28] Bob pulled out all the stops to save her — a sign of the gravity of her illness and of his intensifying emotional dependence on her.

The regional Army hospital could not treat so severe a case; few facilities in the country were capable of doing so. Bob got Thornton to push for Margy's admission to the Army-Navy Hospital in Hot Springs, Arkansas. The air surgeon was told that no civilian facilities were available and that "Colonel McNamara's service during the war has been of exceptional value. . . . The facts above stated make out a deserving case."[29] Finally, McNamara got Margy admitted to a rehabilitation unit in Baltimore.

He was told she would never walk again. Meanwhile, he had a big job and the two small girls to care for. At first, Marie Cling, whose apartment they had been living in, looked after her own and the McNamara children. Then he found an apartment and a babysitter, so he could work his usual twelve-hour days at the base. A week later, he noticed that some sores that had appeared on Kathleen's bottom were worse. He asked the woman if she had taken the child to the doctor, as he had instructed. She replied she had not and would not — she was a Christian Scientist. She was promptly fired. He arranged to send Little Margaret to California to be cared for by his mother, and Kathleen to Canada, where Margy's parents would stand in for the duration.[30]

All McNamara had accomplished in getting out of Annerly Road was now threatened. He had achieved a reputation in business school circles and had had a good war, as the saying goes. But now he was faced with raising two girls with a permanently paralyzed wife. His likely $4,000 yearly pay at Harvard would be consumed by medical bills.

He was decisive without much apparent soul-searching. He says that it was not the medical bills already incurred but the prospect of a life of such medical bills that made him listen to Thornton.

Thornton had concocted a plan for selling the talents of himself and nine other Stat Control men as a team to a single company. He was about to cable young Henry Ford II, who had just left the Navy to take over his grandfather's legendary but failing company. If McNamara went along, he might make $10,000 a year, although Thornton was trying for $12,000 for his men and $16,000 for himself.

McNamara's reaction was that he had planned to go back to Harvard, but Thornton, persuasive as ever, reminded him of his bills, and McNamara agreed to come along.[31]

The student of control was about to apply his lessons not in the classroom or in the laboratory of war, but to the real world.

3

The Legend of Control

MCNAMARA REQUISITIONED an AAF ambulance plane to take Margy to the rehabilitation center in Baltimore. He got himself reassigned to the Pentagon and moved in with his business school friend Eugene Zuckert. Several times a week he went to see Margy in the children's ward, which was the only space they had for her.

Her bed was at the far end of the room. A plaster cast encased her body; her right arm was propped straight up with a brace in a grotesque salute. He had to walk past the children, many of whom were out of bed and partly paralyzed.

"They had learned to drag themselves around on the floor with their hands. They were pulling themselves along on their *hands*," he said years later, crying at the memory of them.

He was teary at the memory of it all, of how threatened his wife was and what she did next. Helped by a therapist — a man with his own tragedy, who had been a victim of poison gas attacks in World War I — Margy set out to cure herself. This required day after day of exercise, calling on all her patience and persistence. "She had a tremendous will, and the example of those kids was fantastic," he said.

By February 1, 1946, when Bob reported for work at Ford, Margy was able to walk. She was brought to Michigan, as were Little Margy and Kathleen. They started a new life, with a nurse to care for the girls and a therapist for Margy. Crosby Kelly, a Ford engineer and neighbor who lived in the same apartment block, recalls coming home from work with Bob. When they entered the McNamaras' apartment, Margy would demonstrate some new feat of movement just achieved. It was a "Robert Browning–Elizabeth Barrett relationship," says Kelly.

The near miss with tragedy and Margy's successful fight to recover had one major effect on their marriage. Hitherto they had been little different from other wartime newlyweds who, when the war ended, started their marriages over again after years of separation. Many other such hasty marriages became strained in due course, but this husband and wife grew closer. Because of Margy's crisis, in the long run they would be closer to each other than to their children.

Her health created an agenda for their vacations. These became centered on physical activity, so that Bob could work off energy and Margy could test her recovery further. She retained a permanent limp, although she went on with her rehabilitation for years. She tried to ski but toppled over in deep powder and nearly suffocated. They tried climbing mountains: Margy would work up to those expeditions through months of preliminary drill. She ensured that their old Berkeley friends joined them. Vacations became ritual reunions and were always outdoors, always vigorous. They were celebrations of her triumph.

Another effect of the crisis took longer to surface and had wider implications. Margy's painful recovery deepened their optimism, their shared faith that applied human effort could achieve almost anything. Afterward, sophisticated people would remark on how naive Bob and Margy seemed; "They were so innocent" when they first moved to Washington, says a former neighbor.[1] People could be scornful of or plain frightened by Bob's naïveté when he would propose ambitious, impossible-sounding schemes. Inwardly, he and Margy could justify their optimism as rooted in Margy's experience: She had faced down nature and won.

To overcome, by force of will, a prognosis of lifelong paralysis is not the same as forcing order out of the chaos of the old Ford Motor Company or reforming the postwar American automobile market. Nonetheless, strengthened by Margy's example, Bob now tested the limits of what his own will and toughness could achieve.

At first it was chancy whether the job, or Thornton's whole plan, would work out. Back in their apartment complex, nicknamed the

Ford Foundation, the men told their wives not to unpack; they might still leave. The wives talked to each other in whispers around the complex, lest the wives of other Ford men who lived there hear what the Thornton men were saying about the place.[2]

McNamara's first sight of the Ford legend had been impressive. For their interview the previous fall, he drove with Charles Bosworth from Wright Field, in Ohio, to Detroit and the nearby city of Dearborn, where Ford was located. Purposefully, they detoured past the great Rouge plant, where a million tons of steel could be forged and transformed into thousands of cars per day.[3] Bosworth remembers how awed they both were by the great hulking buildings and the sheer scale of the place.

The next day McNamara and Bosworth had joined Thornton and the others to meet their prospective employer. Eight of the ten members of the team were present. The men stepped into the rotunda of the administration building in full uniform: a colonel, four lieutenant colonels, two majors, and one lieutenant. They were met by A. G. Coulton, of industrial relations. Last, the twenty-eight-year-old Henry Ford II appeared.[4]

His features were soft, his shoulders sloped. Yet he had the air of a "gleaming figure," in Thornton's recollection. Bosworth recalls that the cocky group felt diminished. They had hoped they would be courted; now they wanted to persuade Mr. Ford to take them.

Although McNamara had visited Wally Haas's wealthy parents while at Berkeley and had shaken hands with Lord Louis Mountbatten while in India, this was his first meeting with the rich elite of the country. Ford Motor Company had $800 million in assets; its voting stock was entirely owned by Henry and a few immediate relatives. With old Henry Ford declining and Edsel gone, Henry would soon be the de facto owner of the entire company.

Edsel had been the first Henry Ford's eldest son. He had had a difficult time establishing himself at the company, between the baronies, the rivalries, and his father's steel grip. When Edsel died, in 1943, President Roosevelt feared for the war effort. The company was the nation's third-largest defense contractor; it had $5.26 billion in wartime business. Yet old Henry Ford was senescent; his Machiavellian aide, Harry Bennett, really ran the place with his gang of hooligans. Edsel had offered hope, but was gone.

So the Navy released young Henry Ford II, Edsel's eldest son, so he could return to Dearborn. He arrived for work at the Rouge in August 1943, effectively alone, with no power except his name. He kept his head low, "moseying around," as he later said.

Henry II had a spoiled youth and a questionable record at Yale but had a good record in the Navy when he was recalled. He knew he was more suited to the role of princeling than captain of a huge enterprise that he did not understand. Although insecure, he showed some of his grandfather's raw will as he set about his task.

His first years were difficult: Bennett and his gang were still in control. Young Ford struggled to win over some of the more competent older men, but his grandfather, still company president, undercut him because he felt threatened by his self-assertion and because he hated the Pope: Henry II's wife was from a prominent Catholic family.

Finally, in September 1945, he got his grandfather and the board to cede the presidency to him. Minutes later, he marched into Bennett's office and fired him. The gesture far from ended the old order, for Bennett's men were everywhere, taking money and goods, committing hidden crimes in the plants. Young Ford wanted some men like himself in age and education, to be loyal only to him and to protect him. So he had welcomed Thornton's offer.

Thornton's men were excited by the prospect, yet they were objects of suspicion and fear. The evening after their introduction to Henry II, John Bugas, one of the old-timers at Ford and a former FBI agent now loyal to the new president, grilled the men at the Detroit Athletic Club.

Next McNamara and the others were made to take three days of IQ and psychological tests — the only time he was ever so tested. He recalls it was easy.[5] He was asked which he would rather be, a coal miner or a florist. He knew what to say. If he answered "Florist," he would be suspected of homosexual leanings. So Robert McNamara wrote down that he would rather be a coal miner. The Thornton men all had college or graduate degrees; many had been star students. They knew that there was hardly a man with a college degree in the company and that the tests were just a trick by the old guard to get something on them. They relished getting even.

McNamara and another of the group, J. Edward Lundy, were the brightest academically. "We just *killed* those tests," recalls Arjay Miller, another of the Thornton men. Some of their scores, they later said, were the highest in the history of the tests.

During their first weeks on the job at Ford, in 1946, they were given intensive orientation to overcome their complete ignorance of automobiles and the company. Each day, Miller recalls, they would visit different shops or plants. They had a blank check to roam anywhere and ask anyone anything. When the group appeared, employees sometimes shook with fear.

McNamara and the other college men, pelting employees with questions, writing down answers, pooling facts, were dubbed the Quiz Kids, after the child prodigies in a popular radio show. But the name that stuck was Whiz Kids.[6]

McNamara had a job — although it was still undefined in those first months. Now he got a teacher. In July 1946, Ernest R. Breech arrived with an office next to young Henry's and a shared bathroom. The title on his door said "Executive Vice-President."[7]

Henry Ford knew the Thornton group could not make over the company for him, no matter how cocky they were. He wanted a senior auto man to mastermind the rebuilding, someone who knew General Motors's management system. He was also hedging his bets on the Thornton group. Ford worried out loud that he was giving too much power to Breech, who was so much older and more knowledgeable than he. But Breech was the obvious man for the job; Ford showed shrewdness in spotting and winning him.

Breech was a small, muscular man with a cocky walk who liked jokes. He was the son of a blacksmith and grew up in the Ozarks. After obtaining a CPA degree in Chicago, he got a job in finance at General Motors installing the new accounting systems put in by Pierre du Pont and Alfred Sloan.

Breech rose at General Motors, making a name for himself as a troubleshooter who could take over ailing pieces of the huge empire and turn them around. He had run several kinds of manufacturing companies, including North American Aviation and Bendix. Sloan said he considered Breech "an excellent prospect for top management." Coming from Sloan, that was saying something.

Breech brought in another experienced man: Lewis D. Crusoe, who had been controller of the Fisher Body Division of General Motors and had retired. Together they persuaded several other senior GM men to come over as well. By mid-1946, Henry Ford had a varsity team.

Thornton was vexed by Breech's appointment. He had set himself up in a good house in Bloomfield Hills; he felt ready to run the company himself. Breech soon knew he had a rival in the talkative, brash Thornton. McNamara, who competed with F. C. Reith as the number-two Whiz Kid after Thornton, faced the prospect of choosing between them.[8]

At first the Whiz Kids worked out of a bull pen in the rotunda of the Schaeffer Avenue building. Then McNamara, along with the two other former teachers among the ten, Miller and Lundy, was taken by Crusoe to work on setting up a financial control system for the company.

McNamara's assignment to finance was inevitable, given his conspicuous skill with numbers. It opened the formative years of his life, years that foreshadowed, for good and ill, his pattern for the future.

Clearly he felt energized by the new challenge, as when he first got to Harvard and when he had started the Statistical Control assignment in England. Crosby Kelly, the McNamaras' neighbor, ran the orientation program for the Whiz Kids. They met at Kelly's office at seven-thirty each morning and fanned out on visits, then regrouped there at three in the afternoon to exchange notes. Kelly noticed that in those first months, McNamara's curiosity was aroused by the size of the task. "He was physically active. His motor was always running a mile a minute. . . . He was a great doer."[9]

The Ford Motor Company was an American legend, the heart of mass production, of the five-dollar day, of capitalism itself. By the time of World War II, it was building one popular car, the Ford, which struggled in third place against GM's top-selling Chevrolet and Chrysler's Plymouth, a distant second. Ford also built the Mercury, an uncertain car in the middle price bracket, and the Lincoln, a prestige car, not to mention tractors and trucks. In wartime it built aircraft, engines, and tanks.

But after his early achievements of the moving assembly line, the Model T, and the Model A, the first Henry Ford refused to modernize management or production. The company had been close to collapse until the war rescued it. By 1946 it had failed to make a profit for eight years. Even during McNamara's first months, as he rushed around for Crusoe, asking questions, getting data, analyzing them, he knew the company was losing millions every month. And it was building few new cars to sell to gain revenue, due to shortages and strikes. The place was running out of funds.

They were a sight, Crusoe and McNamara, as they moved with

determined stride around the administration building or stepped into the Rouge. Tough-looking, stocky "Lewie" in rimless glasses was followed by his lean assistant, dressed and groomed like him. After the war, many young people switched to newer plastic frames for glasses. McNamara continued with the rimless, old-fashioned kind. Crusoe parted his hair severely on one side; so did McNamara. Both had clenched jaws and carried account books, the jaw and the ledgers symbols of the fierce rationalism of the new order. Their role was reform, and their mission holy. There was too much to do, and General Motors could slaughter them anytime.

The varsity team brought "all the GM manuals" along. They stuck them up on walls and tried to implement them directly, recalls Miller, who worked alongside McNamara in those months. Meanwhile, the only certain figure the finance group knew was cash in the bank — which Miller remembers was $117 million.[10] They also knew how much was deposited in the bank each day, which wasn't much. Company funds were dwindling at the rate of $10 million a month, but because the old man had hated banks and borrowing, there was no line of credit to draw on as the cash neared zero.

They could stop paying bills, but no one knew what that would save. To figure accounts receivable and payable, the young men had two methods: One was to lay out the invoices and bills on benches and measure which row was longer; the other was to weigh the two piles on a scale. At Harvard, McNamara had been taught the principles of inventory control. But in the giant Rouge complex, they found thousands of mislabeled parts on stopped overhead conveyor belts that had probably sat there since well before the war. Now he was in the real world of uncontrolled inventory.

Crusoe called the financial situation "incredible." The old men who did accounts were no less remarkable. When the new men asked one old fellow what the financial picture would be in six months, he replied, to their horror, "What do you want it to be?" Yet to Crusoe, his Whiz Kids were little better. He remarked, laconically, that "their knowledge was from books."[11]

There were no common names for things. Ben Mills, another Whiz Kid, was assigned to compile a dictionary of terms, both for automotive parts and parts of the organization. Everyone was ordered to use the new language. Thornton and the men under him worked up a reorganization plan to divide the company into divisions and to separate staff and line, a main organizational principle in the military and at General Motors. One day, as Miller walked upstairs to lunch wearing his suit — the uniform of the new order — he questioned a man he had noticed looking out the window for several days. When the man said his job was to "watch the construction," Miller fired him on the spot.

McNamara remembers the most startling omission. No one knew what it cost to build a Ford car. Yet they needed to itemize all the costs — labor, parts, and capital — so they could start taking cost out, lower the basic price of the Ford, gain buyers, and try to compete with Chevrolet.

A further threat loomed. Because General Motors was more efficient at production, a lower-priced Ford was likely to provoke a lower-priced Chevrolet in retaliation. In its current straits, Ford was in no position to compete in a war of downward-spiraling prices.

"General Motors could have put us out of business anytime," recalls Will Caldwell, who was hired into finance in 1949 and became chief executive officer in 1983. In the early years, he says, "Bob was right to concentrate on costs."[12]

The inquiry into the elements of cost in a Ford spurred a company ritual. They took apart a sample car, piece by piece, to figure out how to reduce cost and hence price.

Years later, at the Pentagon, when the costs of his favorite airplane project, the TFX, were going through the roof, Secretary of Defense McNamara was furious with the Air Force, the Navy, and the contractors for not building it at the planned cost. Frustrated, one day he unfurled the paper plans for the plane and spread them all over the floor. He then dropped onto all fours and began crawling around on the blueprints and announcing which parts could be lighter to reduce costs. The onlooking aerospace chiefs were aghast; the incident became famous in the defense community.

In 1948, Thornton left Ford, having provoked Breech one time too many with his big ideas. In the recollection of some, McNamara loyally offered to go with him. Others recall McNamara's saying he had to stay: He was a poor boy and not a risk taker; Thornton had no job for himself, let alone one to offer McNamara.[13] Thornton went on to become the key figure in the rise of Litton Industries, a giant conglomerate that became famous for being run by the numbers in the 1960s. (It even won a contract from McNamara's Pentagon to build Navy ships in the manner of a Ford assembly line, which was a disaster.) Thornton also figured in Litton's fall, in the 1970s, which disillusioned the public with management by the numbers, when the public was disillusioned with McNamara, too. But back in 1948, their skills seemed golden. Tex had no trouble starting over. Meanwhile, McNamara had learned a lot about power from his Stat Control friend. Now he was on his own.

He helped as Breech and Crusoe, following the General Motors pattern, dubbed each operation a profit center — although in late 1946 this was a wishful term. Breech set up a central Policy Committee, so decisions could be made rationally and openly, on the basis of common information flowing up from the divisions and the line. A rough financial plan was approved in September, but Miller says they knew by the next March that it was "wrong in terms of common sense." They were still experimenting.

"Everyone worked together in the early years. The rivalries came later," says Miller. It could be fun, too. When Miller finished a tentative balance sheet, the others crowded around to learn what Ford's net position was. Remembering the old accountant they had asked before, Miller, a big Nebraskan, raised his heavy eyebrows in mock innocence and asked, "What do you want it to be?"[14]

Since they lacked computers, McNamara's numerical talents were put to good use. He insisted that data come in formatted tables. He specified what the x and y axes should be and that the data be filled in on the grid in neat rows. When someone handed in a table he would peer at it closely for a few seconds. In his mind, he was recomputing the figures.[15] Then he would plop an accusing finger down on a single number and announce it was wrong.

The author of the chart would protest that he had double-checked the arithmetic. No, McNamara would shoot back, it is wrong. Almost always, when the humiliated staffer checked again, he found McNamara's lightning computation had been right.

Meetings were meant to be the ultimate rational forum. Breech had them all reading Peter Drucker's 1946 inspirational book, *The Concept of the Corporation*, which extolled the General Motors system. Drucker, who was already a well-known business analyst, announced that meetings were forums to promote democracy; they offered middle-level men a chance to see policy being made and practice decision making themselves. This was how McNamara used them.

By temperament he was impatient and talkative, but he learned to keep quiet while each of the others around the table spent themselves debating their positions, revealing their weaknesses. Meanwhile, he created suspense by his silence. Finally, Breech or Henry Ford would turn to him and ask: Bob, has the cat got your tongue?

Then McNamara would suddenly blow onstage, shifting in his chair, exuding energy. The husky voice would start in, rolling forth the actions the group should take. The fingers of his right hand would be splayed out while the left ticked down them as he rattled off: one, two, three. When he had finished, Breech would say: Yes, Bob, those are the action points. Does anyone disagree? No? All agreed? Thank you very much, Bob. Meeting adjourned.

These were heady years for McNamara as he built and installed the financial control system under Crusoe, and revolutionary years for the company. McNamara was fascinated by the process of rooting out the old and installing the new. His greater zeal and self-righteousness set him apart from the other Whiz Kids.

Breech, in the meantime, boosted Ford's profits to a respectable level with the 1949 Ford. This was a new car, with futuristic lines, which he produced in a record fourteen months and put on the market three months before the 1949 Chevrolet came out. The car was junk and rattled. But people bought it, 807,766 of them, almost twice the number of Ford buyers the year before. Profits rose from $94.3 million in 1948 to $177.3 million in 1949. The makeover was working.[16]

They took another step to be more like General Motors and created a separate Ford Division, to decentralize responsibility for the company's chief car line. Whoever ran it would produce most of the company's cars and trucks, and would run his own product planning, assembly plants, and distribution and dealer network. Crusoe was made head of this enormous new division. In 1949, McNamara succeeded him as company controller.

In the new system, the job of controller was critical. Monies were centrally managed; budget forecasts and plans were agreed on beforehand between the division chiefs and Breech and Henry Ford, while the controller advised them. Division heads were meant to live up to their proposed performance; Breech had made their bonuses depend on it. McNamara had his first chance at formal power.

As the company inched away from financial collapse, relationships changed. Crusoe, the former finance man, became engrossed in building cars, with the old dream of beating Chevrolet and going head-to-head with General Motors. Breech, meanwhile, was worried about Crusoe's rising star. He had adopted McNamara, while Crusoe adopted McNamara's rival among the remaining Whiz Kids, F. C. Reith. As Crusoe grew more ambitious, McNamara the controller, with Breech's blessing, kept him down.[17]

Thus the legend of control was born; McNamara helped perpetuate it. The legend said the Whiz Kids made over Ford with the tools of modern finance, but this was only partly true. The Whiz Kids did not remake the company on their own. Financial controls, while very important, had not done it alone either. For years the Whiz Kids took orders from the senior auto men, Breech and Crusoe; the other senior auto men Ford hired played key roles, too. Breech's hunches had made a success of the 1949 Ford, and Crusoe's hunches would make successes of the 1952 Ford and the Thunderbird. The control system had prevented Ford from being rolled over by General Motors. But Henry Ford also contributed, by hiring these people and balancing the power centers among them.

The Whiz Kids' fame spread anyway.[18] Breech and Crusoe did not publish in management journals, as did Sloan and Drucker and the business school teachers who publicized Ford's progress in the new era. Breech's network of competent auto men was unknown outside the industry, while the Whiz Kids called their former professors, asked for more graduates, sent out the word that Ford was a good place for a bright young man with ambition. Ford finance would become famous as a management training ground.

And McNamara had played a heady role. As he gained in status, he began to change. The idealism remained, but there was less stiffness and caution. He had seen how Thornton, Breech, and Crusoe used power. Now he would play as they did.

Several other of the original ten Whiz Kids who remained at Ford, as they rose in the company, moved to Bloomfield Hills, the wealthy suburb where the top auto executives lived. Even in the late 1940s Ford's corporate culture was highly conformist, as was the industry.

A man had to live in a certain neighborhood and particular kind of house appropriate to his job. He had to join the right country club and dress according to the company code; he had to have a properly corporate wife. He could risk his career by not voting for the politicians the company supported, because the company knew how a man voted. The saying went that if there was more than one nonconformist at GM headquarters, they thought the place was going crazy.

If a man didn't wear his hat going down in the elevator to leave the office, it was noticed. One's views on every subject were observed by peers and superiors, whether they concerned the shape of the tail fins on the latest Cadillac or the loss of China to the Communists.[19] Lunch table talk, however, was often about tail fins and hardly ever about China.

Deep in the heartland, the men at the hub of the auto industry felt at the center of the country, physically and mentally. The East seemed far away; Washington was off their map; and they never discussed or studied Japan. In the long run, this conformity damaged the industry and the nation. A man was noticed if he drove a rival American car, let alone one of the few foreign ones available, and there were not many foreign cars in Detroit. America was the market and American companies served it, and influenced the oil, rubber, steel, and construction industries to boot.

Even on vacations, company men could commit career-ruining heresies. When the McNamaras descended from the plane taking them to Switzerland to ski, the regional Ford man waited for the viceroy from Dearborn with a gleaming company Ford for his use. To the man's astonishment, McNamara brushed him aside, went to the rental counter, and drove off in an Opel.[20] Horrified word of his action got back to Dearborn, but so did McNamara, who returned from such trips spouting facts and figures about the European competition.

Margy had long since refused to live in Bloomfield Hills, not wanting to play the corporate wife full-time. "We didn't want to raise our children there," McNamara says.[21]

She had more reason to care about the children's upbringing by 1950. Right after the polio, she had an abortion because the doctors said her legs were too weak to carry another child. But in 1950 she had a son — a living sign of her comeback. They named him Robert Craig and called him Craig, which was her maiden name.

Early on, they moved to Ann Arbor, which was the home of the University of Michigan and a thirty-five-minute drive from Ford headquarters, in Dearborn. Margy took up tutoring, and they joined a local Presbyterian church.

Now that Margy was well, McNamara no longer faced a lifetime of medical bills. But the psychic reward of being well paid mattered to him, for money was power. Thus he concealed how different he was in order to win favor with his seniors at the company. He tells a story that was intended to compliment Margy, but that also illustrates his raw drive to get ahead.

When he was relatively new at Ford, he had been invited to have lunch in the executive dining room, which he called the "holy of holies." He sat at one of the group tables and was introduced to a Scotsman who was possibly chief engineer of the company. The man asked him where he lived. He said he lived in Ann Arbor. "Well, I suppose there must be a lot of people named McNamara who live in Ann Arbor," he said. McNamara replied, "Yes, sir, I suppose there are." Meanwhile he was thinking he didn't know of anyone else in town with the name.

The Scotsman got very excited. He talked about a letter he had received from a woman in Ann Arbor named McNamara. The woman was outraged by the fact that Ford test cars were being driven down the public highway at speeds of 120 miles per hour and test braking in the middle of the road, and she told the company to go to hell. As the engineer went on about the explicit language this awful woman had used, McNamara sank in his chair: Only Margy could have written such a thing. That evening he confirmed she had done it. But he did not, in the "holy of holies," tell the Scotsman that the letter writer was his wife. McNamara now sees there was a "deal" in his life: "As long as I produced for the company, they didn't give a damn where I lived. . . . In recognition of that they'd let me live in Ann Arbor. It was never expressed that way but in effect it was a deal: 'We'll let you live in Ann Arbor and vote for Democrats if you will deliver for the company.' "

Although Ann Arbor, as a university town, stood apart from the popular culture, the fads of the 1950s were sweeping the chrome battlements of Detroit and Dearborn. The rounded lines of Breech's 1949 Ford were modest compared with General Motors's first postwar Cadillac. It had tail fins. These became an instant fashion; soon all the major carmakers were offering them on at least some models: small and pointed fins; wide, spreading blades; smooth, low humps; long bulges along both sides of the car. After two world wars and a depression, and once the Korean War ended, in 1953, Americans were ready for frivolity; their taste in cars became baroque.

General Motors had nearly foundered during a previous wave of prosperity, in 1920–21 and in 1924, forcing the du Ponts to intervene, reorganize, and install financial controls. Part of the legend of con-

trol, based on GM's amazing strength since then, was that management systems could protect big corporations from being ruined by
executive whims, in good times and bad. That legend — or
myth — of control was about to be tested in the new Ford Motor
Company. McNamara was about to experience the first Edsel of his
career.

"At first McNamara believed the numbers alone could give him
truth," says Will Scott, who worked for McNamara at Ford in the
1950s. "As he rose, he began to see gray areas." Crosby Kelly recalls
that McNamara tried to use "facts" and his command of figures to
stay out of company politics and above them. But he could not: The
corporate environment at Ford was too political. Kelly says it started
with Henry Ford II himself, who eavesdropped over other men's
intercoms and then confronted them with their private remarks.

As controller, McNamara was no mere bookkeeper, for his nature
was to seize the skirts of power. If he knew Breech or Henry Ford
opposed something, he would develop factual arguments against it. If
he knew they favored a plan, McNamara tempered his objections —
and sometimes fixed his statistics — to stay on the team.

He made himself into a figure of fear as he learned from tough men
like Breech how power works. Fred Secrest, one of the younger
group hired to work in finance, remembers how McNamara terrified
potential recruits. He would give them exactly two and a half minutes
for a job interview. If the candidate talked too long, failed to come
straight to the point, or tried to chat, McNamara refused to see him
again, even if he was hired by someone else in the company.

He kept his staff scared, too. They would stand by meekly when
he did his instant arithmetic to correct their tables and charts. Charles
Ellis, a long-term Ford finance man, says the rule among the staff was
that if you found an error *after* the charts were sent forward, "you
never told McNamara."

He was willing to cross even Crusoe, his former boss and teacher.
Once Lewie began to run the Ford Division, he had "big ideas about
himself," says Arjay Miller. Crusoe began hiring people by himself;
he had them eat with him, apart from the other top executives. He
talked of beating General Motors across the board.[22]

All could not be rationally decided in the new company. Even if
decisions were reasonable, some were not amicable. Crusoe believed
McNamara, now company controller, was refusing to give the Ford

Division enough production capacity to make more cars and more money. Another running battle was over the pace of modernization of the Ford plants: Crusoe wanted to do it faster; McNamara wanted to modernize slower, especially since the Korean War, at the time, required many of the plants to switch to war production, not cars. Over the next ten years, 95 percent of Ford's plants were modernized.

McNamara created considerable anger in others by his negativism. By 1953, Crusoe had become his adversary. Breech, meanwhile, wanted McNamara to be in line for the highest jobs in the company. For this McNamara would need experience in an operating division. The Continental Division had been revived in 1952, but it was tiny and the pet project of one of Henry II's brothers, William Clay Ford. The Mercury Division sold 30,000 cars per year, but it was now the province of another brother, Benson Ford. So Breech persuaded Crusoe to take McNamara as his deputy in the giant Ford Division, which in 1952 built 778,000 cars and 237,000 trucks, 75 percent of all Ford vehicles sold in the United States.[23]

There, they fought over the Thunderbird. Crusoe wanted a jaunty symbol of the carefree leisure Americans imagined they could now enjoy; the spirit of the car, he thought, required just two seats. McNamara argued stubbornly that the two-seat version would make little money, whereas a four-seat Thunderbird had a better profit margin. Crusoe just as adamantly believed that the four-seat model violated the spirit of the car. So the two-seater was approved, although at low production runs. Later, McNamara got the four-seater approved at a meeting when Crusoe was out sick. The year the four-seater was introduced, 48,482 of them were sold, matching the total number of two-seaters sold over the previous three years.[24]

The 1954 Thunderbird succeeded. Riding his triumph, Crusoe moved up in 1955 to a new supermanager job, group vice president for the Car and Truck Division. Then McNamara succeeded Crusoe as general manager of the mighty Ford Division. Crusoe now wanted to finally challenge General Motors head-on in the midprice market. At a fateful meeting, on April 15, 1955, F. C. Reith, McNamara's old rival, who had been on assignment for Ford in France, gave a stunning briefing, complete with statistics, slides, and apparent rationality. It was the culmination of a plan Crusoe had been hatching around the company for some time.[25] Ford should create a new division, a new dealer organization, and a new car, the E car, to challenge GM's

midpriced line, where Ford was historically weak. So great was Crusoe's suspicion of McNamara that he was cut out of the planning
documents.

The plan was approved, although later some noted that it went
through more on the basis of Crusoe's and Reith's advance lobbying
than the numbers on the charts. Only Breech raised a clear warning:
"This could be a great tragedy for this company if it is not a success.
It is a mistake to gamble everything."[26] But Henry Ford was for it;
he had just celebrated the firm's fiftieth anniversary triumphantly. He
hoped now Ford was ready to be another GM. The strength of
Henry II's commitment to the plan showed when he consented to
have the E car bear his father's name: Edsel.

McNamara, like Breech, believed the plan absurdly risky.[27] The
way to match General Motors was to erode its midpriced-car hegemony gradually, by building higher-priced Fords and lower-priced
Mercurys, not to force a direct confrontation.

The price of McNamara's assent was approval for his stretch Fairlane, which sold well in 1957. Meanwhile, the E Car Division was
created, and it designed a curious-looking, flashy car with a horse-
collar-shaped grille. Crusoe cut McNamara out of the reports and
papers on the project, sensing an enemy. For one thing, McNamara
was the head of a competing division. For another, he knew McNamara thought the car was a bad idea.

Crusoe had a heart attack in the winter of 1956–57; his condition
remained uncertain for some time. The E car went ahead. Finally, in
August 1957, McNamara moved up into Crusoe's superjob of group
vice president; he now had direct authority over all Ford cars and
trucks, including the Edsel. The car was in production, ready for
unveiling, and the publicity men were starting a big campaign.

McNamara was literally, then, the man who "brought" the nation
the Edsel.[28] In an August presentation to regional managers, he predicted success based on "the availability of an outstanding product at
a competitive price. Clearly we have it." At the September public
unveiling, McNamara also mentioned the car's fine quality and good
price. Immediately after, someone asked him a question about the
car. He said abruptly, "I've got plans for phasing it out."

The car was an immediate disaster. McNamara's financial controls
were meant to give early warnings of slumps in demand, so production could be cut. But Edsel sales kept falling below the pessimistic

forecasts on their charts. And the worst-case forecasts dropped lower every week. Meanwhile, quantities of finished Edsels flowed off the assembly lines each day and lined up in lots, unsold, burning costs. The new dealer organization was desperate.

McNamara's weekly memos about the unfolding situation read like ones he would later write on another disaster that fell off the bottom of his charts: Vietnam. His attempt at damage limitation even included sudden flying trips to dealerships in Ypsilanti, Michigan; Baltimore; and the West Coast.

On November 27, 1957, he noted, for example, that sales of two of the four models of Edsels, Rangers and Pacers, were so low that the company was "repurchasing" cars from dealers. Edsel Corsair and Citation models on hand were "in excess of needs." He recommended dealer bonuses for Ranger and Pacer sales — but dealer bonuses could do little when the cars were so badly built and looked so odd that hardly anyone wanted to buy them.[29]

On December 4, to the executive committee, McNamara reported Edsel deliveries at 24,900 cars, or well below the 47,600 projected for that period three months earlier. He tried to be upbeat by claiming that "every Edsel sale is a conquest sale," meaning a sale to someone who previously did not own an Edsel. But losses were projected of $20 million to $27 million on a dealer investment of $75 million. Although McNamara attempted to predict just when dealers would go out of business, he added that "many dealers may resign before their working capital is exhausted."[30]

Headquarters commissioned a buyer-attitudes survey, which was even more like Vietnam. Converting potential buyers to Edsel owners and retaining the loyalty of those who had bought Edsels sounds as hard as winning political loyalty in an Asian jungle war. Based on interviews with thirty Edsel owners and more than a hundred midpriced-car buyers, the survey said that Edsel owners were "not highly dissatisfied. . . . However they are not enthusiastic. Their liking has been won but their loyalty is in doubt." As for the hundred-plus potential Edsel buyers, "the problem is not one of indifference. It is one of resistance." The survey recommended shoring up public faith in the car's quality by "testimonials of well-known personalities" speaking "of performance in firmly confident and authoritative tones."[31]

McNamara was strung out, in rages against the Edsel people in those months. Gayle Warnock, an Edsel promotion man who believed ever after that the car could have made it but for McNamara's lack of support, recalls a meeting in late September 1957. At that point the bad reports had only started, although the results were way below expectations.

Leadership would have consisted of bolstering the morale of the dispirited Edsel men. But to McNamara these men were enemies, the other side. He made them write down their estimates of first-year profits for the car. Each wrote down a figure for losses instead. McNamara proceeded to browbeat them about the car, the lubrication system, the compass, the toggle switches, the styling, and other things. The Edsel men went away more depressed than before, and certain that the new group vice president was their enemy.[32]

On another occasion McNamara gathered the men responsible for the Edsel ad campaign for an early morning meeting. He arrived without taking off his galoshes and began walking around the room, pointing at the advertisements they had put on the wall. As McNamara started talking about the ads, he became more and more excited. He climbed up on the leather-covered chairs along the wall and began tearing off the ads and waving them as examples of what the men had done wrong. The admen, their careers already ruined, sat meekly, while McNamara stomped along the chair seats in his wet boots, ripping paper off the wall and telling them off. When it was over, the room looked as if a bunch of vandals had come through, Warnock says. Tommy Thomas, who was there, calls it "the most incredible performance by a Ford executive I've ever seen."[33]

Eventually, on McNamara's recommendation, the Edsel Division was folded into a consolidated Lincoln-Mercury Division. Those dealers still in existence were offered the chance to sell other Ford models to revive their business. A debate went on in the company about how to gracefully phase down production to save face.

Crusoe and Reith's plan to beat GM head-on cost the company $350 million or more. McNamara assigned Reith to his office and then let him go.[34] (Some years later Reith, who had been the most mercurial of the Whiz Kids, killed himself.) The dream of a new, flashy, midpriced car ended with these grim figures. And the dream that the company could be another General Motors died, too.

So the myth that a good financial control system could fend off crippling failure was smashed.[35] Ford had such controls, but the controls did not save it. The most they did was limit the damage as the disaster snowballed.

Had the Edsel been a success, Crusoe and Reith would have been heroes, Ford would have been more like General Motors, and "modern management" would have shared the credit. And the plan's critic, McNamara, would have had less chance of making it to the top of the Ford Motor Company.

It could be argued that Henry II's modern management, his new company's culture of slide shows and data-chocked briefings, had led them astray. But the Edsel was not approved on the basis of data, really, but on Crusoe's and Henry Ford's faith that the moment had come to tackle General Motors. Henry's modern management tools could not save him from poor judgment.

Another myth the Edsel disaster exposed was that Ford's modern management had ended the era of politics and baronies, the infighting that Henry Ford believed had ruined the company in his grandfather's day and contributed to his own father's failure.

But there was politics aplenty, as stories of the fiasco, which now began to circulate, showed. And one of the most proficient politicians at headquarters, Robert McNamara, now had an open field.

4

Organization Man and Mole

B OB IS A COMPANY MAN," says his old friend Willard Goodwin. Certainly as McNamara picked up the pieces of the Edsel disaster in the winter of 1957–58, there was no doubt that the new group vice president, Car and Truck Division, forty-one years old, was exercising his new, wide responsibilities fully and then some.

F. C. Reith's departure and Lewis Crusoe's heart attack eliminated McNamara's major rivals for higher leadership of the company. Ernie Breech, sixty-one years old, the architect of Ford's revival, and Henry Ford's and McNamara's mentor, was now chairman of the board. When he retired, there would be a chance for McNamara to rise further. Although Breech had been the only senior man to utter a warning about the Edsel, Henry Ford now seemed less inclined to listen to Breech. Ford, who was effectively the controlling stockholder, gave signals that he wanted to run the company himself. Pundits at Ford World Headquarters wondered whether the great Mr. Breech, who had guided them for so long, might leave sooner than they had expected.[1]

McNamara was the company man, an architect of the transformation. The fresh young lieutenant colonel had metamorphosed into the sober, hard-charging executive. He had the strongest personality of any of the remaining Whiz Kids; in many ways he seemed to personify the corporate culture of the fifties, and not just at Ford, either.

Yet all along, another side of him fought the values of the company and the auto industry. He disapproved of the industry's promotion of racing; he favored safety; he *liked* test-driving a Volkswagen Beetle. But 1958 was seven years before Ralph Nader would publish *Unsafe at Any Speed,* and racing fueled the public's appetite for faster, sportier cars. Finally, few in Detroit took seriously the odd-looking Volkswagen Beetle, the "bug" that sold just a trickle compared with Detroit's seven million cars per year.

As he became more and more the symbol and leader of the new corporate Ford Motor Company, McNamara grew impatient to impose his own agenda. Success bred further ambition, in his familiar pattern. His preferences were no secret. But they were so different from those of the age that he seemed radical, anti-Detroit, even anti-car in the sense that popular culture defined cars. Would Breech or Henry Ford go along with his schemes? Was his attempt to change the values of U.S. auto buyers a visionary act? Or hubris?

The contradictions had been apparent for some time in his private life. Even as they grew wealthy, Margy and he raised the children not to value money or ostentation. He test-drove luxury cars, but the children made him drop them off out of sight of school lest their friends see their rich mode of travel. Other Ford wives gave teas; when it came to be Margy's turn, she arranged for the ladies to tour the University of Michigan cyclotron. McNamara even met with a young lawyer named Adam Yarmolinsky, who visited him for an hour at his home in Ann Arbor in 1955 while conducting research to identify people accused under a federal loyalty rule.

McNamara resisted the "bagmen" who circulated through company offices at election time to collect political contributions for the conservative Republican local, state, and national candidates the industry supported.[2] He went on voting for Democrats like U.S. senator Philip Hart or liberal Republicans like Governor George Romney. These curious political beliefs were known in a place with little tolerance of dissent. When I once asked him about the level of personal tension he felt during the Vietnam War, McNamara replied that he had begun suffering from bruxism, a condition usually caused by stress, way back in the fifties.

"And let me tell you, Ford Motor Company was stressful," he added. During the late fifties he had extensive dental work to relieve the head pain from the bruxism. "Stress is self-stress, there's no doubt about that," he said.

⁂

His preeminence among the new generation of managers was cemented in the fall of 1959, when the Ford Falcon was introduced. It
quickly became a best-selling car: 400,000 were sold in the first year.
The Falcon was "his," developed during 1957 when he ran the Ford
Division. He hovered over it when he moved up to group vice president. The bird was plain but gracefully styled. It was smaller than
other Ford models; it was lighter, at 2,361 pounds; it had a lower
base price, of $1,624. The only accessories offered were a radio and
a heater.[3] The 1958 recession, which helped kill the Edsel, put buyers
in the mood for a no-frills car.

The Falcon's commercial success catapulted McNamara into that
charmed circle of industry leaders with a proven success, a car they
develop that makes an impact on the national psyche. Breech reached
this nirvana with his 1949 Ford; Crusoe had done it with the 1952
Ford and the Thunderbird, but he had also sponsored the Edsel.
Later, Lee Iacocca proved his special talent with the Mustang. Developing a successful car was the only way a man could make automobile history, now that the business had become so corporate, so
full of men who had to wear the same kind of hats and vote the
company slate.

The Falcon may have convinced McNamara he could reconcile the
values of the industry to his own. The Ford Division, which produced the lowest-priced models made by the company, watched the
low end of the market: Willys, Nash, and the other small American
cars, plus Volkswagen, whose price was $400 less than that of the
least expensive Ford model.

Detroit assumed that if the Beetle was cheap and plain, it must be
bought by poor people. McNamara commissioned a market study,
which found that affluent Americans like professors and doctors were
buying Volkswagens.[4] Further, there was no way even the Ford
Division could build a car that could be priced that low, given U.S.
labor and material costs. So Ford considered introducing a car that
Volkswagen owners might trade up to, one having a similar functional appeal.

McNamara's effort to produce a plain car put him in conflict with
the engineers and designers, who felt they knew the public's taste
better than this preachy young boss. In planning the Falcon, he rode
hard on the designers, engineers, and marketing men as they worked
up the new car's image and hardware. "God, he loved that car!"

remembers Will Scott, who worked on the Falcon in product planning. When a designer once showed him a mock-up of a proposed new car, McNamara remarked that it didn't move him as much as the stained glass windows in Notre-Dame. This was tactless in a place where few had gone to college, let alone visited European cathedrals.[5]

He insisted there be no convertible version of his car — although convertibles were a national rage at the time. He called Scott at home one night to ask how wide the car's door was. Too narrow to install an automatic window crank, Scott told him. McNamara was relieved, Scott recalls; he said how worried he was that someone would screw up the car by putting a useless power window opener inside the doors.

McNamara considered the cars of the time to be absurdly over-powered and ordained that his Falcon have a four-cylinder engine. Why? engineer Harley Copp was asked. Because Bob says a four-cylinder engine costs $13.50 less than a six-cylinder engine, Copp replied. McNamara was getting out weight to keep the costs on budget and get the car he wanted. But small engines were heresy to engineers at Ford and in the industry. It took none other than Delmar S. Harder, the senior operations man whom Breech brought in in 1946, whom even a Whiz Kid could not refuse, to make McNamara agree that likely Falcon buyers might be driven away by fears that the car was underpowered. Thus the Falcon got a six-cylinder engine after all.[6]

He rigidly budgeted in advance the volume and weight of each part of "his" new car. Scott remembers coming up with a plan to enlarge the capacity of the fuel tank from ten to fourteen gallons in the name of the social good of holding more fuel. But this put the tank over its weight budget. McNamara was offended: The weight of the added fuel and bigger tank would add cost. Scott countered that it would mean Falcon drivers got more transportation and would need to stop only to eat or go to the bathroom. Besides, the tank would not be heavier, since most drivers kept their tanks only 60 percent full. The two argued over this; Scott thought his arguments were as rational as McNamara's.

Then the boss reached inside his jacket and pulled out an envelope. Look, McNamara said. Let's decide this by seeing which one of us has a bigger paycheck. It was hardly an appeal to reason, but it decided the fuel tank issue — for good.[7]

McNamara's quantitative discipline drove the engineers and de-signers crazy, but it also ensured that his cars made money. This approach worked for American cars in the fifties, although not later, because their basic engineering was fixed, the last real innovation having been automatic transmission in 1948. In the car business, a single part change could cause rattles in millions of cars out on the road; it was one of the most technologically conservative industries in the country. Scott says, "He had a discipline few of us had, to keep the car simple, to keep the car low-cost . . . fuel-efficient, low-weight. He wanted it to have the spartan attributes that were a mark of his life and his way of thinking and his personal values."[8]

And McNamara was convinced of his righteousness. By building a car with his values, he could persuade others to adopt them. He was willing to build gaudier cars like the Thunderbird and Fairlane, which mass taste demanded. But he wanted, he told me, to "gradually try to shift at least a portion of the market to more efficient products which would provide equivalent transportation at lower cost."

McNamara admits that the Falcon was a car designed to his taste, which he claims was the public's taste, too. "I said: Look. Tastes are changing, they should change in the interests of society. For God's sake, let's not let a vacuum develop that will be filled with foreign cars. Let's fill it ourselves. Let's develop a car that will make money and at the same time provide a social good."

However the Falcon fitted his agenda to change Americans' values, many observers in Detroit did not miss the paradox of McNamara's creation. He *was* the system in the new company; he personally drove the machinery of control, which meant husbanding assets to protect against surprise or bad luck. But this new corporate leader, who helped build a modern company with modern financial controls, marketing, and distribution, produced as "his" car a throwback to the first Henry Ford's Tin Lizzie.[9]

Overall, what McNamara and Ford were striving for in the 1950s was growth, based on the phenomenal rise in Americans' real incomes since 1945. As people bought houses in the new suburbs, lawnmow-ers for their new lawns, and washing machines for their families, they needed transportation, too. The issue, he said in talks around the company, was how much of this growing pie the auto industry in general and Ford Motor Company in particular could capture.[10]

Financial control was an ideal tool for reaching deeper into American pocketbooks. Cost controls allowed Ford to regulate its investment in building a car. Another element of the system was asset control, which the du Pont cousins and Alfred Sloan had pioneered and the first Henry Ford had ignored at great peril. Finally, McNamara invented "revenue control," according to official historians of the company.[11] This meant gathering revenue most efficiently by concentrating selling efforts on goods with high profit margins.

Radios were an example. Originally, Ford installed radios in cars when it guessed people wanted them and were willing to pay extra for them. Then it discovered that a very large number of buyers wanted car radios. Producing more radios lowered the unit cost of making them. So Ford began promoting radio sales. The number of Ford cars equipped with radios thus rose from 37 percent in 1949 to more than 70 percent by 1955. Following a similar effort, by 1955 heaters were installed in 90 percent of Fords, up from 55 percent in 1949.

A fact of life in the auto industry — and one that would influence McNamara's thinking and management style for the rest of his career — was the importance of common parts to efficiency and profits. Ford necessarily had a few basic products, which were very expensive to retool. These were the chassis and shells from which all Ford, Mercury, and Lincoln models, in varying combinations, were made. Yet the age was Veblenesque: Buyers relished being offered endless variations of trim, upholstery, and accessories.

In his professorial way, waving a pointer before slides in his company talks, McNamara termed the growing demand for distinctive goods the "individualization" of the market.[12]

And he capitalized on it. Station wagons, for instance, could be built on standard Ford bodies; they were like an accessory because most Ford buyers bought a station wagon in addition to their regular sedan. Families invested in a station wagon instead of a more expensive TV set or home freezer and thus this revenue to the company was taken away from other consumer goods. Station wagons also had excellent profit margins.

In 1957, the Ford Division under McNamara brought out a two-tone, swept-back car called the stretch Fairlane. It was seventeen inches longer than the regular Fairlane, and buyers were offered more accessories than in any previous Ford car. Sales took off; that year Ford beat Chevrolet. Yet the stretch Fairlane cost only fifteen dollars more to build than its predecessor — the radio, whitewall tires, tinted glass, electric clock, and two-tone finish were all add-ons.[13]

As at Harvard and in Stat Control during the war, *control* was both a personal motto and a management approach. Ford's management controls made McNamara's language of numbers universal in the firm and required that others use it, too. A new language of finance developed, which was now employed to run the company. McNamara pretended never to be swayed from the answers given by his numbers and analyses — except when Henry Ford wanted something different than he did. The role of high priest of financial control suited McNamara. At Ford, as in his childhood, resources were to be husbanded; saved resources, carefully used, would bring him more power.

He had many strengths as a manager. Lee Iacocca, whom McNamara brought to the Ford Division after the salesman's spectacular performance in the Allentown, Pennsylvania, region in 1956, recalls how McNamara taught him to discipline his profusion of ideas. You are a great salesman, McNamara said. But we are about to spend one hundred million dollars on this. "Go home and put your ideas on paper. If you can't do that, you haven't got anything."[14]

McNamara also knew he did not know the sales aspect of the business. He recruited to headquarters Charles Beacham. Beacham was a legendary car salesman, a Virginian who was said to be incapable of adding a bean. But he was unparalleled in his field. Beacham tutored Iacocca and, separately, his boss in the Ford Division, McNamara.

Beacham and McNamara would drive around Ann Arbor on weekends and park anonymously opposite different dealerships. They would sit for hours watching the dealer at work. Beacham would show McNamara how to determine whether the dealer was good, how he used his staff, how he treated customers, how much money he grossed a year, all by watching from across the street.[15]

McNamara seemed a questionable figure to many, however, as he rose, displaying a ruthless drive for winning and for power. He could be generous toward men like Iacocca and Beacham, whom he liked. But he habitually treated everyone else like adversaries to be bullied or manipulated. His meetings with dealers were usually disastrous. He regarded them as weak and corrupt. In his mind, they were missing out on a $170 million market in servicing the millions of new Fords around the country. The number of Fords on the road had increased as postwar sales grew, but Ford dealers' income from re-pairs stayed level. Buyers would come back to their dealers for ser-vicing if the dealers would pull their socks up, he thought.[16]

McNamara was notorious among the design staff, the creative people who wanted artistic sympathy, not math. He once ordered a new car by specifying the weight, dimensions, proposed price, and so on. But what do you want the car to *be?* the designers asked. How should it feel? He had no answer.

His critics were convinced that he purposely wore the Phi Beta Kappa key across his chest on days when he wanted to be particularly fearsome; it glittered there like a small, poisoned dagger. He humil-iated those who could not pick up his language of numbers. He could use "facts" for intimidation more easily than for reasoned exchange. And his instinct of treating all but a chosen few as antagonists, of slighting people who were really his partners in a common effort, hurt cooperation, morale, and his claim to leadership.

He was, in a way, the epitome of a bean-counting manager who understood nothing about engineering cars. Neil Waud, a manufac-turing man, was once explaining to McNamara that, contrary to his wishes, they could not speed up production in the plants, because, among other reasons, the paint ovens were old, dated, and too small for present-day cars. The time required to bake the paint was a bot-tleneck to meeting his production goals. McNamara countered: Why not build the chassis in two main sections, paint them separately, and then weld them together? Waud was appalled that anyone could think a welded chassis would hold together on the road.[17]

The price of control enforced by such a man was fear. Scott recalls meetings held by the product planning committee in the Ford Divi-sion with McNamara every Friday at four-thirty. He was always forceful, yet to run the division, McNamara needed to be told hon-estly what could be built, what could not, what the real problems would be. He kept pressuring them: Are you for this? That? They kept saying yes.

One evening he got a call from Scott, who warned him that not a soul on that committee agreed with him on a particular issue, but they were too afraid to tell him so. Scott remembers that McNamara seemed "dumbfounded" at this.

He raised the issue again at the next week's meeting. But he could not stop himself from being pushy once again. He ticked off the points in favor on the fingers of one hand; he argued loud and hard.

Then, thinking to uncover objections, he asked for a count of who was for and who was against. As he went around, each man said he supported the idea. Again. McNamara looked at Scott as if to say: Are they all lying?

How could McNamara run the company if people didn't tell him the truth and give him true information, whether it came in statistical form or not? On the other hand, how could *he* run the company without making subordinates so frightened they dared not tell him the truth? In 1959, young Robert McNamara did not understand how his system could lead him astray.

The management controls that McNamara, the other Whiz Kids, Breech, and Crusoe installed at Ford and used to run it so profitably were deeply flawed, as would be clear in the long run. But at the time, McNamara and the others rode the crest of a cultural change in American industry, as giant manufacturing companies were taken over by the college set and young men flocked to business schools to learn the secrets of quantitative management. At Ford, McNamara's fellow Whiz Kid J. Edward Lundy built up the new, powerful finance department and made it a training ground for ambitious younger men with economics or business school degrees. Graduates of Ford finance became the entire upper echelon of the company and filled its most senior jobs through the 1980s. Ford was less closed than other big auto companies, so Lundy sent his fledglings into the larger world of American industry, where finance became dominant also.[18]

That some people were swept aside — particularly those in the old engineering culture from which the automobile industry had sprung — seemed not to matter at the time. The engineering of automobiles was fixed, and innovation seemed unimportant. The older engineers were not managers; many were not even bright in the sense that the fresh-cheeked college men were.[19]

McNamara valued quality in cars more than some of his MBA-holding successors. The Falcon was relatively free of the defects that plagued other Ford models of the era. Later, when he sensed the growing consumer preference for higher-quality European cars, McNamara pushed to have the 1960 Lincoln Continental offered with an unprecedented 30,000-mile warranty. This meant they would have to try to build a car that could run trouble-free for 30,000 miles.[20] Mc-

Namara, who seemed the stereotype of the bean counter, was not blind to the growing demand for quality, in fact.

His system, based on Alfred Sloan's, was designed to control resources, assure profits, and decentralize operating responsibility while centralizing planning and control. It did some things well: It redirected resources and effort on a large scale; it maintained financial discipline among the parts of a far-flung and disparate company. It monitored and controlled "throughput": production figures from the assembly lines, and figures showing vehicles distributed, dealer performance, and sales.

Power in the system was concentrated at the top.[21] Only top managers, the gospel went, had enough information to make decisions. And that information was expressed in the common language of finance. The system disenfranchised those who were so important in the early stages of American manufacturing, the foremen and plant managers. Instead of being creators and innovators, as in an earlier era, now their jobs depended on meeting production quotas. They lost any stake in stopping the line and fixing problems as they occurred; they lost any stake in innovation or change. The problems of U.S. mass manufacturing appeared in what on the shop floor was called rework, those vehicles that came off the line too defective to be sold and were set aside for rebuilding. (Many years later, when the Japanese demonstrated an alternative and superior system of mass production that empowers workers and builds cars right the first time, U.S. auto plants with hundreds of cars in rework would become a hallmark of how U.S. managers forced the line to keep running, no matter what.)

Workers became powerless to stop the line or to report problems to superiors; this lack of initiative and low morale, forced on them by the system and top management, proved to be the Achilles' heel of the giant U.S. auto industry. This weakness would allow first the Europeans and then the Japanese to bring the U.S. auto industry to its knees.

In later years, top managers exploited the system of controls for short-term financial gain. After Ford made its first public stock offering, in 1955, the pressure grew to bolster quarterly dividends by manipulating financial data. Such pressure became endemic in publicly held companies in the United States in the 1960s and later, and is a recognized flaw of American manufacturing firms today.

Does this history make Robert McNamara the inventor of the notorious "MBA syndrome" and of the addiction to short-term profits and poor-quality products, for which critics now flail U.S. industry?

The answer is complex. McNamara's personal experience with management controls was *not* centered on short-term profits. He employed them to reorganize a failing institution on a massive scale, for without these controls, the company almost surely would have failed. Subsequently, he and his colleagues used the system to assure a steady flow of profits in fair weather and foul, even to limit losses from the Edsel. He no doubt thought of Sloan's system as a means for radical and enlightened reform, and for wresting stability from the jaws of the chaos of old Henry Ford's company.

Are the perpetrators of a revolution responsible for all that flows from it? McNamara and the other Whiz Kids, as well as Breech and Crusoe, were a transitional generation of managers, moved by the hardships of the Depression to stabilize and control the untrammeled forces in American industry, which had no competition at the time.

But in McNamara's later years at Ford, he and the system displayed the blindness and arrogance that marked the next era of the American auto industry. He used the system as a source of raw power and to exercise his obsessive interest in saving money. It is not clear that he understood how his system was flawed, for, although he was unusually aware of the threat posed by European carmakers and said the answer was for Ford to improve quality, he had also helped make possible the rout of engineers and innovators — men who knew the product — and thus began setting the stage for the later tragedy.

Meanwhile, in 1958–60, as McNamara rose higher in the company, he developed some radical notions for changing Ford, and the automobile business. By late 1960 he was a different man from the twenty-nine-year-old who strode into the rotunda in the uniform of a lieutenant colonel almost fifteen years before. With the years he became angry at how the Big Three — Ford, General Motors, and Chevrolet — manipulated the public, as outraged as Margy that Ford was test-driving and braking cars on the interstate between Dearborn and Ann Arbor.

When he was in the Ford Division, McNamara was "annoyed" and "worried," he told me, by General Motors's promotion of stock car racing. It "appealed to the worst in the American consumer: to their desire for speed," he said.

There was a mad momentum to the race for the hottest car each year. General Motors would advertise Chevrolet as the hottest; then Ford would fix up its car and advertise that it could beat Chevy. Meanwhile, of course, the cars that were raced were little like those in the showroom. Henry Ford abetted this. "Henry Ford liked hot cars," McNamara says, but it was "the wrong way to sell automobiles. So I went to Ed Cole's office in the General Motors Building [Cole was chief of the Chevrolet Division and later president of General Motors] and I said, Look, Ed, this is a lot of damn foolishness. . . . We're appealing to the wrong basis in the buyers. . . . Let's agree that neither of us will advertise speed. He wouldn't agree to it, so I went back and bought the 'hottest cars' and 'hottest drivers' . . . and at least we maintained our own."

He also wanted Ford to promote safe cars, even wanted to make safety a selling point, a positive feature with the public. He got the company to grant $200,000 to Cornell University Medical College for crash-injury research. He says he asked General Motors to come in with Ford to fund it, but GM refused. Also at his urging, Ford sponsored a two-day forum on safety for experts and industry in September 1955.[22]

McNamara made safety an advertising point for selling the 1956 Ford and offered seat belts as an option. His motives for leading on the safety issue were the same as those for leading with basic transportation in the Falcon: He believed he could educate the public to want what he wanted and create a shift in public taste.

When his 1956 "safety car" had been on the market five days he was bullish ("We can report this afternoon that public acceptance has exceeded all our expectations"). But after a banner year in 1955, Ford sales for 1956 proved to be a bust, due in part to the unfamiliar, grim ad campaign. McNamara concedes that "safety is difficult" to sell even today. But he denies his safety campaign hurt sales in a major way: "The reason it didn't go well in 'fifty-six was not that we pushed too hard or too early [on safety], but rather that we had a car — the 1956 Ford — that had less appeal than its competition, the Chevrolet."

Most people in the industry, however, were convinced the safety campaign hurt Ford sales in 1956. It was not an experiment the industry was to try again — not for a decade, until after Ralph Nader and government intervention forced the industry to install, and advertise, seat belts.

As the discouraging sales figures started coming in, McNamara's assistant Paul Lorenz heard a rumor that McNamara had been fired. Lorenz wondered whether to go into McNamara's office and console him. The next day, McNamara was gone. He turned out to have left for a winter vacation. But Lorenz noticed it was a diplomatic time for him to be out from under Henry Ford's eye.[23]

In the spring of 1955, when he would have been pushing his plans for the safety campaign at headquarters, McNamara gave a commencement speech at the University of Alabama. His text was on the same themes he had written about to Cal president Sproul and Provost Deutsch his first weeks at Harvard: the pursuit of profit versus the need for higher ethics in business.

Headquarters forbade McNamara to give the speech; speeches on nonconformity were not encouraged in Dearborn. He gave it anyway and could have read it in the *Congressional Record* on June 16, courtesy of Alabama senator Lister Hill. The dangers of McCarthyism, no doubt discussed in Ann Arbor if not in Dearborn, and McNamara's own bucking of headquarters were the context in which he warned of "grave pressure to conformity" in society and on young people entering business.

> In any corporation, and we [at Ford] are no exception, there is a certain inertia, a tendency to discourage fresh thought and innovation. . . . It takes a degree of moral courage to withstand that pressure, particularly when you are in competition from half-a-dozen eager beavers who eagerly spout the party line.

And he added, possibly with his own situation in mind:

> Sometimes, unfortunately, it also takes a certain dexterity to espouse an unpopular view and still keep your place in the pecking order certain.
>
> The test of your generation will not be how well you stood up under adversity, but how well you endured prosperity.[24]

The hazards of prosperity were mentioned obtusely in remarks he planned to give at the opening of Ford's huge new plant in Mahwah, New Jersey, that June: "In times like these we must be ever more careful not to let the advantages of individual initiative and free choice slip away simply because we are too comfortable and secure to resist."[25]

He criticized the industry again, in a speech to the governors of

New England in November 1958. The country was still in the after-shock of Sputnik; American rockets were failing on the launchpad; and the Soviets were crowing about Communist world domination. Curiously, McNamara's proposed answer to the Communist threat was to improve American productivity. The statistics showing productivity gains in the fifties, he said, masked labor settlements that did not increase worker productivity; management's productivity should be measured, too. He was clearly concerned that the terms on which American business was being conducted would hurt productivity in the long run.[26]

The following March, in a talk titled "Planning and Control" and given at Harvard, McNamara criticized "the lack of imaginative direction in many segments of American business today." Business needed to recognize that "the future will be different from the past," and planning needed to be based on "careful" forecasts and "an adaptation of one's product program . . . to the forecasted changes before they occur."[27]

What he forecast for the auto industry was long-term competition from European cars, which would be built with higher quality and at lower cost than American cars, if American carmakers did not respond soon. This was the blunt thrust of a speech he would give in November 1960.

Henry Ford had finally moved Breech aside and taken the position of chairman himself. Then he had announced in August that McNamara would become the company's next president, a post he assumed on November 9, 1960. The prize was now McNamara's. It was unclear whether Henry Ford realized that his quintessential organization man was also the company's chief radical. McNamara says Ford saw his November speech ahead of time, although he may not have understood its "implications."

At the time, McNamara was promoting a sequel to the Falcon called the Cardinal, scheduled for 1963. The Cardinal was to be smaller and lighter than the Falcon and would compete head-to-head with Volkswagen and other low-priced European imports. The only Japanese cars then in America, practically, were a bargeload of Toyotas that had just reached California. The threat Detroit admitted to was European; the Japanese "invasion" was a decade away.

The Cardinal was to be plain and functional in style. Henry Ford didn't like it much; nor did Iacocca, who by this time had been made general manager of the Ford Division on McNamara's recommendation. The most significant thing about the Cardinal was that it had to be coproduced in Europe, with some parts built in England, and engine and transmission built in West Germany, to make the cost competitive.

Some at Ford may have considered the Cardinal a one-shot car, another experiment of McNamara's like the Falcon. McNamara regarded it as the leading wedge of a new direction the company had to take.

He revealed his vision of the future of Ford — and the industry — on November 21, 1960, at the Greenbrier Hotel, in West Virginia, a retreat of top Ford executives, before the senior managers, including Breech and Henry Ford.[28]

> The industry can take product actions which will push the bottom of the product line down to meet foreign competition, at the same time bettering its relative cost position through design and processing improvements.
>
> In looking to the 1960's, we must face the fundamental question of what actions can the United States automotive industry take to improve its competitive position relative to foreign producers or at least to avoid further deterioration in that position. Should the trends continue [European labor costs declining sharply relative to American labor costs through 1970 in the industry] . . . our domestic passenger car market will be invaded a second time by foreign producers and the second invasion will not be limited to VW type products.

The Greenbrier speech — not previously published — laid out a complete program for meeting the challenge of the imports, of which the Cardinal was but the beginning. McNamara also proposed evolving the company's two car divisions, Ford and Lincoln-Mercury, to compete with each other in all parts of the market, since the market would stay fluid and consumers would become choosier than they had already been. Finally, he complained about the dealers again, criticizing their and the industry's entire approach to sales. It could take nothing for granted, he told them. He quoted a writer named Theodore Levitt to make his key point: For the industry to survive against imports, cars had to be "marketed," not just "sold." Levitt had written:

> Selling focuses on the needs of the seller, marketing on the needs of the buyer. Selling is preoccupied with the seller's need to convert his

product into cash; marketing with the idea of satisfying the needs of the customer by means of a product and a whole cluster of [associated] things.

McNamara warned — before this intimate group of Ford executives in November 1960 — that the American auto industry could go the way of the American railroads if it failed to ask, long-term, what American buyers really wanted. Quoting Levitt, he said: "An industry begins with the customer and his needs, not with a patent, a raw material, or a selling skill. Given the customer's needs, the industry develops backwards, . . . to creating the things by which these satisfactions are in part achieved." Not only was McNamara's description of the problems facing Ford and the auto industry eventually proven true, the solution he proposed in 1960 was the very one industry leaders turned to in the 1980s — once they were almost beaten.

Because McNamara would leave Ford in December 1960, the question remains: Could the industry have taken a different path had he stayed? The Cardinal and McNamara's plan of November 1960 remain intriguing. The car's principal features — smallness, light weight, fuel efficiency, higher quality — were the attributes American buyers found in imported cars and a main reason for the shift away from Detroit in the 1970s. If McNamara had stayed, says Arjay Miller, a fellow Whiz Kid who served as Ford's president soon afterward, the Cardinal would have been produced, and Ford would have been well positioned against the imports. The industry would have been different, Miller says.

Miller fought Iacocca when, after McNamara left, Iacocca took one look at the Cardinal and decided it was a bean counter's dream but hardly right for the 1960s. He killed it.[29] Henry Ford, who hadn't cared for the Falcon, made no move to save the Cardinal.

James O. Wright, who was group vice president at the time and had worked for McNamara, says the Cardinal had to be stopped. True to Whiz Kid form, Wright says "the numbers didn't work" in the end. They could not build the Cardinal cheaply enough to truly compete with Volkswagen. In other words, the race with VW was already lost.

"McNamara would have had to kill it. He wouldn't have ignored those numbers," Wright says, discounting McNamara's subjective side.[30]

For better or worse, American car buyers' tastes changed in the early 1960s. They may not have bought a Cardinal if one had been built. McNamara thought he was changing public taste with the Falcon; but the plain Jane sold well because of the recession. By the go-go sixties, Americans were snapping up sportier models, Chevrolet Monzas and Ford Mustangs. Iacocca put a convertible hood on McNamara's Falcon, making McNamara, who was then in Washington, furious. The world was not ready for his plans to change it.

II
THE PROMISE

5

Sons of the Morning

THIRTY-FOUR DAYS after McNamara won the presidency of Ford Motor Company, he left for a wider horizon, for greater good and greater power.

Ernie Breech, chairman of the board, should have been the man to whom Henry Ford turned after the Edsel came out and after old Lewie Crusoe, who had tied his rising star to it, suffered a heart attack and left. One of McNamara's jobs when he moved into Crusoe's position of group vice president was to limit damage from the $350 million Edsel disaster. And instead of looking to Breech, Henry began consulting privately more with McNamara. He reassured Breech that he was just "using" McNamara more, but Breech knew he was being upstaged.[1]

McNamara's promotion to group vice president coincided with the opening of a new, glass-enclosed, twelve-story building, grandly called Ford World Headquarters. In fact, the crowded old building on Schaeffer Avenue had been better suited for communication and teamwork; on the twelfth floor of Ford World Headquarters, elevator doors opened on a carpeted reception area with security guards. Glass House, as the new building was known, symbolized what the company's historian Allan Nevins called the triumph of collective, rational decision making over individual executive whim.[2] The irony of Glass House was that its secluded offices and hushed halls lent themselves to secret meetings and plots.

More and more McNamara cut a figure around the twelfth floor of

Glass House. He test-drove a luxury Lincoln to work. He wore the corporate uniform of starched white shirt, dark suit, and narrow dark tie. His thick, slicked-back hair gleamed like the hood of a showroom car; his wire-rimmed spectacles set him apart and gave the baby face a look of authority. His jawline was square and determined, but the face was asymmetrical, more so when twisted with anger.

McNamara was not bigger or stronger than other men, but he could by force of personality make himself seem larger, glare down an adversary, wither someone with coldness. He talked in lists, showing off his organized mind. But colleague Will Scott remembers a rare moment of humor when, in a meeting, McNamara rattled off his points, ticking down the splayed fingers of his right hand with his left index finger — "one," "two," "three," down to "six" — and then tried to hit a nonexistent sixth finger, looked down, and caught himself. Everyone laughed, including McNamara.

Henry Ford loved McNamara's organization; it reassured him. The two men would come down the hallway of the twelfth floor, Ford would ask him a question, and McNamara would stand almost at attention, rattling off the alternatives. Henry Ford's thick features would soften as he glanced at another listener with pride, as though wunderkind McNamara were a new toy.[3]

McNamara had spent fourteen years being obedient to Henry Ford. Although he was supposed to embody the rationalism of the remade company's management, he knew where his bread was buttered. McNamara would oversee every detail of the clay model of a new car, but if his boss showed any hesitation upon seeing it, he would quickly say, "Mr. Ford, the reason you don't like this car is that it's one and a half inches too short and we're going to fix that right away."[4]

McNamara's ability to run the company — and to please — paid off. "Ernie, I've graduated," Henry Ford is supposed to have said to Breech in the summer of 1960.[5] He eased Breech out and took for himself the job of chairman of the board. On November 9, 1960, Robert S. McNamara became president of Ford Motor Company, the first nonfamily member to hold the post.

McNamara felt great inner tension as he moved closer to the prize and gained influence on the twelfth floor. Since Harvard Business School he had scorned the "chase for the almighty dollar," but now he was the master of a profit-making machine. He was absorbed in the financial control of the company and in extracting what he wanted from the production lines. The irony was that by 1960, at Ford and General Motors, "progressive and scientific management" was producing the gaudiest cars in history.[6]

In 1958 a little-known writer for *Fortune* magazine, who was working on a book about American society, made a lunch appointment with McNamara. People in the know had told him McNamara was brilliant, a company man who could think and discuss modern corporate organization. Landing in Detroit, the writer tactfully rented a Ford car and drove to Ford World Headquarters. After a thrilling hour-long lunch at which the former professor, who now ran the third-largest manufacturing enterprise in the country, talked impressively, McNamara walked his guest to the parking lot.

Both men could not help noticing that the product of all this erudition was a ghastly cerise and yellow object with tail fins, padded dashboard and steering wheel, and chrome decoration along the sides. McNamara turned sheepish. "Not all matters of design are handled as intelligently as we allowed you to think at lunch. We always have to think of the taste of the consumer," he said to the writer, whose name was John Kenneth Galbraith.[7]

McNamara was mindful, as he gained prominence in the world of automobiles, of his preoccupation since business school with the ethical dimension of business. To spend his life in meetings debating the number of ounces of chrome to be stuck to the sides of 1.8 million vehicles or the number of seats in a Thunderbird was not a virtuous enough job for this Berkeley idealist. Crosby Kelly, who had introduced the Whiz Kids around the company in 1946, when the young men's salaries were $12,000 per year, remembers McNamara's confiding that he hoped to save $100,000 and then go into public service.[8] If McNamara were to make it to the top of the company, he would be one of the highest-paid executives in the world. To boot, Henry Ford had authorized the board's compensation committee to award blocks of Ford stock to the top executives. With each step higher, McNamara could receive ever-more-valuable stock options, too. But as he moved from middle-class insecurity to the safety of wealth, McNamara became restless.

He could solve his inner conflict by using his growing influence to redirect Ford Motor Company's long-term goals to purposes that served society, in his view. Already he had set his sights on Europe, where he wanted the company to coproduce smaller, more functional cars to serve consumers more rationally and stall Volkswagen's advance in the U.S. car market. He had developed a master plan, announced at the Greenbrier meeting just after he became president. But the odds of being free to carry out his plans were lengthened by the growing impetuousness of Henry Ford. Ford's marriage was jeopardized, McNamara knew, because he had started a serious affair with a blond-maned Italian, Cristina Vettore Austin. After firing Breech, he became more dogmatic, saying things like "I am captain of the ship and I intend to remain captain as long as my name is on the bow."[9] Then there was the new constraint of Ford Motor Company's dividends to public shareholders, ever since it began offering stock to the public in 1955. The need to keep producing quarterly dividends could put McNamara's plan to redirect the company at risk.

McNamara's elevation took place at a pivotal moment. In 1960, Allan Nevins and Frank Ernest Hill closed out their monumental three-volume history of the company, which glorified the entwined triumphs of Ford and America, from old Henry Ford the inventor, to the moving assembly line, to the five-dollar-a-day wage for workers, to the wonderful mass-production machine that turned the tide of two world wars and brought postwar prosperity. The historians called Ford a "striking example" of modern America, in which "wealth was better distributed; collective controls had replaced individual power; the social conscience was more sensitive, and government, business and philosophy all felt a larger responsibility for social welfare."[10]

The secret of Ford's success was its rational, modern management, which Ford's new president, Robert McNamara, embodied, said Nevins and Hill. "Individualism is dead," they proclaimed. In fact, neither Glass House, nor McNamara's financial control system, nor the company's management was what Nevins and Hill said. The market was shifting; Henry Ford's whims were starting to rule; individualism, in the form of plots and subplots, was rising again. With unwitting prophecy, Nevins and Hill also quoted the Ford Division chief, Lee Iacocca, who would play a key role in the firm's changing fortunes later on, as saying, "Everyone is playing by ear."[11]

Nevins and Hill's exuberance matched the feelings of many Americans in 1960. The nation was rich and dominated the world economy in a way that was almost unimaginable in the thirties.[12] The growing middle class was moving to the new suburbs as wages rose. Young families were turning the pages of Benjamin Spock's *Common Sense Book of Baby and Child Care* to fathom how to bring up their toddlers. But there was almost nationwide panic after October 4, 1957, when the Soviet Union launched Sputnik, the first man-made earth-orbiting satellite. Sputnik meant the Soviets had rockets powerful enough to carry nuclear bombs to the American heartland in half an hour. And Soviet leader Nikita Khrushchev, who had promised the West "We will bury you," banged his shoe on the table at the United Nations.

Not only Sputnik revealed the unease that lay beneath the surface. Liberals had been appalled at how Dwight D. Eisenhower, the organizer of the Allied reconquest of Europe and president since 1953, had stood aside while Senator Joseph McCarthy hunted supposed Communists in government and ruined innocent men with unproven charges. Now likable President "Ike" seemed to have been lax in spurring America's missile program, and the Communists seemed to be in the lead.

Few issues dominated public awareness and politics as much as the fear of impending Communist victory in the all-out cold war that then raged. Eisenhower was in fact ahead of his time in searching for arms control; his secretary of defense, Thomas Gates, insisted there was no "missile gap." Neither of these positions won much credence, however, and as the 1960 presidential contest approached, Democratic senators Stuart Symington, Lyndon Johnson, and John Kennedy played on these fears. Adding authority to the charge of laxity was Harvard professor Henry Kissinger. "There is no doubt the missile gap exists," he said. [13]

The Republicans nominated Vice President Richard Milhous Nixon. On August 1, in Los Angeles, the Democrats nominated Massachusetts senator John F. Kennedy. Kennedy picked Senate majority leader Lyndon Johnson as his running mate; he needed the well-known southern vote getter to balance his New England political base and his drawbacks as a young, relatively inexperienced, and Catholic candidate. Kennedy's family-based political machine, including his brother Robert and his brother-in-law Sargent Shriver, faced an uphill fight.

Nixon, to distance himself from Eisenhower's supposed weakness on defense, called for greater defense spending and an acceleration of the U.S. missile program. Kennedy hammered hard for a stronger national defense and a more active foreign policy. As for the missile gap, "I say only that the evidence is strong . . . that we cannot be certain of our security in the future any more than we can be certain of disaster."[14] America must "get moving again" and have a "defense second to none." Kennedy squeaked by Nixon in the election, on November 8, by a mere 112,881 votes out of 68.3 million cast. Michigan had been a key state; Kennedy had nailed down the United Auto Workers' support early to offset Nixon's strength with the rich executives of Grosse Pointe and Bloomfield Hills. Kennedy's margin was helped by a vote from a registered Republican living in Ann Arbor named R. S. McNamara.

During the campaign, the Kennedy camp had toyed with the idea of forming a committee of businessmen for Kennedy-Johnson. Neil Staebler, the influential chairman of the Democratic party in Michigan, proposed McNamara to lead it. But Shriver preferred a more visible figure, such as Henry Ford.[15] In any event, the committee plan fell through, and it is unclear if either Ford or McNamara was ever contacted. However, McNamara later said he contributed to Kennedy's campaign.

Harris Wofford, one of Kennedy's chief talent scouts, began compiling files on plausible appointees. He got McNamara's name through Staebler and Adam Yarmolinsky. In 1955 Yarmolinsky was working to help people wrongly accused of disloyalty and happened to visit McNamara in Ann Arbor. Now Yarmolinsky told them that the new Ford president read books like *The Phenomenon of Man*, by religious philosopher Pierre Teilhard de Chardin. McNamara had ties to the university and supported the American Civil Liberties Union. The Kennedy camp also learned that Jack Conway of the UAW had worked with McNamara on the overhaul of the Michigan tax system in 1959–60; Conway respected McNamara all the more because, midway through the debate on the overhaul, McNamara had switched his position to one opposed by his company.[16]

The talent scouts were delighted to find a Republican businessman who had risen meteorically at Ford and who was, at fortyfour, only a year older than the president-elect. They knew Kennedy wanted one or two Republicans in his cabinet. That a young Republican businessman could also be well thought of by labor, be Harvard-trained, support the ACLU, and read Teilhard de Chardin were all bonuses. The clincher came from Robert

Lovett, an establishment banker and Roosevelt's assistant secretary of war for air. Lovett remembered McNamara's work in Statistical Control during the war. He had followed McNamara's career ever since and recommended him.

Kennedy read McNamara's file at his summer home in Hyannis Port, on Cape Cod. He instructed Shriver and Bobby to contact McNamara in the greatest secrecy and offer him secretary of either treasury or defense.

On Wednesday, December 7, in his new, bigger office on the twelfth floor of Glass House, McNamara got a message that Bobby Kennedy had called. He remembered later that he asked his secretary, "Who's Bobby Kennedy?" He returned the call at nine-thirty that morning. Bobby told him the president-elect would like him to meet his brother-in-law Sargent Shriver. McNamara replied: Fine. How about next week? No, Bobby said, the president-elect prefers that you see him today. So the secretary penciled in "Mr. Shriber," rubbing out an appointment with the Ford representative in Manhattan.[17] That she misspelled Shriver's name shows "how much we knew about him," McNamara recalls. Shriver, meanwhile, boarded a plane to Detroit to get to Glass House by four o'clock.

Shriver wasted no time as he stepped into McNamara's office. The president-elect has authorized me to offer you the post of secretary of the treasury, he said. McNamara replied that he wasn't remotely qualified.

In that case I am authorized to offer you the job of secretary of defense, Shriver said. McNamara says he replied again, I'm not qualified.

Well, said Shriver, would you do the president-elect the courtesy of meeting him in Washington? McNamara agreed. They must have talked for some time, because McNamara remembers that it was dark when Shriver left, and he went into Henry Ford's office to tell him what was going on.[18]

But Ford had just left for New York. McNamara took a plane to catch up with him. He says he reassured Ford that night that he would not take the job. He then went to Washington and stopped at the Pentagon to see Thomas Gates, the incumbent secretary of defense, whom he knew because they were both directors of the Scott Paper Company. McNamara asked Gates if he could recommend that

Gates stay on; that way he could remain at Ford, and Kennedy would have a "qualified" defense secretary. McNamara got the impression Gates would not mind staying.

Then McNamara was spirited into a car down a narrow alley in Georgetown and ushered in the back door of John and Jacqueline Kennedy's brick Federal-style home on N Street. He was being hidden from the band of pressmen planted day and night on the chilly door stoop.

McNamara marched through the back door and the kitchen and swung into the living room, near the front of the house. He extended a strong right arm to shake hands with the president-elect. Kennedy was his own height, a year younger than he, and quite handsome, with close-set eyes that riveted with intelligence. Kennedy had a quickness about him, a sharpness of mind that McNamara had rarely encountered at Ford. McNamara may not yet have known that Kennedy was a successful seducer of women, but he clearly felt the man's charm; the presence was undeniable.

McNamara started through his prepared line: He had more influence on interest rates at Ford than did the secretary of the treasury; he wasn't qualified for the job at defense. Kennedy said he knew of no school for presidents, either. Clearly intrigued, McNamara complimented Kennedy on his book *Profiles in Courage*. Recalling a controversy over its authorship, he asked Kennedy whether he really wrote it. Kennedy said he had.

McNamara's coyness did not daunt Kennedy. On the contrary, the Kennedy brothers had been steeped in classical literature and, according to Wofford, fancied that their government would be like Plato's Republic, where the most worthy citizens would be most reluctant to serve.[19] Kennedy got McNamara to agree to come back the next Monday. McNamara departed for Michigan, again through the back door.

The talent search was meant to be secret, but there was a leak. That weekend's *Washington Post* reported that the little-known young president of Ford was Kennedy's first choice for defense secretary. Many such leaks came from Kennedy himself, who delighted in launching trial balloons in the press to test his plans.

In his own version of the story, to me, McNamara said he lied to Kennedy to try to avoid meeting him again. His version implies that he still planned to stay at Ford.

He remembers that it was snowing that weekend in Ann Arbor.

He sat upstairs in the study of their big fieldstone house on Highland Road and talked the offer over with Margy. Leaving Ford meant forfeiting a huge future income, just raised to $410,000 a year, which, with stock options, would come to $3 million or $4 million over the next few years. He says he consulted the two girls about the loss in income. The children and Margy were willing to go if he wanted to.

McNamara sat down and wrote a letter stating his requirements for taking the job. The letter repeated that he was not qualified to be secretary of defense. He would come on two conditions: first, that he be left free to run the department as he thought best and to appoint whomever he wanted, and second, that he not have to go to parties or be "a social secretary."

Roswell Gilpatric, who later worked for him, saw McNamara's letter because Kennedy saved it. "It even had a line at the bottom where the president was supposed to sign," Gilpatric says.[20]

McNamara says he decided to send the letter to Kennedy and then call to tell him that because of a snowstorm, he couldn't meet him in Washington on Monday as planned. There was no snowstorm, and he could have flown. His bald misstatement — to the president-elect, no less — showed his penchant for tactically useful fibs.

He phoned Kennedy in Palm Beach and said he had sent the letter — although he hadn't. When he said he was unlikely to be able to fly to Washington because of the weather, Kennedy said he couldn't get to Washington on Monday anyway. Shall we meet Tuesday? he asked.

On Tuesday, December 13, McNamara strode again through the back door of the brick house on N Street, with the letter in his jacket pocket. In the antique-filled living room, this time he met Bobby Kennedy as well. McNamara began telling the brothers he had to be free to run the department and wouldn't accept political appointees. Earnestly, the big bass voice announced that he had to be granted full control.

The Kennedys' list of qualities they wanted in people included toughness. And tough McNamara was in that second meeting. They had considered keeping Gates for continuity and because he was a Republican, with thirty-five-year-old Bobby as deputy secretary of defense. Bobby would move up when he learned the ropes. But, Bobby told an oral history interviewer in 1964, when they met McNamara, "it was quite clear that he was going to run the Defense Department, that he was going to be in charge and, although he'd clear things with the President, that political interests or favors couldn't play a role . . . [John Kennedy] was so impressed with the fact that he was so tough about it and strong and stalwart that he impressed him."[21]

Sitting in a chair opposite John Kennedy, McNamara pulled the letter from his pocket and handed it to him.

He later said that he knew one didn't make contracts with presidents.[22] But that was exactly what he was doing; leveraging what power he had with Kennedy, positioning himself. He had met the president-elect of the United States only twice and he was already getting the upper hand.

Bobby later said his brother was flabbergasted at the letter. At the time, he glanced at it without expression and passed it to Bobby. Bobby said, "Looks fine to me."

His brother said, "That's perfect. Let's announce it right away." He scribbled some notes on a yellow pad and then swept McNamara out through the front door onto the stoop, where the reporters and a television crew, their breath white in the freezing air, rustled to their feet.

Suddenly, McNamara was in the public spotlight for the first time, standing at attention. He wore a stiff grin that made him look foolish but was really a sign of intense concentration. Next to him, Kennedy looked more like the commander of armies and navies, talking about having a defense second to none and sending tough signals to the Russians, jabbing the air with his hand. McNamara spoke robotically, like a student taking oral exams, telling the reporters the number of shares of Ford stock he owned and computing their value. He said he was a registered Republican. Did he vote for Kennedy? "How I voted is my own affair."[23] It was an odd concealment.

In Ann Arbor, Margy learned from the evening news that they were going to Washington. In Oakland, a reporter caught Claranell as she made a call from a public telephone. McNamara's mother was asked for her opinion and said, "Mercy sakes. I'm glad he's so patriotic." She peered out from under hat and veil as intensely as her son had stared at the cameras a short time before.[24] The spotlight was now on them all.

Henry Ford, meanwhile, sat in the study of his mansion in Grosse Pointe and waved at Charles Cudlipp, a friend of his daughter Charlotte's, to come in and join him. It is not clear when, or how, with

Kennedy's lightning decision, Ford had learned the news was final. Cudlipp saw that Ford had been crying. He gestured for Cudlipp to sit down and poured himself a drink.

"This may be one of the worst days of my life," he said. "I can't believe it happened. You've heard the news about Bob, haven't you?

"Well, I spent years training him. He's the first president outside the family. After all those years of training he's leaving. I can't believe it. Now what do I do?"[25]

Now what to do was a critical question for Henry Ford, who apparently saw no more of his protégé. "I never went back to Ann Arbor, except to get some shirts," McNamara says. Instead, he dived into a new life and a new national and international role — disappointing many at the company and in Ann Arbor, who thought he was their friend, with his ability to yank down the curtain of the past behind him.

Some in Detroit said both Henry Ford and his firm would have fared better if McNamara had stayed. Henry divorced his wife and married Cristina Austin. He set himself up as a potentate among the jet set in Europe. In the early sixties, both Ford and his rising star, Iacocca, seemed in tune with the market. Iacocca's successful Mustang raised doubts as to whether McNamara's plan for functional small cars would have caught on. But the company's renewed investment in Europe, for which McNamara helped lay the groundwork, paid off handsomely, even in the seventies, when Ford's fortunes became erratic, imports invaded the American market, and the inherent problems of American management of mass production came to light. Looking back, except for the Edsel, the company was more stable and successful in the McNamara years.[26]

But at the time, relief was the overwhelming reaction to McNamara's departure at Glass House and the Rouge. And given the difference between McNamara and Henry Ford in temperament and goals, and McNamara's iron rule, many thought he could not have worked out in the long run. A hint of this darker view of McNamara had cropped up in the press that December, when an anonymous Ford official had told reporters, "He rules the place through fear."[27]

McNamara vanished from Detroit as though through a time warp to a new world. He left, partly lured by Kennedy's magnetism. When Arthur Schlesinger asked McNamara in 1964 whether he decided to join Kennedy because of *meeting* him, McNamara snapped, "Yes.

Exactly so. I don't think I have admired any man that I have associated with more."[28]

He left because the national scene appealed to his ambition, which was instinctive in him, and possibly because weighing ounces of chrome and calibrating inches on clay models bored him. He had managed to invest the car business with higher meaning, as his long-term plan articulated at the Greenbrier Hotel showed.

Yet the principal reason McNamara left was Kennedy's promise, for the senator's campaign had not just been an exercise in political manipulation. Kennedy had invested himself and his election with high idealism, which appealed to that side of McNamara concerned with the moral purposes of business and of the nation.

"I believe we Americans are ready to be called to greatness," Kennedy said in the draft announcement of his candidacy in January 1960. In campaign literature sent to clergymen and others, Kennedy warned of America's "dangerous slide downhill, into dust, dullness, languor and decay."[29]

"Our responsibility is to be the chief defender of freedom at a time when freedom is under attack around the globe," he said on September 17 in Greenville, North Carolina. In the pages of *Catholic World* he claimed,

> Pennsylvania Avenue is no longer a local thoroughfare. It runs through Paris, London, Ankara and Tehran, New Delhi and Tokyo. And if Washington is the capital of the free world, the president must be its leader. Our constitution requires it, our history requires it, our survival requires it.

The danger every citizen must rise to meet was not simply Soviet missiles, although Kennedy also promised he would fix the missile gap. Massive retaliation, Eisenhower's stated policy of readiness to fire off American nuclear rockets at almost any Communist affront, was highly dangerous. Influenced by former Army chief of staff General Maxwell Taylor, Kennedy argued that the United States should build up its conventional forces to have the option of large-scale non-nuclear war, or what Taylor called flexible response. Then there was the need to guard against encroaching communism in Africa, Asia, and Latin America. Meanwhile, Kennedy promised to revive stalled talks with the Soviets aimed at a comprehensive ban on nuclear tests. Kennedy was going to stand for strength "second to none" and arms control, too, the sword and the olive branch both.

The call to greatness and preparedness to fight required personal activism. "I believe the American people elect a president to act," he said on September 3, 1960, at the San Francisco airport. His activist presidency would lead Americans to exercise great responsibility, and to great glory. "There is a new world to be won — a world of peace and good will, and a world of hope and abundance; and I want America to lead the way to that new world," candidate Kennedy said. National leaders should not be mired in old political disputes but find solutions in a new era of consensus; he would be a president for all the people.[30]

It was this promise — of more power doing greater good — that drew McNamara to Kennedy like a moth to flame. In fact, Kennedy was arousing what Henry Fairlee, the sardonic British columnist, called the politics of expectation. By making Americans expect heroic deeds on a broad scale by a president who would be more virtuous and more surrounded with excellence than normal politicians, Kennedy excited the hope and idealism forever to be associated with his name. Equally, he set the stage for overreaching, disillusion, and tragedy.

After December 13, McNamara holed up in the Ford company suite in the Shoreham Hotel. He got a large stack of three-by-five-inch white index cards and started telephoning from three phones in the different rooms, running around among them and marking information on the cards. He called early in the morning and into the night.[31] Citizens around the land were sometimes awakened by a rasping, deep voice with a name that many had never heard of. He would ask about another person, or ask for an instant meeting with someone he had decided was qualified for a particular job.

He also investigated the precise extent of his powers as secretary of defense. A prominent panel headed by Senator Stuart Symington had concluded that a new law was needed to strengthen the post. If Kennedy was to request such a law from Congress, it would have to be one of his first initiatives.

The position of defense secretary had been created by the 1947 National Security Act, which formally put the Army, Navy, and Air Force under the umbrella of the National Military Establishment, the forerunner of the Defense Department.[32] But the powers of the secretary were small in relation to the job of mediating interservice fights over roles and missions that accompanied the return to peace. The

struggle for control was part of the stress that caused James V. Forrestal, the first and arguably greatest secretary of defense, to leave the
job in 1949 and commit suicide soon after.

Amendments to the 1947 act created the Department of Defense in
1949 and somewhat bolstered the powers of the secretary. But in
general, none of Forrestal's successors had much impact on the services, which continued to lobby separately for funds for their own
programs from Congress and the Bureau of the Budget.

Sputnik and the destructive competition among the different services prompted Eisenhower to submit further changes to the act in
1958, which vastly strengthened the secretary's power. These also
sheared the Joint Chiefs of Staff — the heads of the Army, Navy, and
Air Force, and their chairman — from the chain of command when
their forces were in combat. The Joint Chiefs' role in war was to
advise the secretary and the president. Now the chain of command
ran cleanly from the president through the secretary of defense to the
unified field commanders around the world, who commanded all the
forces of the different branches in their particular theaters. The Joint
Chiefs' right to bypass the secretary on programs and budget was
curtailed. Finally, the secretary was given seven assistant secretaries
and a general counsel, who were legally his agents and outranked the
military, as he did. The secretary was formally responsible for the
efficient operation of each service through each civilian service secretary. He had new control over research and development, and
procurement as well.

So McNamara dismissed the idea of asking Congress for a new
law. The job had a "full measure of power" already.[33] All that was
needed — it seemed so simple, really — was for him to use this vast
club of power to rational, noble ends.

To fulfill the wish to be a leader above narrow, monetary interests,
McNamara bent over backward regarding his money. He also wanted
to be free of any appearance of conflict of interest. At Senate confirmation hearings on January 17, he announced he had designated the
Continental Bank of Illinois to hold his liquid assets in blind trust.[34]
His yearly income at Ford had been $410,000, which he now gave up
for the secretary's government pay of $25,000 per year. He owned
24,500 shares of Ford stock, estimated at $47 per share. He chose
voluntarily not to exercise options on an additional 30,000 shares the

company owed him on termination, since to sell them would engender a conflict of interest, given that Ford had some defense contracts. The act of forfeiting future wealth was important to him. It was also noted by the Washington press, which glowingly noted his sacrifice as a sign of high-mindedness and excellence among Kennedy's men.

Margy and the children followed him to Washington. They moved into a rented house at 80 Kalorama Circle, in a wooded neighborhood of large homes on a hill above Embassy Row. From the house it was a thirteen-minute ride for his official car, a new Lincoln, along the riverside parkway, across the Potomac River, and into his own parking space under the Pentagon. McNamara's morning commutes were to an office near Thomas Gates's until he was sworn in.

Bob and Margy were taken by "the excitement of the Kennedys, the Camelot side," says Susan Mary Alsop, who with her husband, columnist Joseph Alsop, saw them often in the following years. One of McNamara's conditions for taking the job had been that he not have to go to parties, but the invitations from the White House, or to the Alsops' or other friends of the Kennedys', were irresistible. When Bob and Margy entered a room full of people, Alsop recalls, "he looked so bright, so competent," and Margy was so fine and natural, that "we all felt proud of Jack Kennedy for getting him to come." At some point Bob and Margy would have learned that Jack and Bobby Kennedy had different ideas about marital fidelity than they did. But McNamara refuses to discuss this. As for his own conduct, even among the parties, "Bob and Margy were *so* straight," one hostess says.[35]

The outgoing side of Bob McNamara was drawn to this sophisticated new crowd. "I don't think they had ever been exposed to witty conversation before," says Alsop.

Bob McNamara did have one, characteristically focused way of joining in. He wanted to do the twist. Before going off to the White House, "he told us he would practice at home, in front of a full-length mirror," Alsop recalls. Then "at the White House you would see this very serious businessman dancing the twist. It was touching."

The McNamaras' next-door neighbor on Kalorama Circle, Betty Eisenstein, from her window one day saw Margy climbing over their car with wax and rags. She was amused that the wife of the secretary of defense in this stylish new administration was polishing her own

car. Why are you doing this? she asked. We're going to the White
House later, Margy said cheerfully.

They're so *innocent*, Eisenstein thought.

January 20 was the president's inauguration; the Cabinet as a group
would be sworn in the next day at the White House. McNamara was
but one of a group found by the talent hunt. Among the others
preparing to take their oath were Dean Rusk, a Rhodes scholar and
president of the Rockefeller Foundation, now secretary of state; Mc-
George Bundy, dean of the Harvard College faculty at age thirty-
four and now assistant to the president for national security; Bobby
Kennedy, the new attorney general. Theodore Sorensen, Kennedy's
speech writer, eulogizes the new group as "men with strikingly
successful backgrounds" who were "unschooled in the old pre-war
dogmas" and had seen "the tragedy of war . . . and the new mate-
rialism." But talent scout Harris Wofford more candidly notes what
they were picked *not* to be — neither "too ideological, too earnest,
too emotional, and too talkative," nor "dull."[36]

The pretentiousness of it all seems foolish in hindsight. But at that
moment, many Americans were ready for a new day of national
purpose led by virtuous men. Instructing the talent scouts, Sargent
Shriver even used the phrase "brightest and best," from the 1811
hymn: "Brightest and best are the sons of the morning,/ Dawn on
our darkness and lend us thine aid."[37]

Just thirty-eight days after he agreed to join Kennedy, McNamara
joined this heady elect. The Massachusetts hat industry had been
materially hurt because their own senator had campaigned around the
country without wearing one. So for the inauguration, Kennedy
asked his new company to wear top hats to placate constituents and,
no doubt, to embellish the pomp with which he was surrounding
himself. The young men, wrapped in scarves and gloves to last out a
day in subfreezing temperatures, looked somewhat odd with their
hats. McNamara resembled a thin Teddy Roosevelt, the incongruous
top hat rising above his spectacles and wide cheeks.

They jostled one another in the freezing cold, on a grandstand
erected amid the gigantic columns of the East Portico of the Capitol,
looking out over the bundled crowd, which looked up at them. The
pillars were scant shelter against the wind. White-haired Robert Frost
announced "a Golden Age of poetry and power, of which this noon-
day's the beginning hour."

From his seat behind and above the speaker's podium, McNamara saw Kennedy as he stepped up, hatless, to deliver the inaugural address that would guide McNamara's actions for the next seven years. He saw Kennedy's profile and heard the now-familiar Boston tones deliver the new administration's self-imposed and tragic mandate.

> We observe today not a victory of party but a celebration of freedom, . . . signifying renewal as well as change. . . . [N]ow . . . man holds in his mortal hands the power to abolish all forms of human poverty and all forms of human life. . . .
>
> Let the word go forth from this time and place, to friend and foe alike, that the torch has been passed to a new generation of Americans, born in this century, tempered by war, disciplined by a hard and bitter peace, proud of our ancient heritage, and unwilling to witness or permit the slow undoing of those human rights to which this nation has always been committed and to which we are committed today at home and around the world.
>
> Let every nation know, whether it wishes us good or ill, that we shall pay any price, bear any burden, meet any hardship, support any friend, oppose any foe, to assure the survival and the success of liberty.
>
> This much we pledge — and more.
>
> To those old allies . . . we pledge the loyalty of faithful friends. United there is little we cannot do in a host of cooperative ventures. . . .
>
> To those new states whom we welcome to the ranks of the free, we pledge our word that one form of colonial control shall not have passed away merely to be replaced by a far more iron tyranny. . . .
>
> To those peoples in the huts and villages of half the globe struggling to break the bonds of mass misery, we pledge our best efforts to help them help themselves. . . . If a free society cannot help the many who are poor, it cannot save the few who are rich.

As for the adversary in Moscow, Kennedy asked

> that both sides begin anew the quest for peace, before the dark powers of destruction unleashed by science engulf all humanity in planned or accidental self-destruction.
>
> We dare not tempt them with weakness. For only when our arms are sufficient beyond doubt can we be certain beyond doubt that they will never be employed. . . .
>
> So let us begin anew, remembering on both sides that civility is not

a sign of weakness, and sincerity is always subject to proof. Let us never negotiate out of fear, but let us never fear to negotiate. . . .

Let both sides invoke the wonders of science instead of its terrors. . . .

Let both sides unite to heed in all corners of the earth the command of Isaiah to ". . . let the oppressed go free." . . . [L]et both sides join in creating a new endeavor, not a new balance of power, but a new world of law, where the strong are just and the weak secure and the peace preserved. . . .

Since this country was founded, each generation of Americans has been summoned to give testimony to its national loyalty. The graves of young Americans who answered the call to service surround the globe.

Now the trumpet summons us again. . . .

In the long history of the world, only a few generations have been granted the role of defending freedom in its hour of maximum danger. I do not shrink from this responsibility; I welcome it. . . . The energy, the faith, the devotion we bring to this endeavor will light our country and all who serve it, and the glow from that fire can truly light the world.

In 1968 it was McNamara who stepped up to a dais, this one hammered together by the U.S. Navy on the edge of a dock in Norfolk, Virginia, where the aircraft carrier *John F. Kennedy* was to be dedicated.[38] He escorted Jacqueline Kennedy and her two children, all in white. Behind him in rows, in their summer white uniforms, were senior Navy officers, many of whom had spent seven bitter years fighting him. McNamara gave a eulogy to Kennedy, but this famously tough man broke down. He read out the line "Those who knew him will never again be the same men."

It was true. McNamara never was the same.

6
Power in the Pentagon

THE AUSTERE, five-sided structure of the Pentagon is called simply the Building by the twenty-five thousand people who work there and the American military worldwide. It sits atop a low hill near Arlington National Cemetery, on the Virginia side of the Potomac River. The main entrance looks north across a bend in the river toward the Capitol, the White House, and the stately monuments of Washington. The Building was conjured in 1941 by George Edwin Bergstrom, president of the American Institute of Architects, who produced the design over a long weekend. It was built in fifteen months.

In keeping with wartime austerity, President Roosevelt ordered that no marble be used, so the facade was covered in plain pale yellow limestone. Bergstrom's design was almost a mockery of efficiency: The five-sided plan was meant to allow a person to walk from one point to any other in the geometry in ten minutes. In ten minutes, that is, if they did not get lost in the five stories, five concentric rings of halls, 150 staircases, and seventeen and a half miles of corridors.[1]

The attitude toward the Building among millions of men in the armed forces is as unsentimental as its architecture. Most prefer to be posted at a military base at home or overseas, where they have what they consider real jobs.

They view assignment to the Building as time spent in no-man's-land, pushing papers, fighting office wars on behalf of one's service, looking busy, getting a good mark in one's file. Some in the military relish this bureaucratic life, but many do not. For them, shuffling paper is not what devoting one's life to the country should be, and certainly not for the officers and men who have been in battle and never forget the faces of those who have died. What goes on in the Building seems unreal; yet what goes on there decides everything.

The office of the secretary of defense is a cavernous forty-nine-by-twenty-one-foot room on the third floor on the outermost corridor, or E ring. Room 3E 880 connects through a door to another giant room, the secretary's conference room. In the center is a long polished table; the walls are lined with chairs for "horseholders," the aides who wait on the principal figures meeting at this summit of power with the secretary. The secretary's office has an elevator that leads directly to the Tank, a splendid meeting room used by the Joint Chiefs of Staff. The elevator connects the secretary to the basement garage, his driver and official car, and thence to the world outside.

All this organization belied the true state of affairs in January 1961 when Robert McNamara moved in as the nation's eighth defense secretary. Even when the Pentagon was built, there was not a true, centrally run department of defense, despite the pomp of the big office. In 1949, when the Defense Department formally came into being, the large, baronial postwar Navy retained plenty of power, effectively limiting the civilian secretary. Then the Air Force, born in 1947, asserted itself. The Korean stalemate followed. In 1958, Congress expanded the legal powers of the secretary, giving him near total control over individual service budgets.[2] As McNamara moved in, the issue was how he would use it.

Later the generals and admirals remembered how polite McNamara was at the beginning. "Mr. McNamara seems to be a very fine and able person," General Lyman Lemnitzer, chairman of the Joint Chiefs of Staff, reported to President Eisenhower on January 9, 1961, when McNamara began his work in an adjoining office in the Building.[3]

McNamara's formality belied intense mental activity. In the thirty-nine days between accepting the job and taking office on January 21, he read many reports, particularly the Hoover Commission study of the administration of the federal government and the General Accounting Office reports on the Defense Department. Meanwhile he recruited his team by telephoning furiously all over the country, phoning his future deputy, Roswell L. Gilpatric, the first time at 5:30 A.M.[4] He had most of them hired by the day he moved in.

In the months that followed, McNamara undertook the largest overhaul of the department's budget and administration, the nuclear forces, and the even larger non-nuclear, or "conventional," forces since the United States plunged into World War II. He brought about this revolution with such speed and confidence that "the Building shook," as one civilian participant recalls.[5] To many, especially the new civilians he hired, the shake-up was an amazing feat, and badly needed: They saw McNamara as a crusader in the name of John Kennedy's fine ideals. But in other quarters, the judgment of the little-known businessman from Ford rapidly came into question.

McNamara's first background briefing with members of the press was the evening of February 6 and had been arranged by his new press aide, Arthur Sylvester, to take place in the secretary's conference room. Over cocktails McNamara outlined his plans for a five-year budget system and the various task-force studies under way. The reporters asked whether the Soviets had more operational missiles than the United States. McNamara first said that he had not yet been fully briefed on the situation. The reporters pressed for his initial impression.

McNamara replied, according to several reporters' notes, that the intelligence he had seen so far showed that the Soviets did not have as many operational missiles as the United States previously believed. In fact, there seemed to be more U.S. missiles than Soviet ones at present. Remembers John Scali, who was at the briefing for the Associated Press, McNamara "didn't use the word missile gap," but he did make it clear that he had the impression the United States was ahead.[6]

Scali noticed a lack of reaction among the other reporters taking notes and for a moment wondered if he had heard right. Back downstairs in the press room, Scali filed his story, which went out on the AP wires marked "Bulletin" to get priority over other breaking news. A high-ranking U.S. official was now saying, contrary to everything the Democrats and John Kennedy had stated, that the United States was not behind the Soviet Union in number of missiles.[7] The stories caused an uproar, in the press, Congress, and the White House.

McNamara had been perceptive, in his early reviews of the evidence — such as the first photographs from the Discoverer satellite — to see that the supposed force of hundreds of Soviet missiles could well be nonexistent. He had also been listening closely to his predecessor, Thomas Gates, who had argued in public and private over the previous year that a missile gap favoring the Soviet Union did not exist, although he was not widely believed.[8] But when Mc-Namara then tried to cover up his gaffe, he hurt himself.

The stories attributed to a senior official were readily traceable to McNamara. The day they broke, Pierre Salinger, the president's press secretary, engaged in some "news management" by telling reporters the stories were "wrong," because the Defense Department had no "study" that concluded there was no missile gap. In other words, Salinger didn't deny that McNamara made the statement, perhaps because it seemed likely that he had.[9]

A reporter asked Kennedy what he thought of the practice of having top-level officials hold background sessions with the press. "Well, they are hazardous in many cases, and I think Mr. McNamara might agree with that now," Kennedy said, with a smile. But his irony could not conceal the embarrassment McNamara had caused. McNamara says that he offered to resign over the incident, because it showed he didn't understand Washington and would only create trouble for the administration, but that Kennedy would not hear of it.[10]

Then McNamara denied his statement. John Norris of the *Washington Post,* one of the reporters at the backgrounder, wrote on February 17 that McNamara "declared yesterday that he neither told the newsmen that the United States is behind Russia in missile power nor that it is ahead." He also denied it in a letter to Senate minority leader Everett M. Dirksen: "I have not said with respect to missile power that the United States is either in a superior or inferior position *vis à vis* the Soviet Union," McNamara wrote. The gaffe faded quickly — for congressional Democrats had ridden the missile-gap charge as hard as Kennedy had and were not eager to embarrass themselves or the president. But McNamara, when asked, was either evasive or claimed that the Soviets were really ahead after all. Even though classified intelligence through the spring gave firmer evidence of lower numbers of operational Soviet missiles, on April 7 McNamara told George Mahon, the chairman of the House Appropriations Committee, that the "estimate" showed the United States lagged behind the Soviets in a "gap" that might not be closed until 1963.[11]

The issue died quickly, but McNamara's denials shocked the pressmen assigned to the Building. Warren Rogers of the *New York Herald-Tribune* recalls tracking the story down and deciding McNamara lied in denying his initial statement and may have lied to Kennedy on the matter as well. "He was treating us like the tame Detroit press," Rogers says, "but that sort of thing doesn't work in Washington."[12]

"He came in as a manager," recalls a veteran of the Pentagon's controller's office, Henry Glass, who helped introduce McNamara to the mysteries of the Building in his first months.[13] At first, McNamara turned to the Joint Chiefs of Staff — the heads of each of the three services and their chairman, Lemnitzer. He asked them what changes needed to be made in the budget Eisenhower had left them.

The chiefs' answers proved only a rehash of requests they had submitted to Gates and Eisenhower and not received. McNamara said, "Do they think I'm a fool? Don't they have ideas?" Glass says he suggested that McNamara ask to increase the number of Polaris submarines to be produced. "What number should we ask for?" said McNamara. "Seven," said Glass. "Why seven?" McNamara asked. "That's the number Mahon wants," said Glass, referring to the House Appropriations Committee's venerable chairman. The way the Pentagon had been run, Mahon's wishes were often the starting point for the Building's requests. "That's a hell of a way to build a program," said McNamara. "It's not *logical.*"[14]

A more logical answer lay at hand, to which McNamara now turned. Over Christmas at Aspen, Colorado, McNamara had met at the Brown Palace Hotel, in Denver, with Charles J. Hitch, the long-term chief of the economics department at Rand Corporation, in Santa Monica, California. Rand had sprung from the rich stream of mathematical tools and ideas generated during World War II. While Lieutenant Colonel McNamara had been working in Statistical Control, another set of bright young men, mainly economists, had done "operations research," making mathematical models of military campaigns to evaluate outcomes in terms of lives and effectiveness. Three events — the war's end, the birth of the atomic bomb, and air power's arrival as the chief means of fighting future wars — encouraged many wartime researchers and newly minted mathematicians, physicists, and economists to flock to Santa Monica. Rand's patron was the Air Force, but through its brilliant minds who enjoyed contradicting everything, it often bit the hand that fed it.

McNamara recruited Hitch for the job of controller, which the amendments to the 1947 National Security Act made one of the most powerful jobs in the Building. He had been impressed by a Rand report Hitch wrote with Roland McKean, *The Economics of Defense in the Nuclear Age.*[15] McNamara's mathematical mind lit up like a light being switched on as he read this dry tome. It explained the "program budget" idea that Rand had developed for the assessment and planning of military forces.

Budgeting for the armed services in 1960 was done much as it had been before the Department of Defense was formed. Each service — the Army, Navy, and Air Force — was given a predetermined figure by the White House and left to allot it among different programs as it wished. The relative lack of central control during the fifties, while technology exploded, meant that each service started a smorgasbord of new weapons systems, ranging from a nuclear-powered airplane for the Air Force to a larger aircraft carrier for the Navy.

Rand had proposed an alternative. Instead of letting the most powerful officers in each service divvy up the budget spoils to buy whatever they wished, a system of planning, programming, and budgeting, based on principles of economics and management accounting, could justify decisions on which systems to buy. PPB began by asking what missions needed to be performed and assessed different ways of carrying them out. If the mission for SAC's fleet of fifteen hundred bombers was to destroy targets in the Soviet Union, what did it cost for bombers to perform that mission? What alternative systems — such as long-range missiles — could perform the mission and at what cost? The assignment of costs and benefits created a yardstick for objective comparisons among weapons systems, which could allow everyone to see which systems added to the nation's capability and which performed overlapping missions, and to compare the costs of performing a mission different ways.

Reading the Hitch-McKean report, McNamara was struck by PPB's similarity to management accounting, which he learned at Harvard and had applied to the old Ford Motor Company to beam the searchlight of objective information, the quantitative truth, to determine what elements in a large manufacturing and sales organization did, how effectively they used the resources to reach specific goals. (In fact, when David Novick at Rand first produced a monograph proposing a program budget approach to the Air Force, the paper was banned from circulation, because the plan was too revolutionary and threatening.)[16]

McNamara loved it. Henry Glass recalls that in one of their first conversations McNamara asked, "How do we get our hands around this budget?" Rand's program budget, which it had continued to develop despite the Air Force's cool reception, offered McNamara the natural quantifier with which he could gain control of this sprawling empire and dramatically echoed the approach he had used for the past fourteen years to overhaul and run Ford.

Hitch never forgot the detailed presentation he made to McNamara in the early spring of 1961 in the secretary's conference room. He proposed to spend a year converting the budget arrangements for all strategic nuclear forces — bombers, Polaris, the Army's Nike-Zeus antiballistic missile system — to a program budget. Hitch thought it odd that during the briefing the normally curious McNamara asked no questions.

At the end of Hitch's presentation, McNamara banged his left hand down on the polished table. "That's exactly what I want," he said. He wanted just "one change. Do it for the entire defense program. And in less than a year."

Hitch and his staff filed out of the conference room in "shock," he recalls. They were going to have to install a program budget over a $41 billion program in nine months, in time for the unveiling of the new administration budget in January 1962.

They rushed to divide the entire program into ten program "packages," or missions, such as general-purpose forces and strategic nuclear forces. For this new functional structure, Hitch's men devised a complete statement of all costs over the life of each system. As with management accounting, not only amounts paid out were tallied; other costs, like the operation and maintenance of a weapon over its lifetime, were defined. Hitch and his immediate group worked like crazy and even flew east a whole group from Rand led by Novick, who set up shop in rented offices outside Washington, to get the job done in time.

McNamara had made the decision so fast that he took the budget bureaucrats in the Building by complete surprise. If I had known the secretary was going to take any of you fellows seriously, one of the old-timers complained to Novick, I would have fought you tooth and nail.[17] Now it was a fait accompli; the revolutionaries were taking control, and finally the runaway U.S. defense program would be rationalized — and the nation's defense strengthened, in what John Kennedy called their hour of maximum danger.

McNamara's fast-moving revolution amazed even the widely respected Carl Vinson of the House Armed Services Committee. "How much is enough, when it boils down?" Vinson asked when questioning McNamara in February 1961. "Now will you be in a position to tell the committee, then, from your study, what we need in the field of missiles, aircraft, and vessels?"

McNamara uttered a crisp "Yes sir."

"You will be able to tell us what we need?" Vinson asked incredulously. McNamara said, "Yes sir." "And hardware?" broke in another committee member, Leon Gavin. "Yes sir," McNamara promised.[18] He had been in office a little more than a month.

Enthusiasm over the forty-four-year-old supermanager came from both sides of the aisle in the spring of 1961: from Democrats who had called for a stronger and more centralized defense effort since Sputnik, and from Republicans who agreed that Eisenhower had let U.S. defenses slip. Republican senator Barry Goldwater called McNamara "one of the best secretaries ever, an IBM machine with legs."[19]

After several appearances in which McNamara showed an astonishing gift for memorizing facts and figures, Congress voted three times in 1961 — and again in the next years — to increase the defense budget. McNamara was helped by the fact that Congress was controlled by a few Democratic barons, almost all of them southerners, who believed that foreign policy and national defense should be bipartisan, lest America show weakness to the enemies of freedom in its hour of danger. So from 1961 to 1964 Kennedy and McNamara carried out the largest peacetime buildup in U.S. history and raised the budget from $41 billion to $49 billion; each year's budget was more than the combined national budgets of Great Britain, France, West Germany, and Italy at the time.[20]

Rand in the fifties uncovered many deficiencies in the forces that made them often weak or inefficient, no matter what amounts were spent. The Strategic Air Command's dominance of Air Force programs had caused neglect of tactical air power for fighting wars at closer range. The politics of bargaining within the Air Force had damaged its ability to "lift" Army troops and equipment to the battle theater; lift was, on paper, an important Air Force mission. The Army, bending to the widespread belief that nuclear weapons were the *only* way to fight, had been installing nuclear weapons on many systems: Navy airplanes were unable to carry non-nuclear bombs.

Yet if, as many others argued, the United States would still have to fight non-nuclear wars, armaments must change across the board. Added airlift was needed, and more tactical aircraft.[21]

McNamara issued in March a list of questions that came to be known as the Trombones, because there were seventy-six of them. Among them were "Why does the Navy need a new class of aircraft carriers?" and "What is the basic security policy of the United States?" The chiefs and others were to make studies and provide answers to him within weeks. "We are telescoping a lifetime of work," McNamara said.[22]

It took a person of supreme drive and self-confidence to force the pace of business in the Pentagon. However well led U.S. forces had been in World War II, leadership by 1961 was starting to pass to men who had made careers advancing service interests in the internecine wars over roles and missions in the 1950s. "This place is a jungle," McNamara is supposed to have said as he began closing military bases and proposed sweeping changes in the reserves.[23]

The dumbfounded, defensive responses of many senior military leaders only fired him more. "Decisions are not being made fast enough," he declared to *Armed Forces Management*.[24] By the fall of 1961, when different military factions had appealed his decisions in all 620 subcategories of the new program budget, McNamara made a point of deciding all 620 in a single day.

He claimed to be the objective party in these intramural debates; after all, he had better information than the military bureaus, for he and Hitch were hiring lots of youthful experts from Rand and elsewhere, who were quickly dubbed Whiz Kids, after the nickname used at Ford. "I am not accustomed to making recommendations affecting the life of the nation without investigating them to the fullest extent," McNamara said.[25]

His image as a human computer was positive in those days, for Congress and the public feared the country had been weakened by drift in the Eisenhower years. McNamara announced, "You can't substitute emotion for reason." And he repeated what admirers called a credo: "I would rather have a wrong decision made than no decision at all."[26]

Even John Kennedy, aware of his own shortcomings as a manager, was ready to entrust Defense to the new civilian experts. Kennedy said at Yale in 1962, after a year of enthusiastic praise for McNamara, that some problems are "so complicated and so technical that only a handful of people understand them," forcing average people to rely on "outdated and meaningless slogans."[27] McNamara, said *Business Week,* is a "prize specimen of a remarkable breed in U.S. industry — the trained specialist in the science of business management who is also a generalist moving easily from one technical area to another."[28]

However, there was something about these cocky young civilians and their impatient boss that troubled many in the Building. McNamara responded to reports of dissent by publicly claiming there was no split between civilians and the military. The chiefs have been consulted more than ever before, he said. His statements were true in the narrow sense: His regular meetings in the Tank with the brass were frequent indeed. And military officers were among the Whiz Kids. But he knew, better than any of them, that he was asserting the broad legal powers of the civilian secretary vis-à-vis the armed services more forcefully than ever before. It was an early sign of his pattern of using literally true statements to mislead his audience on the real state of affairs.

McNamara tried to stop the press from reporting on military dissent. He ordered his vinegary press aide, Arthur Sylvester, to take action against leaks. Richard Fryklund, a respected reporter for the *Washington Star,* was shadowed in the Building's corridors. McNamara ordered a crackdown on any off-the-record discussion between military people and the press — an order that was impossible to enforce and one that created great hostility.[29] Recalls AP's Fred Hoffman, "The bad feeling started right away."

He seemed unaware that his credo could be dangerous as he ordered a major strategic buildup that first year. He made his decisions so fast, in fact, that scholars since have searched in vain for the rationality on which he claimed, at the time, they were based. Later McNamara would make the examination of strategic problems and justification for nuclear forces one of his most refined exercises in analysis. But the harsh fact is that in his first months, McNamara ordered a rapid buildup of American nuclear forces to record-high levels just when intelligence estimates of the Soviet force, which should have been the determining factor, kept coming *down.*[30]

As they took office, Kennedy and McNamara looked for ways to quickly repair the supposed missile gap. The immediate threat to U.S. forces, they knew, based on definitive work by Rand, was that

American bombers — which composed the majority of the force — were vulnerable to surprise Soviet attack. The fastest way to fix the missile gap and deter a preemptive Soviet attack was to speed up production of the Navy's Polaris missile.

Polaris was the first twelve-hundred-mile submarine-launched ballistic missile. Sixteen of them could be carried on the new Polaris nuclear submarine, which could stay submerged for weeks in the world's oceans yet knock out Soviet cities on command from Washington. The Polaris missile program was one of the best-run and most technically successful weapons programs in the Building's history. Six Polaris submarines were on duty when John Kennedy took office. On January 30, Kennedy had ordered one speedup; in a March 28 special defense message, a second acceleration, to 29 boats and 464 missiles, was announced. Later, McNamara would further increase the force to 41 submarines carrying 656 missiles. Had Eisenhower's plan remained, the United States, in the next several years, would have bought only 19 boats with 304 Polaris missiles.[31] And in the interim, other branches of the Navy, which saw Polaris as a threat to their budgets, might have successfully beaten this force back to lower levels. This first Kennedy-McNamara reshaping of the force was in place by the end of March.

Now a fleet of big submarines roaming the world's oceans, but staying within striking range of the Soviet Union, was physically impossible for the Soviets to find and disable in a preemptive strike. Polaris could therefore ride out a nuclear war and survive to fire back; it was invulnerable and therefore a "second strike" force. In his first weeks, McNamara heard a briefing, based on a Navy study called WSEG-50, which argued that such seagoing missiles were *all* the United States needed in the way of nuclear forces.[32] The WSEG-50 study computed that only 200 Polaris missiles would deter a Soviet attack for good and assure the destruction of Soviet cities and industry if war ever came.

But McNamara was also listening to men from Rand. On their advice, he agreed that the United States needed more nuclear weapons than a minimum deterrent force; it should have some long-range bombers, which, although they took twelve hours to fly to the Soviet heartland, could then hit Soviet command centers and missile sites with much greater accuracy. He also agreed that they needed some number of land-based missiles, or ICBMs, which were more accurate than submarine-launched missiles and therefore could hit small military targets Polaris could not.[33] The Air Force had been critical of Polaris; the Navy's entry into the prestigious business of fighting nuclear war threatened its monopoly. Since Kennedy had criticized massive retaliation — the doctrine of his predecessor — McNamara favored some ICBMs and bombers to have a flexible across-the-board force that gave more options if war came.

The issue was "how much is enough," the classic question McNamara and his Whiz Kids would pose over and over as they examined the military's requests and supposed requirements. Right away, McNamara and Kennedy decided to retire most of the 1,292 old B-47 bombers and the 19 old B-58s, leaving "only" 500 B-52s, to the surprise and anger of the Air Force.[34] To make the remaining bombers less vulnerable, they ordered them on permanent alert. Some were to be in the air at all times, with others able to take off on fifteen minutes' warning. McNamara often boasted of the United States' trimmer and more alert bomber force; it was a symbol of Kennedy's promise to make America strong, invulnerable, and ready to fight if the cold war turned hot. And the more the Kremlin knew about the young new administration's readiness to fight, the more likely it was to be deterred. That these steps might provoke Soviet leaders, and humiliate them by revealing the inferiority of their forces, seems not to have occurred to these whip-smart young men.

Also on Rand's recommendation, McNamara sped up production of land-based missiles, particularly the small, more accurate Minuteman. Right away, in January, McNamara doubled production of Minuteman missiles from 30 to 60 per month, the most the contractors could build. Their first budget revisions raised the small force Eisenhower planned to 600 Minutemen; by September, McNamara projected an eventual force of 1,200 Minutemen. One Air Force general told Kennedy he needed 10,000; formally the service requested 3,000.[35] McNamara's fight with the Air Force over the ultimate size of the Minuteman force became long and bitter as he moved to make missiles instead of bombers the centerpiece of the strategic forces.

Nothing told Washington faster that McNamara planned to use his legal powers as secretary to the fullest than his fight to hold the Air Force's new bomber, the B-70, in development only.[36] The B-70 was the darling of the Strategic Air Command. It was to fly at three times the speed of sound and use a new material, a titanium compound. McNamara's case against producing the B-70 was, this time at least, based on systematic analysis. A fleet of B-70s would cost $20 billion over ten years, far more than the Minuteman force, and do much of the Minuteman's mission. McNamara and Kennedy proposed limiting the B-70 to two prototypes and no production.

Powerful friends of the Air Force in Congress appropriated more for the B-70 and its reconnaissance version, the RS-70. McNamara proceeded to exercise a little-known but important power he had under the 1958 changes to the National Security Act: He refused to spend the added appropriated funds.[37]

"Uncle" Carl Vinson, the chairman of the House Armed Services Committee, felt Congress's prerogatives had been snubbed. He started to make a constitutional issue of the matter. But the president backed McNamara. In March 1962, Kennedy and Vinson took a walk in the White House Rose Garden and worked out a compromise that still gave McNamara his way. McNamara's diplomacy with Congress on the B-70 had been poor, although Kennedy had coached him to visit Vinson regularly and to work things out slowly and politely, in the traditional manner of politics.

The B-70 fights spanned two years and revealed McNamara's authoritarian side. He seemed disdainful of Congress and the generals who maneuvered to save their pet plane. McNamara saw the B-70 fight as a test of his authority; now "Me-Win" McNamara stepped onstage.

Thus by the summer of 1961, the senior Air Force generals were worried by McNamara; he seemed serious about invading and making decisions about what had long been their preserve. They accused him of planning to phase out bombers altogether.[38] They stirred a publicized and emotional debate over bombers versus missiles that the Air Force and McNamara would fight for the rest of his term. In a prescient column, journalist Joseph Kraft noted that even when McNamara did have good reasons for his policies, he knew how to make enemies.

The Kennedy-McNamara missile buildup was huge. At the time it was criticized mainly for being too slight. The country was in the grip of fear of Soviet aggression. Khrushchev had not only banged his shoe on the table at the United Nations, but in January 1961 he announced that communism would beat the West in "wars of liberation" in developing lands around the world. That August, Khrushchev broke a long-standing moratorium on nuclear tests.[39] McNamara and Kennedy could now counter that they were strengthening America's nuclear forces, not only by slipping Polarises into the sea and adding Minutemen on land, but by reducing the vulnerability of the bomber force to Soviet attack.

In fact, much of the Kennedy-McNamara nuclear force buildup was *illogical,* by national lights; it was an early sign of the dangers of McNamara's instinctive preference for action over inaction. Eisenhower had left plans for a force of about 40 Atlas missiles and six Polarises at sea; in less than a year Kennedy and McNamara planned 1,900 missiles, consisting primarily of the 1,200 Minutemen and 656 Polarises. Counting the bombers, the United States would have 3,455 warheads ready to fire on the Soviet Union by 1967, according to McNamara's secret Draft Presidential Memorandum on strategic forces of September.[40]

Yet in early 1961, new SAMOS photographs and information from Oleg Penkovsky, a Soviet defector, suggested that the Soviets had only 50 to 100 missiles at most. Another then-classified estimate put the real number at *four.*[41] By June, the Army, the State Department's Bureau of Intelligence and Research, and the CIA were lowering current and future predictions of the Soviet force. Although Air Force intelligence continued to hold out for a likely high of 1,450 Soviet missiles by 1966, by the fall the consensus of other agencies was that an eventual Soviet ICBM force would be 850 and, more likely, 450 or fewer.

In the face of intelligence disagreement, McNamara picked a high estimate of 500 to 1,000 Soviet missiles and used it to justify the larger force he and Kennedy had planned.[42] White House advisers Jerome Wiesner and Carl Kaysen tried to convince Kennedy that with the missile gap vanishing, the U.S. force could be as low as 400 missiles or fewer. But McNamara said revealingly at a White House meeting on the matter that autumn that "a thousand Minutemen is the lowest I can go and still get it past Congress." The justification for the Minuteman buildup seems unrelated to the size of the actual threat.

The key to why McNamara recommended such a greatly expanded force, even when he had seen in February that the missile gap might not exist, lies in his sense of obedience and urgent mission as he took office. He had come to Washington to carry out John Kennedy's and the Democrats' mandate. Not just Kennedy, but other well-known figures such as Paul H. Nitze, whom McNamara hired, had been saying that U.S. forces must increase.[43] McNamara apparently did not question this conventional wisdom in the first weeks. He was fresh from Detroit, hiring his team, communing with Rand, and focusing on the defense budget reforms. Once he set the buildup in motion, he made it his own and defended it loyally. The rationalizations then followed.

He had learned a trick at Ford that he used to cut short argument over the proper size of the force. During one meeting to debate the justifications for different levels of missiles and bombers — which were also arguments about the relative power of the Air Force — McNamara asked the participants to state the number of Minuteman missiles they expected to be built when all was said and done. After each man gave a figure, McNamara announced that they had all voted for the very number he himself had written down beforehand: 1,000.[44]

At the time, his planned Minuteman force stood at 1,200; the Air Force was arguing for 1,800 or more, plus the B-70 and other things. McNamara would engage in this debate from every angle until three years later, when he would lower the size of the force to just this number he planned back in 1961. Physicist Herbert F. York, Jr., who was McNamara's first research chief, comments that the final size of the American force was cultural, not analytic. "One thousand is a nice, round number in our culture," says York.

In the excitement of the first year, there was an initial, terrible moment. On February 4 and 5, McNamara and an official party flew to the Strategic Air Command's headquarters, outside Omaha, to be briefed on the Single Integrated Operating Plan. SIOP was the operational plan the generals would execute if Kennedy — and McNamara as second in the chain of command — ever pushed the nuclear button. SIOP itself descended from the original SAC plan of 1951, when SAC bombers were the American strategic force and the Soviets had no striking power of their own. It was known affectionately in Omaha as the Sunday Punch.[45]

The chief of SAC was General Thomas Power, a bomber enthusiast. The plan Power showed McNamara was the one Eisenhower had approved the previous winter. It took account of Air Force intelligence's "discovery" of supposed huge numbers of Soviet missile sites the year before. These added hundreds of new targets to the list. The plan would fire as many as four weapons, sometimes more, at each target.

SIOP was also massive in its retaliation. The bomb that leveled

Hiroshima in 1945 and caused its citizens ghastly destruction was a mere 20-kiloton atomic bomb. A similarly sized Russian city in the new SIOP had four bombs aimed at it: a 4.5-megaton giant and three 1.1-megaton ones in case the big bomb was a dud.

More important than the overkill, from McNamara's standpoint, was that Plan 1-A of the four presidential options called for the United States to fire a preemptive first strike at the Soviet Union, China, and Eastern Europe. Sent across the Arctic on missiles and on bombers would be 3,423 nuclear weapons carrying 7,847 megatons. An estimated 285 million Russians and Chinese would be killed, and millions more in Eastern Europe. The other so-called options in the plan were no better.

Now, the mysteries of fighting a nuclear war, the supersecret controls, the slides and overlays and computers, might have impressed another layman who happened to be number two in the chain of command after the president and who might have to pass on the president's order when the moment came. Not McNamara. His refusal to be "put off" by experts, or "technical problems," as he had said in another context, helped him now.

McNamara interrupted the SIOP briefer to announce that firing four weapons on a single target was wasteful; the fallout produced by such an attack would be "fantastic." Worse, citizens in the entire Communist world would become victims in such an attack, even if Eastern Europe had not lifted a finger against the United States or if China stayed uninvolved.

Among the important targets was a big Soviet air defense radar installation in Albania. General Thomas Power, trying to humor his guest, said, "Well, Mr. Secretary, I hope you don't have any friends or relations in Albania because we're just going to have to wipe it out."

McNamara glared at him. The secretary of defense was a very literal man. Firing the nuclear force was the gravest imaginable action he might have to take, and the generals who supposedly worked for him were giving him no options. It also did not comfort him to recall that Soviet doctrine called for its own massive retaliation on the United States. The Kremlin must have its version of SIOP-62 ready to fire at us, he thought.

After leaving, he gave orders to Alain Enthoven to start the arduous, strife-ridden process of forcing SAC to change SIOP so he could order something less than all-out war. It took one and a half years to draw up guidance, to reprogram weapons and communications. The revised SIOP was ready in June 1962.

Meanwhile, nuclear war could no longer be an abstraction. A glint of reality and fear had penetrated McNamara's facade of logic and reason.

7

Cold Warrior Stepping Up

EUGENE ZUCKERT, McNamara's old friend from business school days whom he made secretary of the Air Force, remembers an early plane ride with McNamara that afforded a rare chance for an extended talk. The round-faced Zuckert drew on his experience in the Truman administration to explain to McNamara that Washington was a town that ran on blurred lines and felt loyalties. McNamara should plan to spend time having drinks with members of Congress, the press, and key diplomats so he would stay ahead of the flow and learn the real agendas, the ones not written in briefing books.

McNamara leaned forward in his seat, momentarily ignoring the sheaves of paper before him, his shirtsleeves glistening white, his coat folded neatly beside him. You don't understand, he told Zuckert with conviction. I'm not going to waste time drinking with congressmen and ambassadors. I'm here to give the president a defense second to none and at least cost to the taxpayer.[1] Zuckert found his zeal admirable, but it worried him too.

Nonetheless, McNamara underwent an important metamorphosis in 1961.[2] His view of his duties broadened as the new team reacted to one crisis after another. But also, his own innate drive pushed him forward, both in Kennedy's councils and as a spokesman for the Western world.

This widening of his role was partly his old instinct for power surfacing, the "Me-Win" McNamara who could not sit in a meeting without wanting to talk and dominate, and who was resented by men who thought their agencies had responsibility for foreign policy. Part of McNamara's strong showing was the personality of Dean Rusk, who tended to hang back, leaving room for the articulate, sometimes arrogant young secretary of defense.

McNamara stepped forward also because he, like many Americans, felt a growing sense of danger that year. The president had spent much of his campaign convincing Americans that the United States was inferior in strategic nuclear arms. He would then launch the ill-fated invasion of Cuba at the Bay of Pigs; he would be threatened by Nikita Khrushchev at a summit in Vienna. As the crises flowed, the activists around Kennedy leapt to meet real — and imagined — tests.

Even as Kennedy announced from the steps of the Capitol on January 20, 1961, that the torch had passed to a generation ready to pay any price in the defense of freedom, the Laotian chief, General Phoumi Nosavan, was failing to be sufficiently active in the cause. Hanoi and Peking sought to control Laos, and Phoumi, who was Washington's only hope for resisting Communist incursion, was not fighting very hard. Laos was about to become a red blob on the map of the world.

On January 19, Eisenhower had warned Kennedy, McNamara, and transition adviser Clark Clifford that if the United States intervened in Laos, "the Sino-Soviet bloc" could hit back with far greater forces.[3] Laos was nestled up against North Vietnam and China, right in the enemy's theater and ten thousand miles from Washington. McNamara says that when he left that meeting he thought, " 'My God, what a hell of a mess.' And I don't recall that in the next ninety days I had any clear solutions to the problem."

By February the Soviets were helping the Pathet Lao, the Laotian Communist insurgents backed by North Vietnam, with an airlift. By March the enemy was capable of a major offensive and was poised to seize the capital and plunge south down the all-important Mekong River valley, thereby splitting the Western-controlled areas of Thailand and South Vietnam in two.

At a meeting at the State Department, McNamara was "vigorous in his advocacy" of arming the six AT-6 training planes the Eisenhower administration had given to Phoumi with hundred-pound bombs. There was an "embarrassed silence" after he spoke. Then

Rusk said that his experience in Asia had taught him that air power without ground troops was ineffective; two bombs on only six planes would make no military difference anyway.[4] It was not a useful discussion, and McNamara's military advice was hardly astute.

At another early meeting, at the White House with Kennedy, McNamara brought along all the Joint Chiefs and all the secretaries of the armed services. The discussion rambled. "It was the worst meeting I ever attended," says Walt W. Rostow, a White House adviser.

General Lyman Lemnitzer, chairman of the Joint Chiefs, briefed the president on war plans for Laos. Lemnitzer said he would need to send 140,000 troops and tactical nuclear weapons to defend that country. "If we are given the right to use nuclear weapons, we can guarantee victory," Lemnitzer said.[5]

Kennedy soon concluded that landlocked Laos was indefensible for practical purposes and "not worthy of engaging the attention of great powers." He moved to arrange a ceasefire and talks on neutralization, although he feared looking weak to Khrushchev. McNamara understood that if Kennedy let Laos become neutral, it would be more important to hold on to its equally threatened neighbor, South Vietnam.

On another front, Kennedy, McNamara, and others were briefed on a CIA plan to deal with the red menace ninety miles south of Florida named Fidel Castro. In 1959 Castro had overthrown dictator Fulgencio Batista and come to power was a liberator. He seized U.S. holdings and turned to Moscow. Cuban exiles in the United States, and many inside government, wanted to get rid of Castro; Kennedy himself had virtually promised to do so in the campaign. Eisenhower had allowed the CIA to train a zealous band of exiles to plan to invade the island, seize key objectives, and spark an internal uprising that could topple Castro. The invasion was supposed to appear as a spontaneous exile action. At that time, covert action and political assassination were accepted by many in the U.S. government as legitimate tools of the cold war, rarely known to journalists or mentioned in the press.

McNamara saw the CIA's invasion plans.[6] He is on record as telling Under Secretary of State Chester Bowles that the invasion could not succeed without American military support. He saw and reviewed the Joint Chiefs' report on the CIA plan. No one, not the enthusiasts at the CIA or McNamara, apparently, noticed the veiled message in this document that the invasion's chances of success were slim without overt U.S. military support. The chiefs, locked into their bureaucratic perspective, let the CIA go ahead.

As the sun sank below the watery horizon off the southwestern coast of Cuba on the evening of April 17, 1961, a flotilla of old ships, with lights darkened and frogmen ready to jump, steamed toward the Playa del Girón. The first piece of bad news was the coral reefs offshore, which the CIA had not mentioned in its plans. These hindered the landing badly. Then a Cuban military jeep drove down to the beach and shone its headlights right in the frogmen's faces; the shooting began; Castro learned of the invasion. He sent his B-26s flying over the scene, and they fired on the exposed landing force. Kennedy's planes, meanwhile, stayed away, on presidential order. One disaster followed another, and soon it was clear that this was not a spontaneous invasion of exiles but a Washington-backed operation that was failing. Castro himself was down on Playa del Girón, spoiling for a real fight and having the last laugh.[7]

Army Secretary Elvis Stahr passed Vice President Lyndon Johnson on the evening of April 18 at a party. Johnson was flushed and excited. He warned Stahr, "There will be blood on the walls" when the president met with his advisers the next morning.[8] Instead Kennedy calmly took personal responsibility for the disaster.

McNamara had contributed his share to it. He had seen the invasion plan and discussed it with the Joint Chiefs. Kennedy later told Arthur Krock of the *New York Times* that McNamara informed him he had tried to get the chiefs to change the plans, but they had assured him they would work "as in Guatemala," where the United States staged a successful coup in 1954.[9] When Kennedy had gone around the table and asked each adviser for his view, McNamara voted in favor. With his penchant for believing he could personally change events, he later decided he could have stopped the scheme. He would tell journalist Henry Brandon and others that the Bay of Pigs was his fault, too.

"It had such a traumatic effect on everybody," says Roswell Gilpatric, McNamara's deputy. "It was bound to shake up any assurance we had in just carrying forward with existing programs or concepts. . . . As far as McNamara was concerned, he became so disenchanted with the military advice he got that he insisted on examining the basic data himself." McNamara told Arthur Schlesinger, "We all learned from it. It was a horribly expensive lesson, however." He says what he personally learned was "Do your own work. Don't rely on advice from anybody."[10]

The humiliation of the Bay of Pigs, then, spurred McNamara to play a broader role. He decided not to trust advice from the Joint Chiefs. Kennedy took away from the crisis the same lesson. When the Laos problem flared up again, in May, he sent General Lemnitzer to that country. The general cabled back a request for thousands of American troops. Kennedy waved the cables at Schlesinger and said that if it hadn't been for the Bay of Pigs, "I might have taken this advice seriously."[11]

A final episode in the Bay of Pigs story boded ill for McNamara's relations with the military services. The press had criticized the chiefs for approving the faulty plan, and Senator Albert Gore had called for their wholesale firing.

McNamara waited for weeks, until Charles Corddry of United Press International asked him at a press conference on May 26 about Gore's demand. McNamara said the chiefs would all stay on. "The Department of Defense was represented fully" in the discussions relating to the invasion, he said, adding, "I am responsible for the actions of all personnel in the Department, both military and civilian. Any errors, therefore, are my errors."[12]

The uniformed military took this defense as so weak as to amount to a public reprimand. McNamara simply did not understand how sensitive the military was to such accusations, or how it looked to civilian leaders for public protection. The incident made many in the military not just hurt, but antagonized.

On the heels of Laos and the Bay of Pigs came Berlin, which was a much greater crisis for the West, the president, and the new secretary of defense.[13]

In 1948, Joseph Stalin had tried to shut off Berlin from the Western allies, even though the city, 125 miles from the border with West Germany, had remained free and accessible to the West since 1945. But the allies' remarkable airlift, run by Air Force general Curtis LeMay, proved the West's right of access, and Stalin backed down. Ever since, the free city, and the autobahn and air lanes that serviced it, had remained, in fact and spirit, the heart of the allies' resistance to the Communist foe.

When Khrushchev met Kennedy in Vienna on June 3, he announced that Moscow would sign a treaty with East Germany — whose legal status was not accepted in the West — by the end of the year. He handed Kennedy an aide-mémoire, which said that once the treaty was signed, Berlin would belong to East Germany and the Western powers would have no rights there. If any Western nation did assert rights in Berlin, it would be violating East German sovereignty and providing a cause for war.

The threat unsettled Kennedy and his advisers, who had to wonder if the supposed Soviet nuclear advantage, the Soviet superiority in ground forces in Europe, Kennedy's sidestep over Laos and humiliation at the Bay of Pigs, had prompted Khrushchev to think he could win a decisive victory. "It will be a cold winter," Kennedy remarked to the old Bolshevik in Vienna.

In Washington, McNamara turned to the war plans. Berlin was isolated deep in East German territory and literally surrounded by East German and Soviet forces. Washington could do almost nothing, given the poor condition of American, German, British, and French ground forces stationed in West Germany, and the small force in Berlin itself. If the Communists blocked access or drew a noose around the city, the only thing to do, it seemed, would be to defend with the crude tactical nuclear weapons along the border, which the United States had been installing since Eisenhower's day.[14]

Kennedy turned for advice to the most commanding figure in Washington on alliance matters, former secretary of state Dean Acheson. Acheson had not only been "present at the creation" (as he titled his memoirs) of the NATO alliance but in large measure had shaped it. By 1961, he believed that American and European willingness to resort to nuclear force — which had been an axiom of Europe's defense from the beginning — was dangerous. Acheson wrote an influential paper for Kennedy in April calling for a switch, by the American government and NATO as an organization, to the alternative of flexible response, in which they would use non-nuclear force for as long as possible before resorting to nuclear defense. Kennedy accepted the paper and adopted flexible response. Dean Rusk and McNamara promoted it. However, in the spring of 1961 it was only a phrase uttered by youthful men in Washington. Alliance policy and arms relied on early resort to nuclear weapons to stop a Communist attack on Western Europe, including Berlin.

McNamara told Kennedy at a National Security Council meeting on June 14 that the U.S. forces in Berlin had enough ammunition only to hold out for eighteen days.[15] Kennedy agreed with Acheson that a much larger conventional (that is, non-nuclear) force was needed to deter Khrushchev or, if Khrushchev moved, to hold on to Berlin without using the nuclear forces. The president ordered Mc-Namara to expand the American Army's eleven regular divisions to sixteen fully combat-ready ones, consisting of almost one million men. General Maxwell Taylor, who had resigned as chief of staff of the Army over the way Eisenhower allowed the Army to grow weak — and rely on nuclear forces instead — may have influenced Kennedy's decision. In his famous book, *Uncertain Trumpet*, Taylor called for rebuilding non-nuclear strength and establishing a million-man army. If Kennedy wanted a policy of flexible response, Taylor now argued, he needed an army capable of fighting.

Army Secretary Stahr remembers that McNamara came back from a meeting with Kennedy during the Berlin crisis and ordered the expansion of the Army. Stahr had the impression he was acting on orders from the president.[16] It was an important moment; the big, revived, ready U.S. Army, of which McNamara would boast and which later was sent into Vietnam, only came into being due to Khrushchev's threat to Berlin and Kennedy's say-so.

Kennedy went on television on July 25 to announce a request for a $3 billion increase in the defense budget, the Army expansion, and the call-up of 150,000 reservists. He also urged the public to buy civil defense shelters. Kennedy said,

> Those families which are not hit in a nuclear blast can still be saved — if they can be warned to take shelter and if that shelter is available. In the coming months, I hope to let every citizen know what steps he can take without delay to protect his family in case of attack.

He warned Khrushchev that Berlin was "the great testing place of Western courage and will, a focal point where our solemn commitments . . . and Soviet ambitions now meet in basic confrontation."[17]

The threat of nuclear force was a clear signal; so was the call-up of the reserves. Kennedy also urged America's allies to prepare themselves to fight.

The pressure mounted on the Kremlin, meanwhile, to do something. The possibility that Berlin would be shut off had caused thousands of East Germans to flow into the city and from there to the West, hoping to get out before Khrushchev made good on his threat and war came. By summer, 3.5 million East Germans had left the country, approximately 30,000 in the month of July alone. At this rate the Communists would soon have no one left to govern. McNamara, the White House, and the Joint Chiefs of Staff studied the war plans.

In early 1961 McNamara did not know much about foreign policy or about the relations among the allies, but he was a very literal man. Fresh from the hinterland and Ford, and from the briefing he had had near Omaha by SAC on what would happen if the United States pressed the nuclear button, he asked questions. He told me, "My attitudes on nuclear weapons were influenced by my very simple — not simple-minded, but simple intellectually — approach to the problem. I asked myself what would happen if we initiated their use."

An airplane crash in North Carolina that occurred in February made a deep impression on him. An Air Force B-47 carrying nuclear bombs went down, and one of the bombs had been released.[18] The controls for arming the weapons had held, but McNamara wondered about this potential accidental nuclear explosion in North Carolina. He recalls:

"One of the first things I asked for was an analysis of the use of nuclear weapons. Well, we got a lot of mumbo jumbo. But we found rather quickly" — he thinks in the first weeks he held office — "that Eisenhower was much wiser regarding nuclear weapons than I gave him credit for."

McNamara discovered the existence of a study Eisenhower had commissioned examining potential nuclear conflict. It was so tightly guarded that, McNamara recalls, there was only one copy.[19] "I read it. What it did was to examine a nuclear exchange. It concluded that such an exchange would destroy the United States." McNamara then realized Eisenhower must have disbelieved in massive retaliation himself, despite the fact that it was widely advertised and perceived as official policy.

Then came the Berlin crisis. In July, on the eve of Kennedy's speech, McNamara and Assistant Secretary Paul Nitze went to Germany. By then, McNamara remembers, he was convinced the military "didn't have any plan to use nuclear weapons that I would ever want to implement. It was clear to me that our use would engender a nuclear response." And he knew full well that Soviet military doctrine called for massive retaliation. "I believed that if the Soviets got into the use of nuclear weapons they would go all out."

In Germany in July, McNamara recalls, he queried the officers in charge of the tactical nuclear weapons that were, thus far, the only way Washington could try to deter a shutdown of Berlin. He asked the officers, "If you use them, what are the Soviets going to do?" They said, "What happens if we don't?" McNamara said, "Well, I understand that if we don't [use our weapons] we are in trouble, but if we do use them, the Soviets will destroy Washington and New York." What would happen next? McNamara asked the officers. They said, "We've got plenty of missiles and bombers; we'll launch them." McNamara says that he thought to himself that "this was just absurd."[20]

Thus by the middle of 1961 the secretary of defense had jumped into foreign policy — that is, into foreign developments involving the possible use of American force, which meant nearly everywhere that year: Berlin, Europe in general, the Congo, Cuba, Latin America. He had even jumped into economic issues where defense allocations affected America's global position, such as the gold drain and the balance of payments. His presence in meetings was stronger, sometimes dominant. Roger Hilsman at State was one of the many who were beginning to be troubled by McNamara's crisp, decisive manner, his lack of self-doubt even though he was roaming beyond his field.[21]

While Nitze and McNamara worked up options, the tension rose over Berlin. Khrushchev announced increases of 3.1 billion rubles in his military budget; he bragged that he had the largest bomb in the world and rockets to deliver it. The flood tide of refugees continued. Kennedy appointed General Lucius Clay, the hero of the 1948–49 Berlin airlift, to command U.S. forces on the scene. Reservists reported for duty. Americans were swamping the manufacturers of civil defense shelters with orders. Kennedy signed an introduction to an issue of *Life* about civil defense.

At half past midnight on August 13 — when McNamara, Nitze, and several other key officials were out of Washington — squat East German T-34 and T-54 tanks appeared along the streets dividing the Soviet-run sector of Berlin from the other zones. East German Vopos stood guard while workmen shoved jackhammers into the pavement. Fence posts went up, then chain link wire, then several strands of barbed wire along the top. Crowds of West Berliners jeered at the soldiers. Others helped relatives or friends make last-minute dashes across. Within days, the barbed wire became an ugly concrete wall, zigzagging like a gangrenous scar through the contours of the city's face. Word of the construction had clattered onto the State Department tickers that night in Washington. American intelligence did not predict the wall.

The wall could quench the devastating exodus. But what were the Western allies to do? "If I had been commander I would have taken a wire and flung a hook over and tied it to a tank and pulled it down," General Lauris Norstad told Lyndon Johnson in Paris on September 30.[22] After the wall went up, intelligence detected the secret movement of troops enveloping the city. On September 1 the Soviets resumed nuclear testing, with some huge explosions; one was 75 megatons, the largest nuclear device ever detonated.

The options McNamara considered that summer, some of which he appears to have endorsed, included the first use of nuclear forces if the enemy pushed further. An unnamed McNamara aide told journalist Stewart Alsop in December 1962, "No matter how you slice it, if we're serious about holding Berlin, we've got to be prepared to go to the nucs."[23]

After the wall went up, Kennedy asked McNamara to look into the effects of their nuclear options. Former Rand staffer Henry Rowen, who worked for Nitze, developed a paper demonstrating that a few SAC bombers, flying low under Soviet radar to escape detection, stood a good chance of hitting all the Soviet missile sites, although a few missiles could survive to retaliate on Europe and the United States. In such a scenario, Rowen's paper said, 34 million people in Western Europe and between 10 million and 15 million Americans would die. According to writer Fred Kaplan, this paper reached the White House over McNamara's signature; Marcus Raskin, who was on McGeorge Bundy's staff, was appalled.[24]

Nitze studied ways that Washington could raise the cost to Khrushchev of continued pressure on Berlin. If Khrushchev started to move, there were things Washington could do to drag out the confrontation for three to six months. Meanwhile, the new Minutemen and Polarises already approved by Kennedy would be entering the force, and the bigger Army would be building up. Within a year the United States could outnumber the Soviets by ten to one in intercontinental missiles alone.

Nitze proposed four "phases" of response, which were discussed at the White House on October 11 and adopted as policy on October

23. NSAM 109, as the policy was termed, shows that Kennedy, under these circumstances, adopted a formal policy of initiating the use of nuclear weapons to hold Berlin, if absolutely necessary.[25] The first three phases involved diplomatic and economic pressure, followed by full mobilization — preparation for war. Only then, if the Soviets moved on Berlin anyway, would the president proceed to the fourth phase:

> *If* despite Allied use of substantial non-nuclear forces, the Soviets continue to encroach upon our vital interests, *then* the allies should use nuclear weapons, starting with one of the following courses of action but continuing through C below if necessary:
>
> A. Selective nuclear attacks for the primary purpose of demonstrating the will to use nuclear weapons.
>
> B. Limited tactical employment of nuclear weapons to achieve in addition significant tactical advantage such as preservation of the integrity of Allied forces committed, or to extend pressure toward the objective.
>
> C. General Nuclear War.[26]

According to Nitze, McNamara showed a copy of the top-secret plan in one-on-one meetings with the defense ministers of West Germany, France, and Great Britain. He handed each of them the paper, read it aloud to them, and then took the copy back.[27]

Sometime in October, the Americans concluded from Soviet hints that Khrushchev might not sign the treaty with East Germany and cut off West Berlin by year's end after all. The crisis receded over several uncertain months. But McNamara's involvement with the nuclear danger had just begun.

McNamara may have had a secret fear that the war plans were "absurd"; yet he was among the president's men who publicly warned the Kremlin that the United States was ready to go to nuclear war if necessary. In the atmosphere of the time, it was controversial if a U.S. official even hinted that America was *not* willing to "go to the nucs." A January press leak that Rusk was studying avoiding the use of nuclear weapons early in a European conflict drew strong criticism in Europe, for example. In September, Maine senator Margaret Chase Smith charged that the new, young president wasn't willing to use nuclear weapons to protect Berlin.

McNamara called Chase's charge "nonsense." The president

would use nuclear bombs in whatever size and quantity were needed to protect vital interests, he said. The *New York Herald-Tribune* quoted him as saying, "It is absurd to think that we would have unbalanced the budget simply to strengthen a weapon we had decided never to use under any circumstances." Bobby Kennedy also said at that time, "I would hope that in the last few weeks he [Khrushchev] would have come to the realization that the President will use nuclear weapons."[28]

McNamara told the allies in May 1962, at a closed NATO meeting in Athens, that U.S. policy was to initiate nuclear weapons if needed.

> As the President has indicated on a number of occasions, the United States is prepared to respond immediately with nuclear weapons to the use of nuclear weapons against one or more members of the Alliance. The United States is also prepared to counter with nuclear weapons any Soviet conventional attack so strong it cannot be dealt with by conventional means.

He also said:

> There is, first, a high probability that in an ambiguous situation the West, not the East, would have to make the decision to initiate the use of nuclear weapons. . . . under some circumstances they may be the only instrument with which we can counter Soviet non-nuclear aggression, in which case we shall use them.[29]

In a speech on November 18, 1963, to the American Economic Club, McNamara said the Soviets "know" that the United States was prepared to reply using "whatever response may be required" to defeat "even nonnuclear aggression at the high end of the spectrum of conflict" if it threatened vital American or allied interests.[30]

Approximately twenty years later, McNamara seemed to take it all back. In a 1983 article in *Foreign Affairs*, McNamara denied he was ready to recommend using nuclear weapons to defend Western Europe in the Kennedy years.

McNamara was now a senior citizen, having retired from the presidency of the World Bank in 1981. He was trying to be a spokesman for the active liberal movement to stop the Reagan defense buildup and talk of winning nuclear war. Now he claimed that "in 1961 and 1962," he had concluded that *nuclear weapons serve no military purpose whatsoever. They are totally useless, except to deter one's opponent from using them.* That is my view today. It was my view in the early 1960s.

At that time, in long private conversations with successive Presidents — Kennedy and Johnson — I recommended, without qualification, that they never initiate, under any circumstances, the use of nuclear weapons. I believe they accepted my recommendation.[31]

Many wondered how McNamara could claim that he had a secret understanding with two presidents that "they never initiate, under any circumstances, the use of nuclear weapons" when publicly and to the allies, he said many times that the United States was prepared to use "whatever response is required" to defeat "non-nuclear aggression."

Many people on both sides of the Atlantic assumed that McNamara must have been lying as secretary of defense — if he was opposed to any nuclear first use then — or was lying now. San Francisco lawyer Frederick Wyle, who worked on NATO nuclear matters in the later 1960s, says if his more recent assertion is true, "we were lying to the allies all those years. I try to judge McNamara as honestly as possible. . . . In my opinion, he made on balance a tremendous positive contribution. . . . But my reaction when I heard him saying he never believed in first use was that this was not constructive." Ronald Reagan's arms control director, Kenneth Adelman, whom McNamara met with regularly in the Reagan years, says: "Either he didn't have this private understanding with Kennedy and Johnson and is making it up now — who knows why, perhaps imagining he can please some people. Or he had this private understanding with Kennedy and Johnson but was telling the allies and the public something different all those years. Either way he's a liar."[32]

McNamara has since tried to explain his evolution. During the Berlin crisis, he told me, he decided that the *allies* "would be the first to say, 'Don't initiate the use of nuclear weapons.'" He recalled a meeting in which a senior allied general suggested using such weapons. Lord Mountbatten was present and reacted with horror, although the British were public advocates of early nuclear first use.[33]

McNamara finally explained the consistency between his public and private statements on nuclear weapons in a long, emotional interview. I had passed him some statements that showed how starkly his public positions in 1961–62 and his later assertions seemed to

contradict each other. "NATO had an established policy at the time
. . . that it would initiate first use of nuclear weapons, if necessary, to
defeat a Warsaw Pact conventional force attack," he began. "Publicly, I couldn't deviate from that policy. And therefore if I was asked
or had to initiate a statement as to what NATO policy was, I simply
referred to the official position." He noted that his official readiness
was also to deter Khrushchev: "The repetition of that NATO policy
was an element of the deterrent policy. We were hoping to deter an
enemy attack by stating publicly that in the event an attack occurred
and we were unable to deal with it with conventional forces, we
would use nuclear forces."

Privately, meanwhile, "I was working on changing NATO policy.
And preparing our leaders, our president, for the contingency that
they might sometime face, i.e., a request from our military for first use
of nuclear weapons, which I felt was contrary to the interests of the
United States and its allies." So, while he recommended to Kennedy
and, he said, later to President Johnson that they never use nuclear
weapons first, McNamara explained, "I couldn't have said that publicly at the time. That would have destroyed the meaning of NATO."

McNamara said he was deeply troubled by his double position. He
went on: "To have a policy . . . that you state publicly but do not
plan to implement is worrisome — not only because of the duplicity
of the statement, but because of the danger that you might have to
implement it." He pronounced the word "danger" with great emotion. The danger, he continued, was in the "mind-set or pressures to
implement" the stated policy; "that's what upset me."

McNamara's staff also had doubts about the advisability of going
to nuclear war. William W. Kaufmann, a Rand expert who worked
with the Office of the Secretary of Defense and who was the architect
of a major theory of nuclear war called counterforce–no cities, says,
"McNamara preferred to say to the allies, that if push came to shove,
he was going to use nuclear weapons. But both I and later Morton
Halperin said it was hogwash about using nuclears." He and Halperin went in to McNamara at one point and urged him to simply tell
the allies he would not recommend that the president use nuclear
weapons first. "McNamara agreed with us, I think, but he declined
to tell them."[34]

So he had become inwardly divided, secretly aware of the dangers of
nuclear war while in public giving the allies the assurances they sought

that the young men of Washington were ready to carry out the American guarantee to use nuclear weapons to defend NATO. Indeed, even with the reserves called up and U.S. reinforcements starting to reach Europe, Kennedy had few alternatives, if Khrushchev turned up the heat that fall, other than to resort to tactical nuclear weapons, as NSAM 109 recognized.

At the same time, McNamara emerged as a formidable figure in the counsels of government. He was doing what an old friend from Cal, Stanley Johnson, calls "coming to the surface."[35] McNamara had evolved a powerful, confident presence in the small study group classes at Harvard Business School and through the committee system at Ford; by now he was so impressive, even dominant, that his ignorance was hidden under a barrage of facts.

It was in his nature to abhor a power vacuum — and fill it. His fateful ascendancy was due to the personality of Dean Rusk.[36] Rusk and the State Department were off to a slow start compared with McNamara and Defense. When, after Vienna, Kennedy asked Rusk for a white paper on the options concerning Berlin, Rusk did not produce it for several weeks, despite growing alarm in the administration.

Rusk was a tall man of southern eloquence. He had risen from dirt-poor roots in Cherokee County, Georgia, won a Rhodes scholarship, and spent critical years of the 1930s in England watching the rise of Hitler. He concluded that the failure of the Western democracies to stand up to fascism had produced World War II. Determination to prevent a repetition of the mistakes of that era led to a dedicated career in international affairs, and his appointment as secretary of state.

Yet Rusk was no administrator; the Berlin paper episode became a pattern. Kennedy's frustration was evident,[37] and inexorably McNamara moved into the breach. He was always deferential to Rusk; he liked him. To me McNamara expressed nothing but admiration for Rusk. The two met every Saturday morning at the State Department, Rusk told me. This means that McNamara got a lot of instruction in the verities of the cold war that first year from a man whose knowledge of the world he respected. Thus outwardly, the newcomer and manager learned from the seasoned cold warrior. It appeared to be an exemplary relationship. Underneath, however, the men at Foggy Bottom — as State's offices are called — became frustrated and alarmed.

When McNamara began issuing his annual posture statements in January 1962, Foy Kohler, a career diplomat who was later made ambassador to Moscow, tried to convince Rusk that "we ought to issue our own foreign affairs summary every year before McNamara gets his out." It didn't happen, with the result that every January, McNamara's annual report became a definitive statement of foreign as well as defense policy.[38]

Other aides recall going in to Rusk to ask him to phone McNamara, usually to get some initiative taken by Defense reversed. Rusk outranked McNamara, and McNamara appeared so deferential to him that surely, the aides reasoned, Rusk could tell McNamara what to do. The aides would hear Dean listen to Bob going rat-a-tat-tat on the other end of the line. Then Rusk would say "All right," hang up, and explain why Bob was right. Kohler said later, "I thought [Dean] let Bob run over him."

McNamara's speed and directness, his organization of facts and force of personality, also impressed John Kennedy. Kennedy said that McNamara would "come in with his twenty options and then say, 'Mr. President, I think we should do this.' I like that. Makes the job easier."[39]

Yet McNamara seemed so certain and dominant that he could appear dangerous. "Bob is the most persuasive man in the cabinet," said Bobby Kennedy, who admired him, "and that frightens me a little."[40] Bobby began making sure that his brother heard other views.

There were several reasons for the power the Defense civilians began to exert around Washington. One was Paul Nitze, who had wanted to be deputy secretary of defense but whom McNamara made assistant secretary of defense for International Security Affairs. Nitze proved well cast as the chief of the Pentagon's "Little State Department." Nitze was older by a decade than both McNamara and Kennedy and was close to Dean Acheson. He had worked at State and knew the skeletons in Foggy Bottom's closets. Nitze rebuilt ISA into a powerful organization in 1961–63, showing a shrewdness that would make him a key player in U.S. defense policy for another three decades.

There were other reasons, too. McNamara favored staff who wrote papers fast and lucidly. Around the Office of the Secretary of Defense, editing draft papers became a competitive sport which the boss also played. Whereas the men at Foggy Bottom waited weeks to get papers cleared up the line, Defense could move nimbly. Explains one of McNamara's civilian aides, "To be the one who initiates the position paper is to control the debate."[41]

McNamara's system of delegation also multiplied his power. Morton Halperin, who came to work at ISA later on arms control, happened to be knowledgeable about the American occupation of Okinawa after World War II. Halperin wrote a paper arguing that the United States should begin procedures to return Okinawa to the Japanese. The paper asked for a meeting with McNamara to discuss whether to pursue this and how to get other agencies on board. McNamara read the paper — along with hundreds of others crossing his desk — and got it back to Halperin the next day. Scrawled on the margin of the first page were the words "No need for meeting. Give it back. R McN."[42]

From then on, Halperin knew he was free to call meetings with State and the CIA and other agencies, and to make up agendas, hand out papers. He could sit in a room and negotiate Defense's positions freely, and McNamara would always back him up, even after the fact. At Foggy Bottom, approving positions took weeks. Halperin and his colleagues had real power, deriving from McNamara. And the men of State grew frustrated.

Yet McNamara's limitations did not go unseen. Seymour Weiss, who worked for Nitze on the Berlin crisis, recalls being in the Pentagon one Saturday. He and Nitze were plotting Warsaw Pact and NATO moves. When they became stuck in their war game, Nitze whirled in his chair and dialed McNamara — who was of course working on Saturday, too. Nitze laid out the scenario: They've done this, we've done that, they've responded this way. Now what do we do?

Weiss realized from hearing Nitze's end of the conversation that McNamara, on the other end of the line, was counting the forces. No, no, interrupted Nitze. I'm not asking how *many* there are. What do we *do?* Bob McNamara had lots of facts that Saturday. But not a strategy.[43]

Few events showed McNamara's growing confidence and power around town that year more than the affair of General Walker. Yet, as with so much else in his seemingly heroic performance, there was a catch here, too.

The temper of the fifties had been vehemently anti-Communist. The John Birch Society, which thought it saw Communists in every quarter, was a significant force in America; the Kennedy men — cold warriors as well — positioned themselves as closer to the center than the Birchites. From his new post as a spokesman for the Western world, McNamara found it alarming how many senior officers gave speeches with political content, often violently anti-Communist in tone. What would the Kremlin think?

Conflict was drawn right away when, in early 1961, a speech to be given by the famous World War II admiral Arleigh Burke was hacked away by a reviewer, infuriating Burke. The speech had had so much political content that Arthur Sylvester, McNamara's press aide, had scrawled at the top of it, "This is a speech that should be made only by the secretary of state." In response Burke called Sylvester a "son-of-a-bitch."[44]

The issue flared up again in April, when *Overseas Weekly,* a tabloid published for troops in Germany, carried a long article about the activities of Major General Edwin Walker, who had been giving "political seminars" modeled on the Birchites' program. Walker saw the broad mass of Americans as dangerously pro-Communist and even attacked the loyalty of venerable Eleanor Roosevelt. He also accused McNamara's special assistant, Adam Yarmolinsky, of being a Communist dupe.[45]

Kennedy called McNamara and told him to investigate what Walker was doing. When, three days later, McNamara had no answer, Kennedy was "on McNamara's back for his failure to produce," says Sylvester. McNamara ordered Sylvester to find Walker in Germany, however he could. Walker's defense of his statements to Sylvester showed him to be on the fringe — although clearly many people shared his beliefs.

There followed a highly publicized crackdown. McNamara, with typical zeal, had many officers' speeches reviewed by an internal committee. The allies of General Walker, the irate Admiral Burke, and Strom Thurmond in the Senate screamed that McNamara was "muzzling" the military. Then Senator John Stennis of Mississippi opened an investigation. The senators demanded all copies of speeches submitted and each edited version. The pile consisted of thousands of documents, which McNamara decided to give to the committee within twenty-four hours of the senators' request. His assistant for legislative affairs rode the Pentagon corridors on a bicycle to get them together in time.

Next the senators wanted to know the names of the reviewers, as well as which reviewer had edited which speech. McNamara was adamant that only he was responsible; he yielded the reviewers' names but would go no further. Kennedy backed McNamara: The principle of civilian control was at stake, along with the president's desire to control his own foreign policy.

At a highly orchestrated confrontation, Stennis demanded the information, and McNamara drew from his pocket a signed order from Kennedy invoking executive privilege. Stennis, a former judge, briefly traced the separation of powers under the Constitution and sustained the executive plea.[46]

What made the episode remarkable was less McNamara's dogged refusal to submit his staff's actions to congressional scrutiny, or even Kennedy's firm backing — although both these aspects were publicized at the time. In fact, one of McNamara's main motives was his determination not to let Yarmolinsky appear before the senators, for he knew they were gunning for him. Almost thirty years after these events, McNamara told me the following story.

Despite the cold war atmosphere of early 1961, McNamara had hired Yarmolinsky from Kennedy's transition team to work as his special assistant. It was a very sensitive job in the Pentagon, for most communication with the secretary crossed his assistant's desk. Yarmolinsky was a liberal, to be sure: McNamara had first met him in Ann Arbor, when Yarmolinsky, then a young lawyer, was investigating cases of people wrongly accused under an executive-branch loyalty rule.[47] When he was fifteen, Yarmolinsky had gone to two Young Communist League meetings but declined to join; Army security had interviewed him in 1948. The FBI in those days created secret files on people on such flimsy grounds. McNamara, when he moved to hire Yarmolinsky, knew the contents of the file, and he asked his deputy, Roswell Gilpatric, whether he thought he should hire Yarmolinsky as his aide. They both decided in favor of it. Then McNamara pointed to Gilpatric and said, in effect, you now have two jobs: The first is to be deputy secretary of defense. The second is to be my lawyer when I am called before Congress about Adam.

Thus the Walker affair — and McNamara's claims of executive privilege — were important in establishing his emerging power. But they were also the working out of a problem he took on from the very beginning, whether from personal courage, because he liked Yarmolinsky and refused to hold an irrelevant FBI file against him, or from some more complex motives of defying the orthodoxy of the cold war, even as he waged it.

When he appeared before the Senate on the Walker issue in September 1961, McNamara stated:

> There is no true historical parallel to the drive of Soviet Communist imperialism to colonize the world. . . . [No dictator] . . . has ever been so well organized, [or] possessed so many instruments of destruction. . . . There is a totality in Soviet aggression which can be matched only by turning to ancient history when warring tribes sought not merely conquest but the total obliteration of the enemy.

He had realized the dangers of "Communist imperialism" back when he lived in Michigan, he said, and read some quotes from Stalin in an issue of *Foreign Affairs* in 1949. He became convinced then that the Communists planned "total obliteration" of free peoples; "If the free world should lose to Communism, the loss would be total, final, and irrevocable. The citadel of freedom must be preserved because there is no road back, no road back to freedom for anyone if the citadel is lost."[48] This was McNamara's mood in the fall of 1961, when he turned seriously for the first time to the problem of South Vietnam.

Kennedy's tactical retreat over Laos made it all the more important to these cold war activists to draw the line in South Vietnam. That country, which adjoined Laos to the east and was being subverted by the same enemy forces, at least had a strongly anti-Communist president.

Vietnam became a significant concern for McNamara during the last week of October. Worry over Berlin still permeated the inner circle, according to William Bundy, Nitze's deputy and McGeorge Bundy's brother, who would be McNamara's adviser on Vietnam for the next three years.

By fall the threat to President Ngo Dinh Diem seemed serious. Kennedy was under pressure. He had not "acted" — in the terms of the day — in Laos or Berlin. Nor, he was publicly reminded, had he taken enough "action" against Fidel Castro, only ninety miles away. So he sent General Maxwell Taylor, his personal military adviser, and White House aide Walt W. Rostow to inspect the situation in South Vietnam.[49]

Taylor and Rostow recommended a partnership with Diem in which Diem would fight the guerrillas and Washington would provide some aid and expert military advice. They suggested sending

8,000 troops to stiffen Diem's force, disguised as a civic action unit to help the government cope with recent floods.

McNamara signed a reply to the Taylor-Rostow recommendations on behalf of himself, the Joint Chiefs, and Gilpatric. Typically, the reply was presented as a series of numbered points. The fact that he was now personally taking responsibility for the advice the chiefs gave the president was significant; when the chiefs' views differed from his, he would include their views in the same memo with his own arguments, thus framing the issues for the president.[50]

McNamara's memo argued that the basic issue was whether the United States shall "a. Commit itself to the clear objective of preventing the fall of South Vietnam to Communism, and b. Support this commitment by necessary immediate military actions and preparations for possible later actions." This was what William Bundy described as the "Berlin-type commitment," which was on their minds at that moment.[51] South Vietnam's strategic importance was not doubted for a moment. In item 1, McNamara affirmed the litany: Its fall "would lead to the fairly rapid extension of Communist control" or "complete accommodation" to communism in the rest of Indochina and in Indonesia, with "worldwide" implications.

Moreover, "the chances are against . . . preventing that fall by any measures short of the introduction of U.S. forces on a substantial scale." The proposed 8,000 troops "will not convince the other side . . . that we mean business" and

> not tip the scales decisively. We would be almost certain to get increasingly mired down in an inconclusive struggle.
>
> 4. The other side can be convinced we mean business only if we accompany the initial force introduction by a clear commitment to the full objective stated above, accompanied by a warning through some channel to Hanoi that continued support of the Viet Cong will lead to punitive retaliation against North Vietnam.
>
> 5. If we act in this way, the ultimate possible extent of our military commitment must be faced. The struggle may be prolonged and Hanoi and Peiping may intervene overtly. . . . I believe we can assume that the maximum U.S. forces required on the ground in Southeast Asia will not exceed 6 divisions, or about 205,000 men. . . .
>
> 6. To accept the stated objective is of course a most serious decision. Military force is not the only element of what must be a most carefully coordinated set of actions. Success will depend on factors

many of which are not within our control — notably the conduct of Diem himself and other leaders in the area. . . . The domestic political implications of accepting the objective are also grave, although it is our feeling that the country will respond better to a firm initial position than to courses of action that lead us in only gradually, and that in the meantime are sure to involve casualties.

McNamara recommended "major units" of U.S. forces *not* be sent unless Kennedy first decided in favor of a clear commitment.

The secretary of defense's support for a Berlin-type commitment and 200,000 troops flickered and then died quickly. Apparently he got a signal that Kennedy was not ready to receive this recommendation. On November 11 a different paper went to Kennedy over McNamara's and Rusk's signatures. It also endorsed a clear commitment, but the proposed actions were much milder and did not involve sending any troops. Instead, the limited partnership between the United States and South Vietnam would go forward in the form of civilian aid to win hearts and minds, as well as American military advisers, guns, helicopters, and barbed wire. The Military Assistance Command the Army had run there since 1954 would be upgraded and a four-star general put in charge. Kennedy signed the memo, except the language committing him to prevent South Vietnam's fall, while keeping most of its contents secret.[52]

McNamara, as with everything, leapt in to carry out the plan. In 1965 he told Columbia University professor Henry Graff that in November 1961, in a conversation with President Kennedy, he had "volunteered to look after" the war in Vietnam.[53]

Kennedy's first year would later be recalled with nostalgia. But the mood at the time was different. By the end of 1961, many ordinary Americans felt fearful about their own survival and the country's. From the steps of the Capitol, Kennedy had beckoned them to engage in the great moral struggle, to bear any burden in the cause of high ideals. But what followed had been crisis after crisis, and ambivalent White House action. Now hundreds of thousands of reservists and their families were rearranging their lives to answer the call-up. As for young children, many would never forget the monthly drills in which they were marched in lines to the school basement when terrible sirens wailed and made to sit against the wall in special poses to brace for the shock of a nuclear blast. In churches, homes, and gathering places, people were debating whether to shoot their neighbors or relatives if they tried to come into their fallout shelters when the real sirens rang.

The call to activism had been thrilling at first. And McNamara was eager for the challenge. But some Americans already were having serious second thoughts.

8

Statistician Against Communism

SOON AFTER ARRIVING in Washington, the Mc-Namaras paid $127,000 for a house at 2412 Tracy Place, a few blocks from the house they first rented on Kalorama Circle. Tracy Place was a curved, shaded street that ran across the slope of the hilly neighborhood known as Kalorama. The architecture was imitation Italian, with a flat, blank stucco facade giving directly onto the sidewalk, small windows covered with grilles, and a pair of oversize double wooden doors; in California it would have passed as fake Spanish colonial.

Georgetown, with its narrow brick sidewalks and rows of old town houses, was probably too crowded and quaint for Margy and Bob McNamara, although the Kennedys lived there and many New Frontiersmen moved there in 1961. Once again, McNamara chose to live apart: Kalorama was across Rock Creek Park from Georgetown. It was newer and roomier, with large, freestanding houses on wooded lots. Kalorama was just the sort of place a prominent corporate figure and Republican would live, whereas Georgetown had a Democratic, New Deal tone. Bob and Margy chose a Quaker school, Sidwell Friends, for the two younger children, Kathy and Craig.[1]

There was anxiety in the McNamara household. The move was a dividing point in the children's lives. Little Margy was the least affected emotionally: She was in college at Stanford, south of San Francisco, and near to family friends and relatives. Kathy was uprooted from high school in Ann Arbor midway through her junior year and found the switch to Sidwell Friends difficult. Craig, at eleven, was found to have dyslexia, so Margy began tutoring him painstakingly. The boy later remembered that in these sessions sometimes "we both ended up in tears."

Meanwhile, the couple were invited out constantly as the social swing of the New Frontier got into motion. They turned down most invitations, to keep their old privacy. When they did go out, Margy could not help feeling different from the eastern Kennedy set: Jackie with her fondness for things French and cosmopolitan, the emphasis on style, on the perfect — and expensive — suit and right pillbox hat. Margy was willing to go to some lengths to coif her hair and wear bright pinks and greens and short hemlines. But her naturalness was not to be lacquered over. Soon after arriving, she told her old friend Mary Joe Goodwin: "People in Washington think I'm stupid."

The previous owners had decorated the Tracy Place house as though they were nobility in medieval Europe. Kathy remembers that the two-story stairwell and front hall had blue walls covered with gold stars; they even found a complete suit of armor. In keeping with the modern styles of 1961 and their own tastes, the McNamaras had the interior painted white throughout; abstract paintings they bought from a Greenwich Village artist relieved the blankness of the walls. They hired a Taiwanese couple to live in, cook, and look after the house. Margy had never been a housekeeper; now that she had to entertain as an official duty as well as see to family needs, the hired couple assured that dinner was served on time and to "Mr. Mac's" liking.

Behind that blank stucco facade, Tracy Place became a house where many lives could go on separately. The living room, dining room, and little library, which all looked out the back into the trees, were separate from the front hall and the stairs to the upper floors, where the children's rooms were. The children could get meals and snacks and come and go without passing through the public rooms or the library, where their father was likely to sit in the evening.

One of the bigger rooms was the low-ceilinged master bedroom, on the back of the second floor. It had its own bathroom and dressing room and led to a small study, which, like the bedroom, overlooked Rock Creek Park and the city and its monuments. It was an appealing suite for people who liked the outdoors and good views. Here Bob and Margy had their privacy. From her study she could run their joint life and her volunteer work.

Margy's personal disorganization was a curious luxury in the household of a man so compulsively organized and obsessed with schedules and time. Friends say it did not bother him, because he considered the house Margy's territory; he would have forgiven any flaw in her, in any event. His old friend Vernon Goodin remembers watching the papers fly off the desk of Margy's study, blown by breezes from an open window. She laughed as she scrambled to hold them down: "I call this my open-air filing system."

The go-go sixties were taking off with great excitement and optimism, sparked by Kennedy and his circle in Washington. But in the McNamara home, Margy worried. She worried that Craig could never be a star student like his father — although with enough help he could do quite well, for he was a bright and cheerful boy. She worried because Kathy was so unhappy and critical.

McNamara had little time for them. He left Margy to cope, thus repeating the pattern of his own childhood, when Robert James had stood aside and let Claranell run the house and raise him and his sister. What Margy and the children saw of him was his well-ordered departure every morning at six forty-five into the back of the black government car, with Mr. West driving him away, and his return after seven-thirty, five days a week and every Saturday. They saw his picture in the newspapers and watched him on television, which was becoming increasingly important with the new half-hour nightly news. At home on Sundays, McNamara watched the political interview show *Face the Nation* with great concentration.

Some days he didn't come back at all, having flown off on his military airplane to Europe and, once a month, to Hawaii. McNamara had a special ability to compartmentalize relationships; he now separated utterly his work and home lives. The children learned not to ask about work — he was terribly important; he was much smarter than they and knew so much more about the world. If he avoided discussing his work with them, who were they to insist?

Looking back later, Craig could say, "My father never shared his real life with us."

As they grew apart in this big house, the one subject they could talk about freely together was the trips: their Christmas ski trip to the Colorado Rockies or California, their forays back to the cabin they kept in Michigan, or the hiking and camping they did with their California friends. But even on those occasions McNamara was often separate, for though he took the whole family along, he would leave them while he and one of the other men set out on their own, testing themselves against nature.

Sometimes in the evening in the little library, McNamara would pull out a piece of paper and write down numbers in rows. He was computing how many ounces and which kinds of food and drink the vacationing group would need and the weight and volume of each item. From these figures he derived charts of the goods each man, woman, and child should carry in their backpack. He imposed limits on their personal gear. He recomputed the numbers several ways to get the optimal mix.

As the date of the trip approached, his hobby reached a special climax. McNamara would go to the supermarket, take a wheeled shopping cart, and plunge up and down the aisles, picking different cans of food off the shelves and examining them, referring to his little chart. He was trying to see if the products that the American food industry created in certain sizes and weights, according to its own logic, matched his careful statistical plan.

By the start of 1962 McNamara had leapt in, with characteristic ambition, as a major foreign policy player in the new administration. He wanted greater control over all nuclear forces. He wanted to end the disarray in NATO about who should have nuclear weapons and under what conditions they would be used. Finally, he wanted to handle the distant guerrilla war in South Vietnam.

Within five weeks, in May and June of that year, McNamara announced his solution to the nuclear forces and alliance issues and made his first flying trip to South Vietnam, where he claimed to have the answers, too.

He relied on quantification extensively. In his first flush of national prominence and power, he believed his techniques were yielding objective answers.

McNamara was overzealous and blind. He did not see the political dimension of the nuclear problem or grasp how deeply the nuclear disputes in NATO expressed underlying national feelings. In South Vietnam, he refused to see that men would pretend to dance to his tune while deceiving him. So along with his optimism and statistical management, McNamara brought to each problem a full — and very American — measure of arrogance and ignorance.

In his first, formative weeks in office, McNamara agreed to be briefed by William Weed Kaufmann, a respected young man, who in 1956 followed Bernard Brodie, the godfather of the nuclear strategists, to Rand. There he became adept at analysis and familiar with game theory and other tools of Rand's formal strategists. An intense man with glittering blue eyes, Kaufmann peered keenly at the new secretary of defense as he approached the huge Pershing desk in his office at three o'clock on February 10, 1961.[2]

Five days earlier, McNamara had been briefed by the generals at Strategic Air Command headquarters outside Omaha on SIOP, the operational nuclear war plan. His alarm bells were going off about what would happen if he ever had to exercise his responsibility, as number two in the chain of command in the free world, and press the nuclear button, an action called for in many of the classified contingency plans he was seeing for the first time.

Kaufmann showed McNamara a detailed strategy for limited nuclear war. He argued that if the Soviets launched a big conventional attack on Europe or a nuclear attack on the United States, the U.S. military could hit back not with the entire nuclear force, as SAC planned, but only with nuclear strikes against Soviet military forces, airstrips, and missile sites away from cities. The United States would announce it was withholding part of its nuclear force to use against Soviet cities if the Soviets did not let up after the first round. The plan, called counterforce–no cities, clearly derived from the theories of bargaining and escalation, which economists and mathematicians at Rand and elsewhere had developed in the previous decade. For in Kaufmann's scenario, it was not the *actual* destruction of Soviet forces, which he assumed Moscow would understand to be only a limited attack, so much as the *threat* of imminent destruction of Moscow and Leningrad and the prospect of many more millions of citizens dead that should make Soviet leaders yield.

The plan could lower the destructiveness of nuclear war and proposed a way to end such a war.[3] And, if U.S. leaders announced they were adopting a counterforce strategy and pointed out how many Soviet lives would be spared by initially declaring cities out-of-bounds, the Kremlin might just be induced to adopt a similar strategy.

Thus the first exchange of nuclear weapons could be limited by the mutual interest of both parties in avoiding their own destruction. A further advantage was that once the United States announced this relatively more feasible way of waging a nuclear war, then its threat to use nuclear weapons would be more credible than it was under the massive retaliation doctrine the Kennedy administration had inherited from Eisenhower and Dulles.

Kaufmann had been working on the idea since about 1958 at Rand and had vetted it in front of "murder boards" of fellow analysts. Rand's sponsor, the Air Force, got wind of the concept. Certain Air Force generals were appalled by massive retaliation and liked Kaufmann's alternative.[4] A longstanding doctrine of air power said that bombing should be selective and aim at annihilating the enemy's military forces and not civilians; U.S. air generals had fought their British colleagues on this point when the Royal Air Force set out to bomb Dresden and Hamburg in World War II. SAC's all-out nuclear Sunday Punch ran contrary to this humane tradition.

There was another reason Kaufmann's plan had special appeal in 1961. Sensitive information from the U-2 flights and new spy satellites were telling Americans for the first time exactly where Soviet bases and installations were.[5] McNamara had ordered more high-accuracy ICBMs capable of quick countermilitary strikes; meanwhile, sea-launched Polaris missiles, which could ride out a first exchange and strike back at Soviet cities, were entering the force by the month. Counterforce–no cities could work.

McNamara was such a fast student that he absorbed Kaufmann's points and fifty-four slides in one hour instead of the four it took everyone else. In characteristic fashion, he adopted Kaufmann's plan wholesale. Counterforce–no cities thus was transformed into U.S. nuclear doctrine at the flick of his pen.

Counterforce–no cities became the basis for the changes in SIOP, the operational war plan for U.S. strategic forces, that McNamara ordered Alain Enthoven to begin working on in the wake of the terrible briefing near Omaha.[6] It also became the basis for the first five-year plan for nuclear forces, issued in late February. McNamara's first Draft Presidential Memorandum on strategic nuclear forces, written as guidance for the next budget and dated September 23, 1961, said:

> [I]n the event of a Soviet nuclear attack, [U.S.] strategic forces would first . . . strike back against Soviet bomber bases, missile sites, and

other installations associated with long-range nuclear forces, in order to reduce Soviet power and limit the damage that can be done to us by vulnerable Soviet follow-on forces, while, second, holding in protected reserve forces capable of destroying the Soviet urban society, if necessary, in a controlled and deliberate way.[7]

McNamara himself said rather little about the new policy. His public statements that winter focused on notifying the Soviets that the United States had a superior nuclear force, thus pounding the last nails in the coffin of the missile gap. Meanwhile the Rand analysts, with their slide rules, computers, and bomb-damage charts, were delighted to acquire such a powerful patron, to be making "real" policy at last. But their sponsor, for the moment, appeared to have other things on his nuclear agenda.

The trigger for McNamara's decision to promote counterforce– no cities was the behavior of the NATO allies in spring 1962.

The Berlin crisis had given the allies every incentive to find alternatives to NATO's historic reliance on the U.S. nuclear arsenal to defend Western Europe. During the crisis, they had spent some money to build up, but it was clear they were not going to go very far toward a true conventional defense.[8] Moreover, the Kennedy administration's preference for flexible response was decried in coffeehouses and parliamentary debates in Europe as evidence that the Americans were weakening their earlier guarantee to protect Western Europe from the Communists. The French in particular were adamant, claiming that since the Americans were backing down on their pledge, a French nuclear force was needed all the more.

Under Eisenhower, it had been American policy to promote the "diffusion" of nuclear weapons to the NATO allies. The commanding general of all NATO forces, American general Lauris S. Norstad, had proposed the creation of a new force of medium-range ballistic missiles (MRBMs) in Europe, under his command, as the nucleus of a future pan-European force.[9]

Charles de Gaulle, at the same time, was maneuvering toward a French-German entente, raising the possibility that his nuclear force could be a bilateral one with the West Germans.[10] Meanwhile Kennedy's foreign policy was aimed at encouraging European unity, economic and political — and, if need be, the formation of some kind of joint nuclear force. Dean Acheson, however, warned that the proliferation of nuclear forces in NATO would be a nightmare. The men in the Pentagon thought so, too.

Kaufmann's counterforce–no cities doctrine had a key corollary: To carry out the strategy, Washington needed central control over all nuclear weapons to orchestrate the sequence and targeting of attacks. Thus the doctrine offered a powerful rationale to stop the spread of nuclear weapons in NATO.

In the spring of 1962 McNamara decided to give a major speech, to tell the allies what U.S. policy *was* and to cut short the confused debate about control of nuclear forces that had flashed around the alliance for years. McNamara's directions to speech writers Henry Rowen and Kaufmann were vague. But by then McNamara had endorsed so many aspects of the counterforce–no cities program that they felt free to develop it fully.[11] Neither McNamara nor Rowen and Kaufmann considered seriously that the speech could backfire or imagined how their ghoulish scenarios would play in the theater of politics. Indeed, McNamara probably thought it was his duty, as the alliance's principal nuclear policymaker, to lay out the policy in detail, since only he had all the "facts."

So he stepped to the podium before a large, closed-door gathering of defense and foreign ministers in Athens in May 1962. American power was almost at its height in relation to Europe: The United States had 6 percent of the world's population and generated 40 percent of the world's product. The budget of the Greek government was $836 million, only one thousand times McNamara's personal net worth. He had not only economic power, but technical expertise — for business schools like Harvard's were nonexistent in Europe, and Rand-style analysis was also unknown there. McNamara thought it was his obligation to instruct the allies in the truths about nuclear war.

Minutes into the classified speech, McNamara was announcing that counterforce–no cities was U.S. policy.[12]

> [T]he U.S. has come to the conclusion that to the extent feasible, basic military strategy in general nuclear war should be approached in much the same way that more conventional military operations have been regarded in the past. That is to say, our principal military objectives, in the event of a nuclear war stemming from a major attack on the Alliance, should be the destruction of the enemy's military forces while attempting to preserve the fabric as well as the integrity of allied society.

Nuclear forces that could attack only cities or "a mixture of civil and military targets" — by which he meant the inaccurate French missile, which could hit only Moscow — had "serious limitations." But attacking military targets while withholding against cities was a "not wholly unattainable" objective for the U.S. forces, he said.

McNamara spent much of the speech disabusing his listeners of the idea that nuclear war was desirable. In European politics the notion of a clean exchange of missiles over the rooftop of Europe had appeal; it was imagined as a lesser evil than another exhausting battle of mass armies on the ground. McNamara tried to dispel this myth by showering statistics on these allied defense ministers and generals — the first they had been given in detail — about the projected human costs on the Continent. If the Soviets aimed for urban-industrial European and American targets, 75 million Americans and 115 million Europeans would die. If the Soviets targeted only military sites, 25 million Americans would die and "somewhat fewer" Europeans. While "both sets of figures make for grim reading," the countermilitary figures were "preferable."

The forces assigned to General Norstad, the Supreme Allied Commander, Europe (SACEUR), would not be capable of knocking out all the Soviet weapons aimed at Europe, he revealed. Western Europe needed other U.S. nuclear forces to launch in Europe's defense. The purveyor of nukespeak went on:

> More than XXX* [U.S.] weapons are scheduled against SACEUR's nuclear threat list. SACEUR plans to assure the destruction of XXX targets on the list with his forces alone. Approximately XXX targets are scheduled for attack and destruction solely with external [U.S.] forces. SACEUR schedules sorties against another XXX more targets with his own forces, but the assurance he will be able to destroy them is not enough to warrant reliance on his attacks alone.

Later in the speech McNamara confirmed Kennedy's promise to dedicate some of the new Polaris missiles to NATO targets. "We have undertaken the nuclear defense of NATO on a global basis," he said, meaning that far-flung U.S. submarines were guarding the allies, too.

Thus he worked up to the need for central control, throwing cold water on the hopes of the French and others: "There must not be competing and conflicting strategies in the conduct of nuclear

* Figure classified.

war. . . . [W]eak nuclear capabilities, operating independently, are expensive, prone to obsolescence, and lacking in credibility as a deterrent."

To the rich American, the higher sums the allies would have to pay to mount an effective non-nuclear defense were worth it, since the result would be to avoid nuclear war; "surely an Alliance with the wealth, talent and experience that we possess can find a better way than this to meet our common threat."

Had McNamara stopped there, he could have been credited with leadership. There was little immediate reaction at the meeting, although Prime Minister Harold Macmillan grumbled in his diary that the call to build up was McNamara selling American arms and condemning European nuclear forces "with equal vigor and clumsiness."[13]

But McNamara insisted that he give the speech all over again in public, at a commencement ceremony at the University of Michigan, using essentially the same text minus the classified targeting data. There followed a debate in the White House over whether this would be politic. McGeorge Bundy warned the president that the passage on "weak" national nuclear forces "might seem to be a continuation of our debate with the French." Curiously, he noted that "Bob" claimed it "does not say anything directly disagreeable to the French themselves" — even though it is hard to imagine more critical language, in diplomatic parlance, than what was proposed.[14]

A sign of McNamara's growing influence on policy was that he got his way without much trouble. He later told me that one reason he insisted on going public was to explain flexible response and counterforce–no cities to the *Soviets*. In the spring of 1962, with the tension with Khrushchev over Berlin still fresh, McNamara wanted to inform the Soviets how both sides could avoid an all-out nuclear holocaust. Counterforce–no cities, after all, aimed to get both sides to limit their attacks to avert massive destruction. "We were trying to influence them," he said. "That was the reason for the Ann Arbor speech."

So he rose, dressed in academic robes, to receive an honorary degree from the University of Michigan in his former hometown of Ann Arbor on June 16 and gave the Athens speech in public. Meanwhile, McNamara's aides briefed the press on counterforce–no cities. A spate of articles followed.

The effect was electric. McNamara's attack on weak national nuclear forces had not clearly exempted the British force, which was justified in Britain as capable of independent use when that nation's "supreme interests" were at stake. Macmillan called McNamara's position an "ill disguised attack upon the determination of Britain." Lord Beaverbrook railed in the *Evening Standard* that "McNamara has given an exceptionally clumsy speech," and that he "lacks the qualities of a statesman."[15]

McNamara's clarification was disdainful. He had his press office issue a statement that Britain's bomber-carried nuclear force had "long been organized as part of a thoroughly coordinated Anglo-American striking force," although "political control remains with the British government." That he was not referring to the British should be "clear to anyone reading the speech in its entirety."[16]

The French were the angriest, however. The Ann Arbor speech heightened French criticism of McNamara, Washington, and flexible response. The French reacted by refusing to even discuss a shift in NATO's formal policy of massive retaliation in key committees. Those in the State Department who wanted Washington to be softer on French nuclear aims and, indeed, believed that having nuclear forces would build political maturity on the Continent were cross with McNamara.

Dean Rusk rushed to Europe to smooth ruffled feathers while denying his trip was occasioned by McNamara's speech. In it McNamara had said that the administration was still considering Norstad's MRBM proposal; soon after Ann Arbor it shelved the MRBM, too. McNamara's blunt insistence on central control flew in the face of General Norstad's plan for an MRBM force for Europe, about which Norstad had been acting like "a proconsul in Outer Gaul," in Roswell Gilpatric's phrase.[17] Kennedy and McNamara wanted more cooperation than Norstad had given them. The president gave a final audience to Norstad. Then the distinguished general, one of the most famous Americans in Europe at the time, crossed the Potomac to see McNamara. McNamara asked him, Well, Lauris, what are your plans? The more compliant Lyman Lemnitzer was appointed to succeed Norstad in Europe. An era was ending.[18]

In January 1963, Charles de Gaulle surprisingly vetoed Great Britain's entry into the Common Market, thus setting back the cause of European unity by years. McGeorge Bundy wrote a rueful memo to Kennedy comforting him that it was not the president's fault; de Gaulle might have done it anyway. But "our lectures to NATO have been sounder in logic than in sweet persuasiveness," he added, in an apparent reference to McNamara's speech.[19]

After delivering the Athens speech, McNamara flew east. He touched down in Thailand "in the black," meaning the trip was top-secret.[20] But his forty-eight-hour visit to South Vietnam would be long remembered for the haste and zeal with which he rushed through it.

Stepping through the plane door at the top of the roll-away steps at Tan Son Nhut Airport, outside Saigon, he encountered the hot breath of the tropics; a waterlogged blanket of steamy air hugging the land, a harbinger of the summer monsoon. Before him were modest buildings; Tan Son Nhut resembled a small airport in the American Midwest. To the side sat some South Vietnamese C-47s, a reminder of war in this provincial scene.

Two men greeted McNamara as he rushed down the stairway with the hustle of a VIP with not a second to waste. The first was Frederick Nolting, the U.S. ambassador, a pinstriper whose measure McNamara had taken. But the second man, General Paul D. Harkins, he had yet to know. The general sported a new, fourth star; he was fifty-seven, and three months into the newly created job of commander, Military Assistance Command, Vietnam (MACV).[21] The president had approved this upgrading of the Army outpost as part of his decision to fight in Vietnam a model counterinsurgency war. As McNamara rushed past the two men toward his waiting car, a cluster of civilians in open-necked shirts called to him, Saigon's tiny American and French press corps.

Kennedy's November 1961 policy of limited partnership with South Vietnamese president Ngo Dinh Diem established that the war was Diem's to fight. Washington would help with increased military advice, funds and equipment, and civilian aid. The advisers picked to help the government forces were to be specialists in counterinsurgency war, heroes in this new arena for fighting Communist "wars of liberation," which Khrushchev had encouraged in a January 1961 speech. Briefly in 1961, Kennedy tried to make increased aid to Diem preconditioned on reforms. But Diem had reacted so sharply to the attempt at a quid pro quo that Ambassador Nolting and others persuaded the president to back off. They rationalized that once Diem was strengthened in his position vis-à-vis the guerrillas, he would be amenable to reform.

McNamara did not realize, as he rushed through the receiving line to be driven to MACV headquarters for a briefing, that handling Vietnam and serving Kennedy's larger interest were contradictory goals in 1962. The situation called not for management controls and statistics but skepticism. The side of McNamara that asked "Why, why, why," as reporter Richard Fryklund puts it, was not in evidence that May.

The trip was called an inspection tour, but it was not a real inspection, since Kennedy had pulled back from directly pressuring Diem and U.S. military aid would rise in any event. McNamara struck the pose of an inspector anyway, as a surviving news photo shows.[22] In the picture, McNamara is seen through the open door of a helicopter. He is in a business suit, his thick hair is smoothly combed straight back, he stares sternly ahead through the wire-rimmed glasses. With his briefcase poised neatly on his lap, he looks more ready to be lifted off to Ford World Headquarters than the front lines of a jungle war.

Behind him sit three plump officers who are laughing: General Lemnitzer, Harkins, and an unidentified Vietnamese. The impression of contrast between McNamara's solemnity and the generals' complacency that spring was not off the mark.

He went by helicopter into the field. As the aircraft lifted higher, he could see a breathtaking green landscape, which appeared completely empty. It was his first sight of Asia since he and Willard Goodwin had hung over the rail of the *President Hoover* off Shanghai while a Japanese aircraft shot at them by mistake.

As the chopper left the red-tile roofs of Saigon behind and headed northwest, the houses and roads gave way to open country of lush green forest and winding rivers shimmering in the sun. With its huge, tall stands of trees hundreds of years old, the land looked timeless. McNamara could pick out the old French rubber plantations when he could glimpse rows of gray-blue trunks beneath green canopy.

The chopper landed in Binh Duong province, where Harkins tramped with McNamara around some model "strategic hamlets," the main innovation of the limited partnership. The strategic hamlet program had started just that February, yet by April Diem claimed that thirteen hundred of the new settlements had been built. The Americans supplied barbed wire and shovels for digging moats so the new homes for villagers would be safe from the enemy.

McNamara was told that the hamlets would spread government

control in areas traditionally contested or held by the guerrillas, since the peasants, grateful for protection and civilian aid, would become loyal to Diem's regime. But he should have noticed the contradictions in these assumptions.

Binh Duong province had been the scene of an appalling episode of relocation.[23] Only seventy of the two hundred people near the village of Ben Cat moved voluntarily. The press had watched in horror as Diem's soldiers began herding the rest at gunpoint and burned down their homes. This destruction was exceptionally shocking because the villagers considered their old homes sacred, as part of their religious tradition of ancestor worship. The reporters learned that Diem was holding up relocation funds meant for villagers. They later discovered that the Viet Cong had influence in the new hamlets anyway. Ben Cat had been a region of intense guerrilla activity for years, and the first, forcible relocation had alienated villagers and in fact strengthened the Communist position. When *Time* magazine published photographs of the brutal operation taken by a Frenchman, François Sully, Harkins had been furious. Sully was later expelled from Vietnam. McNamara knew that the pressmen were unhappy with MACV press policy and would try to get him to change it.

McNamara then lifted off for Dalat, the mountain resort built by the French as an escape from the terrible summer heat. The mountain climber in him would have appreciated the spectacular ridges from which on a good day one could look eastward through clear, cold air to the azure sea. At Dalat, McNamara met Diem for the first time. Like other Americans making the pilgrimage, he received a monologue on the evils of communism, the importance of strategic hamlets, the need for American guns and aircraft to strengthen the government against the Communists.

He was flown farther north, along the coast, to Da Nang, a quiet port with a distinctive wide sandy beach. As he peered down at the teeming coastal villages — a contrast with the empty highlands — he might have computed the numbers: South Vietnam had 14 million people; its armed forces of 170,000 were having a hard time beating 20,000 regular enemy troops. At this ratio the American people would not be safe from the Sioux, as John Kenneth Galbraith noted at the time.[24]

Next McNamara traveled south across the Mekong Delta to the southernmost province of An Xuyen. In summer the new, green shoots carpeted the paddies, growing taller and thicker until they were harvested in the fall. But in May, the endless rice fields were brown still, the seeds still in the muck below the water.

From the air, the delta looked desolate and muddy; canals and tree-lined man-made dikes and huts dotted the scene. McNamara would have been able to see occasional figures in conical hats, bent over and working, a timeless image of Asia.

Only by looking closely could he see the signs that these people, outwardly so tranquil, had been at war for a generation.[25] From the air one could make out triangular fortresses with a lone watchtower on one corner. The maze of bushy dikes linking settlements allowed stealthy communication. The winding canals had banks covered in thick overhanging grass where people and small boats could hide. Next to the bridges he could see guard towers; he may have been told that even armed government troops did not pass through parts of the region, for it had been a guerrilla and staunchly anti-French stronghold for decades.

The *New York Times*'s Homer Bigart, the dean of the Saigon press corps, wrote that at each stop, McNamara was briefed that the surrounding area was now secure. But the Viet Cong told a different story, he informed readers.[26] In 1962, the guerrillas avoided attacking Americans directly, lest an outrage against U.S. citizens bring the United States into the war. The Viet Cong were not ready for direct combat in any event; they were capable only of harassing Diem's troops. Showing well-honed military wisdom, they limited their actions to sending frightening messages to their foe. While McNamara was being briefed at Binh Duong, a convoy of the government's Seventh Regiment was attacked at noon on the main road to Saigon and five people killed. When he visited Da Nang, the enemy blew up a troop train ten miles to the north, killing twenty-seven Civil Guards and wounding thirty.

Under the limited partnership, U.S. military advisers trained Diem's troops to defeat the enemy in battle and lower the military threat to the regime. Harkins gauged success by the percent of the country under government control. Before McNamara arrived, a former intelligence officer in Saigon recalls, he saw Harkins and a junior officer prepare the map to be used in briefing the secretary. Government-controlled areas were covered in blue acetate, and enemy-controlled areas were red. Areas left white were "contested." Harkins told the briefing officer that the map had too much red on it. He waved his arm across it without even looking where he was waving. The officer began tearing red acetate off, randomly, to satisfy his superior. The intelligence officer later witnessed Harkins using the same map to brief McNamara. Appalled, the officer also noticed that McNamara did not question the map.[27]

Harkins was a product of the institutional Army, which had grown bureaucratic and self-satisfied after its victory in World War II and imagined success in Korea. As the more dynamic officers with a real grasp for battle drifted away in the late 1950s (discouraged by Eisenhower's neglect of the service and their colleagues' foolish quest to use battlefield atomic weapons in the next ground war), many of the senior men who remained knew how to succeed only in the narrowest, bureaucratic terms. Would Harkins have supplied statistics — and body counts — no matter who his civilian superior was, or is McNamara solely to blame for this fatal flaw?

The balanced answer is that by 1962, the Army was vulnerable to a civilian such as McNamara, who imposed his own administrative system. McNamara made a practice of sending ahead a detailed list of questions before each of his trips to Vietnam, thus giving Harkins weeks to work up fine-sounding answers and rehearse. This procedure ignited a pattern that would continue throughout the war: Numbers — such as how many weapons shipped, enemy weapons captured, strategic hamlets, enemy and friendly body counts — were used to claim progress.

Years later, a civilian who had watched these terrible, misleading briefings McNamara received in South Vietnam privately took him to task for it. Why did you send a list in advance like that? Why did you give them the chance to lie to you? McNamara had replied: You don't understand. As defense secretary I *had* to let them give me their official line. I could tell when they were lying.

In other words, Bob McNamara was convinced — or had convinced himself — that he had to use the techniques of formal administration to run this war, and being McNamara, administration equaled asking for statistics. He had faith that he could sit through scripted briefings, watching the triumphant march of blue acetate across the maps, and discern truths from lies. McNamara posed as a skeptic and thought of himself as a disbeliever; yet it was his system, and at some level he believed what it told him.

Before leaving Vietnam in May, McNamara met with reporters in the living room of Ambassador Nolting's house in Saigon. He was still dusty in khakis and too rushed to shave. He had "inspected"; he was famous for second-guessing the military. He gave his impressions of the reality of the war. A Defense Department notetaker wrote that McNamara said he was "encouraged," although "no expert." But in forty-eight hours he had seen "a great deal of South Vietnam . . . and . . . acquired a 'good feel' " for conditions in the country.

A reporter asked whether he might feel differently if he stayed longer. McNamara replied, "Absolutely not," that his feelings would be "reinforced" many times over.

He went on to praise the progress of the effort, "using a map . . . naming officers, both U.S. and South Vietnamese." In fortified areas, "attacks have dropped off" and "training is effective." He talked of a "Colonel 'Tong,' " who "impressed" him. Another officer, an ARVN major, was only twenty-one years old but had cleared a large area of Viet Cong and was protecting eleven thousand people. "The Secretary stated he knew of no U.S. officers 21 years old who he thought could do so well."

The reporters asked if force had been used to resettle peasants. "He answered yes, that some of the areas involved in clear-and-hold actions had been under Viet Cong control for 15 years; that older people did not like to move." Had the enemy reinfiltrated strategic hamlets? He said "some undoubtedly had but eventually they would be known through a security check and identification program . . . a screening-over-time phase."

McNamara predicted "no large increase in numbers from those [Americans] now in country." Bigart had asked about Harkins's withholding information. McNamara "gave them the works.

> [T]he United States was not in a war. There were no large scale military actions in which thousands of U.S. young men were being sent out to die. . . . Some things could not be publicized for security reasons, he said. He blamed the press for blowing up other things which caused "grave problems for U.S. policies at home."[28]

In other words, a snow job. Reporters' hopes for some loosening of MACV information policy were dashed. The general-basher from Washington was not going to change Harkins's rules. Bigart mistrusted all officialdom and was not surprised. But a young reporter on the scene for United Press International, Neil Sheehan, who had been in Vietnam only two weeks, wondered how a man as smart as McNamara could be so optimistic so soon.

Sheehan followed the secretary to his waiting car and asked him this question. McNamara turned and gave the young man a sudden glare through his spectacles. He snapped: "Every quantitative measurement we have shows that we're winning this war."

A Marine guard slammed the door.[29] The car raced off to Tan Son Nhut, where McNamara's plane hurtled him east across the Pacific, back to the great Pershing desk and the big problems.

Indochina, the name the Europeans gave to the southeastern tip of Asia, was formed more than 100 million years before Neanderthal man appeared. The drifting Indian continental plate pushed against and under Asia and shoved up the Himalayan Plateau and the enormous mountains that dominate central China. These folded crusts of earth and rock curl east around the Indian subcontinent to form huge north-south rows of mountains. Their highest points in the Chinese interior give rise to all the major river systems of east and southern Asia: China's east-flowing Yellow and Yangtze rivers, the Salween and the Irawaddy, which run south through Burma, and the Brahmaputra, which traverses parts of India and Bangladesh. The Mekong is one of these, rising north of the Himalayas and snaking south and east through Indochina to disgorge at the southeasternmost tip of the continent. Over time, the mouth of the Mekong's waters built up thousands of square miles of river-rich silt, which formed a great flatland. Indochina's eastern region was shaped by the mountains, which wend toward the coast near the central mainland. Just north is a major delta where the Red and Black rivers, flowing southeast, descend from China and the mountains into the Gulf of Tonkin. The Red River delta and the Tonkin Gulf are sheltered from the open ocean to the east by Hainan, the big island that dangles from the southeast coast of China like a giant tear. Where the Red and Black rivers drop down from the high interior to the gulf, a basin was formed of flat country protected on three sides by mountains. It is a natural fortress with routes among the mountain passes north and northeast into China. In this basin long before the first century B.C. settled an offshoot of the Mongol people called the Viets.[30]

They called their kingdom Tonkin for most of their history. The mountains protected them from the more advanced Chinese civilization, to the north; they also linked the two through connecting passes. Vietnamese elephant ivory, spices, and rare woods moved north, as did tithes to Chinese overlords. Southward traveled the

Chinese language, Confucianism, and the art of collective rice farming. Each of these was adapted by the Viets in distinct ways from the parent Chinese culture. Left alone for the time being were the aboriginal mountain tribes and also the Khmer, a people of Indian descent whose cousins to the west would build the temple complex of Angkor Wat and who sparsely populated the southern delta.

For almost a thousand years after Christ, from 938 to 1850, each successive Chinese dynasty tried to overwhelm Viet-Nam (which means Viet to the south). They met sullen subordination, resistance, and bloody revolt. War, like geography, became destiny. The Chinese were superior and foreign; in response the Viets evolved martial tactics of luring the invader to remote places, hitting and running, wearing down the enemy, preparing for the moment of decisive battle and final defeat. They had the advantage of fighting on their home terrain. Their culture glorified not the scholar-mandarin, as did China's, but the soldier-mandarin. National myth extolled war heroes like Tran Hung Dao, who, in the thirteenth century, had driven out the armies of Genghis Khan, and the Trung sisters, who drowned themselves rather than submit after their army was beaten by the Chinese in the first century. The martial tradition reached deep into Vietnamese society; it was prestigious to be an officer in a warrior cult, and women as well as men won honor by showing courage in front of comrades.

The Viets undertook a historic expansion southward along the Indochinese coast from the fourteenth century on. It resembled the Romans' expansion through Italy. In the fourteenth century they absorbed the Champa, a coastal, seafaring people like the Vikings. As they moved farther south, the Viets drove the indigenous tribes deeper into the mountains. They crossed the Saigon River, a southeast-flowing branch of the Mekong, where it empties into the sea at a natural port. Thus they finally reached the great delta on the southernmost tip of the landmass. There the Viets conquered or bought out the Khmer lords and set up colonies of soldier-farmers. They began planting rice, as was customary in their northern homeland, making the once-empty flatland glistening and green.

Thus was formed an ethnically cohesive, mandarin-ruled martial society with a successful tradition of revolt against foreign rule. They were like the Irish in the Western world in their history of resisting conquest. The Vietnamese also resembled the Romans, for once they reached their geographic and administrative limit, along the eastern coast of the region, decline followed. By 1850, they were ripe for quick conquest by the technologically superior French.

France's *mission civilisatrice* in Indochina, although colored by its spread of Catholic churches and schools, was the usual exploitative imperialism. The French hired Vietnamese who converted to the faith to help export natural resources: elephant ivory, precious woods, gems and spices.[31] They planted giant rubber farms. Those Vietnamese who helped the French gained little stature in colonial society, however — as late as the early 1950s it was rare to see a Vietnamese traffic cop in Saigon. The French further degraded their Vietnamese helpers by payoffs in opium and alcohol; they made the Vietnamese brutalize and kill their own people in the name of advancing French control or commerce. Thus, during the hundred years of French occupation there evolved a class of Vietnamese who were dependent on white men's rule and money and had no identification with the masses, who for their part looked on them as oppressors; they had little experience of government, either. Many of the Frenchified elite were Catholic and lived in the north, around the old Tonkinese capital, now taken over by the French, called Hanoi.

Some Vietnamese mandarin families who hated the French practiced political resistance. When one particular scholar-mandarin from Nghe An lost his job because of political activities, the fact made a deep impression on his son, who adopted the name Ho Chi Minh. By the time of World War I, Ho was an anticolonial activist in Paris. He tried to present himself to President Woodrow Wilson during the postwar conference, because Wilson's Fourteen Points for peace rang of an American commitment to the self-determination of subject peoples. But Wilson and the other victors were interested in self-determination only for European whites like the Latvians and Hungarians, and were not about to liberate the dark-skinned peoples of Asia, even one who presented himself to them in morning coat and white tie.

Ho was rebuffed. In 1920 he discovered in Lenin an anticolonial prophet. He became a Communist and spent the next two decades in China, maneuvering among factions to gather a cadre and plan a glorious revolt to retake his homeland. So in the years when Robert McNamara was concluding that he could run virtually any enterprise with management controls and brains, Ho was dedicating himself to a single, focused goal: the liberation of Vietnam from French rule.

Ho's moment came in early 1941, when he and his principal military officer, Vo Nguyen Giap, moved from China down through the mountains to a hideout on the northern slopes of the high mountains bordering China, because the Japanese were moving south, attacking French settlements in Hanoi and down the coast. During the Japanese occupation of Indochina the American Office of Strategic Services found Ho a useful helper. His cadres knew the land; they were expert at disrupting and harassing the Japanese. Meanwhile, some of the French had changed sides and formed a Vichy-style regime aiding the Japanese. But in 1945, the Japanese decided these Frenchmen were about to switch sides again, since Japan was losing. The Japanese launched a bloody crackdown on the French, giving native Vietnamese the eye-opening experience of seeing their white masters killed and maimed. In the meantime, Ho was cleverly using the wartime circumstances in the country to build his cadre. He formed a nationalist political arm called the Viet Minh. In 1941 he had only 5,000 regular soldiers; by 1945 he had 100,000. His political organization was set, his troops ready.

It would be little known in the West for almost thirty years, but in 1945 Ho appealed to the United States for help. Through his OSS contacts he offered to make his nation a free-enterprise zone for American business if the United States would help in the work of liberation. He drafted a declaration of independence based on that of the United States. Both gestures suggest that nationalism was his goal and his interest in communism subordinate to his cause.

The U.S. government in 1945 was preoccupied with more global postwar designs in Europe and East Asia. President Truman adopted what became an American pattern for nine years: rhetorical support for anticolonialism contradicted by quiet, material aid for the French reconquest of their colony from Ho's Communists. Washington's lend-lease arrangements for postwar France specifically allowed it to ship military equipment and men to Indochina, to help with that war; by its end the United States would be paying 90 percent of war costs incurred by the French.

Washington saw Stalin and communism as the overarching threat; the only Communist leader with an independent, nationalist regime was Yugoslavia's Tito, whom Washington regarded as an aberration. Many years later, when Ho's advances to the Americans and the nationalist side of his movement were publicly known, the question begged as to what course Ho would have followed had Washington made good on its anticolonial rhetoric. In 1967, McNamara would list as the first question his staff was to address in the top-secret Pentagon Papers study to derive lessons from history: "Was Ho Chi Minh an Asian Tito?"[32]

Washington's quiet support helped France wage nine years of exhausting war along this remote rim of continent, among the southern-delta rice farms and dikes, and in the treacherous folds of the mountains. Ho and Giap blended the Vietnamese martial tradition with their anti-French cause, playing on their recognized authority as mandarins in Vietnamese society. After 1949 they were helped by guns and matériel from Soviet Russia and Mao Tse-tung, who had driven the American-backed Nationalists and their leader, Chiang Kai-shek, from mainland China.

The advantage of a small but highly disciplined force exploiting native terrain showed in two decisive moments. The first was an ambush of a significant part of the French force in 1950 as it made its way along a narrow mountain road below overhanging rock and jungle, causing a defeat as terrible as Montcalm's when he lost Quebec, in 1759. Washington, however, alert to the spreading menace of Mao's Communists, helped the French keep on fighting.

The second military disaster was the occasion for Washington's most important decision about Vietnam since Truman chose to help the French. In May 1954, the French force garrisoned itself in the western mountains at the border of Laos, at a supposedly impregnable site called Dien Bien Phu. With typical cunning, the guerrillas secretly dragged enormous guns up the surrounding cliffs and opened fire on the camp's airfields with deadly surprise. The siege went on for weeks, but without air reinforcement, Dien Bien Phu was sure to fall. The French and the chairman of the U.S. Joint Chiefs of Staff, Admiral Arthur Radford, wanted Eisenhower to intervene. In a major act of military statesmanship, General Matthew Ridgway, who led U.S. forces in the Korean War and was now Army chief of staff, submitted a memo contrary to Radford's views.[33] Ridgway outlined the tremendous likely costs of U.S. intervention. His argument helped convince Eisenhower not to enter the conflict. Dien Bien Phu fell, ending a nine-year war that cost the lives of 95,000 soldiers fighting for France, 200,000 to 300,000 Viet Minh, and 250,000 to 1 million Indochinese.

Washington still thought it had an urgent stake in not letting Vietnam fall to the Communists. An international conference under way in Geneva fashioned an agreement with a face-saving political settlement for Indochina. The region was declared off-limits to outside military intervention; Laos was created as a neutral state; Cambodia stayed independent; Ho Chi Minh was given the northern part of Vietnam and a temporary capital in Hanoi; Vietnam was divided at its waist, at the 17th parallel. The more Frenchified, southern region was to have a Western-oriented native government. Catholics could relocate to the south, and a huge number, 800,000, moved. In due course, the accords promised, an election would be held to decide the political complexion of all of Vietnam. The accords were a stopgap measure designed to give Paris and Washington time to set up a puppet regime in the South and prevent another part of Asia from turning red. Ngo Dinh Diem, a member of the French Catholic elite whose brother had been killed by the Communists, was installed as president in the new southern capital of Saigon with the help of the CIA.[34] The promised elections were never held. Seven years later, Kennedy inherited Diem, the supposed temporary division of the land, and an increase in activity by guerrillas who had remained in the south and were responding to orders from Ho in Hanoi.

Drawing the line against communism in South Vietnam seemed feasible to the cold warriors on the Kennedy team in the spring of 1962. Although they liked to think they were a new generation, the torch they carried was that of Truman and Acheson, Eisenhower and Dulles. Rusk and the others believed the Communists had invaded South Korea because Acheson, in a speech, had failed to include Korea in a list of U.S. Asian interests. Kennedy had recently decided not to draw the line in neighboring Laos; he was pressured to be unequivocal in South Vietnam and chose the limited partnership, in which Diem fought his own little war with U.S. military advice and matériel.

The press shared the precepts of the cold war. Few reporters or editors — and few Americans, for that matter — knew anything about South Vietnam, let alone about the Communists' long-standing roots in nationalism or the deeper resentment of the peasants for the Frenchified Vietnamese elite. Typical of the coverage was a story by reporter Robert Trumbull that appeared in the February 18, 1962, *New York Times* under the headlines "THREE AREAS OF ASIA DISTURB THE FREE WORLD/ U.S. ATTEMPTS TO STEM COMMUNIST AGGRESSION ARE HAMPERED BY WEAK REGIMES ON CHINA'S FRINGES." An accompanying map showed the Soviet Union, China, and their satellites in black, the United States and Western Europe in white. The crosshatched parts of the rest of the world were deemed "contested" in the great struggle.[35] South Vietnam was crosshatched, on the *Times*'s map and in the American mind.

Carrying out the limited partnership seemed entirely manageable to Bob McNamara. He treated it as a problem in management control and set up what he considered proper resource inputs and measurements of progress to assure line control. This would allow the Army commander on the scene, who reported to him up the chain of command through the commander in chief of U.S. forces in the Pacific, Admiral Harry Felt, to do the job properly and on schedule.[36]

McNamara played a relatively small role in the less quantitative aspects. He helped prevent Edward Lansdale, the maverick CIA agent who had helped install Diem and who knew the country well, from being appointed to a key role on the scene; General Taylor, Gilpatric, and McNamara found Lansdale too odd, too uncontrollable. McNamara clearly wanted deputies who would play on the team. So he acquiesced when Taylor proposed his protégé, Paul Harkins, for the job of MACV commander. Harkins was considered a good choice because he was of the Army; the Army would accept him.[37] As for strategy, Kennedy romantically hoped his new Green Beret special forces would fight a new kind of hearts-and-minds war; McNamara made little effort to see that Harkins really followed such a policy.

Instead McNamara worked to guarantee the flow of new weapons to Diem's troops. Had he been more curious, he might have noticed that these men did not lack guns and that the enemy was significantly underarmed, using old weapons captured from the French and homemade guns. If Diem's lack of battle success was not due to a shortage of weapons, why send new and more powerful weapons? he might have asked. But Harkins wanted them, and the institutional Army wanted them; America's proxies should, after all, have the most modern firepower, they argued. Harkins said, in effect, that napalm could extend firepower in a jungle war, where it was hard to find an enemy soldier in a village. He found herbicides useful; they could open out brushy terrain to make South Vietnam more like the open fields of Europe, where the U.S. Army was trained to do battle. McNamara was not, as far as can be determined, concerned about the lethal effects of these escalations. He asked for statistics to measure how fast

American aid and advisers were reaching Vietnam. He took Harkins's word — and Harkins's numbers — on the uses of these resources in battle.[38]

McNamara committed another mistake in reflexively falling into line with Kennedy's decision to keep the American military role quiet. In this, McNamara crossed over into a moral betrayal of the soldiers whom they were sending to "advise" Diem's troops — and who were inevitably drawn into combat — and of those few who, in this early phase, became casualties. Not until Homer Bigart's stories exposed a policy of not awarding military honors to American soldiers in Vietnam, did Kennedy formally recognize their sacrifice. The Purple Heart is given, after all, for valor in combat, when officially the men weren't.[39]

After meeting with Harkins in Honolulu in February, McNamara claimed that "all" U.S. "efforts" were designed to help in "training" Vietnamese forces. But to the Advertising Council on March 7 he admitted that U.S. advisers were ferrying Diem's troops into battle. On March 15 he said that "to obtain the full range of such training . . . it occasionally takes place under combat conditions." When a reporter asked if this meant American fliers were "firing or dropping bombs," McNamara hedged, saying that they were "under instructions not to fire unless fired upon." But "in a few minor instances they have had to return that fire in self-protection."[40]

By his high profile, his statistics, flying trips, press conferences, and optimism, he identified himself with the war. McNamara gave John Kennedy's limited partnership in this remote corner of the world its aura of invincible, thoroughly American success.

But the stick figure exuding optimism whom Neil Sheehan had followed from Ambassador Nolting's house in Saigon was only part of the man. George W. Allen, a Defense intelligence analyst, recalls a top-secret meeting during the May stopover in Saigon between McNamara and General Lemnitzer, Admiral Felt, Harkins, and Nolting. Allen and the staff sat in chairs along the wall, there to speak if called upon. He saw McNamara set the agenda paper to one side and start talking about his secret stopover in Thailand.[41] Then he said to Lemnitzer: Let's assume the worst, that the enemy drives straight down the Mekong Valley through Laos toward Cambodia. What do we do?

There was a long silence while Lemnitzer fumbled with his briefing book. It became clear that he didn't know what to say until he found the answer in the book. Finally he haltingly replied that this particular contingency called for "SEATO Plan Five," which meant sending U.S. ground troops into Laos.

McNamara then turned to Admiral Harry Felt. Felt used the nickname Don, but McNamara, trying to be friendly, misremembered the name and called him Harry, which irritated the admiral.

Well, Harry, McNamara said, suppose we do what Lem here says and put divisions along the Mekong. What do they do next? Stay there? Move into the country? Felt seemed as tongue-tied as Lemnitzer.

"We can wipe Tchepone off the face of the earth in forty-eight hours," Felt said, referring to a city in Laos.

Allen thought McNamara showed amazing patience with these men, supposedly the cream of the world's finest military machine. The secretary then addressed Harkins: Suppose we do what Lem and Harry say, Paul. How would the enemy position in South Vietnam be affected? Harkins did not know. Nolting broke the silence to utter the cliché that Thailand and South Vietnam were the pillars of U.S. policy and Laos the keystone.

Allen felt embarrassed for McNamara. He was also deeply worried. McNamara was asking good questions and deserved serious answers, not prattle about wiping Tchepone off the map and pillars and keystones. He was also impressed that McNamara had been able to name every major town along the Mekong from north to south. None of these officers in the chain of command and responsible for the region could do that.

The session ended stiffly, with McNamara urging the commanders to work on responses to a Communist drive down the Mekong. McNamara had probed, but not far enough, Allen thought.

By July 1962, McNamara's public statements were more confident than those of May, if such a thing was possible. The statistical indicators were up. Success seemed to be just around the corner.

At Honolulu on July 23, Harkins gave McNamara more encouraging statistics, failing to brief him on a fiasco that had occurred three days earlier on the Plain of Reeds, southwest of Saigon, where one of Diem's officers had the enemy, then let him get away.

McNamara understood that the purpose of the limited partnership was to train the South Vietnamese to fight for themselves, so that the threat would be lowered and the Americans could leave. When would this happen? he asked Harkins. Allen remembers Harkins acting startled, jumping up in his chair. Then he collected himself. The Americans could leave "one year from the time that we are able to get [the Saigon forces] fully operational and really pressing the VC in all areas."[42]

At McNamara's instruction, Harkins produced a plan showing numbers of men, proposed budget by year, and a timetable for rolling up the job. Phases I and II could be complete by the end of 1962. In 1963 would come Phase III, a nationwide offensive by Diem's army, with U.S. reinforcements, to grind away until the enemy was broken as an organized force. In Phase IV, "Followup and Consolidation," Diem's authority would be completely restored and his forces could mop up while the Americans phased out. He dubbed the program Operation Explosion, a name as fatuous as the plan itself. McNamara said: "We must take a conservative view and assume it will take three years instead of one year. We must assume the worst and make our plans accordingly." He understood the political impact of American deaths. "We must line up our long-range programs as it may become difficult to retain public support for our operations in Vietnam. The political pressure will build up as U.S. losses occur."

Did Harkins lie to McNamara? Sheehan, in a later, thoughtful history of the war, concludes he did not. He "willed himself to believe what he wished to believe and to reject what he wished to reject."[43] The same could be said of McNamara.

III
THE USES OF POWER

9

Battling Chaos

I T WAS ELEVEN-FIFTY on the morning of Tuesday, October 16, 1962. Robert McNamara sat at a long table in the Cabinet Room of the White House.[1] On his immediate right was the president; to the right of the president sat Dean Rusk. To McNamara's left sat his deputy, Roswell Gilpatric. Next to Gilpatric was General Maxwell Taylor, chairman of the Joint Chiefs of Staff. Other key advisers, including the national security adviser, McGeorge Bundy, and Bobby Kennedy, were arrayed around the table according to rank, as usual. But the reason for their secret meeting was anything but usual.

Two analysts from the CIA were using pointers to explain enlarged photographs: grainy, black-and-white scenes of a landscape taken from above, showing treetops and open ground. The analysts pointed to hard-to-see details: construction, trucks, transporters, and launchers for missiles. The day before, Monday, intelligence analysts studied film, frame by frame, taken from high-flying U-2 spy planes on Sunday. They concluded that these new photos proved the Soviet Union was secretly installing nuclear missiles in Cuba. This Tuesday morning session was Kennedy's first full briefing on the terrible discovery.

Dean Rusk, the ranking Cabinet officer according to protocol, led off with ideas on how Kennedy should handle the crisis. Then it was McNamara's turn, as the Cabinet's second-ranking member. He had been told of the missiles late Monday evening by Gilpatric, who himself learned the news at dinner at Taylor's quarters and waited for McNamara to finish hosting a Great Books seminar at his house before phoning him with the grim news. At seven-thirty the next morning, McNamara, Gilpatric, and General Taylor studied the photos themselves. They worked up a plan for attacking the missile sites right away.[2] Now, in the Cabinet Room, McNamara's bass voice ticked off the military options: nuclear crisis parsed as cold logic. In a tape that survives, his voice is tense and emphatic.[3]

Before listing "the knowns" or outlining military alternatives, McNamara argued that they had to accept "two propositions." The first was that if they attacked the missile sites, they had to attack before the missiles became operational. "I do not believe we can . . . knock them out before they can be launched." If any missiles were launched, there was certain to be "chaos in part of the east coast or the area, in a radius of six hundred to a thousand miles from Cuba." Second, McNamara noted, any attack would have to include the airfields, as well as aircraft that were hidden and not on the airfields, "plus all potential nuclear storage sites. Now, this is a *very* extensive air strike." Two or three thousand Cubans would die. They could execute the strike within hours if the president wished.

That Tuesday morning the photos did not show actual missiles or warheads, but Kennedy and his advisers had to assume they were somewhere in Cuba. Analysts who had been monitoring ship traffic to Cuba for months now saw new significance in two freighters that had docked in Cuba in September and been riding high in the water. They were built for the lumber trade but were too light to have lumber in their holds. Their hatches were closed; there were trucks on their decks. Probably these ships had ferried sixty-foot-long missiles across the Atlantic, out of sight of American reconnaissance.

McNamara and the others needed desperately to know where the warheads were, how quickly Soviet technicians at the sites could marry them to the missiles, and when the missiles would be able to create "chaos" in the United States. McNamara said, "It's inconceivable to me that the Soviets would deploy nuclear warheads on an unfenced piece of ground"; he was still looking for the warheads, separated from the missiles. Another threat was the MIG jets arriving in crates and the longer-range Ilyushin-21 bombers being uncrated in Cuba; both could drop nuclear or big conventional bombs on the United States. Was Khrushchev planning an all-out attack?

The officials were sure Nikita Khrushchev did not know his gambit had been discovered. The Soviet leader had been bellicose ever since Kennedy's invasion of Cuba at the Bay of Pigs had failed and since the June 1961 Vienna summit. McNamara's twenty-three months in Washington offered numerous outlets for his habitual activism, from Berlin to Vietnam. Now he felt tested as never before.

McNamara later wrote revealingly of the Cuban crisis: "Exposure to danger strips away the protective covering with which each of us guards his inner thoughts."[4]

The men around the table saw Cuba as a pistol aimed at the Western Hemisphere. Since coming to power in 1959, Fidel Castro had transformed his populist revolution into a Communist camp. His growing links to Moscow flouted the Monroe Doctrine barring outside intervention in the Western Hemisphere, which U.S. presidents had preached since the nineteenth century.

Castro's behavior aggravated the American neurosis about communism. He seized huge American holdings, causing dispossessed investors to pressure Washington for restoration and vengeance. Political tensions had grown since the Bay of Pigs. The Kennedy administration secretly authorized Operation Mongoose, a series of covert operations to sabotage Castro's rule.[5] Castro responded by expanding his ties with Moscow to include military "protection." His fears of a large U.S. invasion (he assumed Kennedy would not stumble with another small operation) led him to accept the Soviet missiles in a secret deal in June.

During the spring and summer of 1962, Soviet weapons and military personnel flowed to Cuba, watched closely by U.S. intelligence. Castro claimed they were needed to defend against another American invasion. Kennedy and many others suspected the buildup was intended to arm Communist guerrilla groups elsewhere in the hemisphere, to spread the revolution.[6]

The Soviet military buildup in Cuba became a troublesome political issue for Kennedy. In the congressional campaigns of 1962, Republicans flailed him for not having exorcised the red menace so close to home. The motives behind the Soviet buildup were much debated. New York Republican senator Kenneth Keating said the Soviets were bringing in missiles to be able to attack the United States; intelligence officials interviewed him and decided he had no proof. Alone in the administration, CIA director John McCone — who was also a Republican—privately warned Khrushchev might put missiles into Cuba to fix the missile imbalance, which was now running against him almost four to one.

McNamara and Kennedy were blind to the deep fears they aroused in Nikita Khrushchev by their activism: their huge missile buildup and the U.S. ringing of the Soviet periphery with warheads, such as the Jupiter missiles in Turkey. The Kremlin found McNamara's Ann Arbor speech provocative; in March Kennedy said publicly that Khrushchev should not rule out the chance of a U.S. first strike. Yet Khrushchev also saw that Kennedy tolerated some of his counter-moves: the Berlin Wall and his hints he might put missiles in Cuba. Kennedy did not warn Khrushchev *not* to put "offensive" weapons in Cuba until September — when, unknown to him, the die was already cast.

Now they felt deceived. The Kremlin said, through the Soviet news agency Tass, that the Soviet Union would not put offensive missiles into Cuba.[7] In September, Soviet ambassador Anatoly Dobrynin privately assured Bobby Kennedy that ground-to-ground missiles would not be sent.

The photographs now proved that the Soviets had engaged in "one gigantic fabric of lies," in Bobby Kennedy's phrase. The Cuban pistol was being loaded.

Roswell Gilpatric remembers that that first Tuesday morning, McNamara was not "shaken" but "wearing that sort of taut look that I came to recognize when something came upon him that he just felt he couldn't . . . handle — didn't have any immediate solution for."[8]

The president also was "clipped" and "very tense." He believed the Soviets "meant business in the most real sense, that this was the biggest national crisis he faced." McNamara's attitude was that "nothing else mattered."

From that morning on, McNamara worried if Khrushchev could control his men in Cuba, six thousand miles from Moscow, or whether once the missiles were operational, some Soviet "second lieutenant" could fire them. McNamara told the others, "We don't know what kinds of communications the Soviets have with those sites. We don't know what kinds of control they have over the warheads."[9]

There was a brief debate about whether the missiles changed the overarching nuclear balance. As of that day, the United States could claim 129 operational land-based ICBMs and 144 Polarises, while the Soviets were thought to have only 75 land-based ICBMS. Their submarine-launched missiles were crude, with a shorter range, and were kept beyond striking distance of the United States; they did not compare to the U.S. Polaris.[10]

In fact, the Kremlin's perception of its own nuclear inferiority was a primary motive. Khrushchev and his generals did believe, it is now known, that having a few dozen missiles within a few minutes' flight of the U.S. heartland would redress Soviet shortcomings in the face of Kennedy's bigger, fast-growing missile force.

But McNamara argued that morning and forever after that the addition of twenty to forty missiles in Cuba did not change the U.S.-Soviet military balance. True, the United States had many more missiles than the Soviets, but it could not be sure of destroying the entire Soviet nuclear force in a single strike. So some Soviet weapons would survive to hit back — as would some American weapons if the Soviets attacked first. The fact of Soviet retaliation meant there could be no winners in a nuclear war. Had McNamara stuck to his point and had Kennedy accepted it fully, they could have calmly told the American people they had little to fear, while negotiating a pullout in time. Conceivably this could have been preferable to "the Kafkaesque nightmare" they chose, of risking nuclear war to eliminate missiles that did not harm U.S. security.[11]

All the advisers agreed, however, that Soviet missiles in Cuba were unacceptable to the United States politically. They had to be gotten out. Yet doing so risked general nuclear war.

McNamara came to that Tuesday morning meeting virtually recommending a rapid air strike on the missiles, airfields, and related sites. But after an afternoon in the Tank with the Joint Chiefs, he began to stress the hazards.

The transcript of the advisers' Tuesday evening session, taken from tapes Kennedy secretly authorized of most large meetings, gives a firsthand glimpse of how McNamara's mind worked in the crisis.[12] His dominance in the discussion is striking. That evening, as in several later sessions, Dean Rusk, who should have assumed leadership of the group when the president was absent, was not there.

McNamara ran through three options. The first was the diplomatic protest that Rusk had proposed that morning. McNamara said, "This seems to me to lead to no satisfactory result," because it would warn the Soviets and Cubans and give them time and motive to hide their missiles from attack, thus ruling out effective U.S. military action and leaving the missiles in Cuba. Course 3 was to attack the sites. Course

2 lay between the political course — course 1 — and the military course — course 3 — and was a declaration of open surveillance "and a statement that we would immediately impose . . . a blockade against offensive weapons entering Cuba in the future." Thus did a naval blockade enter the advisers' deliberations.[13]

McNamara outlined the risks of an air strike. The Joint Chiefs believed that it would require "several hundred" sorties and would make the Soviets respond militarily somewhere else in the world, requiring a U.S. military response in turn, perhaps with nuclear weapons. "It may be worth the price. . . . But I think we should recognize that possibility." McNamara added:

"I don't know what kind of a world we live in after we've struck Cuba, and we, we've started it. . . . How do we stop at that point?"

He started organizing the tasks, scribbling down the paper to be prepared for the president the next day.

> Now, could we agree what we're gonna do? I would suggest that we, uh, divide the series of targets up by, in effect, the number of DGZs [Designated Ground Zeroes, or aim points for bombs] and, uh, and, uh, numbers of sorties required to take those out for a series of alternatives starting only with the missiles and working up through the nuclear storage sites and the MIGs and the er, and the SAMs and so on. . . .
>
> But the most important thing we need to do is this appraisal of the world after any one of these situations. . . .
>
> Could I suggest that tonight we actually draft a paper and it starts this way — just a paragraph or two of the knowns. . . .
>
> But then I would follow that by the, the alternatives of, not all of them but the more likely alternatives that we consider open to us. . . .[to people leaving] Just stay a second.

He then started to develop the idea of a naval blockade to stop more missiles and equipment coming in.

> I don't think there is a military problem here . . . and therefore . . . I asked myself, Well, what is it then if it isn't a military problem? . . . Well, it's just exactly . . . that . . . if Cuba should possess a capacity to carry out offensive actions against the U.S., the U.S. would act. . . .
>
> Well, how will we act? Well, we want to act to prevent their use. . . . Now, how do we . . . act to prevent their use? Well, first place, we carry out open surveillance, so we know what they're doing. All times. Twenty-four hours a day from now and forever. . . .

What else do we do? We prevent any further offensive weapons coming in. In other words, we blockade offensive weapons.

Next McNamara added an ultimatum to Khrushchev,

a statement to the world . . . that we have located these offensive weapons; . . . if there is ever any indication that they're to be launched against this country, we will respond not only against Cuba, but we will respond directly against the Soviet Union with, with a full nuclear strike. Now this alternative doesn't seem to be a very acceptable one, but wait until you work on the others.

McNamara's first instinct had been to act; now that he had a better plan, he hung on to it with characteristic stubbornness. During "two and a half hours one day at lunch, after lunch, arranging ourselves, he being the United States and I being the Soviet Union, and making a series of moves and countermoves," Gilpatric says, McNamara was convinced "that this limited form of blockade, quarantine, was the best move. Not all of its details, but it was pretty much set in his mind. He never shifted from that ground from that point on."[14]

Wednesday morning the advisers gathered around the table with the president again. There had been no leak to the press. The CIA's briefing now showed two sites, the first one at San Cristóbal and one nearby, at Guanajay. Both sprouted mobile launchers and twenty-eight launchpads. The blown-up photos now revealed real missiles, the mobile MRBMs and the two-thousand-mile-range intermediate-range ballistic missiles. The IRBMs needed the fixed launchpads now under construction. Since neither could survive attack, both were "first strike" weapons the Soviets would have to use early to avoid losing in a U.S. attack. None was operational yet. When all the sites became operational, some forty warheads could be dropped as far away as Wyoming and Montana. More than eighty million Americans could be killed.[15]

For the moment, the informal circle of advisers Kennedy asked to help in the crisis — including outsiders such as Soviet expert Llewellyn Thompson and Dean Acheson — was code-named ELITE. Only the following Monday did Kennedy make the group an Executive Committee of the National Security Council, or Ex Comm. The ELITE–Ex Comm group met daily in Under Secretary of State George Ball's conference room when they were not sitting in the

White House with the president. Later McNamara would praise the secrecy they had enjoyed for almost a week. In fact, they dissuaded reporters who sniffed out the story from printing it.

On Wednesday the president kept up appearances by campaigning in Connecticut. When he arrived at Yale University, some people turned out to protest the fact that he had not ousted Castro. A placard urged "More Courage, Less Profile."

The ELITE–Ex Comm advisers argued about whether to recommend an air strike and whether it could be kept "limited." An air strike entailed the risk that some of the missiles would be fired, either on Moscow's orders, by panicky Soviet technicians, or even, conceivably, by Cubans. The Soviets could possibly retaliate by attacking NATO missiles in Turkey, where since 1957 medium-range Jupiter missiles had been installed. A U.S. attack on the missiles in Cuba would kill hundreds of Soviet technicians, thereby giving Khrushchev a legal casus belli. The Kremlin took such legalisms very seriously, the group was told.

The problem with the alternative of a naval blockade was that it failed to get rid of the missiles. It even gave the Soviets time to finish making ready both missiles and aircraft and installing any warheads that might already have arrived in Cuba. In addition, a chokehold of Cuba invited Khrushchev to put a stranglehold on Berlin. That, Kennedy had said many times since the tense summer of 1961, threatened NATO at its heart, a vital interest, and would produce a U.S. military response with "whatever weapons are necessary" — a euphemism for possible nuclear war.

Castro figured large in their discussions. As McNamara noted the first day, an air strike and invasion could spark an uprising. It was a beautiful chance to topple Castro, and several members of the Joint Chiefs ardently wished to do so. Whether the men in the Cabinet Room knew it then, U.S.-backed covert actions continued throughout the crisis: Commandos even blew up a Cuban factory. The Senate Select Intelligence Committee investigations in the mid-1970s, headed by Senator Frank Church, concluded that John Kennedy himself was kept from knowing about specific efforts against Castro. McNamara and Bundy were aware of them in general terms; behind this screen of plausible deniability, mid-ranked officials pursued schemes whose effectiveness was mixed at best. The full story of how the men of the Ex Comm viewed Castro in the missile crisis will not be known until the still-classified parts of their deliberations are released.[16]

They did debate whether Kennedy should hold Castro responsible for accepting the missiles, in which case Kennedy could act openly against Castro if they were not removed. But Llewellyn Thompson, formerly U.S. ambassador to the Soviet Union, argued that only Khrushchev had the power to put them in and take them out, and therefore Kennedy should limit his response to Khrushchev.

The notion of a full blockade, which would cut Cuba's economic lifeline and in military terms be an act of war, evolved into a more limited "quarantine" stopping only ships suspected of carrying cargoes relating to the missiles. The distinction between applying military force for military ends, and military force for limited political ends — forcing Khruschchev to remove the missiles — became critical.

Bobby Kennedy recalled that by Wednesday, October 17, McNamara had become "the blockade's strongest advocate."[17] McNamara argued that it allowed Kennedy later options and created a means for Khrushchev to remove the missiles without starting a war. Bobby had also become a passionate blockade advocate. So he and McNamara were on the same side; it was the first time these two, who were later so close, took each other's measure. Bobby's arguments were moral. For the United States to attack a small nation like Cuba was incompatible with American traditions and reminiscent of the Japanese attack on Pearl Harbor. The president was not going to be the Tōjō of the 1960s, said his brother.

"McNamara helped the Attorney General mightily with his now-celebrated argument on 'maintaining the options,' " writes Abel. McNamara maintained that the decision was not "either or."[18] The president could start with the quarantine. If the Soviets did not respond by stopping work on the missiles, he could expand the quarantine by halting tankers carrying petroleum, for example. He could move on up the ladder of military pressure to an air strike and invasion, if needed.

Dean Acheson was a vehement air-strike advocate and thought Bobby's arguments were irrelevant or worse. McGeorge Bundy and Rusk switched positions. Treasury Secretary C. Douglas Dillon, General Taylor, and Paul Nitze favored the air strike with increasing intensity as the hours of meetings ticked by and the pressure grew for firm decision.[19]

Meanwhile, McNamara supervised daily preparations for an air strike and follow-up invasion in case the president chose this course.

They prepared for five hundred sorties, ready to go as of Tuesday, October 23. Their secret still had not leaked.

But troop movements in Florida did catch the notice of some reporters. Kennedy instructed his press secretary, Pierre Salinger, to say there was "nothing to" such reports. On Friday, October 19, a reporter from the *Miami Herald* contacted Arthur Sylvester, Mc-Namara's press aide, and asked point blank if there were missiles in Cuba. "I took it up with McNamara right away," Sylvester said later. "A decision was made to say no."[20]

Sylvester, speaking for the secretary of defense, denied there were Soviet missiles in Cuba. At that moment, Sylvester was one of the few in the Building who knew the secret; even the news bureau chief in Sylvester's office, who handed out the denial, did not know it was a lie.

The Pentagon also said on Friday that no alert or "emergency measures" had been ordered against Cuba. In fact, the alert order had gone out to the Atlantic and Caribbean commands at 1:20 P.M., just before the official denial.[21]

Thursday night the group reached a tentative agreement for a blockade. On Friday, as work proceeded on the missile sites, the men prepared papers, speeches, and presentations to the Organization of American States and the United Nations. They were ready to talk to the president on Saturday. Kennedy cut short a trip to Chicago and returned to the White House. He instructed Salinger to tell reporters the reason for his change in plans was a bad cold. Meanwhile four tactical air squadrons were placed on alert in case the president chose the air-strike option. At the end of the long Saturday meeting, the president decided on the quarantine. If Khrushchev wanted war, he would have to order his ships to run the blockade. An air strike was not so much ruled out as postponed. The advisers discussed how Kennedy should present the Soviet moves to the United Nations and the world. They decided to hold to the tightest secrecy until Monday night. That evening at seven, Kennedy announced on television that there were nuclear missiles in Cuba that could hit Hudson Bay, Canada, or Lima, Peru. He explained the quarantine. His threat of massive nuclear retaliation was explicit: "It shall be the policy of this nation to regard any nuclear missile launched from Cuba against any nation in the Western Hemisphere as an attack by the Soviet Union on the United States requiring a full retaliatory response upon the Soviet Union."[22]

McNamara began sleeping in the Pentagon, on a cot installed in his office. There was a phone extension by the cot, and a lock on the door between the office and the anteroom, where his secretary, Peg Stroud, sat. Only after she checked with McNamara by phone each morning that he was ready would she press a button that unlocked the door. He worked longer hours than ever. Subordinates doing all-night duty would hear their phones ring and a familiar voice bark at them in the middle of the night, when McNamara was supposed to be sleeping. Wags said the reason McNamara could sustain such a schedule day after day was that he operated like that normally.

But he warned his key civilians not to imitate him or hover over the military directly. Adam Yarmolinsky, his special assistant, and John T. McNaughton, general counsel, worked alternate twelve-hour shifts. "Don't be too evident. The military is concerned with civilian interference," McNamara instructed them.[23]

The gravity of the situation and the political dimension of the quarantine justified close civilian control, in McNamara's view. From the Cabinet Room, where the Ex Comm met each day, starting at ten o'clock, McNamara could receive Kennedy's orders and go into an adjoining room to telephone the National Military Command Center, where Kennedy's order would be transmitted to Admiral Robert Denison, commander in chief of the Atlantic Fleet, and thence to a secure telephone on the bridge of the *Newport News* and Vice Admiral Alfred G. Ward, commander of the Second Fleet, the commander on the scene. General Taylor, chairman of the Joint Chiefs, and the other chiefs were only "advisory" to the president and secretary of defense in the chain of command, which ran directly from McNamara to Denison to Ward.

Wednesday, October 24, at ten in the morning, when the quarantine took effect, two Soviet ships were approaching Admiral Ward's line.[24] A Soviet submarine moved in between them, one of four the Navy knew to be in the area. Kennedy sat at the long table with his advisers as they waited to see if the Soviets would charge the blockade; if so, it meant war. The U.S.S. *Essex* required the ships to halt, although Kennedy asked, at this last moment, if they could avoid having the first confrontation with a submarine.

"We must expect that they will close down Berlin — make the final preparations for that," the president said. The "moments of gravest concern," in Bobby Kennedy's words, ticked by. Then they learned that the three Soviet ships had stopped dead in the water.

Yet McNamara's later image of preternatural calm in the crisis was misleading. That evening in the Building, he decided he was not being well informed. Gilpatric, who was by all accounts a steady companion throughout the crisis, says he and McNamara weren't being "told anything. We were just being assured that this overall type of action was being implemented, and the Navy would take care of everything." This fit with the demeanor of Admiral George W. Anderson, the tall, blue-eyed, imposing chief of naval operations, who, when Kennedy ordered the quarantine, had said, "Mr. President, the Navy won't let you down." But when the operation began, says Gilpatric, "we just weren't sure they were operating on the basis of the very latest information. They'd run off a position at 1800 hours and operate on that for the next six or eight or twelve hours rather than constantly . . . adjusting."[25]

So at ten o'clock Wednesday night, McNamara took Gilpatric and marched up to Flag Plot, the Navy's command center.[26] This was a secure room under constant Marine guard. The walls were covered with huge charts of the seven seas, with markers showing the whereabouts of each ship. About thirty men were in the room.

The two civilians began questioning the duty officer. Admiral Anderson entered.

McNamara spotted a marker that showed a U.S. ship off in the ocean by itself, far from the quarantine line. "What's it doing there?" he asked. Anderson later said he did not reply because too many people within earshot were not cleared for this information. Anderson suggested they talk in an adjoining office, which was more secure. There he explained that the ship was tracking a Soviet submarine.

McNamara began interrogating Anderson. What was the Navy's plan for the first interception? Anderson replied that there was no need to discuss it. This was the Navy's operation.

We must discuss it, McNamara retorted. He began lecturing Anderson that the object was not to shoot anybody but to communicate a political message to Khrushchev. The operation must be run to avoid humiliating the Russians, if at all possible, otherwise Khrushchev might start a war.

What were the captains going to do if a ship started through the line? Shoot across its bow? What if it kept going? Shoot at the rudder? What then? What were Anderson's orders to his captains? McNamara demanded. Did each ship have a Russian-speaking officer on board?

Never before had a secretary of defense so cross-examined a member of the Joint Chiefs. Both men were under strain. McNamara was getting emotional. Anderson was red-faced and determined not to lose self-control. Some accounts say Anderson accused McNamara of "undue interference" in naval matters.

Anderson picked up a copy of the Navy regulations manual and waved it at McNamara. "It's all in there," he said.

McNamara answered, "I don't give a damn what John Paul Jones would have done. I want to know what you are going to do, now."

Anderson said, "Now, Mr. Secretary, if you and your deputy will go back to your offices, the Navy will run the blockade."

It was a critical moment in the growing strain and mistrust between McNamara and his senior commanders. Anderson and other Navy men were already convinced that McNamara was a "liar" in his dealings with them, and not the sterling figure he was portrayed as by admirers in the press. Now the civilian had physically intruded on the sanctum of Flag Plot and cross-examined Anderson. Years later, however, the admiral insisted that their exchange had been polite and McNamara's questions legitimate. He had not accused McNamara of "undue interference," he said.[27]

McNamara's invasion of Flag Plot became part of the lore of the Building, a landmark in the annals of civilian control. Even without the later civilian micromanagement of Vietnam, the Flag Plot episode would mark McNamara as the most heavy-handed civilian boss in the military's long and unforgiving memory since Truman fired Douglas MacArthur.

The real issue was whether McNamara's confrontation had been necessary to prevent a shooting war in the Caribbean, where American subs were now chasing Soviet subs, and Soviet and American surface ships maneuvered dangerously close to one another. Gilpatric says that half an hour after they returned to McNamara's office that night, an emissary from Anderson appeared. The officer asked for a list of McNamara's questions and concerns in detail. "From that point on they were submitting, asking approvals," Gilpatric says.

Gilpatric also recalls that as they marched back from Flag Plot through the long corridors, McNamara muttered: "That's the end of Anderson . . . he won't be reappointed, and we've got to find a replacement for him. As far as I'm concerned, he's lost my confidence."[28]

The next morning, Thursday, Admiral Ward's quarantine line intercepted its first Soviet ship. The tanker *Bucharest* was allowed to pass after declaring she carried only petroleum. Then a German passenger ship was let through.

A Thursday morning column by the influential Walter Lippmann created a new problem. Lippmann proposed that the way out of the impasse was for Kennedy to trade the missiles in Cuba for the removal of the Jupiters from Turkey. So good were Lippmann's sources as a rule that the Soviets, particularly the sophisticated ambassador Dobrynin, would assume the article was a trial balloon from the president. But the American leaders dreaded dragging in the Jupiters, at least publicly. Although Polaris made the Jupiters obsolete militarily, no American president could sacrifice the security of NATO — of which the Turks and other allies considered the Jupiters an integral part — to solve a problem in his front yard.

Friday morning, October 26, the president ordered the Soviet ship *Marcula* boarded. Her cargo was inspected and the ship allowed to pass. Back in the Tank, rumor had it that the *Marcula* carried missile electronics but the civilians were too chicken to force the issue and risk war. Right-wing anger was growing in some military quarters in response to Kennedy's supposed half measures.

At the Friday morning Ex Comm meeting, McNamara reported "with considerable agitation," in Elie Abel's words, that some missiles could be operational within hours.[29] They considered a quick air strike. Work was proceeding feverishly at the missile sites. There was a real risk of an incident among the U.S. and Soviet ships and submarines. Apparently without McNamara's knowledge, General Thomas Power of the Strategic Air Command ordered the strategic forces to go to "Def[ense] Con[dition] Two" — the next-highest state of alert — on a clear channel so the Soviets would learn of it and realize the Americans were ready for war. Curiously, Khrushchev's strategic forces were not on alert.[30]

In midmorning, word came from the Caribbean that twelve of twenty-five Soviet ships streaming across the Atlantic toward Cuba had turned back. They seemed likely to have cargoes Khrushchev did not want Admiral Ward's men to inspect. Rusk and others tried to dampen press speculation that Khrushchev had blinked.

Then at six o'clock on Friday night, the tickers from Moscow on the seventh floor of the State Department began typing a long message from Khrushchev with pieces of a deal: Soviet restraint on further weapons shipments to Cuba in exchange for Kennedy's promise not to invade. There was no mention of the Jupiters or NATO.[31]

Khrushchev's letter seemed unedited. It rambled. It made reference to the American "attack" on Siberia in World War II and to pacifist Bertrand Russell. "Only lunatics . . . who themselves want . . . to destroy the whole world before they die" would start a war. He asserted, "We are normal people," and, at another point, "We are both engaged in a tug-of-war, pulling on either end of a rope and thereby tying a knot that, once tied, neither of us will ever be able to undo."

The letter also said:

> What would a war give you? You are threatening us with war. But you well know that the very least which you would receive in reply would be that you would experience the same consequences as those which you sent us. And that must be clear to us, people invested with authority, trust, and responsibility. We must not succumb to intoxication and passions. . . . These are indeed transient things, but if indeed war did break out, then it would not be in our power to stop it.

Khrushchev's strange letter suggested to Dean Rusk that he was falling apart under the strain. But McNamara says he thought Khrushchev correctly saw that both sides were blundering into disaster. He calls it "the most extraordinary diplomatic communication I have ever seen."

The hope that Khrushchev wanted to loosen the rope was dashed Saturday morning, when another message came over the Teletype from Moscow. According to notes made by Bromley Smith of the National Security Council staff, as Kennedy started reading he said, "The statement was a very tough position." Probably the men around Khrushchev were stiffening him up. Or they were trying to confuse the Americans with conflicting proposals, buying time. The new message demanded removal of the missiles in Turkey, and possibly the denuclearization of all NATO, as the price for removing the missiles from Cuba. CIA director McCone told the Ex Comm that morning that some of the missiles were now operational. A Soviet ship, the *Graznyy,* was steaming toward Admiral Ward's line.[32]

Then McNamara and the others learned that an American U-2 plane had been shot down over Cuba by one of the surface-to-air missiles manned by the Soviets. The pilot, Major Rudolph Anderson, was dead. The confrontation was escalating. Kennedy needed more frequent overflights of Cuba to monitor Soviet actions, to watch for signs that they would launch. McNamara was recommending night overflights. If U.S. planes were shot at, the Americans should hit the SAMs. But if a shooting war started, someone might fire the missiles and cause "chaos" in the United States. Smith's notes have McNamara saying, "These offensive weapons must be made inoperable."[33]

Yarmolinsky recalls that McNamara had been "reasonably confident" the crisis could be controlled until Anderson was shot down. Then he became deeply "concerned." Lieutenant General David Burchinal — who calls McNamara a "pacifist" — was in the Tank Saturday afternoon when they got worse news. An American U-2 had strayed into Soviet airspace over Siberia, and Soviet fighters had scrambled. According to Burchinal, McNamara "turned absolutely white and yelled hysterically, 'This means war with the Soviet Union. The president must get on the hot line to Moscow.'" He then "ran out of the meeting in a frenzy." McNamara denies this.[34] (One problem with Burchinal's story is that in October 1962 there was no hot line to Moscow; it was not agreed on until 1963.)

When Kennedy met with the Ex Comm at four o'clock Saturday, October 27, emotions were running high, by all accounts. The president spoke as though an air strike must be undertaken Monday or Tuesday. Kennedy was angry that the Jupiter missiles were in Turkey at all. Since February 1961 he had repeatedly asked for them to be removed. But first Rusk, then George Ball, had not done as Kennedy wished, for fear of ruffling Turkish feathers. That Saturday, Ball stood by his refusal, telling Kennedy that "the Department had decided it could not raise this question with the Turks at this time for fear of disastrous Turkish reaction." Kennedy left the meeting to calm himself by walking around. Returning, he said, in Smith's notes, "We are in a bad position if we appear to be attacking Cuba for the purpose of keeping useless missiles in Turkey. . . . The Turks must be informed of the great danger in which they will live during the next week."

McNamara told the group that he considered a limited air strike "impossible," since U.S. reconnaissance planes were being attacked. They must now look to the major strike, followed by an invasion of Cuba. To do so, he said, they would need to call up the reserves now. If NATO was about to be drawn into war because of the Turkish missiles, the North Atlantic Council, its governing group, needed to meet, and fast.[35]

Again according to the notes of the meeting, McNamara said that if other reconnaissance planes "are fired on, we will attack the attackers." The United States "must now be ready to attack Cuba [deleted]. Invasion had become almost inevitable. If we leave U.S. missiles in Turkey, the Soviets might attack Turkey. If the Soviets do attack the Turks, we must respond in the NATO area."

As he left that grim session, McNamara walked through the White House Rose Garden with George Ball. The fall weather had turned gorgeous, an ironic contrast with the state of mind of these men, staring down the abyss at chaos. McNamara says of that moment, "I wondered if I'd ever see another Saturday night."[36]

On Sunday morning McNamara called more Air Force squadrons to duty. Army divisions in Florida were getting ready for an invasion order, although the decision to bomb and invade Cuba had not yet been made. McNamara was working up a list, this one of ways to ratchet the quarantine tighter.

Shortly after nine o'clock, Moscow announced that the Soviet government had "given a new order to dismantle the arms which you described as offensive." Ambassador Dobrynin strode into Bobby Kennedy's office to confirm that the missiles would be dismantled, crated, and shipped out of Cuba. The deal would include removing the MIGs and Ilyushins. The condition was Kennedy's promise not to invade Cuba. Nothing was said about the Jupiters, Turkey, NATO, or Berlin.

In Washington the relief was total. Yarmolinsky remembers that McNamara's mood was "exaltation, very noticeable exaltation."[37]

The missile crisis did not end that Sunday morning. The missiles and equipment had to be physically dismantled and shipped out, the aircraft recrated and sent back. These operations were monitored by American spy cameras. During the following weeks, the right kept accusing Kennedy of slackness and the Soviets of cheating. The onus lay heavy on the Kennedy men for muffing a chance to overthrow Castro. Charges also flew of mismanagement: Why hadn't they found the missiles sooner? McCone's earlier lone warning that Khrushchev might install missiles was made public and irritated the Kennedys. McCone, a Republican, was blowing his own horn and embarrassing the president. McNamara leapt in to protect Kennedy and sparked a fight with McCone. On February 6 McNamara rushed onto television with blown-up photos to prove to the press and the world that they were monitoring the pullout closely. Bobby Kennedy said later, "McCone was furious about that because they were using stuff from the CIA."[38]

Then McNamara asserted in another television appearance, "I have no evidence that Cuba is being used as a base for subversion directed against other Latin American governments." McCone promptly testified at length on the CIA's extensive indications that the Cubans were exporting revolution — testimony that Kennedy's critics published quickly to embarrass him and McNamara. Said Bobby, "McNamara was very loyal to the President and was doing what he thought was helpful. . . . In fact, he went too far. He didn't have to say what he said, he didn't have to go as far as he did. But of the two [McCone and McNamara], the President was pleased with Bob McNamara. And John McCone frustrated him some."

The chiefs frustrated Kennedy as well. After the crisis he held a pro forma meeting to congratulate them on their performance. Partway through the meeting, Air Force Chief of Staff Curtis LeMay spoke up and said, Mr. President, we failed.[39]

Kennedy was startled. Failed? How?

Castro's still in power. We should have gotten rid of Castro and we failed to do that, said LeMay, in dead earnest.

Kennedy decided he could not work with some of the chiefs. The use of force for limited political ends was just not understood in certain military quarters.

Kennedy and McNamara apparently both wanted to get rid of LeMay and Anderson when their terms expired in 1963. But they couldn't do so without serious political repercussions. They reappointed LeMay for a second term, through January 1965, and decided not to reappoint Anderson. Gilpatric and Navy Secretary Fred Korth were sent to Anderson's grand office to inform him. Kennedy offered to make him ambassador to Portugal. Anderson first was furious, then accepted. Gilpatric notes that Anderson did a very good job in Portugal.

The rumor in the Navy, however, was that it was McNamara who insisted on the ambassadorship, because he couldn't stand to have Anderson anywhere in North America.[40]

In the Pentagon press room, and among some reporters elsewhere, the relief of averting war was offset by anger. Sylvester had arranged for the *Miami Herald* to be assured that there were no missiles in Cuba and no emergency alert when the reverse of both proved quickly to be true. Pierre Salinger had said the president was returning to Washington due to a cold when he was hale and healthy. Sylvester, asked if there was going to be a naval blockade of Cuba, had said no. His answer was true, he claimed later, because he knew it would be a quarantine, not a blockade.[41] The crisis exposed Salinger's and Sylvester's bald deceits, which were their bosses'.

The following March, Sylvester was being roasted at a meeting of the journalism society, Sigma Delta Chi. He was asked about "little white lies" like Salinger's claim that Kennedy had a cold. Sylvester's long-winded reply was to the effect that in times of national emergency, the government should say whatever it has to publicly to protect human life. It was widely summarized as meaning the "government has the right to lie."[42] These would prove to be haunting words for his boss as well.

In March 1987, a wizened McNamara, with untrimmed sideburns and wearing a blue and white polo shirt, sat in a meeting room overlooking the palms at a Florida resort called Hawk's Cay. He had come there to discuss the missile crisis with former colleagues and historians. Harvard's Richard Neustadt opened the session by saying it was possibly "the last time researchers interested in the Cuban missile crisis . . . [could] deal face-to-face with those of you who. . . . had to face the problem of escalation in a nuclear crisis."

The group included Bundy, Ball, and some other Ex Comm survivors. Journalist J. Anthony Lukas judged McNamara, with his "bullet head" and "dyspeptic mood," to be by far the dominant personality in the room.[43]

Although his contributions were mostly positive and accurate, McNamara did seem to contradict his own record in the Ex Comm.

He claimed that the Ex Comm "didn't put much weight on the date at which [the missiles in Cuba] might become operational. At least I didn't. . . . It had no effect on my decisions." Historian Marc Trachtenberg read back to McNamara his words of October 16, 1962, where he stressed the importance of attacking before the missiles were operational to avoid "chaos" in the southeastern United States. That was a preliminary reaction, McNamara replied; he changed his mind soon after. But "time pressure is what makes a crisis," objected scholar Albert Carnesale.[44]

More important, McNamara argued in 1987 and later that they were *not* about to launch a strike and go to war on October 29 and 30, despite the chorus of discussion of such moves in Bromley Smith's notes for Saturday, October 27. "I believe we could have done more with the blockade. We could have continued to turn the screw for quite some time, and I believe that that's what we would have done," he said in a later interview.[45] He also claimed that in a private meeting that Bobby Kennedy held on Saturday night with Dobrynin, Bobby hadn't threatened that the United States would attack right away, even though Bobby himself reported that he had promised immediate action. "Or," McNamara added of Bobby, "he shouldn't have." As on other matters, the older McNamara claimed his past positions were more "dovish" than the record shows.

"The important thing is that the President was not going to war. I know that . . . I'm sure of it." As evidence, he cited the fact that on Sunday morning, he, McNamara, was working on ways to extend the quarantine when news of Khrushchev's capitulation came through.

McNamara's assertion that Kennedy would never have authorized an invasion of Cuba aroused criticism. Pierre Salinger, who attended one of the retrospective meetings at which McNamara made this claim, took McNamara to task in the pages of the *New York Times*. "I have a lot of respect for Bob McNamara," Salinger went so far as to write publicly, but he was judging "the events of 1962 from the perspective of the cooled political climate of 1989 detente."[46]

Historian James G. Blight later questioned McNamara closely on his assertions. He got McNamara to explain why, although the meeting notes of October 27 have him saying that invasion was "almost inevitable," he thinks Kennedy would not have initiated an invasion: "You've got to try to understand the atmosphere in the room on October 27. It was tense. Time seemed short. All sorts of foul ups had been happening. . . . If I actually said it, all I can think of is that

I just blurted out my worst fear, either that the Soviets or us, or both, would soon really believe war is inevitable.

"The functional result for me was to resolve that there was no way the potential war we were looking at was going to be inevitable. No way in the world. And the President felt the same way. Because the President and I both feared that some people might come to believe war was inevitable, we were determined to make sure it never happened.

"No matter how hard you tried, no matter how much rationality you tried to inject into the process, it just never turned out the way you anticipated."[47]

That events "never turned out the way you anticipated" was a crucial admission from a man who spent his life trying to inject rationality into the world around him and to direct vast organizations to specific, rational ends.

Clearly, in the missile crisis, McNamara felt vividly that the nuclear danger could not be controlled or fine-tuned, as he had imagined it could be when he advocated the counterforce–no cities strategy for limited war at Athens and Ann Arbor months earlier. In the missile crisis, as he said later, he believed that "one nuclear bomb on one American city" was unacceptable. "Nuclear war was not at the top of everyone's mind. The atmosphere was serious, very serious. But not wildly emotional."

He was more fearful of a nuclear war than were some of the other men, he said. And he "wondered" about others who "did not feel this way" — an allusion to hawks like Taylor and Nitze, who pressed for an air strike, seemingly immune to the nuclear consequences. "I have a lot of trouble trying to argue the point with people who disagree with me about nuclear strategy. The fear is not a function of some estimate of the probability of nuclear war. Hell, nobody knows what that is. Nobody.

"My concern was [that] the possible consequences . . . were so . . . catastrophic, that I wasn't going to accept even a low probability, if I could possibly avoid it. . . .

"I didn't want to accept any risk of nuclear war. That is the way the situation worked on me. This is the way the missile crisis was affecting my thinking."[48]

McNamara often alludes to Khrushchev's extraordinary Friday night letter, parts of which he can recite by heart. "War ends when it has rolled through cities and villages," Khrushchev wrote, "every-where sowing death and destruction." It is almost as though Mc-Namara was unable to imagine a metaphor himself and planted Khrushchev's in his mind to express his own grave fear.

"I remember it word for word," he told me later. "I'll never forget it. At the time I felt it was the statement of a man under tremendous emotional stress, facing a possible nuclear conflict which he realized could destroy his nation." *Destroy his nation*, McNamara said, the words rising to a crescendo, the intensity of the moment still burning even in the memory of this pivotal moment in his life.

"Khrushchev was talking about *war*," he went on, his voice boom-ing, "*in very clear, blunt terms.*"[49]

10
Untying the Knot

NOT LONG AFTER SUNDAY, October 28, when Khrushchev signaled he would pull his missiles out of Cuba, McNamara's friend and tennis partner Stewart Alsop interviewed the secretary of defense on nuclear strategy in his huge Pentagon office.

The resulting article, which appeared in the December 1 *Saturday Evening Post*, showed Alsop to be positively awestruck at the "new breed" of "defense intellectuals" who are young and "brilliantly intelligent" and toss around words like "spasm response," "megadeath," and "counterforce collateral damage." *Post* readers were invited to delve into the "oddly fascinating reality" of nuclear war scenarios. The confrontation that would occur "the next time Khrushchev makes a wrong move" would be handled by the man with "the highest intelligence quotient of any leading public official in this century," R. S. McNamara.[1]

The article purported to explain the counterforce–no cities nuclear policy McNamara had announced publicly at Ann Arbor in June, which Alsop dubbed the "Doctrine of Controlled Response." In point of fact, McNamara had been backing off the policy practically since he first articulated it, having encountered nothing but problems. They started with London's and Paris's outrage that through it, Washington was trying to nix their independent control of their respective nuclear forces.

The main problem with counterforce–no cities was that it made

McNamara sound as though he were really planning a preemptive first strike, despite official disclaimers. The Kremlin and other critics astutely asked why Washington would wait for the Soviets to attack before it launched its countermilitary attack to disarm Soviet forces. According to military logic, Washington should try to disarm Soviet forces preemptively, before they could begin a strike against the United States.[2]

A second problem was the defense budget for fiscal 1964, then in preparation in the Building. The Air Force asked for added Minuteman missiles and for the B-70 bomber and RS-70 reconnaissance version. The generals also wanted to continue the Skybolt nuclear missile, to be launched from U.S. and British bombers against Soviet ground targets, although McNamara had doubts Skybolt would work. In short, the military was using McNamara's counterforce strategy to justify increases in U.S. offensive forces and even a first-strike strategy, just when McNamara realized that his strategic buildup had to stop.[3] Strategic forces were costing $15 billion, one third of the $45 billion defense budget and one sixth of the federal budget.

But the overarching problem with the doctrine was psychological. The Berlin crisis and Kennedy's promotion of civil defense on television and in the pages of *Life* awakened in the public a gut-level awareness of how horrible nuclear war would be. The insouciance of public discussion of nuclear weapons in the fifties was fading. Berlin and Cuba caused a shift in perceptions of the new age.[4]

In this climate it was politically unwise for the U.S. secretary of defense to adopt the language of "megadeath" and "controlled and deliberate response." McNamara had been saying publicly that if each side followed a limited counterforce strategy and avoided hitting the other's cities, 25 million Americans would die instead of 75 million in an all-out attack, and that the figure of 25 million was "preferable" to the 75 million. He did not insert the word "only" in front of the reference to 25 million dead Americans, but it could be read there by implication. A growing number of Americans were repelled by political leaders' acceptance of 25 million deaths as preferable under almost any scenario. McNamara's larger figures for Western European deaths played no better on the other side of the Atlantic, where a similar shift of mood was under way. Europeans were often schizophrenic: They called loudly for U.S. displays of nuclear willpower (some German leaders were blaming Kennedy for not having gone to war over Berlin and letting the wall stand) while being privately terrified at the prospect of nuclear war.[5]

McNamara sensed the inappropriateness of his fine-tuned strategy even as he tossed around its cold-blooded terms with Alsop. Thus McNamara was parting company with the formal strategists at the very moment he was most publicly identified with them.

The crosscurrents were ironic. McNamara decided privately during the Cuban crisis that one Soviet warhead from Cuba on one American city was unacceptable just when Herman Kahn, the most controversial of the formal strategists, attained his greatest notoriety.[6] Even among the earliest group of superbright Rand mathematicians and economists, Kahn stood out as a crazy genius. He started work on the mathematical problems of the hydrogen bomb but was soon fascinated with analyzing nuclear war.

The combination of Kahn's provocative personality and deadly subject matter resulted in a series of books that discussed nuclear war scenarios with weird abandon. For example, Kahn conceived of a Doomsday Machine, which he claimed was technologically feasible. It would be a giant computer wired to thousands of H-bombs. When the Soviets committed some unacceptable act, the machine would go to war and fire thousands of bombs, covering the earth with fallout and killing everybody. The Doomsday Machine sounded absurd, but it was only a slight exaggeration of military reality, the top-secret Sunday Punch nuclear war plan that SAC improved throughout the 1950s.

Kahn's deeper point was that the Doomsday Machine was a terrible idea. As the alternative, he worked up scenarios for limited nuclear war. His master plan, which drew the most attention, had the combatants starting small, with a few nuclear bombs, and working their way up forty-four "rungs" of a "ladder of escalation," while the two sides bargained to call the whole thing off.

Kahn lectured widely. *On Thermonuclear War* was published in 1960 and sold thirty thousand copies in hardcover. In 1962 he issued another ghoulish and hypnotic tome. *Thinking About the Unthinkable* became a new buzz phrase for what Alsop had called the "oddly fascinating reality" of nuclear strategy. Kahn's writing inspired the 1964 movie hit *Dr. Strangelove*, in which U.S. and Soviet Doomsday machines go to war with each other.

But Kahn's braggadocio, his linguistic abandon and effervescent personality, pushed him beyond the bounds of respectability as the public mood changed. He and his fellow Rand strategists were being responsible in trying to alleviate humanity's greatest threat. But Kahn seemed too detached from the terrible acts he described to a public for whom nuclear war was suddenly real.

McNamara shared Kahn's and his colleagues' ability to keep the emotional horror of nuclear war at arm's length by intellectualizing it. Their formalism and detached language were partly a crutch to control the fears the cataclysm aroused.

The containment of emotion was the precise appeal to McNamara of the Rand strategists as staff advisers and of counterforce—no cities as doctrine. McNamara needed both to prepare himself to act rationally and control his own intense emotions, if war ever came.

Kahn's third book, *On Escalation*, happened to be published in 1965, at the start of the U.S. bombing of North Vietnam, an air campaign that McNamara and others designed on Kahn-like principles of escalation control and bargaining that seemed to work in the missile crisis. What McNamara's fascination with nuclear bargaining scenarios in 1961–62 had in common with his belief in a limited air campaign against North Vietnam in 1965 was that it offered him a way to keep the emotions of war under control.

"War always deeply involves the emotions," wrote the sage Bernard Brodie in 1959 in *Strategy in the Missile Age*. "The collapse of inhibitions in the transition from peace to war does not argue well for the containment of the succeeding violence."[7] It was this "collapse of inhibitions" that McNamara, in his adoption of both limited nuclear war theories and the strategy of controlled bombing of North Vietnam, was trying to check.

Yet by 1962 Kahn was coming to symbolize the irresponsible side of such stratagems. Kahn was deeply stung when a *Scientific American* review of *On Thermonuclear War* called it "a moral tract on mass murder: how to plan it, how to commit it, how to get away with it, how to justify it." Significantly, the managing editor of the journal, Dennis Flanagan, declined to print a rebuttal, telling Kahn, "Surely it is much more profitable to think about the thinkable."[8] Although McNamara never went as far as Kahn in his public language, he went far enough to be criticized for his Marquis of Queensberry rules for nuclear war. McNamara was finding that such talk was not proper for a political leader.

By the fall of 1962, U.S. strategic policy was in confusion. SIOP-63, the revised top-secret operational plan for how U.S. forces were to conduct nuclear war, was now operational and based on counter-force, as McNamara had ordered in February 1961. When he un-veiled counterforce–no cities publicly at Ann Arbor, McNamara told the Kremlin that the United States would execute only a limited attack on Soviet forces in the event of nuclear war. But Kennedy, in his television address of October 22, had announced that if any of the missiles in Cuba were launched, the United States would carry out "a full retaliatory response upon the Soviet Union," a massive attack. Now talking to Alsop, McNamara confused matters more. Of coun-terforce, he said, "I would want to be certain we had other options."[9]

Midway through his interview with McNamara, Alsop told him he possessed leaked information that the Soviets were "hardening" their missile sites to allow some of their ICBMs to survive a U.S. coun-terforce attack. If part of the Soviet force was sure to survive so it could hit the United States in return, were not the days of a U.S. counterforce strategy numbered? McNamara tossed a bombshell back at Alsop.

"His answer [to the Soviet second-strike capability] was in effect, 'the sooner the better,' " Alsop wrote. McNamara replied that the United States already had a secure second-strike capability. Once the Soviets also had forces able to survive a U.S. attack and hit back, "then you might have a more stable 'balance of terror,' " he said.

McNamara's "the sooner the better" view caused a sensation when Alsop published it. The right was aghast. Here was the secretary of defense of the United States, the man responsible for defending the entire free world, who had been eyeball to eyeball with Khrushchev when Soviet deceits brought the world to the brink of holocaust. How could such a man *want* the enemy to survive the decisive blow on its forces for which the Strategic Air Command and others had spent billions of dollars and more than a decade to be able to carry out? How could he want the enemy to be able to fire back? And *"the sooner the better"*![10]

McNamara's remark was not as bizarre as it sounded. Early the previous summer the president had ordered an intelligence review of Soviet nuclear forces.[11] The results, presented to Kennedy at a brief-ing on July 9, concluded that earlier estimates of Soviet ICBM strength, on the basis of which Kennedy and McNamara launched their strategic buildup, were grossly inflated.

The review also confirmed that the Soviets would make some of their ICBM sites "hard," that is, able to survive if a nuclear warhead hit nearby. It stated that the Soviets might build more ballistic missile submarines, which could be difficult for the United States to find and attack all at once. Finally, it said the American people could not really be protected by civil defense, which was still being actively promoted by the administration. A Soviet nuclear attack directed at U.S. cities could kill 88 million Americans, even with civil defense. Thus, both sides were moving toward "parity" in their second-strike ability, which diminished "the prospect of real victors emerging from any major nuclear war."

This review helps explain why McNamara said, when presented with the news of Soviet missiles in Cuba, "I believed, by the time of the Cuban missile crisis, that both sides had parity in their nuclear forces."[12]

The stability of the "balance of terror" was an idea as old as the nuclear age itself. Bernard Brodie had outlined it in *Absolute Weapon*, his earliest work on nuclear deterrence: Once both sides had secure, second-strike forces, each would be restrained from attacking the other first, creating stability. In addition, once such forces were in place, neither side would have an incentive to build more nuclear weapons. Rand's Albert Wohlstetter developed the definitive conditions for stability and popularized them in a *Foreign Affairs* article in 1959. But Winston Churchill expressed the concept best during Britain's parliamentary debate over whether to build an H-bomb, in 1955: "Then it may well be that we shall, by a process of sublime irony, have reached a stage in this story where safety will be the sturdy child of terror and survival the twin brother of annihilation."[13]

"After Cuba, McNamara increasingly wanted to make the point that nuclear weapons had to be limited," Alain Enthoven recalls.[14] McNamara was more and more concerned with stable deterrence. Through his deliberate, attention-getting remark to Alsop he signaled to the Soviets his approval of their buildup of a secure nuclear force, which would lower his own side's temptation to strike first in a crisis. Disillusioned with counterforce–no cities and formal strategy, McNamara sought a Holy Grail, a key to curbing the arms race and creating political stability between West and East.

McNamara's quest would take two years and contribute to a stunning legacy: the congressional votes against a U.S. antiballistic missile system after he left office, the dissuasion of the Soviets from deploying a large ABM system of their own, and the 1972 Strategic Arms Limitation Treaty limiting ABMs on both sides.

McNamara was fascinated by process and sought to weigh explicit rationales, what his Whiz Kids called yardsticks of sufficiency. At the time of the Cuban missile crisis, military leaders in the Building began to see that thirty-two-year-old Alain Enthoven had a strong influence on McNamara's decisions.

Enthoven had specialized in strategic-force issues while at Rand. There and at the Pentagon, he produced papers showing the B-70's cost-ineffectiveness and greatly angered the chief of staff of the Air Force, Curtis LeMay, whose scowling mien, unlit cigar, and unvarnished language made him a formidable foe around the Building.[15]

Enthoven, like his colleagues, rationalized the existence and possible use of nuclear weapons.[16] He was a devout Catholic and had been taught by Jesuits; his religious view was that morally, nuclear war was horrible, and he wanted to devote his work to prevent that calamity. But Enthoven also accepted the existence of the large U.S. force and the growing Soviet arsenal as necessary evils. He had been alarmed when the new secretary of defense, fresh from Ford and knowing nothing about nuclear issues, showed interest in the Navy-oriented briefing on the nuclear strategy WSEG-50, which concluded that two hundred hidden sea-based missiles alone could destroy Soviet cities in a retaliatory strike and serve as a purely deterrent force. Enthoven and Charles Hitch had therefore urged McNamara to hear their Rand colleague William Kaufmann's counterforce–no cities plan.

Thus, Enthoven was no disarmer in 1961. He did not advocate drastic cuts in nuclear weapons or lopping the Air Force out of the nuclear game by limiting the force to a few missiles on submarines. He was more concerned with making the threat to use nuclear weapons credible and how to limit the catastrophe of nuclear war if it happened. Counterforce–no cities had seemed to provide the answer, but by the winter of 1962, Enthoven and McNamara both were ready to look at an alternative. McNamara's second Draft Presidential Memorandum on strategic forces, dated November 21, 1962, announced that the purpose of U.S. nuclear forces was "first, to provide the United States with a secure, protected retaliatory force able to survive any attack within enemy capabilities and capable of striking back and destroying Soviet urban society, if necessary, in a controlled and deliberate way." Its secondary purpose was "limiting damage," that is, "to deny the enemy the prospect of achieving a military victory by attacking our forces."

McNamara's post-Cuba concern with deterring nuclear war was also evident: "The forces I am recommending give any rational Soviet decisionmaker the strongest possible incentives to avoid nuclear attack on ourselves or our allies."[17]

Enthoven proceeded to get to work defining the new first goal, deterrence.[18] If the strategic forces' role was that of "striking back and destroying Soviet urban society . . . in a controlled and deliberate way," how much force was enough?

Enthoven and staffer Frank Trinkl designed a computer program enacting a retaliatory attack that dropped one-megaton warheads on Soviet cities and burst aboveground to destroy buildings and people. Only those killed and wounded immediately were counted as casualties; long-term casualties due to fallout were not included. Their computer calculated the damage achieved by different levels of attack. Thus the number of delivered megatons could be correlated with the percent of Soviet population and industrial floorspace destroyed.

Enthoven knew that in reality, with SIOP-63, the new operational war plan, the vast majority of U.S. nuclear weapons were targeted on Soviet military forces, with only 18 percent aimed at cities and industry. But he decided that this model was valid anyway. As McNamara said in his 1963 Draft Presidential Memorandum, "The calculations [of attacks on Soviet cities and industry] are our best estimates of the results of possible Soviet calculations of what we could do to them in retaliation if they were to attack us."[19]

Enthoven's computer program generated two curves. One showed the percentage of industrial floor space destroyed, and the other the percentage of population harmed. Both were computed as a function of how many megatons were delivered on these two kinds of targets.[20]

Both curves rose sharply as the number of megatons increased. Both then bent and became nearly horizontal, meaning that above certain levels of megatonnage, relatively fewer additional people or industrial targets would be destroyed. The bends, or "knees," in the curves fell at roughly 400 megatons; if 800 megatons were delivered, only 10 percent more people and 3 percent more industry would be destroyed, for example.

But the bends in the curves were approximate. They could have picked 150 megatons as a yardstick of sufficiency because 150 megatons would destroy 60 percent of industry and 15 percent of population. Or they could have picked 500 megatons, which would eliminate 70 percent of industry and 35 percent of population. At 400 delivered megatons, one third of the Soviet population and half of Soviet industry would be wiped out.

Enthoven and Trinkl presumed, of course, that their adversary would be rational, although history does not necessarily bear out this assumption. Many a national leader has launched into war deluding himself that the fatalities on his own side will be low and that the war will be short. On the other hand, since no leader has yet started a nuclear war, perhaps calculations of impending deaths do deter.

In 1963, McNamara reviewed Enthoven's computations in light of the missile crisis, after Khrushchev had written that the Soviets were not "lunatics," in his strange yet ultimately rational letter of Friday, October 26; "we are normal people."

Four hundred delivered megatons became the yardstick for the amount of damage that should deter the other side from starting a nuclear war.[21] But McNamara and Kennedy were buying 656 Polaris missiles and 1,200 land-based ICBMs and already had thousands of megatons that could be delivered by bombers.

McNamara and Enthoven then tripled the yardstick. They adopted a conservative assumption: that any one of the three "legs" of the force — bombers, land-based missiles, and sea-based missiles — should be capable of the Assured Destruction mission alone. In this way they rationalized their larger force.

Analysis had given them a chance to cut the size of the programmed force by two thirds, but they never seriously considered doing so. The implications of the overwhelming U.S. superiority for a possible reduction of U.S. forces were simply not considered closely. McNamara had pushed the enormous buildup in his first year in office; he was wedded to it. In 1963 he was not yet a revolutionary advocate of deep nuclear force cuts.

McNamara now exploited the rivalry among his staff to advance the issue. The public image of his Whiz Kids was of a cadre of like-minded civilians. But, in fact, the rivalry and personal feelings among men hired for their brilliance, rather than team spirit, could be intense. (Indeed, there were military men among the Whiz Kids — to answer the charge of a civilian-military split in the Building, McNamara had asked Enthoven for a list of all the officers who had won

Rhodes scholarships. It was certainly a shortcut to locating brains in the military; and it was another sign of McNamara's preoccupation with the Rhodes as a certification of ability that he himself had failed to win.)

Harold Brown, director of Defense Research and Engineering, had hired an outspoken Air Force lieutenant general named Glenn Kent.[22] Kent often seemed like the right stuff to the fly-away boys of the Air Force. But once he started computing and arguing key points of strategy, Kent was a match for the Whiz Kids, too. True to his background, he disapproved of Enthoven's "antibomber" leanings. He also found McNamara's Draft Presidential Memorandum arguing that the Air Force had a first-strike policy insulting, since no responsible officer would follow a policy contrary to Kennedy's March 1961 declaration that the United States would never undertake a bolt-from-the-blue first strike.

At the same time, Kent was independent of many of his fellow Air Force officers' slavish devotion to counterforce. The object in war, he argued perceptively, was not to destroy the enemy's military forces at any cost, but to limit damage to one's nation and military forces.

The true yardstick of sufficiency of U.S. forces besides deterrence, Kent argued, should be Damage Limitation. Damage Limitation was carried out not only by counterforce systems like the bomber and the Minuteman, but by a smorgasbord of other systems from which McNamara had to choose: civil defense, continental defenses, and the Nike-X ABM system. Kent used this definition to propose Damage Limitation as a yardstick: with it the costs of an ABM could be measured against its effectiveness at protecting U.S. interests, compared with other means of limiting damage, such as civil defense.

McNamara's third Draft Presidential Memorandum on strategic forces, dated December 6, 1963, proposed Assured Destruction as the name for his primary goal of deterrence. He described this policy as "our ability to destroy, after a well planned and executed Soviet surprise attack on our strategic nuclear forces, the Soviet government and military controls, plus a large percentage of their population and economy (e.g., 30% of their population and 50% of their industrial capacity) and 150 of their cities." McNamara added that he would support additional forces for the purpose of Damage Limitation, that is, "if they could further reduce the damage to the U.S. in the event of a Soviet attack by an amount sufficient to justify their added costs.[23]

Kent criticized Enthoven's staff work for another reason. The studies he had seen since coming to Defense failed to take account of likely Soviet reactions to U.S. force deployments. Nor did they account for U.S. force decisions made on the basis of prospective or actual Soviet deployments. Yet both sides spent resources and built more or less effective systems based on perceptions of the other's imminent actions, such as the rumored Soviet ABM. The costs and capabilities flowed back and forth. The nuclear arms race was dynamic.

Kent now proposed a very ambitious study comparing different mixes of U.S. forces in the Assured Destruction and Damage Limitation roles with the costs to the Soviets of responding to different U.S. deployments.[24] Enthoven, taking the advice of his staffer Trinkl, who was engaged in a running rivalry with Kent, argued that the study was not feasible mathematically. McNamara, scanning the methodology with his own practiced eye, overruled Enthoven and ordered Kent to proceed. Given McNamara's powers of computation, he may also have seen, just by scanning Kent's plan, how the study would come out.

In January 1964, Harold Brown carried in Kent's results to McNamara. The secretary of defense pored over the twenty-nine graphs and more than a hundred pages of classified text. He was fascinated.

Kent's graphs and charts showed Damage Limitation to be essentially hopeless as the main goal of U.S. policy. Under some conditions, a combination of systems — civil defense, ABM, attacking enemy forces together — could protect 55 or 60 percent of U.S. industry. But for every dollar the United States spent defending itself from nuclear destruction, the enemy could neutralize that effort by spending only about one third of a dollar in additional offense. Given the enormous expense of the technology for Damage Limitation (except civil defense) and the relatively simple, cheap ways additional warheads could be added to missiles to multiply offensive power, the offense would always win. It was a critical fact of life, given the state of technology both in the 1960s and for thirty years after, even in the era of Star Wars.

McNamara, as he hunched over the great Pershing desk, peering at Kent's ingenious charts and calculations, reached the end of the road that had begun when he heard Kaufmann's briefing on counterforce–no cities in February 1961. He concluded that civil defense or an effective ABM, if one could be built, could protect part of the U.S.

population or industry. But they could not protect sufficiently for a national leader to start a nuclear war and hope his country would survive the enemy's retaliatory blow. "I cannot imagine any scenario leaders would initiate and hope to gain from it," he said. Moreover, he told his staff, with an eye on politics, Congress will never vote the large amounts needed for Damage Limitation knowing how cheaply the enemy can overcome them. So deterrence moved front and center as the prime purpose of nuclear forces in his mind.

McNamara's next move was both a step to build consensus and a bureaucratic trick. With Kent's preliminary results in hand, he now ordered each of the armed services to study the cost-effectiveness of different combinations of systems in the Damage Limitation role and to consider enemy countermeasures and their costs. Harold Brown marched the results in to McNamara in September 1964, just as the fiscal 1966 defense budget was being finalized in the Building.

The services were pleased, believing their work showed that damage to U.S. population and industry could be limited if the United States bought bombers, ABM, civil defense, and air defense. McNamara pointed out that their own studies showed the opposite. As Kent had demonstrated, each level of protection that could be achieved could be overwhelmed by far cheaper offense. Thus deterrence became the U.S. force's primary role, and Damage Limitation secondary as a yardstick to limit damage, imperfectly, if deterrence failed.

McNamara's December 3, 1964, Draft Presidential Memorandum on strategic forces was the most comprehensive discourse on strategic arms he ever wrote. It installed Assured Destruction as the centerpiece of U.S. policy; Damage Limitation now ran a distant second.[25] He invoked the latter to make his final change in the shape of U.S. strategic forces by lowering the proposed final number of Minutemen from 1,100 to 1,000 — the number he had apparently planned to have since 1961.

In January 1965, when McNamara presented the declassified version of this memorandum publicly as part of his proposed fiscal 1966 budget, Assured Destruction made its real debut.[26] It was not invented by McNamara. The core insight occurred when the bomb had just come into being. A further insight, that war-fighting strategies were impractical because the state of technology meant that offense would always win, had been made by scientists Jerome B. Wiesner and Herbert F. York in an influential 1964 *Scientific American* article.[27]

The first irony of Assured Destruction is that McNamara used his bent for analysis, and the formidable analytic talent he assembled in the Building, to arrive at a supposed "truth," which he then put forward as universal law. Assured Destruction reflected that curious pairing in his nature, his intellectual sophistication and need to believe in simple truths, which surfaced over and over in his life.

Thus he elevated Kent's and Enthoven's relativistic findings about the merits of different kinds of offense and defense into a grand simplification: Both sides must refrain from a race in damage-limiting systems, such as ABMs, in order to remain terrified of the mortal blow to their societies that the other side's offense could inflict. Both must construct a posture in which they would forever be afraid of the nuclear fireball that rolls "through cities and villages, everywhere sowing death and destruction."

McNamara would not have evolved Assured Destruction before the Cuban missile crisis for many reasons. And one was that only in the missile crisis — and with the receipt of Khrushchev's remarkable Friday night letter using the above words — did McNamara's own fear crystallize. Afterward, by working through the problem intellectually with Enthoven and Kent, McNamara found a stance from which to project his inner fears into policy, a way to make Washington and Moscow institutionalize the very feelings he had experienced with such force. Thus by stages in his mind did the entire U.S.-Soviet arms race become an extension of "IBM machine" Bob McNamara's own fears — fears that would mark his statements and writings on the nuclear matters ever after.

He knew he could not explain all this in a single speech, remembering the lessons of the Athens and Ann Arbor speeches of 1962; his statements about parting company with people who argue too rationally about nuclear strategy reflect his own disillusion with his earlier, too-rational approach. From 1965 on, he would use the bully pulpit of office to warn of an arms race if the ABM were built by either side and the rules for stability created by Assured Destruction were ignored.[28] No longer did he talk of twenty-five million dead Americans as preferable to other options. He talked of millions of deaths as an inevitable result, a tragedy.

"Scratch McNamara and you have a teacher, a missionary," says a staff aide who helped McNamara prepare his broader, more messianic speeches in the later part of the decade.[29] Enthoven gave background briefings. Reporters like Alsop, flattered by the attention of the man "with the highest intelligence quotient of any leading public official in this century," popularized the ideas. In early 1967 McNamara privately explained the importance of not proceeding with the ABM to Soviet ambassador Anatoly Dobrynin.

He summarized his argument in a speech in San Francisco in September 1967. It was an eloquent appeal for mutual offensive forces, warning that if either side strove for or achieved a defense against nuclear attack — i.e., if either side deployed an ABM — the arms race would be set off again.[30]

Nonetheless, Assured Destruction would remain the centerpiece of U.S. policy for a generation — and was ultimately adopted in some form by the Soviets — because it expressed an underlying truth of the nuclear age. Not only did it give Pentagon managers useful yardsticks for measuring the effects of various proposed additions to U.S. forces, changes in Soviet forces, and the shifting balance between them. It also showed that Robert McNamara, often derided for lacking human insight, had hit on a basic emotional and political truth.

The second irony is that Assured Destruction, although possibly McNamara's most positive contribution to defense policy, was never *real* in military, operational terms. Assured Destruction was never a U.S. strategic "doctrine" in the military sense of the term; it was not put into the war plans. McNamara never went back to change SIOP to allow the president to execute Assured Destruction — a retaliatory strike limited to Soviet cities and industry. Actual targets of U.S. forces remained overwhelmingly programmed for counterforce.

McNamara did not make this abundantly clear in his hundreds of announcements of U.S. nuclear policy in the years that followed. For example, in his January 1965 posture statement, he said he had abandoned counterforce–no cities "for planning purposes" although it remained an option for fighting a nuclear war if deterrence failed.[31] What had really happened was that counterforce–no cities had been superseded for *budget*-planning purposes but was still very much in the *war* plans.

Even though McNamara now announced that U.S. policy had changed to one of making the Soviets certain America would attack its cities and industry, he never ordered SIOP-63 revised to be able to do this.[32] He kept saying he was buying forces for Assured Destruction; but what he had on hand was an enormous offensive force that would rain thousands of warheads on military targets in only a few crude options.

Moreover — and this is perhaps the epitome of his faith in top-down crisis management — McNamara argues that he had improved command and control of the strategic forces enough to allow himself and the president to figure out nuclear strike options once the contingency arose. McNamara says now that if nuclear war had come, he planned to respond ad hoc as the situation evolved. In fact, he told me: "The way I planned to handle it, and the reason I didn't think the SIOP was so dangerous, was that: (a) we had complete presidential control over it; and (b) we knew how, on a rough basis, to cut back the strike options in the SIOP."

He also noted, "You could withhold the bombers, for example, or part or all of the missile force. I always felt, and I specifically checked on this, that we could modify those plans any way we wished at the time. . . . Each one of the plans had weapons you could withhold. So we could go to plan three or plan four and withhold A, B, C, or D. Finally, it became clear to me that it would take more time to modify the SIOP than I had available. To the day I left I never did modify the SIOP to reflect realistic operational alternatives."

In fairness, in the thirty years since, only two secretaries of defense — James Schlesinger in 1974 and Richard Cheney in 1990, after the Berlin Wall had fallen — have seriously modified the SIOP that McNamara signed off on in 1962.[33] But given the enormous attention McNamara drew to his "doctrine" — which was declaratory policy, not military doctrine — one of his close colleagues has a point when he says that Assured Destruction was a "white lie."

11

Controller of Technology

O NLY FOUR MONTHS after the Cuban missile crisis triumph, McNamara became embroiled in a bitter public fight with Congress, the Air Force, and the Navy. The issue was his choice of a contractor for a new fighterbomber that he insisted be built as one plane for the Air Force and Navy. His technical judgment and integrity were questioned, raising the first serious public doubts about his revolution at the Pentagon.

McNamara's intentions were noble enough. In his first briefings on individual military programs, he learned that each of the services wanted its own new tactical aircraft. So, weeks after leaving Ford, he asked, in effect, *why can't all three services have one aircraft?*[1]

Commonality was the key to efficiency and profits in manufacturing automobiles at Ford; McNamara immediately applied this principle at the Pentagon. In 1961 he folded the separate service intelligence efforts into a single Defense Intelligence Agency; he established a single Defense Supply Agency for all the services. The program budget he and controller Charles Hitch installed helped the cause of commonality, by enabling him and others to compare all parts of the giant Defense operation with common, quantitative yardsticks.[2]

Early on McNamara held a "fashion show" in his conference room attended by his civilian and military deputies. The different services' belts and butcher's smocks and women's bloomers were modeled, as were jackets, caps, boots, and other things. As each item was shown,

McNamara decided on the spot which of the versions would henceforth be used by all the services.

In the vivid recollection of Thomas D. Morris, one of the assistant secretaries present, McNamara gave the assembled group a little lecture on the importance of making decisions quickly. It didn't matter which piece of clothing he had picked, he said. What mattered was that he had decided the question and moved on, and not wasted any more precious time on the subject.[3]

As for major weapons systems, McNamara had inherited a smorgasbord, for the Building ran in the 1950s in such a way that many programs were started up and then limped along, fighting for shares of the budget pie. McNamara wanted better planning and careful selection of a few major systems; he wanted duplication only in cases where — as at Ford — managed competition between programs could bring a better result.

In 1961, McNamara set up a common tank program for the U.S. and West German armies. He pushed forward with his predecessor's plan to make the Air Force adopt the Navy's latest all-weather fighter, the F-4 Phantom, instead of continuing production of its own F-105.[4] If these programs could work, he reasoned, why not a common fighter-bomber?

The question was typical of McNamara's studied innocence. He asked obvious questions — and encouraged his Whiz Kids to ask them, too — in the belief that experts and bureaucracy should be able to come back with good answers. His deliberate amateurism was a brilliant executive device in many areas. But it remained to be seen whether a statistically minded executive, with no feel for the physical problems of advanced engineering, could run a demanding weapons program. "I am completely unmechanical," McNamara said in another context.

McNamara also had personal biases concerning technology. He had spent fourteen years in an industry notoriously resistant to technological innovation. Cars with new devices were too likely to have problems on the road; innovation introduced instability and extra cost into manufacturing and reduced customer loyalty. One of McNamara's jobs at Ford was to manage revenue flows, which depended in turn on stable, trouble-free production of cars. These facts of life in the industry inclined him to mistrust new technology. At another level, McNamara was personally suspicious of frills; "his" car had been the plain Falcon, for example.

Another dimension of his personality played out in the drama of the common fighter-bomber. The flip side of the cost-conscious accountant and skeptic of innovation was a naive believer in technological miracles. Thus, many sides of McNamara's character and ideology were engaged in the story of "his" plane, the Tactical Fighter Experimental, or TFX, which flies today as the F-111.

In 1958, John Stack, a legendary aerodynamicist and pioneer in supersonic flight, produced a design for an airplane with variably swept wings that would be able to fly efficiently at subsonic and supersonic speeds. When the wings were extended, the plane would fly subsonically. When the wings swept back against the sides of the fuselage, the plane could accelerate through the sound barrier. A supersonic plane needed to be long and slim, like an arrow, to have the most thrust and least drag.[5]

The enterprising chief of the Air Force's Tactical Air Command, General Frank Everest, saw in John Stack's swing wing a way to revive Tac Air after its years of taking a backseat to the big-bomber boys of the Strategic Air Command. Everest proposed that they base the next generation of fighter-bombers safely in the United States and in a crisis fly four thousand miles subsonically across the ocean. Everest's proposed plane would be able to take off from hidden runways, even unprepared ones made of dirt, fly 600 miles toward the Soviet border subsonically, and then "dash on the deck" supersonically for 200 miles, flying 100 feet above the ground to get past Soviet radar. The pilot would then bomb his target, engage the enemy if needed, and climb to high altitude to fly back to the base.[6]

Thus the mission Everest nailed down in 1960, in a formal Air Force requirement for a Tactical Fighter Experimental, called for the big, heavy arrow to weigh 63,000 pounds, be 82.5 feet long, and do the 200-mile "dash on the deck" at Mach 1.2 with a bomb-bay capacity of 8,000 pounds. To make the plane appetizing to the new administration, Everest added to the nuclear bomb it would hold a capacity to carry conventional bombs.[7]

McNamara was impressed by an early briefing he received on the potential and flexibility of this new, swing-wing plane. He also heard out the Navy's plans for a new fighter called Missileer. This plane would be light, weighing no more than 50,000 pounds, so it could take off from its carrier, dash to its station in the sky, and loiter for hours while a big, new, five-foot radar in its fat nose watched for attacking enemy aircraft. The radar would guide the plane's six new Eagle long-range missiles to hold off Soviet aircraft and protect the fleet at greater ranges than previously possible.

In February 1961, McNamara asked the services to write a "coordinated, specific operational requirement" based on Stack's miracle plane.[8] He ordered Defense Research and Engineering chief Herbert F. York to "establish specifications for a tri-service fighter," i.e., the Army, Air Force, and Navy, the latter including the Marines. York's study, called Project 34, separated the Army's and the Marines' requirement from the Navy's and the Air Force's needs;[9] the result was two planes instead of one. The second plane, designed for close-air support of ground forces and known as VAX, led to the development of the successful A-7.

Meanwhile, Navy and Air Force technical staffs argued that they could build a common fighter only if each relaxed its requirements, but each refused to budge. On August 22, 1961, the secretaries of the Navy and the Air Force reported to McNamara that a joint plane meeting both services' requirements "is not now technically feasible and would place severe operational penalties upon the Air Force and Navy." The Navy's respected assistant secretary for research and development, James H. Wakelin, warned that the "risks" of attempting a common Navy–Air Force fighter were "not consistent with national defense interests."[10]

At this critical juncture, York, who was a distinguished nuclear physicist with a background in atomic weapons, and McNamara the statistician assumed that the engineering problems could be solved and a common plane meeting both requirements built. McNamara especially deemed it important to rebut signs of institutional resistance. Later he explained why he rebuffed technical objections coming from below: "While this attitude, based on years of going separate ways, was understandable, I did not consider it was a realistic approach, considering the versatility and capabilities that could be built into a modern aircraft because of advances in technology."[11]

In short, McNamara concluded the opposite of the military's technical staff. He decided the plane could be built because of "advances in technology" and the "versatility" in modern aircraft. His faith in technology was strong.

Harold Brown was just as bold. Now thirty-three, he had done brilliant work with atomic weapons. He made his DR&E staff dictate the requirements for the joint fighter, after the Air Force and the Navy had said no one plane could meet both requirements.

Rationality and efficiency were supposed to triumph once McNamara signed the September 1 requirement and order. There was much anger and soul-searching down the line; but the Air Force and Navy bureaus involved would at least appear to obey. The new civilians were being very tough. Harold Brown opened one meeting with the comment, referring to the Navy, "What have the bastards done to us now?"[12]

The September 1 directive gave the Air Force the job of running the joint program. It confirmed that the plane would accommodate a three-foot-wide radar, which was less powerful than the five-foot version the Navy had wanted. The wide nose would hurt the supersonic profile of the plane and require more engine power to overcome the additional drag. The plane's length was to be 73 feet, its weight 60,000 pounds. "Changes to the Air Force . . . version of the basic aircraft to achieve the Navy mission shall be held to a minimum," the directive said.[13] It gave the Air Force and the Navy a month to prepare design specifications and a request for proposal, a job that normally required three months. The civilians were hurrying the military, assuming that anything, even this technically demanding project, could be carried out in less time than was usual.

Albert W. Blackburn, a former Marine test pilot who came to work for Harold Brown in 1961, did a back-of-the-envelope calculation, based on past fighter-procurement programs, showing that roughly a billion dollars could be saved by having one plane designed and built instead of two.[14] This figure made a deep impression on McNamara. He cited it for years as the justification for pressing on with the TFX, despite the growing burden of time and trouble. A news headline later posed the right question: "IS IT EFFICIENT TO BE EFFICIENT?"

The data from Herbert York's original Project 34 indicated, curiously, that the Air Force's version of the plane would cost less than the Navy's, even though the Navy's version was smaller and lighter. Yet a basic rule of aircraft procurement is that cost increases with weight. These and other computations from the Project 34 report suggest poor staff work.[15] On the basis of such numbers, however, McNamara plunged ahead and linked the plane's success to his own.

※   ※   ※

The Air Force now ran a competition among contractors. Firms would now bid on the design of one basic airplane, to be modified slightly for each service — in other words, two versions of one plane, with minimum divergence. Thus it was up to industry to square the circle and make the long, heavy "arrow" and the short, light, fat-nosed plane into one.

Six companies submitted plans on December 6. Following Air Force contract-selection procedures, the plans were evaluated by a group of 225 experts, mainly Air Force men, with some Navy men assigned at each level. The evaluators decided that none of the bids met the requirements. They recommended that the two top contenders, Boeing and General Dynamics, be given ninety-day study contracts to resubmit plans. According to later testimony, McNamara told the president that the final decision would be discussed with him before the contract was awarded.[16]

Grazing the technological edge, Boeing had proposed using a "paper" state-of-the-art engine that General Electric had designed but never built. Boeing was now told to use a Pratt and Whitney engine that General Dynamics had already developed for the Navy's Missileer. When the two companies submitted revised plans in April 1962, both designs were worse. The selectors preferred Boeing; but the Navy said neither design was acceptable. The chief of naval operations, Admiral George Anderson, asked that the project be abandoned, to no avail.[17]

The two competitors were given three weeks to correct "deficiencies" and meet Navy requirements. One Navy aviation expert, George Spangenberg, says the contractors knew the task to be almost impossible. But each reasoned that once it won the contract, the requirements would be bent to meet what the hardware could do, as happened with other weapons-development programs. "It became a lying contest," says Spangenberg.[18] The briefings each company gave at Wright-Patterson Air Force Base after this third round were striking. Boeing presented a wholly new plane, an inspired answer to the problem, which it had evidently been working on for some time. General Dynamics, on the other hand, appeared to have "panicked," according to Albert Blackburn. It presented six alternatives and in effect said to the evaluators: Take your pick.[19]

It was now June 1962. Again, the source-selection process favored Boeing. Harold Brown warned McNamara that "many rumors" surrounded the evaluation process, implying that the civilians were de-

manding more rounds for political reasons, to keep General
Dynamics in the race. Blackburn later said the "morale of the evaluation team and of the contractors was low." The Navy's tactic in
terms of interservice politics was to avoid taking the responsibility for
casting a deciding vote.[20]

The men in the middle were the two civilian service secretaries:
Eugene Zuckert, secretary of the Air Force and McNamara's friend
and fellow teacher from Harvard Business School, and Fred Korth, a
Texas banker who replaced John Connally as secretary of the Navy
in December 1961. Under the 1958 amendments to the National
Security Act, the service secretaries had been made the agents of the
secretary of defense in running their departments.

Korth had not gotten involved deeply in the source selection. His
repeated recommendations of General Dynamics may have reflected
concern for his hometown of Fort Worth; the General Dynamics
plant there was scheduled to close down in late 1962 if it did not win
the $6.5 billion TFX contract. General Dynamics's partner in the bid
was Grumman Corporation, of Long Island, a highly successful
builder of planes for the Navy. Boeing's past work for the Navy had
been mixed; its strongest ties were to the Air Force. General LeMay
thinks "Boeing can do little wrong," Blackburn wrote in a memo to
Harold Brown.[21]

Zuckert knew the Air Force well. He was among the Harvard
Business School experts who helped install management controls in
that service soon after it was founded. Zuckert was familiar with the
Air Force's drive to push the edge of technology — and let the taxpayer pick up the extra cost later. Zuckert prided himself on being an
expert on costs and management in the McNamara mold, although
his temperament could not have been more different. Zuckert and
Korth now recommended a fourth round, to the amazement of both
services.[22]

McNamara's deputy, Roswell Gilpatric, wrote a letter to the chiefs
of both companies to explain, as McNamara later testified, that still,
"neither contractor was meeting Navy requirements," and that "my
primary goal was not accepted or fully understood by the contractors." He wanted a common airplane with minimal variation, two for
the price of one, to protect "the savings inherent in a joint program."[23]

For this round, the Air Force project officer, Colonel Charles
Gayle, was allowed to help both contractors meet the conditions,

now restated by McNamara, while not leaking information between the two, since neither had seen the other's designs.

At the end of the fourth round, General Dynamics produced a plane with 84 percent of the parts in common for the two versions; it claimed to meet each service's requirements. The presentation was "inspired," Blackburn later said. Boeing, meanwhile, had refined its third-round design. True to its behavior in past competitions and to the custom of defense contractors, it made sweeping promises for the TFX's performance, while claiming a low cost — lower than the price named by General Dynamics for a much less daring design.[24]

On November 2, Colonel Gayle's evaluators found both designs acceptable. He gave a briefing to higher-ups that provided raw scores; but following procedure, Gayle did not weigh the scores or state a preference. That choice was left to his listeners. The Air Force's Source Selection Board, Logistics Command, Tactical Air Command, Systems Command, Air Force Council, chief of staff, and chief of naval operations all voted for the Boeing plane.

When Zuckert and Korth were briefed, Zuckert noticed several things, he later said.[25] One was that the Air Force evaluators' performance briefing had stressed that the Boeing plane would exceed requirements. Zuckert also thought Boeing's cost estimates were ridiculously low by historical standards. In fact, as major aircraft orders declined with McNamara's bomber cancellations, both companies were under terrific pressure to underbid to get business.

Zuckert had told McNamara on November 13 that he was leaning toward General Dynamics. He now read through the entire file, a "five-foot shelf" of papers.[26] The Air Force secretary found that the General Dynamics model had more common parts; its higher cost estimate showed greater "cost realism" than Boeing's; and it did not promise the moon in terms of performance. Thus it seemed less likely to come back asking for more money to make the plane work at the technological edge. General Dynamics, in short, was more technologically conservative; it had responded to the civilians' new approach.

"McNamara ratified the choice I recommended," Zuckert said then and later. He told me, "McNamara hadn't read all the material" when he accepted his recommendation. Korth concurred also.

On November 21, Zuckert, Korth, and McNamara signed a memorandum that Zuckert had drafted justifying the award to General

Dynamics. McNamara then instructed press aide Sylvester to hold the announcement until the weekend, when the financial markets were closed. The news broke on Saturday, November 24, 1962.[27]

The Boeing camp and the services were thunderstruck. Boeing had effectively won every round in the runoff. It had 75 percent common parts and was "much further down the line in coming to terms with the total design problem," Blackburn said later. Boeing's engineering team was unequaled; if anyone could build this impossible plane, it was Boeing.

The civilians' choice of General Dynamics looked fishy. Blackburn, who was Harold Brown's technical aide for the TFX, submitted some notes favorable to Boeing on November 6. When he learned, after the fact, that the contract had been given to General Dynamics, Blackburn was surprised, he later testified, because there was "no real, supportable case to be made for [McNamara's] choice on the grounds of operational, technical, management, or cost considerations."[28]

Henry M. Jackson, junior senator from the state of Washington, where Boeing was located, met with McNamara about the decision. According to one account, the defense secretary was shockingly rude to Jackson, who was a strong backer of Kennedy's defense buildup and McNamara's Pentagon revolution.[29]

McNamara insisted that the General Dynamics plane was chosen solely on its merits, that Boeing still didn't understand what he wanted. McNamara acted as though congressmen had no business seeking defense contracts for their states and districts; such politicking was not in the national interest.

Jackson was offended. But his and Boeing's self-interest in getting the decision reversed were too obvious. He had one card to play: his good standing as a member of the Government Operations Committee of the Senate. The chairman of this committee and of its Permanent Subcommittee on Investigations was John L. McClellan of Arkansas. McClellan was a populist from a state so poor it had no stakes in the TFX contract or in any subcontract. McClellan, when his ire was aroused, was one of the most feared men in the Senate. His general counsel, Jerome S. Adlerman, was a member of a group of highly powerful Senate staff whose investigation of labor racketeering had been a national bloodletting. Young Bobby Kennedy had worked with Adlerman running the rackets investigation for McClellan. Mc-

Clellan had also let his colleague Senator John Kennedy sit in and ask questions and share the limelight.[30]

But McClellan had no brief for the growing glitter around John Kennedy or the pretenses of McNamara. Someone had to protect the taxpayer. If the Kennedys had rewarded political friends in Texas and thereby cheated Boeing, the deserving winner, of the huge $6.5 billion contract, McClellan could uncover the malfeasance and get the award reversed.

Among the theories of political influence was one that pointed to Kennedy's having carried Illinois in 1960 with the help of Chicago mayor Richard Daley's political machine. Daley was supported by the fabulously wealthy Crown family of Chicago, the major shareholder in General Dynamics. Another charge was that Lyndon Johnson, the former senator from Texas who enabled John Kennedy to carry the South, wanted the award to go to General Dynamics, to help Fort Worth. Kennedy's first Navy secretary, John Connally, was a Texan and was now that state's governor. Navy Secretary Korth had been president of a bank in Fort Worth. But Kennedy had told Jackson that the award was *not* based on political and employment considerations in Texas. Was it a lie? And since McNamara said the same thing, was he lying, too?

McClellan saw that there were troubling sides to the wunderkind McNamara. He had snubbed Congress when he refused to spend funds it appropriated for the B-70 bomber; he had confronted Admiral Anderson during the Cuban missile crisis. An investigation could raise broader questions about who the man was, what he was really doing. As Zuckert says, looking back at that time, "The whole McNamara thing was starting to worry people." [31]

On December 21, McClellan sent McNamara a letter asking that the award of the TFX contract be delayed while his subcommittee looked into the matter. The request brought another McNamara weakness into play. Had he been concerned about congressional prerogatives, had he listened to Zuckert's early advice to take the pulse of Capitol Hill and to note unwritten agendas, he could have agreed to wait.

Instead, Gilpatric signed the letter making the award that same afternoon. The contract with General Dynamics was now set in stone, backed by the full faith and credit of Uncle Sam. McClellan took offense. He could hardly have done otherwise.

✻   ✻   ✻

Adlerman, McClellan's counsel and chief investigator, paid a preliminary call on Gilpatric. Adlerman asked if the president had known the contract would be awarded to General Dynamics. Gilpatric replied, Yes, the president knew.[32]

David McGiffert, McNamara's assistant for legislative affairs, sat in on the meeting and was startled. The first commandment of dealing with congressional investigators was *protect the president*. To say the president knew in advance was to invite Congress's investigators down a trail that could be embarrassing or worse.

McGiffert knew, however, that Gilpatric would have dropped this bombshell only if he thought it would help Kennedy. Perhaps Gilpatric was playing on loyalties, thinking McClellan could be headed off if he knew Kennedy was involved.

But McGiffert had a terrible feeling Gilpatric's statement would only make things worse. McNamara and his men were in up to their ankles already and faced a token inquiry to help Senator Jackson and soothe Boeing. If McClellan set out looking for real corruption, they could be in up to their waists. And, knowing Adlerman and McClellan, they would be wading not in water, but mud.

McNamara perhaps did not sense how dangerous McClellan's investigation could be to him.[33] He was advised to try to get McClellan to invite him as the first witness to testify before the subcommittee. This was a courtesy congressmen normally accorded to heads of Cabinet departments. The advisers told McNamara that if he led off, he could get his facts on the table and shape the story. He could deflect, in advance, any mud McClellan threw later.

But McNamara did not even try to appear first, and McClellan did not ask him. When he opened the hearing on February 26 — saying pointedly that it would last "five or six days" — he and Adlerman had explained their suspicions to reporters; these were amply hinted at in the press.

John Stack, the inventor of the swing-wing design, and Colonel Gayle, who ran the Air Force evaluation group, were the first witnesses. Artful questioning made them state for the record the superior features of the Boeing design. In response, McNamara released the memorandum of November 21 to explain the case for giving the contract to General Dynamics. But that unfortunate document had several errors;[34] McClellan, in pointing them out, implied that the only reason McNamara and Zuckert would make the General Dy-

namics design look better than it was, was to justify a political decision already made.

McClellan was dramatic about finding mathematical errors in a
memorandum of decision signed by R. S. McNamara. "When are we
going to get figures we can rely on?" the chairman thundered to no
doubt delighted listeners.

The president did not like this, and he telephoned McNamara to
ask him to take the hearing seriously. McNamara then overreacted.
He set up two groups, a Red Team and a Blue Team, to work nonstop for days to prepare the brief for his award. The Blue Team,
headed by lawyer Solis Horwitz, was jammed into cubicles in Mc-
Namara's conference room. It could get additional data from General
Dynamics, which was now under contract to the department. The
Red Team, led by McNamara appointee Jack Stempler, another lawyer, put together the brief for Boeing.[35]

March 8 seems to be the day McNamara ordered his staff to return
fire. The vinegary Arthur Sylvester, recently unpopular with reporters for his assertion of the government's right to lie in the missile
crisis, now said, on the record: "Obviously you will hardly get a
judicial rendering from a committee in which there are various senators with state self-interest in where the contract goes."

McClellan and other senators on the subcommittee were furious.
Sylvester wrote a letter intended as an apology. But when McClellan
put Sylvester in the witness chair, under oath, that stubborn fellow
gave the impression that, in his opinion, the hearing was just an effort
by the losers to get the decision reversed.[36]

Gilpatric held a background session with reporters. They then
wrote stories saying that a high-ranking Defense official said he had
been "misled" by McClellan into thinking the investigation would be
brief. Gilpatric admitted he was the source but said he was mis-
quoted.[37]

McNamara could not resist jumping in. He wrote McClellan on
March 9, saying that the investigation "needlessly undermines" public confidence in Defense officials, i.e., himself and his aides. He
claimed the right of an injured party to appear before a congressional
proceeding. Weeks earlier, he had decided not to try to appear first to
get out his side of the story. Now he blamed McClellan for failing to
give the public "an overall framework."[38]

On March 13, general counsel John McNaughton read out Mc-
Namara's thirty-two-page brief. It was a lawyerly document that

invoked the policy goals of commonality, efficiency, and careful planning before making a choice of major weapons systems. In it McNamara denied that other considerations, such as labor conditions in Fort Worth or politics, had affected his choice. McClellan dryly replied that there were "discrepancies" between the new statement and the November 21 memorandum. He said enough to get skeptical quotes into the news articles that reported McNamara's side.[39] McClellan was still shaping the story.

In private, to the Whiz Kids, McNamara could be generous, reasonable, curious. But the McNamara who was challenged by McClellan was a fighter with no holds barred. To his enemies, who now included people in the technical bureaus of the Air Force and the Navy, McNamara seemed cold, an adversary who would stop at nothing to defend himself.

The date of March 21 was set for McNamara to appear in person before the subcommittee. The Red and Blue teams' work was finished. Then Solis Horwitz of the Blue Team asked the technical men on the Red Team, who had written the case for Boeing, to sign a paper saying they concurred that the choice of General Dynamics was sound. But "the professionals" on the Red Team "would not accede to such a proposition." Blackburn, the TFX expert, was appalled at the release of "newly computed data" from General Dynamics to justify the award on new grounds. He was due to leave government soon anyway, and he told his immediate superior, John McLucas, that "I could not, in my conscience, remain associated with the Office of the Secretary of Defense."[40]

Freed from government employment, having had a key role as Harold Brown's civilian adviser and having favored Boeing, Blackburn made a powerful witness when McClellan called on him to testify in May. McNamara was furious, but, in fact, he had brought such angry defections on himself.

When McNamara and Gilpatric arrived on March 21 to testify, McClellan kept the secretary waiting all morning while he grilled Gilpatric about his remarks to the press.

Over the noon lunch break, the afternoon *Washington Star* appeared with an explosive story by Richard Fryklund asserting that two Air Force officers had been so browbeaten by McClellan's staff that after their interrogation, they had sought medical help. The story was based on a report done for McNamara's office and leaked to the *Star*. When McNamara came back to the hearing that afternoon, he said he "nearly had indigestion" when he saw it."[41]

All his plans to regain control of the situation with a statesmanlike defense were abandoned. It was out-and-out war between two enemies who believed not a word the other said.

First McNamara admitted that someone in the Pentagon had most likely leaked the Air Force officers' report, but he said he had not the faintest idea who the leaker was. Then he stressed how hard he was working to keep tempers calm at the Pentagon in the face of McClellan's assault. He was encouraging openness and cooperation, he insisted. No, he was not offended by McClellan's tactics. To prove how responsible he was, McNamara now admitted he had obtained a copy of the report and had it locked in his safe, since a leak would hurt relations with the subcommittee.

But McNamara admitted there were other copies of the report, too, refuting his claim that he had tried his hardest to avoid a leak. He said it was he who told the Air Force men to get medical help in the first place.

If one believed, as did some in that room, that the truth was 180 degrees different from McNamara's version, one could conclude that he had authorized the leak or done it himself.

McNamara had with him the report of the doctors who had examined the officers. McClellan, not to be upstaged, had a transcript of his staff's interrogation, ready to give the press, to refute the charge of browbeating.

The powerful secretary of defense argued over and over that he was acting calmly and responsibly, but he betrayed his fury by body and voice. The more he said he was calm, the more emotional he became. He said: "There is a lot of harm that will come of this investigation. I cannot see any good that will accrue from it. I can see only harm. . . . I think I can minimize the harm."

McClellan: If that were true, I would think the committee ought to quit. Is that what you are suggesting?

McNamara: No sir; I am not suggesting quitting. I am just being realistic. I think there is going to be tremendous harm done to many individuals as a result of this hearing. . . .

McClellan: . . . I regret this as much as you, or anybody else, that this thing has developed and it became necessary, and properly so, for the committee to look into it. But I doubt that more harm will come from clearing it up. . . .

McNamara: Mr. Chairman, I know that is your desire and intention and I hope that is the result. I don't believe it will be.

Last night when I got home at midnight, preparing for today's hearing, my wife told me that my own 12-year-old son had asked how long it would take for his father to prove his honesty.

McClellan: Well, don't you think that is true with all of us in public life?

McNamara: I call it harm and not good.

Amazed subcommittee members and the audience saw that the secretary of defense of the United States, the leader of the free world's armed forces, the walking computer, the famously tough man, was crying.[42]

Afterward, McNamara's office denied that he wept. It told friendly reporters it had been an act, crocodile tears. The year 1963 was the era of James Bond and John Wayne; men were supposed to act cold and hard. According to Benjamin Bradlee of *Newsweek*, who often chatted with John Kennedy, when the president heard McNamara had cried, he became worried.[43]

McClellan would push on through the third week in November. He recessed — temporarily, he said — when the president was shot. He summoned Defense employees — obscure technical experts and senior officials — put them under oath, and made them describe meetings, memos, and nuances of top-level official behavior. The labyrinth of a single McNamara decision lay exposed.

The press joined the fray, too. Leaks from McClellan's closed proceedings were snatched up by reporters, providing months of stories impugning McNamara's decision-making process and raising doubts about his integrity and judgment.

Yet for all his storming, McClellan got no hard evidence of political influence. And the press — which later would be influential in breaking the definitive stories of the My Lai massacre, Watergate, and U.S. intelligence abuses — did little far-reaching investigation of its own.[44] This was the pre-Vietnam press, bound by the conventions of publishing only what officials stated or a document said. The reporters might personally believe that McNamara was lying or that McClellan was making a mountain out of a molehill, but they had no leeway from their editors to dig beyond the public record.

Bobby tried to arrange a truce. He and McNamara visited McClellan on March 27. But stopping the Arkansan was hopeless, Bobby later said: "Our relationship with McClellan deteriorated very badly during this period of time and I had a very bitter exchange with Jerry Adlerman. I mean, Carmine Bellino [who worked on the rackets inquiry] talked to them and they just became impossible about it. They said they were going to run McNamara out of town."[45]

McClellan got two scalps. He found that Gilpatric's former law firm, Cravath, Swaine and Moore, represented General Dynamics on certain matters. Gilpatric had billed $110,000 in fees to General Dynamics before coming to Washington in 1961. But he also did a small job for Boeing and had not charged for it. Most of official Washington agreed that McNamara's deputy was not guilty of conflict of interest. But Attorney General Bobby Kennedy was not pleased at Gilpatric's slight evasiveness before the subcommittee. "Gilpatric was not as open as he should have been," Bobby said later. Gilpatric announced on October 4, 1963, that he would leave government in January. It became known during January that he was returning to Cravath, despite his protests to the subcommittee that he had no such plans.[46]

McClellan's second victim was Fred Korth, the former Fort Worth bank director who as secretary of the Navy ruled for General Dynamics in the source selection. General Dynamics's plant in Fort Worth had taken out a $400,000 loan from Korth's bank. And then it was learned that Korth, while Navy secretary, had an active correspondence with Fort Worth business associates, inviting them to socialize with him aboard the *Sequoia,* the presidential yacht the Navy ran. The Justice Department cleared Korth of a conflict of interest, but Bobby Kennedy felt a resignation was in order. "McNamara opposed it at first, but then went along," Bobby said. So Korth resigned, with a blast at McNamara.[47]

McNamara might have gained in the public arena if he and Zuckert had been able to demonstrate clear evidence for their judgment that General Dynamics was stronger on "cost realism." But when they made this fateful decision, amazingly, neither wrote down a clear record of the choice and the financial reasoning — except, of course, for the faulty document of November 21. Either the decision was politically inspired, so that there were no such reasons to write down, or McNamara and Zuckert were so presumptuous as to think they could overrule the services on a controversial, $6.5 billion contract award without written documentation.

McClellan sent Joseph Campbell, controller general of the United States, who ran the General Accounting Office, to investigate the figures McNamara and Zuckert used. *Newsweek*'s Henry Trewhitt reported that the senators on the subcommittee "rippled with mixed satisfaction, frustration and awe" when Campbell testified about his visit to McNamara.[48]

McNamara had written McClellan that he discounted the Air Force's entire cost-estimation process, because it was "so unreliable." When Campbell and his staff visited the Pentagon to interview McNamara and Zuckert, the two men told the accountants "they were relying upon their experience in the field previously, and that they were able to make rough judgments."

When the GAO men asked for documents, calculations of the sort they usually audited in examining defense contract awards, McNamara announced "he had the figures in his head, indicating that he did not have them on paper."

Hearing this part of Campbell's testimony, McClellan asked him, "Can you audit figures in somebody's head?"

"No," the controller general replied.

So McClellan found smoke but no smoking pistol. He had drawn some blood. He had focused the anger at and mistrust of McNamara that had been growing in parts of the military. But he had not proved his case. By fall his fellow senators on the subcommittee called for a vote of confidence in Gilpatric and won. North Carolina senator Sam Ervin left the investigations subcommittee amid rumors that he was fed up with McClellan's tactics.[49]

McClellan had not succeeded in refuting McNamara's main argument, which was that General Dynamics had responded to the new philosophy put forward by McNamara while Boeing had not. And since the Arkansan found no evidence of a political instruction from Kennedy or Johnson, it remained entirely possible that McNamara and Zuckert had decided for General Dynamics for the reasons they said they had: They wanted to impose the philosophy of commonality and "cost realism," no matter how much the services balked.

By the time the hearings recessed in November 1963, General Dynamics was bending metal for the TFX; the Air Force version was officially the F-111A, the Navy version the F-111B.

It remained to be seen, however, if the newly named hybrid bird, the F-111, could fly.

McNamara could supervise the development of hardware only remotely, by means of the charts and memos crossing his desk for his signature. Yet he had enormous power over the TFX/F-111 and other programs, due to a provision in the amendments to the 1947 National Security Act that let him withhold disbursement of funds for particular research and development items even after Congress appropriated them.[50] General Dynamics, off in St. Louis and Fort Worth, was physically removed from him; but he could cut off its funds anytime. The pressure to proceed with the troubled but high-visibility project was intense.

The physical problems of building the plane surfaced early. National Aeronautics and Space Administration engineers tested the General Dynamics model in their wind tunnel at Langley Field and found the design met only half of the stated requirements for maneuverability, which is critical in a fighter. General Dynamics, however, citing tests made at Cornell University, retorted that the plane would exceed maneuverability requirements.[51]

Through 1963, General Dynamics's regular monthly reports on the plane's weight showed expected gains of a few hundred pounds every two months. Then, in December 1963 — when McClellan's hearings had stopped — the weight of the Navy version leapt by some 5,000 pounds, to 45,259 pounds, from the 40,284 reported in November. The design had not changed that much in a month; the weight had been increasing all along, but the company did not dare report it while the hearings were going on, lest bad news jeopardize the contract award.[52]

The caprices of engineering were at work. McNamara, in his quest for a simple, common weapons system, had actually commissioned a state-of-the-art, Mach 2 fighter-bomber with many complex features. He should have known that the test F-111s would diverge from the "paper planes" he and Zuckert and Korth had approved. Even with the more mundane engineering of automobiles, he knew, as he said later, that "you couldn't change a spark plug or a screw without problems in production."[53] (One explanation for McNamara's insistence that the plane could be built to the stated requirements, even when physical evidence seemed to show it could not, was the background of his advisers. Herbert York and Harold Brown were nuclear physicists. They came from a world of defense engineering in which missiles were complex and difficult to build right. The missile men, in the technology culture of the day, tended to look down on airplanes as easy engineering problems. Some airplanes were; but the TFX was not, thanks to the particular Air Force and Navy requirements imposed.[54])

When word of the plane's shocking weight gain in December reached McNamara, he asked for a status report on the project. The Navy's Bureau of Weapons found that the Navy version, the F-111B, was going to be unacceptably heavy. The bureau insisted that the time for redesign was now, before they got in deeper; meanwhile, the taxpayers' money should be saved by halting work on the Navy prototype.

The Navy bureau men tried to persuade each level in the hierarchy to stick with this recommendation and not water it down in the face of McNamara's and Brown's likely fury. The recommendation to stop production stayed in the draft report right up through the morning of February 14, 1964, the day before it was due to the defense secretary. But by six in the evening, Assistant Secretary James Wakelin gave the bureau men the sad word: The report going to McNamara, and signed by Brown, Zuckert, and the new Navy secretary, Paul Nitze, recommended continuing production for four months, to allow time for "present improving trends" in the Navy version's weight and aerodynamics.[55]

McNamara's stubbornness was creating a fatal pattern. His and Brown's determination that the plane could be built if only the Navy would come to heel, and that General Dynamics had to build it, put their subordinates under tremendous pressure to distort reports and even lie. For example, in March 1964, NASA research and technology chief Raymond Bisplinghoff met with Alexander Flax, the assistant secretary of the Air Force for research and development. Bisplinghoff gave Flax a blunt forecast of the plane's subpar performance and the need for basic redesign. McClellan, who continued investigating the program, later found no written record of this warning; "it apparently was secretarial policy to avoid mention of any TFX problems in written communications," he concluded.[56]

The quick fixes to reduce weight did little good during the four-month continuation McNamara ordered. At the same time, the configuration of the basic airplane — which was a main source of its problems of drag and weight — became fixed. While higher authority denied the seriousness of these problems, the plane's design flaws were being cast, literally, in metal and tooling.

Harold Brown's assistant for the project, Leonard Sullivan, reported in October 1964 that the Navy's F-111B "will not" meet that service's flight requirements and "may not" meet the requirements to take off and land on carriers. Sullivan's report should have reached McNamara through Brown. But the paper that went forward to McNamara omitted these warnings and made only passing reference to "problems" with the plane's weight.[57]

However fine were McNamara's intentions when he started the TFX project, by 1964 and 1965 honesty had gone with the wind. Had he and Brown encouraged the engineers to speak out, had they admitted they had problems and asked for a redesign early on, they perhaps could have had a workable plane, although not the exact plane they ordered back in September 1961. But to admit major error would have exposed the secretary of defense and his aides to more fire from McClellan. Whether McNamara realized it at the time or not — for he was shielded from the truth by favorable reports flowing to him — his pride and stubbornness were preventing him from getting a sound airplane.

The Navy was playing its own game as well. Later, when it developed a fighter it did want, the F-14, it sacrificed all sorts of requirements to be able to go ahead, even when that plane encountered the huge cost and engineering problems so common in weapons procurement. Had the Navy bent the same requirements for the F-111B, for example, it could have gotten a workable plane.[58] What stopped the Navy from cooperating was a fact of institutional life that McNamara had overlooked from the beginning: Because the Navy did not *want* the plane, it would not go out of its way to make the joint program succeed.

By 1965 McNamara was practically fanatical about making "his" plane work. He boasted to McClellan that it was exceeding expectations, even though the first flight tests in 1965 revealed the very problems of high drag and too little power that NASA had warned of the year before. Flight tests of the Navy version reported that pilots found it so underpowered as to pose a "safety of flight problem."[59]

Strangely, McNamara ordered production to start right away on the Air Force version. And in December, he unexpectedly announced a third version, a strategic bomber to succeed the B-52s. The stage was set for the last act of the TFX/F-111 saga.

This was Project Icarus, which McNamara convened in his office on Saturdays, with the heads of General Dynamics, Grumman, the Air Force, the Navy, Defense Research and Engineering, and others.[60] Apparently he believed that if lower-level technical people could not make the plane work, the company presidents could. Meeting with them first at two-week intervals, McNamara delved deeply into the features of the plane — just as he had picked over the plans for new cars at Ford — to try to get weight out.

The blueprints for the plane were spread out all over the rug in his office. The men — most of whom were not engineers but businessmen like himself — stood around awkwardly, trying to offer suggestions and feeling inept, when, to their amazement, McNamara got down on his hands and knees in his pressed trousers and began crawling over the plans with a pencil, calling out instructions that he imagined could force this bird to fly.

The story of McNamara and the TFX contains two great ironies. The first is that although the project, which began in his first weeks and dragged on for his full seven-year tenure, gave a terrible name to his civilian interference in "professional military matters," the fundamental flaws of the TFX could have been unearthed right away by more civilian "interference," in the form of better analysis of the Air Force's requirements. Tac Air general Everest's 200-mile dash-on-the-deck requirement, which remained set in stone throughout, was the real source of the plane's incompatibility with Navy needs.[61]

The second irony is that McNamara, to make his philosophic point about commonality, simplicity, and efficiency, picked an unworkable set of common requirements, and hence a very sophisticated piece of hardware. Those common programs that have worked, such as the Navy–Air Force F-4, have been much less complex and historically have been developed by a single service first, thus not overburdening the procurement bureaucracy when all-important engineering choices are made.

Says Jacques Gansler, a respected expert on military procurement, McNamara, first, "was trying to refocus the system away from the technological edge. He wanted to send a message that henceforth, high-confidence, less risky weapons systems would be deemed preferable, unless going to the edge was critical. Therefore he rejected Boeing's proposal."

McNamara was also trying to make a second point, "which was

that the two services should have one airplane. This made him impose the TFX on an unwilling Navy."

There was a strong element of ideology in this, Gansler observes, as though McNamara knew the points he wanted to make and "said to himself, 'I'll take the first airplane that comes along to make them.' "[62]

12
Dawn and Darkness

MCNAMARA AND KENNEDY seemed to be winning, overall, in the summer and fall of 1963. Mc-Clellan's investigation remained a sideshow, an irritant more than a threat, while the focus of the administration's attention remained on larger changes in the international scene.

McNamara's reputation was buoyed, despite the TFX affair, by a rising tide of public confidence in the United States and its leaders. Americans' diffuse anxieties of the late fifties had sharpened into fears of war during the Berlin and Cuba crises and then changed to relief. Kennedy had muffled his critics on the right by standing down the Soviets; he had stepped leftward when he intervened to support James Meredith's attempt to enroll at the University of Mississippi. From his narrow victory in 1960, Kennedy now stood astride the center of American politics. The Democrats could expect to dominate the nation's domestic and foreign policy agenda for some time.[1]

The economy also gave grounds for confidence. Kennedy's New Economics, which tried to stimulate growth through a controlled federal deficit, was working; as the economy pulled out of recession, unemployment came down to 5.7 percent that July. Kennedy asked Congress for a major tax cut. If it would cut taxes and allow a small deficit, Kennedy argued, they could continue the longest expansion in peacetime history through 1964.

Business was good for U.S. firms. Ford Motor Company was a case in point: In January 1963 it announced record profits of $480.7

million for 1962, which made that year its most profitable since 1955. *U.S. News & World Report* asked in its April 29 issue, "Is a boom ahead for business?" By May, *Nation's Business* had the answer: "COMING: FASTER BUSINESS GROWTH." In the fall another headline asked: "CAN GOOD TIMES GO ON AND ON?"

Apparently they could, although the economy was showing structural weaknesses that worried Kennedy. One was the outflow of a small but steady fraction of the nation's huge supply of gold, which supported the U.S. dollar as the anchor of the postwar currency system. As a senator, Kennedy had fastened on to the gold issue; he continued to worry about it as president, as the gold supply shrank slightly more, due to the United States' $3.7 billion negative balance of payments.[2]

On this issue, as on so many others, McNamara had leapt in with a typically intense focus on quantitative solutions. Both private and government spending overseas caused the payments imbalance. McNamara pegged the cost of supporting more than one million military personnel, and their families and arms, at $2.6 billion. He quickly set up controls to limit defense spending overseas. First he limited the amounts that servicemen and their families could spend abroad. When added U.S. forces were sent to Germany during the Berlin crisis, McNamara concluded an "offset" agreement by which the Bonn government would pay fixed amounts annually to compensate for some of the resulting drain on the U.S. Treasury. He instituted vigorous "Buy American" policies, whereby defense contracts could be awarded to U.S. firms that bid 25 and later 50 percent more than foreign firms. He had tanks and other equipment flown back to the United States for repairs — to avoid spending dollars for repairs in Europe. Finally, an entire Army division began to be rotated, spending half the year in the United States and half the year in Europe, as much to improve the U.S. balance of payments as to practice mobility.

Since 1945, American taxpayers had footed the bill for global leadership by supporting a vast military aid program, but those days of wealth in relation to the rest of the world were numbered by 1961. That year McNamara began converting aid into arms sales, to reduce outlays of government defense dollars and bring revenue into the pockets of U.S. defense companies instead. An arms sales office was established under Henry Kuss, in the Pentagon's department of International Security Affairs, with a de facto mandate to promote American arms sales.[3]

McNamara was as impressed with Western Europe's growing economic power at the Pentagon as he had been at Ford. Now he pressured the NATO allies to buy more American weapons, both to help fix the balance of payments and to standardize weaponry — when he entered office, NATO's armies used fourteen types of small-arms ammunition, while the Soviets used only one. Within a few years Kuss's operation could boast that it was selling $2 billion worth of U.S. arms on average per year. McNamara's export policy mimicked Henry Ford and the Model T: The allies could buy whatever they wanted so long as they bought American.

Over the decade, two thirds of McNamara's arms exports would go to other NATO nations, to strengthen their non-nuclear fighting ability.[4] As for the Third World, Kennedy wanted to curtail major arms transfers to focus those governments' attention on the task of development. But the inexorable pressure of the payments imbalance, and the systematic efforts of Kuss (who even divided his staff into Red, White, Blue, and Gray teams, each responsible to meet quotas in different parts of the globe), pushed exports of arms to the third world up two and a half times, not even counting arms to South Vietnam.

The shah of Iran was deemed rich enough from oil revenues to start paying for his U.S.-built weapons; he had received $387 million in outright military aid since American agents helped him consolidate power in 1953. Kennedy was concerned about the shah's appetites for advanced aircraft for which he had no apparent need. During one state visit, Kennedy sent him across the river to McNamara, who put the heir to the Peacock Throne on a rolling five-year plan of arms purchases, which the administration tried to make conditional on more investment in Iran's civilian economy. The shah did not like being told what he did and did not need; during the briefing with McNamara he looked as though he had "swallowed a persimmon," recalls William Bundy.[5]

McNamara cut a formidable figure, even on the issue of the payments imbalance and the gold drain. He regularly briefed the press and Congress on their quantitative progress at lowering the outflow of defense funds; with his hair slicked back and his straight-arrow part, he embodied the tough, number-crunching solutions the age admired.

The national mood was buoyant. Jack Paar defined the role of a television talk-show host and showed Americans how to stay cool and cocky late into the night. Moviegoers flocked to films that were alternately lascivious, heroic, and inane: *Tom Jones, How the West Was Won,* and *Bye Bye Birdie.* Kennedy's interest in James Bond, the British secret agent in Ian Fleming's spy thrillers, sparked a series of popular movies in which Agent 007 seduced and discarded women while fighting incarnations of pure evil in imaginatively violent ways.

In 1963 the records of a rock group from Liverpool, England, were selling briskly among American teenagers; once the group arrived the following year, Beatlemania would grip the nation's young. Commentators wondered about this most well educated and well-off generation in American history and wrote darkly of "drugs in the suburbs" and "the affluent delinquent." Could the economy expand to provide jobs as the baby boomers came of age? President Kennedy honed the military draft exemptions to encourage college-going youth to stay in school and later enter the professions the nation needed; a side effect would be that the burden of the draft would fall disproportionately on lower-middle-class youth.[6]

McNamara had become a walking symbol of the nation's confidence in science, technology, management, business, and progress. He had cultivated the image of the anonymous, rational executive described by Whiz Kid William Kaufmann, who wrote in a book in 1963 for publication the next year, when McNamara could be Kennedy's running mate: "McNamara has all the best qualities of a professional manager. He has the ability to range over broad areas of interest. He is interested in ideas, has an analytical mind, and a capacity for action. He doesn't worry over details or the possibility of making mistakes."[7]

Kaufmann's paean set the tone for a whole body of literature about defense policy-making in the 1960s that portrayed McNamara as aloof, impartial, and incorruptible. "He wanted all defense problems approached in a rational and analytical way," Alain Enthoven and K. Wayne Smith would write later, furthering the hope that if there were just enough McNamara-style philosopher-kings, and good enough analysis, the Kennedy ideal of objectively derived policy, impartially administered, could be attained at last.

McNamara's own ideal of leadership required him to be out in front of the pack. He often said that he would not be a "judge" who waited "for subordinates to bring him problems for solution or alternatives for decision." Rather, he wanted to be a leader who "immerses himself in his operations, leads and stimulates an examination

of the objectives, the problems and the alternatives." He was much
admired for leading and stimulating the defense program in 1963; at
that time journalist David Halberstam, later one of his harshest critics, wrote, "In my opinion, McNamara may well be this country's
most distinguished civil servant of the last decade."[8]

By the summer of 1963, McNamara was bringing his revolution in
the U.S. defense program, as well as his overhaul of the defense budget
process, home right on schedule for John Kennedy. It seemed not to
matter that he had gone well beyond Kennedy's campaign pledge to
close the missile gap, or that he had exercised the legal powers of his
office almost violently, to their full extent, over two and a half years.
It was not uncommon for his admirers in the press — ignoring other
reporters who strongly mistrusted him — to express the opinion that
McNamara "may be the greatest managerial genius of our time," as the
Washington Star's Richard Fryklund wrote that August.[9]

Right off, McNamara had axed a major military role in space, the
nuclear airplane, and another relic of the 1950s called Dyna Soar. He
ordered an increase in the number of tactical aircraft ready to do battle
over the skies of Europe by one third, since Rand's work in the 1950s
for the Air Force had shown how shorter-range tactical air power
could decisively help ground forces at war — a fact that the men of
SAC who dominated Air Force councils had chosen to ignore for
years. Backed by systems analysis, McNamara stubbornly insisted
that a new close-air-support plane be produced: This became the A-7,
which grew out of the original common-fighter-bomber program that
led to the TFX. But slow and low-flying close-air-support craft were
anathema to the blue-yonder boys: McNamara, backed by Enthoven
and his studies, could prove rationally the need for the plane and could
force it into the budget. As for the kinds of mission the Air Force preferred, that of long-range bombers penetrating deep behind enemy
lines (the sort of mission for which Frank Everest's TFX was originally
planned), Enthoven confessed that many, many studies could not
prove this to be as decisive a factor in a future land war as the Air Force
believed. Finally, Rand analysis had demonstrated the importance of
airlift; McNamara ordered unpopular increases in the Air Force's
cargo planes — and a new plane, the C-5A.[10] He and the Whiz Kids
knocked down Air Force shibboleths left and right — not to mention
the principal fight with SAC over the future bomber and missile
force — in the name of rationality.

At Ford he had played on the competition among divisions; when he left in 1960, he had proposed "managed competition" so Ford could offer a range of models and shift rapidly to meet fickle market tastes. Similarly, in his overhaul of the defense program, McNamara and his band played on competition among the armed services — to force outcomes that would not have been achieved otherwise. The Army, in 1961, had been gearing up to produce a new standard-issue rifle, the M-14.[11] It had been fifteen years in development, weighed nine pounds, and satisfied institutional and traditional demand for power and great accuracy, as though American GIs in the 1960s would be picking off Indians one at a time on the Great Plains. The civilians then learned of the merits of a six-pound spray-fire rifle designed by Eugene Stoner, the so-called popgun the Army Ordnance Bureau spurned. Analysis showed that this was the gun soldiers would need in real firefights. McNamara exploited competition with the Air Force and among Army factions to force wider adoption of the M-16, as the Stoner gun was renamed. It was soon in heavy demand by U.S. advisers in South Vietnam. Without civilian intervention, the troops would have had the M-14, which they literally turned in for the popgun, given the chance.

Analysis also beamed a searchlight on the need to abolish the long-standing taboo — enforced by the Air Force since 1947, to keep its monopoly on land-based air power — on the Army's flying of fixed-wing aircraft.[12] Another imaginative liaison between the systems analysts under Enthoven and the Army group seeking at least a helicopter fleet to move troops around the theater led to tests of a new concept: After 1962, air mobility began proving its worth. In Vietnam this took shape as the Air Cavalry, which would prove vital.

Enthoven and the Rand group had had the least experience with naval problems but knew enough to question the efficiencies of giant aircraft carriers to send air power to roar over distant lands.[13] McNamara had taken office during a historic change in the Navy, just when Vice Admiral Hyman G. Rickover was winning his fifteen-year battle to install nuclear power aboard submarines and major surface ships, and used the Joint Committee on Atomic Energy in Congress to overcome resistance from the Navy's baronies.

At first Enthoven sensed Rickover was an ally; he called on the powerful, diminutive vice admiral in his office, in old temporary buildings along the Mall in Washington, and Rickover had given him the lowdown on the Navy brass, making fun of their pompous conformity. But the issue of modernizing the World War II carrier fleet was pending, and Rickover wanted the new ships to be nuclear-powered, as the submarine fleet was. McNamara gave the green light for the first of the new, larger carriers to be started using conventional fuel; but when he and Enthoven began questioning the need to go to Rickover's four-reactor design for the next two carriers, the battle lines were drawn.[14]

Soon Rickover became a bitter critic of cost-effectiveness, the Whiz Kids, Enthoven, and Robert McNamara. The Navy noticed that the civilians maintained that the Polaris program was not taking funds away from carrier modernization, but it saw large amounts added to its budget for Polaris (about which it was lukewarm at best) while funds for new carriers were being deferred. McNamara claimed that his additional nuclear forces were not competing with general-purpose forces — yet they were. He claimed there was no civilian-military split within the Building — yet there was. He claimed before McClellan that the choice of General Dynamics was purely objective, based on rational grounds — yet he could not produce a single detailed calculation that he had made at the time to support this. By the summer and fall of 1963, with a showdown nearing with Rickover and the Joint Committee on the carrier question, many in the Navy had decided — and told each other — that McNamara was a liar.

But his program was coming together by the fall of 1963; he was making American missile defenses second to none. By the time all the Minuteman and Polaris missiles he had ordered entered the force, the United States would have a ten-to-one lead in ballistic missiles over the Soviets. He had axed the size of the bomber force from 1,700 to 500, but the Soviets "could put only half that number over North America," he said in a speech in November.[15] He had inherited a situation of supposed Soviet nuclear superiority, but now even "the most wishful Soviet planners" contemplating a surprise attack would have to reckon with America's ability to strike back "to destroy the attacker's society."

Perhaps the most important contribution of analysis was the work by Enthoven's systems analysis group and by the office of International Security Affairs in demolishing the myth that Soviet and East Bloc forces numbered 175 effective divisions, compared with NATO's 26. These simple comparisons had convinced the allies over the years that the only way Western Europe could be defended was by quick resort to nuclear arms. Now, by applying other yardsticks to the two sides, McNamara's band demonstrated that Western conventional forces could deploy at least as many resources in an extended war as the Warsaw Pact. Whereas the Communists had 4.5 million men under arms, NATO's active forces numbered 5 million; the fabled 175 divisions were thin in people and equipment, and most were not ready for war. Thus the analysts demonstrated that in a protracted, non-nuclear war, the alliance stood a fighting chance.[16] These findings were publicized by Nitze and Enthoven in speeches and briefings to NATO allies, to try to break down the pro-nuclear mind-set of the time and lay the groundwork for them to formally adopt flexible response and build up their forces.

Despite all this apparent rationalism, McNamara was bounded by the preconceptions of his place and time. Apparently, it did not occur to him that his enormous buildup of strategic forces, his continued installation of tactical nuclear weapons in Europe, and the improvements in the effectiveness of Army, Air Force, and Navy forces for general war could trigger fear in the Kremlin.[17] Americans of the time were preoccupied with having *enough* superiority, not with whether their procurement would trigger a threatening enemy response. McNamara had lectured the Kremlin on Rand-type methods of fighting limited nuclear war at Ann Arbor even as he ordered a vastly superior U.S. nuclear arsenal. The Soviets were meant to accept American superiority as inevitable and desirable. But in fact, the men of the Kremlin reacted emotionally to these warlike signals from Washington. After 1961 Soviet leaders debated a massive nuclear buildup of their own; another response by Khrushchev was to put the missiles into Cuba, to quickly redress his condition of inferiority. So the image of rationality emanating from room 3E 880 in the Pentagon was not believed where it counted most — in Moscow.

Nonetheless, by the summer and fall of 1963, McNamara predicted the defense budget could level off in a year, for frugality and efficiency were the watchwords of his buildup. Even as he gave the services more money than Eisenhower had, he put them on a "cost reduction program" to save money through efficiencies — to the tune of $1.1 billion out of a budget fast approaching $49 billion.[18]

McNamara's goal of a cost-effective military force was the link to the Democratic party tradition of federal spending for domestic well-being that dated back to Franklin Roosevelt. McNamara and Kennedy could boast that they had built a far more powerful and effective defense than the Republicans while freeing every defense dollar they could for social programs. A well-managed defense effort could enhance the party's standing as the helper of the disadvantaged, the working man, the blacks, and the poor.

In reality, John Kennedy as president hesitated to address the problems of civil rights, Appalachian poverty, or housing, despite his early promises, and even though Walter Heller, his chief economic adviser, had proposed an "attack on poverty." But in 1963 Kennedy was pressured to act. He had put the weight of federal law enforcement behind James Meredith the previous September.[19] He sent a major civil rights bill to Congress in 1963, although he was privately prepared to compromise. While the popular mood was go-go, some commentators were worried about the nation's domestic problems and were insisting that the White House address them. There was even a debate about economic "conversion": Once McNamara had bought all the rockets and airplanes he needed, how could defense industries convert to serve civilian production?

McNamara remembered later that they had a plan for lowering the U.S. defense budget on a reciprocal basis with the Soviet Union. He planned to ratchet his defense budget down a notch in a year's time; then the Soviets could reciprocate by lowering theirs.[20] They could play this game of signaling either openly or without admitting it, lest any explicit cooperation bring charges of weakness. McNamara considered meeting regularly in Geneva with the Soviet defense minister to compare budget documents. This was an accountant's fantasy of peace, to be sure, but it mirrored the general mood.

The armed services should have loved McNamara; he was increasing the defense budget by one fourth and turning them into a better-equipped, readier force than ever in Eisenhower's time. Instead, senior service leaders felt tension and anger, while the outspoken generals of the Strategic Air Command were in a state of near rebellion.

Press conventions of the day, and McNamara's crackdown on dissenting leaks, prevented the discontent from being too explicitly reported. But a major event for the Building was the publication of an article by military writer Hanson Baldwin, in the *Saturday Evening Post* on March 9, 1963, called "The McNamara Monarchy." Baldwin had good contacts among senior officers and now spelled out their case that McNamara's "unification" of the services posed "subtle and insidious dangers" that were almost "as great a threat to a secure and free nation" as the coup by rebellious officers popularized in the novel *Seven Days in May*.[21]

Baldwin argued that independent service positions on matters of policy had been beneficial in the past, whereas McNamara's insistence that the services speak "with one voice" represented a real danger. He even blamed the failure to warn of the Soviet missiles in Cuba on McNamara's centralization of military intelligence into one agency and charged that his attempt to streamline the National Guard threatened the republic, too. However self-serving the claims that the military had a God-given right to differ among themselves and in public, Baldwin hit right on the mark when he complained of McNamara's compulsion to prevent contrary voices from being heard: "Objections or dissent . . . are discouraged, muted, or when possible stifled." McNamara had pressured members of the Joint Chiefs to sign written statements attesting to the adequacy of his policies; he had "downgraded, ignored, bypassed or overruled" the advice of Chairman Maxwell Taylor and imposed a "party line" from which no deviation was permitted. Yet "alternatives, variations, disagreements are the breath of life in any organization." The civilians, in the name of openness, were imposing rigidity, a disturbing trend.

Baldwin made another important point in noting that by contrast with the image of efficiency of McNamara's administration of the department, in fact there were now twenty-six deputy assistant secretaries of defense, whereas in 1960 there had been only eleven. The numbers of people working for him had increased by one third, to almost four thousand. The new budget controls had greatly increased the burden of paperwork. And, Baldwin noted, McNamara had "curtailed" dozens of programs while starting very few. Unwittingly, perhaps, Baldwin had pointed to a central purpose of the management controls McNamara and his friends had learned at Harvard and then applied at Ford. One aim of planning and budgeting was to prevent large organizations from undertaking foolish or wasteful projects, just as at General Motors, Alfred Sloan had installed financial controls to end the chaotic initiatives of his predecessor, Will Durant. As McNamara was finding out with the TFX that year, his management system had negative bias — it was better at helping civilian leaders cancel programs than at establishing them and motivating people in the organization to buy in.

Baldwin's article — especially compared with Fryklund's gushing praise — raised the riddle of how a man who seemed so good could have so many enemies, especially if his purposes were as noble as he maintained and if he was as rational as the Whiz Kids said he was.

One clue to the answer was that he constantly felt alone. No one who heard him talk in private, forcefully, emotionally, about all the reforms he was making, about how right he was and how wrong his enemies were, could miss his perception of himself as a lonely crusader. Nor could anyone miss the large number of fronts on which Bob McNamara felt he had to fight. Recounting his adventures later to me, he often seemed proud of how hard others had fought him, as though it made him more virtuous and right. McNamara would glow as he relived the combat. "There was *blood* on the floor," he would say, seeming to relish this sanguinary note.[22]

He told me, "In my experience in executive life, or for that matter intellectual life, at Ford, in Defense, at the Bank — it's a continuing controversy, a continuing battle of ideas. And it is that constant ferment which leads to progress. But the progress is always accompanied by conflict." Thus he rationalized his combativeness.

He put himself at the focus of conflict from strong needs to protect his president and to be loyal down to his handpicked aides. Thomas Morris, a proficient administrator who performed several key jobs for McNamara, including the unpopular closings of hundreds of military bases, recalls how McNamara covered for his staff, took their actions and decisions as his own, and never let them be attacked or criticized.

He also virtually never let his staff testify but appeared himself, particularly if he knew the committee that had called the hearing was hostile. One effect of subsuming all responsibility unto himself was that he had to testify more often as the years went on to defend his unrelenting pursuit of his goals, whether to postpone a new bomber, build the TFX, or close more unneeded military bases.

McNamara usually appeared alone. Black loose-leaf binders next to him, he spoke leaning forward over the polished witness table, with feet hooked around the front legs of the chair as if to stop himself from hurtling across the table at his interrogators.

Sometimes he took the chairman of the Joint Chiefs or the general counsel with him. Mainly his performances were solo acts. McNamara spouted off facts and figures right down to the number of nuts and bolts in a drawer at Fort Dix, it was claimed.

By defending all his aides' actions instead of letting them appear to take the heat themselves, Morris says, McNamara was telling congressional critics: If you attack my staff, you have to reckon with me. The effect was that he took on the increasing burden of being the sole point of contact between his entire staff and Congress.

And criticism grew, because he relentlessly pushed each plank of his program forward. The problems of implementing it would become more complex when under fire. McNamara was creating a catch-22 for himself: By bringing ever more criticism on himself, he became more unyielding and felt more embattled and alone.

Outwardly these performances revealed his close attention to detail, his managerial "genius" and admirable willingness to assume personal responsibility. Inwardly, McNamara was listening closely to any sign of attack and eager to fight back. In a car ride back from one appearance on Capitol Hill, McNamara instructed a naval officer riding with him to write down every charge a particular congressman had made and have a detailed rebuttal ready in the morning. But the congressman was *right,* the officer objected. McNamara would not hear of such a thing, and he no doubt rebutted the congressman at the next opportunity. He has even told interviewers since that he never lost a fight with Congress. But although he may have won many skirmishes with such tactics, in the long run he was positioning himself to lose the larger battle for Congress's trust.

McNamara justified his vigorous exercise of power by saying he was trying to *de*centralize the management of the Building. To Congressman Porter Hardy in 1962, his text was right out of Alfred Sloan: "I don't like to work 14 hours a day, six days a week. . . . I believe in the pyramid theory of decisionmaking, in which decisions are made as low as possible in the chain. I have to take charge, however, to guide the organization through this transitional period." Congressman Hardy replied wryly, "Some of us don't believe that you don't like it, Mr. Secretary."[23]

McNamara wasn't delegating, in fact. He had determined right away that he would review decisions made on every item in the defense program that cost $25 million or more — an astonishing voluntary burden of work in itself. When he did delegate, it was mainly to one of his handpicked civilians or the few senior officers he trusted. His inability to trust the organization below him was a significant flaw. As his monologues showed, he saw himself as alone, often bludgeoning the organization below him into obeying — as though he were not really of the Pentagon or the military, but an outside critic, infuriated by parochialism and resistance to his enlightened truth.

"I know all about participatory management," McNamara would say years later, referring to the theory prevalent in the eighties, based on Japanese manufacturing success, that organizations must change by consensus, not executive fiat. Didn't his tactics alienate the groups he was trying to change? I asked. "Tactics, you must understand, are a function of *time*," he retorted.

Why the rush? Harold Brown recalls that McNamara often told him he planned to stay at the Pentagon no longer than one presidential term.[24] It was naïveté or hubris that made him presume that in only four years he could revolutionize the services, the priorities of the defense contracting community, the defense budget, nuclear strategy, and NATO — and resolve to Kennedy's satisfaction the nagging Communist insurgency in South Vietnam.

It was almost as though McNamara's management genius — his immersion in the administrative system that was the source of his power — got in the way of his larger, noble goals.

McNamara was operating at the head of the West's largest military organization the same way that Tex Thornton had run Statistical Control during World War II and that the Whiz Kids had taken over Ford. He was utilizing a close-knit cadre of like-minded statistical men, operating as a kind of fifth column, to force the organization to change. McNamara spent his time engrossed in the intricacies of his financial system, reviewing stacks of papers formatted to his tastes on a precise daily schedule of reading and meetings. When the reserves had been called up during the Berlin crisis of 1961 and it was publicly suggested that he, as their commander, visit some of the men, McNamara had replied crisply that he could serve the nation better by spending the same time at his desk.

His remark reflected how the system of control — and the fascination with running it — could become an end in itself and could convince a genius-level practitioner of management controls such as McNamara that any operation could be run the same way. To editors of management journals who made the pilgrimage to the great office to ask him his secret, McNamara would say, as he did to *Armed Forces Management* in 1962, "Running any large organization is the same, whether it is the Ford Motor Company, the Catholic Church, or the Department of Defense. Once you get to a certain scale, they're all the same."[25] This precept echoed the statement of purpose of the Harvard Business School in the era when McNamara matriculated there. And, flush with success at Ford and with Kennedy, he believed it still.

Two incidents dramatize the tendency of his moral efforts to lead to bitterness and backlash, and also demonstrate that McNamara saw himself as an outsider and loner in relation to the institution he ran.

William K. Brehm, a civilian who oversaw a small group that assessed land forces under Alain Enthoven, recalls McNamara's frustration as late as 1965, when the Army was unable to give him a complete set of tables showing all the "stovepipes," or job specialties, needed by each division and corresponding tables showing the amount and kinds of equipment required by each group. Comprehensive data were critical for recruitment and training, for equipping the new, larger army in Europe and overseas, including Vietnam. McNamara asked Brehm to expand his group to eighteen analysts to do the job.

But Brehm was concerned about the Army.[26] To have eighteen systems analysts telling a two-million-member institution what its requirements were, right down to two-man well-digging detachments, would not be healthy. Brehm had been appalled already at the bitterness Enthoven's systems analysts had created in the Army. Brehm disagreed with his colleagues' scorn; he believed the Army could do a good job of divining its requirements, if properly led.

So Brehm went to great lengths to get higher-ups to talk to McNamara and persuade him to let the Army figure its requirements itself. The result was a new office in the Army, jointly run by an officer and a civilian. And it did the job well, in due course, changing the way the Army assessed itself. But McNamara had had to be talked into involving the Army at all; his instinct had been to use his shock troops to force reform.

William Gorham, the Rand-trained economist whom McNamara had put in charge, at age thirty-two, of senior generals to work up a military pay study, had a similar experience.[27] Hire whomever you want, McNamara had said when they began examining military pay. The young man eagerly set about investigating the problems of comparability and benefits; no one else in the country was doing such work. Gorham had regular access to McNamara every Thursday at seven-thirty in the morning. The protégé never hesitated to correct or challenge McNamara — McNamara enjoyed being challenged. He liked the intellectual combat Gorham and other Whiz Kids offered. But always in private and on his terms.

Gorham and McNamara figured out a new scheme for military pay and benefits, essentially alone. Even the Bureau of the Budget, which had launched the reexamination in the first place, was not brought into their deliberations. In July 1963, McNamara proposed one of the largest military pay increases in history to a receptive Congress. The 2.7 million members of the armed services should have loved him.

Yet as McNamara stepped into his private elevator to go over to the Capitol to present the plan, he clasped the black binder, the fruit of their labors, to his chest like a baby and said: "Now we've got 'em."

It was an odd remark, Gorham thought. Whom did McNamara think he had "got"? They had not won over the military to their plan, for they had barely consulted the uniformed services. Indeed, the service leaders privately were lukewarm about the pay plan, however generous, because it was not *theirs*. He had not "got" the Congress, except to have the facts to argue down opposition. He had not "got" anything; politically he had hurt himself, despite his fine work. McNamara had found the right answer but alienated everyone.

The flaw of this isolated man of fine intentions, perched atop the Department of Defense and running it intricately through his formal system, was to believe that as a result he understood the real work of the organization, done at the bottom, by ordinary soldiers and their commanders. McNamara made precious little allowance for the possibility that the military as an institution, whose ultimate work is the willed risk of human life, was different from Ford or any other large organization. Nor did he allow for the fact that the Department of Defense, as a branch of the executive, depends ultimately for its mandate on Congress and the political system.

However, by 1963 Bob McNamara was more than immersed in administration: He had revolutionized parts of the U.S. defense program and was trying to reform the alliance. He had seen past all his numbers in the missile crisis; he now knew that he needed to move minds to avert the gruesome danger of nuclear war. McNamara was learning to make simple, clear appeals to Americans, Europeans, and Soviet leaders to pierce their illusions about nuclear weapons. On this score he was trying to emulate his hero, Franklin Roosevelt, whose great contribution, McNamara says, was that "he changed the way men think."

Clearly, McNamara had sincere goals. And he seized an important moment, when the world situation was changing and U.S. security and foreign policy needed fresh analysis and a corresponding overhaul of military roles and missions. In large part, his revolution of the Building was right; his program budget was as necessary to drag the armed services into the modern age as financial controls had been to yank Ford out of feudalism in 1946. The revision of the budget and program was overdue. That both reforms lasted is proof that they were needed. And the analysts' success was more remarkable for having been carried forward when the resources of the nation did not include many foundations, think tanks, or university departments applying systematic analysis to defense problems. Indeed, Enthoven — backed by McNamara — gave an influential series of speeches at war colleges around the country, inviting the military into a new partnership in which they would together — with military art and analytic science — bring a new dawn of reason and objectivity to defense policy. The speeches, along with McNamara's high visibility as an analyst himself, sparked the spread of analytic techniques outside of government and their application to non-defense problems as well. In this sense these conservative men, who had overbuilt the U.S. arsenal and were to some degree readying the country for war, sparked an intellectual revolution that changed American policy-making and public life.

But the tone was set by McNamara's character — his ruthless side, which disdained the institution he was reforming. Although the Whiz Kids' work would be presented in later academic writing and teaching as a dialogue of reason, in their behavior at the time they mimicked McNamara's peculiar scorn.

McNamara had become particularly irked with the Navy during the Cuban missile crisis, when he had confronted Admiral George Anderson, the chief of naval operations, in Flag Plot over the issue of the naval blockade.[28] On one tense occasion, he had begun barking orders at a young captain, Elmo Zumwalt, who was standing in uniform in the defense secretary's big office. As McNamara began listing the things he wanted the Navy to do — one, two, three, rat-a-tat-tat — he became more and more angry. He was also aware that Zumwalt, standing almost at attention, had no way of writing down the numbered instructions he was giving. In a fit of anger, McNamara grabbed a pad of paper from his desk and threw it at Zumwalt. Then he picked up a pencil and threw that at the impeccable blue uniform.

Zumwalt was no more about to defy McNamara, his commander, than Admiral Anderson had been on that fateful occasion in Flag Plot. But he got even anyhow. He stood at attention while the secretary barked at him and indirectly bawled out the entire Navy. Zumwalt refused to bend over to pick up the pad and pencil to make notes, to avoid debasing the Navy. Instead, he memorized the orders and stalked out.

McNamara's "monarchy" was not about the dawn of reason and the application of a broader definition of national defense to parochial military programs; nor was his contribution only about management tools such as the budget and systems analysis. His reign was also colored by moral righteousness and arrogance. In a sense, the Whiz Kids anticipated Ralph Nader and the public interest movement later in the decade. Both were young, fresh, and convinced that history was on their side. Their mistake was to appear contemptuous of the military institutions whose follies they sought to reform. Necessarily, they sought out and promoted military officers in their own mold — men like General Earle Wheeler, who would succeed Taylor as chairman of the Joint Chiefs of Staff in 1964 on the basis of his administrative ability and brains, rather than his operational experience or record in battle.

What I hold against McNamara, says an Army officer who later attained very high rank in his service, after serving two tours in Vietnam in the 1960s, is that he changed the upper echelons of Army leadership.[29] The senior officer corps of the early 1960s included men who had fought in World War II and Korea, who were close to operations, how battles unfold, and the human dimensions of military art. But McNamara and his civilians promoted officers who were number-crunchers like themselves and who would endorse the civilians' program. The institution's response was to build up headquarters staffs, in Washington and around the world, to answer the unending questions and requests for formal reports from civilians. The Army became more bureaucratized and distanced from its roots, its real purpose.

And it became fearful, this officer recalls, looking back on the debacle of Vietnam, which provided enough blame to spread around to everybody concerned. So powerful were this new civilian hierarchy and its demands that people in the institution felt compelled to lie. This, says the officer, is not good situation ethics in any organization, let alone a military organization in a baffling war.

In 1963, McNamara's critics were no happier. McNamara refused to allow the Navy and Admiral Rickover to build the four-reactor nuclear-powered aircraft carrier sought for the next generation of the fleet. The Joint Committee was so mad, not only at his judgment but his tactics, that in its hearing room, right at eye level when McNamara would have to sit facing the dais from the witness chair, it hung a seal inscribed with Congress's constitutional mandate to raise armies and provide for the national defense. The fight over future carriers — and then the nuclear-powered frigates and new attack submarines — would drag on for years.

James Reston, Bob and Margy McNamara's friend, also sensed McNamara's weakness. At about this time, Reston wrote in a prophetic column in the *New York Times*:

> The issue about the Secretary of Defense . . . is his decisive efficiency in putting over dubious policies. . . . He is tidy, he is confident, he has the sincerity of an Old Testament prophet, but something is missing: some element of personal doubt, some respect for human weakness, some knowledge of history.[30]

His habit of operating solo was disastrous in the case of the Skybolt missile affair, which reached its climax just after the Cuban missile crisis and nearly brought down the British government.

In the aftermath of Great Britain's humiliation in the Suez crisis of 1956, Great Britain's Conservative party decided to modernize the nuclear weapons carried by Royal Air Force bombers. Britain had been a pioneer in the development of atomic weapons in the early stage of World War II. The small British nuclear force, supplied under special arrangements with Washington, was a key political symbol of Britain's Great Power status. In 1960, Eisenhower promised the Conservative prime minister, Harold Macmillan, that the British could buy part of the production run of the new Air Force air-launched nuclear missile called Skybolt, which was then in development.

When they first took office, Kennedy and McNamara accelerated the Skybolt program, although its technical problems required that funds be doled out only by the month. In 1962, McNamara asked for two reports on the program, one from Brown and one from controller Hitch. Both suggested McNamara should cancel.

But in the summer of 1962, McNamara was locked in a struggle with the Air Force over the B-70 and RS-70 airplanes, the size of the missile force, and whether the United States had or should have a first-strike policy. To cancel Skybolt directly would anger the Air Force even more.

At an August 24 meeting with McNamara, Hitch proposed that instead of trying to cancel the missile while drawing up the budget in the Building, they should make it disappear. Hitch suggested they carry it in the proposed budget until it reached the final stages in November and cancel it then.

Yet when the new British defense minister Peter Thorneycroft visited Washington in September, McNamara did not notify him of the likely cancellation. Nor did John Rubel of McNamara's staff give the secret away as late as November 3, when Thorneycroft's staff, which had heard rumors, grilled Rubel in London.

Only an urgent message from Thorneycroft, who was growing suspicious, prompted McNamara to seek a meeting with Kennedy, Rusk, and the advisers on November 7, right after the missile crisis. This group discussed Skybolt's cancellation, including the grave consequences for Macmillan. As to the mechanics of a warning, Richard Neustadt quotes McNamara as saying, "I'll take care of it." McNamara then told the British ambassador Skybolt was in "peril" — but not his full plan.[31]

McNamara phoned Thorneycroft on November 8 and said it might be "desirable" to cancel Skybolt. He offered to come to London to discuss the matter before any U.S. decision or any publicity. He "estimated the decision would not be made in Washington before December 10." In fact, he expected to have the cancellation past the chiefs and the president by November 23 and figured he could not stop the news from leaking past the tenth.[32]

Thus word of a possible cancellation reached both Thorneycroft and Prime Minister Macmillan. Macmillan reacted by recalling that Skybolt had nearly been nixed before and might well survive again. Unaccountably, Thorneycroft's defense staff did nothing to work up an alternative, even though modernizing the nuclear force was a key plank in the Conservative party platform.[33]

After this somewhat misleading notice to the British, McNamara did examine alternatives to present to them. The obvious choice was the new Polaris submarine and missile — Britain had a fine navy and a good port in Scotland, which the U.S. Polaris subs used already. But the State Department frantically opposed offering Polaris to the British. George Ball and others were working toward the goal of a joint European nuclear force to promote the unity and political maturity of Europe. To give one ally Polaris to modernize its independent nuclear force contradicted the thrust of State's efforts.[34] McNamara was enjoined from offering Polaris to Great Britain.

On December 4, controller Hitch broke the news to the Air Force that Skybolt would be canceled. The story got some play in the United States but did not reach Great Britain. A week later McNamara stepped off the plane at Heathrow Airport, outside London, and told reporters that he and Thorneycroft would have a "full discussion" of Skybolt, which was "very expensive" and "technically extremely complex." All five flight tests had failed, he added ominously.

The reporters rushed to their phones, while McNamara and his aides sat down in closed session with Thorneycroft and his staff.[35] Arthur Schlesinger calls their exchange a "Pinero drama of misunderstanding." McNamara told Thorneycroft that Skybolt was canceled, but he declined to offer Polaris as such. Thorneycroft recalls being "profoundly shocked." Yet he was not about "to plead on my knees" or "be seen by my people . . . as locked in a struggle with Bob McNamara . . . where I would fail to beat him." So Thorneycroft demanded neither Skybolt nor Polaris.[36]

That evening the London papers were full of a U.S.-British rift. Skybolt was gone, and the Americans had offered nothing in exchange. Macmillan's plans to modernize the British nuclear force, to keep Britain a Great Power, were in tatters.

The news sent a shock wave throughout Britain and hurt Kennedy's sagging relationship with Macmillan.

To save the situation, Kennedy boosted a meeting with Macmillan in Nassau into a hasty summit, where they patched up an offer of Polaris to the British.[37] The upshot of McNamara's worthy effort to scrap Skybolt — which he later called "a pile of junk" to historians[38] — and of his useful application of analysis that uncovered no need for the weapon was a near rift in relations with Britain, severe problems for Macmillan, and the surrender of a more modern and lethal nuclear weapon, Polaris, to another government — not to mention added complications with France, which became more strident in light of the Polaris deal.

Nowhere did the bright and dark sides of McNamara's rule show more clearly in 1963 than on the issue of the nuclear test-ban treaty.

In the aftermath of the Cuban missile crisis, Khrushchev showed new and serious interest in negotiating a test-ban treaty. A comprehensive ban on all nuclear tests had long been a goal of the disarmament movement in the West. Kennedy wanted to talk seriously with the Soviets, too, although the two sides were far apart on many issues, particularly the number of inspections needed to verify a halt to underground nuclear blasts.[39]

Yet both leaders had been changed by the missile crisis. Now both spoke publicly of the need for stability, détente, and greater understanding between the American and Soviet peoples. Kennedy and Khrushchev also corresponded secretly, adding to the hopes of the administration that the thaw in the cold war was real. Exciting signs of a new spring — Khrushchev's liberalization at home, a new "hot line" between the Kremlin and the Pentagon — gave the year a glow of optimism and of achievement to the Kennedy circle.

As defense secretary, McNamara straddled the fence on the issue of nuclear testing in his first two years. His formal responsibilities included setting the requirements for the numbers and types of nuclear bombs needed, in conjunction with the Joint Chiefs of Staff. Actual development and testing were done by the Atomic Energy Commission, over which McNamara had no direct control. The AEC's headquarters often acted as the stalking-horse for the powerful weapons laboratories, Los Alamos and Lawrence Livermore, which exerted wide influence on the military and Congress and on parts of the scientific world. Men like Edward Teller, the Hungarian-born physicist and father of the hydrogen bomb, and a former director of Lawrence Livermore, had the top-secret knowledge that was critical to U.S. nuclear supremacy. A president and secretary of defense ignored Teller and the labs at their peril. And the atomic weapons establishment opposed any test-ban treaty.[40]

Yet by the spring of 1963 the political moment for a treaty had come, after two years of mistrust, rival testing, and tension about faltering negotiations that seemed to be getting nowhere. On June 10, Kennedy gave an important speech calling for peace and an end to the cold war, at American University, in Washington. In the weeks that followed, the Soviets signaled new readiness to reach an agreement. Still, a comprehensive test ban that included on-site inspections to verify a halt to underground nuclear tests seemed impossible to achieve; the administration switched gears quickly, to try to conclude a limited test ban barring tests in the atmosphere, in outer space, and in the ocean, but not underground. A limited test ban would be a great public boon, for nuclear testing in the atmosphere — by the Soviets, the British, and the French, as well as the Americans — was creating outrage worldwide. On the other hand, such a limited test ban would let nuclear weapons development proceed and hardly stop the arms race.[41]

Just as Kennedy was on the verge of agreement with Moscow on the limited ban, the Joint Chiefs objected. As though the issue had just come up, they asked to go back to square one and study whether a limited test ban was in the United States' interest. Rusk told them it was too late, but they would not be deterred.

Explains AEC chairman Glenn T. Seaborg, "I don't think McNamara or anyone had been working that hard on it before April of 1963. They had met; they had exchanged positions. The Joint Chiefs were willing to go along." When there's "no chance of anything happening," he adds, the chiefs are "quiescent."[42] Now that a test ban seemed imminent, the chiefs became dead serious. And Kennedy and McNamara knew that if the chiefs were not on board, they and the weapons labs could block Senate ratification of the treaty.

McNamara later recounted his role with relish. "My recollection is that the five chiefs were unanimously opposed. So therefore I got Ros Gilpatric and the five chiefs and myself into that room next to my office and locked the door." Was the door really locked? I asked. Well, maybe it wasn't, McNamara said. They could leave to go to the bathroom. But it was "in effect locked. I said to them, 'Gentlemen, I have locked the door and it's going to stay locked, not until we agree with each other because maybe we will never agree with each other but until we at least understand each other. I have respect for you as patriotic Americans serving your country at penalties to you and your families. I hope you have equal respect for Ros and me. There must be something we don't understand, because we take diametrically opposite positions [on the limited test ban] and in the process don't seem to understand each other's view. We're going to stay here until we understand why each of us thinks the way we do.' " He added, with a smile of triumph, "When we finally, in a sense, did unlock the door, we were in agreement." It meant "I got every single one of the chiefs to go up [before the Senate] and testify" in favor of the limited test ban. "And that's why the test ban was approved."

McNamara's own testimony to the Senate on the test ban — a succinct case, skillfully argued — revealed new facts about U.S. superiority to reassure the public and disarm the right. Many deemed it brilliant. Theodore Sorensen wrote afterward that McNamara's performance pleased Kennedy most of all.[43] The foes of the test ban in Congress, who were ready to do battle with Kennedy and expected to gain momentum from military testimony, were disappointed. The chiefs did testify for the treaty, because in the locked room they had demanded an enormous price: more funding for the weapons labs, preparation to test quickly in case the Soviets violated the agreement, and other conditions. The net effect was to strengthen the weapons labs, expand U.S. underground testing, and continue the arms race. Nonetheless, McNamara and Kennedy presented the step as a triumph. The administration was winning; the political center was gaining ground, and the right no longer dominated American defense policy.

But the story of McNamara's last-minute bludgeoning of the Joint Chiefs, told with such enthusiasm, reveals a basic flaw in his revolution — his disdain for the military institutions and culture he was presuming to change.

13

Crisis Manager Challenged

VIETNAM BEGAN TO BE A PROBLEM for Mc-
Namara during 1963, as he continued to "handle" the conflict for John Kennedy and to try to get their showcase
counterinsurgency war resolved. Events in South Vietnam
exposed the limits of McNamara's method of running the war, although it was unclear that he recognized them.

On the morning of Thursday, January 3, McNamara learned about
the battle of Ap Bac from that day's *New York Times*. A page 1 story
by David Halberstam, the *Times*'s new correspondent in South Vietnam, described a "major defeat" for the forces of South Vietnam's
president Ngo Dinh Diem and the American military advisers helping them.[1]

Five of the fifteen U.S. helicopters taking part in the action had
been shot down by the Viet Cong with automatic weapons, Halberstam wrote. "Three Americans were reported killed." These were
unheard-of numbers in the distant popgun war to which the defense
secretary had been speeding rifles, artillery, helicopters, napalm, herbicides, and barbed wire. McNamara had been eager to have the
United States make good on its limited partnership agreement with
Diem, which Kennedy had decided on in November 1961. The bargain presumed that if the United States did its part in aiding Diem
militarily, Diem would do his part and beat back the Communist
insurgency to a manageable level.

The battle of Ap Bac showed the reality of the war in the steamy summer countryside to be very different from what McNamara's statistics told him, or what the complacent U.S. Army said about imminent victory.[2]

The envelopment of 350 soldiers of the Viet Cong's 261st Main Force Battalion, concentrated near the Mekong Delta village of Ap Bac, had been carefully planned by some of the American military advisers. By the end of 1962, more than twelve thousand advisers, many of them handpicked experts in counterinsurgency war, had arrived in South Vietnam to give Diem's forces the advice and training that would enable them to win. The unusual concentration of the enemy at Ap Bac offered a rare chance for decisive engagement and for coordinating in battle the helicopters, fighter-bombers, and artillery flowing into the country, thanks to McNamara's efficiency.

In the ethics of war, professionalism and common sense dictate that soldiers help each other in adversity and fight on to win, so the enemy will not live to fight another day. To press the attack even when comrades fall is a personal test of soldierly valor; it is also essential for victory. But when the attack on Ap Bac ran into problems in the foggy dawn of January 2, Saigon time, odd things began to happen on the South Vietnamese side.

The attack was to be a two-pronged surprise by troops of Diem's Seventh Infantry Division, ferried in by U.S. H-21 helicopters, and two companies of provincial Civil Guards, who would simultaneously close in on the enemy from another flank. But the landing of the regular infantry was delayed by early morning fog. Meanwhile, one company of Civil Guards moved into position as planned and met with gunfire. The Viet Cong knew of the pending attack; the night before they took up positions in foxholes along a tree-covered dike running east from the village among the brown paddies.

The second company of Civil Guards declined to move forward to assist the first. The latter, after taking eight casualties, did not press the attack and stopped shooting by ten o'clock. Then U.S. helicopters began landing infantry to attack the enemy position and relieve the trapped first company of Civil Guards. But the enemy had automatic weapons — machine guns and Browning automatic rifles. The H-21 choppers mistakenly began landing within range.

In earlier encounters, the Viet Cong had run in panic before the helicopters, although there had been a battle on the Plain of Reeds the previous October, in which a group of South Vietnamese Rangers had nearly been annihilated by the enemy, who shot at the helicopters as well. Now near the dike at Ap Bac, a first helicopter bearing troops touched down without incident. But as a second hovered to land, it was blitzed by a roaring fusillade from enemy guns hidden in the dike. The South Vietnamese soldiers ran from the chopper and froze behind a low dike; they would not attack. Disaster had struck, and the behavior of the government forces under fire was ominous.

Frustration built by the hour for the U.S. advisers as they saw all their plans and material advantages wasting. They frantically tried to get the South Vietnamese soldiers to move and save their comrades, the Americans trapped in the downed helicopters within range of the hidden enemy guns.

One hope was a company of U.S. armored personnel carriers, M-113s, which was only a mile from the downed choppers and the enemy hidden in bushes in the dike. But the M-113s took all day to move; the South Vietnamese officers' procrastinations infuriated the Americans. Finally the large machines, bearing armed soldiers, drew up to the dike and started toward it. In moments, the vehicles would be on top of the dike, and their soldiers could shoot down at the enemy trapped in their foxholes and save the day.

Suddenly a Viet Cong commander named Dung leapt into the open in front of the first armored machine, hurling hand grenades at it. The code of courage in front of comrades, drilled into the veterans of the long war against the French, propelled the guerrillas to follow Dung. The terrified South Vietnamese, seeing their men atop the M-113s hit by grenades, turned back. The 261st Main Force Battalion survived. The American advisers were furious.

Ap Bac was a decisive moment in a drawn-out countryside war of small engagements that seemed to have no meaning in themselves. It indicated to the American advisers that many of Diem's handpicked officers did not want to seek battle. It also showed that U.S. guns, helicopters, and M-113s, even the flaming napalm the South Vietnamese dropped indiscriminately on their countrymen's villages from the safety of the air, rarely gave the South Vietnamese forces courage or the necessary ethic of fighting for decisive victory.

The officers of the Seventh Infantry Division who performed so ignominiously at Ap Bac — and were later decorated by Diem, for they seized the Viet Cong radio transmitter that afternoon — had been chosen by Diem for their loyalty to him, for coup insurance, not courage or proficiency in war. Neil Sheehan, the young UPI reporter in Saigon at the time, would later learn that Diem had pro-

mulgated a secret order to his trusted officers the previous fall: They
were not to take casualties on their own side. Casualties would make
army service unpopular, and Diem needed a loyal army so his family
could stay in power.

The U.S. advisers were trying to build an army in the American
mold, but their working material was an officer corps chosen by
Diem.[3] Many were former French sympathizers whose interest in
army service was money and status, not getting killed, and who as a
class had little sympathy for the peasants. The October encounter on
the Plain of Reeds and the disaster at Ap Bac convinced some American advisers and reporters, notably Halberstam and Sheehan, that if
the United States was going to win the shooting war against the
Communists, Diem's army and officer corps needed integrity and
professionalism — a real overhaul. The Americans could supply matériel and tactical advice, but they could not force courage on officers
whose culture and explicit secret order induced them to pretend to
fight while arranging to protect themselves. The men of the Kennedy
administration had the choice of believing the young journalists in
Saigon or the military reports coming up through the system. How
well McNamara understood the hazards of believing General Paul
Harkins's battle reports in early 1963 is unclear. Certainly his pressure on Harkins and the chain of command for success, and his own
unshakable optimism, biased those below him to claim great progress.

At least one person who evaluated reports from Saigon says there
was not exactly censorship, but a clear understanding that negative
conclusions were not to be drawn from reports by Military Assistance Command, Vietnam. Says George Allen, a civilian analyst in
the Defense Intelligence Agency at the time of Ap Bac, if one read the
MACV reports between the lines with expert knowledge, one could
see the problems in the field. But when DIA analysts summarized
these reports for others in Washington they were not to draw conclusions contradicting the thrust of MACV's reports. Thus the military bureaucracy conspired to arrange that bad news, in so many
words, did not reach the secretary of defense and the president.[4]

John Kennedy was alarmed by the journalists' reports. South Vietnam began consuming more of his time in 1963, as the situation on
the ground became more complex.[5]

Everything in McNamara's public record suggests that at this point
he believed his statistics and the military reports, not Halberstam's
and Sheehan's reporting. McNamara's experience in Statistical

Control in World War II had been formative. In those years, as a young officer he gained confidence in using numbers to measure key variables in war. When he and General Harkins, the commander of MACV in Saigon, had set up a statistical reporting system the year before, the press in Washington reported that "close attention to battleground statistics" would help the anti-Communists win. "Mr. McNamara hopes that . . . the figures will show him exactly how the war is going day-by-day and which techniques are paying off."[6]

The most prominent statistic was the body count of enemy dead, which had risen sharply after American arms reached the South Vietnamese. A new factor in the body count was Killed By Air, or KBA.[7] Diem and his officers showed great partiality for air power, a preference that Brigadier General Rollen "Buck" Anthis, Harkins's chief air officer, did not discourage. Anthis was an Air Force man, and the Air Force did not want Vietnam to be an exclusively Army show.

So Anthis encouraged the buildup of a South Vietnamese air force, which began regular strafing runs supposedly on fleeing enemy. After each mission, the pilots tallied a score sheet of KBA. Anyone they thought they had killed was added to the body count of dead enemy soldiers, even though the pilots could not see well looking down at trees, shrubs, and grass. The Viet Cong's habit of carrying away their dead gave the pilots a reason to estimate the number that might have been killed but could not actually be seen. One American adviser, Army colonel John Paul Vann, estimated that in the spring of 1963, the body count overall was inflated by 40 percent.

McNamara's statistical control was the ratio of enemy killed in relation to the number of friendly deaths. Progress would be occurring over time if the number of enemy dead increased in relation to the number of friendly dead. On the other hand, such a trend could be badly misleading if the South Vietnamese inflated the Viet Cong body count figures while refusing, as at Ap Bac, to close with the enemy and take casualties themselves.

Even years later, after the body count had become a notorious symbol of the errors of the war, McNamara defended his initial use of these statistics. "People have criticized me for stressing this very brutal concept of body count," McNamara said in the deposition he gave in the libel suit William Westmoreland brought against CBS in 1984. "It was, in a sense, a terrible thing, but if you're secretary of defense and you're concerned about whether you are progressing militarily and it is said to be a, quote, 'war of attrition,' unquote, . . .

then it is important to try to understand whether you are accomplishing the attrition or not."[8]

Risk avoidance by South Vietnamese troops was a known problem to Washington; so McNamara measured offensive-mindedness by charting the number of engagements initiated by the South Vietnamese side. This figure also showed a nice increase in 1962 and early 1963, because as the number of weapons and American advisers grew, the number of actions did as well. The statistic did not reveal whether or when the government side attacked — too often, as in the seizure of the radio transmitter at Ap Bac, it was after it had conveniently let the enemy slip away.

Statistical control measured resources but not the critical matter of how resources were used in battle. The most tragic yardstick of all, perhaps, was the number of guns flowing into the field, pressed on by McNamara's efficiency and the Army's wish to equip its South Vietnamese ally with the best. Emphasis on heavy firepower had been an axiom of Army doctrine since the days of Ulysses S. Grant. It was also a cultural expression of American reliance on superior technology to win wars.

But most of the Communist guerrillas in South Vietnam had also fought the technologically superior French; many were skilled gun thieves. The guerrillas blended in with the countryside in regions like the Mekong Delta, where many villages had been Communist strongholds in the French war and still harbored them and spied for them.

As the American logistical machine sped hundreds of thousands of guns to South Vietnamese government soldiers, more guns leaked to the enemy.[9] There were even cases of villagers or units in Diem's army leaving out guns for the enemy as bribes to avoid attack. McNamara kept statistics on the number of guns the South Vietnamese lost. But American recordkeeping could not change the social system of the Vietnamese countryside or the instinct for self-preservation among a peasantry after thirty years of civil war.

Overall, McNamara's statistical system helped him reject the stories that Diem's men were seriously bungling the conduct of the war. The problem uppermost in the defense secretary's mind through 1963 was one he was better conditioned to recognize: the self-aggrandizement of Harkins and his organization. Saigon was becoming a good posting; in the Army the saying was "Vietnam is the only war we've got." Kennedy and McNamara had turned to the Army to undertake the training and advising part of the limited partnership policy. But a consequence of relying on the mainstream Army was the exploitation of its expanded Vietnam role for its own institutional ends. By 1963 there would be twenty-three generals at MACV headquarters, overseeing a force of sixteen thousand military advisers.[10]

The record reveals no skepticism from McNamara about progress in the shooting war, despite the news dispatches that contradicted Harkins's claims of imminent victory, despite later news accounts showing that the Viet Cong were standing and fighting and that the days of easy killing for the government side were over. The documents do show McNamara's exercising financial control over Harkins's bids for a larger command and more dollars. McNamara's program budget process disclosed that Harkins planned to build up MACV further — even though he and McNamara had agreed in Honolulu the previous year that Harkins would wrap up the job and leave by the end of 1965. On January 19, 1963, at one of the monthly meetings in Honolulu that McNamara used to exert control over Harkins and get the job done for the president,

> Secretary McNamara opposed General Harkins' version of the [country] plan for a variety of reasons . . . too many RVNAF [Vietnamese Air Force] than were trainable and supportable . . . weaponry that was too sophisticated. . . . If the insurgency came under control in FY [fiscal year] 1965 as anticipated, the US MAP [Military Assistance Plan] investment thereafter should be held at no more than $50 million per year. . . . The U.S. phaseout was too slow . . . RVNAF training had to be speeded up.[11]

McNamara pushed Harkins hard to wrap up the training of Diem's forces by mid-1965, as the three-year plan they had developed in secret had proposed. That he believed his statistics, believed that the job was doable, and believed that their strategy had no major flaws was illustrated when the press on May 8 reported that McNamara said, "The corner has definitely been turned toward victory."[12]

Ngo Dinh Diem was a devout Catholic from a mandarin family that had converted and aided the French. One brother was a bishop; the other, Ngo Dinh Nhu, was Diem's right-hand man and chief of security. Diem often talked about how the Communists had killed another brother during the war against the French. He and his brother Nhu and Nhu's wife liked to blame everything on the Communists.

South Vietnamese society was complex. The peasants followed

forms of Confucianism; some were animists. Diem carried out a ruthless massacre of some of the pagan sects in 1955, one reason so many peasants resented him and sheltered the Viet Cong.[13] South Vietnam's two main cities, Saigon and Hue, had large Buddhist populations, which lived uneasily with the Catholic elite. Vietnamese Catholics, mimicking their French masters, habitually discriminated against Buddhists; Buddhists tended to be ordinary people, many in the country's small middle class, many in the army.

A Buddhist revolt in the cities in the spring of 1963 and a bloody crackdown by Diem gave the Kennedy administration pause about its ally. Diem's civil crisis put South Vietnam on the front pages of American newspapers and on television screens, and forced Kennedy to ask if the war could be won with his puppet after all.[14]

In Hue on May 8 — the same day McNamara was quoted as saying they had turned the corner in the shooting war — a crowd of Buddhist activists marched to the radio station to protest a decree by Diem banning the flying of Buddhist flags on the Buddha's birthday. The day was an important holiday, since 70 percent of all South Vietnamese called themselves Buddhists. In the midst of the demonstration, military cars drove up, and some Civil Guards jumped out and shot into the crowd, killing nine people and injuring fourteen. Diem afterward said the incident was started by a Viet Cong throwing a hand grenade. But people on the scene had witnessed a Catholic officer in charge of the firing guards. Protests spread in Hue and Saigon, organized by apparently otherworldly but politically astute Buddhist monks.

On June 11, Quang Duc, a seventy-three-year-old Buddhist monk, sat down in the middle of a Saigon intersection while another monk poured gasoline over his head. The elderly monk then lit a match, and flames roared up his saffron robes. The figure lifted its arms as it turned to ash. Malcolm W. Browne, bureau chief for the Associated Press, photographed the burning figure; Buddhist activists had tipped off the American journalists that something was going to happen.

This blazing symbol of popular hatred for Diem's regime flashed around the world. Then Madame Nhu, Diem's sister-in-law, referred to the self-immolation as a "barbecue." The photograph and a flood of reports about Diem's oppression raised the first questions in the minds of many Americans about what values the United States was defending in South Vietnam.

The young journalists posted to Saigon were appalled by Diem and security chief Nhu's reaction to the peaceful Buddhist protests in this supposedly democratic state. They believed, along with the Kennedy circle and most Americans of the time, that the United States had a mission to check the spread of communism in the world. Halberstam would write in 1964, "I believe that Vietnam is a legitimate part of that global commitment . . . perhaps one of five or six nations in the world that is truly vital to U.S. interests."[15]

Communist tactics, as illustrated at Ap Bac and later, had impressed the journalists, just as they had impressed the young American military advisers who were the journalists' sources much of the time. The journalists were concluding, along with some of the advisers, that for the South Vietnamese to fight and win against the Communists, Diem's whole army and system of promotion had to be overhauled. The journalists knew the war was going poorly in the field; the day of Ap Bac, the reporters had been furious to watch General Harkins acting like a cardboard-cutout general and calling it a "victory" for the South Vietnamese and American side.[16] A running battle had developed between the reporters and Harkins and his briefing officers; the reporters thought MACV was lying, covering up for Diem and his army. By printing the truth from the field, by exposing MACV's lies, Halberstam and the others hoped to get through to Washington, to warn Kennedy he had to change strategies to succeed in South Vietnam.

The Buddhist protests and Diem and Nhu's crackdown raised the related issue of whether the regime could hold the country together, win the people's loyalty, and successfully fight an internal guerrilla foe as clever as the Viet Cong. Diem kept blaming police actions and crackdowns on others, but he and his family were clearly responsible. All summer, Diem avoided taking steps that could have reconciled the two factions — such as a public investigation of the shootings in Hue. He was an Asian potentate, refusing to lose face by conceding any ground to his critics. And his family became bitterly critical of the Americans and the reporters themselves. Peter Arnett of the Associated Press was beaten up by Diem's plainclothesmen, and he and Malcolm Browne were later interrogated by the police. In August, the serpentine Madame Nhu called U.S. military advisers — some of whom had died trying to save her country — "little soldiers of fortune."[17]

Could Washington meet its goal of stopping communism with

Diem as its agent? Was Diem incapable of uniting his society and government? Or was the problem the Nhus, and not Diem? If South Vietnam became riddled with civil strife, the army would be paralyzed; already Buddhist officers were visiting jails to win the release of their children who had been arrested in demonstrations. Would Buddhist soldiers take orders from Diem's handpicked Catholic officers?

Kennedy and his advisers faced a classic dilemma of American foreign policy: whether to back a third world leader for the sake of the anti-Communist struggle, even when the leader is hardly a budding Jefferson. Debate about abandoning Diem was acceptable in the climate of the early 1960s, when "leadership changes" were a common tool of American foreign policy. Indeed, Edward Lansdale, then a CIA agent, had helped install Diem in power in 1954–55, despite the doubts of some of his colleagues as to Diem's competence to govern. Now in 1963, it was in the spirit of the times to consider withdrawing Diem's privilege. If he couldn't be induced to bear any burden or pay any price in the defense of liberty, someone else would have to be found.

"I think the government of South Vietnam is in better control of South Vietnam than it was six months ago," McNamara boomed to Congressman William Minshall on May 15 from the witness table. His listeners may have been surprised, since that morning's *New York Times* carried another grim story — twenty-six of Diem's soldiers had been shot in two enemy ambushes. Nonetheless, McNamara launched into a paean to Diem.[18]

It was a "near miracle" that "one man could have written the constitution, organized a new government," and in less than ten years "moved that country out of near feudalism into the modern world." Diem had tripled the "educational system"; he had "initiated an army" and had brought order even in recent years when he was under "the severest form of attack from the North Vietnamese."

Pentagon statistics made public later were the likely source of McNamara's claims. They showed that whereas 47 percent of South Vietnam's rural population was under "effective government control" in July 1962, that figure rose to 51 percent by December and 54 percent by April 1963 — a steady spread of blue acetate across General Harkins's maps. Other figures in the same report from April 1963 gave the game away: They revealed that despite the guns, armored personnel carriers, aircraft, and napalm, and the thousands of strategic hamlets Diem and Nhu claimed to have built to win peasant loyalty, just seventy-six more villages out of 2,479 had been added to those under "effective" government control. On the basis of such spurious bookkeeping, the crisis manager claimed progress.[19]

Sitting next to McNamara, General Maxwell Taylor, chairman of the Joint Chiefs of Staff, echoed and certified the civilian's optimism. "I have no doubt in my mind we are going to win in South Vietnam," chimed in the handsome hero of Normandy, "that is, if the domestic front here does not accept a tone of defeatism," he added, taking a swipe at anyone who believed the press.[20]

Nonetheless, as Diem and Nhu's repression worsened during the summer, the questions of how to get them to change or whether to abandon them became urgent. Dean Rusk, like McNamara, Taylor, and the military, backed Diem and felt he was needed to win the war. But several officials under Rusk were arguing at least for strong pressures and consideration of "alternative leadership." This faction included Under Secretary of State George Ball; Averell Harriman, under secretary of state for Far Eastern affairs; Michael V. Forrestal in the White House; and Roger Hilsman, director of the Bureau of Intelligence and Research.

Hilsman recalled later how hard it was to dislodge support for Diem in the administration. In meetings with the president, Rusk was frustratingly silent; thus Hilsman and other lower-ranking officials were pitted directly against McNamara.[21] Hilsman remembers that the president sat along the middle of one side of the conference table, with Rusk on his right and McNamara on his left. In the corner was an easel for maps. The official giving the briefing sat opposite the president and McNamara; in 1963 that official was Hilsman, feeling alone without support or comment from his superior, Rusk.

McNamara was an emotional man in these arguments, shooting off facts and statistics about the progress of the South Vietnamese, arguing that skeptics about Diem had no evidence to prove he was a liability.

Hilsman was an intense man, too, who clashed constantly with McNamara. He was a West Point graduate who had fought with Ramon Magsaysay in the Philippines against the Huk insurgency, which was the only successful counterguerrilla war the United States had conducted in modern times. Hilsman was convinced the military men, Taylor and Harkins, with McNamara as their spokesman, were running away with Vietnam policy and fighting the wrong kind of war. He wanted the Americans to train their South Vietnamese counterparts to fight a political war, winning hearts and minds with minimal violence, not dropping napalm on villages and herbicides on local crops. Moreover, popular loyalty would not build for a leader who disdained his own people, Hilsman argued. Hilsman remembers raising some of these issues early on and earning McNamara's enmity thereby: At one Honolulu meeting in 1962, when encouraging statistics were pouring in, McNamara had turned to Hilsman and been very smug. I was right and you were wrong, he in effect said. Now in the White House, on the subject of Diem, he was just as hard to contradict.[22]

Paul Kattenburg, one of the few men at State with long experience in Vietnam itself, spoke up in frustration at a meeting on August 31, although the men around the table outranked him. He said he had known Diem for ten years and had just been to Vietnam. Diem would never reform, and if Washington stayed married to him it would be out in six months, with the anti-Communist cause lost. The officials dismissed Kattenburg's views as "speculative"; later he suffered professionally for having warned that South Vietnam was a lost cause. Kattenburg's reaction, as he later recalled, was that these men were "hopeless." Not a single one "knew what he was talking about. . . . They were all great men. It was appalling to watch."[23]

Nonetheless, the weight of evidence was forcing McNamara to modify his stand in private councils. On August 23, a week before Kattenburg's outburst, Washington received a top-secret message that some South Vietnamese generals wanted to know if the United States would back them in a coup. Harriman, Hilsman, and Forrestal drafted a telegram with a positive reply over the weekend, when the president, Rusk, and McNamara were all out of town.

How this telegram was cleared remains a matter of dispute. Deputy Secretary of Defense Gilpatric signed his approval for McNamara at the Pentagon.[24] Maxwell Taylor, found in a Washington restaurant, gave his approval after Major General Victor Krulak had approved it in Taylor's name. Kennedy, contacted by Ball, said it could be sent if Rusk and McNamara approved. It was sent.

But Monday morning, when Kennedy had returned to Washington and understood clearly the import of the telegram that had been sent in his name to Saigon, he was angry. He convened his advisers and told them they could still take it back; the cable had been a secret instruction for the new ambassador, Henry Cabot Lodge, Jr.[25] They could change the instruction if they did not want to abandon Diem.

McNamara and Taylor at this point equivocated. They wanted to "find a way to get Diem to return to his old position and his old policies." According to meeting notes, they said that Diem, "with all his faults . . . had once been a strong leader and had once been able to command enough support to pursue the war effort."

Nonetheless, McNamara and Taylor added, "in the circumstances" they should tell the coup plotters that "while we prefer Diem to remain — without Nhu — if the Vietnamese deemed otherwise, an interim anticommunist military government could expect American support would continue." Kennedy let the weekend telegram stand, except for giving Lodge more discretion as to how to hint at Washington's policy shift to Diem himself.

The moment proved anticlimactic — the generals backed off. But Kennedy still had the problem of a difficult client. In Washington his advisers were deeply divided; arguments had become bitter. Kennedy sent McNamara and Taylor to South Vietnam to size up the situation. He gave them a stiff letter to present to Diem if they saw fit.

For a second time, on September 25, McNamara rushed down the roll-away stairs off his official plane in the steaming heat of Tan Son Nhut Airport, outside Saigon.[26] Once again there was the official receiving line at the foot of the stairs. Once again a group of reporters stood nearby, watching the signals among leading decision makers about the war. Halberstam saw Ambassador Lodge, the Boston Brahmin and nationally known Republican who had taken charge at the embassy in late August, blocking General Harkins from greeting McNamara. Lodge and Harkins were barely on speaking terms.

McNamara and Taylor rushed off to briefings at MACV headquarters, where Harkins and his men argued that the statistics were still good. There was no evidence, they said, that Diem's crackdown in the cities had hurt his ability to fight, which, of course, Harkins maintained was very high.[27]

McNamara and Taylor spent three hours with Diem. He and Taylor also tried to explore "alternative leadership." They were guarded and escorted everywhere — secret meetings with likely coup plotters were out of the question. So Taylor arranged a tennis match with a key opposition general, "Big" Minh, while McNamara sat at the net watching, supposedly just for fun. Taylor kept chatting with the general between points, but Minh's mind seemed to be on tennis, not a change in government. McNamara listened closely, mopping his brow in the heat. They learned nothing; tennis had been a futile way to try to investigate other leaders on whom the American stake in Southeast Asia might depend.[28]

In the field, McNamara now had with him a very critical report on the shooting war by a civilian, Rufus Phillips, that had been passed earlier to John Kennedy. McNamara waved the report at Harkins's briefing officers and grilled them on why they had not included the negative information in the report in their briefing.[29] McNamara now saw the divisions among American agencies, too — the CIA station chief backed Diem and Nhu; Harkins was addicted to Diem, if not Nhu; and Lodge privately but strongly argued that if the United States did not change leaders soon, its cause in South Vietnam was lost. Lodge worked on the secretary of defense; McNamara even canceled some final trips to the field to talk with him.

The trip had its share of problems with reporters. McNamara's press aide, Arthur Sylvester, had come along. At first he "radiated confidence" and claimed "measurable indices" were running in the Americans' favor. When the savvy Saigon journalists showed no mercy with this foolish optimism, someone ordered Sylvester to shut up. By trip's end the only information he was allowed to give out was the menu at the formal dinner given by Diem: swallow's nest soup and — in a typical gaffe — "shark fin wrapped in shrimp."[30]

The press reported that the visiting Americans had given a "blunt final warning" to Diem. They had found the war to be "going better" and that the political turmoil had "no effect whatsoever" on military operations.[31]

The private report McNamara and Taylor took home contained a similar mixed message. Its sections on the shooting war reflected Harkins's and Taylor's optimism. The military campaign was "sound in principle" and making progress. But it added somewhat inconsistently that "further repressive actions by Diem and Nhu could change the present favorable military trends." It admitted to a greater degree than McNamara or Taylor had said publicly that the political situation was bad; U.S. pressures would be unlikely to "move Diem and Nhu toward moderation."

Hilsman found that McNamara had changed upon his return. "To his everlasting credit," McNamara came back "doubting the statistics he loved so well and grasping that 'unquantifiable' political factors might be 'more important' than he previously allowed." Now Mc-

Namara was heard to say in private councils that they couldn't even persuade Diem to take the most routine military advice — of moving a division — without accompanying it with a set of pressures.[32]

Early in October, Kennedy adopted the McNamara-Taylor report as a new, secret policy of pressures on Diem to reform. It recognized that attempting to influence Diem could provoke a leadership change in Saigon. The move was to be kept completely secret. To Senator Frank Church, who had gotten wind of the policy shift and asked in general about pressures on Diem, McNamara went overboard to imply the administration was keeping its hand out of South Vietnam's internal affairs:

> Yes, it is within our capacity to exert pressures, but it's not within our capacity to assure action in accordance with our recommendations. This is an independent government, and I think it is quite inappropriate to think of it as a colony or expect it to act as a colony.[33]

The McNamara-Taylor report was inconsistent; while admitting that the military situation could become grave if Diem's repressive policies worsened, it proposed that Washington announce plans to withdraw virtually all its sixteen thousand military advisers there by the end of 1965 — the timetable for Operation Explosion, which McNamara and Harkins had agreed on back in July 1962.

William Sullivan, who accompanied McNamara and Taylor on their mission to South Vietnam and helped draft the report, recalls that this withdrawal pledge was in the text at first and subsequently taken out. Then it was reinserted during the plane ride home. When McNamara and Taylor presented their report to Kennedy at a closed meeting upon their arrival, there was some objection to making a public announcement of a plan to withdraw. Finally, the pledge was kept in the report and in Kennedy's new policy. On October 2 presidential press secretary Pierre Salinger stepped in front of reporters at the White House to make the plan public. He announced that a thousand advisers would leave by December 31, 1963, as an earnest token of Kennedy's intention to leave.[34]

The historical question is why. The McNamara-Taylor report brims with optimism that General Harkins could finish the training phase and the heavy fighting on schedule. "We believe the U.S. part of the task can be completed by the end of 1965," it said. Success was defined as "suppressing the Viet Cong insurgency . . . to proportions manageable" by the South Vietnamese government forces. Thus the official reason for withdrawing was that the South Vietnamese would be winning and could contain the Communists on their own. The record shows this was the basis for the negotiations McNamara had had with Harkins since 1962, when Harkins promised early success and McNamara believed him.[35]

Maxwell Taylor noted another reason to plan to withdraw and publicize it: to put added pressure on Diem. Taylor said on the plane ride back from Vietnam: "Well, goddammit, we've got to make these people put their noses to the wheel. . . . If we don't give them some indication that we're going to get out sometime, they're just going to be leaning on us forever."[36]

Yet at the same time, McNamara and Taylor knew that the war effort was in danger of collapsing due to civil strife. McNamara's skeptical questions to the military briefers in South Vietnam show he knew that the war was not going as well as Harkins and his deputies claimed.

McNamara has since told others — apparently in confidence — that Kennedy planned to withdraw *"even if [the South Vietnamese] were going to be defeated"* (italics added). The October withdrawal-plan announcement was part of this strategy, according to what McNamara said later. Deputy Secretary of Defense Gilpatric, with whom McNamara worked closely that fall, later told an oral historian, *"McNamara indicated to me that this [the withdrawal plan] was part of a plan the president asked him to develop to unwind the whole thing"* (italics added). And Daniel Ellsberg, who worked in the Pentagon at the time, recalls that the general counsel of the department, John McNaughton, who was also close to McNamara, told him that McNamara said he had *"an understanding with Kennedy that they would close out Vietnam by 'sixty-five, whether it was in good shape or bad"* (italics added).[37]

In 1986 McNamara told the historian of the Office of the Secretary of Defense, in an interview that he then released for this book, the following: "I believed that to the extent that we could train those forces, we should do so, and having done it, we should get out. To the extent those trained forces could not handle the problem — the subversion by North Vietnam — I believed we should not introduce our military forces in support of the South Vietnamese, even if they were going to be 'defeated.' " He therefore recommended that they announce the plan to withdraw. McNamara told the historian, "There was great controversy over that recommendation. Many in the defense department, as well as others in the administration, did not believe we had fully carried out our training mission. Still others believed that, in any event, the South Vietnamese weren't qualified to counter the North Vietnamese effectively. They therefore concluded we should stay."[38]

McNamara later said to me, "I believed that we had done all the training we could. Whether the South Vietnamese were qualified or not to turn back the North Vietnamese, I was certain that if they weren't, it wasn't for lack of our training. More training wouldn't strengthen them; *therefore we should get out. The president agreed*" (italics added). So he and Kennedy *together* planned to leave. McNamara went on to say, "Then there was an argument over whether we should announce the decision. I thought the way to put the decision in concrete was to announce it. So we did. . . . Those who opposed the decision to begin the withdrawal didn't want it announced since they recognized, as I did, that if it were announced it would be in concrete."[39]

I found myself suspecting, in interviews with McNamara and when reviewing the above quotes for publication, that his sincere belief that Kennedy would have gotten out of Vietnam was something he arrived at later, when the war had become tragic and traumatic for him and the nation. McNamara's reverence for John Kennedy is evident; he is often teary just talking about the man. And the temptation to self-deceive, to believe that his hero and mentor would have wisely guided them out, must still be very strong.

No hard evidence for McNamara's claim has come to light. But it is possible that once McNamara saw how bad things were with Diem in September, he then urged Kennedy to set "in concrete" the withdrawal so they could get out, "in good shape or bad." McNamara, like Kennedy, built a record of public U.S. support for holding South Vietnam, yet he and John Kennedy may have had a different, private agenda.[40]

While McNamara was president of the World Bank, he talked with a colleague about John Kennedy during a long limousine ride through Bangkok. He described Kennedy as "the most remarkable man I have ever met" for the "range of issues which he had thought and worked out in his head." But, asked the colleague, wasn't John Kennedy responsible for the failure of American moral authority in the world by bogging the United States down in Vietnam? McNamara said softly, "Oh no. You don't understand. It was an error of judgment. I know for a fact that John Kennedy would have withdrawn from Vietnam."[41]

Thirty days after Salinger read out the withdrawal pledge at the White House, Diem and Nhu were shot while fleeing a coup in Saigon. The generals who masterminded the coup were led by Big Minh, Maxwell Taylor's onetime tennis partner.

The generals published a photograph of the bloody bodies of Diem and Nhu to convince the people of South Vietnam that they were dead. There was cheering in the streets; girls threw garlands at the officers; Lodge was euphoric. In the countryside, the Viet Cong terrorized and burned strategic hamlets but otherwise laid low. They waited, in the aftermath, to see if the country would fall apart of its own rotten weight.

McNamara now knew the problems of that country were more stubborn and subtle than he had once believed. He had latched on to a simple-sounding answer: withdrawal. But the depth of his commitment to this course had not been tested.

Vietnam seemed distant in the summer and fall of 1963, as McNamara and John Kennedy moved closer toward solving the greater challenge of the Soviet threat. Ever since the Cuban missile crisis, and now with the test-ban treaty, Khrushchev seemed bent on liberalization at home, a freer economy, and had taken steps toward coexistence and communication with his adversaries in the free world.

The autobiography of Soviet poet Yevgeny Yevtushenko had just been published in the West. When the poet visited Washington, Bob and Margy McNamara went to hear him read his poems at the Library of Congress and clapped conspicuously when he came to the line about the meeting of two great rivers, symbolizing east and west.[42] It had been a heady year for these architects of America's global rule, which may be one reason the inconsistencies in U.S. policy for Vietnam did not concern McNamara more that fall.

The day he and Taylor had left on their mission to South Vietnam, McNamara was interviewed by correspondent Harry Reasoner for the documentary program *CBS Reports*, which aired September 26.[43] Reasoner conducted a fairly tough interview, reflecting the new mistrust of McNamara in the press. McNamara did not help himself by categorically denying that Admiral Anderson and General LeMay had not been reappointed due to "their independence." As McNamara ticked off all the good reasons for his decisions on the TFX and the litany of his achievements, Reasoner interjected that one congressman called him "I-Have-All-The-Answers McNamara."

Toward the end, Reasoner threw a soft pitch: What was the defense secretary's prognosis for the next decade? The dreamer in McNamara welled up as he said he hoped "for greater stability" and "lowered tensions throughout the world." How far the Soviets would modify their objective of world domination, "I can't say," McNamara said. "There are signs they are beginning to modify it slightly."

Under the hot klieg lights, McNamara the visionary then pulled out Yevtushenko's book. Peering through his spectacles at the text, he began reading aloud, to millions of television viewers, an echo of his own faith in the ineluctable triumph of reason in the world.

> There's no doubt that it's spring. It's a rough spring, a difficult spring, with late frosts and a cold wind, a spring which takes a step to the left and then a step to the right and then a step back, but which is certain nevertheless to go on and take two or three steps forward. And the fact that winter should hold the earth so desperately in its grip and refuse to give up is also quite in the order of things.

McNamara's own paradoxes were echoed by the Russian poet. He had strengthened nuclear forces for the purpose of never using them; he had urged that they leave South Vietnam even as the military situation there worsened. He quoted Yevtushenko on the hardships of winter as evidence of spring: "But then in the very counter attacks of winter one can sense its growing impotence because times have changed."

In a speech some seven weeks later, McNamara offered the larger irony of his first three years in office.[44] He argued that the reformed administration of the military, the strategic and conventional force buildups, the strong stands on Berlin and Cuba, had changed the "maps" by which policy was charted in the cold war. Now "the wide range of our military resources give us freedom . . . to pursue the peaceful objectives of the free world without fear of military aggression."

He was anticipating the themes of Lyndon Johnson's presidency, which, unknown to McNamara on that day, November 18, was about to begin.

IV
THE TEST

14

Test of a New Leader

T
HE FALL OF 1963 held the prospect of another beginning for Robert McNamara. The Kennedys were looking
ahead to the presidential campaign in 1964, a second term in
the White House, and the future leadership of the Democratic party. But, in fact, Kennedy's legislative program, from civil
rights to the tax cut, was stalled in Congress. Kennedy was needled
by charges of news management and covering up American involvement in Vietnam. The right fumed at him over the test-ban treaty and
prospective détente with Moscow. It was John Kennedy's gift that,
despite such a mixed record, he could create an illusion of heroic
striving and nobility, of promise fulfilled, of leadership in the Greek
ideal.

Three years before, when Kennedy won the White House, Robert
McNamara's world was bounded by Michigan and the auto industry;
his only new horizon was his plan for Ford to leap into coproduction
in Europe. Since then, he had made his own giant leap to national and
international fame. He was now lauded on many continents for management prowess, judgment, and restraint. The Kennedy glow shone
on him, even though he, like Kennedy, had growing problems by late
1963: the TFX, Vietnam, mistrust by the senior military and others.
He had dramatically built up nuclear and conventional forces; he had
rationalized the defense program and reformed its budget process; he
was trying to lower the threat of nuclear war in Europe by pushing
the allies to adopt the strategy of flexible response. His controlled,

threatened use of force in the Berlin and Cuba crises earned him the fashionable sobriquet of crisis manager.

Kennedy and his political advisers, in light of the safe Democratic majorities in both houses of Congress and many state houses, too, expected to win the White House for a second term and prepare the way for another Democratic president in 1968. Lyndon Johnson, after two terms as vice president, would be the logical heir, but the Kennedys wanted to award the honor to McNamara.

Bobby Kennedy later said his brother thought "most highly" of McNamara, "more than any other cabinet member," especially after a crisis like Cuba, "when you can see what can happen to a country and how much depends on a particular individual." Johnson was positioned to be Kennedy's successor in 1968, but Bobby said he and his brother "thought of moving in the direction that would get the nomination for Bob McNamara" as the Democratic presidential candidate in 1968, to be sure the country was "placed in the best possible hands." One path to the 1968 nomination lay through the vice presidency. But they also considered moving Dean Rusk to the United Nations for Kennedy's second term and "appointing Bob McNamara Secretary of State." Bobby had told diplomat John Bartlow Martin that Rusk "wasn't as strong as McNamara." So the Georgetown and Press Club rumor mills said McNamara would replace Rusk in Kennedy's second term. McNamara later did not confirm that such a plan existed. He only said, showing affection for Rusk, "It was always very embarrassing to me to have these rumors going around."[1]

The implications of Kennedy's high esteem could not have been lost on McNamara. His ambition was instinctive, requiring a conscious act of will to rein it in. The modest, unassuming McNamara who appeared at dinner parties was a reversion to the awkward boy from Oakland, new to sophisticated society. This modesty was misleading, for it barely masked enormous confidence and ambition. He had come so far and fast by the fall of 1963 that the presidency could not have seemed distant from his grasp.

He does not admit that either of the Kennedys discussed these options with him. But he did tell Walt Rostow in an interview in 1975, "If I had my life to live over again, I would want to be a politician, an elected official. . . . In a very real sense it is the highest duty one can perform."[2]

Could McNamara have been a political campaigner, let alone won election as president? He had risen to power through the cool, swift, appointive route, by pleasing a single superior and doing what he did well — which was running giant organizations. He used power for ends defined solely by himself or Henry Ford or John Kennedy. He also showed genuine disdain for politics and for many congressmen. Wittingly or not, he decried Congress's right to act in the name of the people; he argued, in effect, that the people had fewer facts and a narrower view of their interest than he. McNamara simply could not have tolerated the messiness and diffuse authority of electoral politics. As a candidate, he would have had another drawback: In the newly important medium of television, he seemed awkward and remote.

How badly McNamara wanted to rise further is hard to guess. He doubtless read with interest the trial balloons in the press saying the Republicans might draft him in 1964 as an Eisenhower-style leader above politics. One story likened Margy to Mamie Eisenhower, as the perfect candidate's wife. Their friends from California were eager for McNamara's advancement, too. "Bob would have been a great president," says his old chum Willard Goodwin.[3]

McNamara got his chance. The mantle of national leadership was thrust on him sooner and more traumatically than the Kennedy brothers had ever planned.

McNamara's calendar for November 22, 1963, listed a "Navy Meeting" from 8:00 to 8:15, "Mr. Bundy" at 9:00 to 9:15, "Sen. Symington" from 12:15 to 12:45, and "Budget Group" starting at 1:30.[4] At 1:30, precisely on schedule, McNamara planted himself in his chair at the end of the long table in the conference room, his back to the connecting door to his office.

This meeting was one of the last summits between the top officials of the Bureau of the Budget and the Department of Defense before the fiscal 1965 defense budget went to Kennedy to review in late November. Before each man lay sheaves of papers filled with numbers they had drawn up with infinite care.

Suddenly, the door behind McNamara swung open and Sidney Berry, his military aide, came in and tapped him on the shoulder. McNamara left and returned a few minutes later, signaling Bundy and Roswell Gilpatric to join him on the other side of the door. The three vanished. The BOB men waited until Gilpatric and Bundy came back through the door.

"I think we had better share with the rest of you what has happened," said Gilpatric. "We have a report that the president has been shot. We're not sure how serious it is."

"Ken O'Donnell is with the president and he hasn't given up hope," said Bundy.

"It looks very bad," said Gilpatric.

Minutes later, McNamara swept through the door, dropped into his chair, looked down at his papers, and began straightening them. This was his usual signal for the discussion to resume, so the others bent forward to restart the ritual.

No one spoke. Instead of resuming talk of dollars and weapons, they sat frozen, like a tableau of government-planning-as-usual at Madame Tussaud's. Bundy said: "I think we better get over to the White House."

McNamara vanished back through the door. The BOB men stood and started stuffing their papers into briefcases. They hurried downstairs to the cars that would take them past the bare trees and stone-cold river. They wondered, in tight-lipped anxiety, could someone shoot at Kennedy, *shoot the president*, maybe *kill* him? What could happen next? It wasn't logical. It didn't fit with the world they understood and planned for. Was it a coup? The Budget men shivered in their overcoats as the cars sped them across the bridge, clutching briefcases filled with plans for a future, which now would be very different.

McNamara's self-control masked storms of emotion that could burst through with lightning force. Yet in moments of crisis, he could be remarkably contained. One general says McNamara took the news of Kennedy's shooting in "shocked disbelief."[5]

He swiftly joined the Joint Chiefs in the Tank. They had been carrying on their own ritual, a summit with West German military leaders. When the chairman, General Maxwell Taylor, was given private word of the shooting, he began passing notes under the table to his American colleagues, hoping the Germans wouldn't notice. Then they informed the Germans of what had happened, disbanded the meeting, and sat with McNamara at the hub of military control to watch worldwide for more violence or further moves against the government, U.S. embassies, or bases.[6]

Major Ted Clifton, Kennedy's military aide, had frantically commandeered the switchboard down the hall from Trauma Room number 1 at Parkland Memorial Hospital, in Dallas. Clifton persuaded a regional Bell operator to patch him into the military communications system. John Kennedy's life was slipping away; the attack on the president might be part of a plot or a coup. Messages were relayed to the nine unified field commanders, ordering them on alert. One went to Defense Condition One, the highest readiness for war. McNamara was the field commanders' immediate superior in the chain of command; his commander in chief was dying.[7]

The minutes ticked by with no sign of hostile activity anywhere. Guards slipped around Eisenhower's farm in Gettysburg, Pennsylvania, in case the former president was next on the presumed plotters' hit list. Dean Rusk was reached on an official airplane headed over the Pacific toward Japan; the plane turned around and started back. McNamara had little to do but watch and wait. He kept in motion in his private elevator between the Tank and his office; he was on the phone, receiving messages, talking with Taylor and the others. He was told by the Defense Intelligence Agency — although he later believed it was the CIA — that Kennedy was dead.[8]

In Parkland Hospital, Lyndon Johnson sat in the minor medicine suite in the back of the first floor. The staff had closed the venetian blinds lest anyone outside see that the vice president was there. According to the Constitution, Johnson became president the instant Kennedy died. When this occurred was never clear. Perhaps it happened earlier, when the motorcade was screaming toward the hospital and, in the open car behind Kennedy's, Johnson lay underneath his own Secret Service agent, who had flung himself across the vice president to block any further bullets. Or perhaps it had not yet happened as Johnson sat in the hospital, waiting. Major Clifton, on his own initiative, ordered the officer carrying the "football," the device for presidential control of the nuclear forces, to leave the whitened figure in Trauma Room number 1 and walk down the hall to the minor medicine suite. But Johnson refused to accept that he was president until he heard from Kennedy's personal staff. He waited until Ken O'Donnell entered and said: "He's gone."[9]

As though waking up, Johnson began to move. The Secret Service had told him they could guarantee his safety only in Washington. So he got to the airport and *Air Force One*, with his own party and the Kennedy entourage. He ordered everyone to keep his movements secret until he was safely aboard the plane and under the protection of the Air Force. Then at three-thirty Central Time, standing between the seats, Johnson was sworn in as president. A photographer captured his raised hand, the Bible, Lady Bird and Jackie at either side. He requested that the picture be distributed as soon as the plane took off, so the world would know the succession had taken place.

From the anteroom of 3E 880 in the Pentagon that afternoon, secretary Peg Stroud had a hard time finding her boss.[10] The door to the inner office was locked. Meanwhile, the secretaries' phones rang off the hook, people kept coming by, and staff watched the television for developments, as did millions of Americans. Television told them that Dallas police had chased a man through a movie theater and arrested him. His name was Lee Harvey Oswald, and he would be charged with the murder of John F. Kennedy.

The afternoon light was failing when the buzzer hummed on Peg Stroud's desk. She picked up the phone to the inner office. A familiar voice asked for two cups of tea, of all things. She prepared a tray and pushed open the door. There sat Bobby Kennedy, looking miserable.

A pretense of normalcy reigned. McNamara said: "Bob, I'd like you to meet my secretary. Peg, this is Bobby Kennedy."

Peg Stroud thought this astonishing but found herself lapsing into formalities. She heard herself say, "I'm so sorry, Mr. Kennedy."

McNamara recalls that Bobby insisted they drive together to Andrews Air Force Base, where the plane was due to land that evening. They rode out in his official car, McNamara recalls, and sat in darkness, waiting for *Air Force One* to land with its grim load and the new president of the United States. General Taylor was in the car, too.[11] As the plane's lights glimmered in the sky, lowering steadily toward the ground, Bobby started to get out and then asked McNamara to come with him. McNamara remembers telling Bobby that he would stay behind; Bobby's errand was "family business," McNamara told him. Bobby vanished in the darkness and found his way on board the plane through the front hatch. A large crowd had gathered; a good number had come spontaneously, but many members of Congress and the diplomatic corps had received word that Lyndon Johnson wanted them there.

The CBS film, watched live by millions, shows an honor guard standing on the ground below the big side door of the plane.[12] The door opens to reveal Kennedy's coffin, Jackie with blood on her suit, and Bobby next to her. A lift is raised to move the coffin off the plane, but it does not reach high enough. The coffin tilts grotesquely as the guardsmen struggle to lower it onto the lift. Then Jackie is helped down and walks slowly to the Navy ambulance to accompany the corpse to Bethesda Naval Hospital. As she reaches for the ambulance's side door and finds it locked, her hand drops in a gesture of exhaustion.

Later that night at Tracy Place, McNamara got a phone call from "someone calling for Jackie" asking him to come out to Bethesda Naval Hospital. So he stood in, helping Jacqueline and the family, after all.[13]

The CBS film of the landing of *Air Force One* also reveals how McNamara choreographed his own public transfer of loyalty to Lyndon Johnson that same evening. The camera is positioned above and behind the dark coats and white heads of the crowd. Slowly the Kennedys move off at stage left, and the camera pans back to the open doorway, where Johnson and Lady Bird step into view, both pale and solemn. Once on the tarmac, Johnson steps to the microphones, his tall, narrow forehead knit with emotion. It is a "sad time for all people," a "loss that cannot be weighed" and a "deep personal tragedy." He promises to do his best. "That is all I can do."[14]

Then McNamara appears in the picture; he shoots through the crowd straight at the new president; his gleaming, straight-combed hair is unmistakable even from behind. The crowd parts without a jostle to let him through. McNamara seizes Johnson's hand, clasping it so firmly and long that the gesture looks rehearsed. He turns and hugs Lady Bird and moves with the new presidential couple off to stage right. He is assisting and deferential, smooth, obedient, and custodial — a physical symbol of confidence and continuity.

As CBS's camera pans back to the crowd and departing ambulance, offstage, the Johnsons and McNamara, as well as Taylor, McGeorge Bundy, and Acting Secretary of State George Ball, board a helicopter to fly to the White House. McNamara is already at the nucleus of a new administration and a new era.

McNamara helped with Kennedy family business after sharing Jackie's vigil at Bethesda Naval Hospital on Friday, November 22. The clan had to decide whether the casket should be open or closed while it lay in state in the East Room and hundreds of mourners filed through. Arthur Schlesinger records that it was Bobby and McNamara who opened the casket and decided that John Kennedy's head should not be on public view.[15]

McNamara remembered and told the family about a walk he had taken with John Kennedy in Arlington Cemetery, on the Virginia side of the Potomac. He recalled that Kennedy had stood on the high hill and admired the view looking back at Washington. On Saturday, November 23, in the rain, McNamara tramped up the slope with Bobby. The family then decided to bury John Kennedy on this site, not in the family plot, in Boston.

Coincidentally, Arlington Cemetery is run by the Army Corps of Engineers, which reports ultimately to the secretary of defense. McNamara took a personal hand in supervising construction of the grave site. It was paid for through a cost-sharing agreement with the Kennedy family, and Alfred Fitt recalled that the project became a caricature of McNamara's problems with other defense contracts.[16] Costs overran; mud slides, stone shortages from the quarry, and other perversities of nature and man threw off the schedule for completion. McNamara followed each detail with his customary rafts of figures and driven oversight. But he had to subdue his czarlike temper to deal graciously with the help of Kennedy friends like Bunny Mellon, wife of philanthropist Paul Mellon, whom Jacqueline Kennedy had asked to help with the flower beds.

McNamara's acquaintance with Lyndon Johnson had been slight. Like the rest of the Kennedy circle, he had paid little attention to the once-powerful former Senate majority leader. As vice president, Johnson was relegated to minor roles like promoting the supersonic transport and running the Space Council, a group McNamara ignored after 1961. Around the Kennedy White House, Johnson wore his insecurities about Harvard, the eastern establishment, and intellectuals on his sleeve. Johnson's aide Harry McPherson watched him slide in his years as vice president. He remembers swimming with Johnson in the pool of the big, ugly house that hostess Perle Mesta had sold him. "He looked absolutely gross. His belly was enormous and his face looked bad, flushed, maybe he had been drinking a good deal. . . . His life was not causing him to come together physically, morally, intellectually, or in any way."[17]

As president, Johnson reached out for McNamara and the other Kennedy advisers. He was still insecure; he felt the job was not rightly his. Harry McPherson says: "Johnson promoted McNamara everywhere. . . . No doubt he was trying to win over" the Kennedy people "as his personal friends and supporters. . . . Rusk was easier to win and more genuinely won because he had been treated not too elegantly by the Kennedys."[18] McNamara, on the other hand, was a Kennedy friend and a bigger prize.

Among Johnson's many compulsions was the telephone. Now that he held the highest office in the land he did not stand on ceremony when he needed to talk, which was often. Johnson deluged McNamara with calls during working hours. He wandered around the White House at night and telephoned McNamara then, too. He telephoned him in Aspen when the McNamaras went on vacation. Thinking he was on a direct line, the president would start talking as soon as someone answered, assuming it was McNamara. A friend once answered the phone at their house in Aspen to hear Johnson talking away, his language scatological. "My God! How that man *talked!*" She shivered at the memory.[19]

Johnson often dragged McNamara and his family to dine with him. Craig was the only one of the three McNamara children at home in 1963 and remembers Sunday as his father's one day with his family. After Johnson became president, his parents and he would be "cooking hamburgers" on a Sunday when the phone would ring. Craig would hear his father repeat, "Yes, Mr. President." Then they would pile in the car and go to the White House for the lunch they were supposed to have had at home. Craig's mother would chat with Lady Bird; his father talked with the president; Craig sat on the edge of the pool. On other weekends the phone would ring and Craig heard "Yes, Mr. President" again, and they would fly in a helicopter to Camp David, in Maryland's Catoctin Mountains. Craig's memory of Camp David was of being left alone in the presidential bowling alley.[20]

But Lyndon Johnson was incapable of moderation in any human relationship. His telephone calls and ceaseless invitations to McNamara to dine and swim stemmed from possessiveness, as though McNamara were a gleaming prize Johnson won in the lottery of life that had catapulted him to the presidency. Aide Jack Valenti remembers Johnson's fascination with McNamara's mental talent for statistics. He recalls meetings at which Johnson asked McNamara some difficult economic question. McNamara, without skipping a beat, rattled out the numerical answer, as if he were Mister Memory in the movie

The Thirty-nine Steps, a robotic individual who answered any question of fact like a machine. Valenti recalls that the president would meet the eyes of the other men around the long, polished table with an expression of pleasure and pride. Valenti took the look to mean *Isn't he amazing? And he is mine.*[21]

Johnson admired McNamara's abilities; like Kennedy, he let McNamara run the Pentagon his own way. Harry McPherson remembers an early phone call from a defense contractor who was probing the new administration to see if White House influence could help win a contract. Not only was the caller told no dice, but the new president gathered his staff and solemnly instructed them that he wanted the Pentagon to continue to run with the integrity Bob McNamara had brought to it. No high jinks, and no White House interference. Johnson respected McNamara as the viceroy who could rule the defense empire — half the federal budget, affecting one tenth of the gross national product — most competently for him.[22] He also knew McNamara could run it in a way that would not hurt him politically and that would leave him free to pursue his large domestic agenda.

But such respect as he held for McNamara was mercurial. Johnson had a vicious tendency to play cat and mouse with appointees who lacked independent power, and McNamara's power depended solely on the president. According to a story, Dean Acheson saw Johnson publicly humiliate McNamara to his face at a meeting. The president "squeezed him like an orange," Acheson had said afterward. Acheson had been so appalled by the president's conduct that he followed Lyndon Baines Johnson into the Oval Office and told him that even a president should not speak like that to a Cabinet officer.

Others who heard Acheson's account were shocked by Johnson's conduct, too. Even if one disagreed with McNamara, as Acheson and many others did; even if one found McNamara too much of an accountant and lacking a gestalt; even if one questioned his truthfulness, as his many critics at Foggy Bottom did; nonetheless, McNamara was a serious fellow and not someone to be criticized lightly. Yet the evidence was that McNamara could stomach this humiliation, out of deference to Johnson or his office.[23]

It was not clear which side of McNamara's complex personality would determine his course with Lyndon Johnson. Was McNamara, after nearly three years as a national and international figure, up to leading the president himself? Johnson seemed to be foisting on him the role of a regent, given Johnson's own insecurity and narrow experience of the broader world. In this new role, would McNamara stand up to Johnson? Or would his habitual loyalty set the tone, loyalty to the office if not to the man?

In those first, awful months after Kennedy was shot, McNamara himself may not have known; he confided to Arthur Schlesinger that he wasn't sure how the relationship with Johnson would work out.[24]

Bobby Kennedy, who drew closer to McNamara in this period, was outraged by McNamara's servility. Talking to John Bartlow Martin when the new administration was only months old, the attorney general complained that Johnson stayed only five minutes at an important meeting concerning strategy options in the event that a U-2 spy plane was shot down over Cuba. However, the president spent an hour and a half at a meeting where he asked each Cabinet member to say what he was doing to cut costs, "turning out lights and things." When the meeting ended, "I heard Bob McNamara say to one of the other Cabinet members, that was a fine meeting. Well, as I say, I might just be sitting there and be mad because I don't like it." Kennedy ranted on about Johnson: "He's able to eat people up, and even people who were considered rather strong figures — I mean, as I say, Mac Bundy or Bob McNamara. . . . They've just — nothing left of them."[25]

Lyndon Johnson was not going to let Bob McNamara think the Kennedys were saints, even as the public and press began to eulogize them. Bobby Kennedy left a tantalizing hint that Johnson told McNamara the contents of the FBI files that J. Edgar Hoover had collected on the Kennedys.

When Johnson became president, Hoover began carrying some of his sensitive files on prominent people to the White House to share with the president. Hoover's files, it has been determined, included information on John and Bobby Kennedy's affairs. The files detailed both men's involvement with actress Marilyn Monroe. Bobby told Burke Marshall of the Justice Department in December 1964: "He [McNamara] used to tell me that Hoover used to send over all this material on me and that Lyndon Johnson would read it to him."[26]

I asked McNamara whether Johnson read or showed him compromising information from Hoover about Bobby Kennedy. "Absolutely not," he snapped.

Bobby also alleged in the same interview that McNamara, "who is having his problems with him [Hoover] now, is convinced that he tried to put a tap on his telephone" to get information "because he thinks there's a conspiracy by McNamara and me to get rid of Hoover."

McNamara told me he did not "think" Hoover bugged his phone. He said that Margy and Lydia Katzenbach, her good friend and the wife of Nicholas Katzenbach, who held posts in the Justice and State departments during the Johnson years, believed both of their phones were tapped. The two women would call each other and tell outrageous stories as a joke to shock the FBI. McNamara added, "I may well have told Johnson he should get rid of Hoover. I thought Hoover was a menace."

Who is to be believed? Bobby, telling an interviewer in 1964 that McNamara has just told him Johnson was reading out Hoover's files "on me" — presumably to torment McNamara with his friend's weak, darker side? Or McNamara, denying it "absolutely" more than twenty years later? And why did he not "think" Hoover bugged his phone, when he admitted Margy did think so? Until hard information on either point comes to light, Bobby's word is more believable.

McNamara may have been uncertain how it would work out with Johnson, and he may have been emotionally bound, despite the shock of the assassination, to stay on out of "loyalty to the office" of this new president who courted him so furiously. But Robert McNamara would stay and serve Johnson for years with his particular brand of loyalty.[27] It is evident that despite Johnson's flaws, McNamara quickly conceived affection and admiration for this long-term Senate majority leader and consummate politician.

In the view of Joseph Califano, who served both men, one link that bound McNamara to Johnson was Johnson's passion on the social issues of civil rights and poverty. McNamara always later spoke of this side of Johnson in a voice that burst with admiration.[28] He later recalled how, when Johnson was vice president, his relations with John Kennedy had been "tense and strained." Johnson had a "huge ego and immense ambition" and "an inferiority complex . . . in the face of the Kennedys' easy social graces." But "he underrated himself. He was a masterful politician in the best sense of the word; in his ability to reconcile those differences among our people . . . so that we could move forward to a common goal and a better life for all of the people." McNamara says that he shared completely Johnson's dream of using federal power and programs to build a "Great Society" — a phrase Johnson introduced in a major speech in May. "That was his great quality. He came upon the scene with that quality just at the time when it was most needed, at the time of the racial conflict which had resulted from a hundred years of failure to deal with the discrimination against the blacks."

McNamara watched the new president's superb performance from a ringside seat. Johnson, from almost his first weeks in office, pushed legislators to adopt Kennedy's social and civil rights bills, which were then stalled in Congress. In speech after speech, meeting after meeting in Congress, and in innumerable White House meetings in which this intense, looming Texan "showed a little garter" to his longtime colleagues, Lyndon Johnson finally won passage of laws that changed the nation, laws that were to lessen poverty, widen education, and expand health care, housing, and voting rights.[29] Clearly Johnson the "masterful politician" fascinated McNamara and allowed him to appreciate Johnson the man.

Further, Johnson's themes resonated with McNamara's past and his own life's struggle. Johnson repeated stories of inequity and poverty from his youth in rural Texas; McNamara's early youth had hardly been one of privilege. Franklin Roosevelt was Johnson's hero for having used government as a turnkey to effect the economic transformation of society; FDR had been McNamara's hero, too.[30]

McNamara himself had risen from poverty, or so he felt. He had seen the New Deal help the depressed Bay Area to its feet. McNamara used his public education at Cal and his abundant good health to transform his own situation in life. Why not education and health for all the poor and underprivileged of the country? As McNamara learned about Johnson through his endless talk of launching a massive war on poverty and injustice, he was impressed.

"If government is to serve any purpose it is to do for others what they are unable to do for themselves," Johnson said in February 1964,[31] a creed McNamara had shared since Berkeley and would later adopt at the World Bank.

Johnson's public performance was as intense as his private one. In his first State of the Union address, in January 1964, he promised an "unconditional war on poverty in America" to be fought primarily through a new Office of Economic Opportunity, which Congress duly voted. He pushed Congress to pass Kennedy's second tax cut, so the nation would grow richer to be able to afford to help its poor. Johnson announced that he wanted Congress to pass Kennedy's civil rights bill *intact*, which was more than Kennedy had hoped to achieve, and which was sure to antagonize Johnson's former allies in Congress, barons of power from Deep South states. The president followed each step in the dance of legislation obsessively, up through the climactic Senate vote in July, which passed the bills.

Racial tempers in the country, already rising in the early 1960s, began to boil.[32] The civil rights movement was suddenly appealing to students from midwestern and northern schools. In March 1965 students and other civil rights workers answered the call to a nonviolent march from Selma to Montgomery, Alabama, targeted as two of the most bigoted cities in the South.

Among the students was McNamara's daughter Margy, who was a graduate student at Washington University, in St. Louis. She boarded a bus heading south with fellow activists, while the men of the Pentagon met with the president on the difficult issue of federalizing the local National Guard as local authority broke down or was directed against the marchers.

McNamara claimed later that he learned the Friday night of the march on Selma that Margy was there.[33] "I called the president," he says. When he told him about Margy, "I thought he was going to tear the telephone off the wall." Johnson had "great misgivings" about federalizing the Alabama National Guard, but "I finally persuaded him to do it. I told him I knew that he loved Margy and he was surely right in calling out the Guard because it protected her on the march."

Califano believes that it was from Lyndon Johnson that McNamara derived his own later passion for addressing social ills. "He [Johnson] changed all of us," says Califano, who was McNamara's special assistant until he left in early 1965 to manage the flood of domestic bills from the Johnson White House. McNamara would draw upon the Great Society — Medicare, Medicaid, Head Start, Model Cities, the Job Corps, community action, school lunches, and myriad others, including the expansion of welfare benefits to non-working poor — for the rest of his career. Johnson's programs were later derided as giveaways, but the economic theory from which they sprang argued for helping the poor directly to make them more productive and, in that halcyon economic era, to bring unemployment down from 5 percent to almost zero.[34] The Great Society in this sense is the clear predecessor of McNamara's later program at the World Bank.

Johnson, in his infatuation with McNamara's talents, was unrestrained in his use of his defense secretary and deputized him to handle almost anything that crossed his mind. It was quickly noticed — and leaked to the press — that McNamara was Johnson's favorite among the former Kennedy advisers who surrounded him. McNamara's power was still derivative, but he had more of it. He was dubbed — accurately — "executive vice president of the United States" by Najeeb Halaby, administrator of the Federal Aviation Administration, and Congress, the press, and even foreign governments knew it.

Johnson wanted to make the federal government sponsor and run broad social programs; the Republicans charged that the government couldn't manage them. Thus the new president — a politician for most of his adult life — was fascinated by McNamara's management and the Whiz Kids. Alain Enthoven recalls being invited to a reception at the White House early in Johnson's tenure — itself a remarkable note of presidential recognition.[35] When Enthoven and his mother came through the receiving line, Johnson took Enthoven's mother aside and launched into an elaborate speech about the wonderful service that McNamara's chief Whiz Kid was performing for the nation.

Johnson even made a largely token effort to export the magic bullets of the program budget and systems analysis to all federal agencies. Yet the idea of rational, objective yardsticks applied to social policy barely took root. Halaby says, "I don't think Johnson had much objectivity or understood the concept of it."[36]

Nevertheless, "systems" became the buzzword of the moment; that good management could solve American society's problems with benevolent federal action was a heady promise. McNamara egged on several Whiz Kids, who undertook the new challenge: William Gorham, who had worked on the military pay study, installed program planning for John Gardner at the Department of Health, Education, and Welfare; Califano himself moved to the White House, where he drafted bills and made at least one speech calling for the application of "systems," as employed at Defense and by the Apollo program, to run society. The president first tapped Adam

Yarmolinsky to be the deputy director of the flagship effort, the
Office of Economic Opportunity. But when congressmen from
North Carolina raised objections, Johnson reversed course and as-
sured them he would not be nominated.[37]

Meanwhile, in the halls of power, observers began noting the almost robotic character of McNamara's obedience to his new boss.
"For some reason, Johnson asked me to help on nondefense issues,
which I did whenever I could," McNamara says. In April 1964,
Johnson made McNamara the czar over federal policy toward the
SST, with far-reaching consequences. Halaby, the FAA administrator, desperately wanted the United States to build an SST soon, lest
the Europeans and Soviets beat out America in this new form of
commercial aviation. Suddenly Halaby had a frightening and wily
foe.[38]

As the new chairman of the President's Advisory Committee on
the Supersonic Transport, McNamara dominated the government debate on whether to subsidize the aerospace industry in building a fleet
of fifty two-hundred-person commercial SSTs to whiz over the
United States, the Pacific, and the Atlantic at three times the speed of
sound. "I haven't yet seen a piece of analysis which will show it will
be economic," McNamara said at the first meeting of PAC.

What followed was a year of McNamara's blistering attacks on the
FAA studies, the Commerce Department, and all who purported to
show the feasibility of this new technology. Califano remembers how
McNamara hung over the numbers like an excited teacher. He would
plop a finger down on a computation done for him and look at
Califano sternly. You haven't put in a factor here for inflation in the
price of fuel, he would say.

Halaby the visionary knew all too well what — and who — had hit
him. McNamara kept destroying all his arguments. The two men's
deputies were like "snarling dogs"; McNamara was accused of causing the loss of American leadership in commercial aviation with his
stick-in-the-mud, Luddite attitudes. He was also deceitful when, finally, Halaby confronted him before the entire committee and
charged that he was out to stop the plane. Oh no, McNamara said
blandly, we have no such intention. "No one in the room believed
him," says a definitive history of the SST.

In fact, the reports McNamara sent to Johnson recited the pros
and cons in exquisite, analytic fashion. But they never said outright

don't build the plane. Halaby later saw the flaw in McNamara's style: An executive vice president who really believes a proposal is bad should say so openly, especially when advising the president.[39]

McNamara demonstrated his loyalty, fine and precise, over the SST. He had also shown an ability to antagonize everyone else on an issue if it helped his goals in serving the president. One result of McNamara's PAC exercise of 1964–65 was the analyses by his men indicating that the planned fleet of SSTs would be uneconomic; another result was the seminal National Academy of Sciences investigation of the sonic boom effects of SST flights. Both sets of findings, after much public debate, killed the U.S. plane in 1971.

Here was a glimpse of how Robert S. McNamara would lead in his new role. Johnson did not moderate McNamara's fighting instincts, as Kennedy had; instead Johnson's own coarseness aggravated McNamara's worst qualities, which the public was soon to see. The 1964 presidential campaign, which preoccupied Lyndon Johnson, showed McNamara's excess of loyalty, his weakness.

The Republican candidate was the ultraconservative Barry Goldwater, an Air Force reserve pilot and friend of superhawk General Curtis LeMay's. Goldwater told a group in New Hampshire, in January: "It's classified information . . . I'll probably catch hell for this. I wish the Defense Department would tell the people how undependable the long-range missiles are. I'm very fearful that we may be caught sometime with our airplanes down. . . . We need to keep up our airplane capability.[40]

This was the first brick thrown at McNamara, who instantly announced that Goldwater's remark was "completely misleading, politically irresponsible, and damaging to the national security." The Joint Chiefs of Staff (including LeMay) said the missiles worked, McNamara asserted.[41]

Goldwater claimed that McNamara favored "unilateral disarmament." He also raised a charge that would stay forever linked to McNamara's name: McNamara was really behind the Edsel disaster at Ford. In Detroit, where McNamara was still often praised, Ernest Breech, who was Ford's chairman of the board, issued a public letter of denial, saying McNamara "had nothing to do with the plan for the Edsel car or any part of the program."[42] But Goldwater and his vocal conservative followers kept repeating the charge. After all, since McNamara promoted inefficient ideas like the TFX, slowed progress by halting LeMay's B-70 bomber, analyzed everything for cost instead of charging ahead, and favored unilateral disarmament, he *must* have brought us the Edsel. Goldwater glued the charge to McNamara's back for life.

Nonetheless, Johnson's strategy was for him to speak often and loftily about the Democrats' enormous military buildup since 1961 — to remind voters that it was Eisenhower and the Republicans who had left the country weak. He deputized McNamara to fight with gloves off.

The president's willingness to play rough was symbolized in a hard-hitting television spot alluding to Goldwater's supposed readiness to use nuclear weapons. It showed a little girl counting daisy petals in front of a mushroom cloud. The only reference to Goldwater was indirect. In another indirect reference to Goldwater, the Democrats promoted the slogan "In your heart you know he might."

But it was McNamara's job to hit Goldwater directly, and he hit hard, on television and off. The public saw the raw, angry McNamara, exaggerating his own arguments to the point of fabrication, to denounce his foe. Insiders, including the military, had seen this harsh, "Me-Win" McNamara. Now the public saw that he was something besides the statesman and rationalist of his image. Meanwhile, the Goldwater camp made reference to his middle name: Strange.

McNamara set up a private office, staffed by Joseph Califano, Daniel Ellsberg, and Alexander Haig, to keep Vietnam out of the campaign.[43] It was only during the week of August 2, when the North Vietnamese attacked a U.S. destroyer in the Gulf of Tonkin and the United States struck back briefly, that McNamara discussed Vietnam in public. Public and congressional outrage died down quickly; McNamara's silence helped keep it from becoming a campaign issue and from being openly debated.

Johnson's popularity rose after the Tonkin Gulf incidents; it looked like the election would be a landslide. But Lyndon Johnson, insecure as always, was not satisfied. He ended the fine American tradition that politics stops at the water's edge, keeping the secretaries of state and defense out of the partisan fray. Johnson made Rusk and McNamara testify before the Democratic National Committee at the party's convention at Atlantic City. The appearances were unnecessary: Goldwater was losing, clearly.

But here McNamara's obedience — and his temper — showed. He attacked the Eisenhower administration's record on defense, saying,

The Defense Department we found in 1961 was one in which each military service made its own plans. We found the Army relying on air-lift which the Air Force was unable to provide. We found the Army envisioning a long war, stockpiling . . . supplies for only a few days.

We found a weapons inventory completely lacking in certain major elements required for combat readiness. . . .

In 1961 we found military strategy to be the stepchild of a predetermined budget. . . . The strategic nuclear force we found was vulnerable to surprise missile attack. The nonnuclear force we found was weak in combat-ready divisions, weak in airlift capability, weak in tactical air support.[44]

In his all-out attack on the 1961 Department of Defense, McNamara implicitly accused his courtly predecessor, Thomas Gates. McNamara knew full well that Gates, who had started to reform the Pentagon and had even tutored McNamara in his first weeks that there was no missile gap, had been the most competent of Eisenhower's three defense secretaries. Now Gates was furious. When McNamara heard this, he sent Gates a telegram claiming he had high regard for him and recalling the complimentary things he had said about Gates over the years. Reports of partisanship were the press's work, not his, he said.

McNamara's telegram made Gates so mad he sent a letter to McNamara and released it publicly: "I am totally unable to reconcile what you told the platform committee with the tone and content of your dispatch to me," Gates wrote. As for McNamara's testimony to the committee, he said, "I cannot believe that you agree with these statements yourself."[45]

From Gettysburg, former president Dwight Eisenhower encouraged Gates and revealed a low regard for McNamara: "Certainly you were very restrained in your attitude and I am grateful you took the trouble to correct some of the distortions in McNamara's testimony. Washington seems to be as filled with demagogues as with starlings; both are noisy and a nuisance, but neither has a great deal of sense."[46]

The McNamara-Johnson strategy of displaying the president as high-minded and peace-loving while his defense secretary talked tough had its uses well beyond the campaign. Larger dangers than Goldwater loomed. All year, intelligence had been reporting that China was preparing to detonate its first nuclear device. A Chinese bomb was expected to upset foreign and domestic order in several ways: It could scotch the nonproliferation talks that China defiantly ignored, widen the Sino-Soviet split to dangerous levels, thoroughly alarm the nations of the Far East, embolden Peking's ally in Hanoi, and, finally, give the right a tangible reason to blame the administration for being soft on communism.[47] (The seriousness with which Johnson and his advisers regarded the imminent Chinese bomb in 1964 is illustrated in a single memo, recently released. On September 15, 1964, the inner circle secretly considered asking Moscow to launch a preemptive attack on the Chinese nuclear test site. The memo shows how strongly the notion of quiet cooperation with Moscow had taken root in the administration; it also indicates the depth of the fears of China. The task was assigned to Dean Rusk, who took no action.[48])

On October 16, China exploded its bomb. McNamara, Rusk, and the president all moved to stress that China had no means of delivering its weapon, that its new capability did not change the world balance of power. Within days Nikita Khrushchev was deposed, and a relatively unknown hard-liner, Leonid Brezhnev, took control of the Soviet state as party secretary.

These two enormous events in the Communist world, back to back, could have meant crisis. Johnson's pose of steadfast leadership and restraint worked. The earth did not stand on its head. The underlying public fears of China remained, but the Kennedy advisers, including McNamara, helped steer a course of calm for the moment.[49]

After Johnson's landslide victory of November 3, Roswell Gilpatric, McNamara's former deputy, who had returned to his law firm in New York and sometimes escorted Jacqueline Kennedy to parties, spoke to his onetime boss. Gilpatric recalls advising McNamara that he could now leave office. "He had fought hard for Lyndon," and Lyndon was now elected in his own right. McNamara had discharged his obligation. It was, in effect, advice to make a clear choice to join the Kennedy camp.

Gilpatric remembers that McNamara told him in November 1964 that he couldn't leave office now — he had to see the Vietnam thing through.[50]

15

The Choice of War

A S LYNDON JOHNSON BURST spectacularly
onto the national stage and used the power of the presidency to turn public attention to civil rights and curing
poverty, McNamara handled Vietnam. The secretary of
defense followed every move and mood of the new president.
Johnson cued McNamara, and McNamara nudged Johnson. During
the fateful year of 1964, McNamara became convinced that the United
States must intervene directly in Vietnam.

The key decisions were hidden from public view. Johnson's political theater featured his pushing Congress to pass the civil rights bill
and tax cut. Johnson burned with ambition to be a great domestic
president; all this required keeping Vietnam under control and off-
stage. There was also time that year for McNamara to ask questions
and put alternatives before the president.

Commentators since, looking over the debacle with so many possible lessons, have called 1964 the "lost" year of the war,[1] the last
point at which a major change of course could have been attempted
and was not. Meanwhile, the situation inside South Vietnam grew
steadily worse. The tangible U.S. commitment increased, from
15,000 advisers there in January 1964 to 26,000 by December. By
December 1965 there would be nearly 200,000 U.S. troops in South
Vietnam and a major air war pounding North Vietnam.

Many military commanders also look back on 1964 as a lost opportunity. North Vietnam lacked air defenses, and its army was not

ready for pitched battle in the South. For example, more than twenty years later, a prominent Air Force officer, retired lieutenant general Robert Ginsbergh, told me with assurance that if the United States had attacked the North by air in 1964, "the war could have been over in three to six weeks."[2]

But McNamara foreclosed choice, discouraged discussion, and talked openly with few people, even though, supposedly, he "seeks alternatives like the Holy Grail," says Whiz Kid William Kaufmann, with typical admiration of the man's supposed rationalism.[3] Yet a completely rational man would have sought more widely and deeply for alternatives than McNamara did that year.

Years later, McNamara admitted that "it was a serious failure on the part of the government to avoid facing the choice" between withdrawal or a greater commitment. "It is said by some that the alternative of withdrawal was fully explored and supported by some — and strongly recommended by some. I don't believe the record supports that." Yet on July 28, 1965, after he helped to shape the terms of America's plunge into war, McNamara bragged to reporters, "Not since the Cuban missile crisis has such care been taken in making a decision."[4]

Johnson campaigned on peace and eight months later took the nation into war. As Americans woke up to the depth of military commitment in 1965 and 1966, many who had voted for Johnson felt betrayed. The outrage would grow in June 1971, after President Richard Nixon ordered invasions of Cambodia and Laos and 150,000 U.S. troops fought on in the South. That month, the Pentagon Papers were published by the *New York Times*. A forty-seven-volume classified history of U.S. decisions on Vietnam, based on documents, the Papers had been assembled by order of a sobered Robert McNamara in 1967, searching out lessons from history.

The Pentagon Papers revealed, the *Times* wrote, the extent to which Johnson and his aides "intensified covert warfare against North Vietnam and began planning in the spring of 1964 to wage overt war, a full year before it publicly revealed the depth of its involvement and its fear of defeat," among other things. They showed that McNamara and the Joint Chiefs had been much more deeply involved that year than the defense secretary revealed at the time, or the public had known.[5]

Yet it has been unclear just why and when McNamara nudged the president, and what Johnson's cues were. (The Pentagon Papers' authors had little access to White House files.) The exact roles of other advisers also remain unclear, from Dean Rusk, who did not put his advice on paper, to John McNaughton, McNamara's deputy for Vietnam from April 1964, who left dozens of draft memos on the war, some of which have only lately come to light.

Most of Johnson and McNamara's communication with each other was spoken, on the phone, at meals, or in the White House pool. Johnson would drag his advisers into the bathroom with him and go on talking. McNamara almost never told his staff how his views differed from the president's. One secret of his power was his pretense that almost all the president's decisions were his own as well, even when he had first advised another course.

When and why did McNamara choose war? He was one of the brightest of the Kennedy advisers in sheer intelligence. He was capable of sound judgment; for example, he had the insight to develop the policy of Assured Destruction, which stabilized the U.S.-Soviet nuclear relationship for a generation. Was his choice of war an aberration in his character and career? Or was it inevitable, given his nature?

Although in fourteen months McNamara's plans for action would be fixed and hard, he didn't start that way in November 1963. The weekend of the assassination, he was still the technocrat, pushing the daily paperwork of government during the trauma of Kennedy's death. The Sunday of Kennedy's funeral, no less, McNamara noticed the new " 'President Johnson tone' for action" in South Vietnam.

The phrase was used by CIA director John McCone in his notes of a meeting the president held with his advisers and Henry Cabot Lodge, the ambassador to South Vietnam.[6] Lodge was in Washington to report on events since the coup that ousted and then killed President Ngo Dinh Diem on November 1. Lodge had encouraged the coup.

McNamara found time on Saturday, amid funeral arrangements with the Kennedys, to dictate a memo briefing Johnson for the meeting with Lodge. McNamara said there was too much "backbiting" among U.S. officials in Saigon. The new government was "clearly inexperienced and unsure of its ground." The president "might have to accept putting in more aid than you would theoretically like," he

said. Less than twenty-four hours into Johnson's presidency, Mc-
Namara was sensitive to Johnson's concern that the current budget
deficit was going to cost him votes on Capitol Hill.

McCone took down Johnson's views. "All too often when we
engaged in the affairs of a foreign country we wanted to immediately
transform that country into our image, and this, in [Johnson's] opinion was a mistake." He "was anxious to get along, win the war — he
didn't want as much effort placed on social reforms."

Johnson had met Diem when he visited South Vietnam in 1961 and
had grandiloquently called him "the Winston Churchill of Asia."
Now Johnson "said he was not at all sure that we took the right
course in upsetting the Diem regime."

The White House announced after the meeting that Kennedy's
policies for Vietnam would continue. But some wondered, no doubt,
if this included withdrawal of the U.S. advisers by the end of 1965,
which had been announced on October 2. Would the United States
stay to be sure of winning? Or would it continue to withdraw?
McNamara had a choice.

He took off for Saigon from Paris after December's annual NATO
meeting — but only after the random violence of the age almost killed
him. The "McNamara Special," the Air Force tanker adopted for
globe-trotting trips in McNamara's usual spartan style, was approaching 140 miles per hour on the runway for takeoff when a
passenger plane crossed its path.[7] Pilot Meredith Sutton swerved the
tanker and slammed on the brakes so hard that a tire burst and began
smoking. William Bundy was sitting opposite McNamara; they felt
the plane lurch. McNamara could not see out, and he asked, "How
far do we have to go?" before they would crash. Once the plane
halted, the VIPs were evacuated down a slide and whisked away from
the tinderbox of the fully fueled tanker and its burning tires. They
took off in another plane.

Landing at Tan Son Nhut in the dank December monsoon and
rushing into meetings, McNamara confirmed the grim news reaching
Washington. Diem's reporting system had dissolved with his overthrow. Now the battle reports were disorganized but more candid;
they showed far greater enemy control than before. Strategic hamlets
were overrun or burned.[8]

The hamlets looked like gray ghosts from the air by day. Many
still smoked from the fires lit by the Viet Cong, who now had free
run of the northern Mekong Delta by night.

In fact, the enemy had planned to fight more openly in the provinces west of Saigon, near the border with Cambodia. This "Ap Bac Emulation Drive" had begun months before Diem fell. The Viet Cong harassed and killed South Vietnamese troops and civil officials in the region yet left alone peasants who cooperated. Such selectivity enhanced the Communists' political appeal, while the random cruelty of undisciplined Saigon troops made the government side ripe to be undermined.

McNamara was irritable. He realized how badly General Paul Harkins had deceived him and how false the reports were on which he had based the plan for U.S. advisers to withdraw by the end of 1965 and leave the mopping-up job to the South Vietnamese. When McNamara tried to question a briefing officer closely, Harkins or his deputy interrupted, but McNamara tired of this game. His face red with anger, he snapped, "I asked that Major the question and I want an answer."[9]

He told reporters only that he had come "to make a few checks" to make sure "we are getting maximum efficiency."[10] But privately he informed the president: "Current trends, unless reversed in the next 2–3 months, will lead to neutralization at best and more likely to a Communist-controlled state." The new government "is indecisive and drifting." Big Minh, who led it, and his generals showed "little talent" for "political administration." Viet Cong progress had been "great" since the coup, but McNamara's "best guess" was "that the situation has in fact been deteriorating in the countryside since July to a far greater extent than we realized, because of our undue dependence on distorted Vietnamese reporting."[11]

McNamara revealed to Johnson that he was arranging the "mapping of the whole Laos and Cambodian border . . . on an urgent basis." He and McCone changed the reporting process to get past falsified Vietnamese statistics and Harkins's self-serving ones. So McNamara manipulated the bureaucracy beneath him. Yet his actions were palliatives compared to the problems he now saw. He could have dug deeper, but he did not do so. He was being the compleat technician, smoothing the way, managing, and not asking the big questions.

Nor did he or General Maxwell Taylor, chairman of the Joint Chiefs, discipline Harkins for having misled them. Strong action could have signaled to the men of the line that McNamara valued honesty and needed it. Dwight Eisenhower, after the early failures of the North Africa campaign in World War II, relieved generals who had brought him good news that proved false; the resulting honesty down the line helped the campaign succeed. There is no greater contrast with Ike's open disapproval than the way McNamara ridiculed Harkins but did not remove him.[12] It is said that to get honest reporting during his interminable briefings in Saigon, McNamara would go to the men's room to collar a briefing officer and demand the truth.

The defense secretary took another step, which was to move ahead with a program of covert action against North Vietnam, called Operation Plan 34A. This program was cued by the president, for part of the so-called continuation of the Kennedy approval of planning for "possible increased activity" against the North, but with no publicity and no negative political results.[13] Johnson's tone was not only to get on with the war, but to do so secretly. The 34A raids would play a fateful part in McNamara's deepening involvement in the war.

Years later, McNamara called the 34A raids "very feeble." They consisted of teams of South Vietnamese and Chinese Nationalists dropped above the border to North Vietnam or raiding its coast. They were approved by the secret 303 Committee in Washington and run by Harkins in Saigon. But William Colby, the CIA station chief in Saigon, recalls protesting to McNamara after the actions started that they were useless and wasting lives. McNamara retorted that more 34A raids were needed, not fewer, and he stepped up the program instead.[14] He supported it on the grounds that they could send a signal to Hanoi, that it should watch out, that the South could fight back.

Part of being Johnson's handyman for Vietnam was managing the news. Back in Washington, McNamara told reporters he was "optimistic on the progress to be made in the coming year." But his annual posture statement released weeks later said that the situation in South Vietnam "continues grave."[15]

His flip-flops provoked skeptical stories, for the press had started to doubt his truthfulness during the TFX hearings the previous year. Hedrick Smith, in Saigon for the *New York Times,* reported the charade by which the administration carried out its October 2 promise to withdraw a thousand advisers by December 31 — it did so using normal rotation. The rest were obviously staying on. The administration had "eliminated the announced goal of withdrawing most of them by 1965," Smith wrote. He was right, although McNamara tried to make policy look unchanged by waffling on this point.[16] The withdrawal plan sank like a stone in water, taking down with it some of the defense secretary's shrinking credibility.

Members of Carl Vinson's House Armed Services Committee grilled McNamara closely in late January. Where did he stand? Was he hopeful or not? Were we withdrawing or not? Who was right, the press in Saigon or the administration?

McNamara appeared in the hearing room armed with a thick pack of all his public statements on Vietnam dating back to October 2. "With hindsight I find nothing inconsistent in them," he assured the congressmen, confident as ever.[17] He gave them an exegesis on why he was textually consistent in supporting Diem the previous September, then hinting Diem should reform, and finally, when that worthy did not change, welcoming the generals who eliminated him. McNamara lectured the committee on why the withdrawal announcement of October 2 was still valid. The announcement had a qualifier sentence, which said Washington opposed "repressive actions" by the Diem regime. These could "significantly affect" military operations. If repression continued, then military operations would be affected and the United States would stay, he said. Therefore, the statement that American forces were leaving and the result that they stayed were totally consistent.

He repeated the Kennedy line that the war had to be won or lost by the Vietnamese. Yet his formal statement, the first that he issued under Johnson, asserted that he could "conceive of no alternative but to take all necessary measures within our capability to prevent a Communist victory." Senator Russell Long asked whether, if the war went "very badly," McNamara "contemplate[d] another Korean war . . . our pouring in hundreds of thousands of troops." McNamara dodged the issue by answering a different question: "We have no plans to introduce large numbers, say hundreds of thousands, of U.S. combat troops into that area."[18]

McNamara's key concealment, however, was his private view that the military situation had been deteriorating since July, well before the worst Diem-induced turmoil and before the coup, but in public he said only that the enemy had gained ground since the coup. Thus he concealed that he knew the extent of the enemy momentum. The

North Vietnamese thought in terms of years; McNamara talked in terms of weeks. "I am encouraged by the progress of the last two weeks," he told reporters on January 28.[19]

The right was not happy to be countenancing a little war in Asia led by a man who turned Whiz Kids loose on the defense program, cut the bomber force, and lied in the TFX hearings, in its view, about the reasons for the contract award. In June, Robert Hotz, who was the editor of *Aviation Week* magazine and an influential voice on the right, wrote a scathing attack on McNamara and press aide Arthur Sylvester called "The Credibility Gap."[20] Reporters covering the Pentagon had learned of a McNamara-Sylvester directive that all military information officers were to speak of the TFX/F-111 as a success, when it was well known in military circles that the plane was having serious development problems. Hotz wrote that McNamara's suppression of truth had become "violent and ridiculous." His "optimistic reports" from Vietnam, "regularly contradicted by events," would hurt the country. The secretary was fanning disbelief at a "critical time," when he needed the public's trust to demand "heavier sacrifices in blood and money" from Americans in Southeast Asia.

Just months before, McNamara had been ready to pull U.S. advisers out of South Vietnam by 1965. Yet in early 1964 he now stressed how vital the U.S. stakes were. McNamara's line echoed American leaders — including John Foster Dulles and even Kennedy in late 1963 — who had committed the United States to keep South Vietnam from falling to communism. In the spring and summer of 1964, McNamara believed in this cause with growing intensity. The time was now, the test urgent. He was convinced by early 1964 that he had almost neutralized the nuclear threats to global peace and survival.

There remained the Third World. McNamara talked a lot in 1964 about China's militant approach to its goal of world domination. All year he readied the public for the likely test of China's first atomic weapon. He saw the growing rift between Peking and Moscow not as weakening the Communist menace in underdeveloped lands; instead, he said, the two giants were vying with each other to lead local Communists to victory and humiliate the West.

"No region is more vulnerable and exposed to Communist subversion than Southeast Asia," McNamara said.[21] The orthodoxy of the postwar foreign policy establishment, which had regarded China as a demon ever since it had been "lost" to Mao Tse-tung's Communist forces in 1949, lay heavy upon him. The great beast of the right had pilloried Truman for losing China and driven supposedly pro-Communist China experts from the State Department. Rusk, Dean Acheson, and Lyndon Johnson also believed China was a serious threat. Equally, they imagined an axis between Peking and Hanoi. Ho Chi Minh's roots in Vietnamese nationalism and hatred of the Chinese were unknown to these wise men of 1964. Thus McNamara reasoned: If Lyndon Johnson chose to draw the line in the sand in South Vietnam to demonstrate to China it could not win, so be it.

He spent the spring hardening up policy and reviewing the military's proposals to do the job with air power. A coup on January 30 displaced Big Minh and the group that overthrew Diem. The new leader was a thirty-seven-year-old, French-trained paratrooper, Nguyen Khanh. Johnson sent McNamara and Taylor to Saigon with the message No more coups. The president "wanted to see Khanh on the front pages of the world press with McNamara and Taylor holding up his arms."[22]

So Robert McNamara traded his business suit for khakis. In March, with the photogenic Taylor and the diminutive Khanh in tow, he barnstormed around South Vietnam in a special tour designed by the embassy press aide. He landed at the bigger towns, stood on rough platforms, wore leis draped around his neck. Ostensibly he was selling Khanh and American friendship to the people; he was also getting Johnson the photograph he wanted.

McNamara the campaigner cut an odd figure. He wore a mindless grin; his eyes looked glazed behind the spectacles; his slicked-back long hair was better suited to the lecture halls of Harvard than a countryside of oxen, sampans, and green rice fields. His public stiffness, which lent him authority when he recited the defense budget to Congress, made him out of place in this exotic world. And his tin ear for language when he repeated "Vietnam moun nam," thinking he was telling the crowd "Vietnam a thousand years," was hardly comprehensible to the Vietnamese.[23] Back at the White House, Johnson, who had been considering McNamara as a running mate, noticed the awkward figure on television and concluded that Bob McNamara was no campaigner.

McNamara treated Khanh to a list of actions he wanted taken, as though Khanh were an assistant division chief at Ford. He pressured Khanh to mobilize the young men of his country for war, for he now wanted to strengthen the South for open war against the North.

He came back with a trip report using the firmest language yet of the U.S. commitment; the passage was adopted by the president and advisers as U.S. policy without debate. He argued against attacking North Vietnam "at this time," because Khanh and the South were "an extremely weak base," which could "collapse" under the weight of open war. Also, McNamara knew before he left Washington that the president did not want to receive a recommendation to bomb. The report showed a flicker of realism as to whether they could ever make the Communists back off ("There may be no practical course within the range of our options"). Neutralization and withdrawal were mentioned and rejected. "Even talking about a U.S. withdrawal would undermine any chance of keeping a non-Communist government in South Vietnam," the report said. William Bundy says he worked up the draft of the document before McNamara left for Saigon.[24]

Nowhere in this report did McNamara state that U.S. military power would be other than decisive. He asked "to be in a position on 72 hours' notice" to launch air attacks on the Laos and Cambodia borders. He referred in passing to the idea forming in his mind — they should be ready to launch "retaliatory actions" and "gradual pressures" against the North.

Briefly, McNamara became a prominent spokesman for this firmer commitment and began to prepare the public for military intervention, and to warn Hanoi. On NBC he called Khanh "one of the most active, most aggressive, most imaginative, ablest" leaders of his country; "he is only 37 years old." McNamara gave a major speech to the National Security Industrial Association at Washington's Shoreham Hotel to announce the stronger Johnson line.[25] Explicitness came naturally to him; now he made clear with blinding pseudologic why the uncommitted nations of Africa, Latin America, and Asia would be saved by America's drawing the line in South Vietnam.

South Vietnam, he led off, had a population almost the same size as California's and in area was "slightly larger than England and Wales." The Southeast Asian peninsula, including Burma and the rest, was the size of the United States east of the Mississippi. If these identifications were not enough, in 1954 the country had been a "fledgling Republic" led by an effective leader, Ngo Dinh Diem. Diem carried out agrarian reforms, spread education, and even formed a National Institute of Administration.

But South Vietnam's national "success story" was threatened by a deliberate decision by Communists in Hanoi "to wrest control" from the "legitimate government." The virtuous Diem had asked for President Kennedy's aid. Aid was given, since in 1954 the United States announced it would uphold the Geneva Accords' provision that Indochina would not be interfered with by outside powers; because an "outside power" — Hanoi as the puppet of Peking and Moscow — was interfering with "legitimate" government, the United States had a duty to take action to stop it. This would later be the official justification for U.S. military intervention.

The speech distorted the history of the place; McNamara failed to say that Diem was discovered and installed by the CIA or that Washington had a hand in overthrowing him. Nor that many South Vietnamese saw the Communists as more politically legitimate rulers than the young paratrooper in Saigon. But McNamara and other officials — and many leading academics and citizens — brushed aside the internal nature of Vietnam's long struggle in favor of demonstrating America's will to fight communism in the Third World. Much later, journalist Neil Sheehan surveyed the wreckage of South Vietnam and wrote bitterly that "for its own strategic and political ends, the United States is thus protecting a social structure that . . . perhaps does not deserve to be defended."[26]

Swept up in enthusiasm, McNamara became glib. When a reporter noted that Senate maverick Wayne Morse called the conflict "McNamara's war," the quick tongue shot back: "I don't mind its being called McNamara's war. In fact I'm proud to be associated with it." Bobby Kennedy remarked soon after, "I don't think, incidentally, [that] was very good politics."[27]

McNamara's instinctive assent in giving the war his name was revealing. When he launched the path-breaking TFX project, McNamara made it "his" plane. As he innovated in shaping nuclear forces and strategy, he made these "his" issues. Ordinary Vietnamese hardly would have called it McNamara's war; to them it was a diffuse, long struggle about ideas, politics, class, religion, nationalism, and anti-colonialism. McNamara reached to make it *his* war to control, to win, and meanwhile to take pride in for the success he saw shining in its resolution.

He raised the stakes while thinking he was keeping costs down. He made a telling remark at an April 22 National Security Council meeting. According to the notes, McNamara said they were "right on the margin in Vietnam and he could not guarantee that we would be there in six months or twelve months from now. Therefore we should pour in resources now because of the terrific cost that would be involved if we had to use US forces."[28]

Yet his impatience grew. Khanh did not live up to the billing McNamara had rashly given him. The paratrooper did not mobilize; he dismissed twenty-three of forty-four province chiefs; he did not pay his civil workers in the countryside. He began talking wildly of attacking North Vietnam — just when Johnson wanted Vietnam downplayed. Obediently, McNamara became publicly silent on the subject.

McNamara rushed to Saigon in May to dampen Khanh's inflammatory talk. "Not all of what he heard was encouraging," says one summary. Again, he could have come home with new ideas for a different course. Instead, he made the orders of the president clear. He told General Harkins and his officers not to "hesitate to ask for anything they need." The secretary "gives first priority to winning the war," say the notes of his military aide. McNamara told the press at Tan Son Nhut, "The progress has been marked indeed" since his visit in March. "The progress has been excellent."[29]

He discussed U.S. military action at length in a meeting Johnson ordered in early June in Honolulu, when Laos seemed about to topple. The defense secretary and the commanders reviewed the old Army operations plans, which called for sending up to seven divisions — almost half the U.S. Army — to fight hordes of North Vietnamese and Chinese. "The possibility of major ground action," McNamara said, "also led to a serious question of having to use nuclear weapons at some point."[30] (This mention of nuclear weapons seems a reference to long-standing Army contingency plans for Southeast Asia, which said tactical nuclear weapons would be needed to stop a large Chinese force.) McNamara also examined the growing list of bombing targets in the North and maps of the Ho Chi Minh Trail serving the battlefield, and heard out John McNaughton, now his principal civilian adviser on Vietnam. A solution to the Vietnam problem, an answer to his own impatience, was taking shape in his mind.

On June 2, while McNamara was in Honolulu, Johnson was asked about Congressman Melvin Laird's assertion that the administration planned to move the war to North Vietnam. The president said, "I know of no plans that have been made to that effect."[31]

*   *   *

But in the summer of 1964, McNamara was considering that U.S. air power could dissuade Hanoi, something two presidents had been unable to achieve through their proxy government and military advisers in the field. McNamara could not pay piasters to civil workers in the countryside, but he could send spy planes over Laos and Cambodia to plot the Ho Chi Minh Trail. The photos and maps told him the enemy was building up this network of routes to carry more men and guns south. As McNamara grew frustrated with the human medium of Khanh and his coterie, he turned to technology.

The Joint Chiefs of Staff had been sending proposals for a direct, major air campaign against North Vietnam to the president all year. Chairman Taylor on January 22 proposed to "arm, equip, advise, and support" the South Vietnamese in bombing "critical targets in North Vietnam and mining sea approaches to the country." While U.S. "resources" would be used under South Vietnamese "cover," Taylor added significantly that "additional US forces" would "support" the "combat action."

On February 18 Taylor tried again and sent McNamara a list of actions, which included "punitive" strikes on the North. The chiefs submitted an extended plan on March 2. As a group, they objected to the lack of a bombing recommendation in McNamara's March trip report.[32]

The secretary of defense took a momentous step. In this report he had recommended that the chiefs be allowed to *plan* for air attacks on the North. He presumed he could control the result, although the machinery of planning had its own momentum.

North Vietnam was so rural that at first the air war experts found only eight targets worthy of the name. The planners added roads, more bridges, "choke points," fuel storage tanks, military barracks and bases, and the North's few industries and power stations. Each target was given a number and its own file. By August 1964, the planning process generated not eight, but ninety-four targets. The intelligence assessments used to justify attacking this "target system" argued — illogically — that since the North had so few industrial facilities, its leaders would care more about losing them to bombs. When the Joint Chiefs adopted this line, they violated the first "fundamental factor" for military success of Sun Tzu, the ancient Chinese strategist: To defeat your enemy, you must first understand him.[33]

McNamara found the chiefs' bombing proposals dangerous. A big air campaign against such a vulnerable country could bring North

Vietnam's army across the Demilitarized Zone and could draw in the Chinese, in a Korean War replay. He had other doubts, expressed in a letter thanking the chiefs for an August study of striking all ninety-four targets. What would be the "effects upon the capabilities" of the North to support the war in the South once all ninety-four were hit? "If the destruction of the 94 targets were not to succeed in its objective of destroying the DRV [Democratic Republic of Vietnam, or North Vietnam] will and capability, what courses of action would you recommend?"[34] Harking back to his days as a Statistical Control analyst for air units in World War II, the secretary of defense was skeptical.

The solution forming in his mind to these dangers was a *limited air war*. He believed "appropriately limited attacks on the North would *not* bring in Communist Chinese air or North Vietnam or Communist Chinese ground forces," he had said in June in Honolulu.

In exploring the possibilities for limited air war, McNamara was nimbly aided by McNaughton, the six-foot-four lawyer with a cutting tongue, wit, and the capacity to convince his liberal friends and colleagues that he was a man of genuine compassion and, later, that he hated the war.[35] But McNaughton's staff work for McNamara was uniformly obedient and limited. Because McNamara relied on him virtually alone to staff out his ideas, and because McNamara was faced with military advice he did not trust, McNaughton bore a heavy responsibility for finding real alternatives for the nation.

In the hands of McNaughton, who was a student of the fashionable bargaining and escalation theories of nuclear war and an expert on legal negotiation, a limited air war was made to look attractive, even promising. For example, one plan he wrote out, in May, would use air power based on the "theory" that "we should strike to hurt but not to destroy." He sketched a "scenario" to "D-Day," which had Congress passing a resolution to enable the president to take broad military action, Khanh delivering an ultimatum to Hanoi, Washington issuing a guarantee to protect South Vietnam against counterattack. Then they would, "initially, mine their ports and strike North Vietnam's transport and related ability to move South and then move against targets which have maximum psychological effect." Washington would call a conference and say the attacks would continue until Hanoi came to heel. In this manner McNaughton tossed around the dice of diplomacy and bombs, as though he were in one more negotiation, and not the lone civilian adviser to the

U.S. secretary of defense preparing to spill American blood in war.

Another McNaughton draft, a "Plan of Action for South Vietnam," dated September 3, had a typical profusion of superficially imaginative ideas. McNaughton copied his boss in assuming that "injecting" some "new element" into the situation could make Hanoi do America's bidding soon. Washington would continue U-2 spy plane overflights to "cause apprehension" in Hanoi; then Washington would do "legitimate things to provoke a DRV response and to be in a good position to seize on that response" and launch increasingly harmful strikes. Hanoi would subsequently go for an "explicit settlement," a "tacit settlement," or it could start to seize South Vietnam. But if the situation became "abominable," McNaughton advised that Washington "disown" South Vietnam, "hopefully leaving the image of 'a patient who died despite the extraordinary efforts of a good doctor.' "[36]

McNamara empowered McNaughton, giving him free rein in the bureaucracy. "I remember John striding around the table where everyone was sitting," recalls William Sullivan of the State Department, who was involved in Vietnam planning in 1964. "He waved his arms and talked about Red Flash Points, and Blue Flash Points [moments of escalation in conflict] and PERT flow charts" as real choices for policy. The others listened to him, Sullivan says, because "everyone knew he had the full confidence of the secretary of defense."[37]

Did McNamara believe, with McNaughton, that Red and Blue Flash Points were relevant in the struggle with Hanoi? Did McNamara consider seriously the "scenario" in which Washington launched an air campaign and then walked away from a fallen South Vietnam like a "good doctor"? McNamara has not commented on the relative positions of himself and his aide.

The true significance of McNaughton's bulging files of cynical musings is that in 1964 McNamara was looking for a solution. He had rejected withdrawal and believed that even talking about it was pernicious to the cause. He feared the Joint Chiefs' bombs-away plans would bring on war with China. McNaughton's Red and Blue Flash Points were less important of themselves, except that they offered McNamara the idea — in fact an illusion — that they could fight a new kind of limited war of managed risk. By the middle of 1964, McNamara the idealist was drawn to the notion that he could save the underdeveloped world by facing down China with a limited war that he could control. He began to think he had the answer. Bit by bit, he became a believer in a cause.

Joseph Califano later said of McNamara's fiery crusades and of the Whiz Kids in general: "Very analytic people, in my experience, get very emotional when they think they have found the right answer."[38]

Almost four bloody years later, the Johnson administration was faced with charges that it had plans in the spring of 1964 to go to war. In February 1968, when a suspicious Senator J. William Fulbright posed the question to McNamara and General Earle Wheeler, chairman of the Joint Chiefs, under oath, both men denied it.[39]

> Fulbright [to Wheeler]: Were there . . . recommendations by the U.S. military at any time from late 1963 until July of 1964 to extend the war into the North by bombing or any other means?
> Wheeler: I don't believe so. . . . There was no thought of extending the war into the North in the sense of our participation in such actions.
> Fulbright: [In 1964] was there any plan for such an intensification of U.S. involvement?
> McNamara: No; none that I can recall. . . . and no plan for the bombing of the North.

Both McNamara's and Wheeler's statements appear to be clear falsehoods: There were "plans" for intensification of U.S. involvement and for bombing the North and "to extend the war into the North by bombing or any other means." Indeed, the purpose of the 34A covert raids that took place during 1964 was to extend the war in the South into the North by "other" means. Fulbright remained convinced — as were many in 1971, when the Pentagon Papers revealed several of these plans — that Lyndon Johnson and Robert McNamara had plans ready and took advantage of — and perhaps deliberately provoked — the Tonkin Gulf "attacks" to launch a retaliation, get the resolution through Congress, and be ready for the wider war they "planned."

Twenty years later, to me, McNamara drew a distinction between the planning he allowed to go forward in the military bureaucracy and elsewhere — which he recalled was not organized and lacked focus throughout most of 1964 — and whether he and the president *intended*, or had an agreed plan for, a wider war. His point is valid, as far as it goes, but it does not address the broader issue Fulbright raised, which was that at some stage of military planning, whether there is one "plan" or many, the executive branch is obliged to consult Congress as to whether to engage in conflict.

"I don't believe," McNamara told me, "that the president, or I, or Dean Rusk, or Mac Bundy were planning, in the sense of anticipating or embarking upon 'overt war' with North Vietnam in 1964. I know that the president didn't intend 'overt war' and I didn't intend 'overt war' in 1964. Johnson didn't have plans for military action other than to continue on as we were. That turned out to be a very, very unsatisfactory approach."

As for the many JCS recommendations for an air campaign or the contingency plans for sending U.S. forces and even tactical nuclear weapons, McNamara said that although such studies existed, they were "not an *administration* plan. We didn't have any plan except to do what we were doing, which was very ineffective. We were examining the possibilities, rather than planning."[40]

Suddenly, in August 1964, Hanoi's navy attacked a U.S. destroyer in the Tonkin Gulf.[41] Two days later, Hanoi seemed to strike again. Now the wise men in Washington had two acts of "unprovoked" aggression they could reply to with air power. Reality now followed the secret scenarios locked away in safes and file cabinets. The Tonkin Gulf "attacks" were almost too useful to be true.

McNamara was in Rhode Island escorting Jacqueline Kennedy to Mass on the morning of Sunday, August 2, when he was told that North Vietnamese torpedo boats were firing on a U.S. ship. He flew back to Washington to learn that the destroyer *Maddox* had been sixteen miles off the coast of North Vietnam on a patrol mission, codenamed DeSoto, eavesdropping on enemy communications and checking coastal defenses. Three enemy PT boats had fired torpedoes and machine guns on the ship in broad daylight. The captain called U.S. planes from a nearby carrier to hit the attacking boats in self-defense.

The president considered whether to order the carriers to send their planes to strike the North's mainland in response. But the ambush seemed peculiar: PT boats were no match for a destroyer. Johnson decided not to hit back. McNamara, explaining this restraint to congressional leaders privately on August 3, mentioned that there had been secret raids called 34A on the coast nearby two nights before. He said the North Vietnamese might have thought the destroyer was connected to the raids.

The *Maddox* and another destroyer were ordered back into the gulf and proceeded along the coast on the evening of August 4. "We are not going to yield to pressure," Rusk cabled Maxwell Taylor (who had replaced Lodge as U.S. ambassador) in Saigon.

At nine in the morning of Tuesday, August 4, McNamara was told that a North Vietnamese message had been intercepted by U.S. intelligence giving the coordinates of two "enemy" ships and ordering its own boats to "make ready for military operations."[42] He got on the phone to the theater commander directly below him in the chain of command, Admiral Ulysses Grant Sharp. Sharp commanded all U.S. forces in East Asia, including South Vietnam. His headquarters was a splendid room in a compound near Honolulu, with big maps on the wall, most of them covered in blue. On his desk was a gold-colored phone that was the secure line to his immediate commander, R. S. McNamara. When McNamara first phoned Admiral Sharp, it was five in the morning in Honolulu and inky night in the typhoon-swept Gulf of Tonkin, seven more hours to the west.

There, Captain John J. Herrick, who commanded the hapless mission, sent encoded messages that flickered through relay points back across the Pacific. "Am under continuous torpedo attack." "Torpedoes missed. Another fired at us. Four torpedoes in water. And five torpedoes in water."

In the White House, Lyndon Johnson was heard instructing someone on the other end of the phone, presumably McNamara: "I not only want those patrol boats that attacked the *Maddox* destroyed, I want everything in that harbor destroyed; I want the whole works destroyed. I want to give them a real dose."[43]

In the Tank, at the Pentagon, the target folders were pulled out. The Joint Chiefs helped to pick North Vietnamese facilities that arguably supported the attack. Since the gravest risk was retaliation by China, U.S. forces in the Pacific were alerted and flexed, just in case the U.S. air strikes would plunge them into a wider war, perhaps within hours.

The uneven mix of analyst and man of action in McNamara determined what happened next, although Johnson's insistence on a hard punchback played a commanding part. The long day of Tuesday, August 4, in Washington was a long night of horror for Captain Herrick and his men. The seas were rough; there was no moon. Lightning storms and mists confused human vision. As the two bulky ships lashed in fast turns to avoid torpedoes, their sonar screens filled with more and more blips, signifying more torpedoes. The young sonarman on the *Maddox* was almost panicked, yelling coordinates as the gunman above fired into the dark, flashing sea.[44]

In Washington, Honolulu, and the east Pacific, the armed forces of a great power lumbered into place to be ready to receive the order to attack North Vietnam for the first time. McNamara managed the preparations through the day, shuttling between the Pentagon and the White House, as he had done in the Cuban missile crisis. The president was unable to resist the chance for dramatic television. It would help to persuade Congress to pass a resolution he had drafted authorizing him to use military force in Southeast Asia. The White House press was told that the president would speak live in prime time.

Captain Herrick now doubted whether the attack had been real. Electrical effects in tropical seas and sharp boat turns, he knew, can cause false sonar signals. His men had seen things, but, he said, it was a "completely dark, and inky black night"; they should wait until daylight to search for debris. Herrick encrypted another cable, which flickered to Honolulu and Washington: "Review of action makes many reported contacts and torpedoes fired appear doubtful. Freak weather effects ON RADAR and overeager sonarmen may have accounted for many reports. No actual visual sightings by *Maddox*. Suggest complete evaluation before any further action taken."[45]

That night, while Johnson and the curious White House press waited, McNamara tried frantically to get Admiral Sharp to confirm the attack. He told Sharp he wanted to be "damned sure what happened"; McNamara needed firm proof before he could advise the president to give the order for the air attack.

The pressure on Admiral Sharp was monumental. His gold phone rang constantly with McNamara barking at the other end. McNamara gave him two hours to determine whether the attack had happened. Meanwhile, two of Sharp's aircraft carriers maneuvered into position in rough seas to be ready to launch the strikes at Hanoi's dawn, hours away, when the order came. Sharp was receiving floods of unconfirmed data from different sources; Captain Herrick was thousands of miles from him, linked to the chain of command through the crude encoding machine on board the *Maddox*.

Sharp tried. He had reports of sightings and the sonarman's reports. He had an intercepted enemy message that referred to a sea battle.[46] He phoned McNamara at 6:07 P.M., Washington time, precisely on McNamara's deadline, and said, "I'm satisfied myself."

McNamara recommended the air strikes, and the president issued the order right away.

Reality foiled McNamara's plans again: The jammed communications system in the Pacific could not reach the carriers. He now waited for confirmation that the aircraft had been launched. Once Johnson spoke on television, the planes would lose the element of surprise and the pilots would be in danger.[47]

McNamara began calling Sharp incessantly to ask if both carriers' planes had taken off. At 11:20 Washington time, Sharp told him they had. Johnson stepped before the television cameras at 11:37 and told the nation that "renewed hostile actions" were the reason that air action against selected targets was now under way.

McNamara gave no hint that there had been any doubt the second enemy attack had occurred, or of how "increasingly ambiguous the reports . . . became as the hours move[d] on," in the words of Senate investigators two years later.[48] He displayed utter certainty. At the time, he was utterly believed. On Friday morning, August 7, Congress, outraged by an enemy so irrational as to attack two times, passed the Southeast Asia resolution, better known as the Tonkin Gulf resolution, ceding to the president its power to make war in that region.

As the United States struck North Vietnam for the first time, Johnson had used the hot line to Moscow to signal that U.S. air strikes meant no wider war. The forces in the Pacific had been put on alert to deter China from stepping in to help Hanoi. McNamara's idea that they could wage a limited air war on North Vietnam without bringing in China seemed confirmed.

What McNamara remembered later of these events was his search for proof. The first attack "seemed such an absurd action that we wanted to be very careful in obtaining the facts." Before he concluded that the first attack occurred, McNamara said, "we actually received statements that pieces of metal that were part of a North Vietnamese shell had been recovered from the deck of our vessel." As for the second attack, he remembered also being "very skeptical" and calling Admiral Sharp to find out what happened. "I certainly was not trying to find an excuse to go to war."[49]

His memory of Johnson's intention regarding the Southeast Asia resolution is important, and it is shared by William Bundy, among others. Johnson, McNamara says, "thought that he might have to escalate and he wanted the Congress in the act. That was the purpose of the resolution. It was never intended as a broad authority to go to war, but rather as authority to carry out additional military action."

Once the Tonkin Gulf resolution passed, McNamara, the president, and the other advisers became publicly silent on Vietnam once again. Secretly, Admiral Sharp pushed hard for keeping up the momentum and continuing air attacks. McGeorge Bundy proposed a "hard look" at the "drastic possibility" of using "substantial US armed forces . . . against the Viet Cong." But he said McNamara was "very strongly against" even landing any Marines. Johnson, campaigning in Texarkana, Texas, criticized those "who want to go north." He said, "We are not going to start another war, and we are not going to run away from where we are." Limited bombing became the topic of the moment in the inner circle, although one of the Whiz Kids saw the flaws in the prevailing logic, warning that the bombing "might well fail to be effective short of a larger US military involvement." Nonetheless, through spreading self-hypnosis, the image of a short, antiseptic war was taking hold.[50]

After the Tonkin Gulf episode, Johnson had asked how they could "take" the "ball" with "maximum results and minimum danger." One result was that in September the DeSoto patrol was sent back into the Gulf of Tonkin, once again in international waters, and once again as live bait. During the morning of September 18, 1964, messages flashed from the far Pacific signaling an attack on the ship. Behind the scenes, McNamara questioned the evidence sharply. The president decided they were not sure there had been an attack. Perhaps lightning, currents, and darkness had confused the crew.

The press had heard reports of a new provocation at sea on September 18. McNamara first cut short an ongoing news conference that day, then canceled a speaking appearance. The next day he rushed into the Pentagon briefing room in a gold sport coat, read a mild statement, and ran out again in less than a minute.[51] There would be no retaliation. In fact, they were waiting for a clearer chance.

On October 5, McNamara was told that Benjamin Read of the Department of State wished to see him in person. Read handed McNamara an envelope. Inside was a cover letter from Under Secretary of State George Ball and a thick document.[52] "I am enclosing my scep-

tical thoughts on the assumptions of our Viet-Nam policy," Ball's
cover letter said. It said five copies of the memorandum existed: one
each for McNamara, Rusk, and McGeorge Bundy, and two for Ball's
safe. McNamara knew that Ball was a passionate believer in European
unification and the multilateral force and had long been critical of any
deeper U.S. involvement in South Vietnam.

When he sat down with Ball's sixty-seven-page handiwork, Mc-
Namara read: "Within the next few weeks, we must face a major
decision of national policy." Since the Saigon government was crumbling, Washington could let itself be forced out of South Vietnam. Or
it could take over the war with "substantial U.S. ground forces" or
bomb the North to "improve our bargaining position." Their fourth
option — the one Ball clearly favored — was to get a political settlement without further U.S. military involvement.

Ball conceded that South Vietnam was "of considerable strategic
value" to the United States. But the "primary motive" behind U.S.
policy was "political . . . to make clear to the whole Free World that
we will assist any nation that asks us for our help in defending itself
against Communist aggression." Moreover, the case for defending
South Vietnam was not clear-cut, as was the U.S. intervention to save
South Korea. Ball asked: "Should we move toward escalation because
of the weakness of the governmental base in Saigon?" He urged that
they now "undertake a rigorous balancing of accounts" to measure
the "costs that might result from the widening of the war" against
"the costs of a carefully devised course of action designed to lead to
a political solution under the best conditions obtainable."

Ball argued that an air campaign against the North, which the
other advisers increasingly looked to as a way of bettering the U.S.-
Saigon position, would not improve the cohesion or effectiveness of
the South Vietnamese "unless it was followed by the fact — or even
the promise — of a military invasion of North Viet-Nam [sic]." As to
whether air attacks would reduce the ability of the North to wage war
in the South, Ball's paper was the only high-level document to cite
the "Sigma II" war games played in the Pentagon in September (in
which McNaughton participated, but not McNamara). The Sigma
games had shown that Hanoi could fight on even if the entire target
list was hit. Ball knew that most top military and civilian leaders had
ignored the ominous results of these games. But his main point was
that since bombing would have little military effect and would not
benefit the South's performance either, it would not improve U.S.

leverage in a political settlement and therefore should not be undertaken.

Moreover, Ball predicted that Hanoi's reaction to an American air campaign would be to escalate the fighting in the South through more infiltration or an outright invasion. "Each party would choose to fight the kind of war best adapted to its resources," he warned. "The North Vietnamese would be clearly tempted to retaliate by using ground forces, which they possess in overwhelming numbers." This would cause the United States to commit land forces. U.S. troops would bog down in a ground war, which was George Ball's nightmare, since he had seen the French disaster in Indochina as an adviser to Paris in the 1950s. "We would find ourselves in *la guerre sale* with consequent heavy loss of American lives in the rice paddies and jungles."

China's "substantial interests . . . would be jeopardized" by U.S. air strikes. China would need to avoid the "loss of face" of not aiding a Communist neighbor under attack. And Hanoi was supporting Peking in the Sino-Soviet dispute. China might come in to "safeguard its own security," which would be "menaced" by U.S. military action in Southeast Asia, and to protect the rail line linking Kwangtung with the inland province of Yunnan, through North Vietnam.

Ball cautioned that there was "a *fair chance* that China would intervene [Ball's italics]." He added that Douglas MacArthur and President Truman had discounted the chances of China's entering the Korean conflict, to their later regret when Chinese troops crossed the Yalu.

The United States would thereafter not be able "to control the process of escalation." Ball wrote:

> It is in the nature of escalation that each move passes the option to the other side, while at the same time the party which seems to be losing will be tempted to keep raising the ante. . . . Once on the tiger's back, we cannot be sure of picking the place to dismount."

Through escalation, America would be deploying "substantial U.S. land forces" and creating a totally different relationship to the war as U.S. casualties mounted. It would put itself in the former position of the French, "with all the disastrous political connotations of such a posture."

Thus the United States would be stalemated against North Vietnamese and Chinese forces.

At this point, we should certainly expect mounting pressure for the use of at least tactical nuclear weapons. The American people would not again accept the frustrations and anxieties that resulted from our abstention from nuclear combat in Korea. . . .

Our employment of the first tactical nuclear weapon would inevitably be met by a Communist accusation that we use nuclear weapons only against yellow men (or colored men). . . . There would be a profound shock around the world . . . among nonwhite nations on every continent. . . .

At the same time our action would liberate the Soviet Union from inhibitions that world sentiment has imposed on it. It would upset the fragile balance of terror on which much of the world has come to depend for the maintenance of peace. Whether or not the Soviet Union actually used nuclear weapons against other nations, the very fact that we had provided a justification for their use would create a new wave of fear.

The consequences of all this cannot be overstated. . . . Prospects for disarmament and other measures for lowering the general level of world anxiety would be destroyed. . . . The first firing of a nuclear weapon (whether tactical or strategic, it makes no difference) would revive a real but latent guilt sense in many Americans. . . . While no one can be certain, the best judgment is that the Soviet Union could not sit by and let nuclear weapons be used against China.

Ball followed these scenarios with a section arguing that U.S. military intervention, instead of increasing U.S. credibility and prestige with allies and other free nations, could cause instead the lowering of "confidence in American judgment." Obviously influenced by his French colleagues' intense criticism of the American involvement to that date, he claimed that U.S. allies believe "we are engaged in a fruitless struggle . . . we are bound to lose." Asian neighbors would be lukewarm, while other, less developed countries would "strongly oppose" an air offensive. In Europe, "our influence depends not merely on the defense efforts we are making, but on European confidence in our judgment and restraint."

The final section of Ball's memo proposed his "political solution": Washington should renew its policy of preconditioning U.S. aid on South Vietnamese performance and "desire" for U.S. help. To the extent the South Vietnamese did not perform — as seemed likely — the United States could build a "juridical and political basis" for leveling off American effort, and for withdrawing if "the Vietnamese people . . . no longer desire our help." The threat of a U.S. departure could make the government more responsible, or it could hasten the trend to neutralism. ("We would almost certainly accelerate existing covert probing of the possibilities of a deal with Viet Cong elements," he said. Among various "settlements," Ball clearly countenanced "a government largely dominated by Communists" or a neutral regime, as in Laos, while the Communists held sway in the countryside.

Original to the end, Ball's lengthy memo flouted the "domino theory," which dominated the imaginations of McNamara and many others. At many points in this argument he warned starkly of the menace of Peking and subscribed to the notion of a Peking-Hanoi axis, but he seemed sanguine about letting South Vietnam go neutral or Communist, although he did not address the point directly. He noted, for example, that Thailand would need more American support and that Malaysia could be a problem. But Burma, Cambodia, and Indonesia — which others regarded as dominoes likely to topple once the reds controlled the South — "would no doubt be happier with a political solution out of a simple desire to see the 'mess' in South Vietnam disappear."

"McNamara, in particular, was absolutely horrified" by the memo, Ball said later. "He treated it like a poisonous snake." Ball found that "Rusk and Bundy were more tolerant . . . than Bob was. He really just regarded it as next to treason, that this had been put on paper."[53]

The meeting that Ball sought to vet his idea and decide whether the paper should be shown to Lyndon Johnson did not occur until almost a month after McNamara received his memo, November 7. McNamara, Rusk, and Bundy met with Ball that afternoon, a Saturday. Ball hoped for serious discussion. He was ready to give the paper to the president if any of these three more powerful men showed interest. But the discussion went nowhere. A second meeting Ball hoped to have on the matter was never held.

As for Lyndon Johnson, all he knew of Ball's warning came from a leak to Joseph Alsop, who reported the existence, although not the substance, of Ball's dissent. Johnson was as furious at the leak as McNamara had been with Ball for writing down his views.[54]

* * *

Why was McNamara so rude to Ball? Why did he commit a worse crime than rudeness, which was to push away from him the substance of Ball's warning, as though it were "a poisonous snake"? McNamara's rebuff that fateful Saturday meeting on November 7 was, in a sense, the climax of his year-long evolution on Vietnam. Just over twelve months before, he had been busily organizing the phased withdrawal of U.S. advisers to wind down American involvement, until the deaths of Ngo Dinh Diem and John Kennedy in November 1963 had scotched that plan. McNamara then obeyed Lyndon Johnson's "tone" for "action" in the shooting war; Johnson had made clear that he could not afford to lose South Vietnam to the Communists, so McNamara had deftly managed a backdoor effort to hold on to it — and with minimal publicity, in keeping with the president's wish. The result was a cascade of plans and covert action, but no firm policy. As McNamara grew frustrated (and he would later remember his impatience with the lack of clear policy), he was reluctantly planning stronger action with McNaughton and McGeorge Bundy, working up an active answer to a problem. He was following his deep personal instincts for activism and, unwittingly, the very management advice he liked to recite to others: Any action is better than no action; it is better to make a wrong decision than no decision at all. The curious analyst in McNamara who sought alternatives was hardening into the driven man of action.

Now here came Ball, whose paper, on its face, defied two key assumptions McNamara held dearly. As he read closely the final recommendations of Ball's long memorandum, it was clear that Ball was willing to let South Vietnam gradually turn Communist — although the memo didn't quite say so. And Ball seemed sanguine about the consequences for the region, even though he accepted the conventional wisdom of the menace of Peking.[55] This flew in the face of McNamara's own dark fears of China as well as Johnson's instruction to McNamara that he not lose South Vietnam, not doom Lyndon Johnson to a political fate like Harry Truman's when he had lost China in 1949 and thereby kill not just the Great Society but the greatness of LBJ.

Ball also flouted another premise that McNamara had come to believe by November 1964. "Once on the tiger's back, we cannot be sure of picking the place to dismount," he had written, and then proceeded to outline several lurid, Korea-like scenarios: First, Washington would send large numbers of ground forces. (Ball would later argue it would go to half a million, and McNamara would tell him that he was crazy, that using such a number in the discussion was "dirty pool."[56]) Then the Chinese would cross the DMZ. The war would stalemate, the public become restless, and he, Bob McNamara, would then face pressure from the U.S. public to use nuclear weapons on the battlefield to break the deadlock. It seemed preposterous, because McNaughton had been outlining to McNamara a much more fine-tuned campaign, an air campaign of controlled risks.

McNamara had been through his own epiphany about the value of nuclear weapons by November 1964; he had long since resolved never to recommend that a U.S. president initiate their use. The use of tactical nuclear weapons first in combat, in Europe, had been studied extensively; and at Honolulu in June, he had reviewed the Army's old contingency plans, dating back to the 1950s (and in reaction to the Korean stalemate), which called for their use. By November he was sure he would never let Ball's scenario happen.

So McNamara, riled at these affronts and now confident he had the answer, sloughed off Ball's paper — not just those two clear weak points, but the points made that later would show Ball had understood how intervention could cause America to weaken its position with allies and friends, and how its supposed military advantages could be nullified by the other side. Yet these arguments also seemed so limited, because they clearly drew on the French humiliation, that Bob McNamara thought he could afford to dismiss them, too.

"I never got the impression McNamara was particularly . . . impressed by the French parallel, which was of course a great part of George's argument," says William Bundy. "I don't recall Bob's being that impressed by people saying, 'This is how this nation has behaved historically.' He is very much a doer and a builder. And arguments that this is the way we've always done it, at Ford I am sure, practically made him show the door to whoever was saying it."[57]

The president gave steady cues that he was moving toward stronger action as the situation in South Vietnam deteriorated. On November 1 he cabled Ambassador Taylor in Saigon, asking if U.S. "air and ground units" should be sent to South Vietnam to protect American citizens. Taylor was "greatly surprised that the offer of ground troops was made so casually" by the president. He did not want them.[58]

Then on November 1 the Viet Cong staged a powerful attack on the American air base at Bien Hoa, a deliberate slap in the face of the giant. The Joint Chiefs urged quick retaliation, but now Johnson demurred. After his landslide victory, the chiefs tried again. They pressed hard for a "sharp knock" air attack on the entire ninety-four-target list. The enemy was sending troops southward. The time to strike was now. Admiral Lloyd Mustin tried hard to convince the civilians that a war could be short and decisive if it was undertaken with great force, hitting all the targets, bombing the infiltration trails in Laos, mining the ports. Meanwhile, civilians in the Office of the Secretary of Defense disagreed. McNaughton peddled his flash points and signals; Ball urged avoiding a military commitment.

Over at the Building on the other side of the Potomac, Joseph Califano recalls a "feeling" that the subject of possible war became very secret and therefore serious. One of the Whiz Kids working for Enthoven, going over the next year's budget, noticed the amounts for ammunition were up.[59]

Johnson behaved in contradictory ways. He said on December 1 that stable government in South Vietnam was a prerequisite for direct U.S. action. The same day he approved Barrel Roll, the secret bombing of the trails in Laos. This decision flowed from his obsession with secrecy. The press was not in Laos, and the planes were based off-stage, in Thailand. So reporters in Saigon would never know about the bombing. They found out in January, in fact, when one of the planes crashed and the wreckage came to light. Johnson also agreed "in principle" that, at a later stage, they should move to "Phase II," in which they would bomb North Vietnam. "Day of reckoning coming," the president said ominously.[60]

He sent another startling cable to Taylor in Saigon. Every recommendation he got, Johnson complained, called for "large scale bombing. I have never felt that this war will be won from the air." What was needed "is a larger and stronger use of Rangers and Special Forces and Marines, or other appropriate military strength on the ground and on the scene. *I am ready to look with great favor on that kind of increased American effort* [italics added]."

Taylor protested. In his months as ambassador, he had become a convert to striking the North with bombs to avoid bogging the Army down in jungles and rice paddies. The support for bombing, coming from so famous a military man as Taylor, carried weight with the president.

McNamara's impatience won. In January 1965 he made his choice a matter of record when he associated himself with a brief, pivotal memo McGeorge Bundy sent to the president on January 27.

As national security adviser, Bundy hitherto had limited his role to that of gatekeeper, seeing that views and paper flowed to the president as needed. Now Bundy injected his own strong views into Johnson's mind, in the name of McNamara and himself. They were a powerful combination, these two Harvard men, veterans of Berlin and Cuba and friends of the Kennedys'. Now they told Johnson what course they preferred.

They asked for a meeting with the president the same morning the memo was delivered for "a very private discussion."

> Both of us are now pretty well convinced that our current policy can lead only to disastrous defeat. What we are doing now, essentially, is to wait and hope for a stable government. Our December directives make it very plain that wider action against the Communists will not take place unless we can get such a government. . . . Bob and I are persuaded that there is no real hope of success . . . unless and until our own policy and priorities change.

In South Vietnam, Bundy and McNamara told Johnson,

> our best friends have been somewhat discouraged by our own inactivity in the face of major attacks on our own installations. The Vietnamese . . . see the enormous power of the United States withheld. . . . They feel we are unwilling to take serious risks. . . .
>
> We see two alternatives. The *first* is to use our military power in the Far East and to force a change in Communist policy. The *second* is to deploy all our resources along a track of negotiation. . . .
>
> Bob and I tend to favor the first course, but we believe that both should be carefully studied and that alternative programs should be argued out before you.
>
> Both of us understand the very grave questions presented by any decision of this sort. . . . But we are both convinced . . . that the time has come for harder choices. . . .
>
> McNamara and I have reached the point where our obligations to you simply do not permit us to administer our present directives in silence and let you think we see real hope in them.
>
> McG. B.[61]

In January 1965, McNamara was at the peak of his power and influence: a veteran of two nuclear crises, a potential vice president or president. He had experienced no serious failures, in his own mind or in that of Lyndon Johnson. It is hard to understate the weight of his record and sheer force of personality in that fateful meeting with the president.

After twenty-seven years of public silence, private soul-searching, denials, and bitter reminders, McNamara offered a view of his mistakes of 1964 and 1965:

"It is very difficult for anyone to examine his own failures, particularly when they are very painful to think about," he told me. "The greatest failure of all was Vietnam . . . at the start of the Kennedy-Johnson administrations' engagement in Vietnam, we surely did not foresee that it would turn out as it did. We failed in that sense.

"We misjudged Chinese geopolitical objectives. If you read what Lin Piao [China's defense minister] said, China sounded like a terrible threat. If you saw what the Chinese did in Indonesia and you saw the support they were giving North Vietnam, they appeared to be a threat. But I now question whether the Chinese leadership had as their objective achieving hegemony in Asia. At the time, however, we assumed that this was their objective.

"The misjudgment of China was a serious error, one of many. We misjudged as well the capability of the South Vietnamese to maintain a government that was independent of North Vietnam.

"We — and I would say our society — were captives of a view of the Soviet Union which I think was either incorrect or at least only partly correct. We believed we were containing an expansionary communist force."

McNamara then tried to comment on the fateful memo of January 27, poring over the brief text for some sign of the doubts that, after twenty-seven years, loomed large in his memory of his state of mind as he plunged toward war.

He recalled that he "joined with" Bundy in writing the memo and denied that Johnson cued them to recommend military action that morning. McNamara composed this sentence: "It was difficult to support any one of the three options considered but a choice had to be made."[62]

16

Intervention and Promise

MCNAMARA, wrapped in the illusion of American power, committed himself to a military solution in Vietnam on January 27, 1965, when he let McGeorge Bundy's memo, urging the president to unleash "our military power in the Far East and to force a change in Communist policy," speak for him.

When the two men met with the president from eleven to twelve-fifteen, Johnson told them: "Stable government or no stable government [in Saigon], we'll do what we ought to do. . . . We will move strongly." Thus he abandoned the previous policy, that Washington would wait for a viable government before taking military action.

Johnson directed that U.S. dependents leave South Vietnam. He ordered another DeSoto patrol into the Gulf of Tonkin; U.S. forces in the Pacific were to be put on alert to be ready to strike back if the patrol was attacked.

The president also decided to send McGeorge Bundy to South Vietnam.[1] The press noted that Bundy's trip, his first to South Vietnam, could signal a change in policy. Bundy took along John McNaughton, McNamara's aide.

The standard picture has been that the Kennedy advisers pushed a "reluctant" Johnson into war. But Bundy's aide Chester Cooper says of the trip: "The problem was that Johnson had already made up his mind. For all practical purposes he had dismissed the option of de-escalating and getting out, but he didn't want to say that he had, and

so the rationale for this trip was that this was going to be decisive."
But "he damn well had decided already what he was going to do."[2]

McNamara by late January was tortured by the inconclusiveness of
American policy. His impatience shows in notes McNaughton made
on a "Draft" he prepared for a twenty-five-minute meeting with Mc-
Namara at seven forty-five on the morning of January 27. McNaughton listed three courses for Washington in light of the "deteriorating"
situation in South Vietnam. Where McNaughton wrote "Striking the
DRV might, but probably won't" help, McNamara disagreed and said
air strikes could "help the actual situation."[3] Inaction was McNamara's enemy that morning, or so he imagined. His cure for "drifting"
would be the most politically fine-tuned bombing campaign in U.S.
history, against a real enemy who was immune to it.

On the afternoon of Saturday, February 6, in Washington, a message
ticked into the Pentagon's National Message Center that an American
barracks at Pleiku, in the heart of the highlands of South Vietnam,
had been blown up. Eight Americans had been killed and more than
sixty wounded. The event shook Bundy, the detached rationalist, and
crystallized his feeling that Washington had to demonstrate its commitment by military action. He urged that they hit back.[4] Johnson
convened the National Security Council at seven forty-five Saturday
night at the White House. All, including McNamara, voted for a
limited reprisal on similar targets in North Vietnam.

Forty-nine American planes roared off carriers and landing strips
to bomb and strafe a barracks above the DMZ at Dong Hoi in an
operation called Flaming Dart. McNamara and Ball met reporters in
the Pentagon press room armed with photographs of wrecked helicopters at Pleiku.

In his staccato manner, McNamara waved his pointer over the
maps and unfamiliar Asian names. The part in his hair was narrow
and straight, like the contrails of the jets venting official anger ten
thousand miles away. One purpose of the briefing was to tell the
enemy that presidential policy had shifted. "I wouldn't wish to char-
acterize this as a tit-for-tat raid," McNamara said to Hanoi through
the cameras. "It is a clear and necessary response to a test and a
challenge of [our] will and purpose and policy. We wish to emphasize
we seek no wider war. . . . The key to the situation remains the
cessation of infiltration from the North into the South."[5]

A "test and a challenge" by Hanoi? Reporters were skeptical. *New*

York Times reporter Charles Mohr wrote that if, as the administration said, the size and intensity of the attack were directed by Hanoi, why was the raid carried out by a mere company of local guerrillas? "This is not a large Vietcong assault. Many are much larger," Mohr wrote. He proposed that the Pleiku attack took place not due to specific Hanoi direction, but due to the failure of the South Vietnamese to guard the base. Mohr also asked why all three attack carriers of the Seventh Fleet had been within striking distance of North Vietnam at the time, when the fleet was normally dispersed. The press, reading such tea leaves, concluded that the administration had had something bigger in mind, well before Pleiku.[6]

On February 10, the Viet Cong obliged with a second attack on a base for U.S. military advisers, at Qui Nhon. The president met with the National Security Council for three and a half hours. McNamara, with Admiral David L. McDonald, chief of naval operations, at his elbow, urged a retaliatory strike on related targets in North Vietnam. Flaming Dart II hit the skies immediately. The White House hinted that future attacks might not be tied to specific enemy outrages in the South. They were moving — to McNamara's relief — to the so-called Phase II of more regular air "pressures" that the president had approved "in principle" on December 1, 1964.

The enemy was given a signal of a wider war, but Americans were not supposed to hear it too plainly. The Eighty-ninth Congress convened in the Capitol on January 4. It included many new Democrats elected on the coattails of Johnson's November victory. Lyndon Johnson had big plans for "his" Congress. He sent it five special messages even before his State of the Union address, in January. By April he had submitted more than two hundred bills, from voting rights for blacks to Medicare and higher education, and was working frantically to get them passed. The deficit reached a new low; the economy reached a new high. In February, while the war planners debated bombing targets in secret, Johnson persuaded the Senate to vote more than a billion dollars to help fight poverty in Appalachia, a harbinger of votes to come.

Ironically, the document revealing McNamara's motives and plans for an air campaign against North Vietnam was McGeorge Bundy's trip report, dated February 7 and partly drafted by McNaughton.[7] Summarizing McNamara's evolution on the war over the previous year, it foreshadowed how he would justify the air war.

Bundy's report urged that the United States launch "sustained reprisal" air attacks against North Vietnam, which would be "justified by and related to the whole Viet Cong campaign" in the South. The administration would make it clear that the bombing was not aimed at destroying North Vietnam as a sovereign state, but at preventing Peking and Moscow from jumping in to save Hanoi. Washington would offer relief from the "pain" of the bombing in proportion to Hanoi's de-escalation of the war in the South.

Bundy argued that "pain" inflicted from the air could induce Hanoi to hold back in South Vietnam. As the enemy lowered its attacks, Saigon's forces could make military progress. Morale would be lifted, and the "effectiveness" of the Saigon regime would increase. Echoing his and McNamara's January 27 assumption that U.S. military action could influence South Vietnamese behavior, Bundy said that as the South Vietnamese saw how the bombing helped them, they would defer more to U.S. advice. Thus an air campaign could end the indecisiveness of the war for Washington, even if the fighting dragged on for some time at lower levels.

Bundy proposed they move into this bombing campaign with great subtlety and rationality. He said that at first they should hit the North after "the assassination of a province chief" in the South, "but not necessarily" after "the murder of a hamlet official"; after a "grenade" was thrown into a "crowded cafe in Saigon," but not due to a "shot into a small shop in the countryside." Then they would move up to "sustained" air attacks to "correspond" to the "level of outrages in the South." Meanwhile, Washington would keep offering to reduce or stop the bombing "when outrages in the South are reduced or stopped."

Bundy stressed that he was not urging that they "wage offensive war." He said, "The object would not be to 'win' an air war against Hanoi, but rather to influence the course of the struggle in the South." There is no more succinct definition than this of McNamara's aims in Rolling Thunder, the name of the bombing campaign based on Bundy's report that the president approved right away.

Rolling Thunder derived, clearly, from the intellectual theories of signaling and bargaining among adversaries in nuclear war and of ladders of escalation and de-escalation that had guided McNamara out of the nightmare of massive retaliation in 1961–62. But in February 1965, these crisis managers did not notice how different Ho Chi Minh's situation was from Khrushchev's. The Soviet leader had agreed to take the missiles out of Cuba because he had feared nuclear war that would roll "through cities and villages, everywhere sowing death and destruction."[8] Ho Chi Minh, by contrast, could fight on despite almost any gradations of pain. And if Washington seemed to be edging toward total war, Ho could threaten total war in return by calling on his backers in Moscow and Peking.

McNamara may have imagined the bombing campaign as a balance sheet, with the number of enemy targets hit in one column and measures of enemy activity in the South on the other. Bundy's report even proposed a yardstick: They could publish "weekly lists of outrages" in the South corresponding to the level of "pain" inflicted in the North.

McNamara confirms that his goal was political. "I had been an Army Air Force's officer during World War II, and I knew something about bombing. I never did believe bombing could win wars. And I didn't believe bombing could stop infiltration or destroy the war-making capacity of North Vietnam.

"I did not believe it was likely we could win a military victory. I did believe that the military action should be used as a prod towards moving to a political track: to increase the chance of initiating or achieving movement on the political track."[9]

McNamara now had what he needed: a plan for quick action that offered hope of changing Hanoi's mind soon. The plan required that he and the president keep control of the action. He had a set of mechanical images — a ratchet moved up and down, a spigot turned on and off — to describe what he was doing. Clearly the plan resembled counterforce–no cities, his first strategy for fighting nuclear war. Both were based on limited attacks and the threat of greater pain; both required masterminding by the secretary of defense and the president. Both presumed an enemy would react rationally to the other side's power to hurt. Finally, for McNamara, both performed the same emotional function, of keeping the random brutality and chaos of war at a distance.[10]

Lyndon Johnson liked the plan, too. On February 13 he secretly approved it as "a program of limited and measured air action against selected military targets," which would gradually escalate. "Sustained reprisal" was much more than a rationalist fantasy, as far as the president was concerned. It answered several practical problems. Johnson did not want war with the Soviet Union or China; he believed U.S. military strikes on the enemy could shuffle the cards in

America's favor; he needed to control the publicity from a wider war to manage his relations with Congress. It is questionable whether Robert McNamara would have recommended a bombing campaign that he did not control minutely, given his misgivings about air power and his nature. As for Lyndon Johnson, this campaign offered a chance to wield military force — a president's highest duty and test — as domestic and geopolitical theater.

Did McNamara push Johnson again? After February 13, the president may have hesitated. Bundy wrote Johnson on February 16, "Bob McNamara repeatedly stated that he simply has to know what the policy is, so that he can make his military plans and give his military orders. . . . It seems essential to McNamara . . . that there be an absolutely firm and clear internal direction of the U.S. Government."[11] Rolling Thunder began on March 2, delayed by Nguyen Khanh's resignation in Saigon.

Whether or not McNamara and Bundy pushed him, Johnson was not displeased, as recently released meeting notes by Bundy illustrate. "Where are we going?" Johnson asked in his typically sweeping way after three weeks of bombing. McNamara said, "Our message may be getting thru," in Bundy's notes. Bundy recorded Johnson saying: "Do they know we're willing to talk. You can revisit targets. I dont wanna run out of targets + I dont wanna go to Hanoi. I was a hell of a long time gettin into this. But I like it."[12]

Two things then happened, presenting McNamara with a new choice. The first was that nothing happened: Hanoi gave no sign it would pull back in the South.

The second was that the military insisted that the bombing campaign continued to be run according to principles it recognized. When McNamara asked the chiefs for a plan on how to continue, he was briefed on a twelve-week "interdiction" campaign of attacks that would "walk" steadily northward toward Hanoi.[13] By week eleven, after three thousand sorties would have been flown, the noose would be ready to close on Hanoi and Haiphong; then Washington would instruct Hanoi to do its bidding and, if it refused, tighten the noose in week twelve.

But McNamara and Johnson were not about to delegate twelve weeks of bombing to the military. On April 6 the president signed an order that regularized Rolling Thunder and called for increasing or slackening the pace if the enemy let up in the South. A specific provision ordered pilots to avoid hitting the M-19 aircraft bases near Hanoi, on the rationale that if the Chinese technicians there were hurt, China might come into the war. The president declined to take out a surface-to-air-missile site under construction, even though the SAM, once finished, would threaten U.S. planes. And targets were to be approved *slowly,* for one or two weeks at a time, decided on in the White House by the commander in chief and his second in command, R. S. McNamara.

This single decision by McNamara and Johnson set the tone for the entire air war. When his and Bundy's plan had no effect, McNamara could have opted for the military's way, with swift and violent strikes against all ninety-four targets. McNamara avoided rejecting this preference outright, lest leaks rebound against them. He made the choice of gradualism piecemeal.

The strongest advocates of air power among the senior military registered heartfelt complaints. Gradualism, they feared, would not dint the will of fanatics in Hanoi. China was not a danger, they thought. Furthermore, over time, the North could build up air defenses, which would make the campaign costly in U.S. pilots downed and captured. The chiefs saw their chance to end the war quickly slipping away.[14] Years later, when North Vietnam had built up one of the most intensive air defense systems in the world — one that downed many U.S. pilots — air commanders remembered these early civilian directives, which bought the enemy time, with great bitterness.

McNamara won handily over those officers who objected to a gradualist bombing campaign. One reason he did so was the character of General Earle "Bus" Wheeler, whom McNamara helped to promote over several more senior officers for the job of JCS chairman in 1964, when Taylor went to Saigon as ambassador. Wheeler had risen through the staff route. He was cool, intelligent, articulate, precise. "Bus left each night with a neat briefcase," says his friend Army Secretary Stephen Ailes. "Bus also was a big admirer of McNamara."[15] Both were administrators rather than strategists.

When he became chairman, in July 1964, Wheeler laid down two rules for dealing with McNamara. One was unanimity: Under him the chiefs began masking internal disagreements, to block McNamara's ability to divide them and win. Wheeler's second rule was to work things out, to broker between military and civilian viewpoints. It was a course McNamara loved, for it guaranteed harmony with the chiefs.

To some other officers, it reinforced their scorn for Wheeler as "a political general."

Had a different man stood in the chairman's shoes, he might have spelled out forcefully the long-term costs of gradualism to civilians. As principal military adviser to the secretary and the president, the chairman could have sent a strong message with blunt advice. But Wheeler acquiesced to civilians' wishes. For years many commanders blamed McNamara for imposing gradualism on them. Only recently have a few said publicly that Wheeler shares the blame for not cleanly rejecting it.[16]

The adoption of gradualism resulted in a patient ritual, which dragged on for years. General Wheeler and McNamara would bring target folders to the White House. They would sit with the president and some others — Bundy or his later successor as national security adviser, Walt Rostow. McNamara would advise, Wheeler would hunch forward, peering over his glasses as he did when he was worried, which was most of the time. Lyndon Johnson would put down a long finger on an Asian name on a map. They told one another that this choice of target, or that one, would make a difference in Hanoi's calculus of war.[17] And Wheeler would go back alone to the Tank, to explain the latest refinement to the chiefs. In the end, Wheeler served longer than any other chairman of the Joint Chiefs in history, for six years, through July 1970. When he left, the war still raged. The job and the war cost him two heart attacks, and ultimately his life.

McNamara adored him. He said after Wheeler's first attack, "I would rather have Bus Wheeler after a heart attack than anybody else before one."[18] McNamara meant the comment as praise, but it also revealed how few soldiers in the Building he trusted, even after years on the job.

"It doesn't look like our escalation message is getting through," a reporter said to McNamara on March 8, when the first claps of Rolling Thunder produced no letup in enemy activity.

Optimist McNamara was undaunted. He admitted their new air policy had not caused enemy aggression to stop. But "what they will do in the future, we can't say."

By April 26, he claimed the bombing was successful, using the new rationale that it hurt the North's ability to carry on the war. With map and pointer he showed bridges struck in the southern region, roads hit. "We have slowed the flow of men and materiel and this has adversely affected the Viet Cong, although I don't wish to overemphasize the degree to which it has affected them so far." Prisoner interviews showed it hurt enemy morale in the South. He did not claim the bombing had improved South Vietnam's government or military effectiveness or had increased U.S. influence, but since those early hopes had been top-secret, the press did not know they had not been realized. McNamara conceded at least one fact that ran against this hopeful report: Enemy infiltration was increasing. Thus South Vietnam could be in more danger, not less, in the months ahead.[19]

Robert McNamara refused to give the Joint Chiefs the big air war they wanted, but he was eager to give General William C. Westmoreland American troops. Westmoreland was a tall, bushy-browed, smooth-featured soldier from a South Carolina military family.[20] He was so much of the mainstream Army of the 1960s, and so closely shared its ideas and preconceptions, that he came to be called "the inevitable general." He made the right connections at West Point and rose swiftly. Maxwell Taylor helped get him appointed as General Paul Harkins's deputy in 1963. As Harkins lost favor with Washington, Westmoreland won a fourth star and Harkins's job of MACV commander. At first McNamara worked smoothly with Westmoreland; both were corporate men who prided themselves on getting the job done. Neither, as it happened, had a feel for this particular war.

At a meeting on February 26, 1965, "with no work by any staffs outside the Pentagon," William Bundy says, the president heard and approved Westmoreland's request to land thirty-five hundred Marines at Da Nang, the coastal city giving access to the northern neck of South Vietnam just below the DMZ.[21] Their mission was to guard Da Nang air base, now a likely terrorist target since it was used for Rolling Thunder. The instant decision caused the Marines to wade ashore on March 8, dressed in full battle regalia, in a useless display of bravado. The door Eisenhower and Kennedy held shut when they had refused to send combat troops now suddenly swung open.

There is no record that McNamara dissented; he probably backed the move. But John McNaughton — the negotiator — had tried to change the "signal" sent by this first deployment of troops. McNaughton wanted Westmoreland to take a less conspicuous unit, the Army's 173rd Airborne, instead.[22] Westmoreland, however, got his way, a sign of how power was starting to shift to the commander in the field.

Yet McNamara remained squarely in the saddle. He had "very substantial personal advantages" in those days, recalls Chester Cooper, McGeorge Bundy's aide for Vietnam. "He was a very forceful guy." When he expounded his views, he was "all souped up" with "a lot of fire." He was "exhausting to listen to." He came in with "briefs, numbers, ratios, estimates, and projections that sounded good and maybe had more verisimilitude" than the presentations of others who used "adjectives and adverbs."[23]

Protocol seats the secretary of defense at the president's left elbow in formal meetings. McNamara's closeness to the president was no mere formality as decisions gained momentum in the spring of 1965. He enjoyed special access and influence.

His full bush of hair now sported a military shave at the temples. As the decisions grew bigger, as the moral stakes grew, his intensity and self-control gave him an air of command. The boy wonder was gone, and the senior military and other advisers saw instead a commander being tested and testing himself — a commander in a hurry.

McNamara had the bit between his teeth. Enemy infiltration was rising; secretly, the administration knew the enemy planned to cut South Vietnam in two by the end of the year. The rainy season was ending, and the enemy could act soon. McNamara wanted to take whatever military action was needed, in his opinion, to turn the tables in the war soon. His bureaucratic adversary, who thought this course could be disastrous, was Under Secretary of State George Ball.

Ball waited three months to put his warnings against escalation directly before the president after that Saturday in November 1964 when McNamara, Bundy, and Rusk had unanimously refuted his sixty-seven-page "tiger's back" memo of October. Ball in his memoirs calls it "bureaucratic casuistry" that his colleagues had decided that bombing the North would stop revolving-door governments in the South. Nonetheless, he held off handing his memo to Johnson during the pivotal ninety days when Johnson decided on December 1 to secretly bomb the trails in Laos and "in principle" to hit North Vietnam later, and when he ordered the Flaming Dart attacks after Pleiku, in early February.[24]

Ball first put his argument before Lyndon Johnson on February 13 — the day Johnson ordered that the bombing of the North be regularized, in fact. That day they discussed a paper Ball coauthored with Llewellyn Thompson, the former ambassador to the Soviet

Union. The Ball-Thompson position opposed escalation (but endorsed limited air strikes), in contrast to a McNamara-Bundy position. The latter Ball says he wrote to "smoke out my colleagues." McGeorge Bundy responded to it by scribbling in the margin to the president, "*Not* our view" (Bundy's italics). The Ball-Thompson argument was that Johnson could "not long continue air strikes against North Vietnam" without engaging Chinese MIG fighters deployed there. "Once our planes have been engaged heavily by MIG aircraft, you will be compelled . . . to face the decision to mount an air effort to eliminate the major MIG base . . . near Hanoi." U.S. attacks on the North would trigger a North Vietnamese buildup on the ground in South Vietnam, Chinese aircraft based in China entering the war, and U.S. attacks on China. The memo dwelt less on the risks of a drawn-out ground war than the horrors of escalation: deployment of 300,000 U.S. troops, fighting against Chinese troops, and "the question of using tactical nuclear weapons against the Chinese." The president, Ball remembers, "read the memorandum quickly, then asked me to go through it point-by-point. He thanked me and handed the memorandum back without further comment."[25]

Sensing the growing momentum, eleven days later Ball showed his "tiger's back" memo of October to Bill Moyers, the White House press secretary, who shared Ball's fears. Moyers gave it to the president, who found it "fascinating and wanted to know why he had not read it before," Moyers told Ball. The memo was formally discussed with the president at a meeting on February 26 — the same day and, it appears, the same meeting when Johnson decided to send the Marines to Da Nang.

Ball remembered later that Johnson referred to points by page number and seemed closely attentive to what he was saying. McNamara "produced a spectacular display of facts and statistics to show I had overstated the difficulties we were now encountering and that the situation was much better than I represented — suggesting, at least by nuance, that I was not only prejudiced but ill-informed." Rusk also made a "deeply felt" argument about the "dangers of not going forward."[26]

Why did Ball wait so long to approach the president directly? Ball later said that since he was a second-ranking officer, he did not "treat with the president on an *ex parte* basis"; he was ready to send his memo to Johnson only if McNamara, Bundy, or Rusk encouraged it. And his warnings "seemed to irritate everybody."

Also, George Ball had other issues on his agenda that winter with Johnson, McNamara, and Bundy. A colleague from the State Department remembers that Ball had a vivid ambition to be appointed secretary of state when, after the November election, Johnson moved Rusk out of the post, as some had expected. Ball saw Bundy as a rival for the secretary's job; their relationship was uneasy in this period.[27] Also, Ball was a firm Atlanticist who wanted to keep U.S. foreign policy focused on Europe (one reason he dreaded the United States' getting bogged down in Vietnam). And all through 1964 Ball was the leading American proponent of the multilateral force, or MLF. This plan, originating with a group in the State Department some time before that revived it with Kennedy's apparent blessing, would have created a "force" of surface ships loaded with Polaris missiles, to be operated jointly by the NATO allies, with firing decisions taken by committee. Now, the MLF made little military sense — it was anathema to most of the Pentagon, for example — but Ball and others argued that if the West Germans could be made to accept it, it could siphon off Bonn's ambition for its own nuclear force. And the jointly run fleet and committee could promote European unity, which was almost a sacred cause to George Ball and others at Foggy Bottom at the time.[28]

The MLF planners hit a sudden obstacle in December 1964, almost a month to the day after Ball tried to win Bundy, McNamara, and Rusk over on the subject of Vietnam. The president finally looked at the MLF proposal closely, because the British prime minister was arriving and a firm U.S. position had to be taken. He learned, in meetings with advisers on December 5 and 6, that Kennedy hadn't been strongly for the plan after all, and that the West Germans, although publicly in favor, were unenthusiastic. Johnson was further disturbed that his advisers thought Congress could be made to agree to such a nuclear-sharing arrangement; Congress was not ready at all to vote for it, he complained. An outside adviser who attended the sessions recalls that Johnson was "angry" with Ball for overselling the plan to him. "He thought he had been misled."[29]

In that session, as throughout the winter, McNamara was Ball's ally in saying the president should support the MLF plan. McNamara agreed with his colleagues in the Pentagon that it made little military sense; yet he also realized it could solve a basic political problem of Western Europe's wish for a say in when and how nuclear weapons would be used. "Bob McNamara was very good on the MLF. . . .

He and I sort of fought shoulder to shoulder for it," Ball remembers. Bundy, on the other hand, wrote a key paper airing the problems with the MLF and gave it to the president while failing to show it to Ball in advance. "For the first time . . . I got really angry at Mac Bundy," Ball said later, but he added, "Bundy was extremely fair in all his dealings" and "this was the only time I ever got really angry at him."[30] Bundy's paper — and the unsatisfactory answers the advisers gave on December 5 and 6 — caused Johnson to decide not to go all out for the MLF. He would let it die quietly or would come out in support in the unlikely chance the allies demonstrated that they wanted it.

Thus in January and February, while Bundy and McNamara were pushing Johnson to launch a limited air campaign over North Vietnam, George Ball was trying to salvage the Atlantic orientation of foreign policy, including the MLF, which he still hoped to make happen. Ball needed McNamara's support, as he had in the past. Thus, although his concerns about the dangers of an extended ground war were heartfelt, Ball limited his objections, strained by the four-way relationship between himself, McNamara, Bundy, and, above all, Lyndon Johnson after the contretemps of December.

Ball would try again. At Johnson's request, he produced the plan for diplomatic withdrawal, with Dean Acheson, on very short notice in April. In June, he argued against going above 100,000 U.S. troops, lest too many white faces make it an American and not a Vietnamese war. In late July the president asked Ball to debate McNamara again with set-piece papers, but even then, Ball modified a stronger draft that favored withdrawal; the others pressured him into arguing for a "compromise" result.[31] By July 21 the exchange went: President: "Can we make a case for this — discuss it fully?" Ball: "We have discussed it. I have had my day in court. . . ." President: "George, you have pointed out the danger but you haven't really proposed an alternative course. . . ." Ball: "I would not recommend that you follow McNamara's course."[32]

McNamara did his share to fill the debate with illusions that they were really examining options; yet he contributed to Ball's isolation. Moreover, his ear for Ball's important political and historical arguments was fatally weak: He heard Ball saying that escalation could not be controlled — and the one thing Bob McNamara was planning to do that spring was to *control* this little war. There was no real debate, or as two recent scholars of the debate have written, there "was no sustained attention to issues and no follow-up." Ball was forced to become a policy entrepreneur, seeking allies, pulling his punches to win hearings. "The impact of advice became a function of skill and resources in bureaucratic politics."[33]

And on this turf, Bob McNamara outgunned almost any adversary, especially a lawyer like Ball who had no operational plan, jumped late into the debate, lacked bureaucratic allies of McNamara's caliber, and did not start task forces and action plans on his own. Finally, since Ball's boss, Dean Rusk, did not protect and advance his right to be heard before the president, Ball was left, somewhat unfairly, to deal with McNamara and Bundy alone.

Thus it was not that McNamara's proposed escalation was objectively wiser; tragically, it appealed to the president because McNamara had worked it all out. He had the forces ready to deploy, he had the chiefs in line (and was bringing formerly dissident voices on board). He was promising to contain expansionary communism and not let South Vietnam fall, while holding China at arm's length. He was promising a limited and fitting war that would not expose the president or the nation to too much political risk. It was precisely these qualities, which made Bob McNamara so useful, and such a symbol of management and excellence, that caused Lyndon Johnson to buy in to his greatest mistake.

So McNamara wanted action and needed consensus within the bureaucracy. His conduct was never simple as he set about his goals. Ball told me that when McNamara got one of his memos that was due to be discussed before the president, "Bob would always call me right away and come to see me, bringing McNaughton with him." He always came to Ball's office as "a matter of courtesy."

In these meetings McNamara "would appear to be quite sympathetic. These discussions would end by him saying, well, we must find a negotiated solution." McNamara would talk with Ball "as though we were fundamentally in agreement." Then, in front of the president, "he would shoot me down in flames with all these new statistics I hadn't heard before. He tried to give the impression I didn't know what I was talking about."

McNamara's visits to Ball were probably a stratagem to flush out the dissenter ahead of time, to be better able to refute him before the president. McNamara would not comment on Ball's version of this bitter and fateful debate. But Ball, for one, seems convinced the secretary of defense was being "honest" and did see the problems Ball raised, even though he had chosen another course. "It wasn't deliberate. If anything he's a very honest man," Ball says. "It reflected his own schizophrenia."

Ball also became convinced that McNaughton — a principal architect of Rolling Thunder — was a closet dove. "He used to say to me privately that he agreed with me," Ball says.

The doubts that McNamara seemed to share with Ball in their private meetings surfaced on the evening of March 5, seven days after he had shot down Ball in front of the president over his memo. That night, McNamara had a long, secret, and pessimistic talk with Rusk and McGeorge Bundy. Bundy reported to the president the next day:

> Last night for the first time Bob McNamara said what many others have thought for a long time — that the Pentagon and the military have been going at this thing the wrong way round from the very beginning: they have been concentrating on military results against guerrillas in the field when they should have been concentrating on intense police control from the individual villager on up.

McNamara was pessimistic about the South Vietnamese political situation. Bundy reported that there was "no evidence" that the new government has the "will, skill and human resources" for a "turnaround."

McNamara and Rusk felt "it was important to show that we are ready to talk about Vietnam." McNamara went "further" than Rusk in thinking "we should find a way to have real talks in an international meeting." Bundy added that McNamara's idea was "We will need a conference table if things get worse, as he expects."

The three met with Johnson on March 10 at Camp David. Bundy had told the president, "McNamara particularly thinks it a very good idea to have a quiet talk this way." At Camp David, Johnson held firm that formal negotiations would be unavailing "because we haven't done anything yet." Johnson said, in meeting notes,

> Nearly everyone chose to forward this more than LBJ but I did cross bridge in my own mind in December [1964].
> If you can show me any reasonable out I'll grab it.

> To give in = another Munich. if not here — then Thailand. Come hell or high water we're going to stay there. beg borrow or steal to get a government.

Talking about withdrawal was still considered near treason. Nothing in the record shows what happened to these advisers' plan to prepare for South Vietnam's collapse. Bundy had promised the president their planning would be "very privately" held. "This mission will not exist anywhere except in this memorandum."[34]

McNamara could talk as though he understood Ball's points; he could confess privately to Rusk and Bundy that they were putting too much stress on a military solution in Vietnam. But he was just as convinced that some military action was needed to stop Vietnam from falling to the enemy. Intelligence indicated that the enemy planned a decisive drive in the South. So he was ready to dispatch U.S. troops and roll over anyone who opposed him.

At their secret session on March 5, McNamara, Bundy, and Rusk considered sending "a large allied force" into the highlands below the DMZ "as a show of force and deterrent." They knew that a few days earlier the president had summoned General Harold K. Johnson, chief of staff of the Army, to the White House for a rare interview. He told him to go to Saigon. "You get things bubbling, General," said the tall commander in chief as he poked the officer in the chest. The general flew to Saigon and came back with a twenty-one-point plan and a recommendation to send one division.

HK, as General Johnson was called, was a man of strong opinions, but obedient. In complete secrecy, he told Lyndon Johnson that a ground war in South Vietnam would take five hundred thousand troops and five years.[35] It was a remarkably accurate forecast, which the president conveniently neglected to mention in his memoirs.

Westmoreland now upstaged General Johnson by requesting, at almost the same time, a *three*-division force, of which two would be American and the third made up of regional allies.

McNamara seconded General Johnson's one-division force and took the larger request to the president. And when Westmoreland asked permission to send any troops he had into combat and the president agreed, McNamara obediently hid this historic shift in mission until another official leaked it in June.[36]

Maxwell Taylor had rushed to Washington to argue against the growing momentum for troops. Taylor had been U.S. ambassador in Saigon since July 1964 and had had time to cast a professional eye on the military problem of securing a long, narrow country whose native force was weak and corrupt. Taylor now opposed letting the U.S. Army he helped to rebuild in the early 1960s bog down in an inconclusive war. He came to Washington, argued, and left, thinking he had slowed the momentum.[37]

During Taylor's ten months as ambassador, this experienced soldier gained a healthy respect for the enemy; "his tenacity and ability to maintain morale are absolutely amazing," he said. Taylor preferred that U.S. troops not be sent to Vietnam at all. But if they were sent, they should adopt an "enclave strategy," which experts later said might have worked. Taylor saw no point in using troops to seek battle in the hinterland, because South Vietnam's long, wilderness border adjoining enemy sanctuaries in Laos and Cambodia gave the enemy the advantage. Instead, U.S. troops would help South Vietnamese forces defend coastal areas, or "enclaves," where 90 percent of the population lived. As the enemy was driven and kept away from the coasts, Saigon's writ could be said to govern the country, and the Americans could declare victory and leave.[38]

Once Taylor was back in Saigon, McNamara "bombarded" him with cables showing "eagerness . . . to rush in troops now that the official reluctance had been breached." The general — formerly a close colleague of McNamara's — felt betrayed. McGeorge Bundy warned the president, "Direct orders . . . would be very explosive right now." Taylor was a famous man and a friend of the Kennedys'; a resignation in protest would be very awkward. McNamara flew to Honolulu to meet Taylor on April 20 and nail down a "consensus" for sending the three divisions, which would raise the number of American troops to 75,000.

What McNamara said to Taylor is unrecorded. But the general fell into line, smartly, with a "consensus" report by McNamara from Honolulu recommending troops. Bundy's comment to Johnson reveals Taylor's collapse: "Max thinks we can get a favorable settlement in a matter of months rather than in [as McNamara says] 'perhaps a year or two.' "[39]

Taylor continued to propound his enclave approach to any prospective ground war. But when McNamara hauled him into line at

Honolulu, he effectively silenced this useful voice. McNamara also knew that Taylor would not serve another year as ambassador. "Max has been at times dangerously rigid," McGeorge Bundy sniped in a memo. In fact, had Taylor been more rigid, had he fought harder, he would have served McNamara, the Army, and the nation better.

At a press conference on April 26, McNamara, although claiming the bombing of North Vietnam had been "effective," also announced that 39,000 enemy troops had infiltrated to the South since Rolling Thunder began. He thus built a case for further U.S. military action but kept the "consensus" decision to raise U.S. troops to 75,000 secret.

In April, the economy was in its fifty-first month of expansion. The Eighty-ninth Congress was passing a whirlwind of Great Society programs. Professors criticized the war; on April 17, fifteen thousand students and others protested outside the White House. Dean Rusk called left-wing protests "nonsense," reflecting the administration's scorn for the left-liberal fringe. A week later, when the president sent U.S. troops into the Dominican Republic to forestall a supposed Communist coup, the public backed his move. Johnson's popularity soared.

A hint of the feared enemy offensive in Vietnam came during the first week of June, when 1,000 guerrillas overran the district capital at Dong Xoai and attacked a U.S. Special Forces camp ninety miles north of Saigon. The South Vietnamese counterattacked but lost at least 900 men in four days of fighting. McNamara told the president at the White House on June 5 that Hanoi now believed it was winning the struggle.[40]

On June 7 General Westmoreland gave Washington the final push. He secretly requested that U.S. troops be increased to 150,000, or thirty-four battalions, "as rapidly as is practical during the critical weeks ahead." The chiefs quickly finalized the request by raising it to 175,000 troops, or forty-four battalions: thirty-four American units and ten from South Korea and Australia. The urgency grew days later, when the Buddhist who had been running a chaotic government in Saigon was thrown out and a new group took power, led by Nguyen Cao Ky.

McNamara at first hesitated. William Bundy recalls that he urged sending up to eighteen battalions, which was more than the thirteen agreed upon in Honolulu, putting 95,000 Americans in the country, but fewer than the chiefs had asked for. Bundy also recalls that Mc-Namara urged that they make this commitment public with a major presidential address.[41]

The question of whether to send a much larger force and Americanize the war pressed on McNamara in the third week of June. Enemy attacks were cutting like a dagger eastward from sanctuaries in Cambodia, across the central provinces above Saigon, through peaceful-looking hills, and toward the sea. The country could split and fall like rotten fruit.

For four years it had been McNamara's and the Army's job to prevent outright defeat. Now that the crisis had come, long-standing problems in McNamara's administration of the war came to the surface. He — and the Army — needed a strategy by which U.S. troops could succeed. He and the Army needed open and honest debate. A serious inquiry would have exposed the self-serving way General Paul Harkins had run Army operations in Saigon since 1962: the false statistics, the preoccupation with body count, the overload of senior officers, the misleading stories of success. McNamara had tried to address some of the problems. Yet by avoiding bloodletting and by his fascination with statistics, he added to them.

One honest voice was that of HK Johnson, the Army chief of staff, whose duties included oversight of Army operations and strategy. The general always carried around a bulging briefcase of unfinished work. He was an original, smart soldier who had seen the darkest side of the Asian land war during World War II. HK had made the Bataan Death March, where severed heads of Filipinos marked the trail; he then spent the rest of the war in Japanese prison camps. He had been critical of the Army's tactics and firepower in Korea.[42]

General Johnson doubted the Army could be effective if it fought in Vietnam the way it had in Korea and Europe, in large-unit frontal battles stressing firepower and attrition. When forced to recommend sending a division, the general asked that it be used experimentally before a bigger force was sent.

In May 1965, HK responded to the growing pressure for substantial forces. He drew up a plan for sending a large force and calling up the reserves. A significant force was needed, first to show Hanoi immediately that it could not win. Johnson thought the Army should adopt a low-firepower strategy and disperse itself throughout the country to pick off the enemy skillfully and quickly. He also wanted the reserves called up so the American public would know the full extent of military commitment, the supreme sacrifice being asked of its sons. McNamara valued General Johnson for his brains and insight but, curiously, made no comment on the general's plan.

Instead, McNamara swiftly supported the strategy of attrition war put forward by Westmoreland, apparently without debate. Westmoreland planned to use whatever U.S. troops he had to take the offensive and engage the enemy's main forces — not the guerrillas, and not the infiltrators in South Vietnam's coastal cities. He wanted to fight in the frontal, decisive style that had characterized U.S. Army tactics since the days of Ulysses Grant. Bombing would "strangle" the battlefield and isolate the enemy inside South Vietnam, while American troops would grind down the North Vietnamese regulars, whose numbers were growing in South Vietnam. Meanwhile, the South Vietnamese forces, advised by Americans, would carry out the slow, defensive job of securing populated areas and cities. Westmoreland's deputy, William DePuy, explained the plan simply: "We are going to stomp them to death."[43]

The critical debate over strategy did not take place. McNamara was in a hurry by the third week of June to send forces to stop the collapse of the government in Saigon. Taylor had been effectively silenced. General Johnson was unwilling to contradict Westmoreland, the field commander. Thus unopposed, McNamara endorsed Westmoreland's "concept of operations," the forty-four-battalion force and attendant request to call up the reserves, which had been assumed. Nothing in the record explains what pushed McNamara over the top from his stated wish, just weeks before, to hold the line at 95,000 troops. A riverboat restaurant in Saigon was bombed; an American prisoner was executed by the enemy. But these events were not unusual enough to have changed his mind.

McNamara may have been influenced by an analysis of "force ratios" that Westmoreland's staff in Saigon produced in the third week of June.[44] Counterinsurgency war doctrine held that friendly forces needed to be ten times greater than the enemy in order to win. (This was the basis of the estimate made by General Johnson in March that 500,000 troops would be needed to win a ground war.) But Westmoreland knew the president was not about to send half a million troops. He needed to justify a lower number.

The MACV staff decided to count only the 50,000 regulars in South Vietnam as the main opposing force. Thus it cut another estimated 100,000 Viet Cong irregulars from the roster. This produced a figure of 72 enemy battalions in the country. Counting each South Vietnamese battalion as the equal of each enemy battalion, the South Vietnamese had 133 battalions to the enemy's 72. Since American units had more firepower and were better trained and led, each U.S. Army battalion was counted as equal to two of the enemy's, and each Marine battalion was counted as equal to three of the enemy's. In this way the staff could tally 172 friendly battalions to the enemy's 72, or a 2.4-to-1 force ratio. Given that Communist regulars were the principal foe, and that the Americans wanted to fight a conventional battlefield war, Westmoreland's staff argued that they would fight what Ho Chi Minh's doctrine called Third Stage war, where a 2.4-to-1 force ratio would do just fine.

McNamara bought the notion of a quantitative war. His June 24 memorandum to the president began: "The VC are winning now largely because the ratio of guerrilla to anti-guerrilla force is unfavorable to the government." In other words, by redressing force ratios, the Americans could shift the balance. Justifying his recommendation to send up to 175,000 troops, McNamara told Johnson, "The number of US troops is too small to make a significant difference in the traditional 10-1 government-guerrilla formula, but it is not too small to make a significant difference in the kind of war which seems to be evolving in Vietnam — a 'Third Stage' or conventional war."[45]

Thus McNamara supported attrition war on the conventional Army model, and the usefulness of firepower and other "force multipliers" in this curious setting. They fit his presumption that America's technology and resources would help it succeed. His dismissal of his poorly armed yet strangely effective enemy was typical of the time, although McNamara, like the generals advising him, bears special blame for being so cocksure. General Wheeler called the enemy "raggedy-ass little bastards." And the U.S. Army, in its wisdom, failed to translate into English the French account of their own nine-year struggle and defeat against this enemy, until 1968.[46]

Also in June, with equal haste, McNamara sent another force multiplier into battle. As Westmoreland dispatched his troops to stalk the highlands, the enemy proved very hard to find and, when found, to see and shoot. The enemy hid, moved, and ambushed with terrifying skill in that hilly terrain, overgrown with brush and darkened by the canopy of high trees. Instead of adjusting tactics to counteract the enemy's unique skills, Westmoreland asked to unleash a technology that lay close at hand and was tantalizingly underused.

Nearby, on Guam, were squadrons of B-52s, the pride of the U.S. strategic bomber force. Their wings stretched 185 feet across; each could carry thirty-seven thousand pounds of nuclear or conventional bombs for seventy-five hundred miles. Their real mission was to destroy the Soviet heartland with nuclear bombs. But some had been moved into the east Pacific in June 1964 in anticipation of a Chinese response to any exchanges between the United States and North Vietnam. The big bombers were given no role in Rolling Thunder's strikes on North Vietnam, for if one went down in enemy territory, Moscow would have a free sample of the American strategic arsenal to pick over.

The Alice-in-Wonderland result of Westmoreland's request and McNamara's quick approval was that in mid-June of 1965, the B-52s began raining maximum loads, fifty iron bombs per run, on "suspected enemy concentrations" in *South* Vietnam.[47] The first strikes made headlines; billows of orange flame roiled brush and huts. Then friendly villages were bombed by mistake. The press learned that in many cases, commanders radioed for air strikes without watching where they fell or even having seen an enemy in the region at all. "Unobserved" air strikes became notorious.

These excesses of proportionality were terrifying to the enemy, to the South Vietnamese, and to some American observers. Yet McNamara, in ordering up the B-52s, continued the error he and Harkins made in 1962 when they encouraged the South Vietnamese to napalm and strafe their own villages. A Parkinson's Law of war was now at work — as more destructive power was available, it was used.[48] Later in the war, Victor Heyman, one of McNamara's Whiz Kids, asked Westmoreland's deputy DePuy why they used the B-52s at all. DePuy looked at the civilian calmly and replied, "Because they're there."

On June 24, McNamara recommended that Johnson send the forty-four battalions into Vietnam right away, to "reestablish the military balance by the end of December," and that he call up the reserves.

But, he warned, the president should be ready to send additional troops the next year, 1966.[49]

As to strategy, the U.S. troops would be "a quick reaction reserve" engaging enemy main forces. Somewhat contradictorily, McNamara said they would also be "hounding, harassing, and hurting the VC" even "should they elect not to stand and fight." He cited force ratios to demonstrate that the proposed number of U.S. troops could be effective.

McNamara appears to have stapled together all the Joint Chiefs' suggestions; he also included mining North Vietnam's harbors, destroying rail and highway bridges leading north from Hanoi to China, and hitting the routes leading to China. "Destroy the war-making supplies and facilities of North Vietnam wherever located," he proposed. Also, "expand strike program against bridges, ferries, railroads"; "be prepared to destroy airfields and [surface to air missile] sites as necessary." Frank contact should be made with the enemy to offer to talk anytime, and to keep Moscow and Peking calm.

The memo smacks of panic, although a footnote carefully advises Johnson that he need not decide on the expanded air war right away. In fact, McNamara's sword waving may not have been spontaneous. "The president mentioned to me yesterday his desire that we find more dramatic and effective actions in South Vietnam," McGeorge Bundy told McNamara on June 18.[50] McNamara may have been showing the president what an all-out military effort involved, for several military leaders had argued that an intensive air war, plus an injection of troops and a reserve call-up, would do the job right away.

"Rash to the point of folly" is how McGeorge Bundy described McNamara's plan. Bundy pointed out its many weaknesses. "I see no reason to suppose that the Viet Cong will accommodate us by fighting the kind of war we desire." Also, it was a step onto "a slippery slope toward total US responsibility and corresponding fecklessness on the Vietnamese side." McNamara had not examined the "upper limit of US liability. If we need 200 thousand men for these quite limited missions, may we not need 400 thousand later?"[51]

McNamara, Westmoreland, and Bundy warned formally, in print, that the war could be long and inconclusive. Westmoreland pegged it as lasting three years, reflecting Army preconceptions: America had fought World War II in three years and had been involved in Korea for the same length of time. Through the memos and meeting notes, however, there runs a clear sense that in the short run, U.S. intervention would be decisive, not to win in the military sense but to turn the tide in Saigon's favor soon. After all, U.S. escalation in the Berlin and Cuban crises had precipitated a quick response from Khrushchev. Impatience was deeply ingrained in McNamara's nature; by late June he was pressing for fast U.S. action and was equally eager for quick results.

More than twenty years later, an older, changed Robert McNamara told an oral history interviewer, "I never did believe that a military victory, in the narrow sense of the word, was possible." He made similar statements in public, under oath in the Westmoreland trial. What he remembered of his state of mind in the spring of 1965 was that the choices were "difficult" and the situation grave, because it involved the imminent fall of South Vietnam.[52] In his memory, doubts and regrets dominate, although at the time, in the inner circle, Robert McNamara was supremely intolerant of the doubts of others.

"It wasn't clear to me that we could avoid defeat by any action in our power," he said, looking back. He recalled that a key part of his belief that military intervention would work was what he called the political track, a drive to communicate with Hanoi to reach a settlement. In his mind, the Vietnam crisis of 1965 was like the Cuban missile crisis, when Kennedy and his advisers escalated with the naval blockade but signaled to Khrushchev a way out with diplomacy.

McNamara's Vietnam memos from the spring of 1965 bear out his recollection. In April, June, and July he recommended a serious political effort to accompany military intervention. For example, the conclusion to his July trip report said:

> [T]he course of action recommended in this memorandum — if the military and political moves are properly integrated and executed with continuing vigor and visible determination — stands a good chance of achieving an acceptable outcome within a reasonable time in Vietnam.[53]

In Vietnam in 1965, he later recalled, "if we were to expand militarily we must expand the political track as well, because it wasn't at all clear that military action alone could achieve our objectives. . . . It was not at all clear to me that military action would lead to substantial political movement. Therefore it was a very difficult situation."

But the "great sense of uncertainty about achieving a military victory," which he recalled articulating in the memos of spring 1965, does not appear in his public statements of the time. Publicly, McNamara did not say they would "win." He mainly said that sending troops and bombing would "blunt" the enemy drive or buy time for the South Vietnamese to defend themselves.

The confusion and anger that many veterans had about McNamara's later statements is partly justified. War, at the level of the platoon foray, the battalion action, or the bombing run, seems a simple matter of win or lose, kill or be killed. McNamara sent them to fight in a cause he fervently believed in at the time: to contain China, to stave off the defeat of an ally to whom four presidents had given their word. But he never told his soldiers, in so many words, that on the battlefield alone they could not "win."

Naturally, Lyndon Johnson sent McNamara to South Vietnam in July, as the situation grew worse there, and forced him to choose a new course. McNamara whirled around that country, saying to the television cameras with a hint of autobiography: "These have been two of my most impressive days since I have been Secretary of Defense."[54]

The American presence had changed Saigon. Journalist Robert Shaplen found the pretty, provincial city now full of cars and exhaust. Its merchants and government officials were "bristling with greed" at the imminent arrival of more American troops. Many in Nguyen Cao Ky's government, including the family of chief of state Nguyen Van Thieu, operated major networks of graft: Province chiefs were appointed only if they kept supplying money, funds that came from American aid.[55]

Bui Diem, a former ambassador to Washington, sat in on the meeting between McNamara, Thieu, and Ky.[56] Diem found the former Ford chief uninterested in the members of the three-week-old government sitting opposite him. McNamara had sent over in advance a list of twenty-five questions; now he started asking them. The answers were exactly what he wanted to hear.

How many allied troops would South Vietnam need between now and the end of the year? Answer: forty-four battalions plus one more to guard Saigon. Would the people of this country "readily accept a presence of this magnitude?" Answer: "Most Vietnamese did not consider the US as having any colonialist aspirations." However, the impact of American troops would be minimized if they operated "in less populated areas," which happened to be Westmoreland's plan.

McNamara was "precise but affable, scribbling on a yellow pad" and firing questions about "numbers, organization, management, and logistics as though he was bent on finding all the factors and components for the solution of some grand mathematical equation," Bui Diem recalled.

McNamara made no effort to size up Ky, who was sitting across the table. In fact, McNamara first saw Ky at a dinner earlier on the trip. Ky had arrived late, wearing a tuxedo and red socks and looking like a bandleader in a cheap Hollywood movie.[57] McNamara had been shocked. Possibly he was uncomfortable because he realized the new U.S. troops could add $8 billion to his $50 billion defense budget, all to legitimize a leader who dined in red socks.

While in Saigon, McNamara received a cable from Deputy Defense Secretary Cyrus Vance in Washington, who reported on his talk with "highest authority" — i.e., the president.

> 1. It is his current intention to proceed with 34 battalion plan.
> 2. It is impossible for him to submit supplementary budget request of more than $300–$400 million to Congress before next January.
> 3. If a larger request is made to Congress, he believes this will kill the domestic legislative program.
> 4. We should be prepared to explain to the Congress that we have adequate authority and use of funds by deficit financing . . . to finance recommended operations until next January. . . .
>
> I asked highest authority whether request for legislation authorizing call-up of reserves . . . would be acceptable . . . and he stated that it would.
>
> I pointed out that we would have great difficulties with Senator [John] Stennis concerning this course. . . . He [the president] said we would just have to bull it through.[58]

Leaving from Tan Son Nhut Airport, McNamara continued his public hints of a bigger U.S. commitment. He flew home, where preparations were under way to announce the major deployment and call-up of the reserves. As usual, McNamara's trip report had been drafted before he left for Saigon.

McNamara's return sparked a week of White House meetings,

which were advertised as a comprehensive review that would help Johnson make up his mind. The time seemed right, noted McGeorge Bundy, for "a major statement" to Congress and a "fireside chat" by the president.

As the hour for launching the wider war drew near, McNamara became bellicose. At a crowded White House meeting on July 22 that included the president, the military chiefs, and the service secretaries, unreality reigned. Johnson asked — rightly — why putting in 100,000 men would make a difference. Admiral McDonald said, "Sooner or later we'll force them to the conference table." What if the Russians or Chinese come in? the president asked. General Johnson paused and said, "If so, we have another ball game." McNamara was almost rabid on the imminent Communist takeover of the Third World if they did not make their stand now. He said:

> Laos, Cambodia, Thailand, Burma, surely affect Malaysia. In 2–3 years Communist domination would stop there, but ripple effect would be great — Japan, India. We would have to give up some bases. Ayub [Khan, leader of Pakistan] would move closer to China. Greece, Turkey would move to neutralist position. Communist agitation would increase in Africa.[59]

At a meeting the next day, Friday, July 23, McNamara endorsed what was now called Plan I, a public commitment and the reserve call-up, with a $2 billion near-term budget request for sending 100,000 more troops starting November 1.[60]

But Lyndon Johnson could humiliate Robert McNamara. Others at this session saw the president differ openly with him; Johnson said abruptly that he preferred Plan III. This would send the same number of troops but *without calling up the reserves.* The supplemental appropriation they would ask for would be $1 billion, not the $2 billion sought in Plan I.

Thus McNamara learned, in front of others, that the president would not take the steps that he and the Army had said were a basic prerequisite for a U.S. ground war in Asia. Johnson would make them fight not as past wars had been fought, with the public fully aware of the commitment and behind the fighting man; they would tiptoe into war.

Says one who was there: "McNamara's reaction is not known, but the President, not wanting to discuss the subject further," avoided McNamara by slipping out a side door. He said to speech writer

Horace Busby as he left, nodding toward McNamara, "Think we'll
get a resignation out of him?"[61]

Johnson was well aware that McNamara socialized with Bobby
Kennedy. If McNamara was tempted to resign, Bobby might push
him into going through with it. The president deftly invited McNamara to Camp David the next day, Saturday, perhaps figuring Mc-
Namara was safer in the Catoctin Mountains under his own eye and
that of the Secret Service, where the Kennedys could not play on his
loyalties.

McNamara now knew that he had lost on the reserves. By Saturday he probably knew he had lost on the equally critical issue of how
they would pay for the war. Top-secret estimates placed the added
cost in the fiscal year that had just begun on July 1 at $8 billion to $13
billion.[62]

McNamara has since said that "the initial draft of the July 1965
Vietnam paper presented to the president" contained recommendations for a call-up of the reserves and a tax increase.[63] Without a tax
increase or wage and price controls (the two means the government
used to finance past wars), a large deficit, inflation, or both could be
created. Yet the president, according to Vance's cable to McNamara
in Saigon, wanted to ask for only $300 million to $400 million and no
tax increase. In McNamara's account, Johnson overruled him, saying: " 'You know so goddamned much about it, you go up there and
you get the vote count and you come back down here and give me the
names of the people who will vote for it. Obviously you don't know
anything about politics. You say you would rather try [to pass a tax
increase] and fail than not to try at all. Well, I'll tell you what is going
to happen. We'll put it forward; they are going to turn it down. But
in the course of the debate they'll say: "You see, we've been telling
you so. You can't have guns and butter, and we're going to have
guns." ' "[64]

By that Saturday at Camp David, therefore, McNamara knew the
president wanted to pay for the war by stealth, or at least postpone
paying for it as long as possible. McNamara had lost, but he did not
consider resigning. He had developed the plans, he was committed to
action, he was manic about the dangers of letting South Vietnam fall.
And he was not about to part with Johnson during this crucial test of
his presidency.

The draft of McNamara's Vietnam trip report that has been released, dated July 13, does *not* contain a recommendation for a tax increase.[65] McNamara explains that he took care that this difference between himself and the president did not come to light. He says, "The draft memo had an *x* for the size of the appropriation required. During my trip to Vietnam, the *x* kept getting larger. I therefore had typed in a request for a tax increase to cover the larger appropriation required. When the president rejected the recommendation, the memo was retyped without the recommendation."[66]

Clark Clifford, the Washington lawyer and member of Johnson's kitchen cabinet, had been alarmed by McNamara's views of impending disaster in Asia. Clifford feared Johnson was being hounded into war by his advisers. To Clifford, as to George Ball, the president seemed "reluctant" to go to war; Clifford was unaware of the many cues he had given of his readiness. Briefly at Camp David, Clifford sat opposite McNamara with the president and made the case against intervention. McNamara listened without a hint of his feelings.[67]

It was a moment when McNamara could have taken Clifford as an ally and argued that the United States should not go in unless it notified the country through a reserve call-up and arranged for the war's hefty annual price tag through a tax hike or price controls. McNamara could have threatened to resign if Johnson would not act more responsibly.

Instead, he argued in favor of Johnson's decisions. He chanted the litany: China was testing them; they had to make a stand in South Vietnam or face terrible consequences elsewhere. Whatever inner struggle McNamara was engaged in, Clifford saw only the hard-driving executive vice president of the United States on that round. He had engineered the plans, and even if they were flawed he would carry them out and defend Lyndon Johnson's choices — and his own — with utter loyalty.

The president announced at midday July 28, during a crowded news conference, that additional troops would be sent. He gave no fireside chat to the public or major address to Congress. Then and for the next six months, Johnson and his advisers would hide the size of the force they were sending; they said they were raising troop levels to 125,000, instead of the 175,000 actually agreed upon. They made no mention that they were preparing to send another 100,000 troops in 1966. Instead, they stated that more would be sent "as needed."

The decision was unveiled as a choice of *not* going to war. Prominent columnists and editorial writers were relieved that Johnson also announced a new peace effort through the U.N. and that he was not calling up the reserves. Photographs from the space probe of Venus filled the front pages.

Robert McNamara testified before Congress on August 4 that they were sending additional troops only to "block the Viet Cong offensive" and give the South Vietnamese "time to strengthen their government." He did not claim the Americans would win. He explained with great persuasiveness why they did not need to call up the reserves. He asked for immediate funds of $1.7 billion — more than the $1 billion Johnson wanted, but less than the $2 billion he had sought.

Echoing Johnson, and despite private preparations to send more forces in 1966, McNamara told the congressmen, "We have no desire to widen the war."[68]

17

Two Enormous
Miscalculations

FROM THE AIR, the broad plain descending from the high mountains and the long, exposed coastline made North Vietnam look like a bombardier's dream in the summer and fall of 1965. The country had few real roads. Its only highway, the former Route Coloniale from Hanoi to the southern boundary, ran along the coast like a glittering ribbon, adorned along the side with rail tracks. The country's two cities, Hanoi and the port of Haiphong, were its hub, yet they were small, having few factories, oil tanks, and power plants. They were reached by big iron bridges built by French civil engineers. From Hanoi-Haiphong, a few rail lines and roads splayed like the spokes of a wheel north and east up through the mountains, forming vital links to China. There were few air defenses. It would be a mathematically precise task to bomb this poor country, reasoned military planners far away in Washington.

The mountains of adjoining Laos harbored a network of trails that linked North Vietnam's south- and west-running roads to the Laotian plain, South Vietnam, and Cambodia, which was neutral and officially off-limits to American ground operations. In December 1964, Lyndon Johnson ordered planes based in Thailand to begin the secret bombing of the Laotian trails to warn Hanoi and limit enemy infiltration. Operation Barrel Roll remained unknown to the American public for months.[1]

In South Vietnam, Washington's decisions of July 1965 had unleashed a war machine that was meant to devastate the enemy but that

devastated the country even more. Reports of enemy "concentrations" converted patches of rural ground or entire villages into targets. Over the hills and highlands soared B-52 bombers, built for
nuclear war on the Soviet heartland, which now dumped thirty thousand pounds of high-explosive bombs on a single run, turning whole
villages into flames and cratering the green ground. Operation Ranch
Hand planes sprayed herbicides to kill crops and defoliate trees. Tear
gas was sprayed into huts and tunnels to rout supposed enemy. Napalm was widely used. The people whose hearts and minds were to be
won over to American ideals began to flee their homes and ancestral
graves and shrines to become refugees in squalid camps on city
fringes.

What General Westmoreland's command considered the necessities of war deeply shocked many reporters. News stories focused on
villages bombed in error, on South Vietnamese and Americans firing
on friendly forces, and on enormous overkill for meager body counts
of enemy dead. "There comes a time in every war when men tend to
become indifferent to human suffering," wrote columnist James Reston after traveling around the country. "We may be reaching that
point in Vietnam." But "punishing the civil population" in the South
"with blind shooting and bombing is obviously unnecessary and stupid."[2]

McNamara, meanwhile, geared up the machinery of the war with a
certain pride. The challenge of counting everything in a 1.2-million-
man army was a massive inventory flow problem like those he had
handled with such facility at Ford.

Helping him count and move objects and people at the right place
and time, to Hawaii, Guam, the Philippines, and Thailand, was Paul
Ignatius, assistant secretary of defense for installations and logistics.[3]
Ignatius felt deficient as a statistical manager. He would work all
night to meet a polite request from the voice on the other end of his
special phone; the next morning, carrying in the tables, cross-eyed
with little sleep, he saw a fresh, energized McNamara eager to meet
the new day. "We moved 100,00 men 10,000 miles in 100 days,"
McNamara often bragged.

Not only was his managerial activity heightened, but his optimism, too, was at fever pitch. On television he announced that the Viet
Cong had "withdrawn" in past months. On August 11, the body
count looked good — he said the enemy had lost 7,000 between May

and July, whereas his side lost only 3,000. Using the media to talk to Hanoi, he offered to cut back the bombing of the North if Hanoi pulled its 325th Division from South Vietnam. This was the signaling game meant to resolve his limited non-war.[4]

Three weeks later, Peking dented his illusion of power. On September 2, Marshal Lin Piao, minister of defense of China, issued a rare official statement that seemed to say the Communist powers would fight the Americans forever. Lin Piao called on the "rural areas of the world" — Asia, Africa, and Latin America — to rise up and encircle "the cities of the world" — the United States and Western Europe. Vietnam was "the most convincing example of a victim of aggression defeating U.S. imperialism by a people's war."[5]

Lin Piao predicted correctly that America's nuclear and technological superiority would prove a "paper tiger." "Everybody" could "see that the U.S. aggressors are unable to find a way of coping with a people's war." The Vietnamese (that is, the Vietnamese Communists), "though apparently weak and small," are "more powerful than U.S. imperialism."

McNamara and most top American officials read Lin Piao's statement as a promise of "unshakable" support for Hanoi. "The Chinese people will do everything in their power to support the Vietnamese people until every single one of the U.S. aggressors is driven out of Viet-Nam," Lin said. Hanoi seemed to take heart from Peking's support of Vietnam as a model for world revolution. Meanwhile, North Vietnamese prime minister Pham Van Dong announced that Hanoi was ready to fight for twenty years.

McNamara likened Lin Piao's statement to Adolf Hitler's *Mein Kampf.* He told Jack Raymond of the *New York Times* that the most "significant" challenge for America was "greater proficiency" in combating the "so-called wars of national liberation. It is perfectly apparent that we will be facing more such wars in the years ahead." Cyrus Vance, McNamara's deputy, issued the administration's rebuttal in a speech that urged North Vietnamese leaders to separate their "interest" from Peking's and consider the costs of the endless war Peking was urging on them.[6]

Had McNamara known better, he might have taken heart from Lin Piao. An article by Murray Marder of the *Washington Post* described a Rand Corporation analysis of Lin's speech showing that it actually said the opposite: Peking was telling Hanoi to fight on on its own. In fact, virtually no one in the West then saw the huge trouble brewing in the closed society of China; Mao was having domestic difficulties and foresaw that he would have to keep the Red Army at home.[7] At the time, however, neither McNamara nor most Americans discerned Mao's potential weakness, only his strength and threatening army of millions.

Other developments troubled McNamara. In early 1965, Washington had evidence that Hanoi had ordered its forces — regular army units moving south, guerrillas, and political cadres — to smash South Vietnam in two, starting from the sanctuaries in Cambodia and advancing east to the sea. These orders lent urgency to McNamara's rush to deploy U.S. troops that spring. But by September, Hanoi's orders had changed; now the fighters were told to gird for a long war.[8]

McNamara and the other advisers almost turned back. At a previously unrevealed "difficult and inconclusive" session on Saturday, September 11, McNamara, Dean Rusk, McGeorge Bundy, and George Ball exchanged doubts about their course.

Dean Rusk questioned "whether we really need to move up to 200,000 men," although "McNamara continues to feel that we do," Bundy reported to the president the next day. What if the enemy continued to refuse to do battle? Might the Americans bog down in jungles and rice paddies after all? Rusk, McNamara, and Bundy then met with Johnson and sent a remarkable "Eyes Only" cable to Henry Cabot Lodge, now reinstalled as ambassador in Saigon. It said: "Informal high-level review over weekend . . . leaves us with feeling situation has more major uncertainties, variables and possibly occasions for changes in our actions." It seemed likely that "increasing US ground strength is driving Hanoi/VC to avoid major unit actions and in effect revert to pattern of placing primary emphasis on small scale actions." This raised "a residual question whether further increases in strength at presently planned pace are wise, or whether we should in some small degree defer further increases."[9] Previously, when Westmoreland had asked that the initial deployments be raised from 175,000 to 210,000, McNamara had recommended approving the request. Now there were second thoughts.

The situation cast doubt on the usefulness of the bombing. The advisers proposed to Lodge that they arrange a study group like the famous Strategic Bombing Survey, which exposed the lack of effectiveness of the Allied bombing in World War II. The cable reached the grim conclusion that, in effect, the only way Washington could save South Vietnam was the old, uninspiring task of inducing Saigon to win the loyalty of the people.

But Lodge, who had been a maverick on policy in 1963, was now a hard-liner. He cabled back that they had plans to make the bombing "more effective"; there was no need for outside review. As for the fact that the enemy had not engaged large military units, this was a "big dividend," because it allowed U.S. forces to concentrate on pacification.[10] Thus Lodge blocked criticism at a key moment when the war machine could have been turned around.

McNamara now heard from a man whose views on the enemy he respected greatly, Llewellyn Thompson. Also previously unreported, Thompson headed a review of the Vietnam situation in early fall 1965. The conclusion of his study, reached in October, was that the enemy would "probably decide in the near future to break up most of their large units" and limit itself to terror and sabotage or fade "into the woodwork." Only when Hanoi was convinced that the United States would stay the course, and pacification had succeeded in most of the country, would Hanoi's mind change. The Thompson report suggested that the way to convince Hanoi was less by increasing U.S. troops than by building a more effective South Vietnamese force. McNamara read these conclusions just when the infiltration numbers leapt upward; more evidence that he had made a colossal miscalculation in July.[11]

Protests against the war were still scattered in the fall of 1965. Among the most active were antiwar groups in the three communities McNamara knew best — Ann Arbor, Berkeley, and Oakland. In New York, a twenty-two-year-old relief worker named David Miller burned his draft card in public to invite arrest for breaking Selective Service laws.

Administration leaders did not take these protests seriously. Rusk, McNamara, the president — and most adult Americans — assumed that Vietnam would be like other American wars; young people would enlist or submit to the draft, notwithstanding their new fads of Beatles songs, bell-bottom jeans, and long hair.

In the early evening of November 2, during rush hour, McNamara was in a meeting in his office at the Pentagon. He was told something was happening outside his window. Moving to the big curtains and looking down into the dusk, he saw a knot of agitated people, and ambulances and smoke. Medics were covering something in blankets.

McNamara's eyes widened as he heard the shocking news that a thirty-one-year-old Quaker pacifist had drenched himself in kerosene and burned himself to death. A column of orange flame leapt twelve feet high as the clothes and flesh burned. And Norman Morrison — for that was the young man's name — had chosen the parking lot below the window of McNamara's office to send a message to him. Before he left his home in Baltimore to drive to Washington, Morrison had asked his wife: What can I do to make them stop the war?

McNamara saw two ambulances below. He was told the man had been holding his infant daughter when he started to burn. Was one life snuffed out, or two? As the flames stretched up his body from his shoes, on which he had struck the match, amid the sweet smell of burning kerosene and flesh, Morrison tossed the baby away from him. Had she been caught? Hit the pavement? People, some in uniform, ran toward the scene, but it was too late. The baby was put in the other ambulance. McNamara was told her fate was unknown.[12]

Later, as protests spread around the United States, Norman Morrison's name was almost forgotten. Miraculously, the baby survived unharmed. Hanoi made Morrison into a martyr, mounted exhibits about him, and sent a letter to his widow. To Huu, a North Vietnamese poet, wrote of the baby's redemption "at the cruel edge of your five-faced cathedral of violence." He said in a poem addressed to McNamara:

> *Mr. Secretary, you were looking another way*
> *When grief stalked to your window to forgive you.*

McNamara and Margy sporadically attended Washington's Presbyterian church on New York Avenue, known as Church of the Presidents. In Ann Arbor he had been made an elder in the Presbyterian Church. The Catholic-Protestant conflict in his own upbringing sparked his interest in moral theology, a subject he liked to read about and discuss. The earliest antiwar protests included liberals in several denominations, and McNamara made a point of seeming open to their views.[13] Probably their arguments against the war genuinely interested him.

But the Quaker Norman Morrison was different. That a young American — in photographs he has close-cut hair and a square, high brow — had volunteered for a horrible death and risked his daughter's life, too, shocked McNamara.

Years later he would barely discuss it. He only termed what he had seen from the window "awful," in a very low voice. The suicide was "a personal tragedy for me."[14]

Sobered by Lin Piao, the enemy buildup, the possible futility of his air and ground war strategy — and the carnage beneath his window — McNamara sent a fifteen-page single-spaced memo to the president on November 3. In 1971, the Pentagon Papers revealed its conclusion but not its length or the extent to which it showed him starting to see the problem of Vietnam through new eyes.[15]

Their decisions to bomb and send troops "make sense only if they are in support of a long-run United States policy to contain Communist China," he told Johnson. He likened China to Germany in 1917, to Germany and Japan in the 1930s, to the Soviet Union in 1947, when it launched the cold war. China was capable of "mobilizing the people and resources of Asia" against the West. Thus "the role we have inherited and chosen for ourselves" was to use our power to "move the world . . . in the direction we prefer." This could not be done if "some powerful and virulent nation — whether Germany, Japan, Russia or China — is allowed to organize their part of the world according to a philosophy contrary to ours."

McNamara reassured the president that the U.S. infusion of "ideas, aid and manpower" had "frustrated" a decisive Communist takeover of South Vietnam. But the war continued at a "high pace." South Vietnam's economy was "deteriorating." Ky had made no political progress since the summer. Meanwhile the enemy was "savagely" destroying rural authority. The "base of political support" necessary for a viable non-Communist society was not developing.

He seized upon the enemy's continuing "vigor," which was contrary to their expectation of July, that flexing American might would bring change by the end of the year. That summer the size of enemy regular forces increased from 6,000 to 71,300; the number of cadres increased by one third, to 40,000; and the number of guerrillas increased by one fifth, to 110,000. U.S. deployments of July had been based on friendly-to-enemy force ratios that were now obsolete.

The defense secretary drew grimmer conclusions than Lodge, Rusk, or Westmoreland, who had the same information. His instinct for singling out a key fact, which helped him see through the alleged missile gap in 1961, for example, now helped him penetrate the orthodoxy that American power and technology would quickly turn the tables in this war. Now, the "investment" they had made in military force was bound to diminish over time, he told the president. They could "increase our investment," or they could compromise, get out, and let South Vietnam go.

McNamara quickly rejected compromise, arguing that they had gone too far to turn back. Moreover, winning "public acceptance" of lowered sights would be hard. If they compromised now, they risked "political humiliation" and "more costly confrontations later on."

To avoid "stagnation" and "disintegration," McNamara said, they were "left . . . with the need to deploy additional US or Free World forces." They should try a bombing halt of several weeks to test enemy willingness to talk and also to show the world they had tried to find a way out. This would be followed by a second phase of troop deployments in 1966 and a wider bombing campaign in the North.

The once-confident optimist was now guarded. Success, he warned the president, required that the political and military situation in South Vietnam "snowball" in America's favor. But the snowball could roll back. "The odds are even that, despite our efforts, we will be faced in early 1967 with stagnation at a higher level."

In November 1965, McNamara learned of the first large engagement between Westmoreland's troops and enemy regulars in the valley of the Drang River, near the Laos border. The Americans fought skillfully and won; new helicopter units were decisive. But the body count claimed 240 Americans dead versus 2,262 enemy. McNamara told Johnson on November 3 that by early 1967, after another eighteen months, "US killed-in-action can be expected to increase to 500-800 a month." Now almost half of the lower number had died in one engagement.

Westmoreland and the chiefs were elated. Even the normally skeptical chief of staff of the Army, General Johnson, said, "After the battle of Ia Drang, the worst was behind us."[16]

As reports of the battle reached the Pentagon, staffer Henry Glass noticed how close the Drang River valley was to the Laos border. Westmoreland was supposed to be using his troops around Saigon. What are they doing way the hell over near Laos? he asked McNamara as the reports came in. Whatever his private doubts, McNamara said calmly, "We can't run this war from Washington; let West-moreland run it."[17]

McNamara was moving inexorably toward a moral choice on a scale that few people, and few high officials, face in their lifetime. He had made an enormous miscalculation in July when he promised, in effect, that the U.S. intervention would be limited and controlled. Now what to do? Westmoreland hastened his growing anxiety on November 23 by cabling Washington with a request for many more troops, just as McNamara was off to NATO meetings in Paris. The general wanted forty battalions to be sent in the second phase, through June 1967, instead of the twenty-eight battalions McNamara had already recommended. The secretary of defense flew from Paris to Saigon for his seventh visit.

There he saw how the decisions of July were changing the country. He toured the huge concrete structures of a new naval facility at Cam Ranh Bay; he saw warehouses, fuel depots, helicopter pads; he saw the C-130s now flown by the Air Force to support the Army in the theater and to bring out bodies in brown, slick bags stacked for loading. From the air, the verdant landscape northwest of Saigon was now pockmarked with craters from the B-52 strikes.

Westmoreland, tall, even-featured, humorless, said he needed twelve more battalions to do the job right, the Army way. The general's spit-shined briefers told their civilian superior that the enemy "buildup rate is predicted to be double" their previous estimate.[18] Friendly-to-enemy force ratios would shrink to as low as 2.1 to 1.

McNamara heard how the general proposed to use the force to engage the enemy in the central region, where Communist regulars had been detected; to open the highway from Saigon to Vung Tau, on the coast. U.S. troops could block Viet Cong recruits from delta villages from reinforcing new enemy units near Saigon. In fact, West-moreland was proposing a version of General Paul Harkins's old three-year plan, based on the Army's institutional lore that infantry war — in Europe, Korea, or Southeast Asia — was all the same: build a killing machine, turn it loose, "attrit" the enemy, and win.[19] But attrition war would be slow work; Prime Minister Ky told McNa-mara that after two years of this kind of war, his government would control 50 percent of the country, down from the 65 percent Ky had estimated when McNamara visited in July.

✳   ✳   ✳

McNamara's public remarks hid his most pessimistic thoughts, but reporters picked up a new mood in the congenital optimist. "Mc-Namara finds Hanoi's build-up means long war," said a *New York Times* headline; a *Columbus Dispatch* headline proclaimed, "Toughness of Viet Cong amazes McNamara."

"He looked different" when he came back from that Vietnam trip, recalls Chester Cooper, McGeorge Bundy's deputy on Vietnam. Cooper remembers seeing McNamara step into Bundy's office on his return. At a glance, Cooper saw that McNamara looked "concerned" and "grave, either about what he saw in Saigon or about the upcoming meeting giving the news to LBJ, or both."[20]

McNamara carried in to Johnson on November 30 a three-page "supplement" to his long memo of November 3. The middle of page 1 warned of "dramatic recent changes," of "the increased infiltration from the North and the increased willingness of the Communist forces to stand and fight," as at Ia Drang. The enemy could have 150 battalions in South Vietnam by the end of 1966, when "hopefully his losses can be made to equal his input."

He recommended sending the extra battalions Westmoreland wanted for Phase II, putting 400,000 Americans there by December 1966, and added that "further deployments (perhaps exceeding 200,000) may be needed in 1967."

But "deployments of the kind I have recommended will not guarantee success. US killed-in-action can be expected to reach 1,000 a month, and the odds are even that we will be faced in early 1967 with a 'no-decision' at an even higher level" of casualties.[21]

On December 6, McNamara dispatched to the president a grimmer version of this memo. "The United States must send a substantial number of additional forces to Vietnam if we are to avoid being defeated there," he said. He did not mention raising taxes; he said more troops could be sent without calling up the reserves.

He closed with a statement that is startling in light of his public optimism at the time and his later claim that he believed the war was "militarily unwinnable."

> If the US were willing to commit enough forces — perhaps 600,000 men or more — we could ultimately prevent the DRV/VC from sustaining the conflict at a significant level. When this point was reached, however, the question of Chinese intervention would become critical.

Hanoi and Peking might at that point yield and

> salvage their resources for another day; but there is an almost equal
> chance that they would enlarge the war. . . . and bring in large num-
> bers of Chinese forces . . . the odds are about even that, even with the
> recommended deployments, we will be faced in early 1967 with a
> military standoff at a much higher level, with pacification still stalled,
> and with any prospect of military success marred by the chances of an
> active Chinese intervention.[22]

Robert McNamara looked into the abyss and saw three years of war
leading only to stalemate, and he warned the president.[23] He went
through the motions of considering compromise but rejected this
course. He saw his miscalculation but stuck with the war that winter;
he was committed to it, politically, publicly, and emotionally. Giving
up was not in his program or his temperament. And he believed the
cause was just: To contain Lin Piao's expansionary China was "the
role we have chosen for ourselves," the duty of American power.

Henceforth, McNamara's public promotion of the war and private
skepticism would have a tense moral dimension. As long as the war
went on — and two and a half years was very long on McNamara's
time scale — as many as 1,000 young Americans a month were going
to die. In November 1965, the toll of Americans lost in Vietnam since
1961 passed the 1,000 mark.[24] He once told me that those rising
numbers were one of his deepest concerns. "Numbers, as you know,
are a language to me."

McNamara could have gone public and revealed that he thought
the military situation was worse than General Westmoreland and the
Joint Chiefs of Staff said it was, that they might have to send 600,000
American troops instead of the 200,000-plus so far announced by the
administration, and tried to turn the war off by speaking out. But
support for the war still ran strong; his naysaying could have brought
escalation in the hopes of a quick win. Had McNamara's voice caused
a pullout and spared American suffering, South Vietnam would have
suffered — and fallen.

For many of McNamara's critics on the left and right, his performance, after his supposed moment of disillusion in late 1965, was
fraudulent because he went on publicly supporting the war and the
fighting men when he knew the war would be more frustrating and

bloody than Westmoreland or the administration as a whole was saying. He should have stepped out of government and stopped it; therefore, by staying he caused needless U.S. casualties. David Halberstam wrote in 1979, for example, that McNamara's "entire role contradicts his image of a man who will sacrifice his career for moral purposes. . . . The real McNamara is someone who says one thing in public and always follows the mandate of his superiors in private."[25]

Hesitantly, on the record, McNamara offers a partial explanation of why he chose to stay in his job and went on supporting the war, in public and in his memos to the president, after the fall of 1965. First, McNamara disputes the popular notion that he was disillusioned about the war in late 1965, because, based on his memos of the spring and own recollection, he had not been convinced they could gain a military victory even in July, when he recommended sending troops.[26] The purpose of the U.S. intervention was to force Hanoi to pull back, which would be a political result, not a military win.

Therefore "it was not in vain" to press on with the ground war, even though he — but not the chiefs and Westmoreland — saw it evolving toward stalemate. "We were trying to press the war in the field and achieve at the same time our diplomatic objective. . . . I thought pressure in the field, pressure militarily, would increase the likelihood of movement on the political track. The linkage between the two tracks was that large-unit military action was exacting a cost.

"And that cost was the stimulus, we hoped, or I hoped, to progress on the political track. It was important that the North Vietnamese believe we could continue that cost through the large-unit actions. *So the fighting was not in vain*, even though I was pessimistic about how well we were doing in the field."

The fact that McNamara's memos were privately pessimistic was part of his duty, he says, in effect. "In my memos to the president, I tried to give the pros and cons of our position, and then end up with my judgment [that] I had real doubts as to whether we could win militarily, and I wanted him to understand that."

As to the moral balance between continuing to expend American lives in what, with hindsight, many would see as the hopeless cause of propping up South Vietnam, McNamara, like many other people during the late sixties, believed Asian communism was expansionary and aggressive. He answered the moral point at the time, more than once, when reporters asked, for example in October 1966, whether sending more Americans was worth it: "I would rather expend a limited number of American lives if it saves millions of South Vietnamese and other Asian peoples," he shot back.[27]

As McNamara headed toward widening the war, he contacted the Kennedy camp, which was becoming critical of Johnson and the conflict. The day he returned from Vietnam, he asked his secretary to get Arthur Schlesinger on the phone. The Harvard historian's new book, *A Thousand Days,* had just come out, based on the diary Schlesinger kept while he worked in the Kennedy White House. The book made headlines by revealing Kennedy's dissatisfaction with Dean Rusk and his plans to make McNamara secretary of state in his second term.

On the phone McNamara said "he wanted some fresh thinking," Schlesinger wrote in his diary on January 21, 1966.

Schlesinger arranged a dinner at his Georgetown house on January 6 with some other former Kennedy advisers: Carl Kaysen, Richard Goodwin, and John Kenneth Galbraith. Schlesinger recorded that

> the subject was, of course, Vietnam. Bob combined frankness about issues with discretion about personalities in his usual fashion.
>
> McNamara said, as he had before, that he did not regard a military solution as possible. The military advantages of the bombing, he seemed to feel, were marginal and outweighed by the political disadvantages. The infiltration rate had increased steadily (fourfold?) since the bombing had started.

McNamara seemed "skeptical about the value of enlarging our ground forces." When Schlesinger asked "whether the North Vietnamese had increased their commitment in response to or independently of American action, he said flatly the first." When he was asked about U.S. goals, McNamara defined "his objective in South Vietnam as 'withdrawal with honor.' "[28]

The phrase "withdrawal with honor" was literally consistent with McNamara's private advice to the president that their goal should be to force the enemy to stand down and get a favorable settlement, even if it took years and 600,000 American troops. But in the jargon of the emerging doves that winter, withdrawal with honor meant leaving soon in any form that did not immediately cede turf or government control to the Communists. The exact makeup of a government in the South that Washington was prepared to leave behind was the nub of the debate.[29] At Schlesinger's house that night, McNamara seemed to favor the "compromise outcome" scenario he had rejected in memos to the president:

"One gathered that he might even be prepared to consider Viet Cong participation in such a [neutralist] government — presumably on the Laos model," Schlesinger records.[30]

As for McNamara's emotional state, Schlesinger found him "oppressed and concerned at the prospect of indefinite escalation." He wondered, in his diary, why McNamara had sought him out, since the group "had very little to offer" besides "moral and intellectual reinforcement." McNamara clearly used the session to forewarn these men that escalation was on the way. "He may be assembling support among his liberal friends," Schlesinger speculated, but dismissed this thought as "too Machiavellian."

Maybe he had only wanted an evening of "unfettered and far-ranging speculation," Schlesinger went on. "In any case, we all left with increased admiration for his intelligence, openness of mind, and inextinguishable decency."[31]

McNamara was looking for "fresh" ideas when he returned from Vietnam in November, and he was handed one in particular — for a technological "barrier" — that would play a major part in his attempt to redirect the war. Economist Carl Kaysen, who had worked in John Kennedy's White House and then returned to M.I.T., recalls visiting McNamara twice in December 1965 in his office.

It was common for leading university scientists and other experts to work on military problems during war, in a long and important tradition dating back to World War I and before. In Cambridge in 1965, there evolved a "floating crap game," Kaysen says, involving a few Harvard and M.I.T. faculty — some with formal Pentagon ties and some without — to brainstorm on ways to resolve the war. Since Hanoi said that an end to the bombing was a precondition for talks and a settlement, the Cambridge group asked "what the bombing was supposed to achieve." It was supposed to lower infiltration; the group then asked if there were other ways to achieve this. Thus the idea arose of the "electronic fence," or "barrier" — later as notoriously linked to McNamara's name as the TFX and the Edsel.

Perhaps America's technology could be used to advantage in the jungle after all, Kaysen's group told McNamara in December. A string of new devices — tiny sensors that detected footfalls, air-dropped mines, remotely guided air and ground fire — could be installed starting at the coast, following the 17th parallel, running inland and continuing straight on across the waist of Laos, intersecting the trails that ran north-south there. Along the border between North and South Vietnam, the Marines could build strongpoints to be aided by remote sensing and could kill anything coming across. Kaysen says the group told McNamara the best a barrier could do was to cut infiltration, not stop it altogether. But if the line imposed enough of a penalty on the enemy, the bombing could become redundant and could be stopped. Hanoi might talk. Meanwhile the United States could continue physically blocking enemy movement south. McNamara's reaction showed his frustration — and too-eager embrace of technological promise.

"McNamara was ready and waiting. He just loved the idea. His attitude was: Great. Get me a proposal," says Kaysen.[32] John McNaughton attended Kaysen's second meeting with McNamara; the former Harvard law professor would become a strong advocate of the barrier. In a memo actually drafted by Harvard law teacher Roger Fisher and retyped on McNaughton's letterhead in January, the plan sounded seductive: "The general theory is to convert the contest from one of will (in which the DRV and VC have as much reason to outlast us as we do to outlast them) to a contest of physical capability in which we are superior."[33]

The plan for the barrier went forward in secret. Scientists in a secret group called the Jason Division of the Institute for Defense Analyses would bring in parallel studies to McNamara by the fall of 1966 — one on the inutility of the bombing, and the second on the practicality of the barrier.[34] McNamara, by then running a much larger war, would still be enthusiastic.

In December 1965, the defense secretary reached for the lever of a bombing pause to induce some enemy response, some lessening of military activity or signal for talks — and thus slow the treadmill of escalation he saw looming.

McNamara's November 3 memo pushed hard for a bombing pause and associated diplomatic and political efforts. Among his arguments was that since the bombing did not affect the pace of the ground war in the South, stopping it would make no military difference to the war there. McNamara still believed that Hanoi might react to shifts in the "pain" from bombing, that the enemy would respond to such supposedly rational signals.

In mid-December, McNamara told the president, "The military solution to the problem is not certain, one out of three or one in two. Ultimately we must find alternative solutions. We must perforce find a diplomatic solution." Johnson said:

"What you are saying is that no matter what we do militarily, there is no sure victory."[35]

"That's right," said McNamara. They had been too optimistic in believing American power would work. "We need to explore other means. Our military action approach is an unacceptable way to a successful conclusion." They continued to talk. The president stood up, yawned, and said, "We'll take the pause." He left the room.[36]

But what kind of pause? Stopping for a few days — as they had in May for the Tet holiday, with no result — for Christmas? It was policy not to announce changes of military plans in advance, so reporters and governments around the world waited as the skies cleared on Christmas Day and the bombers stayed grounded. A thirty-hour ceasefire had been declared, too.

Johnson's closest advisers were in the dark about what would happen next. On December 27, McNamara flew from Aspen, where he had spent Christmas, to the president's Texas ranch. Johnson and Lady Bird greeted him at the hangar. The three dined on quail, rice, peas, and coconut pudding, according to assiduous presidential recordkeepers.[37] The records do not divulge what McNamara discussed with the president from 8:05 to 10:55 in the ranch house living room. But it seems likely that McNamara took advantage of the absence of Dean Rusk, who was a foe of bombing pauses, to work on Johnson to continue the ban on bombing and make a major diplomatic effort toward Hanoi.

Johnson made dozens of phone calls that night. Immediately, American diplomats began flying around the world, conveying the president's supposedly sincere desire to talk, albeit without offering concessions. The "peace offensive" was reported as genuine, although later, when the Pentagon Papers revealed the cynicism of high-level memos on the matter, many concluded it had been a sham.[38]

Hanoi took military advantage of the letup. "The stuff just poured down there [into South Vietnam] during those thirty-seven days," Clark Clifford said later. On January 10 McNamara argued for extending the bombing hiatus to give Hanoi more time, but General Wheeler countered: "Every day increases their capability in the south." On January 25, George Ball wrote that if they resumed sustained bombing, it "will more than likely lead us into war with Red China — probably in six to nine months."[39]

The pause failed. Ho Chi Minh sent a defiant answer to a secret letter from Johnson. William Bundy recalls that the president was infuriated by Ho's tone. From then on "it was a new and tougher ball game."[40] On January 30 the planes lifted off to bomb again. But McNamara signaled Hanoi, through the press, that this was a "soft" resumption, not an escalation. They were striking at "approximately the same level in terms of volume as the average day in the period just prior to the pause."

Privately he could say the bombing made no overall difference to the tempo of war in the South. Publicly he claimed the bombing had an effect in raising the costs to Hanoi. Only the closest textual analysis can determine if the public and private McNamaras are contradictory on the question of the bombing's utility. He told reporters, "We, by photographs and other means, can, I think, prove . . . that we have dramatically increased the cost of infiltration . . . I think we have reduced the flow; we guess we have reduced the capability, or the capacity of the system by perhaps half."[41]

McNamara had pushed for a long suspension in the bombing against near-unanimous opposition from the other advisers, and it hadn't worked. He had left the president open to criticism for putting steel in American boys' backs. Later Clark Clifford, an adviser who was a hawk opposed to the pause, said it was "an emotional issue." When the suspension didn't work, Johnson "felt he had been kind of suckered into it and nothing had come of it and that he'd gotten bad advice on it." The thirty-seven-day pause, therefore, was the beginning of the split between a chastened Robert McNamara and Lyndon Johnson on the war.[42] Later on, Johnson used to refer to it as "the Communist pause."

The bombing hiatus should have been John McNaughton's finest hour, the moment his influence rose and he would be widely seen as McNamara's successor.[43] McNaughton, like his boss, continued to recommend bombing pauses on the grounds that even if this one hadn't worked, later ones might. Insightful yet strange draft memos fairly flew from McNaughton's pen that January, many newly released. How many went to McNamara, and how they influenced him, are unclear.

On January 19, 1966, McNaughton outlined a position opposite to the Vietnam-is-a-vital-interest argument, which had been the basis of his earlier stance in favor of intervention.

> In Vietnam, the Communists probably think their vital interests are involved (and it takes some sophistication to see how the area automatically involves ours). It is not clear that we dominate the area militarily at the subnuclear levels, and honest opinion is split as to who is "right" in the controversy. *We therefore have in Vietnam the ingredients of an enormous miscalculation* [italics added].

McNaughton went on to countenance some "compromise outcome." He noted that "[it] took us almost a year to take the decision to bomb North Vietnam; it took us weeks to decide on a Pause; it could take us months . . . to get us in a position to go for a compromise."[44]

Later, McNaughton would be eulogized by some of his liberal colleagues as a man of great principle. But the McNaughton of these memos is a negotiator, grazing the realities of war and politics. Few of his colleagues would have recommended the following scenario for starving the North Vietnamese *slightly* that McNaughton penned January 18.

> Destruction of locks and dams, however — if handled right — might (perhaps after the next Pause) offer promise. It should be studied. Such destruction does not kill or drown people by shallow flooding the rice; it leads after time to widespread starvation (more than a million?) unless food is provided — which we could do — "at the conference table."[45]

McNamara's decision to stick with the war, and the slim results of his pause, left him facing pressures from the Joint Chiefs to widen the bombing, gain momentum, and force a change of enemy will by destroying its military-industrial complex.

North Vietnam had no oil supplies of its own; it imported 175,000 metric tons of oil a year, mainly delivered by Soviet tankers unloading in the port of Haiphong. Fuel was needed for the trucks and cars to move war matériel to the South. From January 1966 on, the commanders asked to bomb the North's petroleum, oil, and lubricants (POL in military jargon), 97 percent of which were concentrated in only thirteen major storage areas and which constituted a spectacular target system. Results were promised; the Joint Chiefs on March 1 argued that a fast attack on POL would be more damaging to the

Above left: Claranell Strange McNamara, Robert James McNamara, and Bobby, c. 1918, at the beach. *Above:* As an Eagle Scout. *Left:* At right, with friends on the Berkeley campus, c. 1936. *Below:* In an electrical storm on Mount Whitney, California, 1937.

Margaret Craig McNamara on a honeymoon boat trip, 1940.

Accepting President-elect
John Kennedy's offer to be
secretary of defense,
December 13, 1960, at the
door of Kennedy's
Georgetown home.
McNamara had just handed
Kennedy a letter naming his
conditions; Kennedy put it in
his pocket, unsigned.

The nation's eighth secretary
of defense working at the
nine-foot desk that belonged
to General John "Black Jack"
Pershing. Behind McNamara
is a portrait of the first
defense secretary, James V.
Forrestal.

With President Kennedy (in
sunglasses), inspecting a silo
being built to hold the new
Minuteman missile at
Vandenberg Air Force Base,
California, March 23, 1962.
On Kennedy's left is General
Thomas Power, chief of the
Air Force Strategic Air
Command.

Left: Refusing to answer further questions from reporters on February 6, 1963, after McNamara called a press conference to insist that the removal of Soviet missiles from Cuba was adequately monitored. *Below left:* On February 6, 1961, McNamara told reporters at a background briefing that he saw no signs of a missile gap favoring the Soviets, and embarrassed President Kennedy. *Below:* Senator John McClellan held well-publicized hearings in 1963 investigating McNamara's award of a $6.5 billion contract for his new Navy–Air Force fighter-bomber, the TFX.

"You Can Say One Of Our Missile Gaps Has Been Closed."

'ME NAME IS McNAMARA, I'M THE LEADER AND THE BAND . .'

Copper Calhoon, a character in *Steve Canyon*, snickers at McNamara in this strip reprinted in *Time* on May 31, 1963, as doubts about his policies and judgment grew.

Meeting with Ngo Dinh Diem in Saigon, September 29, 1963, to pressure him to reform so the country could better carry on the war. On Diem's left are U.S. ambassador Henry Cabot Lodge and General Maxwell Taylor.

Pessimistic news reports from South Vietnam in 1963 by David Halberstam of the *New York Times* (left), Malcolm Browne of the Associated Press (center), and Neil Sheehan of United Press International contrasted sharply with official optimism.

Hearing a military briefing given at the residence of a province chief in September 1963. Ambassador Lodge listens skeptically. The portrait above is of President Diem.

Conferring with President Lyndon Johnson on Saturday, November 23, 1963, while John Kennedy's body lay in state in the East Room.

Below: Briefing the press during the night of August 4–5, 1964, as U.S. planes hit North Vietnam for the first time.

Left: Barnstorming around South Vietnam in March 1964. President Johnson instructed McNamara to show the people that the new leader, Nguyen Khanh, had Washington's full support.

Right: Awarding a Purple Heart to Captain Paul V. Daugherty at a U.S. Navy hospital in Saigon, July 17, 1965. *Far right:* Studying a map showing government- and enemy-controlled areas in the vicinity of Bien Hoa Air Base, July 20, 1965.

Speaking to the president after touching down from Saigon on the morning of July 21, 1965. George Ball is at far left. Next to Ball is Secretary of State Dean Rusk.

Hiking in Zermatt, Switzerland, with the Matterhorn in the background, August 1964. From left are Margy McNamara, Willard Goodwin, Craig McNamara, Mary Joe Goodwin, Peter Goodwin, McNamara, and Willard Goodwin II.

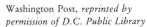

Touring LBJ's boyhood home of Johnson City, Texas, in the president's white Cadillac, April 1965. In the rear seat, with the Johnsons' dog, are Margy McNamara and Lady Bird Johnson.

Having a word with Bobby Kennedy at the entrance to the McNamara home on Tracy Place, during the wedding reception for the McNamaras' elder daughter, Margaret, in September 1966.

Associated Press

Associated Press

United Press International/Bettmann

Telling Senator John Stennis of his conviction that heavier bombing of North Vietnam would escalate the war without resolving it, August 25, 1967.

Briefing reporters on his plan to build an electronic fence to cut infiltration into South Vietnam, September 7, 1967.

Looking from the window of his Pentagon office during the evening of October 21, 1967, at fifty thousand antiwar protesters demonstrating below.

Associated Press

At Medal of Freedom ceremony at the White House, February 28, 1968. The McNamara family is to the right of the president. Incoming defense secretary Clark Clifford (hands clasped) is seated at left.

McNamara's Pentagon departure ceremony, February 29, 1968.

L. D. Warren and Cincinnati Enquirer

Washington Post, reprinted by permission of D.C. Public Library

The *Cincinnati Enquirer* captured the antigovernment, antitechnology mood of the country, and McNamara as a symbol of failure, in this cartoon, which appeared on February 6, 1968.

Courtesy World Bank

Left: McNamara is at the center of the group (in white shirt) viewing a rice field in Somalia. *Below:* Describing how the World Bank would meet the needs of Africa to reporters, September 1968, when he gave his first address to the Board of Governors. *Below left:* Margy McNamara in the Colorado Rockies in 1976.

Associated Press

Courtesy Robert McNamara

Associated Press

Testifying before the Senate Foreign Relations Committee, December 1990, in favor of continuing sanctions against Iraq instead of early military action. At right is Arthur M. Schlesinger, Jr.

enemy's ability to wage war "than an attack against any other single target system."[46]

McNamara refused to endorse the proposal; hitting North Vietnam's fuel stocks would make no difference, he thought. On background, he had told Stanley Karnow and other reporters in his hotel room in Honolulu that February, "You cannot bomb an agrarian society into submission."

Yet all spring he was urged to undertake this significant escalation. When the North began importing more trucks and dispersing its POL, and when he was handed an opinion by the CIA favoring a big air campaign, McNamara finally recommended that POL be hit.

In June, the order went out. McNamara stepped under the klieg lights at the Pentagon, in front of his gold curtain, to report on the critical new step.[47]

He had become a classic sight, his gleaming spectacles and square forehead and rapid-fire voice, his lower jaw jutting out in determination. He spoke and moved almost robotically, while statistics poured forth like the computer of his public image. He personified the war machine even as he fought it from within.

The effect of the escalation was to greatly expand the air war McNamara ran; sorties doubled during 1966 as a result, with a corresponding increase in cost, including bombs to be produced and paid for. But all that happened was that the tempo of enemy fighting in the South increased, although the commanders made sweeping claims of success. And now McNamara made little secret, even in public, that this wider bombing achieved little.[48] His open anger came partly from guilt, since he had suspected it wouldn't work at the time he approved it. The war was ratcheting upward instead of down. So were Robert McNamara's emotions.

Nineteen sixty-six was a year of disillusion and confusion for McNamara, as indeed it was for the country. The war manager who seemed so certain before the television cameras was inwardly lost.

If his first miscalculation was the scale of the conflict, his second was the war's likely cost. A bigger, longer war could ruin the chances for large-scale aid to Appalachia and other victims of poverty, for medical care, housing, cities, and all the other issues on which Lyndon Johnson wanted to go down in history as a great president. But Johnson's political instincts told him Congress would not vote for his domestic bills if major new funds or a tax increase was needed for the war. The president's game now was to avoid making Congress or the country face this choice.

So McNamara the master accountant became a key player in decisions that, combined with poor economic choices by the next administration, created the inflation and weaker U.S. economy of the 1970s. Indirectly, in an ironic twist, this chain of decisions strengthened Europe as an economic power, which would be very important to McNamara at the World Bank.

McNamara has argued that he wanted the war to be paid for by open and honest accounting. But such was his loyalty to Johnson that he set to work hiding the full cost — until it was too late and the wild horse of inflation had run from the barn.

Meanwhile, his suspicion of the military had not abated. He feared the services would use the war as an excuse to insist on programs and funds he thought unwise. As Lyndon Johnson said later to biographer Doris Kearns, McNamara enforced a "requirement" — which the president endorsed — that the Joint Chiefs "were not to receive one nickel" for the war "without a plan."[49]

When McNamara visited South Vietnam in July 1965, he learned from Cyrus Vance's top-secret cable that the president was ready to send Westmoreland up to 175,000 troops and call up the reserves but insisted he could ask Congress for no more than $300–$400 million in new funds. McNamara protested, as McGeorge Bundy wrote to Johnson, that gross understatement of the costs would get them in trouble. The full costs — which were then pegged at an additional $8 billion in the current fiscal year — "will be sure to come out pretty quickly, especially if he looks as if he was trying to pull a fast one."[50]

In preparing the defense budget within the Pentagon in late 1965, McNamara instructed his new controller, Robert N. Anthony, to apply the rule used in the Berlin crisis — when the reserves were called up, the country faced war. Anthony and the services were to build a budget on the assumption the Vietnam War would end by the last day of the fiscal year, that is, by June 30, 1967. This was arbitrary but made sense when the government faced a crisis, no one knew the outcome, and hundreds of people in many agencies had to plan and allot funds on some common basis. The purpose of the cutoff was to let the military pay for its immediate needs but disallow long-lead-time items justified on possible levels of conflict that were not certain. A very important dimension of budgeting for Vietnam, to McNamara, Anthony, and others, was that federal law made misestimation a crime. Thus a simple, uniform assumption, so long as McNamara said it was arbitrary, kept him and hundreds of government workers within the law.[51]

McNamara promised the president and, in effect, the public that "Vietnam would be the most economically fought war in history."[52] They would not make the mistake of the Korean War, when Congress in the emergency spirit of fiscal 1951 appropriated an enormous sum, and at war's end there was $65 billion still unspent, which made fiscal control impossible in the years immediately afterward. McNamara's assurance and expertise were welcome, for Johnson feared to the point of paranoia that a debate over war costs could not only jeopardize the Great Society but also put the hawks in Congress in command.

Most Americans in the fall of 1965 did not realize Lyndon Johnson had taken them into war. There had been no reserve call-up; there was no enemy baiting or flag waving; administration spokesmen mentioned only that 125,000 men were being sent (and not the full 175,000 planned or the increase to 210,000 agreed on in late fall). The administration explained that it was sending soldiers into combat as an expedient to turn the tide, to stop a full defeat of South Vietnam, although it hinted that more troops could be sent and that U.S. soldiers might have to "remain" for some time. But there was no public mention of the plans to give Westmoreland another 200,000 men for Phase II by December 1966, which Westmoreland began pressing for that winter. Thus, 400,000 Americans were likely to go to Vietnam, and the country did not know it.

The business community, and some in Congress and the press, speculated on how big the war could become and what it could cost.[53] The issue was real: A big deficit or a tax hike, or wage and price controls — which were the options for financing a major war — could wreck the American economy, then charging along at the peak of the American Century. For years, unemployment had been dropping and was now close to 5 percent; inflation was virtually nonexistent, and the booms in investment and consumer spending sparked by the tax cuts of 1962 and 1964 were taking hold. Could the war go to 500,000 troops and $10 billion, as rumored?

Gardner Ackley, chairman of the respected independent Council of Economic Advisers, which had shaped these successful policies, was due to give a speech on September 9. Ackley pressed McNamara on how high the bill could go.

McNamara assured him they were thinking nowhere near the $10 billion figure. So Ackley scotched the rumors publicly.[54] Four months later, when the president and McNamara revealed that the war bill for fiscal 1966 would be closer to $12 billion, Ackley was furious. He never trusted McNamara after that.

Accounts of McNamara's deceit of Ackley at this moment have not noted that the incident happened before September 9. That is, McNamara was assuring Ackley that the cost of the war was under control before the enemy buildup of October-November, before the "difficult and inconclusive" night meeting of September 11, when McNamara, Rusk, Bundy, and Ball considered not even going up to 200,000 troops in the first wave, before Ia Drang and the grim intelligence on future enemy escalation. However, McNamara's later downplaying of the war's costs to other officials in government was not so defensible.

McNamara had quickly opened new production lines for bombs and ammunition. The bills were coming due that fall, but the fiscal 1966 budget then governing disbursements had been passed nearly a full year before, without the war in mind. A very senior civil servant in the controller's office recalls the problem.[55]

Legally, McNamara could not approve payment for items for which Congress had not appropriated funds; this harness on executive deviation from legislative will was a principle of the republic dating back to the Boston Tea Party. But Defense needed money fast.

Joseph Hoover — the senior budget officer in the controller's office — proposed an answer. While it was a criminal offense to *transfer* funds among appropriations accounts, perhaps they could *borrow* from other accounts, saying they would give the money back later.

Maurice Lanman of the general counsel's office was upset; the tactic was illegal. McNamara cut him short. "Don't tell me I can't do it. Tell me how I can do it," he ordered.

Thus began a raid on other parts of the defense budget. For example, items with long lead time, such as shipbuilding accounts whose funds had been authorized years before yet were still unexpended, were used. The Treasury Department knew about the maneuvers. It is very likely that McNamara privately informed congressional leaders to gain legislative approval and stay within the law.

Then came the fall 1965 enemy buildup, the battle of Ia Drang, and McNamara's terrible insight that they were on a treadmill of escalation likely to lead to 600,000 U.S. troops in Vietnam by mid-1967.

His November 3 memo estimated the cost of Westmoreland's first infusion of troops at $13 billion.[56] He knew a steady, large expansion of defense orders would strain U.S. companies, which were going full tilt to meet domestic consumer demand. The risks of inflation were high, unless consumer demand was slaked by a tax hike. Worse, many of the added billions would be spent overseas, causing the U.S. balance of payments (which McNamara had worked to keep favorable since 1961 by selling American arms to the NATO allies) to start hemorrhaging red ink.

"Bob McNamara had a better grasp of economics than anyone I have seen in the Cabinet," recalled Walter Heller, the former CEA chairman who was the nation's most prominent economist at the time.[57]

But McNamara's understanding of the ballooning budget problem made him no more open with others. He continued to be obtuse with Ackley and the CEA and with Henry Fowler, the secretary of the treasury. He said he didn't know what the total war costs would be; he claimed a low figure could be $11 billion, a high $17 billion, the median $15 billion.[58] His vagueness on the high figure is more shocking considering that, in a separate channel unknown to these economic officials, McNamara was simultaneously predicting the escalation to 600,000 American troops by mid-1967, despite the assumption that the war would end by June 30 of that year, now the basis of budget estimates. Anthony told me later that he was not instructed by McNamara that winter to revise the assumption.

So the key debate was restricted to a tight group involving the president, McNamara, and a few others over what lump sum to plop into the budget and announce in January 1966 as the estimated cost of Vietnam in fiscal 1967, and over whether to press for a tax hike to head off inflation. Ackley and Fowler felt like outsiders; that they were the responsible economic officials in the land didn't matter, apparently.

Where McNamara really stood was not clear. Walter Heller said McNamara wanted to raise taxes right away and thought he could persuade the president to announce a tax hike in January 1966. Heller had been summoned by the president to the ranch in December and debated the need for a tax increase, which Heller favored. Johnson seemed "genuinely persuaded he couldn't get it out of Congress," Heller told me later. After the visit, he telephoned McNamara. McNamara "gave me the feeling that there was a good chance we could persuade the president to go for a five percent surtax." When Heller sounded doubtful, McNamara repeated, "I think we'll be able to persuade the president."[59]

But in other circles, apparently because he knew the president's mind, McNamara spoke out against a tax hike and overruled the objections of the less articulate Henry Fowler, for example. It was an all-too-familiar side of McNamara: loyal to the president, arguing an unwise position, which he privately disagreed with, to help Johnson maneuver. An associate of Fowler's says, "The country was not well served by Bob McNamara that winter." Adds another participant in the discussion who was part of this debate and also acquiesced in the president's wishes on taxes, "It was not our finest hour."[60]

McNamara even may have encouraged Johnson's reluctance to state a high figure for Vietnam and ask for a tax increase. The debate took place in December and January, when he was urging Johnson to prolong the bombing pause and claiming Hanoi might respond. McNamara may have transformed a faint and unrealistic hope for early resolution into some sort of assurance to Johnson that he could resolve the war soon, within a year, for example.

This explanation is advanced by Arthur Krock, the formidable former Washington bureau chief of the *New York Times*. Krock knew the president fairly well. "Why did Johnson think he could escalate the costs of the Vietnam war on such a scale and still believe he could get away with no call for increased taxes?" Krock wrote to a friend in 1972. "The answer . . . is *McNamara's prediction of a clear out by June, 1966* [sic]. . . . LBJ was so eager to believe McNamara that he abandoned his own usually sound comprehension that you have to pay for what you buy" [italics added].[61]

And finally, as the January deadline neared for releasing the budget, announcing the estimated costs of Vietnam, and stating whether he would ask Congress for a tax hike, Fowler, Ackley, and Schultze told Johnson he could postpone asking for a tax increase in January and press ahead with his domestic agenda in Congress. "It may only be feasible to propose higher taxes later in the year," they said. Even Wilbur D. Mills, chairman of the House Ways and Means Committee, gave such advice. The president could come back later for more funds and a tax hike if "the acceleration in expenditures continues," Mills told Fowler.[62]

Clearly Johnson wanted to procrastinate. He unveiled the proposed fiscal 1967 defense budget in January, seeking a record $57 billion for defense, of which $10 billion would be the cost of the war. In a typical subterfuge, the president asked for a very small tax increase, which Congress rejected, since the $10 billion figure offered no urgent case for passing one. Now Johnson could whine that Congress would not go along with a big tax hike.

McNamara, ever helpful on this matter, proceeded to defend the $10 billion estimate in public and explain his "arbitrary assumption" that the war would end by June 30, 1967.[63] Neither he nor others discussed their plan to raise troop levels to 400,000 that year or the chance that there could be 600,000 Americans in Vietnam by the proposed end of the war.

In most accounts, Johnson and McNamara are supposed to have sacrificed proper financing of the war to save the Great Society. But Schultze, who is as responsible as McNamara for what happened and has rarely discussed it in public since, offers an important explanation of Johnson's reluctance and fears. The president avoided asking for a major tax increase because he feared the generals, Schultze explains. "He couldn't have gotten a tax increase on economic grounds alone; you can't sell Congress on tax hikes. He could have gotten it by wrapping himself in the flag and declared Hanoi despicable and sought wage and price controls and called out that National Guard. I recall Joe [Henry] Fowler telling him, Mr. President, if you make it a war tax you'll get it. But — people forget this — Johnson at that time was a dove. He knew that to get a tax hike he'd have to call it a war. As Toynbee says, it's easy as hell to get a democracy to hate somebody. He literally was afraid he'd lose control."[64]

Through 1966 McNamara was the president's hard-nosed servant. He deflected questions and speculation about the future scale of the war and its cost. He displayed an amazing ignorance of whether the war would get larger or smaller, whether it was likely to end sooner or later. Since he didn't know, it would be "irresponsible" to name a figure. He answered questions on future troop numbers artfully, steering clear of any hint of a wider war. He avoided lending any credence to those who suspected — rightly — that Johnson was in it deeper than he said and was going deeper still.[65]

When, on one occasion, a reporter pressed too hard on the point, McNamara exploded. He snapped that the reporter's figures were wrong and that he didn't know what he was talking about. It was the same display he used to deflect the nation's top economic officials, who were faring no better.

Before the House Appropriations Committee's Subcommittee on Defense in February 1966, when McNamara was repeating that he couldn't give a firm estimate lest it be shown to be a miscalculation, Chairman George Mahon said to him, Look, our commitment in Vietnam now is far bigger than you predicted a few years ago. "Where have we miscalculated?"

"I do not know if you should call it a miscalculation," McNamara replied solemnly.[66]

Still, in 1966 the economic damage was not great, although the signs of inflation began to show. Prices of domestic goods began rising, and workers began to demand higher wage hikes to keep pace with the rising cost of living.

McNamara tried to run the war frugally, but his holding back on costs opened him to charges from Congressman Gerald Ford of "shocking mismanagement" and major claims of "shortages" that were hurting the war effort, voiced through writer Hanson Baldwin. John McNaughton's trips to Europe to buy back bombs from the allies, which McNamara's energetic arms sales office had sold them earlier to help the U.S. payments balance, was a striking symbol of the much-discussed mismanagement of the war. McNamara's frugality, and zeal for control, ran completely against the grain of the traditional conduct of American wars, in which the public and Congress heap money on the armed forces in the belief that added dollars will spare American lives.

Thus arose the ugliest military-civilian conflict of the era, the charge by senior officials that civilians were nickel and diming the fighting forces and thereby needlessly drawing out the war, expending more American lives rather than fewer. The counterargument from McNamara and his staff, that the services were playing tricks and causing shortages by hiding things in warehouses,[67] using the war to "get well," held no comparable political clout, for Congress and the public saw a frustrating war and wondered if the answer wasn't just to pay more and win.

At the time, McNamara was personally tormented by the charge of shortages. He would talk on for fifty minutes in a meeting, nonstop, proving that the shortages did not exist.[68] He was becoming hurt and angry, because his humane purposes in fighting a limited war, in keeping it limited, were being lost in public and private debate.

The moment that liberals and conservatives turned decisively on McNamara and his boss, when the charge of liar took hold for good, was November 30, 1966. That day, at the Johnson ranch in Texas, the true cost of the war in the fiscal year was acknowledged to be not the $10 billion or $12 billion McNamara had put forward earlier, but $20 billion. And the federal deficit, instead of being $1.8 billion, as announced in January, would reach a shocking all-time high of $9 billion.

Not by coincidence, the Eighty-ninth Congress had gone home, having passed a second landslide of Great Society programs and without having taken up a major debate on the war, which the revelation of its true likely cost and the request for new taxes would have provoked.

The press speculated openly now that Johnson and McNamara had systematically understated the real costs of the war and left the country a substantial deficit. Tom Wicker, in a December 8 column in the *New York Times*, charged McNamara with mismanagement. An angry McNamara called him to say he had not misestimated the cost; he had known the total expense would not be $10 billion or $12 billion for some time. He had abandoned the end-of-fiscal-1967 assumption the previous April. But Mr. Secretary, you didn't tell us until now, Wicker said.

Johnson did not push hard for a tax rise until the summer of 1967. His political calculation had been accurate. His "moment" of power to pass controversial domestic programs had been fleeting. Not only did Congress now balk at his domestic programs, but Congressman Mills and others dallied on the tax increase until mid-1968. By then inflation had started to rise, as the price the nation paid for another congressional session's worth of Great Society legislation.[69]

The historical issue is whether the initial inflationary twist was unavoidable. Taxes or wage-price controls could easily have enabled the United States to fight the war without major economic distortion, since the war at its height, in 1968, consumed only 3 percent of the gross national product.[70] The cost of Johnson's policies was inflation. But had he sought a war tax in 1966, most people think now (as they did then), he could not have had the stream of programs passed by Congress in the interim.

In their miscalculation of the ultimate length and costs of the war, McNamara and Johnson could be accused of short-term horizons and a fixation with minimizing costs on the bottom line — a charge often leveled at McNamara's brand of management in other contexts. This is what the distinguished pilot and North Vietnamese prisoner of war Colonel James Stockdale meant when he angrily denounced the Vietnam War as "a misguided experiment of the Harvard Business School crowd."[71] And Johnson's obfuscation and concealment on money matters set a new standard for later presidents, who felt freer to decouple their short-term political needs from those of sound fiscal management.

But McNamara's and Johnson's many critics rarely specify what they would have been willing to sacrifice to have had Vietnam paid for as it unfolded and funded more generously, so the fighting men felt less demoralized and shortchanged. And the crucial debate a tax request would have sparked might not have led to quick withdrawal, but a wider and longer war.

Ironically, Lyndon Johnson's judgment holds up well with time. Had he submitted a sizable request for funds and taxes in early 1966, the country could have had a bigger war and less inflation, but fewer of the social programs that benefited the country in the long run.[72]

McNamara's illusion that he could control the forces starting to shake the country raised his hyperactivity to new heights. Hiking on their family camping trips, he and his old friend Willard Goodwin would go off on their own, after camp was made for the night.

"Dad and Willard wouldn't come back for hours, until after dark. Everyone would be worried," says his daughter Margaret.

Craig found his father so agitated that, being loyal in his own way, he avoided asking him about Vietnam, which was, of course, the main topic on his own mind as he approached draft age and, like all young people, wondered about the war's values and implications. But McNamara was uncommunicative at best on the matter.[73]

On November 6, 1966, McNamara visited Harvard. His welcome at the business school was cordial. Then he was driven across the Charles River to speak to a group at Quincy House, one of the

Harvard undergraduate houses. Harvard, like other campuses, had seen antiwar protests since March of the same year.

McNamara emerged from Quincy House and started to get into a campus police car on Mill Street. A crowd estimated at eight hundred surrounded the car, prevented it from moving, and then began rocking it. McNamara jumped out, climbed on top of the car, and said, "OK, fellas, I'll answer one or two of your questions. . . . We're in a mob and I don't want anyone hurt — I also have an appointment on the other side of the river in five minutes."

Michael Ansara, a leader of Students for a Democratic Society, then a little-known protest group, produced a microphone and asked for questions from the crowd. Someone asked why the administration insisted that the war resulted from the aggression of Hanoi after 1957.

McNamara retorted that the "aggression started after 1954, not 1957." They knew it "because the International Control Commission wrote a report that said so. You haven't read it and if you have you obviously didn't understand it." Someone shouted that he had read it. "Why don't you guys get up here since you already seem to have all the answers," McNamara answered.

A student asked why the government didn't publish the numbers of South Vietnamese civilians killed.

We don't know how many South Vietnamese civilians have been killed, McNamara shouted, that's why we don't publish the figures.

A policeman scrambled up on top of the car to protect him, but McNamara shoved the man off. Running through his mind were the student protests he saw as an undergraduate at Cal in the midthirties. Later he would say of the Harvard incident, "It was a terrible situation. There was a great danger of people getting hurt or actual loss of life. I was under tremendous stress and trying to calm the crowd, to reduce the uncontrollable and uncontrolled emotions that existed."

In fact, at the time, he taunted the students. "Listen. I spent four of the happiest years of my life on the Berkeley campus, doing some of the things you're doing here," he yelled from the top of the police car. "But there was an important difference. I was tougher and more courteous.

"I was tougher than you and I am tougher today."[74]

By the end of 1966, Bob McNamara found that being tough, mentally and emotionally, was getting harder.

18

Utopia Postponed

BOB MCNAMARA needed to believe he was a virtuous man, and he needed others to believe it, too.

At a commencement ceremony at Amherst College, in Massachusetts, in June 1966, a number of graduating students wore black armbands signifying their protests of the Vietnam War. McNamara sat on the podium as the graduates received their diplomas and took note of a startling fact. Later he asked one of the graduates why more summa cum laudes wore armbands than any other group.[1]

It was a disturbing observation by the man who raided universities and think tanks of their best and brightest. The war was alienating McNamara from the sort of youth with whom he had felt at ease.

In less tumultuous times, he would have been completely welcome at Chatham College, in Pittsburgh, as guest speaker at his younger daughter Kathleen's graduation, but picketers hooted at him there, too. It was hard for any member of the Johnson administration to appear on campus, so rapidly were students and professors shifting against the war.

After he was shouted at or reviled by a mob, he would return to his office, shrug off questions, dive into his room, shut the door, and stay there alone for a long time.

During 1966, McNamara began to answer his accusers. He was suddenly on fire and burning with zeal to fix America, the arms race, and NATO. His was no backstage effort; he charged into these tasks visibly, theatrically, as though he were yanking up a blind to let the world look through at the real Robert McNamara.

Home was uncomfortable, too. He needed Margy more, as his inner agitation grew.[2] Meanwhile, along with other parents of the 1960s, the McNamaras found that providing three children with affluence and opportunities beyond any they themselves ever had did not create domestic tranquillity. All of the children were affected by the spirit of rebellion that marked their generation, and by the peculiar circumstance of being the children of the perpetrator of Vietnam. Their name was on the war, and their peers noticed.

Daughter Margaret was least affected; she was older than most of the student protesters and in the group that the war passed by. Shier than either parent, Margaret avoided putting herself forward in school or student groups "because of my name," she says. "People attached such importance to my name." She left Washington University, in St. Louis, in 1966 to marry a young reserve officer, Barry Carter. The McNamaras gave her a big church wedding, and Lyndon Johnson threw a party at the White House for her.

Kathy was less insulated; she was in college just when the antiwar movement took hold. Sharp, articulate, and confident, she had inherited her father's temperament. She rebelled strongly against both parents, defying them on matters of dress and decorum and thereby rocking the household. Kathy's rebellion, say family friends, was against everything; it did not spring only from conflict with her father.

In the summer of 1966 she went to work for Bobby Kennedy and became a good friend of Sam Brown's, the antiwar leader. She even had Brown over to Tracy Place for dinner, and the articulate activist faced an entire evening of trying to convert the secretary of defense.

Says Brown: "There was a great effort on the part of all to maintain cordiality. But the arguments became bitter rather early. I was a proselytizer of a cause, and if I could have any influence on a man of McNamara's power I would try. We discussed the war at some considerable length and heat." But Kathy remembers thinking Sam was holding back. She could not tell if he was getting through to her father.

McNamara remembers, typically, the only word of praise dropped by the scruffy, commune-living accuser with whom he spent three hours fighting. On the doorstep, Brown turned to McNamara and said, "Anyone who loves the mountains as much as you do can't be all bad." Brown says, "Yes, I said it."[3]

Margy McNamara bore the brunt of her husband's dependency; even when the children were home, she and Bob spent much time alone, he monopolizing her with his talk. The children had to compete with him for their mother's time, but she was always generous. As their troubles grew, she extended herself more and more. Margy also had her work with Cabinet wives to keep her busy.

In 1966, she was tutoring a child in the district schools, reading from one of her own children's books, when the child asked if he could have the book. Margy agreed, of course, and got the idea for a reading program for the city. With the help of some friends — and later a grant from the Ford Foundation — Reading Is Fundamental was born, and the tiny, cheerful woman now had a career, a board, a budget, volunteers, and even employees, and a mission to send vans around the city so that children could be given the books in them and learn to read. As Margy was pulled several ways, she grew tenser. She was fond of Bobby Kennedy and his disaffection with the war disturbed her, too. Then there was the strain of the war on her husband, who was now grinding his teeth in his sleep. She was quite sick in 1966 but concealed it. Her doctor told her to slow down, but, looking back later, it is clear that she didn't.[4]

Craig, however, now at St. Paul's, an elite boarding school in Concord, New Hampshire, bore the heaviest brunt of Bob McNamara's self-absorption and inability to reach out to his own children. McNamara was emotionally incomplete. He could be paternal to bright young Rhodes scholars and others in his own image, but he could not reach out to Craig, who still had problems reading and who had no talent for statistics. He had none of that aggressive ambition that marked his father's youth: getting A's in school, becoming an Eagle Scout.

While at St. Paul's, Craig began seeing a psychiatrist every Wednesday in Boston. He went to a meeting at which some Quakers said how wrong the war was. Craig telephoned his father at the Pentagon and asked for some information about the war. Surely, he thought, his dad could explain why it wasn't as wrong as these people said. But the written explanation of Vietnam from Dad never arrived in Craig's mailbox.[5]

Did Bob McNamara note Craig's growing crisis? One of his

daughters says, "Dad only noticed when he saw the American flag upside down in Craig's room."

McNamara's debut as public moralist consisted of a powerful speech in May 1966 in Montreal to the American Society of Newspaper Editors, in which he downplayed military force as an instrument of U.S. foreign policy. It was sparked by an argument that he had with Congressman Otto Passman, a critic of foreign aid, who asked McNamara if it wasn't true that American military aid to foreign countries caused wars in them. To answer Passman's questions, Mc-Namara's staff found some World Bank figures on the number of violent outbreaks in different countries and the amount of U.S. aid given to each.[6]

McNamara made these numbers the nub of his speech. On May 18 he strode before the editors in Montreal with the following assertion: "We still tend to conceive of national security almost solely as a state of armed readiness: a vast awesome arsenal of weaponry. . . . We are still haunted by this concept of military hardware." But for the United States, military hardware was a "negative and narrow" means of security. The essence of security, McNamara said, is "the character" of a nation's "relationships with the world," the "fund of compatible beliefs" and "shared ideals," which made relations with Canada so secure, for example.

His focus, however, was on "the developing nations," the "roughly 100 countries," mainly in "the Southern Hemisphere," that were "caught up in the difficult transition from traditional to modern societies." They represented a "sweeping surge of development, particularly across the whole southern half of the globe," which "has no parallel in history." The poorer these societies were, the more they tended to violence: "There is an irrefutable relationship between violence and economic backwardness. . . . The trend of such violence is up and not down," he warned, citing some statistics.

> In a modernizing society, security means development. Security is not military hardware — though it may include it. Security is not military force — though it may involve it. Security is not traditional military activity, though it may encompass it. Security is development. Without development there can be no security. A developing nation that does not in fact develop simply cannot remain secure.

Remarkably for the man who had seen the hand of Peking and Hanoi behind every guerrilla mortar attack in the highlands of South Vietnam in 1964, McNamara downplayed the role of communism. It was a "gross oversimplification" to regard communism as the central factor in every conflict throughout the underdeveloped world. The turbulent process of modernization was an ideal environment for Communists to manipulate the "wholly legitimate grievances" of developing societies for their own ends.

The United States' role was to "help provide security" to developing nations who "need and request our help" and who were "willing to help themselves." McNamara stressed civic action, that is, "using indigenous military forces for non-military projects, education, public works, health, sanitation, agriculture." He commended the work of American civic action teams around the world and underlined the importance of U.S. economic aid. "The president is determined that our aid . . . should deal directly with the roots of underdevelopment, and not merely attempt to alleviate the symptoms." He called on the allies to do more to aid the Third World. McNamara sounded a softer note than the administration had heretofore when he appealed for "building bridges" to U.S. adversaries — the Soviet Union and China — "to create a community of interest" in the long run.

McNamara's emphasis on constructive alternatives to war set up his surprise ending, when he proposed universal national service. His staff had not expected him to keep it in the final text. He suggested that "every young person" in the United States give two years of service to the country, either in military service, in the Peace Corps, "or in some other volunteer work at home or abroad."[7]

A striking element of McNamara's Chatham and Montreal speeches was their personal overtones, coming from a man who "refused to be known" after five years in Washington, as one journalist puts it.

At Chatham, McNamara alluded to the fears that society "has fallen victim to bureaucratic tyranny of technology and autocracy" and to "Dr. Strangelove sitting at the computer's console." But "the real question, clearly, is not whether we should have tools. But only whether we are becoming tools."

He quoted a sign carried by a demonstrator at Berkeley that said, "I am a human being; do not fold, bend, or mutilate," and added, "It is a sentiment we can all emphatically agree with."[8]

At Montreal he spoke of man's

halting but persistent effort to raise his reason above his animality. He draws blueprints for Utopia. But never quite gets it built. In the end, he plugs away obstinately with the only building material really ever at hand: his own part-comic, part-tragic, part-cussed, but part-glorious nature.

Robert McNamara was announcing he was not a "tool" or an "IBM card" or even Dr. Strangelove at the controls. He was a builder of Utopia, who was not finished building it — not yet.

McNamara had chosen a gathering of hundreds of news editors to good effect; newspaper readers around the country could not miss what Bob McNamara's priorities were. The Montreal speech was reprinted in full by the *New York Times,* and the Chatham speech also got wide coverage.

Columnists drenched him in praise. Mary McGrory claimed that "the real Robert McNamara" had "stood up" at Montreal. "The Secretary of Defense has suddenly started talking in public the way he has increasingly talked in private." This "real" McNamara was "lofty and far ranging and liberal beyond any dogmas." She wrote that he was a "book-lover, idea-fancier and humanitarian."

Was this the same "cold computer" that Congress complained of, the man who spoke of "kill-rates"? His two dazzling performances — quoting Greek philosophers, saints, poets, a dramatist, and Abigail Adams — were "entirely too much for the simple politicians of the city," McGrory said.[9]

James Reston, who had recently castigated McNamara in print for lying about Vietnam, issued a panegyric: "McNamara is reaching beyond the draft, beyond the Pentagon, beyond administration policy, beyond the present, even beyond the concept of sovereign nation states. . . . He is searching for a unifying principle." Pentagon adviser Townsend Hoopes wrote to Adam Yarmolinsky that the Montreal speech was "educative" and "courageous" and "a discreet declaration of independence from the rigidity and growing irrationality of official policy."[10] A young man who danced with Margaret McNamara that summer remembers that she mentioned the Montreal speech. "*That's* what my father is really like," she said.

McNamara's savoring of the moment was cut short. Lyndon Johnson was furious at his defense secretary for upstaging him and for straying from the White House position on draft reform, which did not countenance universal service. Moreover, says Johnson aide Eric Goldman, McNamara's universal-service notion "smacked of the speeches being made by Edward M. Kennedy."

The hoopla over the Montreal speech caused Johnson, from pure pique, to cancel a planned appearance before the United Auto Workers in Long Beach, California, where he had expected to announce the formation of a blue-ribbon commission to study reform of the draft, a statement that would have won the interest of every youth in America. Instead, the White House released the plan quietly on July 2.[11]

Any satisfaction McNamara gained from his burst of freedom was soured by his own divided nature. In November at Harvard — after the confrontation with students in the afternoon — McNamara attended a small dinner given for him at the Institute of Policy Studies. Someone asked him why he had given the speech in Montreal. The secretary of defense blurted out:

I just felt I had to give it. It was for someone else to do really. But they weren't doing it. So I felt it had to be said. But I shouldn't have done it. It was childish of me. I am the secretary of defense. It is my job to motivate men to fight. It's not my job to say to colonels that their profession is irrelevant. It was very childish of me. But I felt it needed saying. So I did it.[12]

In August 1966, McNamara made another startling announcement, garnering more attention because he chose the most hostile possible audience, the Veterans of Foreign Wars, in front of which to unveil his new plan. As pro- and antiwar demonstrators marched outside, McNamara told the VFW that he was going to uplift the "subterranean poor" by taking into the military each year 100,000 young men who would normally be rejected. Again, he spoke in a new voice, presumably that of the "real" Robert McNamara: "Poverty is a social and political paralysis that atrophies ambition and drains away hope. It saps the strength of nations . . . because it withers and weakens the human potential necessary to development."[13]

The law required that all boys turning eighteen take the Armed Forces Qualification Test, or AFQT. Each year about a third, or 600,000 of the 1.8 million who took it failed because, McNamara said, "they are victims of faulty education or inadequate health services." McNamara announced that approximately 100,000 of those who failed the test could be accepted and, through "the application of advanced educational and medical techniques," be "salvaged," first for "productive military careers and later for productive roles in society." He also promised that the military could absorb this number of low scorers with no loss of "efficiency."

The premise of Project 100,000 (whose intellectual father was Daniel Patrick Moynihan, who wrote a report called *One-Third of a Nation* when he was assistant secretary for policy in the Labor Department) was that military service was the catalyst that would allow men to return to civilian life "with skills and aptitudes, which for them and their families will reverse the downward spiral of human decay," as McNamara said.[14]

A smaller-scale program called STEP had been tried when John Kennedy was president, but Congress had cut the funding, reflecting the resistance of the career military to accepting low-aptitude recruits. Project 100,000 was structured so as to circumvent congressional approval, and it was launched in October 1966. "New Standards" men began entering the service in October, as draftees and volunteers in equal numbers; the following year 100,000 were brought in.

In his haste, McNamara overruled at least one of his closest manpower experts, Alfred Fitt, who wanted only a 3,000-man, low-key program, which could have greater odds of success and thereby convert Congress.[15]

McNamara set out to benefit the largest number of poor in typical style, working alone in the big office with a single, trusted aide, Thomas Morris. Morris was the most proficient administrator among the Whiz Kids, "relentless rather than brilliant," one former colleague says.

Like so many other McNamara initiatives, Project 100,000 was adversarial, designed to prove somebody else was wrong. In this case Morris and project director Irving Greenberg decided they could demonstrate that low-aptitude men could be "fully satisfactory soldiers" by keeping their commanders ignorant of which men they were. Project 100,000 would be a blind experiment run on a 1.5 million-member organization. Or so the social engineers in room 3E 880 hoped.

They decided to fool, in effect, the trainers of the New Standards men. Draft boards and recruiting centers were instructed to have 22.3 percent of all recruits be "Cat Fours," men who scored in Category

Four of five on the AFQT. The boards and centers were told to single out, within the Cat Fours, a certain number of men with specific characteristics that marked them as victims of poverty. These project men were to be identified as part of the experiment only by a secret code in their file.

Did McNamara and his fellow social engineers know that the majority of project men would be assigned to the Army and to that largest of Army "occupational specialties" called combat? Thus, that the project men had a higher risk of becoming casualties in Vietnam than other entering servicemen who qualified, usually on the basis of higher scores, for noncombat jobs? "We realized this could happen," Morris says. He added that he and McNamara tried to "offset" this possibility by requiring that more project men be taken into the Navy and Air Force, where they would be less likely to be exposed to combat.

But again, the designer of Utopia would be accused. As it happened, McNamara's announcement of his Great Society program coincided with the publication of a number that confused and angered many. Official statistics released in early 1966 showed that fatalities of black soldiers composed 23.5 percent of American deaths in Vietnam in 1965, a death rate more than double the percentage of blacks in the population, which was then roughly 10 percent. Journalist Neil Sheehan concluded in an early, brief article on the program that since most project men were black, "it is evident that most Project 100,000 recruits will go into combat and many to Vietnam."[16]

The high black death rate ripped wider the wounds of civil strife. Some black leaders continued to argue that the military was fairer than American society at large. (In fact, the 23.5 percent figure reflected the higher proportion of blacks in the career Army, whose speciality was combat, and in 1965 the first units sent to Vietnam were made up of career men, not new recruits.)[17]

But Martin Luther King, Jr., called on blacks to refuse to serve and compared Vietnam to Nazi concentration camps. Although he later retracted the remark, he and many other black leaders denounced the military and the Vietnam War as tools of oppression and racism. Thus McNamara, instead of being praised by black leaders for his help to their people, was criticized for supposedly luring the poor and black into the service with promises of better jobs and then using them as cannon fodder.[18]

Meanwhile, most training camp commanders and NCOs thought they knew who the project men were, despite McNamara's and Morris's efforts to conceal them in the influx of Cat Four recruits. Commanders claimed to have cracked the codes in the men's folders. Many simply branded any low-performing recruit as one of "McNamara's morons."

McNamara sought praise but was pilloried for tricking the underclass. While the death rates for blacks in combat came down from 1966 on, and overall the death rate for project men was no higher, fury persisted for years over the 23.5 percent fatality figure and "concentration camp" charge.

Some of the project men stayed on to make careers in the service; others suffered emotionally and physically, as did many Vietnam-era veterans. "Many weren't even on a fifth-grade level," says Herb de Bose, a former first lieutenant who works with veterans. The Army was supposed to teach them a trade, but they had "no skills before, no skills after," says de Bose. "I think McNamara should be shot."[19]

Years later, McNamara seemed shocked to hear the accusation that the project men formed a disproportionately high percentage of casualties. Possibly he was ignorant of the charge, since the controversy over their subsequent problems arose mainly after he left government, in early 1968, and severed himself from the public debate on the war.

McNamara remains proud of Project 100,000. He said to me, "It was launched as an experiment. The first year we took only forty thousand and their performance was carefully evaluated. There was tremendous opposition to bringing the 'disadvantaged' into military service. But Johnson and I believed, based on studies from World War II, that the 'disadvantaged's productivity would be improved by military discipline and military training. Also, it increased the equity of the draft."

Was it instituted in response to the need for a larger force for Vietnam? Or as a social program? McNamara replied: "If the question is, would I do it again today" — in peacetime — "the answer is yes."[20]

For McNamara, one incident leavened the public attacks on him in his early years at the World Bank, when his appearances in public sparked demonstrations, violence, and police action. As he debarked from a plane, a black soldier standing at attention saluted. Beneath his cap the man beamed a wide grin; his eyes flashed in recognition of R. S. McNamara.

McNamara noticed the soldier looking straight at him. He pulled himself up and greeted the man.

"Proud to meet you, sir," said the man, still at attention and smiling. "I'm one of your morons." McNamara pumped the man's hand gleefully. He was now gaunt, his suit was loose and flapping; his hair was grayer and wispy. He rushed off still laughing at this brief moment of appreciation.[21]

McNamara followed the launch of Project 100,000 in 1966 with an April 1967 announcement that Realtors in communities around military bases in Maryland would be required to rent to black soldiers and their families. Neighborhoods near military bases were usually prosperous and white; black servicemen were forced to live in poorer housing, far from the base, in black neighborhoods. In 1963, the Kennedy administration had declined to act vigorously on the issue of discrimination near bases, and then McNamara seemed to concur. "I strongly agree that military personnel and military resources are provided for purposes of national security and are not instruments of social change," McNamara wrote Senator Fulbright at the time. But in January 1967, possibly at Johnson's urging, he acted differently.[22]

Management control was now unleashed to effect social change. McNamara enlisted Thomas Morris to inventory all Realtors within a radius of each military base in Maryland. Then Morris and Cyrus Vance met with the Realtors and warned them that unless they stopped discriminating, the base commander would declare their businesses off-limits to *all* servicemen, black and white — a potentially devastating blow. The Realtors were given a schedule for compliance, and black servicemen were instructed to report if they had any problems. McNamara and Morris's juggernaut rolled across Maryland, achieving more desegregation of housing in a few months than the state had seen in years.

McNamara next turned his desegregation system on other military bases, in California and elsewhere. The program gained momentum, yet in a speech in November he castigated himself for failure.

There are thousands of our Negro troops, returning from Vietnam, who are being discriminated against in off-base housing. . . . The

Negro serviceman has been loyal and responsible to his country. But the people of his country have failed in their loyalty and responsibility to him.[23]

And later he said:

I get charged with the TFX. It's nothing compared to my failure for four years to integrate off-base military housing. I don't want you to misunderstand me when I say this, but the TFX was only money. We're talking about blood, the moral foundation of our future, the life of the nation when we talk about these things.[24]

Just after starting the integration program, McNamara issued a credo in another speech: "Management is the gate through which social, political and economic and technological change . . . is rationally and effectively spread through society."[25] Even as he confessed to failure, his faith in management was unshaken.

McNamara was equally zealous to cement the gains in nuclear stability he believed he had made with the Soviets in 1963–65.

He also worked very hard in this period to get the Soviets to adopt his own policy of Assured Destruction and to prevent them from escalating the arms race by deploying antiballistic missile systems. But that zeal for specific outcomes — so admirable in forcing organizations to respond to his will — didn't wash with his enemy. McNamara could claim he knew better than the Soviets what was objectively safest for them both and tick off the most *rational* force posture for both sides to adopt. But his own less-than-rational buildup of the U.S. missile force in 1961–63 to a terrifying American advantage, from the Soviet point of view, now began coming home to roost.

Thus his own actions undermined the very stability he sought to preserve, in the long term. Yet there is also no doubt that McNamara's growing moral urgency in the late 1960s — perhaps emotionally driven by his miscalculations in Vietnam — shaped the debate over the ABM of 1969–72 and laid the foundation for the Strategic Arms Limitation Treaty of 1972 and subsequent nuclear arms control.

The story unfolded in two parts. The first concerned the American ABM program and the issue of how to respond to intelligence reports of Soviet ABM deployments.

From the mid-1960s on McNamara lectured publicly and privately on the dangers of either Soviet or U.S. deployment of ABMs. Alain Enthoven's staff analyzed scenarios of nuclear exchanges, war gaming to try to predict what would happen with different force levels and defensive ABM systems.[26] McNamara's yearly memoranda to the president on strategic forces, drafted by Enthoven, became path-breaking documents.

He knew that his client, the president, was no strategic analyst. It appears that Lyndon Johnson could not bring himself to read these elegant, abstract papers himself. He would lie down and have someone else read them to him aloud.

McNamara told me: "Johnson was not by any means an expert on nuclear strategy. He and I had quite different views on the ABM. He rather leaned in favor of the ABM, certainly initially, and I was strongly opposed to it." Morton Halperin, who worked on the ABM question at International Security Affairs, says that Johnson cared about the ABM issue mainly because so many other people around him felt so strongly about it.[27]

So McNamara proselytized, with analysis and sheer force of personality. To lower the heat caused by the possible Soviet ABM program, he approved development of a top-secret, cheap, bug-free technology called MIRV (multiple independently targetable reentry vehicle). With this system, multiple warheads were placed aboard a single missile and were designed to separate and guide themselves to targets as far as seventy-five miles apart with high confidence.[28] By the mid-1970s, once the United States deployed MIRV aboard most of its land- and sea-based forces, the number of U.S. deployed warheads shot up, from 5,045 in 1966 to 12,386 in 1986. The Soviets deployed their MIRV as well, pushing warhead levels up from 1,047 in 1966 to 10,054 in 1986.

McNamara later regretted his position on MIRV. He told me the administration was correct in continuing MIRV development as a hedge against a possible Soviet ABM, but he also said: "We could have said: God! Don't go ahead with MIRV if the Soviets stop their ABM! We could have put it in neon lights with some warnings, to assure that the whole government would be alerted to just how dangerous MIRVs would be and if we went ahead with them. . . . We could have said, Mr. State Department, Mr. CIA, Mr. Science Adviser, we want to alert you in advance that under no circumstances should we proceed with MIRV one minute beyond the time the Soviets curb their ABM."[29]

He also recalled warning that the Soviets would build their own MIRV. His November 1965 draft memorandum predicted that "a Soviet MIRV deployment could pose a serious problem to the survivability of our land-based forces." But at the time, the American MIRV was years away from deployment, and the program was top-secret; a Soviet MIRV was also years away. So in late 1965 his comments about MIRV were positive; he embraced the U.S. program as a cheap, reliable hedge against greater-than-expected Soviet threats.[30]

Meanwhile, the signs that the Soviets were pushing ahead with ABM increased the pressure on McNamara by the Joint Chiefs to deploy an American ABM as well. By the fall of 1966, as military frustration with McNamara's management of the war turned bitter, within the Pentagon, the military's drive for ABM deployment became a litmus test of whether men in uniform could ever win against "monarch" McNamara. The defense secretary and the chiefs flew off in December 1966 for the final showdown during budget talks at Johnson's ranch.

McNamara and Vance sat at the president's ranch house holding firm against the ABM deployment while the chiefs took the opposite side. McNamara told me, "The chiefs, all five of them, presented their views to the president. The president called on me to respond. I responded by saying that I totally disagreed. I strongly opposed proceeding with an antiballistic missile defense and advised him in the strongest possible terms to refuse to support the chiefs' position. It was one of the few times I left the president in a position where he had to choose in the starkest terms between one of the recommendations of the chiefs and my own. . . . It was a very uncomfortable position for him, and, in effect, it was for me."

McNamara and Vance proposed a deal. They would do as the chiefs wanted and ask for initial ABM deployment funds in January, but they would also announce that they would not spend the money if the Soviets showed signs of considering talks on limiting ABMs on both sides.

"The president seized upon this formula, agreed to it," McNamara says, although Johnson agreed more because it seemed to pacify warring factions than because he concurred on issues: "Johnson did not see what I believe was a fact then and today, that one could not move to agreed-upon limits on offensive forces if either or both sides were deploying defensive forces."

McNamara returned to Washington eager to contact the Soviets. He chose as his agent Anatoly Dobrynin, Moscow's long-standing ambassador to the United States. McNamara says: "A series of meetings took place, including a meeting with Dobrynin at my house, just Dobrynin and I, discussing in very candid, frank ways the nature of the nuclear problem, what each side was doing with the nuclear forces, the strategy each was following, the risks which confronted us, the reasons why I felt it was in our interest to initiate discussion on ABM as well as on offensive forces. That was totally unpublicized."

Dobrynin would put McNamara's proposal to his government; in the annals of SALT this was the approximate moment that serious work on U.S. positions began, at State, CIA, and the Arms Control and Disarmament Agency.[31] A sign of McNamara's urgency on nuclear arms control in 1967 is that it was he — not Rusk or William Foster, the ACDA director — who dragged Dobrynin to lunch at his home to explain the dangers and the need for restraint.

But McNamara's effort seemed to have disappeared in Moscow as though swallowed up by the earth. Publicly he and others repeated the January formula: If the Kremlin was willing to talk about ABM limits, it could prevent Washington from spending funds for ABM deployment. Then in June 1967 came the Six-Day War, and Soviet-American relations became very strained.

In mid-June McNamara got a phone call from the president.

"Bob, what are you doing about Glassboro?"

"Glassboro, Mr. President? What do you mean?"

"You're in charge of this. What have you done?"

"In charge of what?" asked McNamara.

"You've been pushing me for a long time to meet with Kosygin. By God, I'm going to meet with him and you haven't made any preparations for it?"

McNamara said he didn't know anything about it. Johnson replied, "You better darn well get the place fixed up" — an apparent reference to security arrangements.

"Mr. President, where is Glassboro?"

"It's in New Jersey."[32]

On June 23, McNamara was sitting at a cramped dining room table in a modest white house at Glassboro State College, a site picked because it was midway between the United Nations, where Aleksey Kosygin, the Soviet premier, was, and Washington, where Lyndon Johnson was.

McNamara had about one day's warning and brought a brief paper to talk from, no more. The Middle East dominated the agenda.

Dobrynin later told a Western reporter what happened next from his and Kosygin's viewpoint.[33] After Dobrynin had heard McNamara's exposition of nuclear dangers over lunch at Tracy Place, he had gone to Moscow and told Kosygin that McNamara was a genius. Dobrynin led Kosygin to expect the American defense secretary to give him a major briefing, with tables and charts on the arms race and ABM.

So Kosygin was startled when at lunch, with about twenty-five people in the room including aides and interpreters, the president turned to McNamara and said, "Bob, why don't you do your thing now. You've got fifteen minutes." So McNamara burst forth on the danger of defense, the safety of mutual offense, the importance of neither side's trying to gain a first-strike capability against the other. Arms control on offensive weapons was meaningless without limits on defensive systems, which were the real danger.

Aleksey Kosygin had deep suspicions of the West and knew little about Americans and their casual ways. Nor did he care to learn, since he planned to spend the next day, Saturday, visiting Niagara Falls. He would get a view of nature but no insights into the arms race or Johnson's habit of bringing up earthshaking matters at crowded lunches.

"When I have trouble sleeping at night, it's because of your offensive missiles, not your defensive missiles," Kosygin said after McNamara spoke at lunch. Kosygin brushed off the suggestion that they talk about limiting the ABMs. The communiqués issued afterward said nothing on the matter.[34]

McNamara couldn't have his Utopia free of defensive arms if Kosygin didn't get the basic argument. He recalls that when he came home that evening, he instructed Margy to try to get Kosygin to come to dinner the next night. Margy got on the telephone and tried to track down Kosygin. Finally she found he was at Niagara Falls and unavailable for dinner in Washington.[35]

McNamara remembers the episode vividly because days later, a stony-faced FBI man pressed his way into his office with a personal sealed message from J. Edgar Hoover. Hoover's phone tappers had been busy. His message informed McNamara that a woman identifying herself as Margaret McNamara had telephoned Soviet individuals all over town and around the country. Hoover made it plain that the wife of the secretary of defense had no business talking to Communists, calling them far and wide.

McNamara's effort to get the Soviets to see reason and talk about ABM limits had failed. He was trapped, by the terms of his deal at the Johnson ranch, into having to deploy the ABMs. Utopia would have to wait.

The Pentagon said officially the matter was undecided, right through August.[36] Meanwhile, McNamara's staff prepared a major speech on the arms race, to be given on September 18 in San Francisco. At the last minute Morton Halperin, one of the drafters of the speech, was told to add a pro-ABM ending to the speech, whose entire burden was to explain the arguments against it.

McNamara could simply have said that none of the ABM systems at the present or foreseeable state of the art would provide an impenetrable shield over the United States. Or that if the United States deployed even a partial ABM system, the Soviets would be likely to build more offense to overcome it.

But this was not McNamara's mood in September 1967. Instead he put the ABM issue in the context of runaway technology and the "mad momentum" of the arms race, which only acts of high-minded restraint by enlightened leaders could check.

> 'What is essential to understand here is that the Soviet Union and the United States mutually influence one another's strategic plans. Whatever their intentions or our intentions, actions — or even realistically potential actions — on either side relating to the buildup of nuclear forces necessarily trigger reactions on the other side. It is precisely this action-reaction phenomenon that fuels an arms race.[37]

The speech displayed the paradoxes of the "new" dissenting, morally concerned McNamara. On the one hand, the end of his speech, with its lukewarm endorsement of a "thin," anti-China ABM, both made clear what official policy was and made him its spokesman. But the whole emphasis of the carefully argued case, linking ABM to larger themes with wide appeal, made his real position clear, too. It would be reprinted for years and, together with the work done by Enthoven, and even McNamara's lecture to Kosygin at Glassboro, inched both sides toward the ban on ABMs clinched in the SALT accords of 1972.[38]

Thus McNamara seemed to fail in his quest for a stable world free of ABMs, although over the longer run it would be clear that he had used the bully pulpit well in the cause of restraint. The second part of the story, however, was more ominous. For in his zeal to build up Kennedy's ICBM force, face down Khrushchev over Cuba, and plunge into Vietnam, Robert McNamara did not closely consider the emotional and political effect of these actions on Moscow.

The years during which McNamara put Assured Destruction at the center of American nuclear policy happened to be years of little activity in the Soviet missile program. The Soviets had only 75 operational ICBMs at the time of the Cuban missile crisis and still possessed only 224 by mid-1965. Meanwhile, the United States was building up toward the force McNamara planned, of 1,054 land-based ICBMs and 656 Polaris missiles at sea. The Soviet submarine-launched force remained at 27.

When McNamara capped the U.S. force in 1963–65, he adopted extremely conservative planning assumptions about the future Soviet force. And he took pains to dramatize just how conservative his assumptions were.

This was the origin of another McNamara planning device, the greater-than-expected threat. GET "is a projection of Soviet strategic capabilities which assumes the Soviets develop and deploy their forces to a degree which we believe is only remotely possible," he said. GET served as a red flag, warning the public just how unlikely it was that Soviet forces would ever be that high. GET also gave McNamara political room. It emphasized his awareness that serious threats existed but were improbable and let him work with the more likely, midrange projections of future enemy forces.

Thus, McNamara spent much effort warning against a repeat of the overestimation of future Soviet forces that led to the earlier missile-gap hysteria. Meanwhile, median intelligence projections of Soviet missiles came downward in the mid-1960s. In April 1965 McNamara said to *U.S. News & World Report*:

> They do have the ability to catch up [with the United States in strategic nuclear forces] by 1970. Therefore, I cannot give you any final estimate what their 1970 force will be, because next year they

could change their plans. But I can say that their rate of expansion today is not such as to allow them even to equal, much less exceed, our own 1970 force.

Then he made the great leap, hoping the "rational" course he wanted the enemy to follow — which loomed in the forefront of his own mind and imagination — was at the forefront of his enemy's mind as well. The evidence, he said, "means that the Soviets have decided that they have lost the quantitative arms race, and they are not seeking to engage us in that contest. It means there is no indication that the Soviets are seeking to develop a strategic nuclear force as large as ours."[39]

But in June 1966, American spy photographs showed that the Soviets seemed to be building up a larger missile force after all. There were new signs of work on the big SS-9, each one of which, with its 25-megaton warhead, could destroy three U.S. missiles, which were deployed in groups of three.[40] The Soviets also started work on fifty-four new missile sites. That October, U.S. intelligence projected that the Soviets would have between 805 and 1,010 missiles by mid-1966, instead of the final force of 500 predicted earlier. By late 1966, they had actually deployed 320 missiles.

The public was alarmed, but McNamara reassured it by alluding to new technology (in fact, the still-secret MIRV) that would enable the planned U.S. missile force to keep an easy lead in warhead megatonnage, even if the ratio of U.S. to Soviet missiles shrank.

However, his adversary was reacting to him not with intellectual logic, as McNamara wanted, but with an eye toward crude considerations of power. Kosygin had said he couldn't sleep at night because almost 2,000 missiles were pointed at his force of 300. Now he was doing something about it.

More than twenty years later, a very much older McNamara would claim quite freely that his and Kennedy's missile buildup, not to mention his mishandling of MIRV, caused the arms race of the 1970s — as though to have Vietnam on his conscience was not enough. In fact, he began blaming their early buildup for later Soviet actions in his ABM speech in San Francisco, although scholars disagree as to which American moves triggered the Kremlin's decision to seek nuclear parity with the United States.

Scholar Lawrence Freedman, for example, concludes that the

Kremlin decision was made after the internal debate over guns versus butter in 1963–65. Hard-liners won a commitment to build up the missile force because the American invasion of the Dominican Republic, in April 1965, and intervention in Vietnam that year seemed evidence that the United States was using its nuclear superiority to throw its weight around in the world.[41] Freedman's view makes McNamara responsible for the devastating Soviet missile buildup, but not in the way he thinks.

McNamara now says that if he had had the "intellectual sophistication," he could have stabilized U.S. missiles and warheads at a lower level. "I could have said to Senator Russell, we have got enough superiority at 4,000 warheads. I could have asked for less."

We were finishing a series of interviews on his nuclear evolution. McNamara had a leprechaunlike air as he danced behind his desk, picking up charts of nuclear force levels and talking nonstop.[42]

He imagined he was God in heaven judging the lifetime performance of Robert McNamara on earth by comparing numbers of Soviet and American warheads. The chart he held showed that the Soviets were very slow to build up warhead levels to match the huge growth in U.S. warheads brought about by MIRV in the 1970s. "The fact that they held down as much as they did just amazes me. My God, it's amazing to me they didn't all lose their heads. Up here, someone should have said: Why in the hell didn't you, Mr. Ustinov or General X, why didn't you back here [points to earlier year] get yourself ready so we didn't have this terrible deficiency there [points to later date]?

And the converse ought to be said to me. What in the hell were you doing, McNamara? You must have ordered those things [MIRV] back here in 1965. Why the hell did you do that? You not only wasted our money, you stimulated an arms race!"

McNamara had positioned himself as philosopher-king of the arms race. At the same time, on his frequent trips to Europe, he pursued his crusade to force all fifteen nations of NATO to adopt the quintessentially rational doctrine of flexible response that Washington had urged since 1961.

McNamara's problems with allied leaders were not only that his hard-hitting style — although it may have helped France's defection from the military side of NATO in 1966 — created resentment. He also faced the bills now coming due on his and Kennedy's sweeping promise to bear any burden in the defense of liberty. The pledge assumed vast American wealth, enough for the United States to pay the lion's share for NATO and meet forty-odd other treaty obligations around the world.

As the costs of Vietnam mounted, the United States moved into an era of "strategic overstretch," in historian Paul Kennedy's phrase. The sun was lowering on American world hegemony. The late 1960s were a pivotal moment when, militarily and economically, today's Europe was born, and R. S. McNamara played a leading role as midwife.

Lyndon Johnson regarded the larger NATO allies much as he regarded his "allies" in the Senate, as friends for whom he did a lot and who should prove their friendship by returning the favor when asked. Johnson had nothing of Kennedy's sense of drama or symbolism about the grand alliance. Johnson was more interested in manifesting America's destiny by saving a poor country of brown-skinned people than in paying to defend rich Europeans who could afford to defend themselves.[43] His lack of subtlety on the point managed to lose America's closest friend on the continent — in Bonn.

Worried about the payments balance, in 1965 Johnson in effect appointed Bob McNamara bill collector for West Germany. In 1961 the Kennedy administration had made an ingenious "offset" agreement with the Germans whereby they would buy U.S. military goods and services equivalent to the dollar costs to the U.S. Treasury of military expenditures in that country, or about $650 million per year. The U.S. Seventh Army there was the Germans' main protection on its long, exposed border to the east. But paying more for defense was not too popular with the Germans, every year Bonn balked — and paid.

Ludwig Erhard, the genial economist who succeeded the venerable Konrad Adenauer in 1963 as chancellor and leader of the ruling coalition, had been the first chief of state to visit President Johnson's ranch. Erhard came in December 1963. The two men had gotten along famously, and back home, Erhard bragged of his closeness to the Americans.[44]

Then the United States lost popularity somewhat. The German air force had agreed to buy ninety-six Lockheed F-104 Starfighter jets back in 1959. By the mid-1960s these were crashing at an alarming rate; an anti-American Starfighters widows' group was active in German politics.[45] Washington's appeals to Bonn for aid in Vietnam were largely futile. Another problem with West Germany was the nonproliferation talks promoted by Washington. These could produce a multinational treaty recognizing East Germany, a West German nightmare. By early 1966, Erhard was saying he could not meet the required offset payments and asked his friend Johnson to let him off the hook.

Meeting with the Germans, McNamara might as well have been chief of the mighty Ford Division bent on enforcing a contract with some beleaguered supplier. His tool was the club, not the rapier. He had told Adenauer's government in 1963 that "the United States wanted to leave its forces in Germany but would not be able to do so unless there was a continuing full offset agreement," according to the notes taken by the U.S. ambassador to Bonn, George McGhee. When Erhard visited in December 1963, McNamara repeated that "the United States simply could not continue to maintain forces in Germany without full offset payments."[46]

Erhard came to the United States again, in December 1964, to warn that his defense budget was being cut. After a state dinner honoring the chancellor, Johnson took him upstairs to "a small darkened room," according to McGhee. Erhard tried to explain his problems, but Johnson towered over him, "gesticulating and speaking in a strong strident voice.

" 'Now we're going to find out who our friends are,' " Johnson said darkly. The communiqué issued afterward said Bonn would make the full payment, but it cost Erhard at home.

Erhard returned in September 1966, when the costs of Vietnam were creating a record deficit and the U.S. payments balance was negative for the first time. Meanwhile, Erhard's defense budget was still being cut; the Starfighter widows were trying to defeat him. According to McGhee, at one hastily arranged session called to make Bonn shape up, Defense Minister Kai-Uwe von Hassel represented the chancellor and McNamara spoke for the president.

Hassel was a "perfect gentleman, soft spoken with a well modulated voice." He was "no match for McNamara," who was "confident and quick to respond with the right fact or figure." McNamara spoke in "rapid staccato phrases" and injected "a note of the United States's moral right to offset payments, whereas Hassel, asking for leniency in fulfilling an acknowledged obligation, was disadvantaged. Hassel became increasingly embarrassed and appeared to give up."

The communiqué issued after this visit also said Bonn would meet its offset payments. But in West Germany, Erhard was finished. The burly economist, the father of the postwar German economic miracle and leader of the party most emotionally bound to Washington, was defeated by the left.

Erhard's fall meant the end of the long period of West German political incubation tended by America and the beginnings of independence.[47] By treating a loyal friend brutally — because of underlying panic over the economic situation caused by the Vietnam War — Johnson and McNamara helped spark the rise of Ostpolitik, the turning to the east, which has been a key feature of German foreign policy ever since.

Both America's and McNamara's credibility were sinking in Western Europe — from coffeehouses to parliaments to by-election campaigns — because Washington was distracted in Asia.

McNamara had lectured and bullied, ever since the Berlin crisis and his Athens and Ann Arbor speeches of 1962, to make the NATO allies build up the full twenty-nine divisions needed to hold off a Warsaw Pact invasion without early use of nuclear weapons. To him, flexible response was urgent and rational; to the Europeans it was merely expensive. Charles de Gaulle denounced it as a plot to abandon Europe.[48]

Meanwhile, McNamara and his energetic arms sales office told the allies what to buy. Arrogance was chronic. "We don't expect them to buy anything from us they don't require or which they can get elsewhere at a lower price, higher quality, or with better delivery terms," McNamara said.[49] But American-made arms were the best in the world, and McNamara could present charts showing each ally's "needs" better than any of them could. Washington was overplaying its hand again.

And when large U.S. troop deployments were sent to Vietnam, many in Europe decided that McNamara and Johnson were more concerned with distant Asia than with them.

McNamara kept urging the allies to adopt flexible response formally and to buy the necessary arms just when American forces in Europe were being transferred to Vietnam. The Seventh Army, the five-division backbone of NATO's ground force, filled up with raw recruits as its more seasoned men were sent east. Europeans were certain Washington was weakening the force.

But McNamara denied the charge forcefully. "I believe we are in a better position to meet our worldwide commitments today than at any time in recent years," he affirmed on August 25, 1966.[50] In fact, while the quantity of American forces in Europe remained the same, the quality diminished. The chronic shortage of experienced officers and NCOs over time made the Seventh Army an institution in crisis, plagued by racial fights, drugs, officer fraggings, and other signs of demoralization. Because it was so green, the Seventh Army was particularly vulnerable to problems spreading elsewhere in the Army, and in American society.

McNamara now loosened Western Europe's tether to America in another way. Under stress, he could be very creative; 1967 — which at home was the year of his greatest trials over the war — proved his most constructive yet in Europe, paradoxically while his credibility plummeted.

McNamara's counterparts in other NATO defense ministries clung to the alliance's formal policy of early resort to nuclear weapons if any member of the alliance was attacked. In part this reflected long-felt dependence on the American nuclear guarantee; also, since a nuclear defense was far cheaper than the massive conventional force buildup called for by McNamara at Athens in 1962, the allies stuck to the old doctrine to avoid the costs of a buildup.

In addition, possession of nuclear weapons was seen in Europe as a symbol of the world-power status that France, West Germany, and Great Britain at least all sought in the postwar world. Each allied country wanted either its own nuclear weapons eventually or at least "a finger on the trigger" with Washington. Fear that a revived West Germany would demand its own nuclear force had produced the U.S. plan for the multilateral force advocated by George Ball and others. Meanwhile, Charles de Gaulle dangled before the West Germans the bauble of a bilateral agreement in which Bonn might one day share control of France's nuclear *force de frappe*.

McNamara had become convinced that the allies' illusions about the usefulness of nuclear weapons were dangerous. He was, for better or worse, an unflaggingly literal man. While many in Europe thought that tactical nuclear weapons, used early, would protect them, McNamara's analyses showed that in almost any scenario, the damage would be worse to the allied side. He needed to make them understand this. By the time McNamara stepped off his plane for a regular meeting of NATO defense ministers in May 1965, he had a scheme to achieve this through a novel organization.[51] The Nuclear Planning Group's real inventor may have been John McNaughton; Denis Healey, the Labor defense minister of Great Britain; or Harlan Cleveland, U.S. ambassador to NATO. Many have claimed to be the father of the idea, but the actuality was brought into being thanks to McNamara's drive to effect literal outcomes fast. He said later: "Whenever I want to be really efficient, I get a building about half the size that anybody wants and say that's what we're going to build Ford cars in or that's what we're going to have for the Navy or whatever it may be. Well, we followed the same procedure [in NATO]. . . . Now, this sounds childish, but it isn't childish. There's a very direct inverse relationship between the number of participants and the degree or extent of accomplishment"[52]

Normal meetings of NATO defense ministers were formal affairs, comprising the defense ministers, the professional military, and their staffs and interpreters. They were large and politically diverse gatherings that dwelt mainly on procedure.

McNamara persuaded the allies to set up three working committees, of which one, Working Committee III, would have the sensitive job of planning for nuclear forces. He insisted that a small number of prominent allies be members of this select group. After March 1966, when France announced it was withdrawing from NATO's military command, McNamara could set the group's nuclear agenda.[53]

He ordered a special five-sided table built. He established rules: Only the minister could sit at the table; only the minister could speak. Now McNamara had a small, controlled forum in which he could lead the allies over time to his own views of the nuclear problem.

It was a sign of some maturity, for in 1962 he had tried to convert them by preaching from the podiums at Athens and Ann Arbor. Now he used his considerable personal skills with a small group — and his power, for he had his finger on the nuclear trigger, and, except for the British, they did not.

McNamara remembers that at the first meeting around the table, he asked for an agenda and got "dead silence." Then he said, " 'Well, you've all been talking about whose finger is on the trigger. Let's make that the first agenda item!' " They said, " 'Oh my God no,' " he recalls, because each country "wanted only the U.S. and its *own* finger on the trigger." He then proposed the first item to be "a discussion of a plan for initiating the use of nuclear weapons." He assigned the West German defense minister, Kai-Uwe von Hassel, this job. When von Hassel protested that he knew nothing about it, McNamara said, "That's why we have established this committee. You can learn." McNamara told him he could have any expert he needed, and von Hassel went to work.[54]

The actual discussions are still classified, but McNamara's points concerning the uselessness of nuclear weapons to defend NATO are shown in his now-released presidential memorandum on European tactical nuclear forces. It asked what the general who commanded all NATO forces in Europe, who was always an American, would do once the huge enemy force invaded the West.

> Although SACEUR has an airborne command post . . . the rest of his command structure would remain in jeopardy during a theater-wide nuclear war. Consequently, we must anticipate that control of the nuclear battle would become *directionless* in very short order [italics added]. . . .
>
> Since SACEUR has no major reserves, except for forces from the United States which would have to be brought in through ports and airfields that might already have been destroyed, his front would collapse rapidly.

The alternatives? McNamara's memo noted that NATO's official policy denied "the feasibility of nonnuclear war." The French had "no concept of limited war" to defend Europe. The British favored a "brief conventional delaying action" that, if it failed to block the enemy, should be followed by "selective use of a few nuclear weapons . . . as a necessary link to general nuclear war." The Germans wanted "prompt use of tactical nuclear weapons" to stop the loss of territory at the border.[55]

And McNamara the teacher went to work. One staffer remembers a discussion in which McNamara ran through the basic scenario with map and pointer. Here is the enemy blitzkrieg driving across the Central Front; it quickly penetrates the NATO line, McNamara said, moving the pointer, from here to here.[56] To contain these enemy armored divisions, NATO approves the smallest nuclear strike it can make. We detonate a 20-kiloton weapon, targeted to minimize civilian casualties . . . here. McNamara's pointer came to a rest.

"My God," cried out von Hassel. "That's my district." He leapt from his seat and rushed to the map to read the labels more clearly. The teacher's lessons were being learned.

The confidential discussions in the Nuclear Planning Group were one of the key factors in getting NATO to adopt flexible response in the military committee in May 1967, and by the respective governments in December that year.[57] So useful was the NPG that the group lives on today as the critical working forum for discussions of the most divisive issues. It is a tribute to McNamara's insight and persistence — and to the moment, for historically the Europeans realized that nuclear weapons were not the be-all and end-all of nationhood — that flexible response has remained NATO policy ever since. The issue that dominated European politics for a decade was largely laid to rest, freeing the continent to focus on the issues that still define nationhood and community in Europe today: trade, technology, finance.

McNamara's record in Europe — his early insight into the dangers of nuclear weapons and forceful drive to cement an agreed safer policy with NATO — seemed to fit his image of restraint. Certainly this image helped him in later years, as conventional wisdom on both sides of the Atlantic came to view nuclear weapons with far more skepticism than was prevalent in the 1960s.

But McNamara's real role is more complex and even contradicts the image of nuclear restraint. First, he did not succeed in getting the allies to adopt flexible response as he defined it originally in his Athens and Ann Arbor speeches of 1962. What he sought was a strong enough non-nuclear defense of NATO to contain an enemy non-nuclear attack to thrust on the Kremlin the terrible decision to use nuclear weapons first. But the NATO allies balked from the large conventional-force buildup this policy required: Britain in the middle 1960s was trying to draw down its Army of the Rhine, and Bonn was leveling its defense budget. They argued, moreover, that if the war was going to go nuclear, a massive conventional defense would become irrelevant soon anyway. So why build it? Thus the text adopted in 1967 allowed only enough conventional buildup to delay the resort to nuclear defense. McNamara admitted in a private memo to the president in January 1968, "There are some situations (which are highly unlikely) where if deterrence failed we would have to initiate use of nuclear weapons. After years of effort this is the most ambitious strategy we have been able to convince our Allies to accept."[58]

There was also the contradiction between McNamara's stated admission that they would have to resort to nuclear weapons, given the inadequacies of non-nuclear forces in place at the time, and his private conviction, held apparently all through the later 1960s, that he would never authorize the first firing of a nuclear weapon. In meetings of the Nuclear Planning Group, recalls Harlan Cleveland, the assertion that the United States was prepared to use nuclear weapons was like "litany in church." And a German military officer told scholar Catherine Kelleher in the late 1960s, "There's not much serious doubt that the Americans will eventually use nuclear weapons and that McNamara, whatever else he has done, has increased the stockpiles" — a view that was a given among senior commanders of the time.[59]

McNamara publicly and in private justified deployments of tactical nuclear forces in Europe. Yet later he claimed that he had private understandings with both Kennedy and Johnson in which he expressed his belief they should never use nuclear weapons first. When author Greg Herken asked McNamara if this understanding included an overwhelming enemy invasion of Europe, McNamara said yes. To me he has explained that he had to uphold the policy in public and to allied governments, even though he thought it flawed and dangerous, while educating them to move away from it.[60]

The stranger aspect of McNamara's record on this matter is that while he was bullying the allies about the dangers of nuclear defense of Europe, it was his policy to *increase* the number of such weapons all through this period. He and John Kennedy had inherited commitments made by President Eisenhower to build up the nuclear defense of Europe. When McNamara took office there were 2,500 tactical nuclear weapons in Europe; by the time he left there would be 7,200 there. According to Colonel Frank Camm, who was a key tactical nuclear planner in Enthoven's group, a judgment was made that "breaking existing agreements" would wreck the allies' receptivity to arguments for flexible response.

So McNamara added the theater nuclear forces as Eisenhower had planned, to assure the allies that the U.S. nuclear guarantee was still firm. In fact, he decided in 1963 to cut off the buildup, which duly leveled off a few years later and would have gone much higher than 7,200 had the cutoff not been taken. Meanwhile, he tried to convince the allies how useless these weapons were and privately was resolved not to exercise the American nuclear guarantee if he could avoid it — even though he affirmed it in public.

His buildup of tactical nuclear weapons was therefore political: McNamara did not believe in these weapons or even want them for

military purposes. By allowing the buildup to go forward — and
even publicizing the fact of it to give extra reassurance to the allies, he
avoided complicating his fight for flexible response, with what would
have been a bruising fight over "denuclearizing" NATO. Later, of
course, he could claim that he fought hard for nuclear restraint and
even regretted allowing the buildup ("We should have stopped the
increases," he said later). But at the time, he had barked at those who
accused him of planning to "denuclearize" Europe: "Let me once
again assure you that this is not true. Nuclear weapons are flowing in
at about the same speed that these erroneous reports are flowing
out."[61]

"His pressing on the NATO front gave him an intellectual focus
which distracted him from his agonies over Vietnam," says Timothy
Stanley, Harlan Cleveland's deputy. NATO headquarters had been
moved lock, stock, and barrel to Brussels by the spring of 1967.
Stanley and his wife lived in a modest house there.

McNamara took Margy along on his NATO trips, and they sometimes stopped at Stanley's house. At night McNamara would sit with
Stanley in the little walled garden, talking on and on about Vietnam.

Perhaps the privacy of the enclosed garden or the remoteness of
Stanley's household from the mainstream of their lives made McNamara talkative. In their garden talks, McNamara sounded off. His
mental engines ran on overdrive, and he seemed depressed. "He told
me that he had advised the president to raise taxes and been overruled," Stanley says.

"Bob presented the facade of the human machine. I got beyond
that and saw him reflecting doubts about the wisdom of our whole
course in Vietnam."

Margy seemed unhappy with the whole situation, although Stanley saw no outward sign of the ulcers that would cause her hospital-
ization in 1967. But Margy told Stanley's wife that she wasn't sure
how much longer her husband could hang on.[62]

19

Hawk and Dove

INSTITUTIONS TREMBLE when a new idea appears," wrote the philosopher William James. By early 1967, McNamara had spent six years propounding the goal of an American defense policy based on consensus and above politics, echoing John Kennedy's ideals. But after six years, almost anyone in the military who expressed admiration for McNamara jeopardized his chances of promotion. The most vocal senior brass were embittered by the endless fights and mutual accusations of dishonesty, which accompanied the civilians' carrying forward their new age of reason.

A still uglier notion percolating in some quarters of the Building was that McNamara's quantitative management techniques had not only hurt the armed forces but had caused the inconclusiveness of the war in Vietnam.

Instead of consensus and civility, McNamara's seventh year saw idealism replaced by anger; the bipartisan coalition on security that he inherited was rent by deepening division in Congress and the nation. Many, unwilling or unable to speak of their own failures, blamed the man they were allowed to hate: Robert Strange McNamara.

McNamara had promised that the United States would use its power only in "limited and fitting" ways, but instead he rode a juggernaut of entrenched Navy and Air Force interests in widening the war.

Still to come were the My Lai massacre and actress Jane Fonda's trip to Hanoi. Meanwhile, the growing antiwar movement portrayed the North Vietnamese as patriots, fighting for national ideals, and the South Vietnamese as corrupt tories. At St. Paul's School, in New Hampshire, Craig McNamara, after hearing some Quakers make the antiwar case, concluded, "We were on the wrong side."[1]

McNamara was publicly upbeat about the precision of the air war and the toll the ground war was extracting on the enemy. "Ho Chi Minh is a tough old S.O.B. but I'm as tough as he is," he would say. But a close-up photograph taken at a news conference on February 16 shows the ragged, spotty pallor of the skin, the sleek hair flecked with gray. One eye only is visible; it is shadowed, catlike, rolled sideways, looking out of the rimless glasses through which he had viewed the world for so long. His hand conceals his mouth in an uncharacteristic pose of doubt.[2]

He still gave dozens of briefings before the blown-up maps of Vietnam, with chart and pointer. But now his voice sometimes broke, and he put his hand up to his mouth, apparently to cough but really to catch the confused tide of emotions surging within.

He gave a speech on February 24 at Millsaps College, in Jackson, Mississippi.[3] Pale against his dark suit, McNamara at the podium looked sepulchral, flanked by flowers and the college's sedate guests.

He spoke as leader of men at war, paying tribute to the fighting spirit of a heroic regiment of Mississippians who upheld their flag at Gettysburg. Not a man escaped alive, he said. He coughed.

McNamara's main topic, management, was not off-limits to his inner stress. He read the speech, glancing down and up and swiveling his head from left to right to look at the audience. "Under-management" of society, he said, was "the real threat to democracy." To "under-manage reality" is to let "greed . . . aggressiveness . . . hatred . . . ignorance . . . inertia . . . [or] anything other than reason" shape reality. McNamara came to the line "If it is not reason that rules man" and then stopped for a second, gulped, and went on: "Then man falls short of his potential." When the film of this moment is run at slow speed, his face can be seen in a terrible convulsion — mouth open, eyes shut, grimacing as though a knife were twisting through him — until the reflex of control stills his features and lets him speak again.

Friends chalked up his condition to six years of twelve-hour, six-day weeks and punishing plane trips. But his physical stress signaled deeper problems.

At the rational level, his career and place in history were at stake, as were the nation's health and future. If he relaxed his control even slightly, the war would widen, the Chinese could come in, and the Soviets might be forced to react. Then all his work toward cooperation and arms control would go up in smoke, not to mention his self-respect.

But the stakes were emotional, too. To cope with war, military professionals learn to accept the brutality and randomness of it, war's chaos. McNamara, however, was horrified by the random aggression of war. These were qualities he feared in organizations, in his life, even in himself. Emotionally, he could not make "the transition into war," in Bernard Brodie's phrase.[4] He was making an exhausting effort to control not just the war, but also his emotions.

Bob McNamara and Margy continued to see Bobby Kennedy and his circle, even though the president now hated Bobby. The Kennedy camp was moving to the left on Vietnam, starting to murmur that John Kennedy would have gotten the United States out of the conflict.

Publicly, Bobby avoided criticizing Johnson or the war; instead he criticized the bombing, the peace efforts, and the toll on South Vietnamese civilians. He avoided an open break lest he be accused of sabotaging the party and the war effort.[5] Privately, the schism was deep, which made McNamara's treks to the White House by day and Hickory Hill by night more questionable.

The Kennedy name was magic, and many people hoped Bobby would run for president in 1968. McNamara could not have overlooked the strong odds that he would have a major role in a new Kennedy administration. People in Bobby's circle believed then, and believe now, that McNamara was one of them and served Johnson only out of sufferance.

"McNamara was extraordinarily indiscreet to be telling Bobby the war wasn't working out," says a friend of the family.[6] Washington was full of rivalries, and for a sought-after figure to play to several camps was not unusual. But McNamara was second in the chain of command in a war that his president was more determined than ever to fight. McNamara led men at war. No matter what he actually said to Bobby over drinks or dinner or tennis, the result was that Kennedy's circle believed he had lost faith in the war. His position as war leader seemed compromised.

To me, McNamara maintained he was careful never to speak against Johnson or the war in his evening sojourns. He could not help it if others heard what they wanted to hear. "Bobby Kennedy was a very emotional person," he stressed.

"We frequently met at his home or my office or whatever, and it never bothered me. I recognized Johnson probably knew about it and wondered whether I was in effect being disloyal to Johnson. I wasn't being disloyal to Johnson, but it was clear to me that Johnson might think so. But that didn't stop me."

So there was some defiance in his visits to Hickory Hill, some breaking away from the president who controlled his working life and his telephone. They were also a sign of inner confusion about who he was, hawk or dove.

McNamara's off-the-record self provoked comment. The title of a profile piece by Lloyd Shearer in *Parade* summarized the growing issue of his identity: "Will the Real Robert McNamara Please Stand Up?"[7]

If he believed the war was "unwinnable militarily," why did he stay on and urge more fighting? By December 31, 1965, a total of 1,636 Americans had died in Vietnam and another 7,665 had suffered wounds. Through March 1968, another 19,255 Americans would die and 120,687 would be wounded. Was McNamara needlessly responsible for this added bloodshed? Could he have turned it off? Was he trying to do so? He says now he believed in the value of fighting on: "We were trying to press the war in the field and achieve at the same time our diplomatic objective," which was to maneuver a response from Hanoi that could lead to talks.

"My belief was that we were having difficulty militarily, but we still had a chance of progressing on the political track as a result of our military pressure. If I didn't believe that, I should have strongly recommended withdrawing from Vietnam, and if the government wouldn't do it, I should have resigned. There's no question about that in my mind."

In short, the only way to get the war resolved — that is, to persuade Hanoi to talk — was to keep fighting, even if the fighting was inconclusive and the war unwinnable in the military sense. This is why after the fall of 1965, McNamara had embraced the high-technology barrier and the thirty-seven-day bombing pause, urged diplomatic contacts, and capped Westmoreland's troops — all to gird the United States for the long haul.[8]

McNamara also argues that he worked to limit the war to hold *down* U.S. casualties because he thought the struggle would be inconclusive until Hanoi saw that the United States could fight on indefinitely. Gradualism, which many officers blamed for prolonging the war and increasing U.S. casualties, was pushed by McNamara to minimize loss of American life, he now says.

Clearly he thought what he should do was to stay in office and help the nation fight on, paradoxically, to end the war sooner. Whether his aim was realistic is another matter.

On Christmas Day, 1966, page 1 of the *New York Times* carried a dispatch by Harrison Salisbury, whom Hanoi granted a visa days after claiming that Americans had bombed twice inside the "hole of the doughnut"; in other words, in Hanoi proper. Washington preferred to communicate with the enemy by force, and no announcement was made of a ratchet upward in the air war. But Hanoi screamed — and many around the world believed — that the two strikes meant that America's war machine was closing in for the kill. Salisbury's series from "behind the lines" ran day after day over the next two weeks. Barry Goldwater and others denounced him and the *Times* for printing enemy propaganda.[9] But for many, the stories were their first ground truth about what America was really doing to its enemy.

In photographs and stories, Salisbury described bombed-out churches; he went to Hanoi's Van Dien truck park and Yen Vien rail yard, hit in the December raids. He saw rows of nearby houses damaged. Story after story implied that not only were enemy civilians hit accidentally, but that American planes were targeting people and civilian life. Salisbury visited Nam Dinh, a city of ninety thousand on a rail line fifty miles southeast of Hanoi. The gray stucco cathedral, flying red banners at Christmastime, overlooked "block after block of utter desolation." Salisbury interviewed the mayor, who told him the Americans had attacked the town fifty-one times but never admitted having done so. Bombs had struck the silk factory at the hour when the shifts changed, killing forty-nine. The mayor claimed Nam Dinh was "a cotton-and-silk textile town containing nothing of military significance." Salisbury's quotes of official U.S. denials that the town had been attacked only suggested that Washington was lying.

Philip Goulding was a lanky, affable former reporter who had replaced Arthur Sylvester as McNamara's assistant secretary for information. Goulding admired McNamara, which is why he had come to work for him. But he realized that McNamara's habit of over-statement had set the trap that Salisbury now sprang on them. The secretary often boasted how careful the bombing was, how few enemy civilians suffered, due to the precision of Rolling Thunder. McNamara regularly added that there would be collateral damage, that some enemy civilians would be hit; but this was in the fine print. Goulding says, "We had been gradually convincing the people of the United States that all our bombs always fell upon the targets at which they were directed, that we killed no civilians. . . . We should have known better."[10]

McNamara was furious about Salisbury's reports. He, General Wheeler, and President Johnson were still engaged in the dreary pattern of picking bombing targets almost weekly. They attempted to avoid signaling a wider war by hitting "civilian" targets, by recognizing a "buffer zone" along the Chinese border, and by steering clear of MIG fields and the ports. Henry Glass remembers McNamara's asking why the planes could not fly along the river to attack a bridge, instead of crosswise from bank to bank, so that the bombs that missed would fall in the water instead of on houses clustered on either bank.[11]

Yet part of Salisbury's message served McNamara's larger purposes in early 1967. After the number of air raids per month doubled from six thousand to twelve thousand in 1966, McNamara warned more openly of the "marginal inutility" of more strikes. His January 1967 posture statement — overshadowed by Salisbury's stories — contained his most skeptical public remarks to date on the bombing; he was building the case for restraint, more pauses, and a stand-down if the barrier worked.

Salisbury painted a graphic portrait of a disciplined people, carrying on "briskly, energetically, purposefully," thanks to the "Vietnamese fighting tradition of struggle against long odds, of unyielding battle against powerful enemies."[12]

He had been taken at night in a Soviet-built Volga sedan down the main coastal highway. The Americans attacked by day; at night, traffic rose to a peak. The road was crowded with trucks and cars moving steadily, camouflaged on top with huge tree boughs. Hundreds of people on bicycles carried large loads. Salisbury was shown how, when a bridge was hit, the North Vietnamese swarmed to the riverbank and lashed their long canal boats together sideways and laid planks over the top. In a short time the new "bridge" supported large trucks and cars. Spare railroad ties were artfully scattered near the tracks frequently hit by U.S. bombs. Dispersal prevented the repair materials from becoming targets. The North could fight on forever while the Americans spent millions in a futile air war. This was exactly McNamara's point.

Admiral Ulysses Grant Sharp, who from his headquarters in Honolulu commanded all U.S. forces in the Pacific, including the air war, demanded that more sensitive targets be released to follow up on the momentum of the December strikes. But McNamara was opposed, and the additional targets stayed off-limits, to Sharp's and the pilots' frustration. The civilians were pandering to enemy propaganda and prolonging the war, they muttered.[13]

McNamara, meanwhile, was trying to get the terms of the air war changed by building his barrier — a series of strongpoints across the neck of South Vietnam and electronic sensors and systems in Laos. When it failed, it would go down in history as "McNamara's line," along with the Edsel and the TFX. But for the moment, in 1967, the barrier went forward because William Westmoreland, worried about enemy guns north of the Demilitarized Zone, wanted it.[14] So the Marines were digging in, and the electronic-sensor work went forward, all in secret. McNamara used the barrier to hang on, restrain the bombing, until the system was built and could replace the expense and cost in lives of the air war.

McNamara had turned to Alain Enthoven to gain leverage over the ground war. In 1965, the systems analysis shop started a basic statistical control operation for troop deployments. A year later McNamara empowered them to do much more. Enthoven, the chief Whiz Kid, who had had nothing to do with the earlier Vietnam decisions, became involved.

"I thought — but never knew — that McNamara had a deal with the services. They would let us run all over the rest of the defense program and ask a lot of nasty questions and overturn assumptions, so long as they were left alone with their war, without unwanted civilians poking around."

Enthoven says he did not seek a role in the war because "I didn't know anything at all about it. If I barged into an area where I knew nothing, I would be attacked. I was under attack already from many fronts. I was vulnerable." As the war turned to stalemate and frustration, the devoutly religious Enthoven wondered whether, had he and his analysts been consulted sooner, they could have seen the flaws in the decisions and averted the tragedy.[15]

McNamara authorized the analysts to ask questions about every aspect of Westmoreland's troop requests and to uncover the games the bureaucracy played to puff up "requirements." One of the analysts recalls, "We were amazed at how little real planning lay behind the requests."

Using Enthoven's work, McNamara was able to get Westmoreland to agree on a cap of 470,000 troops, to contain the scale of the fighting and put an upper boundary on future casualties. Enthoven's office assembled a data base on actions in the ground war and began some analyses, using the Pentagon's big computers.[16] One study uncovered the alarming fact that, although the Army kept asking for more mines, one fifth to one third of all U.S. deaths were caused by these devices, while they killed relatively few enemy in exchange. A very influential paper looked at representative firefights in 1966. It showed the enemy could control his losses within a wide range and took casualties mostly when he chose to fight. The significant conclusion was that the rate of loss of enemy life — the so-called body count — was controlled by enemy tactics, not U.S. or South Vietnamese ones. The office even started a newspaper to disseminate facts and studies throughout the theater. Some officials tried to block it, but *Southeast Asia Report* was an instant publishing success — classified, of course.

However, the analysts started late, and their influence was limited. Enthoven's men were resented for so many other reasons that the Army in Vietnam hardly considered them its own. And through his notorious role in downsizing military budget requests, Enthoven became a scapegoat for causing "shortages" that were "losing" the war.[17]

Even with Enthoven's help, McNamara succeeded in containing only the *quantitative* side of the ground war. By 1967, he had had little impact on the qualitative issues, although the pilot studies showed promise and he was beginning to wonder if the Army's concepts were wrong. McNamara said later: "I had some gut feelings — but no way of knowing the process of analysis by which we could establish what I think was fact — that the military tactics being pursued by the U.S. were ineffective in that situation.

"How we would have known these things at the time is not clear to me."[18]

Both McNamara's attempts to innovate — the pilot studies on tactics, and the barrier — suffered from the flaw of being introduced from the top down. But military organizations faced with failure in war must adapt from the bottom up. When the German army was stalemated in the trenches in World War I in 1916, the overhaul of tactics was run by a brilliant tactician, Colonel Fritz von Lossberg, whose handpicked general staff group traveled to shaken unit commanders and coaxed from them "the burdens of their hearts" as to what had gone wrong in battle. A massive, seven-month reform based on the findings, presented as though it came from the field commanders, produced a reversal, and tactical success in the spring of 1917, although of course it was not enough to prevent the Germans from losing the war.[19] In Vietnam, neither the Army nor the office of the secretary of defense went systematically to the bottom of the chain of command, to coax "the burdens of their hearts" from perceptive commanders and arrange tactical reforms, as if from below.

Yet McNamara was determined to fight on, half-seeing and half-blind, believing, rightly or not, that he could somehow persuade Hanoi. His resemblance to James Forrestal, the only previous strong secretary of defense, whose fight against impossible odds and service opposition drove him to suicide in 1949, was striking.

William Brehm, who ran the deployment controls for Enthoven, recalls that he sat late one afternoon in McNamara's great office opposite the nine-foot Pershing desk and the portrait of Forrestal. Brehm and McNamara were computing an order of ammunition for Vietnam.

The defense secretary was pacing back and forth on the carpet, between Brehm's chair and the intense, angular face of Forrestal. "Let's see. That would be two thousand rounds for every enemy infiltrator," McNamara said. "That oughta be enough."

McNamara stopped pacing and looked straight at Forrestal's portrait, which gazed back at him through blank eyes. His body suddenly shuddered violently. He was crying, Brehm realized, as though he could never stop.[20]

*   *   *

On March 23, four days after U.S. planes struck North Vietnam's only iron and steel plant, at Thai Nguyen, McNamara learned that Westmoreland wanted to break the agreed troop limit. The general asked for an "optimum" force of 210,000 more men and ten more tactical air squadrons to foray into Cambodia and Laos and to increase action in South Vietnam's Mekong Delta. His backup request was for a "minimum essential" force of 80,000 more troops and four to five tactical air squadrons.[21] If McNamara and Johnson refused the request, they would no doubt be accused of not supporting their field commander and of delaying victory.

McNamara thought sending such a number would add $10 billion to the galloping defense budget, split the United States politically, and create a "major national disaster."[22]

Three weeks after he learned of Westmoreland's troop request McNamara faced a new choice. He received George Woods, president of the International Bank for Reconstruction and Development, known as the World Bank, into his private dining room for lunch.[23]

Woods had asked for the meeting. McNamara did not know Woods or his reason for coming. Woods began by praising McNamara's speech in Montreal the previous May on development and security. It sounded just the call to action by rich nations that Woods himself had been trying to issue from the Bank. Then Woods came to the point. His term was up in August; by charter the U.S. president, who represented the Bank's largest source of funds, nominated an American for the post. Johnson would have to send names over soon. Was McNamara interested?

McNamara said later he told Woods he would stay on at Defense as long as the president wanted him; he said he reported the conversation to Johnson, who was noncommittal. Woods, a secretive and difficult man, did not reveal his approach to McNamara to anyone else.

The allure of the World Bank presidency must have been palpable to McNamara instantly. The post offered a quick escape from the Gordian knot in which he was entangled. It offered a new subject, a new constituency, and an outlet for his and Margy's Berkeley-honed idealism.

The advantages must have been equally clear to Johnson. Aide George Christian says the president was concerned in 1967 about McNamara's haggard condition. He thought the Bank would be an ideal forum for McNamara's talents. As the weeks and months went by, and McNamara's secret positions on the war became blunter, Johnson surely noticed that the president of the World Bank was an international civil servant who must impartially serve all 106 member governments and is barred from commenting on the domestic politics of any one of them. As Bank president, McNamara would be barred from speaking out about the conduct of the war.

McNamara went out of his way to avoid telling Johnson he wanted the post. Johnson concealed his interest in making the appointment from McNamara. Two men who communicated dozens of times daily, who were almost indistinguishable in their public roles and power, could not talk to each other about separation.

Westmoreland flew to New York in April and told an Associated Press lunch that the military picture was "favorable." Addressing both houses of Congress, he claimed his forces would "prevail."[24] Behind the scenes, Westmoreland and McNamara fought over the still-secret troop request.[25]

In a key exchange, McNamara turned the tables on the general. Westmoreland had argued that they were about to pass, or had passed, the "crossover point" at which enemy losses exceeded additions. More troops would make his "meat grinder" attrit the enemy faster.

McNamara then asked what would happen if the general didn't get even his "minimum essential" force.

Westmoreland replied that they would not be defeated, but it would be "nip and tuck" to counter likely enemy reinforcements. This amounted to admitting that the president did not have to grant the request.

McNamara asked how much shorter the war would be under each alternative. Westmoreland said: "With the optimum force about three years, with the minimum force at least five."

In other words, the fighting war could not be conclusive before Johnson went before the voters in 1968.

Westmoreland thought Johnson was inclined to grant the request, but McNamara was reluctant. The general flew back to Saigon empty-handed, for the moment.

Enthoven went to work on Westmoreland's request. The minimum requested force would increase weekly kills by 139 per week and the optimum force by 431 a week.[26] In both cases it still would take ten years to kill all the enemy. The analysts also found that 90 percent of

large firefights were still initiated by the enemy, which strongly refuted Westmoreland's claim to hold the initiative. In addition, they
discovered that MACV's own tables did not show they had reached
a crossover point.

John McNaughton also reviewed the request for McNamara. By
1967, the staff of his office in International Security Affairs was one
of the strongest groups in the entire government in favor of extricat-
ing the United States honorably from the war. McNaughton himself
seemed as dovish as anyone. One staffer heard McNaughton say,
"This war is shit." McNaughton urged that McNamara, instead of
granting the troop request and having the general come back for more
later, stand and fight "the philosophy of the war" then and there. He
wrote:

> A feeling is widely and strongly held that the "Establishment" is out
> of its mind. The feeling is that we are trying to impose some US image
> on distant peoples we cannot understand (any more than we can the
> younger generation here at home) and we are carrying the thing to
> absurd lengths . . . [T]he increased polarization . . . [signals] the worst
> split in our people in more than a century.[27]

On May 19, 1967, McNamara handed the president an explosive
twenty-two-page single-spaced memorandum opposing the troop request.[28] He was becoming more open in his pessimism, a mole inside
the war machine.

> This memorandum is written at a time when there appears to be no
> attractive course of action. The probabilities are that Hanoi has de-
> cided not to negotiate until the American electorate has been heard in
> November, 1968. Continuation of our present moderate policy, while
> avoiding a larger war, will not change Hanoi's mind, so is not enough
> to satisfy the American people; increased force levels and actions
> against the North are likely to get us in even deeper in Southeast Asia
> and into a serious confrontation, if not war, with China and Russia;
> and we are not willing to yield. So we must choose among imperfect
> alternatives. . . .

In the United States, the Vietnam War was becoming

> increasingly unpopular as it escalates — causing more American casu-
> alties, . . . more distress at the amount of suffering being visited on
> non-combatants in Vietnam, South and North. Most Americans do

not know how we got where we are, and most, without knowing why, but taking advantage of hindsight, are convinced that somehow we should not have gotten this deeply in. All want the war ended and expect their President to end it. Successfully, or else.

This state of mind in the US generates impatience in the political structure of the United States. It unfortunately also generates patience in Hanoi.

He repeated to the president, as he did so often in public, that Westmoreland said he was having success in the large-unit war.

The "big war" in the South between the US and the North Vietnamese military units (NVA) is going well. . . . "In the final analysis," General Westmoreland said, "we are fighting a war of attrition." . . . General Westmoreland believes that, as of March, we "reached the cross-over point" — we began attriting more men than Hanoi can recruit or infiltrate each month.

But the "other war" against the VC, pacification, was "still not going well." There was too much corruption and too little government control, or "rot in the fabric." The political structure of South Vietnam was "moribund," the population "apathetic," and ARVN, the South Vietnamese army, "tired, passive, and accommodation-prone." The enemy believed the United States would not be able to "translate our military success in the 'big war' into the desired 'end products' — namely broken enemy morale and political achievements by the Government of Vietnam." As for the diplomatic track, whether or not the recent initiatives had much substance to them, "it is clear that Hanoi's attitude currently is hard and rigid. They seem uninterested in a political settlement and determined to match US military expansion of the conflict."

It was quite an evolution from this former proponent of signaling-and-bargaining war.

McNamara told the president that if they followed "Course A," it meant giving Westmoreland 200,000 more troops, calling up the reserves, and adding $10 billion to the defense budget. Course A would also mean bombing North Vietnam's rail, road, and sea imports. It "could lead to a major national disaster; it would not win the Vietnam war, but only submerge it in a larger one."

Would granting the request for troops "polarize opinion" in the United States to the point of "massive refusals to serve, or to fight, or to cooperate, or worse?" McNamara thought not, although Congress could get into a "divisive debate."

Would the added forces "make a meaningful military difference?" If they had passed the crossover point, as Westmoreland claimed, could they not do the job without the added troops? he asked shrewdly. Even with a larger U.S. force, could not the enemy conduct "terror from the bushes" and nullify the troops' impact? Now, "the enemy can and almost certainly will maintain the military 'stalemate' by matching our added deployments as necessary."

McNamara recommended "Course B." He would give Westmoreland "no more than 30,000" additional troops and would forbid incursions into Cambodia and Laos. The administration would push a "cool drive to settle the war" by "clarifying" U.S. aims, which could be explained as only preventing outside interference with South Vietnamese self-determination, not ensuring a "free and independent" South Vietnam as current policy said. They would limit the bombing of the North to below 20 degrees north latitude. Meanwhile they would "press on energetically with the military, pacification, and political programs," with "periodic peace probes" involving "a role in the South for members of the VC."

There were risks: The South's government could fall apart under the strain; the country could become neutral like Finland or Cambodia. It could become Communist, but this evolution would take three to five years, McNamara claimed.

His conclusion was very guarded: Course B "will not win the Vietnam war in a military sense in a short time," but it would "avoid the larger war" of Course A. It would be part of "a sound military-political/pacification-diplomatic package that gets things moving toward a successful outcome in a few years. More than that cannot be expected."[29]

Much has been made in later years of McNamara's secret pessimism, which differed so starkly from what he seemed to say publicly and what the president, Wheeler, Westmoreland, Dean Rusk, Walt Rostow, and others told the American public at the time. When many of McNamara's private memos became public with the Pentagon Papers in 1971, and when the full May 19 memo was declassified in 1984 in connection with Westmoreland's libel suit against CBS, McNamara was criticized as a liar and deceiver for having concealed his gloom from the public and for saying they could "win." He explained to me why he kept his darkest prognosis from public view: "In my memos to the president, I tried to give the pros and cons of our position and then end up with my judgment. I had real doubts whether we could win militarily and I wanted him to understand that."

He went on to say that because he was in a minority among the advisers and the president, he did not believe he should reveal his pessimism too openly. He added a very important admission: Robert McNamara was gloomy, but he wasn't sure his gloom was justified. He told me:

"You have a tremendous obligation as an officer of the government dealing with an issue of national security, to be careful that you don't press on the president views that carry the risk of substantial error. . . .

"There are differences of view among presidential advisers at any point in time. And there is a question how far an adviser should go in publicizing his personal opinion when it differs from the majority view.

"You can say I should have resigned. But to the extent I didn't get out I had an obligation to recognize that I was in a minority and that I may be wrong."

I may be wrong, he said. He was indeed, but he did not see the alternatives as black and white. "The situation was full of grays," he said. He added a key point as to why he did not recommend outright withdrawal that spring: "I saw no *low-cost* means of withdrawal."

"The Washington papermill broke all previous records," when Mc-Namara's secret May 19 memo reached its select recipients, noted the authors of the Pentagon Papers; memos commenting on it fairly flew into the Oval Office. McNamara had one ally, the under secretary of state, Nicholas Katzenbach. But Walt Rostow was critical, the Joint Chiefs were apoplectic, and William Bundy, a strong hawk whom McNamara by now had stopped consulting, called the memo "a fig leaf cover for withdrawal." Johnson had to contend with this fracas, as well as a request from the Joint Chiefs the next day to escalate the bombing and step up military commitments worldwide. This in turn caused McNamara to fire off a counterblast on June 12 calling for restraint in the bombing and more pauses. The president needed to bring his official family together, and so he sent McNamara to Vietnam — again.[30]

*   *   *

Within the Building, the mole, who happened also to be its monarch, rummaged for candid answers. Having suppressed dissent for so long, he now had to scrounge for new people brave enough to give him unorthodox views.

One afternoon McNamara greeted a man sent by the director of the CIA to brief him on the war, George Allen.[31] Allen had been in Saigon back in 1954 and was one of the agency realists — pessimists — on the war. McNamara's regular briefer from the agency, George Carver, was part of the hawk faction. Carver was unable to come, so Allen had been sent to give Carver's briefing.

Since it violated the code for a briefing officer to deviate from the prepared line, Allen stepped into McNamara's office ready to give Carver's briefing.

McNamara the tight-jawed despot had vanished. Instead Allen found an openness and personal magnetism he had not seen in the secretary before. McNamara indicated that he didn't need to hear the briefing; they could just talk. Allen replied crisply that if the secretary did not want the briefing, he would leave. McNamara said no, he had thirty minutes scheduled.

An informal talk would get him in trouble with CIA director Richard Helms, Allen said. Don't worry, I'll take care of Helms, McNamara said. Then he asked:

"What would you do if you were sitting here?"

Allen was shocked — but not as surprised as he might have been, given the rumors about McNamara's private position. For a full hour they talked freely, understanding that the talk was private. Within his self-imposed prison, McNamara was trying to break free.

It was not the tortured, haggard figure of two lives and roles who bounded down the stairs of the big tanker at the Tan Son Nhut airfield, outside Saigon, on July 7. McNamara loped down the receiving line looking cool in pressed khakis. His shoulders swung with his big-power, self-important walk as he raced into his ninth trip as the president's viceroy and arbiter of policy.[32]

He was there with the authority to hammer out an agreement acceptable to Westmoreland, one that did not grant either the minimum or optimum request. When McNamara's official car pulled up at MACV headquarters, he could see the sign on the door to the meeting room that said "High Noon."[33]

His trips had acquired the character of royal processions. Westmoreland and Admiral Sharp had their officers rehearse their briefings for McNamara for weeks. Robert Komer, who was now chief of pacification, had been asked by Westmoreland to send over Komer's briefing officer for a run-through. Komer replied he would brief McNamara himself. Westmoreland was astonished.

Look, McNamara has this idea that the line officer in charge should know his own program, Komer said. He'll like it better if the person in charge answers for his program. Westmoreland was taken aback. Then he decided Komer had a capital idea. Soon he had the officers in charge briefing their own programs — a simple idea of direct responsibility that it had taken nine trips from the secretary for the new MACV command to figure out.[34]

In fact, McNamara found few surprises in the briefings; he was there mainly to hear out Westmoreland's case and ratify some figure less than even Westmoreland's request to take home.[35] The new ambassador, Ellsworth Bunker, told him, "The situation is not a stalemate." MACV's intelligence officer admitted that the crossover point was "a nebulous figure," but said they might have passed it. Admiral Sharp, in from Honolulu, pitched for a wider air war. General Wheeler took Sharp aside afterward: McNamara snubbed you, he said, because you didn't stress *restraint* in the air war. That's the theme he wants.[36]

In the field McNamara was shown Potemkin villages of the fighting. From a helicopter guarded by four A-4s, and wearing earphones that looked like Mickey Mouse ears, he watched flashing artillery of a battle near Con Thien, near the DMZ. The commander of a Special Forces camp explained their need to hit the Cambodian sanctuaries. McNamara saw one of the war's more fantastic construction projects — a U.S. barracks built on floating oil drums, which allowed U.S. forces in the watery Mekong Delta to sleep at night safe from the enemy, after six years of "progress."[37]

The High Noon summit was inconclusive; Westmoreland broke it off to go home because his mother was dying.

As he left Vietnam, McNamara sounded upbeat about the shooting war. He had "clear indication of the success of . . . large unit actions." He avoided repeating Westmoreland's claim that they were "winning."[38]

McNamara said political progress within South Vietnam had been "dramatic" (in his May 19 memo he had said only that it was moving "as well as can be expected"). He said pacification "is progressing, but the progress, I must say to be candid with you, is very slow indeed" (his memo had said the "other war [pacification] is still not going well").

But his gloomiest views stayed hidden. He did not tell reporters, as he had in his secret memo, that "the war is achieving a momentum of its own which must be stopped." Nor did he make public his scathing characterization of South Vietnam's forces or regime. And he concealed his recommendation for Course B, a "cool drive to settle the war," and his willingness to countenance a neutral or Communist South Vietnam free of Chinese domination.

Many journalists picked up his relative gloom anyway. The press was by 1967 bitterly divided as to whether the war was criminal, futile, or merely taking longer to be won than expected. Reporters read different things into McNamara's stance. Reuters wrote as McNamara returned home that he saw "more progress . . . in the war in the last nine months than in the previous six years." A *Washington Post* headline noted, "MCNAMARA SEES SURGE IN VIET WAR'S PROGRESS." But the *Baltimore Sun* said McNamara's remarks "wisely lack the tone of excessive optimism that characterized a good many earlier reports." Neil Sheehan, who had gotten very accurate leaks of Westmoreland's minimum and optimum requests, quoted an unnamed official as saying that McNamara "took the most hard-nosed line I've ever seen him take out here." And the *St. Petersburg Times* wrote that McNamara's reported determination to hold the line on troops will "revive credibility in the United States in a war of limited objectives and ultimately work its pressure on Hanoi." Some members of the press, at least, were getting his point.[39]

Yet right after that trip, McNamara said twice that the United States could "win" — the word he avoided on thousands of other occasions when he was baited to use it. To *Newsweek* he denied the situation was a "stalemate" — whereas the May 19 memo had used the term to describe the shooting war.[40]

In a White House meeting on July 11 he said: "This is not a military stalemate." Clark Clifford then asked McNamara whether "public sentiment" was right in thinking the war "couldn't be won." The meeting notes say: "For the first time Secretary McNamara said he felt if we follow the same program we will win the war and end the fighting."[41]

*   *   *

In Saigon and Washington, McNamara was adamant that West-moreland needed few added troops and could use the ones he already had to get more combat power. There were 1.3 million men under arms in the region, but only 50,000 to 60,000 were engaged in combat. Enthoven and his crew had been studying how to correct the low ratio of combat to support troops, for which MACV had proposed no solution since 1961. McNamara stressed that he would recommend giving Westmoreland any troops he "required." But now he asked what was "required."

Westmoreland and McNamara fought again over the matter in Washington. Then Westmoreland left for Saigon.

On August 3, the White House announced quietly that only 30,000 more troops would go. There was no mention of hooks into Cambodia or a reserve call-up.[42]

McNamara had won, and contained the war again. But he had not fought the "philosophy of the war" or changed it. Instead of gaining momentum, he was losing it. Senator John Stennis of Mississippi, a close ally of the senior military, had announced that hearings on the bombing policy would be held in August. Worst of all for McNamara that summer, his private phone to the president stopped ringing.[43]

On the eve of McNamara's July departure for Vietnam, Margy's ulcers required that she be hospitalized.[44] She checked into Johns Hopkins University Hospital, in Baltimore — near where, twenty-two years before, she had lain in the children's ward for five months with polio. In 1966 she had seen a doctor, who told her to slow down. Since, she had had to deal with Margaret's wedding, Kathy's graduation, Craig's troubles, and her husband's mounting problems. It was said that McNamara's stress was so great that his teeth grinding kept her awake at night. Meanwhile, her main project, Reading Is Fundamental, was getting off the ground, demanding her time.

She tried using an assumed name at the hospital so the press wouldn't accuse Bob of being an impersonal "computer" leaving her for Vietnam when she was sick. She would not be seen in public until a brief appearance in mid-August. As had been the case with her polio, she was weaker than she let on. "Bob has all the problems and I have the ulcer," she joked before one operation. "Margy got my ulcer," he said.

Friends noticed that her illness had a bigger impact on him than all his other problems. His normal hyperactivity became frantic; he insisted on making the forty-mile trip to Baltimore every night — a curious repetition of the crisis over her polio. He appeared at the Pentagon each morning punctually, but unshaven and haggard.

McNamara picked up the phone in Margy's hospital room on July 19, to hear Colonel Robert Pursley, his military aide, tell him that McNaughton was dead. He, his wife, and their eleven-year-old son had just taken off on a Piedmont Boeing 727 from Asheville, North Carolina, and collided with a private Cessna aircraft. All nineteen people on board the Boeing plane were killed. Another son, age eighteen, who was not with them, was the family's sole survivor.[45]

McNamara was "very controlled" when he heard of his protégé's freak death, Pursley says. But afterward he and Margy grieved, alone in the bare hospital room. Suddenly they were no different from thousands of other couples who had lost loved ones to the rising violence of the age. Wanton death had been unleashed on those two lonely people in a hospital room in Baltimore, and not all the trappings of office could protect them from it.

White House aide John Roche claims the cumulative shocks of the summer and his precarious position led McNamara to be "disturbed" and near a "nervous breakdown." Roche occasionally crossed paths with McNamara.

"By the summer of 1967 McNamara was in very serious psychological condition," Roche says. "It was my judgment, based on a certain amount of intuition and a certain amount of experience with people who are disturbed, that Bob McNamara was hanging on by his fingernails. What I'm saying here is not intended as a characterological criticism of Bob at all, because I have immense respect for the man. He did, in my judgment, just about everything wrong. But there's no question that before he deceived anybody else he deceived himself, for he was a completely sincere and dedicated guy.

"[H]is wife was in the hospital with an ulcer as I remember it, and he was, I thought, in terrible shape. Oh God, he looked awful. You see, nothing worked. Everything he believed in was being knocked on its ass in Vietnam. Here was a guy who really believed that the truth is what you get out of the machine when you ask for it. You know, what will we do about x? and here comes the answer, the organizational truth. It just wasn't working. The heat was terrific. He was, I think, a very disturbed guy and I think the President was aware of this also.

"I heard the Forrestal reference used two or three times by others.

Harry McPherson and I talked about it at the time after one particular session with McNamara where he just sat there and his jaw quivered, and two or three times he looked like a man in just terrible shape."[46]

McNamara calls Roche's claim that he was near the breaking point "absolutely absurd. Any time a Cabinet officer is in that condition, the president should get rid of him, quick." As for the evidence of the frozen jaw and inability to speak, McNamara claims his bruxism was much worse at Ford. But then the inner man appeared, unbidden, when he added, "Stress is self-stress, there's no doubt about that."

George Christian, another presidential aide who saw McNamara at the White House often, dismisses Roche's claim as overblown. McNamara "wasn't irrational. He was campaigning for a change in policy," Christian says.[47]

The president was worried. Roche stepped into the Oval Office one day to find Johnson talking to Margy McNamara on the phone. She was still in the hospital. It was August.

"He hung up the phone and turned to me and looked at me and said, 'You know, he's a fine man, a wonderful man, Bob McNamara. He has given everything, just about everything, and, you know, we just can't afford another Forrestal.' "[48]

McNamara appeared at the doorway of the office of Joseph Califano after a Cabinet meeting that summer.

He asked Califano, Can I talk to you about a personal matter? Sure, said Califano, surprised.

McNamara said that if his name came through as recommended to succeed George Woods at the World Bank, he was interested. "Would I please *not* tell the president that he was indispensable as secretary of defense," Califano recalls being asked. The aide agreed to cooperate, but when the president said nothing, and he saw no list, Califano had no more to do with the matter.[49]

According to another source, Johnson was handed a list of possible candidates for the World Bank job. Woods's term was up but had been extended while Johnson procrastinated. The president was startled to see McNamara's name on the list. Then he commented that he didn't know McNamara was interested. He added, in this version, if Bob wants it, he can have it. He can have whatever he wants.[50]

Jack Valenti had lunch with Johnson during this period. Valenti asked in passing whom he was going to name to the Bank. The president launched into a long monologue about what a great job it

would be for Bob McNamara. Valenti recalls that Johnson went on
and on about the possibility so gleefully and playfully that Valenti
thought he was joking.[51]

On August 9, Senator Stennis opened his hearings on the air war. He
was part of a very powerful faction — Senators Richard Russell, Stuart Symington, Barry Goldwater, Howard Cannon, and others —
that argued that civilian restraints were losing the war. Stennis had
arranged to call the senior military commanders first; everyone knew
they would be asked for their personal views and thereby be able to
state, behind the closed doors of the hearing room, their objections to
Johnson's and McNamara's restraints on the air war. They would
assert over and over to sympathetic senators that the quick way to
victory — which was therefore more humane than civilian-imposed
gradualism — was to hit the whole target list in a strategic bombing
campaign like that of World War II. Stennis, with his personal authority, his powerful Senate allies, and the senior commanders, perhaps even the Joint Chiefs, behind him, could take the president and
McNamara hostage.

American planes bombed the huge Paul Doumer Bridge in Hanoi
for the first time on August 13. The next day U.S. planes attacked
inside the buffer zone along the Chinese border, previously off-limits.
Richard Nixon declared the time was right for "massive pressures";
the New York Times warned that the dikes could be the next targets,
to flood the rice paddies and ordinary citizens. There was a sense in
those weeks of August that all-out war was imminent, that the balloon could go up.[52]

McNamara was to appear before Stennis on the twenty-fifth, after
the military witnesses had many days to testify. Clearly it would be
a kangaroo court. Secretly, meanwhile, McNamara was telephoning
Harvard professor Henry Kissinger, whom he had arranged for the
president to send on a secret mission to Hanoi with two Frenchmen,
to see if talks could begin in exchange for a bombing halt. His faith
in negotiation was undiminished, and he hoped the leaders in Hanoi
would bite, even though Lyndon Johnson, because of Stennis, was
bombing more sensitive targets each day.[53]

"We intended all along to have you," Stennis said as McNamara
settled his tense, underweight frame into the witness chair at ten-
ten on the morning of August 25. His eight-page statement had

been handed to the press minutes before, written and released to have maximum impact. In the hearing room, it was Christians and lions.

The secret dove and dissenter had refused hitherto to state his full skepticism about the air war in public. Now, intense pressure and personal unhappiness brought out his creativity. He was losing on the bombing — and he had lost on the ABM. His seminal speech on the ABM was prepared that August, too, as he worked up his bombing testimony. If he couldn't convince the government on the inside on either matter, he would take his case to the people.

Before Stennis, McNamara argued his strongest case yet against widening the air war. The bombing had "always" been a "supplement to and not a substitute for" an "effective" land and air "campaign in South Vietnam."[54]

The volume of bombs the United States was dropping on North Vietnam was approaching that dropped on Europe in World War II. Yet the enemy could sustain the war on *15 tons per day of imports.* He added that even if the enemy required 75 tons, "a few trucks" could sustain it. Meanwhile, the capacity of the transportation network for moving matériel south was more than 200 tons per day. Bombing "has and is hurting North Vietnam's warmaking capability," but there "is no basis to believe that any bombing campaign, short of one which had population as its target, would by itself force Ho Chi Minh's regime into submission."

The military witnesses had argued that the civilians should allow them to hit the entire target list, to do the job right. McNamara devoted much of his testimony to the fifty-seven remaining "unstruck" targets on the list, showing how trivial they were: a plant producing thirty tires a day; nine fuel sites that held less than 6 percent of the North's fuel; a vehicle repair shop of forty-eight thousand square feet, smaller than a garage on a side street in Alexandria, Virginia. The value of all industrial targets hit in the past year was $44 million; McNamara contended that hitting these remaining targets would not make any difference.

> Our air attack has rendered inoperative about 85 percent of the country's central electric generating capacity, but it is important to note that the Pepco plant in Alexandria Va. generates five times the power produced by all of North Vietnam's power plants before the bombing.

He opposed bombing the ports, reasoning that very little incoming fuel was needed to keep the war going. The risks of hitting foreign ships, especially Soviet ones, were high indeed.

McNamara argued that they had not increased U.S. casualties by bombing gradually over time, rather than conducting the short and humane campaign the generals wanted. "No analysis" by "any agency" showed there would have been fewer casualties had there been a big initial air campaign; in fact, analysis showed the casualties would have been greater. He warned against impatience:

> The tragic and long drawn out character of that conflict in the south makes very tempting the prospect of replacing it with some new kind of air campaign against the north. But however tempting, such an alternative seems to me completely illusory. To pursue this objective would not only be futile but would involve risks to our personnel and our Nation that I am unable to recommend.

The hearings ran for seven hours. Under questioning by Senator Strom Thurmond, McNamara asserted that his strategy was "not no-win." And he cited military experts who said they were winning: "I think from what you have heard from General Westmoreland and General Wheeler and the other Chiefs . . . [is that] each of them firmly believes we are winning and will continue to win."

Nearly twenty years later, CBS lawyers made much of this testimony when they cross-examined McNamara under oath. Aren't you a damn liar, sir? How can you say you believed the war was militarily unwinnable when you said to Thurmond it was "not no-win"? The judge in the case interpreted CBS's line of questioning to be aimed at the point that the "witness is not a truth-teller."

McNamara's appearance in Westmoreland's 1984 libel suit against CBS was supposed to be a field day for all those who resented his lengthy silence, who wanted him to account for his actions in lying and deceiving the public. Now they had him under oath and could show the world who he really was.

McNamara looked haggard. He had come to the courthouse in a rumpled raincoat just off a plane from Europe. As he sat in the witness box he traced the circle a Styrofoam cup had made on the polished surface. The fullness in his features that had made him look so boyish in the old days was now gone; the face was a mass of lines and a tight jaw.[55]

He spoke haltingly, in bursts, dueling with his interrogator and his own temper. Gradually his old combativeness rose; he wanted to dominate the room, but he was cornered. In 1967, McNamara said, he told Thurmond the war was "not a no-win program" and *Newsweek* the war was not stalemated because at the time, a top-secret mission he arranged with Kissinger was going to make a fresh offer to Ho Chi Minh. Even though he thought the war was militarily "unwinnable," military pressure and this political track "appeared to offer the opportunity of . . . a win . . . situation." But "these are rather hairline distinctions," he said.[56]

McNamara later explained to me that his verbal tactics were deliberate: "I tried to be very careful. I was skating a very narrow line." When referring to the military situation, he intentionally quoted Westmoreland or the chiefs and avoided saying *he* thought the fighting war could not be won.

He did think pressure on the enemy from Westmoreland's campaign "would increase the likelihood of movement on the political track." The "cost" to the enemy "was the stimulus, . . . I hoped, to progress on the political track." He added, *"So the fighting was not in vain."*

And he said in a characteristic note that it was the numbers, his blessed numbers — the numbers that had blinded the men on the line from qualitative judgments on the war — that warned him the fighting would not work.

"By 1967 we had a lot of information on the number of men who had infiltrated, the number killed (from the body count) and current enemy strength. By then it was clear to me that the figures did not add up; if the body count was correct, then the figures were wrong. That's why I was losing confidence in the figures and in the optimistic military reports.

"My whole point was: Don't let's kid ourselves that we are making progress."[57]

When Stennis's hearings broke for lunch after the first hours of McNamara's testimony that August, he appeared in the hallway, eyes glazed, but grinning at the press, and responded to questions.

> Reporter: Senator Symington charges your policy differs from the military commanders'. He says if you are right we should get out of Vietnam.

McNamara: Symington . . . is completely wrong. My policies don't
differ with those of the Joint Chiefs and I think they would be the
first to say it. Their strategy for winning in South Vietnam is exactly
the same. . . . I think there is some misunderstanding as to the basis
of the argument over the bombing campaign in the North.[58]

McNamara claimed, when asked by another reporter, that his differences with the chiefs were "very narrow." But that was not how
the chiefs saw it in August 1967.

His testimony was a remarkable ploy. Newspapers around the
country reprinted his eight-page statement; many editorial writers
grasped that his real message went beyond the case against bombing
a few more targets. Without actually saying so, McNamara had explained with far more authority than Harrison Salisbury could that
the bombing had virtually no impact on the struggle in South Vietnam. The conclusions were inescapable that the North could fight on
indefinitely and that escalating the bombing would be dangerous.

He had made a case to gather support for his private agenda, which
consisted of more bombing pauses to induce movement toward negotiations in Hanoi, and perhaps to one day turn the bombing off, if
the barrier, then being built, worked to limit infiltration so America
could fight on without an expensive and politically costly air war. Yet
he had officially supported the present bombing campaign. The conflict between private and public selves was plain.

His stock of power shrank. Califano says of McNamara's testimony, "Believe me, Johnson was mad."

The next day the president effectively disavowed McNamara's position before the press. McNamara felt "hurt," says reporter Henry
Trewhitt. Yielding power was not easy.

After McNamara testified in official support of the current bombing
campaign, the Joint Chiefs met in the chairman's office. In complete
secrecy, late into the night, they considered a joint resignation — an
unprecedented act. Leading the discussion was General Earle
Wheeler. They had all known the bombing policy wasn't working.
For McNamara to claim that continued gradualism would exact a cost
from the enemy was to them a bad-faith defense.[59]

After years of compromising with civilians, Wheeler was determined to pose starkly the military issue: The United States should
"make an unambiguous stance in Vietnam — or get out."

Wheeler told his staff he would take calls from the president and no one else. They had no contact with the waiting staff down in the Tank, not even with duty shifts changed in the evening. Inside his office, Wheeler faced the others from a chair pulled in front of his desk. He said he thought they should resign "en masse" at a press conference the next morning. Thomas H. Moorer, chief of naval operations, said he hadn't been surprised by McNamara's testimony. John P. McConnell, chief of staff of the Air Force, said he would do what the group wanted; he would do anything to help his flyers. The strongest proponent of resignation was Army chief of staff Harold Johnson. The general now deeply regretted that he had not resigned when the president and McNamara declined to call up the reserves back in 1965. The military was being blamed for a war they had no control over, he said.

The Joint Chiefs agreed to call a press conference for the next morning. They took an oath of silence, promising to tell no one, and went home.

Early the next morning, Wheeler returned from his quarters. He had been having chest pains in the previous week. The conflict between the apparent usefulness of a resignation and his military oath of obedience tore at him. Now he thought resignation was the wrong course. The press conference was never held. And despite a few rumors, not until the 1980s did the story emerge. This manifestation of the major schism in modern civil-military relations — the cumulation of McNamara's poor relations with the military and an unsuccessful war — went unreported, even to McNamara.

Johnson, meanwhile, sensed the brooding discontent of the chiefs and invited General Wheeler — or, when he was out (for he had a heart attack that fall), one of the other chiefs — to their regular Tuesday lunches: the hub of power.

McNamara's position, which began in late 1965 as a heartfelt urge to restrain the war, had become by October 1967 a tangled mass of honesty and concealment.

One of the few doves left in the administration was David K. E. Bruce, the U.S. ambassador to the Court of St. James's. At a meeting in Washington at about this time, Bruce argued for himself and the British Labor government (which officially supported the war) that the president should minimize the commitment and get out.

Back in London, Bruce was surprised to get a phone call from

McNamara. Bruce spoke to him and afterward put the receiver down with an amazed look. He told Thomas L. Hughes, of the State Department, who was with him, that McNamara had called to say that, despite the fiery argument they had had in Washington, at which McNamara with his usual pyrotechnics had put Bruce down, "I just wanted you to know that I agree with everything you said. But in my position as secretary of defense I can't give any hint of it."[60] McNamara's reputation for integrity was already near rock-bottom with many. When this story made the rounds of the well-established anti-McNamara network, it sank lower.

Possibly what caused the nervous tension, the tears, the bruxism, was not just the strain of trying to manage a limited war, but going against the grain of American wars by keeping both the military and public emotions in check so they could fight on for years and win the test of wills with Hanoi. Part of what was metamorphosing McNamara was the thought — which some in the Kennedy camp were voicing openly — that the intervention had been unnecessary in the first place, that Robert McNamara had been utterly and totally wrong and now people were dying for his error.

Many, during the 1960s and after the publication of the Pentagon Papers, came to the conclusion that he did think the war was wrong or unneeded; but this is not, in fact, what he said publicly or in the memos of the time, or what he says today.

He saw then they had misjudged China and that the geopolitical stakes — the domino effect — were smaller than he believed in 1964 and 1965. "I knew we had made mistakes," he says, although he does not specify if he thinks intervention was one of them. "That's why I set up the Pentagon Papers. . . . By then it was clear we had made a number of mistakes, which scholars — through the Pentagon Papers — should have the ability to analyze and draw conclusions from."

But to McNamara in 1967, "past mistakes were irrelevant" in the conduct of his job. "The relevant points were: we were there; what should we do?"

Joseph Califano, his former special assistant who in 1967 worked in the White House, offers a candid view of the change in McNamara: "The whole thing affected him personally. No doubt at a lot of levels. He had come in with a view that you could measure with some precision victory in a guerrilla war and there was some rational, calibrated way you could raise the level of escalation. And it affected everybody, the whole question of the multisided nature of communism. Personally, it took its toll."[61]

McNamara, meanwhile, spurned the growing antiwar movement, which announced it would march on the Pentagon and shut it down on October 21. The sight of Norman Mailer, high on LSD, leading the crowd, the general disorder and mental sloppiness of the protesters, offended him. But the religious man in him was drawn to the marchers as he saw them speckled like a long snake, winding up the drive to the lawn below his window. There were fifty thousand of them.

The marchers declared the North Vietnamese to be oppressed patriots. "The real enemy is Lyndon Johnson."

McNamara was at his window; some of the marchers and photographers could see him, looking ghostly through his curtain. As dusk fell, the procession coiled down the highway and gathered on the lawn face-to-face with cordons of National Guardsmen. No one knew when or how violence might start. The Building was filled with troops. He said to me later, "Actually, there's no way to protect the Pentagon."

To the marchers below he was still the symbol of militarism, technology, mindless computers, herbicides, napalm, white shirts, narrow ties, combed hair, corporations, obedience, lying, and government run amok. A press release issued in his name defended the Dow Chemical Company for its service to the free world in making napalm.

From the window, McNamara imagined how *he* would lead the march. In his speech at Millsaps in February he had said modern society was "under-managed"; clearly the antiwar movement was. He later told an interviewer, "Girls were rubbing their naked breasts in the soldiers' faces. They're spitting on them; they're taunting them. God, it was a mess."[62] To have power, protest must be orderly, he stressed, with some knowledge of the matter.

"There was no question I would be up there. You don't delegate something like that. Christ, yes I was scared. You had to be scared. It's terrifying. . . . They did it all wrong, I mean the marchers. The way to have done it would have been Gandhi-like. Had they retained their discipline, they could have achieved their ends. My God, if fifty thousand people had been disciplined and I had been the leader, I absolutely guarantee you I could have shut down the whole goddamn place. You see, they didn't set up proper procedures."

Their disorder compared unfavorably with his own escalation control. "You know, there wasn't one shot fired. I'm very proud of that to this day. Our troops didn't have any ammunition in their guns."

Perhaps everything I and Dean Rusk have tried to do since 1961 has been a failure, McNamara blurted out to a meeting of wise men convened by the president on October 31, ten days after the march on the Pentagon.

That same day at lunch, McNamara "stated my belief that continuation of our present course in Southeast Asia would be dangerous, costly in lives, and unsatisfactory to the American people," as he wrote to the president the next day.[63]

Attached to the note was the most radical proposal that McNamara had given the president yet, for what would become under President Nixon the "Vietnamization" of the ground war. If the administration kept to its present course, U.S. casualties would reach 700 to 1,000 a month, bringing the total in the next fifteen months — Johnson's tenure in office — to "10,900 to 15,000 additional Americans dead." This would bring the total killed in action to between 24,000 and 30,000, which was close to the "Korean total." Any widening of the war would add to casualties.

To avoid this, McNamara proposed, the president should stabilize deployments at the 525,000 level and turn more of the fighting over to the South Vietnamese. He should unilaterally and indefinitely stop bombing North Vietnam. Since the bombing did not affect the war in the South, a halt would not raise U.S. casualties. Death seemed to be on his mind. The paper got nowhere with Johnson; McNamara's power seemed to have run its course. The president "was honestly worried McNamara was letting his emotions get into it too much. Clark Clifford, he regarded as stalwart and unemotional," says George Christian.[64]

It was as though McNamara could not cut the tie to Johnson directly but had to engage in a series of more and more extreme positions to force Johnson to do it himself. The bombing halt and troop stabilization paper may have been just too much. Or, as Rostow's former military aide, Lieutenant General Robert Ginsbergh, believes, Johnson decided McNamara was a traitor, a friend of the Kennedys' and not of his.

Without telling McNamara, on November 13 Johnson called Treasury Secretary Henry Fowler and told him to get busy over at the World Bank.

McNamara learned suddenly, in late November, that the *Financial Times* of London reported that Her Majesty's government was being asked to approve the nomination of R. S. McNamara as the next president of the World Bank.

The news hit Washington like a cyclone. McNamara rushed to the White House and was closeted alone with the president.

McNamara returned to the Pentagon, and Bobby Kennedy hurried to room 3E 880 — just as he had on the afternoon of his brother's murder.[65] The two were alone while the outside world raged in confusion, again.

Bobby was urging McNamara to make a statement saying he could no longer serve the government in good conscience and to decline to become Johnson's appointee to the Bank — to use this moment for the cause of stopping the war. In effect, to tell the world who he was. Robert Strange McNamara now had a choice.

20

The Modern Public Servant

BOBBY KENNEDY apparently believed that McNamara opposed the war just as he did. Kennedy was becoming emotional on Vietnam, although an open break with the president was months away. When Kennedy had called for a show of hands at a Catholic girls' college and saw that the majority favored more, not less, bombing, he blurted at them, "Do you understand what that means? . . . Don't you understand that what we are doing to the Vietnamese is not very different than what Hitler did to the Jews?"[1] That fall of 1967, Kennedy was overtaking Johnson in the polls and emerging as the most prominent voice of the small but coalescing liberal wing of the Democrats; the president, however, commanded the center and the right and was thought unbeatable.

During that autumn, reporter Neil Sheehan asked Kennedy if it was true that McNamara had turned against the war. Bobby confirmed it and told Sheehan "in detail" what he claimed were McNamara's feelings. But Sheehan did not believe it: A transformed McNamara meshed too smoothly with Bobby's presidential plans.[2]

When the London press broke the story of McNamara's impending appointment to the World Bank and Bobby raced to his Pentagon office, the Kennedy camp told reporters that the defense secretary was leaving over the war. Clearly Kennedy believed McNamara had a higher loyalty than to the president. All he had to do was make a statement saying he differed from the administration over policy and could no longer carry out his duties. Then he would be free to fly to

Kennedy's nest, and the covey of doves would gain immeasurably.

Confusion reigned that night, aided by the fact that presidential press secretary George Christian had denied to reporters that afternoon that McNamara was leaving; Christian was not privy to Johnson's maneuvers with the Bank. Johnson received the president of the *Washington Post,* Katharine Graham, and also the *Post's* executive editor, Benjamin Bradlee. Both were friends of McNamara's and demanded to know if he had been fired. Columnist James Reston, working his phone, tried to get the straight scoop from the president, who shunted him off to speak to Califano.[3]

Meanwhile, Bobby sat in McNamara's office, probably pressuring him to make a statement. McNamara was on the phone with Califano at the White House. At about nine-thirty that night Califano rang the buzzer on John Roche's desk. Come here, Califano said. What are you doing? Roche asked.

"I'm trying to keep from going insane," Califano said. Roche joined Califano and heard one side of the torrent. "Johnson wasn't talking to McNamara, and McNamara wasn't talking to Johnson, but they were both talking to Califano, like the good friend in the divorce case sort of caught in the middle of it," says Roche.[4]

When I asked McNamara if Bobby came to his office that night, the blind dropped abruptly. "I don't doubt he did, because we were very close," he said. He would not say directly what Bobby asked him to do, or whether he was speaking to the president or not, as Roche says.

"Bobby would have been very happy to see me resign with a hell of a blast at Johnson, but I wasn't about to do anything that wasn't in my opinion in the national interest." Then he retreated to an assertion he has made over the years: "To this day I don't know whether I resigned or was fired."

The assertion seems plainly untrue, given that his strong memo of the previous November 1 flew in the face of what the president was prepared to do or wanted to hear; he had been asking to be fired, without saying it, and he was.

McNamara said to me, "I don't think Johnson told me he was circulating my name" to the Bank's member governments. I asked whether 106 governments knew his name had been placed in nomination but he didn't. "Yes," McNamara said. "That was Johnson, typical Johnson."

On the evening of November 29, Kennedy joined Arthur Schles-

inger, Pierre Salinger, and others at about eleven at the King Cole Bar
in New York City. According to Schlesinger's diary, Bobby told the
group that McNamara said he had "*not* had any intimation that
Johnson had sent his name up for the Bank." He had heard from "a
leak in London" that "he was on his way out."

Over drinks, Schlesinger "expressed incredulity" at McNamara's
"apparent acquiescence" in Johnson's dumping him. "Wouldn't any
self-respecting man, I asked Bobby, have his resignation on the President's desk half an hour after he heard the London bulletin?" But
McNamara didn't need to make a "public clamor," Schlesinger went
on. "Why does he not resign quietly and go back to private life? Why
does he have to fall in with LBJ's plan to silence him and cover
everything up?

"Bobby listened silently and a little gloomily," Schlesinger noted.
"Then he ventured that that was what he thought would finally happen — that Bob would not take the World Bank job and instead
would quietly resign from the government.

"Obviously this is what Bobby had been urging him to do."

They broke up "around 1" in the morning and bought copies of
the morning *Times*. The headline read: "MCNAMARA TAKES WORLD
BANK POST." Schlesinger wrote, "Bobby was evidently surprised and
sad about this."[5]

On November 29, all 106 governments had completed the appointment process, and immediately McNamara darted into the Pentagon pressroom, which was jammed with reporters.

He sat squarely in front of the gold curtain. His hair was combed
straight back, and his clear eyes focused into the television camera
from behind his spectacles. He looked more like the full-cheeked
wunderkind of 1961 than the haunted figure reporters had seen of
late.

He read a statement: In less than sixty days he would have served
seven years as secretary of defense; he was glad to have served his
country and the president; he would stay to prepare the next budget
and leave on February 29 to take up his duties at the World Bank on
April 1.[6]

He said nothing about why he was going, whether he had been
fired, whether he differed with President Johnson on the war, or
anything of substance. He rose and rushed from the room, avoiding
questions. The White House issued its own statement, which contradicted McNamara's on a few details.

"I just have this sense of two guys who bungled the public relations," says Califano.[7] But it was more. McNamara had turned down a chance to step forward and, by speaking out, radically change his own life and that of the country. But he was not ready to take such a course.

For the majority of Americans that December and January, events piled on each other in surreal juxtapositions. Martin Luther King, Jr., winner of the Nobel Peace Prize, was shot at as he marched for open housing in Chicago. A Strategic Air Command B-52 on full alert lost its hydrogen bombs in the Greenland ice, reminding Americans of the grave risks they ran having 5,856 nuclear warheads deployed in the name of liberty around the world.

In South Vietnam, General Westmoreland's 1967 "progress" campaign with the press and public was bollixed by the enemy's siege of the Marines at Khe Sanh. Americans had been repeatedly told there was light at the end of the tunnel. Now, instead, they found an impending humiliation at Khe Sanh that could be as devastating as the French defeat at Dien Bien Phu.[8]

Then, on January 23, another small Communist state humiliated the American empire. The North Koreans abruptly seized the Navy ship *Pueblo* and its crew, valuable papers, and codes, for the *Pueblo* had been on a mission like the destroyer *Maddox* in the Tonkin Gulf in 1964, which was to eavesdrop on enemy messages indicating military capabilities. That the *Pueblo* could be snatched up without U.S. protest or retaliation was a shock to a country that had voted $73 billion for defense, a sum larger than that spent by the government of the republic between 1789 and World War I. Lyndon Johnson's inaction was "LETTING US BE NIBBLED TO DEATH," screamed one angry headline.[9]

The case for strategic overstretch — that the United States had obscenely overstepped the limits of its power — was being built by the left. Foreign aid came under fire, and several congressmen called for bringing U.S. troops home from Europe to force the Europeans to pay for their own defense. Eugene McCarthy, Senate poet and iconoclast, announced that he would challenge the president for the Democratic nomination on an antiwar plank. Insiders gave McCarthy very long odds; only Bobby Kennedy was thought capable of denting the Johnson machine, and he remained undeclared and waffling.

The intellectual leader of the emerging left was J. William Fulbright of Arkansas, chairman of the Senate Foreign Relations Committee, "secretary of state of the Senate," and a longtime Johnson confidant. After endorsing the deployments to South Vietnam, Fulbright gave a series of speeches attesting to his scholarship and thoughtfulness. He argued that cold war verities were passé; China was not the threat heretofore imagined, and the United States should withdraw from Vietnam honorably soon. Above all, Fulbright — feeling betrayed by Johnson — pounded on the theme that the executive-military complex (Johnson and McNamara) had usurped Congress's power under the Constitution, lied to elected officials, the press, and the people, and violated public trust.[10]

In August 1964, Fulbright had worked to get the president's Southeast Asia resolution adopted by the Senate, believing Johnson's announcement that the enemy had attacked U.S. destroyers not once but twice in the Gulf of Tonkin, on August 2 and 4. But an Associated Press investigative story in 1967 awakened Fulbright to the possibility that U.S.-backed commando raids had struck the enemy nearby on the night of July 30–31; the story also reported that right after the supposed second attack, the captain of the destroyer task group, John Herrick, doubted it had happened. Through the fall and winter, Fulbright's staff gathered evidence that fed their growing convictions that the United States had provoked the attacks — contrary to Johnson's word — and that the second attack had never occurred, also contrary to Johnson's word. In short, the emergency that was the basis for Congress's ceding its war-making powers to the president had not occurred, meaning that Johnson's legal basis for the war was built on a lie.

Fulbright had regretted his role in the 1964 affair; he believed he had been duped and had apologized to the Senate. Now he planned a hearing for February 1968 to call McNamara to account under oath, for it had been McNamara who testified in 1964 that the attacks were unprovoked, McNamara who certified that the second attack took place. If Fulbright could say his public mea culpa, McNamara could, too.

In the early hours of the morning of January 31, Saigon time, enemy rockets flared and mortars burst in cities and towns across South Vietnam. The Communists struck an incredible thirty-nine of forty-four provincial capitals simultaneously during the traditional Tet holiday cease-fire. By nine forty-five in the morning, the press reported, the enemy had penetrated the U.S. embassy compound in Saigon. The stunning breadth and scope of the attack came as an utter surprise to U.S. forces and constituted a massive intelligence failure.

The shock of the Tet offensive rippled instantly through the United States. Millions were appalled as television relayed images of spectacular defeat, contradicting official reports that the *enemy* was being defeated.[11]

McNamara was less shocked than many in the upper reaches of government. His mathematical mind had long since reckoned that the enemy was not being killed off at anything like the rates Westmoreland had claimed. "You couldn't reconcile the number" of enemy, "the level of infiltration, the body count and the resultant figures. It just didn't add up. I never did get the answer," McNamara said years later in a deposition for the Westmoreland-CBS lawsuit. In his posture statement released that January, he warned of a future enemy buildup in the South.[12]

As images of the Tet carnage were beamed into American living rooms, the president offered Westmoreland more troops to avert a U.S. defeat. General Wheeler began a series of steps exploiting presidential fears to obtain the reserve call-up and reinforcement of troops worldwide that the military had wanted for so long. Wheeler lobbied for sending 200,000 troops; McNamara tried to head off this new madness. In the moral arithmetic of war, if he allowed 700,000 Americans to fight in Vietnam instead of the 500,000 already there, casualties would increase by 40 percent. McNamara had been struggling to stave off needless additional U.S. deaths for more than a year.[13]

But his power was running out daily, almost by the hour. McNamara's successor, Washington lawyer and superhawk Clark Clifford, would determine the choice with the president, not McNamara.

McNamara was losing energy. His last weeks saw no letup from the dreary pattern of argument over the merits of bombing targets. Alfred Fitt recalled a meeting in which the generals were thumping away, plugging to hit harder, when McNamara surprised them.

He waved his left arm in a gesture of exhaustion. "All right," he said, "bomb it if you want. One more or less won't make any difference." McNamara's passivity was startling. Moreover, it was the first time he had ruled on target policy without paperwork.[14]

His self-possession was only sporadic; now the inner strain showed. As he posed for photographs with Clifford, McNamara's eyes were glazed, his face jowly, his collar loose. Harry McPherson recalls a meeting at the State Department of the top advisers: Rusk, Rostow, Under Secretary Katzenbach, and Clifford, who was preparing to take over.

Suddenly McNamara launched into a harangue, banging his hand on the table as he talked. McPherson had "never heard him speak with such terrible emotion." There were tears "in his eyes and in his voice," he says. McNamara ranted about "the goddamned Air Force with its goddamned bombing campaign that had dropped more bombs on Vietnam than on Europe in the whole of World War II and we hadn't gotten a goddamned thing for it," McPherson remembers.

McNamara went on for a full five minutes in "rage and grief and almost disorientation." Dean Rusk seemed uncomfortable. Clifford, meanwhile, looked from one of them to the next. His gaze seemed to say: Here is your co-leader. See where he has gone. Is this where you are going?[15]

The tears came more often and involuntarily now. To avoid their being seen by visitors to his office, McNamara would turn away to appear to be looking out the window. One of his secretaries told a friend, "He does it all the time now. He cries into the curtain."[16]

There was some question in his mind as to how long he could hold on. To the press McNamara remarked that he was "counting the days," adding how fortunate it was that his last month had only twenty-nine of them.[17]

American liberals in early 1968 were struggling with disillusion still and felt weighed down by the responsibility for the war. Vietnam had taken 16,022 American lives, lasted longer than the Korean War, and led to military humiliation and economic weakness, as both inflation and the foreign trade deficit grew. The media covered antiwar statements by clerics, professors, and artists, although most of the public supported the Vietnam commitment. Yet to come were President Nixon's escalation of the bombing, *his* weakening of the U.S. economy, and publication of the Pentagon Papers, in 1971. McNamara was leaving the political stage at a precarious moment, when the polarities that would define the next decade were just emerging.

The cautious, grim tone of McNamara's seventh and last posture statement echoed the shaken public mood. Soviet military spending was up by 3.9 billion rubles to 16.7 billion rubles by 1968, its land-based missile force continued to grow, and there had been a serious risk of war over the Middle East in June 1967. McNamara still held out hope that Kremlin leaders would behave like rational adversaries; he claimed that they had "to confront the fact that they too have an interest in stability."[18] But the Sino-Soviet split was creating a militant rivalry between the two all over the Third World, one that was further aggravated by China's impending nuclear might. Inside China, the violent Cultural Revolution was in full swing. A change in leadership seemed likely, but McNamara warned this could bring to power a more militant regime, which could "confront the free world with a new and even more severe threat."

McNamara's prognosis for Vietnam was sobering, and his stress on the need for fundamental political progress and pacification was seen by commentators as realistic. "The secretary's swan song," said *Newsweek,* "made franker and far less rosy reading than any of its predecessors."[19]

He confirmed that he believed in the war. Collective security, he said in the statement, had had "a particularly high price, both in lives and in wealth, first in Korea and now again in Southeast Asia. So the American people have a right to ask: were the achievements worth their cost. . . . I think they were."[20]

He also defended the sacrifice because it kept South Vietnam free and "purchased time" for the other nations of Asia to become steadier and more able to defend themselves against communism. He argued that a sign of this progress was the Association of Southeast Asian Nations, an agreement formed the year before among Thailand, Indonesia, Malaysia, the Philippines, and Singapore — the very dominoes whose toppling the U.S. intervention was meant to prevent. This rationale for the American sacrifice in Vietnam would be one of the enduring justifications later, when the Asian economic "miracle," barely visible in January 1968, took off.[21]

McNamara's parting statements gave the lie to any speculation that he was retreating into isolationism. South Vietnam was a "vital interest" because the United States "is a Pacific country." America might have felt disillusioned with the turmoil in the world, but "of all nations, we have the most at stake. The existence of an open, outward-looking, humane society in the United States depends upon the vitality of similar societies elsewhere." And he said, "Our burden is large, because our capacity is large." He was upholding, in effect, the premises of the American Century.[22]

His gloom over Vietnam was not seen as perfidious, just realistic compared with the bombast that had come from other advisers, the president, and Westmoreland before Tet. A profile in the *Washington Post,* citing his rumored disenchantment, noted, "There are no Georgetown circuit stories of expressions of self-doubt by Rusk or Rostow."

McNamara signaled obtusely that there had been self-discovery and personal change. Quite possibly he was seeing his basic errors during the war, and his own capacity for misjudgment, for the first time. Before reporters he found an excuse to quote T. S. Eliot's "Little Gidding":

> *We shall not cease from exploration*
> *And the end of all our exploring*
> *Will be to arrive where we started*
> *And know the place for the first time.*[23]

He telegraphed his sense of failure in his own Morse code. On February 4 on *Meet the Press,* alongside Dean Rusk, McNamara interrupted a question on another point to announce that he had erred over the Bay of Pigs invasion back in 1961: "I have never said publicly and I want to say today, that when President Kennedy assumed full responsibility for that action he didn't say what he might have said, that every single one of his advisers, me included, recommended it. So I was responsible for it."[24]

The reporters doing the interview were startled that he had admitted to being wrong at all — let alone on the Bay of Pigs, which now seemed so many mistakes ago. One asked whether he thought he had been wrong at other times.

"I can think of far more than time would permit me to list," McNamara retorted. Defending U.S. goals in Vietnam later in the same program, he added, "I don't by any means suggest that we haven't made mistakes over the many, many years that we've been pursuing those objectives."

When journalist Peter Lisagor visited the defense secretary's office, he made a point of monitoring the books on the shelf behind McNamara's chair to guess his thoughts. He noticed a copy of Roger Hilsman's book *To Move a Nation.* Hilsman had steadfastly opposed the militarization of the U.S. program in Vietnam while he was in government and had fought with McNamara over it. His book argued that the military escalation was in error.

Lisagor asked McNamara, "You're reading Hilsman's book? I thought you two didn't get along."

McNamara replied, "I won't speak against Roger. Turns out he was right all along."[25]

McNamara gave one of the most revealing interviews of his career to Saul Pett of AP, which was published on February 4 and widely reprinted.[26] Pett asked how he dealt emotionally with the casualties. McNamara said: "Sleeping pills help. . . . It also helps to believe in what you're doing and to know that the men who are fighting the war also believe clearly in what we're doing."

Pett read McNamara a quote, attributed to him, suggesting failure. It said, "I've been given all the resources I've asked for to solve the problem in Vietnam and I've failed. Perhaps it's time for someone else to try." Pett wanted him to comment on this admission, but McNamara responded, "I have not said that."

The reporter asked whether Vietnam had taught him that all problems cannot be solved by quantitative analysis. At first, McNamara ceded no ground: "There are a number of factors about Vietnam on which it has been difficult to get enough information," he said stiffly. Then came the big concession: *the attitude and thinking of the North Vietnamese, for example*" (italics added). Was he saying that he had utterly misjudged the enemy? He swung back to safer ground: "I believe the problem of Vietnam must be attacked rationally, but the results will be imperfect because we lack certain facts."

Pett returned to the question of errors in general. The rationalist answered, "Most decisions, once made, do not bother me in the slightest." He said he could tolerate an error of $10 million or $15 million, but he did not address errors involving lives. McNamara went on: "On the really major issues, I would hope that our mistake level is at an absolute minimum." He did not say that on the "really major issue" of Vietnam he had made two mistakes — first, of escalating the war without making the enemy yield, and second, of trying to contain the war to get it resolved. Nonetheless, Pett was amazed — as were the many who read and wrote about this interview — that R. S. McNamara admitted any error at all.

He did not reveal exactly what was tearing at him. Publicly, he had said "I believe" that the sacrifice had been justified. Were his regrets only about tactics?

His wife, Margy, who knew his secrets better than anyone, hinted at part of his burden: "It's not over yet," she said to the press in a rare public comment.[27] Margy said this more than once, implying that her husband's guilt came from his sense of not having finished the task of containing or ending the war. The manager who demanded results from others had failed to achieve them himself.

McNamara's solution to the conflicting perceptions of his real position was silence. He said to Pett, "I will make no comment on Vietnam now. It's not yet possible to look back on it with any wisdom. Perhaps in two or four years but not now."

While McNamara's emotional self-control diminished in the count-down to February 29, so did the momentum of his effort to run U.S. security objectively, using the yardstick of analysis.

"Nobody should be under any illusions as to what his departure means," columnist Joseph Kraft said in a valedictory column about the end of McNamara's tenure. "It expresses a failure in the mana-gerial faith, a crisis of the whole postwar generation," Kraft wrote, showing a sense of history rare in daily journalism. McNamara might be the "foremost American public servant of the postwar era," but he was leaving office "under a cloud that casts a dark shadow across the qualities and values of the best men" in the country.

> He embodies perfectly the change in outlook which took place in this country with the transition from depression to prosperity.
>
> The mean pickings of the depression had bred an emphasis on harsh philosophical disputes . . . along fundamental lines of political and moral conflict. But prosperity meant enough to go around for every-body if only a way could be got round the embarrassing conflicts of yore.
>
> In the dawning atmosphere of success, accordingly there emerged a faith that transcended ideology. That faith — the pre-eminent faith of the postwar generation — was a faith in manipulated settlements that went beyond old-fashioned conflicts, in arranged solutions that took all interests into account. It was faith in the manager.

John F. Kennedy and other postwar leaders shared this faith, Kraft pointed out, but McNamara at the Pentagon was "its Daniel come to judgment."[28]

In the surreal early months of 1968, that judgment could well appear to be running against the "managerial faith," the integrity, and even the competence of Robert Strange McNamara. Everything he had touched seemed to be going sour, not just Vietnam.

The M-16, the lightweight automatic rifle promoted by McNamara and the Whiz Kids, had been exploding in Vietnam when the trigger was pulled, maiming and even killing some American soldiers. During the summer and fall of 1967, the House Armed Services Committee ran an extensive, highly publicized investigation of the M-16's development. The investigation faulted the Army more than McNamara for sabotaging the effectiveness of Eugene Stoner's brilliant prototype. Others blamed McNamara more than the Army, arguing that his ordering the service to speed up development had "politicized" and "rigidified" the final design.

He was unable to resolve this tragedy before leaving, although he did manage to stop production of the IMR ball propellant that experts saw as one cause of failure. A year would pass before the problems with the gun were resolved so it could become the successful standard rifle it remains today.[29] But in February 1968, McNamara could not claim a clear win; even this well-intentioned effort was stained with American soldiers' blood.

While his gun was exploding, McNamara's pet airplane, the F-111, crashed. Overall the crashes of the planes occurred in no greater proportion than those of other new military aircraft. But they revived the stories about McNamara's dictatorial management of the F-111 program; meanwhile, he denied a top-down salvage effort was under way. He lied in making sweeping claims for the plane's success, which by 1967 was obviously not succeeding.[30]

Senator John McClellan resumed hearings. He had amassed a thick file of alleged McNamarian mismanagement and deceit, and an encyclopedia of discontent from the Navy over its version, the F-111B. Meanwhile, the British government, which had committed to buy the F-111B, was getting nervous and eventually canceled its order. McNamara's other project, to have the U.S. and West German armies build a common tank, had been abandoned. The only clear win for his principle of efficiency through common technology remained the F-4. And even it didn't really fit the principle, since the Navy had developed it and McNamara had to force the Air Force to take it on.[31]

All told, McNamara ordered up seven variants of the F-111 — the F-111A for the original Air Force mission, the F-111B for the Navy, the F-111C, the F-111D, the F-111E, the F-111F, and the F-111K.

Of them all, only the A's and C's entered service, and they had very different capabilities from those which McNamara had laid down in 1961, and for which he had sacrificed his reputation as a manager of technology.

But even twenty years later McNamara clung to his faith in multiplying the benefits of a technology by finding simple items that could be replicated at the lowest practical cost. At the World Bank he would try to achieve these efficiencies all over the Third World with pumps, wells, farming practices, high-yield strains of rice and wheat, and other technology. He told me that had Vietnam not intervened in his second term, "there was tremendous opportunity for commonality. So I would have done more of that in my second term."[32]

Senior Navy officers and McClellan did not wait for McNamara to leave to begin getting rid of the plane that they now hated, it is safe to say, as much as they hated him. What was wrong with his whole style was not the process of executive decision or the principle of commonality, not the idea of an Air Force–Navy fighter-bomber — all of which were legitimate and achievable. What was wrong were the man's preference for abstraction and his disdain for the realities of hardware, and his immovable fixity of purpose once he had decided on his goal. Finally, the atmosphere of oppression he created prevented warnings of trouble from reaching him. Too often the services were excluded as meaningful decision makers.

Kraft put his finger on a key lesson: A "central weakness," which had caused "the managerial faith" to fail, was that it had been "confined among a small group of initiates, not . . . broadcast among [or sufficiently shared with] . . . the armed services."[33]

Nine days after succeeding McNamara, Clark Clifford was asked by Senator Richard Russell how he felt about the Navy's controversial F-111B airplane. Russell's fellow senators and the bemedaled senior officers, who accompanied the new secretary to this maiden hearing, listened attentively.

The suave, tall figure, whose long record as a behind-the-scenes influencer of presidents, including Johnson, fairly oozed reassurance. He said he would reevaluate projects with an open mind and not merely carry on where his predecessor had left off. The noted military commentator Brigadier General S.L.A. Marshall, who would not have missed this hearing for all the wars in the world, wrote, "The occasion appears to have been vastly enjoyed by all present."[34]

A month later the Navy's TFX, the F-111B, was dead.[35]

McNamara also appeared to have been wrong in another area. In his January 1968 statement, he announced that in the past year alone, the Soviets had doubled their ICBM force to 720 — a rate at which, if maintained, they would surpass the United States' 1,700-missile force in a few years. Neil Sheehan commented that McNamara's willingness "to accept parity" in missile numbers troubled some people — even though McNamara, in fact, promised that the United States would stay ahead in warhead megatonnage by deploying MIRV when it was ready.[36]

McNamara's approach to negotiating with the Soviets, of tolerating their missile programs while capping his own and trying to reason the Kremlin into moderation, suggested misjudgment in early 1968. The enemy was not listening to him. Thus, he made the Democrats easy targets for charges of vulnerability on global security issues, including the siege of Khe Sanh, the apparent enemy victory of the Tet offensive, and McNamara's "losing" the war through piecemeal bombing policies. The politics of the 1970s and 1980s was taking form, in which Republicans would flay Democrats as the party of weakness.[37]

The backlash against McNamara was so severe that Congress's long-standing discipline in fiduciary matters was breaking down. L. Mendel Rivers, the rabidly pro-Navy chairman of the House Armed Services Committee, who was a friend of Vice Admiral Hyman Rickover's and of nuclear propulsion and who hated McNamara, was wreaking havoc with the fiscal 1969 authorization bill.

Rivers had been enraged by McNamara and Enthoven over the issue of building nuclear frigates. He did something with few precedents in the disciplined Congress of the 1960s: He threatened to hold up action on the defense budget request until the frigate money was restored, a move that foreshadowed the congressional assertion of power and tinkering with minutiae of the defense budget of the next twenty years. One of McNamara's greatest services, in fact, had been to act as a buffer between congressmen and their constituents seeking military contracts. A stubborn defense secretary made it easier for congressmen to give their districts bad news. Rivers's action signaled the me-first defense politics now stirring.[38]

McNamara refused to yield to the Navy right down to the end. In February he announced a decision to stop construction of nuclear attack submarines to block Rickover, the father of naval nuclear propulsion, from getting the entire new class of attack submarines he wanted (which Enthoven had priced at $2 billion). McNamara was determined to have his way — to the last. Or, as he said to me once of his fights with the Joint Chiefs and senior men like Rickover, "What was I supposed to do? Wait for them all to *die?*"

His final coup was to ax the entire program with no compromise, standing firm on his analysis, which showed the new fleet not to be worth the cost. McNamara had withstood Rickover's demands for a year, but Rickover was ready for him. The Joint Committee on Atomic Energy did the admiral's bidding and issued a report before McNamara left office attacking systems analysts and their conclusions. By June, sums for the ships were added to an already large deficit- and inflation-producing defense budget, to start buying Rickover's new subs.[39]

Alain Enthoven became the sacrificial lamb for McNamara's judgments, right and wrong. It was easier for senior officers to charge that Enthoven and McNamara knew nothing of war or were dishonest than to confront the serious issues the civilians kept trying to raise.

Rivers requested that Enthoven appear before his committee in June 1968, after McNamara had left the scene. Clifford did not interpose himself between the chief Whiz Kid and the often drunk committee chief.

"McNamara always protected us and went up to testify himself. Even when we made mistakes he would go before the press, the military, or the Congress and defend us and never let them blame us directly," says one of Enthoven's closest colleagues. This had been the secret of his power. "He was saying, if you come after my staff, you have to fight me." McNamara was self-centered, assumed sweeping responsibility, and gathered power too firmly in his own hands. One positive side of these traits was that he held himself personally responsible for his staff, and he protected them.

Even though "we told him he didn't have to go" before Rivers's committee, says Enthoven's associate — "someone else could go" — Enthoven did appear. There followed one of the most vitriolic cross-examinations in congressional memory.

The associate fears that Enthoven was deeply scarred by the experience. "He felt he had given seven years of service to his country, and now he was being pilloried for upholding values in which he deeply believed."[40] The same could be said for his boss and patron.

McNamara's managerial revolution gained international momentum just as the most virulent backlash set in at the Pentagon. Every defense secretary since has been closer to the logrolling school of management. Even those who have tried for central leadership have distanced their images from that of McNamara, lest the military brand them as another devil, like the one who said he was serving the public interest and lost the war.[41]

Wrote Kraft, "The bell that now tolls for Secretary McNamara tolls for the group that has supplied this country with its most enlightened leadership."

Senator Fulbright and his fellow members of the Senate Foreign Relations Committee prepared to confront McNamara on the twentieth of February, hoping that the man, who was in so many ways an honorable public servant, felt some compunction to clear the record before he departed.

Fulbright was now armed with sonar reports and statements of sightings and the arguments that these were dubious evidence of the second so-called attack on U.S. ships on August 4, 1964. Above all he had Captain John Herrick's critical message sent that night from aboard the *Maddox* saying that earlier reports were "doubtful" and asking for a "complete evaluation" before any action was taken. He was convinced that the attack had probably not happened and that McNamara had concealed this at the time to continue the emergency atmosphere and get the resolution passed. Hadn't Johnson and McNamara tricked them?[42]

On the morning of February 20 the secretary of defense swung through the painted white doors of Fulbright's chandeliered hearing room with the same overbearing presence with which he had dominated American security policy for seven years. General Wheeler was at his side; only a few staff members accompanied him. As usual, McNamara spurned his privilege of appearing with a retinue of splendidly uniformed officers; he appeared solo with Wheeler and the same old flat yellowed briefcase, a symbol of the notion that his power rested, not on his retainers or even in his files, but under that sleek hood of hair, now thinning.

Fulbright's weathered face looked hard at McNamara, the light eyes intense, the lilting southern accent lending dignity to his words. They were neighbors up in Kalorama; the senator admired Margy.

Fulbright said his purpose was to "review the decisionmaking process of our Government in time of crisis." He wanted to establish the truth.

"If this Nation cannot learn from its past performance and acknowledge where it has been wrong or insufficient to the task, then the United States will become servile to its past — and suffer" for it. He read McNamara two lines from Eliot's "Little Gidding":

> *History may be servitude,*
> *History may be freedom.*[43]

There was some sparring over an internal study McNamara refused to release to the committee and a staff report the committee had declined to give the Office of the Secretary of Defense. Fulbright and McNamara skirmished over whether McNamara could release his formal statement that morning, since both sides knew that shaping the news was key and that reporters were waiting outside. Then McNamara launched in.

"Even with the advantage of hindsight, I find that the essential facts of the two attacks appear today as they did then, when they were fully explored with this committee and other members of Congress." The *facts* were *fully* explored with Congress? Fulbright knew McNamara had not told them of Herrick's skeptical message or his request that they delay further action until the facts could be established. The defense secretary was claiming something that was not so.[44]

McNamara argued that the "weight of evidence" at the time made the existence of the second attack "incontrovertible," despite Herrick's telegram. He cited the search for evidence he had ordered that afternoon and his documented order to Admiral Ulysses Sharp in Honolulu that they defer any retaliation until they were "damned sure" what had happened. He listed the visual sightings and radar and sonar — although the committee knew that excited sailors can see luminescent flashes in the water in typhoon-ridden seas. He placed special weight on the facts that Captain Herrick, later that night, had confirmed that some attack occurred (while adding that its nature was unclear) and that Admiral Sharp, a seasoned commander and McNamara's deputy in the chain of command, had concluded the same.

Bit by bit, this master of the witness chair led the senators back to the intercepted enemy messages, which, he said, were unequivocal proof of the second attack. At one point he asked that the room be cleared of the committee's staff. He then showed the startled senators — who by definition were permitted to view top-secret material — the intercepted messages and described them. The senators, not experts in intelligence, had no way of disputing him.

Fulbright was keenly disappointed. He did not agree that the "incontrovertible" evidence of the intercepts was proof. The evidence was "uncertain" even with the intercepts, he said to McNamara, yet in 1964 "your statement and General Wheeler's was without any doubt, any equivocation that there was an all-out attack."

But "if I had known of that one telegram, if that had been put before me on the 6th of August, I certainly don't believe I would have rushed into action. . . . All my statements were based upon your testimony." In trusting McNamara's evidence to get the resolution passed, "I did a great disservice."[45]

Fulbright said, "I regret it more than anything I have ever done in my life." But McNamara claimed utter certainty, as he does today, and expressed no regrets whatever.

When the ordeal was over, the press photographed McNamara and Wheeler through the door of their limousine. In the picture, Wheeler smiles, and McNamara's grin is wider. He seems to be laughing, although it is the laughter of exhaustion. He had told Fulbright from the witness chair that while he would love to help the committee further, he saw no way in the next nine days to fit another visit into his schedule. The door of history slammed shut.

In 1964, and apparently in 1968, McNamara did not doubt that the intercepts were good evidence of the second attack, although in fact they were not.

It appears that the messages McNamara took to the hearing were *not* North Vietnamese reports of an engagement with U.S. destroyers on August 4; two reported on the destroyers' movements, and two other messages were from the sea fight two days before, on August 2. Later, expert analysis of the time and date signatures on the bits of paper, and the times they arrived in the Pentagon, and their content, revealed that they were no proof at all. *

---

* McNamara read to the committee four intercepted enemy messages, after Fulbright's staff left the hearing room (though McNamara's staff were not required to leave). The first intercept gave the location of the *Maddox* and *Turner Joy* and was sent to a Swatow-class North Vietnamese boat at five o'clock in the evening, before the so-called second attack. The second message was also sent that night from shore

On August 2, intelligence functioned normally, but on August 4, messages found their way to McNamara and Admiral Sharp in chaos and confusion. Unanalyzed intercepts helped to form McNamara's case that fateful night that a second attack had occurred. When, three and a half years later, Pentagon staff began preparing for Fulbright's hearing, the still-secret, translated messages were pulled from the files. McNamara and some key subordinates, such as Deputy Secre-

---

to two Swatows and instructed them to "make ready for military operations." Although McNamara called this one an "attack order," Senator Albert Gore quickly got him to admit that to "make ready for military operations" could be an order for defensive or surveillance movements, not to attack. Since Swatows have only machine guns and do not fire torpedoes, it is hard to see this message as an order for two small boats to attack the big, heavily armed U.S. destroyers twelve miles from shore.

In the third intercept McNamara read that the "North Vietnamese vessels stated they had our ships under attack." It reported an "enemy vessel wounded" and "an enemy aircraft falling," that is, a U.S. ship hit and a U.S. plane falling. Yet the destroyers sustained no damage during the alleged attack of August 4, and none of the Navy aircraft overhead malfunctioned, whereas in the daylight battle of August 2, the *Maddox* was hit by enemy fire and one of the Navy's aircraft wavered for a time, thinking it had been hit. Thus the third intercept "fits" the first attack better than the alleged second one. Moreover, this message reporting the attack reached the Pentagon while the August 4 attack was supposedly under way; yet enemy messages from Southeast Asia normally did not reach the Pentagon that fast. Further, an eavesdropping van on board the *Maddox* picked up no enemy radio traffic during the alleged attack; and if this message was sent at the time, the *Maddox* would have heard it. Thus, the third intercept seems more likely to be an exaggerated report from the attack of August 2, which only reached the Pentagon two days later.

The fourth intercept was relayed "immediately after the attack ended," according to McNamara. It said the North Vietnamese lost two ships in the engagement. This message could be taken as conclusive proof of the August 4 attack, since some U.S. radarmen reported, on the basis of blips on their screens, that two enemy boats had sunk. However, the ships' radars were notoriously fickle during that nighttime "engagement," and no enemy ships were reliably seen by eyewitnesses, let alone any sinking ones. North Vietnamese public broadcasts disputed there had been an attack, much less that they lost any ships. In contrast, on August 2, in daylight, two North Vietnamese ships were seen to be damaged and a third was burning; a captured North Vietnamese naval officer in 1967 admitted that three ships sank after the August 2 encounter.

McNamara claimed these intercepts were "incontrovertible proof" of a second attack; but in 1968 Fulbright did not believe they were proof at all. While being able to put his investigators onto this evidence, Fulbright found it hard to pursue this issue after the hearings. Later examinations, one by Anthony Austin of the *New York Times* in 1970–71 and another by Ray Cline of the Bureau of Intelligence and Research of the Department of State, concluded that McNamara's "proof" fit the events of August 2 rather than August 4, that the messages must have been jumbled when the records were stored, and that normal intelligence checks did not clarify the error when McNamara's testimony was prepared. (Anthony Austin, *The President's War;* "The Phantom Battle That Led to War," *U.S. News & World Report,* July 23, 1984; and interviews.)

tary Paul Nitze, apparently still believed they were hard evidence of the second attack. If any experts at the time noticed that they did not fit the events of the second attack and so were not proof, it appears that McNamara was not told.[46]

Thus emerges the tragedy of the Tonkin Gulf affair, caused by McNamara's and Johnson's impatience. During the night of August 4–5, McNamara used raw intelligence in the form of the messages to decide that the enemy had attacked. He did order a search at the time to be "damned sure," as he said to Sharp, that an attack took place. But he misled himself — and was misled — by haste, confusion, and his own unwillingness to wait and check with experts who, had they analyzed the messages, might have caught the error. His philosophy of management — that leaders can decide anything, that procedures and experts can be bypassed to get things done — caused him, the chain of command, and the nation to stumble.

And in 1968, McNamara, believing the secret intercepts were conclusive, showed his usual preference for turning arguments that were gray into black and white.

He also maneuvered for the president's political advantage. Clearly the president had enough problems that February. Had McNamara expressed doubts about the second Tonkin Gulf attack, or admitted that the executive branch had had "plans" to bomb the North in the spring of 1964 (which he also denied in the hearing), Kennedy, McCarthy, Fulbright, and the rest of the growing left wing of the party could have made an issue of deceit in Johnson's conduct of the war and raised Cain with his bid for the nomination. McNamara's hardline case helped the president contain the Tonkin Gulf investigation as a political issue.

His choice was a portent of the politics of a later era, with presidents affirming their right to lie or distort — not for national security but for immediate political gain.

And for McNamara personally, his choice fitted the logic of one of his several personae. He was no more about to bequeath the president of the United States a messy campaign fracas over the Tonkin Gulf in 1968 than he had been ready to admit on the record in February 1961 that there was no missile gap. It was, to be sure, one definition of public service.

Massive energy propelled him forward as he counted the days to the close of business on February 29. There was a strange scene on February 28 at a ceremony in the White House at which the president awarded him the Medal of Freedom.

Johnson said that McNamara "may not have accomplished the impossible, but he achieved the unlikely." He had made America "the strongest, most efficient military power in history." At the World Bank he would now "try to build the kind of world that alone can justify that strength." The president's affection for him shone.

"If I may be very personal," Johnson said, turning to McNamara, who stood soldierlike beside him, "I am giving the world the very best that we have to win the most important war of all."

McNamara accepted the medal and stepped to the lectern. Behind him was the president, Margy, Little Margy, Kathy, and Craig all in a row. Before him was an audience sitting in ballroom chairs, a *Who's Who* of Democratic Washington: Alice Roosevelt Longworth, Chief Justice and Mrs. Earl Warren, Bobby and Ethel Kennedy, Edward and Joan Kennedy, General and Mrs. Maxwell Taylor. Even Mendel Rivers came.

Suddenly, McNamara could not speak. He coughed, drew his hand to his mouth, and blinked tears.

"I think — I think I better respond on another occasion," he said. He turned and looked plaintively at his wife. A reporter noticed the look on Craig's face. The boy "stared at his father as though for the first time."[47]

The ceremony ended, and there was one more day. The elevator got stuck, and it rained, as though nature were taking its revenge on McNamara for trying to control it. Even his F-111s could not fly overhead in formation to thank their creator; clouds caused the flyby part of the ceremony to be scrapped. Then he was out, and packing for Colorado, focused on the weeks of vacation before he would confront the Bank on April 1.[48]

"Had he been the subject of a novel instead of a figure in American history for the last seven years, one could expect to find him now either a sputtering basket case or a martyr screaming in the night on a pyre of politics and special interests," Saul Pett had written in his profile.

Pett captured not only McNamara's conflicting moral signals and ambiguity, but his habit of living in the present and fixing on the future while denying or simplifying the past.

"There he still is, Robert Strange McNamara, . . . still visibly intact of body and soul and psyche after seven years." On a Saturday morning in his office, McNamara reminded Pett of "a happy scout-master" with "a galloping zest for challenge that one imagined accompanied Theodore Roosevelt into a herd of buffaloes."

The reporter tried to get McNamara to admit that Vietnam had shaken his faith in logic and reason, but McNamara wouldn't play. So Pett concluded with an accurate reading of the man who, after a month off, would take over the World Bank and dominate the development scene for thirteen years as he had dominated American security for seven at the Pentagon: "He leaves with what he came, a continuing faith in reason and logic and the processes of objective analysis."[49]

Robert Strange McNamara ended his towering role in American security and in Washington with his core faith "in the processes of objective analysis" unchanged. But the man himself had changed. The McNamara of 1961 who made his debut in Teddy Roosevelt–style top hat on the steps of the Capitol would not have beat his breast on television about being wrong. By 1968 McNamara had seen that he was capable of huge misjudgments and that he had wrought much suffering in the name of good. "I was wrong" were not words that the public or private McNamara uttered in the days of his own Camelot.

By 1968, he had become a divided man to the point of terrible inner confusion. The old tension in him between the needs to have power and to display the promise of a better dawn had become a deep schism.

The dark side to Joseph Kraft's eulogy of McNamara's managerial faith was his equal belief that a handful of players at the top would have the best information, and that only they could make decisions that were really in the public's interest. McNamara said later about one of his key achievements, the Nuclear Planning Group, where a few men huddled together could serve the general good: "I have always believed that the more important the issue, the fewer people should be involved in the decision."

His reform of the Pentagon and U.S. forces from January 1961 onward had benefited from his faith in a small group of men with the best information deciding the fate of many, for McNamara the intelligent novice from Michigan and his Whiz Kids could ask the big questions and brandish their power as a needed counterweight to military tradition and parochialism. McNamara's other great achievement, of beating back the military's and NATO's faith in nuclear weapons and changing the forces and war plans to avert nuclear war, was also carried out by a small group of powerful men with superior information. After all, the knowledge that debunked the myth of the practicality of nuclear weapons — that there was no missile gap, that the war plans were dangerous, that the Warsaw Pact armies were not ten feet tall — was secret information.

McNamara had piled triumph on triumph through the fall of 1965 due to two traits: his faith in and use of a particular style of management, which concentrated power at the top, and his loyalty to his boss, his source of power, which was so reflexive as to be blind to Lyndon Johnson's poor judgment. Both carried Bob McNamara and therefore the country into war in Vietnam. And both prevented him, when he saw the enormity of the mistake, from speaking out. Indeed, after the fall of that year, McNamara played a classic insider's game to rein in the war, to hide his most serious disagreements with the administration, for the sake of the higher good — as he saw it. All the while he was more torn by consequences raging beyond his control.

He had changed, but not enough. Vietnam humiliated him and shocked his conscience: He now saw he could do harm. But caught up in action, as always, he did not know how he had changed or what to do about it. He could cry. He could read T. S. Eliot on television. He could commission the Pentagon Papers for history. But this unreflexive man could not look into himself and find answers.

So he could not change enough to make the emotional transition into a member of the political opposition, to go public, join the marches, and hurt Johnson, whom he admired and had served. McNamara told me, "I didn't want to bomb Hanoi; I didn't want to withdraw. I didn't have the answers. All I knew was we were in a hell of a mess." But not enough of a mess for him to radically change his style and entrust the voters and the world of politics with his full views, to let the country decide. Thus he only talked of his regrets very quietly and rejected Bobby's urging that he speak out. He retreated into silence, confusion, and remorse, which would propel him into his next life and world; in denial instead of self-knowledge.

When February 29 released him at last, McNamara, Margy, and Craig flew to their house in Snowmass, Colorado. Exhaustion was relieved temporarily by the energizing whiteness of powder and long ski runs. A friend telephoned the house to hear an excited voice bark gaily, "Come on out. It's just wonderful."[50]

V
THE WORLD

21

"McNamara Yanqui"

THE MCNAMARAS' COLORADO HOME was located near Aspen, in the town of Snowmass. Bob and Margy bought the place in the 1960s to use as a home for winter reunions with their old California friends. The cedar house had a big porch and a stunning view of mountain slopes; nothing could seem more different from Washington. For years the house served as a pleasant refuge for the couple, and McNamara was one of the Aspen community's distinguished citizens.

By the winter of 1967–68, Aspen had become a fashionable winter retreat for mobile, well-off youth with liberated life-styles and liberal politics. McNamara began to be hounded even there. Clumps of people shouted at him; protesters rocked his lift and heckled him on the slopes; in a lodge dining room, one woman came up to him as he poured catsup on his hamburger and yelled that she hoped it reminded him of human blood.

Once someone set fire to their house when the family was away. "I'm so mad since the doves tried to burn down my house in Aspen, Colorado, yesterday," McNamara told the president back in Washington.[1]

Brock Brower, a writer, tried to sit down next to McNamara in an Aspen lodge but was almost shoved away by McNamara's old friend Willard Goodwin, who thought Brower was another heckler. Only after Brower explained that he was on assignment to write a profile of McNamara for *Life* did Goodwin let him sit down.

Brower was struck by how subdued McNamara was. He seemed very absorbed with Margy and concerned with her health, which had not been good. During a long interview by the huge fireplace in their home, McNamara sounded "highly concerned about the budget-busting bill for the war," which he said he had not expected to go so high. "He did not go so far as to say he disapproved of the war but all the indications were that he considered it was not viable," recalls Brower. McNamara discounted a political future for himself; he said he was going to an international institution and that was that.

Brower skied the Big Burn with them; McNamara shepherded the group down the long run as though nothing else were happening in the world. He and Margy skied close together, as one; Brower could sense their almost supernatural closeness. Craig straggled behind. Brower saw little communication between father and son. He thought that to Bob McNamara, it was "as though Craig was not there."[2]

Craig had his mother's features but was taller and more strongly built than either parent, strong enough to make the football team at St. Paul's School, where he was now a junior. He also had a with-drawn air, born of inner uncertainty that weekly visits to the Boston psychiatrist had not resolved. "I was in a lot of trouble academically," he said later. It was hardly surprising, however, that the son of a secretary of defense gained entry to Stanford in the fall of 1969, the university to which families in the Bay Area who had "made it" sent their children. But within a year, Craig would be standing in a draft line in Oakland, in pain from the ulcers that had dogged him since high school and not knowing whether his father, off somewhere trying to save the disadvantaged of the world on a massive scale, knew he was there.

McNamara swung through the doors of the shining black facade of the World Bank main building at 1818 H Street, in Washington, early on the morning of April 1. Rainer Steckhan, the young German who had been George Woods's special assistant, had also arrived early, to be ready for his new boss. McNamara suddenly burst into Steckhan's little office, which adjoined the large, formal president's office, and came at him, hand extended. The German was surprised. This was not how men of great authority were supposed to act. Whoever McNamara might be, he was not what Steckhan expected.[3]

The four previous presidents of the Bank — Eugene Meyer, John J. McCloy, Eugene R. Black, and George Woods — had been a businessman, a lawyer, and bankers, respectively. All were impeccable establishment figures accepted on Wall Street and by the U.S. Treasury, which was very important to the Bank. The Bank's senior staff worried that Lyndon Johnson had dumped a political liability on them; McNamara was an architect of the Vietnam War, which was unpopular the world round; to boot he was rumored to have been fired. Another anxiety among the close-knit staff was that McNamara would descend on them with a phalanx of Whiz Kids and turn the place inside out, as he had the Pentagon.

In McNamara's mind that morning, however, were thoughts about his new mission. "Everything we have done in Vietnam won't count for a thing if Indian democracy goes down the drain," he once remarked to Chester Bowles, the U.S. ambassador to India during the sixties.[4]

The populations of the Third World were growing faster than their gross national products. Echoing the view of experts, McNamara had forecast that the globe south of the equator would become "a hemisphere in turmoil." In his 1966 Montreal speech, McNamara had argued that the United States and Western Europe had an overwhelming interest in addressing these problems. But the small, quiet institution through whose halls he had just raced seemed an improbable vehicle for carrying out that mission.

On the coffee tables in the anteroom to McNamara's new office lay the morning papers, with big, bold headlines blazing the news that Lyndon Johnson was out of the presidential race. The night before, in a television address with a surprise twist that shocked the nation, he had announced he would not run for reelection that year and was drastically reducing the bombing of North Vietnam.

Clearly McNamara's long hours in the Oval Office arguing that the bombing of the North was inconsequential to the course of the war in the South and an obstacle to starting talks had taken hold in the president's mind, although at the time the signs were that McNamara was losing his case. Now Johnson announced he would only bomb south of the 20th parallel, that is, the southernmost part of the North's territory, the exact move that McNamara recommended the previous November only to meet outrage from the other advisers and be rejected by the president. Now, in absentia, McNamara had won.[5]

The man who on the record persuaded Johnson to take this historic step and ratchet up the search for peace was the new defense secretary, Clark Clifford.[6] Johnson had turned to Clifford as he began to wonder about McNamara's positions, loyalty, and mental state. Clifford took office on March 1 utterly committed to continuing the war; yet within weeks he decided the United States had to de-escalate and had won over the president. Clifford achieved in weeks what McNamara had not accomplished in two years.

There was a connection, however, between McNamara's many arguments in the inner circle and Clifford's fast conversion once he took McNamara's job. McNamara's civilian staff work on the war had been done by Paul Warnke and Morton Halperin of International Security Affairs. By 1967, ISA was the most eager group in the Building to find a way out of the war. Its staff helped Clifford see the war in a new light during the critical weeks of March, while McNamara was in Aspen. "McNamara set it up by putting us in place to brief Clark," says Halperin.[7]

Johnson's announcement that he was out of the running had tremendous implications for McNamara's own situation. Exactly two weeks after Johnson's address — and two weeks after becoming an international civil servant — McNamara made a statement to be shown on television praising Bobby Kennedy, who was now a declared candidate for the Democratic nomination.

McNamara claimed, then and later, that he was only speaking for history on Kennedy's role in the 1962 Cuban missile crisis. He said of Kennedy that in the period "of the most intense strain I have ever operated under, he remained calm and cool, firm but restrained, never nettled and never rattled." He praised his friend's "shrewd diplomacy" as well. Clearly the statement could dampen the public's impression of Bobby as John Kennedy's emotional younger brother who lacked experience in foreign affairs.

He denied any political intent in making the commercial, but even his close staff had warned him not to do it. At least one member of the viewing public, Brock Brower, the *Life* writer whom McNamara had just told in Aspen that he was renouncing a role in U.S. politics, was shocked. Brower took the commercial as a very serious decision by McNamara to throw his support to Bobby, even if McNamara denied it.[8]

The television statement raised a hue and cry of understandable criticism. The *New York Times* wrote that since McNamara was now an international civil servant, he had "displayed poor judgment and poorer taste." His gesture "shakes, if it does not destroy, confidence in his sense of the political proprieties."[9]

The affair underscored a truth about his new life. Free as he now was to roam the earth and talk to anyone, McNamara would be judged in his own country by the standards and values of the American political scene.

McNamara's commercial for Kennedy hurt India, which in the spring of 1968 was counting on receiving millions of dollars in import credits from the World Bank's affiliate, the International Development Association. The funds for regular Bank loans came from Bank borrowing in private markets; in contrast, IDA obtained the money for its concessional loans to the poorest countries from government appropriations. The United States government normally provided 42 percent of all moneys lent by IDA. Now, as McNamara well knew, Congress's growing isolationism was causing it to sit on funds that would "replenish" IDA for five years. Meanwhile, IDA was running out of funds to lend. The Kennedy commercial only gave Congress more excuse to dally.

An ongoing, serious problem for the Bank and IDA was that its largest donor was reluctant and often late in providing funds. McNamara's appointment could make the problem worse, because he had such a long and unfortunate history with Capitol Hill. The senator who controlled the IDA replenishment bill was J. William Fulbright, who, just weeks before, had confronted McNamara over the evidence of a second Tonkin Gulf attack in 1964 and decided McNamara had misled him, with disastrous consequences.

McNamara tried to recoup his standing on the hill — and help India — by writing to Fulbright, "Perhaps if you are going to be back in Washington for a while we can get together; we have a lot to talk about."[10]

His dependence on Congress and the treasury was integral to the founding arrangements of the Bank. In the town of Bretton Woods in northern New Hampshire in July 1944, Harry Dexter White, assistant secretary of the U.S. Treasury; John Maynard Keynes, the British economist; and others worked out basic arrangements for the postwar financial system designed to prevent any return of the inflation and protectionism that destabilized Europe after World War I.[11] The group invented the International Monetary Fund, the Bank's sister institution, and the International Bank for Reconstruction and Development, which is the formal title of the World Bank. The idea's evolution reflected the disposition of power during the era: the Americans made the basic proposal, which was imaginatively elaborated on by Keynes and the British party as they crossed the Atlantic aboard the *Queen Mary* en route to the meeting.

The Bank was conceived as a means to help devastated Europe rebuild. At that moment, the United States was stepping into its new role as the economic giant of the world; Europe was destroyed, and Britain and its empire were still considered a great power. East Asia was being ravaged by war; southern Asia and Africa were still colonial turf. Although Latin American nations came to Bretton Woods, the conferees saw Europe's reconstruction as the Bank's primary task; the other continents were on the margin of their mind and of the actual plans.

The men of Bretton Woods decided to have a Bank with a capital base made up of subscriptions from member countries (20 percent paid in, the rest guaranteed), which would serve as collateral for it to offer bond issues to raise the necessary funds. The Bank would lend these funds out as long-term, fixed-interest-rate loans, whose repayment would be guaranteed by borrowing governments. The Bank's Articles of Agreement specified that all loans "shall, except in special circumstances, be for the purpose of specific *projects* of reconstruction and development" (italics added).

The Bank would be run by a Board of Governors, who would be the finance ministers of the subscribing countries. Their voting power was proportional to their country's capital subscriptions. Thus the United States, which paid in the lion's share of the Bank's first capital, had the largest voting share, at 37.2 percent; Great Britain was second, with 13.8 percent. While the Bank president was given broader powers than most CEOs, he was "subject to the general control of the Executive Directors," who represented the member countries and who were to be in residence at the Bank's headquarters.

Because its loans would be unusual, to rebuild roads, power plants, and the industrial nerve system of Europe, the Bank's articles included a key rule: The Bank would have to obtain prior approval from the government of any country in which it wished to raise private funds. Thus the Bank needed approval from the U.S. Treasury each time it wanted to offer bonds in the United States to raise funds. And New York was the center of the financial world.[12]

Crop failures, mounting debt, war, and economic mismanagement in the 1950s led to the creation of the International Development Association, an affiliated organization operated by Bank staff and run from the Bank's offices in Washington. IDA was formed to make long-term concessional loans — at no interest, and with fifty years to repay and no repayment due for the first ten years — to the poorest countries, mainly India and Pakistan, which could not qualify for regular Bank loans.[13]

The funding for IDA credits, as these special loans were called, came from replenishments paid by member governments. Since the United States government supplied the bulk of IDA funds and the Bank could deal with Congress only through the treasury, that department had the power to hurry up or slow down Congress's action for money for this key part of the Bank's work.

Thus the treasury habitually treated the Bank as its ward.[14] McNamara quickly sensed that the institution felt limited by this inferior status. Right off he asked the staff why the Bank did not lend to Indonesia or Egypt or the poorer African nations. He was told that Indonesia was a pariah to the American government; Egypt was unpopular with Congress; Africa was too backward to benefit from the Bank anyway.

He asked why the Bank didn't borrow and lend on a larger scale. The staff said Congress and the treasury were not sympathetic to a bigger Bank and would not approve more private borrowing or a bigger IDA.[15]

McNamara still did not know how the Bank could address the problem of the hemisphere in turmoil he had outlined at Montreal. But he knew he would need independence and power, no matter what course he charted.

Among the staff he inherited was an Englishman hired by Woods named William Clark. Clark had been a press officer for Prime Minister Anthony Eden but resigned in disillusionment over Eden's handling of the Suez crisis. Clark then took up with the Fabian-inspired wing of British Laborites who invented the concept of development and terms like "developing world" from their observations of India and other places where the Union Jack was coming down. Clark was well traveled; he made a point of knowing everyone who was anyone in the field of development, and in the world, for that matter. He was an incurable name-dropper. He made no secret of being a homosexual. Clark's comment about Bob McNamara when he came to the

Bank was that despite his flying trips to Europe and Vietnam, "he didn't know the *world*."[16]

Clark checked around town to find out what people thought of McNamara. Clark knew former Illinois senator Paul Douglas. "Douglas thinks he's a liar," he noted in his diary.[17]

But Clark hit it off with McNamara and thus was given a tempting chance to be close to a second famous man. He prepared assiduously for his morning chats with his boss. He also fell in love with Margy, if the term can be used; her wholesomeness and utter loyalty to Bob made it easier for Clark to befriend her than if she had been a more seductive type of woman. Margy was as endlessly focused on Bob as Clark was; they were parallel supports in very different ways.[18]

The trio's early trips were a wild success. Margy felt delighted to share a life with her husband again, and Clark showed off amusingly. He knew the personalities and the gossip of the many capitals they visited. Bob would race around, visiting dams and agricultural stations, and then meet with finance ministers and officers of the national bank with Clark. Margy toured, and the three joined up later for dinners and plane rides. "Wherever he went, William went out of his way to arrange a hotel room right next to Bob and Margaret's," says one of McNamara's aides. Clark wrote of McNamara in his diary, "He was my superior and father figure. I was determined to avoid an Oedipus situation." Clark confessed to wanting "to win his favor and so be made a school prefect."[19]

Clark recorded the most important early meeting McNamara convened, of a group Woods had established called the President's Council, which met every week. After a typically long and inconclusive session, during which Clark noticed the sky darkening outside, McNamara became frustrated with these slow-talking and, to him, slow-thinking senior men. At the end he said: "I am going to ask you all to give me very shortly a list of all the projects or programs that you would wish to see the Bank carry out *if there were no financial constraints*" (italics added).[20]

The shock of his announcement was followed by the shock they found when the meeting ended. The city of Washington was ablaze and rioting; the darkening sky had been caused by smoke. Martin Luther King, Jr., had been assassinated in Memphis. Many black people whose hopes he had aroused had taken to the streets. It is not clear if America's failure to quell the poverty and injustice that fueled the violence that afternoon gave McNamara pause in his plans to attack poverty worldwide. He had just given an instruction that would lead to a more ambitious plan than even his own country had undertaken.

McNamara knew he wanted a big Bank before he knew for certain what to do with it. His wish was instinctive, and much of it, no doubt, was ego: The Bank's annual borrowings were $735 million in 1968, which was the unit cost to the Pentagon of a few F-111 fighter-bombers, or less than one month's fighting in Vietnam. "At first he kept talking in billions and then he would correct himself and say 'I meant millions,' " says a Bank staffer.[21]

To enlarge the lending program, he had to borrow more, however. An early meeting with some bankers in New York flopped. Their view was that as a result of the administration's mismanagement of the war's costs, the country was in its worst economic condition in two decades. The bankers gave little sign that they trusted him.

But McNamara was computing how many billions the Bank should lend. The treasurer, Robert W. Cavanaugh, warned that rapid new offerings would hurt the Bank's AAA rating from Moody's. Irving Friedman, the Bank's economist, was "getting ulcers," thanks to McNamara's plans and demands, according to Benjamin King, one of the Old Guard. McNamara in June won approval for new issues. An offering was made in Switzerland, which failed. It was an unheard-of humiliation for the Bank, and a red flag to the doubters among the Old Guard. McNamara "gratefully" accepted Ca-vanaugh's resignation, in Clark's words, and looked for someone congenial.[22]

A career lawyer at the Securities and Exchange Commission in the fall of 1968 received a phone call from McNamara, apparently from the blue.[23] What do you know about international finance? McNamara asked. Nothing, said the lawyer. Have you ever studied accounting? No, the lawyer said; he had studied English literature, history, and trial law.

McNamara asked what the man thought of investment bankers; he replied that he was trying to indict most of them under the Sherman Antitrust Act. What do you think of commercial bankers? They're guys who sail around on Long Island Sound in the summer, the lawyer said. What do you think about the problems of poverty? asked the new antipoverty czar of the world. The lawyer said poverty was one of those things you could spend your life at and still not succeed. Then McNamara asked him if he would accept the post of treasurer of the World Bank.

The lawyer's name was Eugene Rotberg. Others recall how the tall, philosophically inclined lawyer rushed around the stuffy institution in his first months, in early 1969, "like a chicken with his head cut off." In fact, Rotberg's work at the SEC had been exceptionally imaginative; his studies of the markets and of firms' behavior were famous in certain circles. Now his imagination and prescience — and newness to the topic he was hired to master — paid off, literally. McNamara gave Rotberg an almost biblical instruction when he began work at the Bank: Find where wealth exists in the world and bring it to me, that is, to my Bank.

Rotberg and McNamara traveled to Bonn and persuaded the government of Willy Brandt — who knew McNamara from NATO days — to approve the first Bank bond issues in West Germany. They flew to Kuwait, where they raised more funds. McNamara told Rotberg to borrow funds at the lowest possible cost, "because any mistakes you make will be borne by the poorer countries." So Rotberg took off for Japan. The Bank had lent to Japan after World War II; the Japanese appreciated the Bank. Rotberg's studies forecast explosive growth and continued high savings rates in Japan; that Japan had no bond market did not stop him. He persuaded the Japanese to lend to the Bank, at low rates, to help the poor. McNamara asked him, "Do you think we can raise a billion dollars a year?" Rotberg replied, "Sure, why not?" Within a year they had done it.[24]

McNamara's flights to West Germany to raise funds symbolized the cresting of the American Century. In the 1950s, the United States had produced 40 percent of the world's output. The dollar was tied immutably to the price of gold, of which the United States had the commanding stock; the dollar was the world's currency. All the Bretton Woods arrangements were based on these bedrock assumptions. But by March 1968, the weakening dollar was causing foreigners to buy up gold, inflation was drawing American dollars overseas, and the positive payments balance and trade position the United States had enjoyed for decades had plummeted to zero — heading toward negative balances on both counts.

March 15, 1968, would be known as a fateful Ides of March for the world's financial system. That day President Johnson tried to block the tide of U.S. dollars flowing abroad by imposing controls on direct transfers of funds by U.S. companies to subsidiaries abroad.[25]

Johnson's move stemmed the flood only a little, since many U.S. dollars heading overseas came from his own defense budget, still at a record high to fight in Vietnam and support U.S. forces in Europe and other regions. The American Century was getting too pricey for the United States to afford.

The long-run effect of the president's move, however, was the growth of parallel financial markets in Europe and later in Japan. The attractiveness of investment in the United States declined when the rush on gold at the official price that March produced a new dual price for gold. This would lead, in 1971, to the unlinking of the dollar from its historic anchor in the official price of gold, and, in effect, the end of Bretton Woods.

These consequences were to expand the economic clout of Europe after March 1968. Now R. S. McNamara, who helped trigger the chain reaction, behaved like other U.S. investors and was going where the wealth was.

In June 1968, McNamara was attending a meeting in West Germany when he was passed a note saying that Bobby Kennedy had been shot in Los Angeles. He continued the meeting but then flew to Idlewild Airport, in New York, where he saw the haunting spectacle of security guards around his own plane's landing area. As in November 1963, the Secret Service could not be sure there was not a plot against the Kennedy men. McNamara was trying to start a new life, but violence and death stalked him.

Television newsmen stopped him on the sidewalk outside his Washington office while Kennedy lay dying. In outtakes of the film, McNamara swerves to avoid the cameramen. Then he submits to an interview while tears stream down his cheeks. He stutters that he hoped Bobby would live and that the nation needed to observe the values for which Kennedy stood. Then he rushes into the building, overcome, past a Bank security guard.[26]

McNamara wept as a pallbearer at Bobby Kennedy's funeral in Saint Patrick's Cathedral, in Manhattan. Alfred Fitt, still at the Pentagon, with responsibility for Arlington Cemetery, remembered the phone call he got from McNamara, saying in the same barking, authoritative voice as in November 1963, "Come on, Alfred, we've got to do this burial thing all over again."[27]

Jack Kennedy was dead; Bobby was dead; McNamara was doomed to survive and see their reputations tarnish, not to mention

his own. He not only lost a political future in the resurgence that
Bobby Kennedy might have engineered, but also both of these brothers, who brought out the best in him. Now McNamara's political
future with the Kennedys could come only with their younger
brother, Ted.

For years, the big second-floor hall of the house at Tracy Place
would be dominated by a sketched portrait of John Kennedy and one
of McNamara done in the Camelot years. The walls of Margy's study
were covered with photos of Bobby. They kept the memory bright.

Kennedy's death was one more void for McNamara, one more
unresolved piece of his complex inner mosaic. Friends noted his
moodiness and the martinis, which worried them. Margy would call
Wally Haas and his wife in California and urge them to stop over
when in Washington, spend the evening. Bob needs you; we all do,
she said.[28]

He tried to recapture Camelot when the aircraft carrier *John F.
Kennedy* was dedicated that September. Caroline Kennedy was to
christen it, and McNamara agreed to make the dedication speech.
The Kennedy family and Navy brass flew into Norfolk, Virginia, for
the dockside ceremony. In ABC film footage, Jacqueline Kennedy
sits on the dais with young Caroline and John, all three in immaculate
white. Behind them sit Ted and Joan Kennedy, looking young and
attractive, and tiers of Navy officers in summer-white uniforms. Mc-
Namara is in a dark business suit, seated between Jacqueline and little
John, and being fatherly and gentle with the boy. He steps to the
podium to speak.

"Those who knew him will never again be the same men. It is thus
not only for us few, but for the multitudes of others the world
around," he says, that John Kennedy was "the embodiment of a new
hope that reason, and civility, and sanity might prevail. That the
rigidities of extremism might give way to the realities of accommodation. . . . That human diversity be accepted not simply as a fact but
as a value. That gaiety and grace and composure be not merely the
mark of civilized men, but the mark of civilized civilizations as well.

"The life of this ship may not always be as" — here he stops and
coughs, skips a word and picks up — "as the life of him for whom it
was named. May it sail with his integrity. May it sail with his valor."
McNamara's voice becomes halting. He looks down, pauses, and his
hand goes up to his mouth. Finishing quickly, he whips down from

the podium to return to his seat, snapping one leg over the other in a rapid gesture of anger. The admirals look shocked at their former tyrant's public breakdown.[29]

McNamara knew he might not be able to deliver the speech. As he had walked up to the reviewing stand he had abruptly shoved at a surprised secretary of the Navy, Paul Ignatius, a piece of paper that was a copy of the speech. "If I don't get through this, finish it," McNamara snapped in his familiar bossy tone.[30]

McNamara sought out for particular attention the largest poor nations, as well as those that were borderline between the East and West and potentially unstable. He had long had his eye on Indonesia. In his 1964 speech justifying the U.S. commitment to South Vietnam, McNamara called Indonesia "the greatest prize of all" for Communist domination, with its "resources, territory and the world's fifth largest population" and its "strategic location" across the gateway between the Indian and Pacific oceans.

When he had been at the Bank only a few weeks, McNamara asked to see Bernard Bell, who had prepared a critical report on the Indian government's errors and needs, and then negotiated with India during its crises of the midsixties. McNamara told Bell he wanted him to move to Jakarta to set up a resident mission. Bell was reluctant; his daughter was nearing college age, and unless he and his wife stayed in the United States, she might not get into Boston College, which was her goal. McNamara buzzed his secretary. Get me Eunice Shriver, he said. Bell heard McNamara instruct John Kennedy's sister, who was a trustee of Boston College, to help admit a young lady he would send to her. What's your next objection? McNamara asked. Bell said his daughter would need help with her studies. McNamara said Margy could coach her. Send her to my house on Saturday, he ordered.[31]

McNamara disposed of Bell's other objections, and Bell and his wife moved to Jakarta. Bell's move there represented a major policy shift. Sukarno had broken with the Bank in his last years and the feeling was mutual; George Woods had refused to even meet the Indonesians. Suharto had come to power in the fall of 1965, in the aftermath of one of the bloodiest massacres of modern times, sparked by an attempted coup. Reports later claimed five hundred thousand had been killed, including tens of thousands of Chinese, who were tagged as Communists.[32] Suharto began to court the West and installed some young Indonesian economists trained at McNamara's alma mater, Berkeley, to do something about the country's economic collapse (its debt was 20 percent of its gross national product). Bell knew the Berkeley Mafia; soon he and the Bank were helping remake the economy.

McNamara decided to make Indonesia the first client country to visit, although the trip was delayed because of Bobby Kennedy's assassination. When he and his aides debarked at the airport in Jakarta, the whole Indonesian cabinet turned out to greet them. "He seemed so happy to be welcomed by these people," Bell recalls. "He was very happy we were going to work out this very full relationship. He had no reservations, no ambivalence whatever."[33] When a group of American embassy wives tried to corral Margy for the duration, they were politely rebuffed and told that Mrs. McNamara wanted to see the country. So Margy, too, immersed herself in these wild, lush, tree-covered islands.

Before leaving, McNamara had a long discussion with Suharto. When Suharto, currying favor, bragged about his anticommunism, McNamara cut him off and asked how he planned to integrate the thousands of Chinese still in Indonesia after the massacre; your Chinese are the backbone of your commerce and future development, McNamara said. The remark showed how far he had come since his warnings of Chinese Communist expansion in the past.[34]

Bell later reflected on the spectacle of the lone American and his wife who arrived to bestow money and respectability on this outcast nation and were cheered by crowds in colorful clothes. The case for a major Bank effort in Indonesia was strong on its merits, but for McNamara personally, Bell says, "I always thought it was redemption."

McNamara was greeted with suspicion and violence on his trips, too. He visited India in late 1968 as the crisis in IDA funding dragged on. McNamara went to Calcutta, notorious for its overcrowding and slums. As he entered the city he was met by an unruly mob, running in the streets and burning buses.[35]

He was ferried to the governor's house, from which he could see the crowd filling the streets below. They held up a banner with the words "McNamara Yanqui." Above their heads they waved an effigy of McNamara as Uncle Sam. It had painted blue pants and a red-

and-white-striped jacket. The head had dark straight hair and spectacles.

The effigy tilted wildly and then began to burn. The smoke and flames and shouting men made a strange contrast to the tiers of ornate blue-shuttered windows lining the boulevard. McNamara had to be evacuated by helicopter. Even the *New York Times* reported this distant riot and warned in an editorial that there would be more violence in the Third World if McNamara's mission of peace and aid failed.[36]

In fact, the Bank seemed an unlikely vehicle to fix the slums of Calcutta or the sprawling mess of Jakarta. The 767 staff members McNamara found were overwhelmingly Anglo-American, with an admixture of Dutch and Belgian workers. There was only one high-ranking officer from the Third World, a Pakistani; men from the former colonies were overwhelmingly anglicized, often seen in blazers. Meetings of the Oxford-Cambridge Society were announced in the Bank's newsletter. The place had the air of a boarding school such as Eton.[37]

For most of its history, the Bank made loans to Europe and Latin America for dams, power plants, mines, railroads, and roads — projects that were clearly certain to meet an economic rate of return. The staff hovered over each project, required infinite detail, and took months to make decisions. Later what William Clark called its "leisurely perfectionism" would be remembered nostalgically by the Old Guard.[38] In fact, this handcrafted approach took a long time and was patronizing toward the new nations. "We made a loan to Ghana," recalls one of the older staff men, "and then waited for years to see how it came out before making another."[39] Others remember the Bank's demanding to pick local officials to staff a water authority in Pakistan and taking months to decide whom to choose. All these habits, including the preoccupation with economic rates of return, stemmed from the Bank's inbred insecurity about its standing as a bank.

McNamara was temperamentally incapable of operating this way. At this rate, progress in the Third World would be snail-like at best. He found the Bank underutilized or, as Clark said in his diary, "an inefficient way to run a planet."[40]

"I have always regarded the World Bank as something more than a Bank, as a Development Agency," he said in his September 1968 maiden speech to the Board of Governors, putting them on notice.[41] Privately McNamara was more scathing; if I had only been concerned about loans, he said, I would have gone to a *bank*.

He announced that he wanted the Bank to lend in many places previously off-limits, like Indonesia and Egypt and southern Africa; he wanted the Bank to be in every developing country, which then numbered about ninety. He was disturbed by the geographic asymmetries: The Bank lent a lot to Brazil and Argentina but not to Ceylon or Nepal.

McNamara also reported that the list of projects the Bank might undertake if money were no restraint led him to compute the Bank's real needs. This was the list he had asked for that fateful April afternoon of riots after Martin Luther King's death. He had a "development plan" for each developing country, which, to carry out, would require a doubling in the Bank's lending in five years.[42] It would double its lending to Latin America and triple its lending to Africa. IDA's programs would expand to help the poorest. His numbers were in place, even if the content was vague.

McNamara often said that if a manager wasn't taking risks, he wasn't doing his job. To the governors he referred to the biblical parable of the talents, which "illuminates the great truth that all power is given to us to be used, not to be wrapped in a napkin against risk."

The leisurely old Bank culture changed — not without resistance. Only a few people saw the new boss; they carried out his orders, phoning around and asking for reports by deadlines. McNamara found aides who were good with statistics and filled in tables for him. He asked for five-year projections of what countries needed and what the Bank could lend. John Blaxall, a "runner" assigned to dredge up statistics for McNamara's seven master tables, recalls that McNamara demanded to use only tables and no graphs. The tables had to all be upright on the page, so he would not have to rotate them to look at them sideways. They had to be filled in in pencil, so as the numbers changed he could neatly erase and fix them.[43]

What if we don't *know* the right number? the staff asked the few aides with access to the new president. Make an estimate, the aides replied. This euphemism avoided telling the staff to guess. It meant: Give us the best you can by our deadline; when you get the real figure, call.[44]

The old Bank ran on committee meetings; McNamara installed

line control. Certain people were given telephones with a green light for the line that went directly to McNamara's desk. They were expected to phone Zeus directly anytime.

The system drove John Adler crazy, recalls one of his staff. McNamara had made Adler chief of the new program planning and budgeting group, which was a powerful job. Adler, however, was so compulsive that the green light was not a privilege but a torment. He hardly dared leave for the bathroom lest McNamara call. He did not call McNamara directly; instead he would telephone his secretary on another line and ask whether McNamara was free to take a direct call.[45]

Given McNamara's stormy relations with Congress in the old days, he might have been expected to encounter rough seas with his new "legislature," the thirty executive directors of the Bank. Together they represented all the subscriber countries; they lived in Washington for their appointed terms, meeting weekly to vote on all Bank loans and IDA credits proposed by the president and staff. The EDs, as they were known, represented the real power of the Bank; the U.S. executive director, for example, was the treasury's agent and voted the American share, now at 23 percent. (If American sugar producers opposed a Bank project that would enhance a borrowing country's sugar production, for example, the U.S. director needed very few allies on the board to block the loan.) George Woods's relationship with the EDs had been terrible, and they in turn often paralyzed him.

Once again in his career, Robert McNamara exploited the authority of others to acquire power for himself. At the beginning, he called on each of the EDs in turn, in their offices, tactful and gracious. His rapid grasp of detail and their individual concerns put him intellectually above Woods right away.[46]

He ran their Tuesday meetings with polish, and in a much more businesslike manner than Woods had, a change that was greeted with relief all around. Meetings started at nine and ended at two. No one could wander out to get coffee, which was served at eleven sharp, and lunch was timed equally exactly. As in the NATO Nuclear Planning Group, McNamara induced the EDs to become fully responsible for their portfolios; no substitutes were allowed, so each had to come prepared.

Soon it became clearer what his goal was, besides orderly management. McNamara had understood that the EDs had the power to block him; his power derived from them. Thus he treated them the way he had treated presidents. Every possible objection was discussed in advance. He was leading them to accept his proposals, one at a time, to achieve a perfect record of board approvals.

The result was, predictably, no dissent. Directors of the institution, the president made clear, were not really meant to debate at the meetings, let alone raise new, serious objections. One of the aides remembers an early session when a substitute sat in on a meeting. When McNamara called for discussion, the man began to *discuss* the point at issue, even to object, as though this were a free-floating meeting. The others all grew tense as he talked on, ignorant of his blunder. McNamara gave his aide a note, which the aide carried around the table, asking, "Who is he?" The reply came back: "He's a substitute." Afterward, McNamara reissued his rule of no substitutes — in other words, no one should break through the ritual and try to make the discussion genuine.[47]

In this way he built an edifice of personal power. The Old Guard hated his deadlines and his barked orders and gossiped that he was not to be trusted. McNamara's determination to radically expand the Bank added to the staff's insecurities. So the story started, sotto voce: McNamara is ruining the Bank.

McNamara also said publicly right off that he wanted to lend for population planning. "More than anything else, it is the population explosion which, by holding back the advancement of the poor, is blowing apart the rich and the poor and widening the already dangerous gap between them," he said in his speech to the governors in September.[48] Growing populations in cities and rural areas "first eat up a portion of the present scarce supply of capital" and hence can "defeat a nation's efforts to raise living standards overall."

McNamara chose to lecture on population to a press association meeting in Buenos Aires; he and Margy were spat on at the airport as they left. In 1969 he gave a major speech on the population issue, at the University of Notre Dame, the United States' preeminent Catholic college. Both speeches, to such potentially hostile audiences, made headlines, as he intended.[49]

McNamara the prophet talked as apocalyptically of the population explosion as he had of the dangers of nuclear war. In his 1968 address to the governors, he proclaimed, "Casting its shadow over all this scene is the mushrooming cloud of the population explosion."

"Thousands of human beings will die today . . . of . . . hunger.

. . . Most . . . are children," he said at Notre Dame. "They are not mere statistics. They are human beings. And they are dying, now; at this very moment; while we are speaking. And they are dying needlessly."

The children who were dying were "fortunate," for millions of those who "live languidly on" were "stunted in their bodies, and crippled in their minds." They then had malnourished, stunted children, forging "a chain of conditions that only spiral the total human performance dismally downward." The world faced "mass starvation" or "political chaos." Many experts agreed that population was a problem, but the public McNamara was becoming a man of darker visions — perhaps privately, too.

It sounded almost nutty to the Bank staff and some others. Where was McNamara getting these ideas? *Lend* for population? How would you compute a rate of return? Lend systematically to higher-risk countries in Africa and South Asia? One staffer told journalist Henry Trewhitt soon after:

> We wondered what this guy who had produced the Edsel and the F-111, and who had engineered the Vietnam thing, could know about much of anything. This was all mixed up with the feeling that he had been forced on us by Lyndon Johnson.
>
> On top of that was the notion that this was a man of quantity, not quality, and that all this talk of human consideration in development was cheap expiation for Vietnam.[50]

As he took the reins of power at the Bank, McNamara seemed more cautious than before. He admitted into his one-on-one conferences Perry Sellon, a former journalist hired by Woods to take soundings in Congress about the IDA bills and other matters.

"We are going to have one hell of a problem on the hill and you are it," Sellon says he told McNamara to his face. They always had trouble with Congress, but "it's going to be tougher because of your situation and the Vietnam War."[51]

He had said it, to McNamara's face — the forbidden word, *Vietnam*, which the others, knowing his sensitivity and silence, dared not utter.

A sign of how McNamara had changed, however, was the fact that he did not throw Sellon out. Instead he saw him several more times. McNamara knew he had imprisoned himself behind a wall of yes-men before; he sensed he should listen to odd messages. It remained to be seen if he could protect himself against illusion and overoptimism this time.

Craig got through St. Paul's and off to Stanford without a reconciliation with his father; instead it was Margy who worried about him constantly. Bob McNamara, the habitual seeker out of bright young men and admirer of protégés in his own image, could not relate to the shy and less articulate boy who was his own.[52]

Craig wanted his father to notice him, to treat him as an equal, to talk about his concerns and then hear out Craig's. He felt hurt, not just by his father's apparent indifference to him. Craig wanted the approval of his friends and teachers, but many of his peers considered his father a war criminal.

"It was like being a child of Speer," says one of the children's friends, a reference to Adolf Hitler's technocratic aide Albert Speer. Craig wondered who he was. "I felt like an egg without a yolk," he says.

Obedience brought Craig little reward from his father, except an occasional impersonal talk about skiing or their trips. Defiance brought rage, as in the incident when McNamara found the American flag hanging upside down in Craig's room.

Friends say that Bob's relationship with both Craig and Kathy deteriorated as the children grew up. Kathy was opposed to the war politically; she was defiant toward both parents on matters of dress and other things. She argued with her father and took Craig as her ally. McNamara sloughed it all off and left the burden of communicating with them to Margy.

McNamara had a series of special assistants who were smart, multilingual, and all from Northern Europe. They were replicas of the cool, precise men McNamara adopted as protégés at Defense: Nordic Whiz Kids.[53] With them, he could be fatherly. Sven Burmeister, who was McNamara's aide in the later seventies, recalls that one of his duties was to find out how each executive director was going to vote in advance of the meetings. Once, when Burmeister told McNamara he had a "hunch" how a particular vote would go, McNamara retorted:

"A hunch? You sound like my kids! I don't want to hear about hunches. I only want facts." When the directors voted as Burmeister forecast, McNamara, grinning, asked him: "Have you got any more hunches?"[54]

At Stanford, Craig was influenced by Professor Bruce Franklin, a prominent antiwar radical. Craig went to antiwar demonstrations; he ran through the streets breaking windows; he read the names of war dead at the airport. "I was so confused by the contradictions in my life and the country," he recalls.

But when he tried to become "a spokesperson" against the war, Craig found he couldn't speak in front of a crowd. Being only a follower was another reason for self-doubt.

In 1970 he was classified 1A and was likely to be called to military service. He phoned his sister Margaret's husband, Barry Carter, who helped him prepare his file. Craig had had ulcers since high school; Carter saw to it that this would appear in the file and be taken into account. Then Craig stood in the draft line in Oakland — his father's hometown — shivering. "I didn't know if my father knew I was there," he says. Between his psychiatric history and the ulcers, he was reclassified to 4-F.

Craig did not realize his own strength. He had inherited both of his parents' instinct for self-preservation. In 1971, he set out with friends on motorbikes for South America. In 1970, Salvador Allende, a Marxist, had been elected president of Chile, promising to empower the poor. Craig decided to see the revolution firsthand.

He and his friends biked through Texas, Mexico, and Panama. By the time he got to Colombia, Craig was tired of being stared at by peasants as they roared through villages "in leathers, on big bikes." He had to sleep beside the bike to be sure it would be there in the morning. Craig parted company from the bike and his friends and traveled on by himself.

"My life just changed in radical and wonderful ways," he recalls. It was the first time "I had been truly, unutterably alone, without girlfriends, school, the family" — and without his father.

When he reached Santiago in October, he remembers, the energy and enthusiasm of the celebrations of Allende's first year overwhelmed him. His own "spirit of hope" was buoyed when he laid eyes on Fidel Castro.

The Cuban leader was making a state visit to honor this new bastion of Marxism. Craig stood in the hot sun and listened to Castro talk for three hours. "I was grasping on to every word."

The atmosphere in Chile during Allende's first year was heady. Craig recalls feeling "incredibly optimistic and extremely idealistic." Because he didn't want to take a job away from a Chilean, he went to Easter Island and found work running a dairy farm. He could be useful, and his name did not brand him. There, at least, "being Robert McNamara's son was not bad."

Their destinies were similar at that moment; Craig living monastically and devoted to helping the islanders, while his father flew around the world, economy-class, determined to make loans in every developing country.

Craig could escape to Easter Island; McNamara could orbit the Southern Hemisphere. But Richard Nixon kept the United States in Vietnam, as the economic, social, and political devastation of the war spread through America. After Nixon's election as president in November 1968, the antiwar movement built to a crescendo, including students, professors, artists, and many middle Americans. The "national disaster" that McNamara had forecast in May 1967, which would follow from a wider war, had come to pass.[55]

Nixon claimed his goal was "peace with honor," but he prided himself on being tough.[56] He secretly launched the bombing of neutral Cambodia in 1969, to show Hanoi he would not be shackled by self-imposed restraints like his predecessor. Nixon maintained that he was "de-Americanizing" the war by giving masses of arms to the South Vietnamese and starting to bring American soldiers home. McNamara had in fact proposed Vietnamization back in November 1967, only to see his idea angrily rejected by the other advisers. Negotiations dragged on while the fighting and bombing raged, but no settlement could be agreed on so long as Nixon ruled out allowing a coalition government that included Communists. Nixon then ordered the invasion of Laos, a move that Johnson and McNamara had rejected in 1967. It proved only a costly draw, despite official claims of success. "De-Americanization with all deliberate speed" would come at the price of another 21,000 American lives, 53,000 more Americans seriously wounded, and wider anger against the government at home.

Nixon called student protesters "bums." On May 4, 1970, National Guardsmen shot into a crowd of demonstrators at Kent State University, in Ohio, killing four. In reaction, more than four hundred colleges and universities across the country shut down. The following spring, a group of Vietnam veterans denounced their war crimes in front of the White House and threw away their medals before a crowd. An estimated 30,000 members of the "Mayday Tribe" descended on Washington to try to block access to the city, only to be arrested, on presidential orders, on trumped-up charges. The son of Robert McNamara, despite his special burden, was just one of many Americans enraged with the abuse of American power.

McNamara's World Bank office was only blocks from the White House, where Nixon and his national security adviser, Henry Kissinger, made their fateful choices. McNamara tried to distance himself from the war, but his past now caught up with him in a spectacular way that was traumatic for him and the country.[57]

Unknown outside of a very small group, a highly classified, forty-seven-volume study, "United States–Vietnam Relations, 1945–1967," was finished in January 1969, eighteen months after McNamara commissioned it. The study's director, Leslie H. Gelb, took one of the fifteen copies of the work to McNamara at the Bank.[58]

During the eighteen months, Gelb and McNamara had had no direct dealings; McNamara had avoided substantive involvement and ordered his assistant secretary for International Security Affairs, Paul Warnke, to do likewise. The study was carried out in Warnke's organization. As the Gelb group started collecting documents to make it "encyclopedic and objective," following McNamara's original guidance, it made an important decision to not only include documents but write analyses and summaries. Thus Gelb described the final study in his letter of transmittal as "not so much a documentary history, as a history based solely on documents."[59]

Avoiding bias in examining anything so wrenching as Vietnam was "a treacherous exercise," Gelb's cover letter said, especially for a task group housed in the agency prosecuting the war. The task force had thirty-six writers on loan to the project at different times. "Almost all the studies had several authors," Gelb noted.[60] Among the anonymous authors who worked on the study were many military men, including Paul Gorman and Robert Schweitzer; among the civilians were Daniel Ellsberg and Richard Holbrooke.

In early 1969 McNamara received Gelb and a military officer at his

office. The visitors set some boxes on a low table. Gelb pulled one of
the volumes from a box and handed it to McNamara; each had a light
blue cover and plastic binding.

Brusquely, McNamara glanced at the sample volume and shoved it
back. He said he didn't want to keep the study at the Bank. He told
Gelb to take it back to the Pentagon. There was nothing more to say,
so Gelb and the officer left with the boxes. They had been with
McNamara five minutes.

McNamara paid a high price for his unwillingness to accept a copy
of the study and read it calmly at his leisure. His refusal stemmed
from his ahistorical nature, and the vehemence of his effort to push
the war away from him. It was also typical that he seemed to have no
sense that he could hurt the morale of the task force or its director,
who had labored in the belief that McNamara, having invented the
study, would care about the result and share their pride in it. "We
had a sense of doing something important and of the need to do it
right," Gelb wrote in his cover letter, which McNamara now declined to read.[61]

Another of his protégés would force McNamara to read the study
when it won world fame as the Pentagon Papers. Daniel Ellsberg had
been among the most brilliant Rand Whiz Kids that surrounded Mc-
Namara in the early 1960s.[62] After graduating summa cum laude
from Harvard, Ellsberg gravitated to the Rand Corporation, to be at
the intellectual center of the important military problems of the day.
At age thirty in 1961, Ellsberg discovered that the Air Force's Strategic Air Command's operational plans for nuclear war would automatically blow up the entire Soviet Union and China. He ran around
the Pentagon, repeating how dangerous the plans were to whoever
was cleared for the information. McNamara also was appalled by the
SAC war plans, once he saw them for himself at SAC headquarters in
his first weeks as defense secretary. McNamara had assigned Alain
Enthoven and young Ellsberg the job of supervising SAC's repro-
gramming of the nuclear force, to give the president at least some
crude options if war came.

Ellsberg rose in McNamara's circle at the Pentagon, but by 1965
he became obsessed with Vietnam. He got himself transferred to the
State Department so he could go to Saigon in 1967 as a civilian adviser
at the embassy; he was the equivalent of a lieutenant general in civilian rank. Ellsberg was now thirty-six; he would be remembered
later by many as wearing a Marine uniform and carrying a revolver in

the streets of Saigon, his deep blue eyes gleaming with drive to whip the Communists. His tour in Vietnam qualified him to help Gelb's task force when he returned.

By 1969, Ellsberg was back at Rand with his top-secret clearances and an impeccable record as a hawk. He now read the entire study. He also learned through friends on the National Security Council of Nixon's secret bombing of Cambodia. Ellsberg's road to Damascus came in August 1969, in San Francisco. He heard a speech at a meeting of the War Resisters League and was so moved that "I went to the men's room and sat down on the floor and cried for about an hour."

"Zealotry is a constant in the character of a man" even when his opinions change, *Times* reporter Neil Sheehan wrote later of Ellsberg. The former hawk was now convinced that the American cause in Indochina was wrongheaded and that Nixon's slow Vietnamization was a "bloody, hopeless, uncompelled and surely immoral prolongation of U.S. involvement." In the fall of 1969, Ellsberg decided to violate federal law and risk a life sentence in prison in order to smuggle the huge study — bits at a time — past the security guards at Rand, copy it, and sneak it back in. Ellsberg wanted the inside story of U.S. involvement to be read by the world.

By 1971 the United States had been fighting an undeclared, medium-scale war for six years — twice as long as U.S. troops fought in World War II and in Korea. Black Power and the Black Panthers had supplanted Martin Luther King's nonviolent approach to the civil rights struggle. The Weathermen and Students for a Democratic Society dominated the antiwar movement. The politics and culture of what is now called the sixties in fact reached their peak in the early seventies. Also, the ethics of public service changed when several civilians and even military men felt that higher loyalty compelled them to leak classified information to see that the truth was told.

Journalism changed, too. The editors of major news organizations began to realize that Vietnam was not like past American wars, when there had been a journalistic obligation to support the cause.[63] More and more, the media printed open criticism of the president and senior officials; the big story became abuse of power and government lies. Nixon and Kissinger, obsessed with secrecy, only whetted the press's appetite to expose government secrets. More and more, James Reston's early statement that Lyndon Johnson was taking "the country into war by stealth" reflected the pattern for the war; the *Times* was one of the leading established organizations questioning officialdom. Ellsberg chose Sheehan at the *Times* for his act of higher loyalty.

Thus the paper obtained the still-classified Pentagon Papers in the spring of 1971. The rest is well known — the resignation of the *Times*'s lawyers who refused to defend the paper if it printed the study, the sequestering of Sheehan and other staffers in New York's Plaza Hotel to read and excerpt the huge work and write interpretive articles on what it meant.

Less well known is the fact that Robert McNamara, the study's progenitor, knew the *Times* had it. Bob and Margy were friends of James and Sarah Reston's.[64] During an informal evening at Tracy Place in June, when the editors had decided to publish, Reston told McNamara that the *Times* had the study. He did not ask McNamara if the paper had acted properly in accepting the classified document. Nor did he divulge the source. He asked: Now that we have it, should we print it?

McNamara replied: Yes. Reston even showed McNamara a letter the *Times* had drafted to rebut the expected challenge from the Justice Department. McNamara, with his usual concern for detail, proposed some word changes. Had he known what the *Times* writers holed up in the Plaza were going to say, he might have given different advice.

Thus did McNamara condemn himself to read parts of his own study, apparently for the first time, in the pages of the paper and in the context of what the *Times* wrote that it meant. Day after day through June and July, the excerpts and articles filled entire pages and became the talk of the nation. Nixon's administration tried to block further publication, and the case went to the Supreme Court. Not since John Peter Zenger in the eighteenth century had a free-press issue so galvanized opinion. In the furor, McNamara called Paul Warnke to see how they could track down the leaker.[65]

The *Times* quoted the summary, analysis, and narrative sections written by the Gelb task force. It also quoted and reprinted some of the documents in the study. It then wrote articles saying what the study meant. Although the *Times* articles stated that it was not going beyond what was in the study, the articles and much of the commentary they sparked around the nation accused the architects of the war of having ignored sound intelligence advice against the bombing and of having misled the nation about the depth of commitment and the danger of defeat.[66] Sheehan summarized the lessons the *Times* drew from the study in the preface to the book version, *The Pentagon*

Papers as Published by the New York Times, which it published that year to satisfy the enormous American and worldwide demand.

> To read the Pentagon Papers in their vast detail is to step through the looking glass into a new and different world. This world has a set of values, a dynamic, a language and a perspective quite distinct from the public world of the ordinary citizen and of the two other branches of the Republic — Congress and the judiciary.[67]

In this world, "clandestine warfare" was considered a normal mode of operations, and the leading decision makers — including McNamara — "emerge as confident men — confident of place, of education and of accomplishment." The "written language of these men . . . is the dry, sparse language of problem solving." "Only once in the history," Sheehan writes, "do two of the leading participants" — McNamara and his aide John McNaughton — "express emotional and moral qualms." Sheehan says this occurs in a "personal letter" from McNaughton to McNamara in May 1967 and the subsequent May 19 memorandum "both men drafted," which "stand out as lonely cries against the human cost of the war."[68]

But in Sheehan's introduction and the writings of others, McNamara was accused of misleading the public, of using illegal means, of overconfidence. Moreover, because the Pentagon Papers revealed for the first time the depth of his disillusion with the military side of the war, the extent to which he concealed his gloomiest thoughts from the public was also known.

At the Bank, McNamara appeared for the most part calm. The first installment ran on a Sunday, June 13. On Monday at the regular meeting of the President's Council, McNamara spoke with "obvious concern, in measured tones" about the background of the study.[69]

He declined to respond publicly to the allegations about him appearing in print, giving as his reason, "I cannot be President of the World Bank and defend my record as Secretary of Defense." To the staff and member governments this seemed the right response: McNamara was putting his obligation to serve Bank member governments impartially ahead of his self-interest in jumping into America's maelstrom.

"Frankly," another friend told journalist Trewhitt, "I was worried about him during most of that first week, and I was not alone." But the moodiness that went with his rage continued, as did the "fondness for a good martini — or several," in Trewhitt's words. That summer, says Kathy McNamara, "Dad got the shingles. And it wasn't the World Bank that was giving him shingles."[70]

Gelb's documentary history had been based for the most part on McNamara's and McNaughton's files. And the *Times's* interpretations, although claiming to stick to the anonymous authors' views, showed the scope of McNamara's private advice to the president that the war could not be won militarily. By quoting official optimism and private pessimism from McNamara and other officials, the *Times* disclosed, with seeming authority, that McNamara led a war he did not believe in and lied to the people.

"My God. Does anyone think I would have commissioned this if reasonable men could have concluded that I was a deceiver and a liar?" Trewhitt quoted McNamara as saying privately that summer. McNamara was deeply upset by the accusations. "Gelb skewed the study," he is supposed to have said.[71]

He sometimes claimed the task group had exceeded its mandate, apparently forgetting that he approved the decision to include narratives and summaries. "The form was to be raw material, and all raw material," McNamara informed the historian of the Office of the Secretary of Defense in 1986. In 1975, McNamara told Walt Rostow that commissioning the volumes demonstrated his concern for history, but he added, "They didn't quite take the form I had in mind when we started the project."[72]

Robert Komer, one of those to whom McNamara expressed his displeasure, notes that to have a serious documentary history come to light in the sensational, accusatory form it did "was the opposite of what he had in mind." Gelb, meanwhile, was offended at hearing that McNamara considered him a dove, a biased historian. Gelb had tried to make the narratives and summaries unbiased and nonaccusatory, and he particularly intended the write-ups to be "neutral." Indeed, many of the authors of the analysis sections strongly favored the war.[73]

McNamara now faced a tidal wave of accusation, to which he chose not to reply. But his inner fury showed when, after Ellsberg came forward and was charged with his crime, one of his defense lawyers called on McNamara. The defense wanted McNamara to testify that publication of the study had not harmed national security. I know you are a liberal, the lawyer told McNamara in his World Bank office, because your liberal friends say you are. So you should help our cause.

McNamara burst out in a rage at the man and drove him from his office.[74] He hated Ellsberg for having switched sides and for violating his security oath; he hated what he thought were the Gelb study's conclusions; he hated having accusations of deceit ricocheting around in the press. He did not testify in defense of Daniel Ellsberg.

McNamara hated being accused, but at another level he brought the role of pariah on himself. In the early 1970s he was not willing to face his accusers or the country. During the national debate that followed the leak of the Pentagon Papers, or earlier, McNamara could have turned to face the demons of Vietnam eye to eye.

McNamara was moving leftward as he left office; his November 1, 1967, memorandum to the president urged a unilateral bombing halt, and he developed the San Antonio formula, which allowed, at last, talks to begin with Hanoi. Alone of the most senior advisers he foresaw that continued prosecution of the war would make the United States lose the "will to persist" and split the country. McNamara was prescient, despite his often deaf ear for politics.

Little known is that McNamara regularly met with Henry Kissinger in the immediately following years, when Kissinger was security adviser to President Nixon. Kissinger writes that in this period McNamara "missed no opportunity to press on me courses of action that those who were vilifying him would have warmly embraced."[75] These, of course, Kissinger did not follow; in his wisdom he escalated the air war instead. It seems likely that McNamara knew about the secret bombing of Cambodia but chose not to protest in public.

Had McNamara had a more open, direct character or had he more faith in the political process, he could have stepped into the public debate to curtail the U.S. role as early as 1968 or after January 1969, when Johnson left office. McNamara knew how to use the bully pulpit: He could have spelled out the real odds of the struggle in the same compelling language he had used privately with Johnson since November 1965. He could have made the public understand — long before the *Times* revealed his doubts in June 1971, in an accusing, unflattering way — how much better he understood the issues for the United States in the war and how pessimistic he was.[76]

Whether he could have turned the war off for America by speaking out is another matter. His successor, Defense Secretary Clark Clifford, had a major impact on public debate when he wrote publicly about his own change of heart in *Foreign Affairs* in the summer of 1969. For McNamara, who was even more closely identified with prosecuting the war, to speak out, too, would have added greatly to the pressure on Nixon to withdraw U.S. forces faster. But McNamara stayed silent.

Rational factors in his choice were his concern for the Bank and his plans to help the poor. The years 1969–71 were before Watergate, years when Nixon and his men used all methods at their disposal to hurt those on their "enemies" list. (They took revenge on Clifford for his article, for example.) To speak out on the war, McNamara would have had to quit the Bank before serving even one term, to protect *it* from Nixon's vengeance. He would have had to break with his friend Henry Kissinger, who continued to give the impression to McNamara — as Kissinger did with Fulbright and all real and potential critics — that he truly listened to him. He would have had to break with the establishment, the intimate halls of power, for the uncertain turbulence of left-liberal politics. And, of course, there would be no hope of a second term, that is, a ten-year run at saving the poor and transforming the Third World.

In his mind, this last consideration may have been the deciding one. He had confided to Willard Goodwin during their long sea voyage after college that his life's goal was to help the largest *number* of people. He was now shaping a program of dazzling ambition, using the Bank as his instrument, to carry out this goal. The Green Revolution, which was just taking off, had the potential, for example, to change the lives of millions — with proper management. McNamara was just grasping these possibilities when the Vietnam debate broke over him in 1971. Which should he do, relieve the suffering of his own countrymen and perhaps save thousands of U.S. soldiers' lives, and cleanse his own reputation, or stick with the establishment, the levers of power he already knew, and enhance life — literally, nutrition, health, longevity — for millions? History will judge whether, on the scales of five, ten, or twenty years, he made the right moral choice.

On the heels of the Pentagon Papers, in 1972, David Halberstam published *The Best and the Brightest*. It was a book waiting to be written, one that reflected the disillusion and anger of the time. The story revolved around a few principal actors, the Kennedy advisers and key military men, who were advertised as the best of their generation and who through overconfidence and ignorance led the nation on a deluded journey into Vietnam.

The public read, in this immediately successful book, the rich lode of anecdotes and lore that many in the press corps who covered the war had known for years but had been unable to print under the old rules of narrow fact and direct quotation. In a series of profiles in *Harper's* that led to the book, Halberstam had adopted the "New Journalism," which allowed the writer to tell unconfirmed stories, even depict the presumed motives and thoughts of public figures. Robert McNamara, along with McGeorge Bundy, was a major target, and the story of the press's bitter frustration with the man came pouring out. The McNamara of Halberstam's profile is not the best and brightest, as he seemed at a distance, but narrow, dishonest, unwilling to lose a bureaucratic fight.[77] He and Bundy embody the flaws attributed to the nation's leaders, men who pretended to be smart and tough but disdained real knowledge.

Over and over the book tells in haunting, almost biblical tones the tales of virtuous men at State or in intelligence who warned, who pitted themselves against the superficial Bundy and McNamara, William Bundy, Walt Rostow, and others. Halberstam seems to say that but for these flawed men, the slide into folly could have been stopped. The Pentagon Papers had revealed some of George Ball's memos from the spring of 1965; in July 1972, *The Atlantic* revealed Ball's sixty-seven-page warning of October 1964.[78] Thus Halberstam lionizes Ball as a man of moral courage while terming McNamara a "liar," a "fool," and "unwise." His summation said:

> Lyndon Johnson had lost it all, and so had the rest of them; they had, for all their brilliance and hubris and sense of themselves, been unwilling to look to and learn from the past and they had been swept forward by their belief in the importance of anti-Communism (and the dangers of not paying sufficient homage to it) and by the sense of power and glory, omnipotence and omniscience of America in this century.

Johnson here, as throughout, is relieved of the main burden:

In a way Lyndon Johnson had known better, he had entertained no small amount of doubt. . . . He and the men around him wanted to be defined as being strong and tough; but strength and toughness and courage were exterior qualities which would be demonstrated by going to a clean and hopefully antiseptic war with a small nation, rather than the interior and more lonely kind of strength and courage of telling the truth to America and perhaps incurring a good deal of domestic political risk.[79]

Victor S. Navasky, in a review on the front page of the *New York Times* Book Review, pointed out that a close reading of *The Best and the Brightest* shows its argument to be unclear at the heart. The scathing, perceptive profiles and intense personalization of the story give the impression that the flaws of these individual men drew the country into war. But, Navasky added, "the assumption that if you switched the 'players' you could change the outcome of the game — seems to be at war with the very thesis of the book that somehow the 'best and the brightest' were not good enough, were victims of history, the bureaucracy, of the cold war — of the fall of China, the rise of McCarthy, the war in Korea."[80]

By the early seventies Robert McNamara's life had reached a point 180 degrees opposite from where he began. In the 1930s, he had admired Roosevelt and the benevolent power of the state; he idealized public service as a more moral use of his talents than the "chase for the almighty dollar" in business and therefore had given seven years to the country and four years to the World Bank. Now he found himself a walking symbol of the misuse of power, the man who ruined the liberal promise for the nation, for younger, once-idealistic reporters like Halberstam, and for his son's generation.

His position was even more strange because he had commissioned the Gelb task-force study for history and because he had seen some of the errors of the war and written them down to warn the president. Now blamed for having concealed those insights, he was held far more to account than Rusk or Walt Rostow, who had no doubts at all. McNamara had been sincerely concerned and brave enough to write it down, yet he was now pilloried for insincerity and lack of moral courage.

Halberstam's criticisms of McNamara grew with the years. In 1979, he wrote the *Times* attacking James Reston for having written favorably about one of McNamara's speeches. McNamara's "crimes against the public weal" included his silence after 1969, when Mc-

Namara chose to "criticize the war in very private conversations with very selected journalists" and spoke "more to enhance his own slipping personal position rather than be part of a painful national debate." Thus the added charge that McNamara's silence on the war in the early 1970s prolonged the war. "In that period 18,000 young Americans and countless thousands of Vietnamese died," Halberstam added, laying the blame for Nixon's war dead on his preferred target, McNamara.[81]

The issues raised were fundamental to McNamara's life and nature. Had he been merely a victim of history? Would another man in the same job in the 1960s, as Navasky asked, do as McNamara did and accede to the growing military involvement to stop South Vietnam from falling? Or were his errors of his own making, deep in his character, his love of secrecy, his curious mix of intelligent focus and blindness? Gelb, for his part, felt so strongly that the tragic result in Vietnam was not caused by flawed men deceiving the public that he wrote a book to counter the Halberstam thesis. In *The Irony of Vietnam: The System Worked*, Gelb argued that in fact even the dissenters agreed, in the end, after they said their piece, that the overriding need of U.S. foreign policy was to prevent South Vietnam's collapse. McNamara and the other leaders were upholding the foreign policy consensus of their generation.

McNamara, had he spoken out, is unlikely to have taken refuge in history or the postwar foreign policy consensus as an excuse for his mistakes. He clearly believed he was personally responsible for the mistakes made; he believed, when he was at Defense and in his new work at the Bank, that it is a leader's job to be ahead of the consensus, to see its flaws and redirect it. But as the contradictions rose up to haunt him, he stayed silent. Fear of further attack, fury at his accusers, the conviction that he had acted rightly — and some wish to fly from the maelstrom, the horror of it — perpetuated his silence.

Around the Bank, *The Best and the Brightest* became required reading. Keeping it hidden in briefcases and desks where the boss or his aides could not see, the international staff read this excoriation closely. William Clark, whose duties included easing McNamara's relations with the press, moaned in his diary that they would be worse than ever. Those men have long memories, Clark noted, although he also complained that McNamara tried to manipulate the press too much and invited mistrust. "He shaved the truth," Clark wrote in a revealing entry.[82] Others at the Bank, lured to work there by the clarion call of McNamara's speeches, his apparently sincere drive to help the world's poor, and the new, efficient organization he was building, read the book and wondered: Are we engaged in a great moral and technical challenge with a chance of success, as McNamara says? Or is there something inexorable about the man that leads to failure?

McNamara had a chance to feel literally how much some people hated him during the fateful year of 1972. That summer, as he rode the ferry to Martha's Vineyard, he was sitting in the cabin with a friend when a young man told him there was a phone call for him and guided him outside.[83]

On the narrow side deck, the young man struck McNamara repeatedly, pinning him against the railing in the night as the ship churned steadily through the dark, echoing water. The man had McNamara up against the rail, about to push him over, but McNamara, at fifty-six, was in good physical shape. He flung the youth back and staggered into the glowing cabin. He entered with his hair ruffled, his glasses askew.

Soon the captain appeared.

Do you want to press charges? he asked.

McNamara said no. The other passengers in the cabin who overheard this remarkable exchange realized that the tough Bob McNamara was vulnerable. "McNamara was very, very shaken," says a good friend. "But he'll deny it, of course."[84]

The Bank, meanwhile, was not immune from the widespread mistrust of American power spreading through domestic and international politics. Since Salvador Allende had come to power, the World Bank had made no loans to his regime. In April 1972, McNamara went to Santiago to give a speech and meet with Allende's men to chart a path by which the government could file applications for loans. McNamara's explanation for the Bank's apparent cutoff of Chile was that it had received no applications from the new regime. Now he professed to be trying to help them, although still, he says, Allende did not apply. In the context of the isolation of Allende's government by commercial banks, criticism aimed at it by the International Monetary Fund, and Chile's mounting debts, the Bank's actions were considered suspect by many.[85]

McNamara did not visit Craig in his self-imposed sanctuary on

Easter Island. But Margy, who was deeply concerned about the boy's safety and stability, made the trek. "When she left," Craig says, "she thought I was never going to leave the island."

By 1973, Craig was disillusioned with the Easter Islanders, who seemed to crave television sets and American protection, and who did not like Allende at all. On the mainland, Allende was embattled; his regime's future was uncertain, and word came from Washington of a forthcoming Senate investigation of whether the CIA and the ITT Corporation were plotting to overthrow him.

Craig came home.

On one of his first evenings in Washington, Craig was taken into his parents' social world. In the home of *Washington Post* publisher Katharine Graham, Craig got into an argument with his father, contending that the Nixon administration was trying to overthrow Allende. McNamara refused to admit that the government was attempting any such thing.

A short time later, Allende was assassinated in a military coup. The boy's fury and mistrust rose again. "That's why I'm still cautious about my father to this day. . . . If they [McNamara and Graham] didn't know what was going on in Chile factually, they must have known it intuitively. But they wouldn't say so."[86]

Craig was no different from millions of other Americans who in the early 1970s read the Pentagon Papers and *The Best and the Brightest* and now thought they knew the "real" Robert McNamara; Craig and the public drew from that moment of national disillusion the continuing mistrust of power and of American military intervention that has marked national politics and the Democrats ever since.

McNamara's inability to communicate with Craig was representative of his larger inability to come forward and explain when the crisis of confidence broke nationwide.

Thus McNamara compounded his problems, and the country's, by his decision not to answer or speak out in a way the country or his son could understand or accept.

22

The Promise of Development

MCNAMARA'S INTENSIVE PROGRAM of traveling to and studying each developing country paid off. At first "the world was not at ease with him," says Leif Christoffersen, who was McNamara's special assistant in the early years at the World Bank. But many trips later, Christoffersen "saw the developing countries line up behind him." McNamara could almost hypnotize certain people with his sincerity and professionalism. "He can expand his personality to meet the occasion," says another senior aide.

The growing admiration of leaders in Africa, Asia, and Latin America formed the paradox of McNamara's first five-year term: He won a new constituency in the developing world and among development experts while his reputation sank at home with the publication of the Pentagon Papers and bitter public criticism of his role in the Vietnam War.

Meanwhile, he re-created the Bank on a size and geographic scope to make it "a critical mass of power," in William Clark's phrase.[1] McNamara felt challenged by his self-set requirement to raise money on an unprecedented scale, to expand the staff; his new economics department, headed by Hollis Chenery, a Harvard economist, put the Bank at the cutting edge of research in development economics.[2]

McNamara had changed. He was no longer the happy figure of 1961, new to national power and propelled by creativity and self-confidence. One sign was the relative slowness of his first appointments; another sign of change was the language of his early speeches. In 1968, for example, he said that the prior six months had been "the half year in my whole life in which I have felt myself the most challenged," and he referred to the "deep sense of frustration and failure" he attributed to others in the development field.[3]

He never talked about Vietnam. During a trip, however, if a foreign leader raised the subject, McNamara would call the war a "tragedy" and say "enormous mistakes were made," recalls Christoffersen. "He left the impression the errors were fundamental," although Christoffersen does not remember that McNamara discussed what the errors were.

The charge made in books and articles that followed publication of the Pentagon Papers — that McNamara hypocritically kept quiet about how grim the war's prospects were — was mirrored by the claim that he was talking about poverty at the Bank just to look good, in compensation for Vietnam. The accusation that he was insincere in his new role could have been answered by almost anyone at the Bank in daily contact with the man. Most people at the Bank feel a moral commitment to the cause, notes one staffer. But they hide it behind a veneer of detachment. It was therefore almost embarrassing to sit with McNamara in meetings, the staffer adds, and watch him banging his left hand on the table and talking fast and emotionally, even crying sometimes, as he pushed to get things done.[4]

He was not posturing; McNamara believed he could get results — that is, improve the condition of the poor around the globe — by applying his lifelong brand of quantitative, top-down, results-oriented management. In this respect he had not changed.

He was unchanged in another way. As with U.S. defense policy and nuclear strategy, and even earlier at Ford, McNamara searched now for what he liked to call an "intellectual foundation," a philosophy of what his Bank would do.

By the fall of 1973, as he ended his first term, the Bank was lending a net of $1.2 billion a year, or one tenth of all official development assistance being transferred from rich nations through bilateral aid and multinational groups such as the United Nations.[5] In the prior five years the Bank had committed $13.4 billion to be spent over the lifetime of projects, or twice the amount it had committed in the five years before he came. The total debt owed by developing countries was high, McNamara noted in fall 1973. But since half of it was owed to official agencies (including the Bank) that were helping the countries use the money to create economic growth, he had positioned the Bank as a lever to influence what happened in the Third World.

The missionary was surfacing, emerging from the chrysalis. McNamara still had his computerlike air; he relished his and treasurer Eugene Rotberg's financial feats. But he regularly spoke of the Bank as "a development agency." He bragged as early as 1969 about the Bank's loans to education, adding what good rates of return they were getting on these loans. However, a staffer candidly told Edwin Dale, Jr., of the *New York Times* that no one knew really what the returns on education loans were. The staffer believed in McNamara's sincerity anyway. "I think you can say that he suffers for the poor of the world," he said.[6]

At an early joint meeting of the Bank governors and the directors of the International Monetary Fund, while the limousines for this distinguished, dark-suited group waited outside the luxurious meeting hall, McNamara told them, "Four to five thousand years after the introduction of the written word, more than a third of adult mankind still remains illiterate." Twenty percent of the male labor force of the developing world was unemployed; major cities were doubling in size every ten years.

A Bank employee says of McNamara's hopes to solve these problems, "He's really sort of a Norman Vincent Peale, you know — positive thinking on everything. He has a propensity to say yes."

But suffering for the poor and articulating his concern about overpopulation, illiteracy, and Third World cities did not constitute a program. McNamara was slow, by his own past standards, to develop his philosophy. And no matter how much he immersed himself in data on aid and trade, he still read about the ongoing war in the newspapers and was still heckled in public. His long days at the Bank were a kind of cocoon from reminders of the war. Not until later, when a unified Communist Vietnam tried to woo him for loans, would McNamara be faced with the V word in his closed new world. Although depressed, he reached for a new star to follow. William Clark noted in his diary, "He can always find a cupful of wind for his sails."[7]

The act of will, battening down all reference to his pain and inner depression, could make him seem oblivious to his past. Early in McNamara's tenure, a Bank photographer tried to shoot publicity photos of the new president at work. Hold a paper and look at it, the man instructed. McNamara picked up a document and gazed at it while the photographer honed his angle. Then the photographer noticed that the paper was a letter from one of the Kennedys. Hold a paper relating to *Bank* work, he said.

Next he asked McNamara to pose on the sofa and arranged some objects on the coffee table for the foreground. But he found symbols of war, not souvenirs of a man of peace: an oriental sword; the fragment of the shell that he and Willard Goodwin saved from the *President Hoover* back when it was fired on by the Japanese in 1937; and one of the caltrops — grim-looking iron forks — that the Danish police had strewn in the streets in Copenhagen in 1970 to hinder movement by horses or vehicles and quell the riot that broke out on McNamara's arrival.

The man of peace who systematically combed the developing nations of the world found himself sometimes in strange company. William Clark recorded their visit with Emperor Jean-Bédel Bokassa, head of the Central African Empire, who had himself crowned emperor in the style of Napoleon to the tune of $90 million in French funds.[8] Bokassa was one of the most ruthless leaders in Africa; he was later indicted in absentia for cannibalism. Clark called him "criminally insane." All afternoon McNamara sat with the cabinet, hearing its grandiose schemes. Near the end, he protested, "You can't do that. You must realize that you are really bankrupt."

The finance minister replied with a smirk, "But how can you say that? We control the printing presses."

The emperor heard the afternoon meeting had gone badly, so he commandeered the state dinner for McNamara that night. He fired the finance minister midway through it. Clark recorded that he wangled a seat next to this minister — before his dismissal — "to be sure I mightn't be assassinated during the meal."

Afterward, Robert McNamara, the straight boy from Oakland, Margy, and Clark were treated to the emperor's idea of entertainment: "a lot of dancing girls, very scantily clad apart from their high thigh boots, coming in and singing, '*McNamara et Bokassa sont frères, sont frères.*' "

McNamara's quest for a program, a formula for winning the fight against poverty in the Third World, took five years. It ended in another of his great simplifications. It changed the world of development and in some sense changed the world.

The field of aid had indeed been experiencing "frustration" and "failure" when McNamara parachuted into it in April 1968. The accepted model for how the new countries of Africa, Asia, and Latin America should modernize was based on the presumed lessons of the Industrial Revolution and on Western Europe's recovery after World War II. All societies were presumed to go through stages, from subsistence farming to large-scale agriculture, to a bourgeois, small-business phase, to heavy industry. Only in the last stage was enough capital saved and pooled for reinvestment, which could generate more industrial activity and profits; this was the "takeoff point" at which growth became self-sustaining and the benefits of growth would "trickle down" to the poor. The text advocating the "stages of economic growth" theory was a book of that title, written by Walt Whitman Rostow, who later became Lyndon Johnson's national security adviser and a proponent of bombing.[9] Rostow had been McNamara's nemesis in his last year in office, and now McNamara learned to criticize his theory of economic growth as well.

The World Bank had followed the stages-of-growth philosophy, not because of its intellectual depth, but because it could be used to justify large loans for dams, power plants, industrial activity, telecommunications — in other words, the kind of lending the Bank knew how to do. For much of the 1950s and 1960s, the theory seemed to work: The gross national product of the Third World grew in the 1960s at an average of 5 percent per year, which slightly exceeded American and European economic growth.

But theoretical stages of growth and trickle down were not working, as any visitor to India or Africa could see by the late 1960s. Officials who dealt with the repeated tragic famines in India and Pakistan, and the hectic emergency shipments of wheat from Alberta, Canada, or Kansas to prevent mass starvation, knew that GNP growth could hardly be an accurate measure of progress. Population was increasing so fast in such areas that it threatened to swamp any gains from GNP growth; the poor were getting poorer, absorbing resources for roads or sanitation without contributing to growth. A world of overpopulation and frequent famines was hardly one of progress, no matter what the GNP figures were.

Thus, McNamara's early stress on the population problem did not stem just from inner gloom or his obsession with numbers. He had indeed found the single most important factor in the ill-understood economics of the developing world. He grasped that only if these societies attacked population growth (necessarily in keeping with their mores and religious customs) could the specter of advancing poverty be kept at bay.

His early speeches mentioned the need for education, health care, and curing malnutrition, although health was a topic the Bank had previously left to U.N. agencies.[10] And he began talking about the large numbers of impoverished people who were not sharing in growth, the "widening gap" between elites who benefited from industrial loans and operated huge plantations growing crops for export, and the masses of poor whom he saw on trips.

Each fall, the Bank's Board of Governors, the finance ministers of member countries, would meet. Between the ministers and staffs, and the senior staffs of the World Bank and the International Monetary Fund, which would hold its annual board meeting at the same time, the gatherings numbered six thousand people. McNamara chose to make his annual speech to the governors the major way he laid out his thinking and goals for the Bank — thus identifying the Bank and its program with his person. To the Board of Governors in Copenhagen in 1970, while demonstrators shouted outside, McNamara stressed the moral obligation they had to ensure that aid reached the poor. He argued that the rich were not the enemy; the real enemy was poverty. Answering anger among many Third World regimes at affluent nations, McNamara in the fall of 1971 called attention to "the bottom 40 percent" of humanity — 800 million people in the developing world — who needed to be helped because GNP growth had passed them by.[11]

The left-liberal critique of entrenched power that was now popular in the United States had spread among many Third World leaders, whose nations depended on exports to the wealthy nations for hard currency. The regular sessions of the United Nations Conference on Trade and Development had become strongly political; at one, Salvador Allende carried the banner for poor nations in criticizing the First World. McNamara, on his visit to the UNCTAD meeting that Allende hosted, in Santiago in 1972 — the same trip during which he did not visit Craig on Easter Island — sympathized with the resentment of these Third World states. He made headlines by charging it was "wholly illogical" for wealthy nations, after twenty years of aid to the Third World, to maintain high tariff walls against Third World exports, which those nations needed desperately to grow. But he also warned Third World rulers and elites that unless they focused on the bottom 40 percent of their people, through major reforms, aid alone could not save them from the disaster that would follow.

Instead of "fruitless confrontation between rich nations and poor nations," he said, there should be agreement by "all of us" on "practical measures which are conceptually sound, financially feasible, and which can command the requisite public support."[12]

In other words, McNamara urged these leaders to adopt a managerial, objective solution. His insistence that there *were* technical answers — ways the poor could gain a share of the economic pie without revolution — showed that his old faith in management burned strong. In fact the Bank, as a matter of policy, refrained from requiring that member governments engage in large-scale land reform as a precondition for receiving Bank aid; there were limits on how much political change could be forced by an outside technical agency — already seen as an agent of Western capitalism.

At the landmark U.N. Conference on the Human Environment in Stockholm in June 1972, McNamara defined the task of development very broadly as providing "fundamental human dignity" for the 2.75 billion people in the world who were poor. The Stockholm conference organizers aimed at making the industrial world aware that it was polluting fragile planet earth. A related debate concerned whether poor nations should sacrifice industrial growth — for many aspired to build steel or paper mills to "advance," in economic terms — to lessen global pollution. Most Third World leaders resisted any suggestion that they should slow their advance while the developed nations were contributing most to environmental degradation and were doing so little themselves. At Stockholm, McNamara claimed somewhat rashly that there need be no contradiction between growth and environmental goals for developing nations; again, he maintained — in advance of the facts — that technical answers could be found.[13]

In the fall of 1972, he gave another black-suited performance to the Board of Governors, calling on Third World governments to "redirect their development policies to attack directly the personal poverty of the most deprived 40 percent of their populations." They "must" establish "growth targets" for meeting "essential human needs," even if the cost was some "reduction of the pace of advance" in "narrow" and "highly privileged sectors."[14]

Poverty was not a "symptom" of underdevelopment, he now said. Rather, it was "a condition that must be attacked." Although he also blamed political factors — unfair laws, inequitable land distribution, bureaucracy, and corruption — he focused on poverty as the real foe.

And, as in 1965 against an earlier perceived foe, McNamara felt a driving moral urgency to succeed fast. "Our clear duty for the remainder of this decade is to face up to mass poverty for what it really is, determine its dimensions, locate its whereabouts, set a limit beneath which we will not accept its continuance."

As for the timetable, McNamara said they should "set a threshold of human dignity and decency which is achievable within a generation." But he had still not completed his program to meet these goals.

The Board of Governors, even many in the Bank, wondered where McNamara's ideas were coming from, says Hollis Chenery, the Bank's leading economist after 1970. Did they stem from the Delos conferences on the earth's future that the Greek community builder Constantinos Doxiadis held on his yacht? Was McNamara advocating education loans because Margy's organization, Reading Is Fundamental, was successfully growing and lending books to disadvantaged children?

In fact, McNamara found his way to some of his ideas through William Clark's address book. Clark was part of a group in Britain that had been angered by the way London acted toward its colonies ever since India and Pakistan won independence with the help of Lord Mountbatten in 1947. This group in a sense launched the concept of development; its political philosophy reached back to the Fabian Society of Beatrice and Sidney Webb.[15] The Fabians sought to use government as an equalizer of wealth in Great Britain. However, since the new governments in the former colonies were not ready for such roles, the Fabians turned to outside programs that would develop the new nations more equitably.

Clark and his friends attacked the aid establishment and its policy of supporting the elites in the new nations. They were outraged that in many places the small group that had already cornered the national wealth should prosper from aid given in the name of helping the poor. In the 1960s in the United States, the best-known spokesperson for this critique of the aid establishment was Clark's good friend Barbara Ward, Lady Jackson. Clark jealously kept his own unique status with McNamara; but he also made sure McNamara consulted Ward often.

McNamara said that he first heard Ward speak to a group of

Kennedy Cabinet members at Hickory Hill, Bobby and Ethel Kennedy's home. McNamara claimed she kept them "spellbound for hours." Indeed, she had a musical voice, having trained as an opera singer; she had made weekly broadcasts for the BBC throughout the war. This quick-witted daughter of a Quaker and Catholic had adopted the Pope's faith, read economics at Oxford, and was working for historian Arnold Toynbee when she applied for a job at the *Economist* and discovered her talents as a journalist. She helped write the magazine during World War II. By war's end, between her columns and BBC broadcasts, she was, in her early thirties, well known in Britain.[16]

Ward's experience covering the Marshall Plan for Europe turned her into an admirer of the United States and a believer in the potential of aid. In 1949, the United States gave 2.79 percent of its GNP to Western Europe. That money, technology, and a dose of capitalism could achieve so much appealed to her deep Catholicism: The United States had exercised the moral duty of the rich to help the poor. A strong moral sense infused her arguments; in fact, she was passionate on the issue.

Ward lectured at Harvard in the early Kennedy years; she and her husband, Robert Jackson, persuaded Kennedy to support Kwame Nkrumah, Ghana's president. The titles of her books reveal her evolution and prolificness: *Development and Dependence in Emergent Africa* (1959), *India and the West* (1961), *The Rich Nations and the Poor Nations* (1962), *Why Help India* (1963), *Women in the New Asia* (1965), *The Decade of Development* (1965), *Spaceship Earth* (1966), *Nationalism and Ideology* (1966), *The Lopsided World* (1968). Ward had been a supporter of the Vietnam War and liked Lyndon Johnson for his directness, more than she had John Kennedy. Her best American friend was Adlai Stevenson, although the Kennedys, John Kenneth Galbraith, Hollis Chenery, and Bob and Margy McNamara were high on her list.

Ward's British expatriate friends cattily called her a glib journalist and passable economist. Ward did not claim to be original, but she catalyzed and simplified ideas in the way McNamara needed from 1968 on. While Chenery influenced him on the technical issues, Ward convinced him that the Bank could direct resources at the bottom 40 percent — the largest *number* of the poor — and make them productive. She became a kind of beacon during the years when McNamara was a pariah at home and searching for an intellectual foundation for the Bank's program — a star to steer by.

"She influenced me more than anyone in my life," he said of Ward later. David Runnalls, who worked with Ward when he was a graduate student, recalls her saying that McNamara talked to her about Vietnam, which was a sign of his trust. Clark remembered McNamara's sending Ward drafts of his speeches, "shy as a 17-year-old schoolboy."[17]

A turning point for McNamara came at a conference Ward organized at Columbia University, in New York, in 1970, which brought together Young Turks critical of the aid establishment to discuss a study chaired by Lester Pearson on aid. Ward persuaded U.N. Development Program director Paul Hoffman to come and Johannes Wittveen, director of the International Monetary Fund. She invited Maurice Strong, who ran Canada's aid program, and, of course, McNamara.

McNamara was in classic form, recalls Runnalls. He was in shirtsleeves, making notes, firing questions back at these wild young men who hurled angry charges of oppression and corruption and who spoke of the need for justice. McNamara had been a Young Turk himself, way back at Ford and when he first charged into U.S. defense policy, in 1961. One of his favorite stances was that of the bright newcomer shoving aside old fogeys. So his curiosity was piqued. He barraged the younger men with questions: How would you reach the poor directly? Why would that work? Give me a number.

Some at the meeting wouldn't sit in the same room with him. After all, it was 1970. Massive student protests at Columbia in 1968 set the pattern for demonstrations taking place all around the country. As McNamara stepped out of Low Library, overlooking the college green, he told William Clark he would like to have a look around the campus.

Clark and Runnalls exchanged horrified glances. If Columbia students learned that the "butcher of Vietnam" was in their midst, they could start a riot. In the 1968 protest, a policeman had been paralyzed; McNamara would not be safe here. The two escorts talked McNamara out of his proposed walk.

Then they asked how he planned to get to the airport. By subway, said the frugal McNamara. This was not wise either, Clark and Runnalls thought. They relaxed only once they had edged the president of the World Bank into a yellow cab and saw it sail up Broadway, knowing that no one on the crowded sidewalks knew who was inside.

Also attending the Columbia conference was a Pakistani named Mahbub ul Haq, an intelligent and angry man who had been on his nation's planning commission for thirteen years and had come to the United States "to reflect on that experience," he later said.[18]

Ul Haq was appalled by what the Western aid establishment had done to hurt his people. The Bank had helped divide the waters of the Indus River system in 1960 and subsidized large irrigation and power works — which benefited relatively few. Aid made some cotton and rice farmers fabulously rich; Pakistan's aid-supported heavy industry grew 13 percent per year in 1960–65. But by 1970, after war and the systematic robbing of East Pakistan by the West, the nation's twenty-two richest families still owned everything. Meanwhile, the village-based Comilla project in East Pakistan, which worked miracles among the poor, got no support. The elite kept the masses miserable to keep them powerless; aid was a tool of repression, in ul Haq's view.

"I had seen people stoning the development projects I had built up with such care," he said. He talked of taking aid directly to the people.

During a temporary stay at the Bank, ul Haq attacked McNamara's plans for the expansion. His encounters with McNamara were "very unhappy"; McNamara "suggested to me that this kind of belligerent questioning of growth at a time that the World Bank was committed" was "totally uncalled for."

Ul Haq decided to go home, but McNamara, interested in the man's defiance and drawn by his charisma, called him. McNamara "asked me to write down coherently all the arguments that I could marshal in favor of the thesis that we must focus directly on poverty and on the poor sectors and certain target groups and that 'trickle down' would not work."

The young man suspected a trick. "I felt that probably he wanted me to commit myself in writing and so demonstrate just how shoddy some of the arguments were. But this was the measure of the man I came to appreciate. He always used to rethink issues.

"His belligerence was often an invitation to sharpen your own arguments and to be professional, and until he had come to terms with something in his mind, he would keep rethinking it and coming back to it."

So ul Haq and McNamara, along with others, coined many terms about the bottom 40 percent and its condition. "He wanted facts and figures"; for example, that whereas Brazil as a whole had grown by 8 percent, its bottom group grew by only 1 percent. Ul Haq said, "During this period [McNamara became] convinced that growth was not trickling down."

Thus McNamara, who steered clear of so many other angry young men — his son, the Vietnam veterans who were coming home in increasing numbers in those years, reporters who tried to call him to account over the war, even Bank employees — was excited by one-on-one combat with this appealing adversary, who spoke so pointedly for the mass of people he sought to help. Ul Haq came to enjoy much favor; the Bank staff worried that he was becoming "a guru" to McNamara, says analyst Robert L. Ayres.

A final influence on McNamara was the group of scientists who were ushering in the Green Revolution in Pakistan, India, the Philippines, and Mexico just when he came to the Bank. The first phase of exportation of high-yielding varieties of rice and wheat from research centers in Mexico, Japan, and the Punjab had been carried out by large landowners, who received fertilizer, credit, and aid from the United States, the Ford and Rockefeller foundations, and elsewhere. The Bank could play a role, he was assured by experts, in redirecting the benefits of the Green Revolution to small farmers who had thus far been shut out.[19]

McNamara had found among the Bank's senior staff some extraordinary men who knew the Green Revolution firsthand. Among them were the Australian agricultural expert Sir John Crawford; Peter Cargill, a tall, hard-drinking Briton formerly in the colonial service in India; and Montague Yudelman, a South African expert on African agriculture. They guided McNamara to the idea that the Green Revolution could be brought to small farmers, who, as he would say, tilled "a handkerchief of soil" and who, given enough aid, could grow their family's food and perhaps a bit more to sell at market. Small farmers were a potential key to improving the economic condition of the lower strata.

McNamara at first resisted the idea of concentrating on small farms because he disapproved of old Henry Ford's romantic visions of autoworkers cultivating little farms, recalls David Hopper, a Bank expert on India and Pakistan. One of the inventor's indulgences had been to build Greenfield Village, a reproduction of the early settlers' simple life, which the elder Ford held out as an ideal for all Americans, even in the age of mass production. But McNamara, a modern man, scoffed at Ford's idea; it was silly to try to turn back the clock.

McNamara's resistance was broken, Hopper recalls, by the argument that building modern industry in poor lands was not benefiting poor people — the message McNamara heard from Chenery, Ward, and others loud and clear. The millions in Mexico or India who left rural areas to squat near cities did not find industrial jobs or become productive, and they left many others behind, destined to remain in the countryside and stay destitute. McNamara concluded that if the cycle of insufficient food, poverty, and overpopulation could be broken where it started, in rural areas, the indigent could be made productive and sustained economic growth could begin.

Thus by the fall of 1973 McNamara had a polished speech ready — honed in his usual way, by phoning around the Bank for data to support his case and numbers to set the quantitative goals for his program. Appropriately, the annual meeting of governors that year was to be held in Nairobi, Kenya; poor farmers were a major new target in his strategy, especially those in Africa. On September 24, 1973, McNamara made the word "Nairobi" synonymous with his own approach to development, the summation of his five-year quest.[20]

Early in the speech he defined his foe. The target for attack was not poverty in general or what he termed "relative poverty," which he defined as the fact that some people in a society are always better off than others. Rather, they should be concerned with "absolute poverty," which was "a condition of life so degraded by disease, illiteracy, malnutrition, and squalor as to deny its victims basic human necessities." He assigned a number to those in absolute poverty: "Nearly 800 million individuals — 40% out of a total of two billion — survive on incomes estimated . . . at 30 cents a day in conditions of malnutrition, illiteracy, and squalor. They are suffering poverty in the absolute sense."

In a "typical country" served by the Bank, McNamara announced, the richest 20 percent of population got 55 percent of the national income, whereas the lowest 20 percent of the socioeconomic ladder got only 5 percent. The growth in GNP in the developing world had occurred among the top 40 percent, who lived in or near cities, while the remaining 60 percent, in the countryside, were for the most part getting poorer.

The key insight was McNamara's link between rural poverty as a distinct phenomenon and the potential of the Green Revolution to raise small farmers' productivity and incomes. Past GNP growth in these countries had been propelled by the "mining, industry, and government" sectors, while the livelihood of the small farmer had stagnated. Although millions of rural poor migrated to cities, the huge numbers left in the countryside and faster rates of population growth there meant, McNamara said, that more than half of all people in the developing world would still live in rural areas in the year 2000.

"Within rural areas the poverty problem revolves primarily around the low productivity of the millions of small subsistence farms," he said. Their improvement in past years was so small as to be "unacceptable" — a word McNamara the missionary used more and more.

No matter what else the Bank and developing nations' governments did, such as building more industry or improving cities, McNamara argued, "without rapid progress in smallholder agriculture throughout the developing world, there is little hope either of achieving long-term stable economic growth or of significantly reducing the levels of absolute poverty." Past development programs, by the Bank and other agencies, had given little serious, sustained attention to the program. Now he wanted to confront it "head-on."

Then McNamara took a leap and proposed a sweeping goal: In twelve years' time, by 1985, "production of small farms" should increase so they would be expanding at 5 percent a year on average. Their past growth rate had been 2.5 percent. McNamara put in some qualifiers and then rushed on.

> Clearly this is an ambitious objective. A 5% rate of growth has never been achieved on a sustained basis among smallholders in any extensive areas of the developing world. Smallholder production has risen on average only about 2.5% per year in the past decade . . . but if Japan in 1970 could produce 6720 kg. [kilograms] of grain per ha. [hectare] on very small farms, then Africa, with its 1270 kg. per ha. and Latin America with its 2060 kg., have an enormous potential for expanding productivity.

He announced, "Thus I believe the goal is feasible."

The program was ambitious also in that it focused not only on farming. McNamara suggested that national governments, the Bank, and other aid groups concentrate on packages of service to rural areas — "small feeder roads, small scale irrigation and drainage systems, storage and market facilities, community schools and health centers, and other facilities which make use of local labor." The major emphasis would be on land reform — which, he admitted, would take political courage by governments — and on credit, agricultural-extension water supply, and public services. Also they would build "new forms of rural institutions," which would promote "the inherent potential and productivity to the poor as is generally given to protecting the power of the privileged."

And McNamara the missionary repeated the moral argument, echoing Ward. "The whole of human history has recognized the principle — at least in the abstract — that the rich and the powerful have a moral obligation to assist the poor and the weak." Once the "facts" about the present low levels of official aid were understood, he said, he could not believe that "people and governments of the rich nations will turn away in cynicism and indifference." He closed:

> All the great religions teach the value of each human life. In a way that was never true in the past, we now have the power to create a decent life for all men and women. Should we not make the moral precept our guide to action? . . . You and I — and all of us in the international community — share that responsibility.

The cheering and applause from rows of people, many in bright African dress — and the Nairobi speech itself — were perhaps McNamara's finest hour. The speech certainly ranks, along with his repeated descriptions of Assured Destruction while he was at Defense, his 1967 speech against the arms race, and his August 1967 testimony arguing against wider bombing of North Vietnam, as one of his most important contributions. McNamara only *seemed* to be a new man; in fact, he had learned to command a podium years before and could still do it.

It was not the plan of a humble man. "Development's task," McNamara said near the end of the speech, was to "deal with" the "extremes of privilege and deprivation."[21] This was a huge goal, and one unlikely to be met, in fact. Nor were McNamara's assault on the largest *number* of poor and his claim that they could end poverty in a generation modest either.

The sheer scope of the Nairobi program may have stemmed from the vilification he had experienced in the previous two years at home. It was McNamara's pattern that the more he was stung by accusations over the war, the louder and more publicly he would speak to show his virtue and do good. The pace of his activity was suggestive: In 1972, the year after the Pentagon Papers were published, he gave three major speeches instead of his usual one; in 1973, the year after *The Best and the Brightest* appeared, he arrived at the Nairobi platform. And his faith in using the potential of agriculture, technology, and human organization had an autobiographical air, harking back to the Bay Area valley whose agricultural economy blossomed during his youth.

Then there was the lurid language he used to describe poverty, a "condition of life so degraded . . . as to deny its victims basic human necessities." These and other phrases describe the poor as trampled on by circumstance, neglected and abused, paralyzed and unable to realize their potential as people, and, as he began to say often, denied "human dignity."[22] It is noteworthy that this definition of the poor as those denied human dignity came at a time when in his own life he was "degraded" by abuse over his role in Vietnam, still sometimes physically attacked by angry people in the street, boycotted at the tennis courts on Martha's Vineyard. For some summers during his years at the Bank, hippie protesters would gather outside a house the McNamaras had bought on Martha's Vineyard and stare at them through the big picture window.[23] The physical conditions of McNamara's life in no way resembled those of the masses he now sought to help, but the conclusion is inescapable that at some level he took up the cause of the absolute poor so passionately because he identified with them. Certainly, he would have invented the same program — in economic, social, and managerial terms — had he not waged the humiliating Vietnam War in his previous life, for the Nairobi program both echoes the Great Society and flows logically from the reform movement in the field of development of the time. But the driving emotional energy McNamara focused on their plight was linked to his own experience of humiliation.[24]

Finally, the spectacle of northern California in the early twentieth century may have hovered in McNamara's imagination as he spoke glowingly at Nairobi of the potential of small farms. He had seen that kind of wealth creation firsthand; McNamara had even uplifted himself from the relative poverty in which he was raised. It is hard to believe that a Bank president from a more privileged, urban, or even East Coast background would have thrown himself into the cause of rural poverty as did this once-poor boy from Oakland. In McNamara's imagination, if northern California could pull itself up, if Bob McNamara could pull himself up, then the rural poor of the world could pull themselves up.

The Nairobi program was one more of McNamara's grand simplifications. In reality, it was not clear that what worked for small rice farmers in Japan could be replicated by tribesmen growing maize or groundnuts in Africa. It was not clear that rulers of Third World countries would redirect money and scarce talent to the politically powerless rural poor. It was not clear that, once the "facts" about how little official aid rich countries gave the Third World were known, affluent governments would contribute more.

Yet from the welter of problems and proposed solutions, McNamara had concocted a simple scenario to solve the largest possible problem he could have tackled. Says Stanley Please, a British expert whom McNamara tagged to carry out the program in Africa: "I never knew whether McNamara really believes all those simple truths he expounds with such force, or whether he knows he is simplifying on purpose in order to act, lest he admit things are complex and get bogged down, as all intellectuals do." S. Shahid Husain, a Pakistani who was a loan officer for Brazil when McNamara came to the Bank and rose steadily during the McNamara years, says: "I believe that people's strengths are the source of their greatest weaknesses. McNamara's great strength is his phenomenal ability to take any issue and focus on it to the exclusion of other things, to the point that other things don't even exist for him."[25]

McNamara would focus on concrete actions and drive for results in his antipoverty war, although "rural development," as the Nairobi plan to help smallholder farmers was termed, was not necessarily something the old Bank's organization or culture was geared up to carry out. There had been resistance to it among the staff even as the speech was drafted. The Bank was used to overseeing projects with explicit, economic rates of return, physically large projects with obvious economic benefits. It was unaccustomed to funding many small agricultural projects, to improving long-term yields, or to providing complex packages of health, education, and community aid with hard-to-define returns.[26]

McNamara himself saw no obstacle; many years later, when the long-term lessons of his antipoverty war were known, it was remarked at how he made little organized effort to educate the institution or adapt it to his mission. He seemed confident that his authority was complete, that he need only give directions and set goals. This was, after all, the same man who in 1962 had told an interviewer that "running the Department of Defense is not different from running Ford Motor Company or the Catholic Church, for that matter. Once you get to a certain scale, it's all the same." It was the philosophy based on Alfred Sloan and the du Pont cousins' financial control systems and the approach of the Harvard Business School, that any type of business can be run with common techniques. It remained to be seen whether a system of management that evolved to serve large American manufacturing enterprises, transplanted to a bank, could usefully enable that institution to make inroads against rural poverty.

But to the doubters who worried about the financial and institutional risks — and the risk that the Bank would leave the poor nations stuck having to repay the loans even if the "new style" projects did not succeed — McNamara would respond with his parable of the talents, saying that power was not given to him to be "wrapped in a napkin against risk." Around the Bank, he was paraphrased as stating, "If you are not taking any risks, you are not doing your job."

Within weeks of the Nairobi speech, the mainly Arab members of the Organization of Petroleum Exporting Countries, which controlled most of the world's oil supplies, jacked up the price of oil. Prices, which had been $2.40 a barrel, quadrupled, to $9.60 a barrel. The news hit the industrial world like a Richter scale–15 earthquake. "We cannot ever expect a return to normality," said a memo McNamara found on his desk upon his return from Colorado on New Year's Day.[27] His just-announced plan to save the world was turned inside out.

Gas lines formed in America. Public panic was widespread over the high cost of gasoline, home heating, and industrial operations. Another price rise came in December 1973, which hiked prices another 130 percent and which resulted in an OPEC embargo on oil shipments to the United States that lasted until the following March. The success of OPEC at holding a gun to the head of the industrial world led to sweeping fears that other exporters of raw materials would form cartels and raise prices. Inflation, already high, was rising.

McNamara went to one of the meetings of development officials at Tidewater, Maryland, right after the oil price rise. Clark noted, "RSM tries reason. Let's get the figs and use very small percentage of Arab funds for aid/dev."[28]

By December, Hollis Chenery produced an internal Bank analysis that disputed the popular idea that other Third World countries besides OPEC nations would grow rich off raw-materials cartels. Instead, Chenery predicted that the prices of other raw materials would remain unstable, while the collective bill for higher-priced food and fertilizer (the latter made from oil) would raise the debt of developing nations that imported oil by $20 billion a year.[29]

Yet even this greater indebtedness — horrendous for poor nations — was a drop in the bucket compared to the $300 billion OPEC could accumulate in a few years, which would slosh around the global economy. The oil-exporting states would ultimately invest much of that money in affluent nations, and perhaps in the more creditworthy developing nations. But even if private borrowing and lending took place on this unprecedented scale, the poorest countries still had a slim chance of competing for loans needed to buy scarce foodstuffs, fertilizer, and other essentials, because the value of their exports would decline.

OPEC's actions had another consequence for McNamara's plans. Already, the governments of well-off states and the financial world were preoccupied with their own problems; the new global economy meant that it would be harder for McNamara to put his concern for the poor at the top of rich nations' agendas.

The billion people in the poorest Third World countries, primarily in South Asia and East and West Africa — now called the Fourth World — would be harder hit; their development prospects had been delayed a decade. And the developing world — that tidy, postcolonial entity visualized by the Fabians and Ward — would now split into groups: the OPEC nations, including Mexico and Venezuela; the non-oil-exporting nations with diversified economies, like Brazil or Thailand; and the poorest, the Fourth World.[30]

But McNamara did not retreat despite this unexpected blow. At Nairobi he had announced plans to increase the scale of Bank lending yet again; he still planned to carry through, to borrow more and lend more, $22 billion over the next five years. His assumption had been that this scale of lending could help the developing nations grow on average 5 percent per year; now the prediction was that the poorest would grow by 1 percent.[31]

McNamara's logic was sound up to a point: Bank project lending, particularly for food and other basic needs, would make the borrowing nations able to grow in ways in which they might not without his Bank's program. Thus, Bank loans, including IDA credits, would be the answer to creating future wealth, one of the few ways poorer countries could generate real growth and reduce debt in the long term.

McNamara took off on a prearranged trip for Australia. Meanwhile, Munir Benjenk, a Turk who was the Bank's vice president for Europe, the Middle East, and North Africa, flew to Tehran to show Chenery's draft paper to the head of Iran's central bank.[32] Did the shah not realize, he asked, when he had cemented OPEC's joint price rise that he was hurting poor countries? The head of the central bank scoffed at first and then listened. Benjenk got in to see the prime minister. The higher Benjenk took his case, the shorter his paper became. Finally, the plea on behalf of one billion of the world's poor was boiled down to a single page.

"I will show this to the shah in St. Moritz tomorrow," said the prime minister. Mohammed Reza Pahlavi was skiing while these earth-shattering results of his actions played out. The shah got Benjenk's one-page paper and agreed to meet McNamara in Tehran.

McNamara's meeting with the shah, in February 1974, produced one of the most remarkable schemes of the era — one that suited McNamara's purposes fine. The shah proposed that OPEC and the Bank establish a new fund that would recycle billions in OPEC oil moneys to the poorest countries on concessional terms, to aid growth. The Bank would administer the loans, but one third of the fund's governing board would be from poor countries, one third from OPEC, and one third from the First World. Page 1 of the *Washington Post* ran a photograph of McNamara with a story about this sweeping plan; in effect, he was running the planet.[33]

William E. Simon was a dedicated free marketeer who had watched warily as McNamara's Bank grew. In the fall of 1973, Simon was the point man for the Nixon administration's response to OPEC. Simon hated McNamara's scheme for two reasons: It gave McNamara and the Bank too much power over the global economy, and it diminished the United States' clout in Bank affairs and its control over R. S. McNamara.

Simon, furthermore, had a low opinion of the holder of the Peacock Throne. William Clark recorded in his diary what McNamara apparently told him: "Bill Simon: 'the Shah is a nut.' "[34]

Finally, McNamara's scheme recognized that OPEC was a new global power player. Simon and the Nixon men wanted to break OPEC that winter. Their response to OPEC's challenge was raw power, reflecting America's insularity as its domination of the world's economy began to wane. Simon and Nixon refused to take these white-sheeted sheikhs seriously and presumed Washington would end up in control. While no one gave McNamara high marks for diplomacy with the Arab world, he was right in October 1973 and more perceptive than the Nixon men in recognizing OPEC's real strength and in trying to seize this new wealth of the world and bring it, through him, to the poor.

McNamara and the shah's proposal foundered quickly. Simon and Henry Kissinger simply said that the United States' 23 percent vote on the World Bank's board would be cast in opposition. The shah was also stabbed in the back — other OPEC leaders were angry that he had concocted and publicized the plan without consulting them.[35] Had McNamara and Reza Pahlavi been less arrogant and impatient, the fate of the world economy would have been different.

Still, McNamara did not give up. Kuwait and Saudi Arabia recognized some obligation to offset the effects of their action, and Reza Pahlavi had been sold already. Benjenk, McNamara, and others pushed hard to build up these nations' bilateral programs; by August of 1974, Eugene Rotberg had arranged borrowings of $1.15 billion from OPEC nations such as Iran and Saudi Arabia and added the largest single offering ever, for $500 million, from the newly rich OPEC nation Venezuela. Simon continued to object, but McNamara was at least gaining petrodollars, if not on concessional terms.

The picture was depressing nonetheless; that fall, McNamara reported to the governors that Official Development Assistance from the First World had declined to 0.3 percent of their total GNPs, thus falling away from the 0.7 percent figure agreed to in 1970 and 3.4 percent established in 1973.[36] His Nairobi program specified that poor nations needed to borrow $16.7 billion for the rest of the decade to grow at 5 percent; if they borrowed only that amount, the poorest nations' growth would decline. He thus postulated that the total borrowed should be $24 billion. "It is obvious that no attempt to increase the productivity of subsistence agriculture can succeed in an environment of overall economic stagnation." To combat economic stagnation, he argued convincingly, a bigger Bank was needed.

William Clark made McNamara sound scoutlike about the grim fact that instead of winning the war on poverty within a generation, all he could hope to do was to stem poverty's spread. "Bob [is] determined," he wrote in his diary, "to keep up the Bank's work. If you feel responsible for the Third World . . . you do 'your share,' however inadequate."[37]

So McNamara pressed on with his antipoverty program, although the terms of trade kept shifting, working against the poorest regions and countries as months and years passed. He was nothing if not systematic, for the style of control he had established could direct resources — to get a "throughput" of economic benefit and greater "human dignity," as he put it.

Looking over the loan commitments to Brazil in one of his statistical tables one day, McNamara picked up the phone and called Montague Yudelman, his expert on agriculture for Africa and other dry regions. I see we have a billion in loan commitments for Brazil, said McNamara. But only $100 million is for antipoverty work.

Can't you arrange to have at least $600 million go for antipoverty work? McNamara asked. Yudelman complied, and before the Bank's economic study of Brazil's poverty-stricken Northeast was even finished, projects to help small farmers were begun, with the Brazilians putting up most of the funds.[38]

He searched out the enemy, poverty, and quantified it. He and his staff at the Bank were trying to identify the 700 million "absolute poor" in the fall of 1974. "We do not now have all the information we need to identify the different groups in individual countries," he said. But they were building a data base with "present and potential levels of productivity of individuals in each category." Some in the Bank objected that counting and classifying people as absolutely or relatively poor was a poor exercise, so to speak. "We did a lot of body counting in those days," remarks a staffer, not without irony.[39]

"We cannot simply turn our backs on half the total population this institution serves," McNamara said in the same fall 1974 speech. Says another staffer, looking back, "It must have been the pain of his life to see the poor get poorer."

And there was a contradiction, overlooked for the most part in his soaring speeches. His central insight at Nairobi was that economic growth could be created in rural areas by giving technical aid to small farmers — those who tilled "a handkerchief of soil," in his fine phrase. But people with land were, by definition, not landless and not the absolute poor, who, by his announced income criterion, had almost nothing. McNamara was rushing past a sociological fact of most of the societies he sought to help, which was that the very poor people were landless or squatters with no title to land. Those with farms existed in "relative poverty"; he counted them separately from the 700 million. Who, exactly, was he planning to uplift? wondered a few experts at the time.[40] The problem would haunt him later.

McNamara's systems approach, however, would prove in at least one case to be of overwhelming importance. He had displayed all his life both skepticism of advanced technology and an underlying faith in technological miracles. McNamara, explains one of the Bank's senior statistical experts, was looking for what economists call a "production function, a standard approach so powerful and efficient that it could be easily transferred from one situation to others and between countries.

"One couldn't help [but get] the impression that he had the belief that if we prototyped in a few places, we could go off and put it onto the production line."[41]

McNamara arrived on the scene at the right moment, therefore, as far as the Green Revolution was concerned. The miracle strains of high-yield wheat and rice that would thrive in parts of Asia and Latin America had proved themselves.[42] As a trustee of the Ford Foundation from April 1968 onward, McNamara had a front-row seat at the breakthroughs pioneered by the four research institutes that were supported by Ford and by the Rockefeller Foundation and that created the Green Revolution. He got to know the remarkable people of the Green Revolution, such as Norman Borlaug and Forrest ("Frosty") Hill. "McNamara had an intellectual's fascination with the hands-on, land-grant guys," remarks Yudelman.

The Green Revolution was becoming the victim of its own success. Between them, the two foundations bankrolled the four institutes, the first one in Mexico, where Borlaug did his seminal work with Mexican semidwarf wheat; one in the Philippines; one in Colombia; and one for tropical agriculture, in Nigeria. The annual budgets of the four centers were climbing toward $11 million; although the foundations had made several unusual long-term grants to keep them going, it was not clear that long-term financing could be arranged. Compounding the problem was the rising demand for advice and extension, the mechanism by which new agricultural knowledge, seeds, and farming techniques spread to specific localities and are taught, one on one, to local farmers. Eleven million dollars was a drop in the bucket to convert the hundreds of millions of rural farmers in India to better farming practices, to remove the threat of famines and raise incomes above fifty to seventy-five dollars per year.

At a meeting at the Rockefeller Foundation's conference center at Bellagio, Italy, in 1969, after a "homespun presentation" by Frosty Hill on how the new varieties were transforming India's Punjab, McNamara proposed a "consultative group" of several organizations and aid donors to jointly provide funds for the institutes on an ongoing basis, says Warren Baum, a key player.[43] Immediately John Hannah, the director of the U.S. government's aid program, suggested that the United States provide 25 percent of the funds for a joint group. McNamara's idea, swapped around the meeting, became the answer.

His faith in management drove him to find the right organizational vehicle by which to disseminate the Green Revolution on a scale commensurate with its potential. The Bank's executive directors, however, had reservations: Why not regional groups to support the far-flung institutes? Why not have the United Nations food agency take the lead? Why should the World Bank provide the secretariat and organizing functions, as McNamara recommended? Supporting agriculture research at the increased level that McNamara encouraged, in different regions and new, specialized institutes, would be a huge enterprise, and what about the diversion of Bank staff time and funds? McNamara pointed to Rotberg's successful investment of the Bank's liquid funds to answer the last objection: The Bank would pay for the operating costs of the group secretariat in Washington from profits on invested funds, he said. As for why the Bank should take the lead, McNamara noted that the directors already had agreed to plans to lend $4 billion for agricultural projects in coming years, projects whose total value over time would be $10 billion, yet the research base to validate this investment did not exist.

McNamara's approach to running the planet, in Clark's phrase, was to determine overall needs and then find resources to meet the needs. This approach seemed bold, if not rash, when he talked of population growth or of reaching all of 700 million absolute poor. Yet it was right for the situation of agriculture in 1969–71. The weakness of his management style — overcentralized direction, overemphasis on resource inputs and the "production function" — were strengths in this case.

M. S. Swaminathan, one of the deans of Indian agriculture, recalls that McNamara convened the experts at a dinner party at his house on Tracy Place in 1971.[44] Swaminathan remembers McNamara's banging his hand on the dining room table as he told them that their plans were too *small*. Instead of scrounging for $11 million per year, the institutes needed to spend $100 million per year by 1980, he said.

The experts were stunned.

Meanwhile, the Bank's executive directors were still balking, and the foundations' string was running out. But the consultative-group format was being developed steadily into a mature plan, and in 1972 the unglamorous-sounding Consultative Group on International Agricultural Research came into being. Its headquarters were in the World Bank's offices, while its technical advisory committee was housed in the Food and Agriculture Organization. CGIAR had a troika of expert directors — Hill, Swaminathan, and Sir John Crawford — and funds to run the research centers, pledged by eleven donors and totaling more than $160 million; its annual grants would rise toward $100 million during the decade.

By the early 1980s, more institutes had been added and hundreds of new strains had been exported successfully to Asia and Latin America, although with less success in Africa, on the whole. The institute in the Philippines assisted China for years, despite the fact that China was neither recognized by the international system nor a member of the Bank.[45]

By 1983, eighteen years after the first successful new strains grew in India and Pakistan, 58 percent of the rice land in the developing countries — which lies mainly in Asia — was planted with the new varieties of rice. Also by that time, the new varieties of wheat and rice distributed from the research centers were estimated to have provided fifty million tons of additional food per year, enough to meet the cereal needs — that is, the caloric requirements — of 500 million people, "impressive numbers by any standard," says one evaluation.

Swaminathan says, "McNamara's personal conviction of the crucial role of research was a very important factor in CGIAR's gaining momentum." Would the larger, more organized structure and vastly greater funding levels have been achieved without McNamara and the Bank? Swaminathan thinks not. "Without the Bank's indications that it would be central, the thing would not have moved."[46]

McNamara and Margy were touring a town in the West African nation of Mali, south of the great, dry region of the continent called the Sahel, when they noticed about eight adult men walking along, holding on to a pole; a small child held the other end of the pole and led them along.

Why? the McNamaras asked. The men were blind, they were told; 20 million people in seven countries in West Africa, from Senegal to Niger, faced a terrible choice: farm and risk blindness, or barely scrabble a living off parched land away from the river.[47]

The scourge was a disease called river blindness, or onchocerciasis, spread by a black fly that bred in river rapids. A farmer on the banks might be bitten a thousand times a day when the flies were buzzing and thus be implanted with worm larvae. As the worms grew, they caused terrible internal pain and itching; people had committed suicide to end the agony. The dead worms built up in the human eye and caused blindness.

"Margaret in particular was affected by this," recalls David Bell, former head of the U.S. Agency for International Development. Margy asked her husband why the Bank did not do something about it. McNamara explained that the Bank left health programs to the World Health Organization. But Margy wouldn't take no for an answer, and Bob McNamara decided his wife was right.

McNamara the moralist often said that not to act is tantamount to action and carries equal responsibility. There was no preventive inoculation against the disease at the time, so the only solution was spraying. The Bank justified project loans to fight river blindness on an economic rate-of-return computation of how much more productive the people of the region would be if more retained their sight.

The remaining problem was the lack of expertise or organization in the many countries where the disease struck — African countries often had modern city hospitals but rarely organized health care in rural areas. The Bank's first lending to fight the disease, in 1974, went to a supergovernmental group, mainly staffed with European and American experts, that could fly helicopters along rivers, crossing provincial and national boundaries.[48]

River falls were sprayed with pesticide in breeding season; the disease receded somewhat; the flies adapted; the pesticides changed. McNamara's war raged on.

Only years later, when a vaccine was found that could prevent the disease, was the war on river blindness really won. In January 1992, the Bank could say that its program "virtually eliminated" river blindness in the original area. Mechanisms were in place to prevent a resurgence. Some 450,000 people a year were being vaccinated. As with CGIAR, the Bank played an administrative and coordinating role with other donors.

Even McNamara's severest critics, who later argued that the Bank as a whole suffered under him, admit that CGIAR and the river blindness campaign were true successes.[49] Yet at the time, some staff worried about the amount of funds being lent to end a disease for which there was no medical cure, and about his use of non-African experts and outside institutions. The repeated helicopter raids spraying pesticides were reminiscent of both McNamara's earlier war, and of his belief that technology and money could conquer the foibles of man and nature.

McNamara reflected the mood of America in the middle 1970s as he roamed the Third World, trying to understand and engage it, while he fought off inner doubts and sought resolution and peace. Americans were turning inward, too. The OPEC oil-price hikes of 1973 represented a catalytic event that made many aware of the power of the Third World. The nation's vulnerability had been driven home earlier, with the Tet offensive and seizure of the Navy ship *Pueblo* in January 1968. Americans became aware of the Third World as never before in the 1970s; meanwhile McNamara traversed it and preached to annual governors' meetings about its importance and power.

Back at the U.S. Treasury, down the street from the Bank, William Simon was now secretary. Gerald Ford, who as House minority leader had criticized McNamara for mismanaging and losing the war in Vietnam, now occupied the White House. Simon represented another side of America: the conservative philosophy that America should put its national interests first and had no business bleeding for the poor, ungrateful Third World. The Nixon administration had supported the Bank and multilateral aid. Now Simon, backed by Ford, felt McNamara was dancing out of his control.

McNamara had by 1976 launched a second major initiative to call attention to the plight of urban areas in the Third World. But the terms of trade were worsening for poor countries, and international discussions of commodity agreements and buffer stocks had reached little resolution. He concluded by 1976 that he needed a still bigger Bank. The Bank and IDA would commit $7 billion that year, the most ever. To go any higher McNamara required either more paid-in capital by member governments or a change in Bank rules to allow a higher level of borrowing against existing capital paid in. In either case, McNamara needed a green light from the treasury and the Ford administration.

Simon didn't like the idea;[50] he argued that lending more to poor countries in such a volatile international economy could produce defaults — although the Bank had never had a default in its history and retained its AAA rating. Moreover, the Bank's Articles of Agreement required it to lend no more than its paid-in capital at any time, a remarkably conservative rule given that most banks' ratios are twenty to one. As negotiations began between the Bank and the treasury, the House of Representatives voted to lower the U.S. contribution to IDA to $320 million. As in 1968, slow congressional action could have disastrous consequences for the poor countries. It was the treasury's job to lobby congress to move; Simon seemed to be holding the IDA appropriation hostage to force McNamara to lower his demands. According to Bank senior staff, in one summit meeting Simon said to McNamara: Why are you always holding a gun to my head? Coming to us with demands and then making us out to be bad guys if we don't do what you want?

In another exchange, when Simon alluded to the crippling effect of the U.S. delay in appropriating funds, McNamara made up, on the spot, a new rejoinder the staff had never heard before. He told Simon they had ways of running Bank operations smoothly, no matter what Congress did.

The confrontation came before the Bank's resident executive directors, who guided the president on behalf of member governments. On the board, Simon controlled the United States' 23 percent vote. Clark recorded that Simon had worked the phones; McNamara had also worked the phones. Simon won agreement that the capital increase would be limited to $8 billion; McNamara wanted five times that amount. In addition, the executive director representing Japan resigned from the board, with a rare public blast at McNamara[51] — apparently to curry favor with the Ford administration. Wrote *Bar-*

ron's, "There is more than a personality clash involved in this power contest. The Bank's efforts to generate economic improvement in the poor countries involve government planning, [and] a redistribution of wealth and resources from rich to poor." Simon added a new complaint to the controversy: The Bank didn't need all that money because the staff was overpaid.

McNamara and Simon made a deal, or so Simon thought. Simon would allow some increase, although not as much as McNamara wanted, as long as the Bank adopted more "prudent" lending practices, such as shorter maturities and higher interest rates charged to borrowers.

At the following annual meeting, in the fall of 1976, the presidential election was weeks off. McNamara took advantage of the popularity of former Georgia governor Jimmy Carter. He calculated that the Republicans would not be in power much longer. And in his speech, he argued for a huge further increase in the Bank's capital.

Simon felt betrayed.[52] McNamara can't be trusted, he told the press. But a few weeks later, Carter won; McNamara had timed his political moves shrewdly, and another large increase in his program was approved soon after the Democrats took office.

Independence and power had been McNamara's goals from the beginning — so he could shape policies and programs in the Third World. Now he had them — again.

23
Management Is the Gate

M CNAMARA LOVED the expanses of southern Africa, the jewel-like islands of Indonesia, the tiered green terraces of the Punjab set against stunning mountain backdrops. The open horizons of the Third World recalled the topography of his boyhood, the scale of the San Francisco Bay, the sweep of farmland in the valley. They revived the sense of limitless possibility that stamped Robert McNamara's imagination all his life.

Now, in his new incarnation as the helper of the greatest number of people in the developing world, McNamara directed his management control system to bring about social and economic change. His system had been invented for the era of mass production and taught at Harvard Business School; he had used it to overhaul Ford and then the Pentagon. That it had failed him in Vietnam did not restrain him now. McNamara had said in his little-noticed speech at Millsaps College in 1967 that "management is the gate through which social and economic and political change, indeed, change in every direction, is diffused throughout society." At the Bank, his management controls were sculpted by his idiosyncrasies, his compulsive quantification and need to act. Despite the bad news from OPEC, he still hoped to beat back his new foe, poverty, in a single generation.[1]

To engineer change across three southern continents, McNamara traveled. He traveled to run his system, negotiate project terms, check up on progress made, and pull the levers of power with national governments. His travels had an escapist quality, although they were anything but leisurely.[2] On his first visit to West Pakistan, McNamara had been taken to a distant dam site. During the ride, he was subjected to hours of monologue by one of his hosts. Afterward he instructed his staff never again to put him in a position where he could not control his time.

Thereafter, he set a hectic pace of appointments, field visits, instantaneous arrivals, and rushed departures, which raised the same issue as had his flying trips to Vietnam: whether the whirligig allowed him to learn of real problems and complex truths. On one occasion, he descended in a white helicopter on a remote African village, resisted being stuffed into a litter to be carried to a project site, and was taken there on a motorcycle. He returned to the village soon after and took off again. To what purpose? asked an oldtime Bank staffer who observed the frantic scene.

He also traveled to cement a partnership between the Bank and the Third World. When his aide William Clark had warned that local people could resent Western institutions like the Bank dictating to them, McNamara had objected, saying, "The Bank is of the Third World," Clark wrote in his diary.[3]

He strode through teeming cities, such as Calcutta, where he had to step over the bodies of emaciated people barely alive. Once he and Margy motored into a cluster of villages in tropical northeast Guinea, in French West Africa, where the Bank supported villagers who tended some pineapple farms. People for miles around heard that the man who had been helping them was coming. When he and Margy were driven into the main town, hundreds of Africans in long white robes filtered out from among the tall trees and huts to see him. They began clapping when he arrived. McNamara seemed embarrassed, recalls Timothy Tahane of the Bank, who was there; he quickly darted into the large hut for his meeting.

In his journeys, McNamara moved through the Third World as an intellectual leader following his 1973 speech at Nairobi, where he put forward the Bank's new agenda to lend for smallholder agriculture, or rural development, as well as for traditional projects like power plants, dams, and railways.

He claimed to be only a partner, but he came as a partner bearing gifts in the form of long-term loans at competitive, fixed rates. He offered credits to the poorest nations, such as India and Tanzania, that is, loans with no interest, only a 0.75 percent yearly surcharge, and fifty years to pay, offered by the International Development Association, the Bank's in-house affiliate run by its staff.

He encouraged needy nations to borrow more, in the utter conviction that more lending would create economic growth, especially among the lower strata of their societies.[4] All his efforts in the 1970s were driven by growth: The Bank and IDA committed $2.7 billion a year on average in McNamara's first term for 152 projects per year; by 1978 he planned to commit $8.7 billion a year for almost twice as many projects.

McNamara's management controls at the Bank determined the volume of resources spent and imposed deadlines; he set targets for the sums to be dispersed by type of loan and region, for each year. This was throughput, the pivotal concept put forward by Donaldson Brown — the inventor of management controls at Du Pont and General Motors — which was used by top managers to gauge the efficiency of mass-production operations. McNamara measured not just the direction and volume of resources, but the numbers of beneficiaries reached and the rates of return achieved at a pre-set five-year mark compared with the targets set when the project was approved.

McNamara still stopped off in the First World, in London, Paris, or Bonn, although he was "ill at ease in Europe," recorded William Clark in his diary. McNamara left the fund-raising side of the Bank more to treasurer Eugene Rotberg, who became the largest nongovernment borrower in the world and used this leverage to assure ample funds for McNamara's crusade. Rotberg scanned the Bank's charter and found nothing that barred them from trading the liquid assets on hand. He opened a trading floor in the Bank's offices in Washington and soon was trading the assets on hand at yields that rivaled the best commercial banks. By decade's end, the sleek, high-tech "pit" in a space-age-looking room adjoining the office was earning 8.8 percent or $835 million a year on liquid assets of $9.5 billion.[5] Profits from the trading floor paid for the Bank's physical expansion, helping CGIAR, so the Green Revolution would spread, and other projects that aided the world's most backward places and people.

The Bank offered bonds in Japan, Kuwait, and elsewhere. McNamara viewed Western Europe mainly as a source of wealth to be tapped rather than as the revered parent culture. He had displayed this attitude toward Europe at Ford, when he recognized the long-term growth potential of European carmakers; he showed it at the Pentagon when he insisted the European allies should spend more on defense — and buy more American weapons. Now he repeatedly asked the European countries and others, including the United States, to increase their share of aid.

He was oblivious to the pomp of old Europe. In one meeting with the aristocratic French president Valéry Giscard d'Estaing, seated in priceless Louis XV chairs in a splendid formal French drawing room, McNamara pulled a card from his pocket lined with rows of figures in his own cramped scrawl. When Giscard showed interest, McNamara hitched his chair closer to Giscard's. As they talked further, McNamara kept yanking his chair across the rich Aubusson rug until the two chairs were askew, next to each other, and the two men's faces were side by side, peering at the card of numbers as though nothing else in the world mattered.[6]

In the overall scheme, everyone should win. He would direct resources — Bank loans and IDA credits — for projects expected to bring rates of return of 10 percent or more, which was the official cutoff point for approval of any project by the board. A government that borrowed from the Bank in 1977, for example, paid around 8.5 percent fixed interest on its loans;[7] if the project earned 10 percent or more, the loans were creating net real growth of at least 1.5 percent. Some projects achieved rates of return of 15 or 20 percent or even higher, such as when a dam opened a new region for farming or when farmers, receiving new seeds and technical advice, could sell their new crops for many times what they earned for their old ones. An IDA credit lent to a country at zero interest for a project that earned 10 percent or more created a wider margin of growth.

Borrowing governments owed the money back even if the project failed to generate the projected rate of return. These governments were committed another way, for the Bank lent only when there was cofinancing for a project from other sources: other aid agencies, private concerns, or the borrowing government itself. A third factor protected the Bank — its founders required that the net value of outstanding loans could never exceed the amount of paid-in capital and retained earnings, whereas commercial banks normally lend twenty times their capital. Furthermore, the Bank's paid-in capital was only one tenth of what it could "call" from member governments in an emergency. Thus the backing for McNamara's lending program was strong indeed.

From this bastion of fiscal prudence, McNamara could seed investments around the world. Viewed from one perspective, the

Bank's program added to the borrowing governments' debt; viewed from another, it was the single most organized way a borrowing state could assure real economic growth.

McNamara demonstrated his attraction to power, among other things, on his flying trips. He set great store by one-on-one meetings with each nation's leader. After this contact, says an aide, "the country, to his mind, is the prime minister or the president." He first had met Indira Gandhi when he and Margy went to India in 1968, on the trip when he was burned in effigy in Calcutta. The daughter of Jawaharlal Nehru was still shy, still filling her father's shoes. But she knew her silence kept others on edge and used it skillfully. Her aides were astonished, therefore, when she opened up to McNamara, talking and smiling, the two of them getting along, says one Indian hand, "like a pair of old shoes."[8]

McNamara appeared to find another soul mate, in Tanzania, the stunning East African nation famous for its Serengeti Plain and snow-capped Mount Kilimanjaro. McNamara expected a difficult first session with Tanzania's president, Julius Nyerere, in Dar es Salaam, the capital on the Indian Ocean.

Nyerere and his officials arrayed themselves on one side of a long table; McNamara and his group sat on the other. "The feeling was ice," according to Leif Christoffersen, McNamara's personal assistant.[9] The Tanzanians were expecting McNamara, the terrifying American war minister, to "lash out" at them over the Tan Zam railway project, which they had built with Chinese help and which had been a sore point with George Woods.

As they started, Nyerere smiled politely at his visitor. Nyerere had led the country since it gained independence in 1961 as Tanganyika. He was one of the most engaging men in the world. But tension was high; his smile did not defuse it.

McNamara asked to say a few words before they started. He said: I see my role as looking into the future and assessing the development needs of Tanzania. Now that the railroad is under way, what is the next priority? Is it the port? At this the ice broke; the Tanzanians were amazed that McNamara was willing to erase the past and that he would even ask what they wanted.

The meeting gained momentum as the two leaders discovered each other's better side. McNamara had been unprepared for this gentle man with a philosophic turn of mind who quoted Shakespeare. Nyerere, for his part, was surprised to find how accessible McNamara was. At the end, the two principals rose, and their staffs stood back to let them walk out together. As they moved through the doorway Nyerere smiled at McNamara; the smooth lines of his handsome brown face made the smile electric. The leader of Africa's most promising socialist country took McNamara's arm as they walked out, as if to say, This could be the beginning of a beautiful friendship.

In the early 1970s, Tanzania was the darling of many liberal donor nations, such as Sweden and the Netherlands. Unlike other postcolonial African leaders, Nyerere lived simply and spurned wealth; he wanted his people to have education, health, and greater equity by gathering in small communal towns called *ujama'a*. Politically, he wanted Tanzania — and Africa — to be open to east and west. Tanzania, created in 1964 by the union of Tanganyika with the island of Zanzibar, possessed abundant natural resources, including good soil and a strong export crop of sisal. Its per capita income of $267 was high for Africa at that time. Tanzania seemed promising to McNamara and many others.

But Nyerere turned out to be not as enlightened toward his people as he seemed; he would teach McNamara that creating economic growth took more than resource input, throughput, targets, and appraisals. Many years later, when a city resident failed to show up for an appointment with an aid official in Dar es Salaam, as the capital was crumbling and Tanzania, shaped by Nyerere, was crippled with poverty and debt, someone remarked that the missed appointment had been a TP — a Tanzanian Promise, or a promise not kept.[10]

The Bank staff rushed during those heady, idealistic years to find antipoverty projects — which were termed "rural development" projects — to carry out McNamara's Nairobi program. The Bank's traditional loans for such undertakings as power plants, dams, and port construction also grew, constituting 60 percent of all loans in the 1970s. But "rural development" was the buzz word and goal of the new, younger staff, many from the Third World, who had been lured to Washington by McNamara's call. They bustled up and down the corridors of a new, modern office building next to the old headquarters at 1818 H Street and flew "on mission" to borrowing nations. "Mission" was an apt term, for the Bank's new pose was messianic. "In the old Bank, we were rewarded for finding reasons not to lend," says one of the old-timers. "Under McNamara, we were rewarded for finding reasons to go ahead."[11]

A likely target was Brazil's Nordeste, or Northeast, a region of parched soils and bare coast that forms the horn of Brazil protruding into the windy mid-Atlantic. Once, the coast had been green with brazilwood trees. The Portuguese, who arrived in South America in the sixteenth century, cropped these for export while importing Africans as slaves to labor on big sugar plantations. Shifts in the sugar trade and the discovery of gold and better land to the south drew later colonists to what became São Paulo and Rio de Janeiro. As southern Brazil grew over the next three hundred years, the bleak Nordeste sank into obscurity, and generations of descendants of African and Indian slaves scraped out an existence amid dust storms and heat so stifling that it regularly killed their cattle.[12]

McNamara visited the Nordeste on his first trip to Brazil, in October 1968. Brazil by then had a large, diversified economy: ranches, mines, steel mills, even an auto industry. It had been growing overall at 8 percent a year and was expected to take off economically, as South Korea was doing.

Brazil was a huge, complex country; inland from its extended coast rose the dark curtain of the Amazon rain forest billowing across most of a continent. A group of generals who took over in 1964 had supplanted Brazil's democratic institutions and made economic choices that widened the gap between rich and poor. On his first visit there, McNamara was struck by the disparity in incomes between the elites of São Paulo and Rio, with their new office towers and luxury hotels and tony beaches, and the pathetic inhabitants of the Nordeste, which formed the biggest concentration of poverty in Latin America.

The Bank's plans to lend for projects in Brazil's Nordeste were well along by late 1973. An economic study of the region was undertaken, but it was typical of McNamara's pressure to get moving that he didn't wait for this study to be finished to sign the first of ten project loans.[13] These projects were supposed to provide feeder roads, rural electrification, crop storage, research, extension, credit for farmers, health services, and cleaner water. Legal obstacles, such as the fact that many small farmers there lacked titles to their plots, would be dealt with later. The Brazilian authorities seemed enthusiastic.

In Tanzania, once McNamara sensed Nyerere's commitment to "equity" — that is, improving the incomes of the rural people — similar rural development projects were arranged. The East African savanna, laced with forests and fed by warm, heavy rains, seemed to offer many good sites for the new communal villages Nyerere was creating. McNamara's drive to install packages of uplifting services in the countryside — health care facilities, schools, wells, farming advice — fit Nyerere's plans like a glove.

McNamara said in his 1974 speech to the Board of Governors, for example, that the Bank had just voted a $10 million IDA credit for "one of the poorest regions in Tanzania" to "enhance the productivity, incomes, and living standards of some 250,000 people — roughly half the entire rural population of the area" in "135 newly established villages" in the Kigoma region. Their aim was "doubling the per capita incomes of the villagers over a twelve-year period."[14]

He also helped expand a Mexican government project aimed at the rural poor: PIDER, as it was called, would "integrate" several rural development needs at once by providing "labor-intensive feeder-road construction, water and soil conservation projects, and support services for . . . Mexican land reform," as well as "rural schools, water supply, health facilities and electrification." He admitted the Mexican adventure was "the most complex program" the Bank had ever been associated with. But while "the risks of failure are greater in rural development, for the first time we are beginning to see substantial income and employment benefits within the reach of very large numbers of the rural poor." Agriculture lending alone would bring "economic returns in excess of 15 percent," he said confidently.

Like Tanzania, Malawi was one of southern Africa's poorest countries. Malawi had been part of the former British colony of Rhodesia; it is landlocked and rises west of one of southern Africa's major lakes, Nyasa. Malawi's Lilongwe region was the site of an earlier Bank-supported project aimed at the poor, which seemed successful enough to be a model for rural development projects elsewhere. The Lilongwe project was expanded and similar integrated projects started in additional areas. Other aid groups added funds, until one fourth of Malawi's land area was being helped by foreign aid.[15]

The Bank underwrote a Green Revolution experiment to bring irrigated rice farming to Lake Alaotra, one of the few wetlands regions left on the island nation of Madagascar.[16] In Kenya the Bank supported tea and coffee farms; it financed the production of cotton, an important cash crop, in Cameroon, Nigeria, and elsewhere in West Africa.

In the early and mid-1970s, Asia was the greatest challenge. South Asia contained half of the world's absolute poor. India, with 550 million people, was the region's largest nation and one of the poorest. "India *was* development," says a Bank staffer without irony or exaggeration.

It was fortunate that McNamara had hit it off with Mrs. Gandhi, because India had experienced regular disasters from monsoons and famines; it was also moving toward a tie to Moscow. The Bank could play a pivotal role in improving India's condition and possibly slow its slide into communism. Thus Mrs. Gandhi, when she met McNamara, held some cards, too.

But most of India's land area seemed unable to support its huge population.[17] All but 15 percent of its arable land was already farmed, and it imported 10 million to 12 million tons of foodstuffs annually. Cattle and buffalo were widespread sources of milk and protein, but the nation's stock of 54 million cows and 26 million buffalo met less than half the milk requirements of the nation. Geography shaped the destiny of India's people. The alluvial soils of the continent-sized peninsula did not retain water from the monsoons, so the small farmer's lot was either drought or devastating rains. India's political traditions were split between the heavy-handed state socialism of Nehru and the simple village ethos of Mohandas Gandhi. It was not clear whether or how, technically and politically, India's growth could be raised above the depressing 2 percent a year it had averaged since independence, in 1947.

By the late 1960s, however, many in India's federal government and society had concluded that it could no longer afford to focus exclusively on building heavy industry, as Nehru had stressed. Thus, India's fourth five-year-plan, for 1969–74, focused on rural employment and aid to small farmers. The fifth plan continued the new emphasis. When McNamara met her, Mrs. Gandhi was considering help for the rural poor for political reasons — to defuse the growing discontent in the lower strata of the nation. She also knew that the "benefits" of past industrial investment had not trickled down; something else had to be tried.

McNamara made a commitment to Mrs. Gandhi: He would *manage* the flow of IDA credits from Washington to Delhi, so that there would be a steady flow of funds to this largest of IDA borrowers, even when Congress balked during the periodic fights to refinance IDA.[18]

The Green Revolution had already succeeded in India, with large farmers in Haryana and the Punjab. Rainfall was low in these imposing, tiered hills, slung between the Indus River system of West Pakistan on the west and the Himalayas on the east. But the ground held moisture well; the large irrigation works built cooperatively by the governments, AID, and the Bank in the 1960s had transformed the landscape into a kaleidoscope of green.[19] Many of the region's farmers were Sikhs, India's most energetic and mercantile group, who produced miraculous yields and profited handsomely. McNamara arrived on the scene eager to spread the benefits of irrigated agriculture both geographically and to the poorer farmers, at a time when this need was recognized at the federal and local levels there.

The timeless picture of India's countryside — the lone farmer with his plow and buffalo — began to change in the 1970s, partly due to the Bank's emphasis on rural development. Millions more farmers had some form of irrigation and planted the shorter, broader miracle rice strains. By decade's end the average Indian's cow was more likely to be one of the new breed, which gave seven hundred gallons of milk a year instead of the fifty gallons ordinary cows gave. New breeds of buffalo yielded similar dairy gains. Life expectancy increased with improved nutrition: By the late 1970s the average Indian could expect to live to age fifty, whereas in the 1950s the average Indian lived to age thirty-two. The common apocalypse of mass famine faded.[20]

Agriculture inched forward in West Pakistan, whose elite had a long history of involvement in development issues, if no particular interest in social equity. By the end of the 1970s, more than half of Pakistan's rice farms were using miracle strains. The prime minister, pressured from outside, adopted a national strategy to grow high-yielding wheat, which was adopted widely as well. However, says Joseph C. Wheeler, the head of the AID mission in Pakistan at the time, the government was still flying by the "seat of its pants" in health care, education and population control.[21]

During the war in which Bangladesh broke off from West Pakistan, McNamara went on lending to India, despite pressure from the U.S. Treasury to halt such loans since the American government favored Pakistan. In 1971 the war gave birth to Bangladesh, a new nation that was crowded, often devastated by cyclones, and had a strong Communist movement. IDA lent for wells for small farmers and aid to cotton growers, and it advanced the first general-purpose, nonproject loans, to help the government pay its rising oil debts after 1973. McNamara could try to slow Bangladesh's slide into deeper poverty; he could not reverse it.

In Indonesia, McNamara's emissary Bernard Bell had had much leverage with the regime of President Suharto in 1968, during its early days, when Suharto needed the Bank's Good Housekeeping seal of approval to win respectability in the outside world. Indonesia's external debt then stood at $2.1 billion, or 20 percent of its gross domestic product; with over 200 million people, it was one of the world's poorest nations. Bell's staff in Jakarta worked to set up new national institutions; IDA credits helped to reclaim the old coconut and palm oil plantations, which were the largest tree estates in the tropics. The Bank also actively supported the spread of irrigated rice farming. Here, too, the specter of famines faded.

Suharto gets the credit for Indonesia's early progress, but, notes a Bank report, "in the absence of IDA assistance . . . it is hard to see how such development efforts would have progressed as rapidly as they did."[22] Indonesia passed a major test of economic capability after the 1973 oil-price rise, when it became one of the few very poor nations able to win contracts from oil companies to explore and develop offshore oil and gas deposits.

Through the decade, however, the Bank staff was under pressure to find more projects in Indonesia to meet McNamara's pressure to expand loan volume and the numbers of beneficiaries helped. By 1980, the Bank and IDA would have sunk $3.9 billion into ninety-six projects in Indonesia in a mere twelve years. One of the more common area development projects it lent for was "transmigration" — so people from overcrowded islands could "benefit" from clearing and farming in outlying islands. McNamara knew that Suharto's resettlement program was politically inspired and entailed some brutality, but the role McNamara had carved out of a partnership, of making the Bank "of" the Third World — and his everlasting zest for action — propelled him to buy in to the program. To influence it, he hoped.[23]

On his travels, McNamara paced through Third World cities and their slums. These were growing in a pattern peculiar to the late twentieth century. Marginally better conditions in the countryside allowed more people to leave rural areas and seek new lives in the

city. The exodus created acres and acres of shantytowns on the out-
skirts of urban centers, made of cardboard and tin sheets. They were
packed with people having a shade more schooling and slightly fewer
children than their rural cousins, but the new urban settlers were
beyond the reach of city services and had no hope of finding jobs.
"Roughly 200 million" of the absolute poor lived in cities, McNamara said in a major speech on urban issues in 1975. By the year 2000,
"three out of every four Latins will live in a city," as would "one out
of every three Africans and Asians."[24]

McNamara proposed to attack the "pathology of poverty" in these
cities with packages of integrated programs to create jobs among
small employers, extend credit, and support small manufacturers of
export goods. Water and sewer systems, roads, and housing would
form the bricks and mortar. So the Bank plunged into Jakarta; Mexico City; Lima, Peru; and elsewhere, but it found that people destroyed the houses built for them and that local authorities and
national leaders feared that helping their urban masses would foment
political unrest. A year after McNamara launched his urban campaign, the Bank was embroiled in the Philippines in a controversy
over who would represent the beneficiaries of a Bank-sponsored
project in the Tondo area of Manila.[25] The contending groups were
a grass-roots organization that claimed to represent the people but
that was accused by strongman Ferdinand Marcos of being pro-
Communist, and Marcos's handpicked agents, known locally as Marcos's "eyes and ears." Aid became a political pawn, and by decade's
end the Bank had done little of substance there.

The Bank staff, meanwhile, especially the middle ranks, was increasingly tense at having to devise ever-more projects to meet the higher
lending goals that McNamara stipulated for his mass-production
lending machine. And once McNamara's desired doubling in the
Bank's capital was approved — finally, in 1979 — he would require
the staff to double the volume of lending. Where, they wondered,
would the additional projects be found? How to staff them, in Washington and in the poor countries themselves? How to be sure of
getting adequate rates of return?

McNamara's slick new institution, whose staff had grown to four
thousand, was becoming a bureaucracy; it now had country departments, a new rural development division, a powerful economics
group, and, of course, the program budget boys who rode herd on

the numbers. As problems in the new rural and urban projects became known, headquarters set up more specialized offices; coordination was to take place in the field.[26]

The old Bank, with its handcrafted approach to project lending — do one project at a time and risk little — submerged itself in this new bureaucracy. But the values and culture of the old Bank persisted, such as the chronic anxiety about getting the exactly predicted rate of return from projects, and the obsession with quantitative respectability. The old hands, now spread out in the bigger organization, complained of the rush to meet timetables and deadlines, and of the guesswork that went into figures flowing up to McNamara and the board. The clubby spirit of the old Bank — which also made it patronizing toward the borrowing nations — was traded for the clout of the new lending machine. What McNamara's Bank gained in raw financial power was being lost in inner integrity, they griped. Thus their refrain that McNamara was ruining the Bank.[27]

Bank employees noticed something odd about their boss. The Bank was a small enough place, with internal dining rooms and its own bookstore, so that everyone saw each other often enough. But they never saw McNamara, whose idealism had lured them there and who defined their careers.

In fact, every morning at eight he entered and ran up eleven flights of stairs to his office. At seven in the evening he would trot down the stairs again. Anyone who felt lucky to encounter him in the stairwell was mistaken — he did not stop to chat. They never saw him in the cafeteria, or in the executive dining room, since he lunched in his own dining room, on the top floor. "He always lunched in his own dining room because he didn't want to be seen," wrote William Clark in his diary.

A remarkable rumor circulated, which was hard to check out politely: The man in the elevator hidden behind a newspaper *was* McNamara. This man stood in the back with the paper completely unfolded and held close to his face. There was no doubt that McNamara was physically in the Bank each day; he signed directives and barked on the telephone. Yet he avoided contact with the employees he trusted to carry out his work. His conduct reminded one of his protégés of the saying:

"He loves humanity more than he loves human beings."[28]

* * *

There was a sequel to the elevator puzzle. After McNamara had headed the Bank for a number of years, people began complaining about his indifference. Joan Braden, a friend of his and Margy's who was a guest in his private dining room in the late 1970s, brought it up with him one day, relaying complaints she had heard through a woman who worked at the Bank.

McNamara turned to her, almost angry. A muscle tightened in his cheek. He said: "Look, I can do one of two things. I can either run the Bank as an international institution or know the names of all these people's wives and children. I am going to do the former." End of conversation.[29]

Margy had already stepped in. She formed an organization of the spouses of Bank employees, who were mostly wives. These were women of many different nationalities, some new to America, for whom Margy was a magnet in her own right. She would come to a meeting, plop down in a chair, kick off her shoes, and be informal and sympathetic. Her efforts with the Bank wives, putting them to work on good causes, were highly constructive. Yet her husband's weakness as a manager was to offload the problem of institutional morale onto his wife.

"He never talked with us," remarks one of the Bank's experts on Brazil who traveled with McNamara to Latin America many times.[30] McNamara kept staff members busy feeding him information and work; they rushed to keep up with him. He flew economy-class and preferred a front-row seat, where he slept, worked, or talked with Margy or William Clark. When the plane landed for stopovers, he sped out the door ahead of everyone and vanished into the airport. Until, that is, the exact moment the plane was due to take off again, when he reappeared miraculously and dashed back to his seat.

Thus he could travel with knowledgeable people for days and not know them. An exception was the last evening of the trip, when he would take them all to dinner, become informal, and even ask about their families. But, this staffer noticed, he was informal only on the last night of the journey, when he knew he wouldn't see them at close range again soon.

McNamara had built an ideology of impersonality, rooted in his own discomfort around people and his wish to be above ordinary folk, to be, literally, *extra*ordinary. For him to ask about wives and children, to share the average experiences of life with subordinates, would be to fall back into the ordinariness from which he had yanked

himself up in Piedmont, at Berkeley and Harvard. His rejection of
emotionalism was not only a fear of his own emotions; it was a
deep-seated desire not to show the foibles ordinary people share.

This was a great flaw in McNamara the supermanager. He said in
the 1967 Millsaps speech that "management is the most creative of the
arts, for its medium is human talent itself." But in his drive to exploit
his uniqueness to the utmost, he denied the human qualities of those
far below.

His pattern was to develop brilliantly the talents of a few people
around him. No one can deny that McNamara evoked some tremendous performances at the Bank — just as at Defense he had inspired
a trusted few to do remarkable things. But in his compulsion to be
extraordinary, McNamara disdained those he found average, including many at middle and lower levels. Like the managers of the U.S.
auto industry at the time, McNamara ignored the workers on the
line, whom he and his system treated as cogs in his great machine.
And like his fellow leaders in the auto industry, McNamara hurt
himself, and hindered his fight against poverty, by not communicating more with subordinates. Thus, the system and the man almost
guaranteed he would rush on, blind and alone, and fall short of the
accomplishments he would claim.

William Clark alluded to the problem in a rare diary entry in
which he confessed to sometimes being demoralized by McNamara's
impersonality. Clark wrote:

> Bob always believed that people were dedicated to development and
> so would work for it with [his] sort of devotion. Part true: they were
> often dedicated in front line but those further back were more con-
> scious of the struggle for career [and felt] driven. Explanation in the
> Bank was very weak. There were rules and plans but they usually
> emerged from Mount Olympus, which was cloud covered.[31]

There was a contradiction, it seemed, between McNamara's goals
of combating poverty in myriad social systems throughout the world
and the management system he used to fight this war. Says Barbara
Ward's colleague David Runnalls, "There was a real question as to
whether, given what McNamara wanted to do in the poverty field,
the Bank was the best institution to carry it out." India's S. Guhan
notes that antipoverty lendings totaled about half the dollar amounts
of traditional loans — for dams and power plants, for example — yet
were "three to four times more demanding" in terms of staff time and

effort.[32] It was difficult for the Bank staff to administer loans for social projects from Washington and assure that they met their expected rates of return. Staff also had to see to it that funds were not misused and that local national agencies carried out these intricate plans with McNamarian vigor.

Staff members worried that the borrowing nations could not administer more projects than were already in the pipeline and that, as their oil debts grew, there would be problems of repayment. In other words, the limits of the poor nations' "absorptive capacity" would soon be reached. When these doubts were raised, McNamara countered with his own quantitative fixation: "Absorptive capacity was not the issue," he said, because project lending produced real economic growth.

Roads became popular, for example, because the Bank staff could claim that maintaining a road helped the landless who lived nearby. Area development — such as the cutting and clearing under way in Indonesia — also fit the rubric of economic growth, since people without land would now produce crops. However, the rush to fund farmers in Brazil's Nordeste meant that Bank-funded credits went to those who already had title to land. These tended to be owners of larger farms, and not, by a long shot, the poorest farmers. The staff expedited the extension of loans and the disbursal of funds; "new style" projects went forward without delays — and without much adaptation to local constraints.[33]

Meanwhile McNamara's runners kept counting relative and absolute poor, to give him some quantitative sense of whether he was winning his war.

"You can see Vietnam," said a staffer interviewed in 1975 about McNamara. "All that dedication and drive, that hope and assurance that you can deal with a problem by laying it out logically. . . . The difference is that now it's pointed in the right direction," he said.[34]

He maintained tight financial control in the ironfisted manner he learned from Lewis Crusoe, his mentor at Ford in the late 1940s. Crusoe had uttered the motto of cost-conscious mass production when he said, "Around here, we'll kill for a nickel." At the Bank, McNamara sought to lower the unit cost per beneficiary or beneficiary family of poor people, so more could be uplifted for a given cost. Says a program budget officer, "If you told [McNamara] that local constraints would cost fifty dollars more per family, at that point he'd become the most stubborn manager you could have encountered."[35]

Bank employees supplied him with figures, even when they knew they were shaky at best. One sign of the fear that the man atop Olympus inspired was the story — told years later, still with resentment — of the time McNamara made someone return from vacation to dig up one figure.

B. S. Braithwaite captured the mood in a "Hymn to the President":

> *O President — to us below*
> *Look down and put us in the know*
> *Teach us to study and comply*
> *With memoranda till we die.*
>
> *And if the tempter seeks to give*
> *Us feelings of initiative*
> *Or if alone we go too far*
> *Chastise us with a circular.*
>
> *Through missions, meetings, flights, and storms*
> *Give us the strength to fill up forms*
> *Thus may your staff their whole life through*
> *Report the way you want them to.*[36]

Says S. Shahid Husain: "Without knowing it, he manufactured data. If there was a gap in the numbers, he would ask the staff to fill it, and others made it up for him. The practice was not widespread, but it was habitual." Thus the system and the man created ignorance of problems in the field, where reality was playing out. The system was customized to the man, and the man was the system.

The system helped the man to become more certain, rather than less. A Bank official told Joseph Lelyveld of the *New York Times* in 1975, "The more I deal with poverty, the more distressed I feel, the more unsure. With McNamara, it's exactly the reverse."[37]

Meanwhile, the poor were getting poorer. As McNamara's reign moved toward the ten-year mark in 1977–78, he found himself in a very different position from that reflected by the glowing predictions he made in his first years.

On the one hand, the Bank was active in more than a hundred

developing countries; his loans and credits flowed out precisely by continent, region, and type of project. Repayments flowed back without defaults. The AAA rating that was so key to the Bank's success was untarnished. Moreover, the Bank was powerful in a way that the old Bank could never have been. It had become the foremost actor on the world development scene. It had a commanding position for centralized data collection, and it published research on development questions. Beginning in 1978, McNamara also launched an annual stocktaking, the *World Development Report,* used by other agencies and scholars. Pakistan's Javed Burki says in admiration: "McNamara made aid credible."[38]

However, the pivotal position McNamara hoped he and the Bank would occupy at the fulcrum between the First and Third worlds eluded him. So did his goal of ending absolute poverty in one generation, that is, seventy years. Even the most optimistic assumptions projected the numbers of absolute poor, which in 1975 were counted at 770 million, to decrease only to 600 million by the year 2000.

The world economy had changed, sidelining him. In his first years, the Bank disbursed $1 billion a year in loans and credits, or roughly one sixth of the $6.2 billion external debt increase of developing nations. But with the piling up of petrodollars in Western banks after 1973, the balance of financial power shifted to the private banks. These were proffering several of McNamara's Third World clients commercial loans at better interest rates and with very few conditions — albeit with maturity periods often as short as five years. By 1978 it disbursed $2.8 billion in new loans, yet the Third World borrowed $58 billion from other sources that same year. "If the Brazilian government didn't like what McNamara told it to do, it just borrowed the money commercially at better rates and with no strings attached," says John Lewis of Princeton University and the Overseas Development Council.[39]

A new world economy was emerging, one very different from that envisioned by McNamara at Nairobi. Growth was slowing overall in the First and Third worlds as money went to pay OPEC for oil instead of being productively invested, as it had been in the halcyon 1960s. But even the increases in official and commercial lending would allow middle-income developing nations to grow 3.4 percent per year over the next decade, while the poorer developing nations would grow at 2 percent or less. However, if the First World changed the terms of trade for Third World exports, it could at any moment quash even that marginal growth. Agriculture grew at only 1.5 percent a year — a far cry from the 5 percent per year McNamara had set as his planetary goal at Nairobi.[40]

There were good signs: Population growth had slowed a little, and incomes had improved in fourteen poor nations, allowing them to graduate from poorest-country status and qualify for Bank loans, rather than IDA credits. But conditions were only getting worse in places like Tanzania and Bangladesh; the markets for their few exports were shrinking. McNamara's plan for substantially lowering poverty depended on overall economic growth to succeed, as in the 1960s: instead, the poorest countries faced disaster.

Moreover, many regimes were following ruinous economic policies at home. For example, many still discriminated against poor farmers by holding down prices they could charge for foodstuffs, in order to keep urban food prices down and their regimes popular. Thus farmers, even with bank aid and new seed varieties, had little incentive to grow more food. Africa's ability to feed itself was diminishing, in fact, despite infusions of aid.

In too many cases, regimes signed covenants in Bank loan documents, in which they promised to change certain policies, solely to please aid donors.[41] The tendency was to state good intentions when McNamara visited, and then not carry them out after he left. As countries grew poorer, altruism was in shorter supply; leaders were concerned with staying in power and staying in business — which were often the same thing.

McNamara was faced with a choice. He could enforce all the conditions that went with his loans but that might cause national leaders to tell him to go home, or he could be lenient and keep the projects going, and lend for other purposes, even inefficient industries, to shore up his clients' payments imbalances.

For years the Bank had advised Kenneth Kaunda, the paternalistic head of Zambia, to diversify away from copper. Copper was Zambia's only export, and a source of great wealth in boom times. But Kaunda never managed to set aside funds to serve as a cushion against the inevitable cycles of bust. When world copper prices plunged for good, in 1976, Zambia veered from wealth to bankruptcy; the Bank maintained its support, funding three agricultural projects that were unsuccessful. It even signed off on a "program loan" to help Kaunda through his fiscal crisis. McNamara did not pull the plug.[42]

The dangers of direct Bank cutoffs were shown in Ethiopia after

1974, when a coup led by military officers overthrew the emperor and resulted in the redistribution of land. The Bank had warned for years that land reform was essential to improving the lot of ordinary farmers, so initially Bank lending to Ethiopia doubled. Then the new regime refused to compensate the owners whose property had been seized. Since Bank rules prevented lending to regimes that nationalized property without compensation, the Bank cut its aid.[43] This heavy-handed pressure may have hurt moderates: Ethiopia then suffered dictatorship and mass starvation.

Even McNamara's conversation mate Indira Gandhi cracked down. Not only did she declare a state of emergency in 1975, but also, apparently at the instigation of her son Sanjay, her government ordered a forced vasectomy campaign. Men were yanked off buses at random and selected for operations — a brutal perversion of the principles of mass education and expanded personal choice, which McNamara supported. The campaign stirred worldwide publicity and set back the cause of population planning internationally. Here, too, McNamara went on lending.[44]

Instead of walking away from the game because Third World leaders would not play as he wanted, McNamara chose to stay and keep dealing. As at so many other junctures in his life, he was more concerned with sins of omission than commission. He believed so strongly that official aid, properly managed, would induce economic growth that he found it more important to try and fail than not to try at all.

One rationalization he offered for pressing on with loans to difficult regimes was the doctrine put forward by the Bank's economist Hollis Chenery since 1974, that the poor could gain a larger share of the national wealth without political and social upheaval or without seriously depriving local elites.[45] McNamara was hardly alone in such rationales; it was a strange paradox of the entire aid community in the 1970s that liberally inclined donors — such as the Swedes and Norwegians — aided some brutal regimes, claiming that things would be worse for the poor without their benign outside influence.

McNamara informed the Board of Governors in 1978 that if the Bank curtailed its program, developing countries would face the "critical dilemma" either "to reduce their growth rates" or depend further on "potentially volatile private capital flows." Ergo, more official aid was needed.

"It is sometimes argued that the costs will simply be too high; that the world just cannot afford it," he told the governors. "But the truth is really the other way around. What the world cannot afford is procrastination and delay, while dangerous social pressures build."[46]

When the newspaper *Europa* asked him in 1975 why he was pressing on in light of continued high oil prices, inflation, and rising protectionism, McNamara cited "civilized societies' acceptance," for hundreds of years, "that the strong shall help the weak." He added, "If one doesn't wish to accept the moral foundation for aid, one can point to national self-interest, because interdependency is more than a word; it's a condition of life." McNamara was echoing Henry Luce's call to the American Century, in which he argued that America had a moral obligation as "a good samaritan" to feed the world's hungry and buy its goods.

McNamara told *Europa* that some in America said "the world is a lifeboat with a capacity of 100, [and] there are 125 people in it, and if anyone is to survive, 25 must be sacrificed. I totally disagree with that."[47]

Where McNamara's plan succeeded, it did so magnificently. The most striking trend of the seventies was the growth in agriculture, especially in South and East Asia. Overall, Bank lending for agriculture earned rates of return of 14.2 percent. McNamara had set a goal of 5 percent agricultural growth per year. Production in East Asia — South Korea, Taiwan, Indonesia, and other nations — grew by 6.5 percent in 1978. Agriculture in South Asia, including India and Pakistan, grew by a record 8.4 percent in 1977. More typical increases were 4 percent, and India achieved an average of only 2.2 percent for the decade.[48]

But the Bank's focus on multiplying small farmer incomes proved worthwhile, on the whole. Many farmers saw their incomes jump six times, benefited by the match between timely research that produced new crop varieties and the spread of such results. There was some success in Latin America, too, although agriculture grew there at just 2 to 3 percent.

Africa was different. Droughts racked the sub-Saharan region in the early part of the decade, and war and famines in the Sudan and Ethiopia followed. Gradually it became clear that foreign-aided attempts at irrigated farming had backfired; irrigation could salt up local water supplies and force farmers to move on, deforest more land, and thus enlarge the desert. Much foreign aid to Africa in the

1970s proved misdirected: wells built with the intent of making no-
mads more stationary only caused overgrazing and increased desert-
ification. And the Bank was not immune to funding white elephant
projects — demanded by regimes to employ state workers or "develop" the local capital.[49]

McNamara had been too optimistic in his faith that the benefits of
the Green Revolution would be replicable in Africa. Few of the
miracle wheat or rice varieties would grow in that dry climate, and
the new technology had not improved production of sorghum and
millet, Africa's principal food crops. Too many regimes refused to
give farmers an incentive to grow more by raising prices for their
food crops. Thus, overall sub-Saharan agriculture, which grew by a
scrawny 1.7 percent in the early 1960s, dropped to 0.1 percent growth
in 1976. Although it recovered somewhat, rising to 1.6 percent in
1977 and to 2.9 percent in 1978, these rates of production were
nonetheless far below those for other regions.[50] African agriculture
was a different problem, and the Bank and other donors had been too
hasty in assuming that what worked in Asia would work there. "Typically the packages [of seeds and fertilizer] had not been tested in the
project's environment," said a later evaluation report by the Bank.[51]

Although the numbers looked good for selected projects, many could
see by the late 1970s that parts of McNamara's programs were not
working. The irrigated rice project in Lake Alaotra, on Madagascar,
was one of the few acknowledged failures. Farmers in Brazil's Nordeste were resisting using the new seed and fertilizer packages that
development officials presumed would work; the Bank often proposed growing one new crop instead of a safe mix of traditional ones.
And since few of the poor had land titles, the "benefits" of aid were
corraled by those in the local hierarchy who were already better off.

In Tanzania, reports came back that the gentle Nyerere was having
rural people moved into the new *ujama'a* at gunpoint and that many
new communal villages were not working out.[52] Nyerere demanded
that his ever-generous aid donors prop up inefficient state agencies
and industries; the Tanzanian markets board used the talents of ten
thousand government employees to go on setting thoroughly inequitable prices. As Nyerere's balance of payments got worse and his
position less secure, he resisted painful but needed national reforms.
Many of the *ujama'a* were barren, and their inhabitants, who once
farmed their own little plots with pride, became apathetic; instead of

being enlightened by African socialism, the system was crushing them.

By 1977 and 1978, the pattern was clear. McNamara's management scheme had forced the Bank to grow and meet physical targets: money lent, miles of roads repaired, irrigation works completed, and so on. Meanwhile, local social and political factors — which were critical to success in difficult environments like sub-Saharan Africa or the Brazilian Nordeste — were bypassed. Given McNamara's personality, word of these problems had trouble reaching the top.

McNamara's antipoverty loans to India, for example, did well due to features of the reporting system. There was considerable confusion about what constituted "new style" loans to aid the poor. McNamara had first used the term "rural development"; a January 1975 Bank policy paper on the new approach referred to "integrated rural" development; a variant on these was "area development" projects. But another definition said a project was "new style" if more than 50 percent of those who benefited were below the Bank's poverty line.[53] Since most Indian irrigation works were designed to aid smallholders, the staff could count most agricultural projects in India as antipoverty loans. And since irrigation projects were a subject of great expertise in the Bank, they often showed good rates of return.

India's success in the 1970s in spreading local health and education benefits was due to a cultural advantage it had over most of sub-Saharan Africa. Despite the cumbersome federal structure bequeathed by Nehru, India's villages enjoyed active local governance, a legacy of Mohandas Gandhi and democracy. The Bank could work with these local groups and could also arrange with many nongovernment groups to deliver services. So whereas McNamara tossed integrated packages of aid into an organizational void in the countryside in Tanzania, the Indian system of Panchayati Raj — government by village councils of five — was able to administer his funds.

McNamara had been too ambitious; overcomplexity dogged the entire rural development program. Many staff believed that, to qualify, projects had to integrate social services and agricultural extension to a given group of beneficiaries. Even in the United States, government agencies do not deliver integrated packages of services and agricultural aid to the poor — yet McNamara presumed that in the hinterlands of three continents, these could be dropped into place.

A main source of anxiety to the Bank staff was where to find people to run these projects who were powerful enough locally to make them succeed. It could employ experts, and outsiders, or the few indigenous college graduates in a place like Kenya, for example. But marshaling a country's scant "human resources" to make a Bank project work meant depriving them of the chance to work on their country's other urgent problems.[54] This worry among Bank employees only grew as McNamara pressed from 1976 on to double the Bank's capital so they could loan even more; staff had to make projects larger, to soak up more funds, or stack more projects on ones just started. Area development projects were another solution; the average size of these loans grew four times during the seventies.[55]

As for the borrowing governments, as their oil debts grew they were too willing to accept more projects loans, whose funds they needed sorely. And as depression spread in Africa and Brazil, for instance, national leaders could point to enclaves of the poor being helped by foreign aid.

Thus the conditions were set for success in some places — and for failure in others. "The tendency towards complexity and large size" made rural development projects hard to manage, said a later Bank evaluation; "governments have frequently not been able to implement such complex projects effectively." Pilot projects were scaled up too fast to meet quantitative targets, and local authorities, such as the Mexican government, which ran several PIDER projects with Bank aid, "proceeded in the top-down manner to which they were accustomed." Said this same 1988 evaluation: "It is now clear that the Bank's PIDER projects were overly ambitious, given the lack of technical and institutional experience in Mexico in the 1970s."[56] Meanwhile, back in Washington, the Bank grew top-heavy itself.

McNamara's personality was reflected in these arrangements. His presumption that he could reproduce integrated projects on a mass scale; his faith in resource input as the catalyst for uplifting the poor; and, most of all, his impatience with local bureaucracy and eagerness to designate outside agencies to do the job stemmed from long-standing habit. He had had the heady experience of bypassing the military chain of command in Stat Control in World War II; he relied heavily on his Whiz Kids instead of regular military organizations at the Pentagon. His disdain for normal government showed at the Bank. There were long-term costs to this obsession with efficiency.

In Malawi, for example, the overall numbers looked good through the decade, for even in recession the market for tobacco stayed strong worldwide. Malawi's gross domestic product grew at 10 percent a year, while the economies of other black southern African states stagnated; model schools seemed successful. The agriculture experts — mainly foreigners working through an outside agency — tried to get small farmers to adapt new strains, but after years, the farmers continued to reject them. The Malawian government, thus uninvolved, had learned little about helping its own poor. Malawi's president for life, Hastings Kamuzu Banda, kept on skewing economic policy against poor farmers and in favor of big tea and tobacco growers. The rich farmers were regularly allowed to take land from the politically powerless farmers whom the Bank was trying to help. The Bank had not reformed Banda's government or done much to help its institutions mature; its work there had been "relatively expensive and management-intensive," said a later summary. And when the project ended and the foreigners departed, what would Malawi have left? It would still owe the money that funded the projects; it would still have its poor. The impact on agricultural production, said the same report, "has been negligible."[57]

Although the results of McNamara's program seemed mixed at the time, a decade later the Bank's Operations Evaluation Department came in with its verdict. The Bank's "non-rural development" projects from the 1970s "failed" at a rate of 11 percent — that is, 11 percent earned less than the 10 percent rate of return required for approval. But 37 percent of McNamara's rural development projects "failed" by earning less than 10 percent rates of return.[58] McNamara's critics say this figure illustrates that he failed overall. And the OED study candidly aired the problems of overcomplexity, too little staff time per project, too little attention to market pricing and to other policies of national regimes. But McNamara's defenders would say that having six of ten work is real success, given the untried nature of his experiment. Even the OED report noted that successes occurred within projects that "failed" according to the official rate-of-return yardstick.

The lessons were reaped for the next generation of rural projects in the 1980s.[59] Today the Bank supports simpler projects; it lets one local agency take the lead for field trials for maize, another for providing health clinics or schools. Project designs are less ambitious, since the Bank now recognizes the limited absorptive capacity of local governments. The board approves projects more on the basis of "sustainability" — what will be left when the project people leave — than on assured quantitative returns by the five-year-appraisal mark. And the economic upheavals of the 1980s have led all aid donors, including the Bank, to place more responsibility on borrowing regimes to manage their societies and help their poor.[60] This put less faith in Great Society approaches, which McNamara's were, to a large degree.

By the late 1970s, area development was becoming notorious to the growing environmental movement. Over the cries of environmentalists and charges of brutality in Suharto's regime, the Bank went on sponsoring transmigration in Indonesia, long after McNamara left.

In Brazil's wideswept Nordeste, the lack of results for small farmers frustrated many. The Bank's efforts strengthened local agencies — they should have, since the Bank was working through four layers of government. But the 1988 OED report would conclude that despite some small-scale successes where local authorities ran with the ball, "few of the poor of the region benefited from the Bank's programs."

The generals in sleek but crumbling Brasília — itself a symbol of the nation's failed ambition — had another solution. Instead of helping the poor where they were, why not move them into the Amazon to farm? The last of the ten projects from the McNamara era for the Nordeste was to settle the western Amazon in a place called Alto Turí.[61]

Meanwhile, in southern Brazil, the Bank made several loans to aid large livestock ranches. The trend of expansion of big ranches was displacing small farmers in the region. So the generals reasoned they should move these into the Amazon, too, to Rondônia province. In 1979 the Brazilian government asked McNamara whether the Bank would be interested in lending for a road through the rain forest to tame the wilderness.

Is management the "gate" by which change is diffused in developing countries? Or is politics the main agent of change, whereby land is redistributed to the poor, markets are freed, currencies are floated at international rates, and nations lurch painfully forward into modernism? Was McNamara wrapped in a technocratic dream when, on his travels, he saw the problems of trying to wring change from a bad economic environment, unscrupulous rulers, and slow-moving local government?

For most of the 1970s, the criticism came mainly from the Old

Guard, furious at how McNamara had supposedly ruined the Bank. By the later years, however, liberal activists charged that he was not really helping the poor anyway, but lending for cash crops like cotton and displacing the poor, clearing forests, expanding the desert, and cutting down tropical rain forest.

But consider the alternatives, said McNamara's supporters. Could the old Bank, with its leisurely perfectionism and afternoon-tea atmosphere, have been a real player in the brave new world of the seventies? It might have funded fewer antipoverty projects and taken longer with them, and learned a bit more on a very small scale. Not pretending to be a partner to every Third World country, the old Bank might have picked up its marbles and left when a nation's economic environment became hostile to its project goals. It might have had a 90 percent success rate on a few dozen rural development loans, instead of a 63 percent success rate on several hundred. McNamara would argue that the old Bank's sins would be those of omission: Millions of poor whom he reached would have gone unhelped.

Yet no one who visited Dar es Salaam in the 1980s and saw the clogged railroad, the nearly paralyzed port, the big state office buildings, and who had shopped for days for a light bulb or visited the pathetic, baked-earth *ujama'a*, would say the promise of aid of the early 1970s had been fulfilled. Again, reality fell short of McNamara's claims.

William Clark advised McNamara against seeking a third term. "Quit while you're ahead," he said, sensibly.[62] Denis Healey, who had been the minister of defense for the British Labor government in the 1960s, visited McNamara when the reappointment process was starting. Healey had a powerful personality and intellect, and was the only one of McNamara's counterparts in NATO's Nuclear Planning Group who sparred openly with him. Healey admired McNamara's insights on nuclear policy but thought he lacked political sense.

Healey happened to arrive in McNamara's big office before he did. With practiced one-upmanship, Healey walked over to McNamara's huge desk and sat in his chair to await him. His coat was off, but then, to improve the joke, Healey put his coat on and sat again in McNamara's chair, to look more imposing as the supposed president of the World Bank. McNamara entered and was relegated to the role of visitor.

I hear you're seeking a third term, said Healey. McNamara replied disingenuously that individuals and institutions needed periodic change.

Come on, Bob, said Healey. I know you'd love to be reappointed. McNamara then explained that with Democrat Jimmy Carter just elected to succeed Gerald Ford, he had a sympathetic administration at last. If he began a third term in 1978, he would have at least two more good years.

But Healey had a better political ear, which was how he had stayed near the forefront of British politics for so long. The winds of conservatism were rising in Britain. Healey rose to give McNamara back his chair and warned, "If you get yourself reappointed, you are building your own coffin."

On April 24, 1977, McNamara was formally named by the member governments to a third five-year term as president.

Within two years, Iranian oil stopped flowing to the West, and OPEC raised world oil prices. Again.

24

The World Takes Its Price

I N 1977, at the time McNamara was working with the Carter White House to be nominated for a third five-year term, William Clark, his press aide and friend during the past nine years, decided to leave the Bank and return to England.

Clark was discreet about his reasons for leaving. But one of Mc-Namara's aides noticed that when McNamara went on his official trips, he left his traveling companion behind more and more. McNamara had needed Clark in the early years, to acquaint him with who was who in the aid community and the developing world. But as he became knowledgeable, he needed Clark less.[1]

The other reason Clark left the Bank was that Barbara Ward was now quite ill; Clark was the logical successor to run Ward's organization, the International Institute for Environment and Development, in London. IIED was a useful platform for Lady Jackson to advance solutions to international poverty and ecological issues. Now she had a small lump in her throat that would prove to be malignant, an ironic fate for one whose fame rested on her musical voice and speaking ability. Once an admirer gasped: "Barbara, you speak so movingly. You sound like Mother Teresa!" Ward snapped back, "Well, I have to work at it much harder than Mother Teresa. Our Lord leans over her shoulder and tells her what to say, but *I* have to work it up *all by myself.*"

Ward still flew to the United States to see her influential friends. There she would talk and write, and if her voice rasped, she said,

"I've caught an olive in my throat." She still could captivate her American patrons and stayed sometimes at the Tracy Place house of Bob and Margy McNamara.

By the end of the decade in which she had helped to steer McNamara's approach to development in both its moral dimension and its focus on the bottom 40 percent, Ward was exhausted. She would take the night flight back across the Atlantic, wrapped in blankets, and be met at Heathrow by her friend and secretary, Irene Hunter, who would drive her through London's foggy streets to Hunter's house. Ward would use this as a way station until she was strong enough to be taken to her own home, down in Sussex. There she would rest and recoup to carry on her crusade, not just against the rich nations' neglect of the poor, but against apartheid in South Africa. This was a cause to which Bob McNamara also soon turned.[2]

Did Ward notice when she stayed at Tracy Place that Margy was tired, too? She still worried constantly about her three children. Little Margy's marriage had ended unhappily, and she was now divorced; Kathy was working toward a degree in forestry at Yale but was still not close to either parent. When a Yale faculty member tried to befriend her by asking if she was related to the famous Robert McNamara, Kathy flinched and said, "He's my uncle."[3]

Craig, after returning from Easter Island, enrolled in agricultural school at the University of California at Davis. He was still ignored by his father. He and his friend Graham Wisner would try to argue with McNamara at dinner; everyone would get mad. McNamara acted as though his son didn't know what he was talking about. But Polly Wisner Fritchey, Graham's mother and an old friend of Bob's and Margy's, noticed that McNamara seemed "proud," even as he got cross, that the boys were taking him on.[4]

McNamara had a hard time understanding a son who was so different from himself and who looked to him for encouragement. His distance from Craig was part of his inability to create the emotional bonds of a leader with those below, which hurt him in the long run at Ford, with the military, with the Bank staff; ultimately it hurt him with the Vietnam veterans.

Craig generally stayed out of politics in the 1970s, after the emotional tumult of the antiwar movement faded. However, in the late 1970s in California he became alarmed about Jimmy Carter's plans to deploy the MX missile. Craig decided to come to Washington to lobby his congressman. He called his father and asked: "Dad, what would you do? What should I tell this guy?"[5]

McNamara told him, "Stay out there." In other words, don't get involved, don't bother. From McNamara's Olympian perspective, one congressman wasn't going to change the MX vote, then or ever. But Craig says he felt "humiliated" that his father would not encourage him to be politically active. Weren't those the values his dad and mother stood for? It did not occur to McNamara, meanwhile, that he was putting Craig down.

"My mother was an essential ingredient who always helped me, even in the darkest times, when I was being very frustrated in my communication with Dad," says Craig. "She would say, 'Dad supports you even though he didn't show it at the moment.' It was those times with Mom that did keep me going."

Being the intermediary was a big burden for Margy. Friends recall that Bob simply ignored the boy. "Once in a while he would jump in" and announce what Craig should or should not do. But then he would back off and leave Margy to cope. Says Craig: "Mom helped me through the worst of times. . . . When I think of all she did for me . . ." Daughter Margy remembers, "She would always ask about me. I never thought to ask her how she felt."

Margy's daily business was Reading Is Fundamental, of which she was chairman of the board. RIF now had programs in almost all fifty states and a full-time staff in Washington. Bringing books by van to lend to children in poor neighborhoods, it was politically popular as a low-cost way to improve literacy.[6] Margy ran the Bank spouses' group. She traveled with Bob constantly. All told, it was not an easy life, or a very private one.

Globe-trotting with her husband, Margy took along her preoccupations. Ruth Graves, the executive director of RIF, always knew where she was. Like Hansel and Gretel's trail of bread crumbs in the forest, Margy left a white trail of her travels. Into RIF's office would pour letters from Nepal, perhaps, quickly followed by letters from Delhi, in India, and then Lahore, in Pakistan, then Kabul, Afghanistan, as Margy and Bob moved from one place to the next in a few days. The letters came from officials in each of these locations and asked for information about the RIF program, for Margy talked about their literacy campaign in America to politicians and bureaucrats she met wherever she went. Through Bob, she made sure that the Bank lent for primary education, which was too often more a political slogan than a reality in the Third World.

The McNamaras still took hiking vacations with the Goodwins and other friends; in 1973 they made a memorable 150-mile month-long trek in Nepal, to base camp on Mount Everest, where Margy rode a yak. The members of the party wrote their own comments at the end of a little book about the trip that Mary Joe Goodwin wrote and illustrated;[7] McNamara, who had grabbed his wife's camera and become so enthusiastic about it that Margy never got to take a shot, wrote of the "forbidding majesty of ice-shrouded peaks" and the "grace and hospitality of an ancient people" who have "one tenth our literacy and one half our life expectancy," but "humor and dignity" nonetheless.

He wrote that he had spent thirty years trying to "place the problems of our own era — an era of mounting economic chaos, political controversy, and tensions among nations — in some form of historical and philosophical perspective," and the trip helped him. He repeated the lines from T. S. Eliot that he had quoted to reporters when he left the Pentagon:

> *We shall not cease from exploration*
> *And the end of all our exploring*
> *Will be to arrive where we started*
> *And know the place for the first time.*[8]

As for Margy, their mountain treks were triumphs of her recovery from polio and of her physical strength. McNamara later recalled, tearful at the memory, that on her forty-eighth birthday she had rappeled 120 feet in the Grand Tetons. The trek to the base camp of Mount Everest took her to 16,000 feet at the age of fifty-eight. And as late as 1980 she would retrace with them an old silk and salt caravan trail in Nepal.

McNamara's insistence on her constant company had a cost. A friend recalls seeing her crossing the airport in Frankfurt, all alone, with a big backpack on her small frame. She was traveling to join Bob someplace to go hiking. She looked so frail that the friend thought: What kind of a man lets his wife travel around alone like that? But Margy was so cheerful as she crossed time zones and countries — economy-class — just to be with him that the friend thought: Bob is lucky to have her.[9]

*   *   *

If there was ever a human being who believed that applied intelligence, organization, and resources could mold reality to suit his will, it was Robert McNamara. By his third term at the Bank, his outlook was global. Meanwhile his rigid, autocratic side was ever more apparent to those who dealt with him daily.

Forbes magazine captured him in a photograph taken close up at an international meeting, in profile and wearing earphones.[10] His head is set back; the eyes glare, the jaw juts forward, clenched in a typical pose of tension. The earphones and dangling cords are so prominent that his rimless glasses are hard to see. McNamara habitually experienced such meetings wired, for after ten years as head of a major international institution he spoke no language other than English. His hands are clasped in front of his chin. The photograph seems to be of an inner man, appearing to listen but really deep in his own world.

Timothy Stanley, McNamara's colleague from the 1960s, when they had set up the Nuclear Planning Group in Brussels, remembers lunching with McNamara around this time. The table in his private dining room at the Bank was covered with a pink tablecloth. By each place was the usual yellow pad and pencil. McNamara dived into the olives and carrots, arranged in little dishes in the center, and started talking about population. Across the street, the director of the International Monetary Fund, who was always a European, served the best wines and cuisine — real international bankers' lunches. But a repast with R. S. McNamara began with olives and carrots, and a thimbleful of sherry if his guest dared to ask.

McNamara went on about the population issue, Stanley recalls. He had given a major speech at M.I.T. in 1977, saying that at present growth rates, the world's population would level off at 11 billion beginning in the year 2020; this represented a slight slowing in growth from earlier scenarios, which showed the world's population racing upward to 15 billion and more. The gist of McNamara's speech was to urge international agencies and Third World governments to keep working to slow the rate of growth more, so population would stabilize sooner at a lower level, such as at 8 billion starting in 2000. Even then there would be the question of whether the planet could sustain two times the present 4 billion people. How could enough food be produced? What about the stress, crowding, and frustration, and social and military instability?

As he explained these issues to Stanley over lunch, McNamara

scribbled some numbers on his yellow pad. Needing more room, he
began writing on the tablecloth. He became more carried away and
stood up. Still talking, McNamara moved along the table, writing
figures on the pink cloth. There was no stopping his verbal torrent or
his emotion. When the hour allotted for lunch expired, Stanley had
heard more about the population question than he needed, he
thought. And the tablecloth, ringed around with hieroglyphics in
McNamara's southpaw scrawl, looked like an artifact left by an ancient visitor from another world.[11]

The worst real-world threat yet struck a body blow at the Bank and
McNamara's program in 1978 and 1979. Iran had been a good Bank
client over the years: It had borrowed $1.2 billion to build schools,
aid farming, repair roads, and fund other projects. But modernism
turned tail there in the fall of 1978 when Iranian fundamentalists
revolted against Shah Mohammed Reza Pahlavi. Widespread strikes
and violence began pulling Iran apart. Iran's oil stopped flowing to
the West. The price of oil from other OPEC suppliers shot up.

President Jimmy Carter faced the grim choice of propping up the
shah — or having to mount a large-scale military intervention if Iran
crumbled and the Soviet army crossed its northern borders.

By February 1979, oil cost $14 per barrel (in contemporary dol-
lars), and the spot price was $23 on the barrel. OPEC agreed that
producers could add "surcharges" to even these prices — which
would make the import bills for everyone else rise still higher.[12]

All through 1979, Americans felt the shocks of the revolution in
Iran. The shah was diagnosed as having cancer; he was flown to
Egypt, Morocco, the Bahamas, and Mexico, seeking refuge, and in
October flew to New York for treatment; Ayatollah Ruhollah
Khomeini left exile in France to return to Tehran.

All year, McNamara tried to break the deadlock in Congress over
the funds needed to replenish the International Development Association and the $3.2 billion American share of the Bank's major cap-
ital increase. Aid was needed more than ever, he argued, because the
non-oil-exporting Third World states faced a doubling of oil debt,
already steep.

But while the Bank and other aid agencies portrayed the Third
World in images showing noble-looking peasants working amid their
cotton, priming wells, or tilling fields behind oxen, that year Amer-

icans saw it on their television screens as shouting mobs denouncing the United States as the Great Satan.

America's sense of powerlessness was driven home on November 4, 1979, when Iranian "students" invaded the U.S. embassy in Tehran and took some sixty American diplomats hostage. The mighty United States, long-term protector of Iran and largest financier of the Bank and IDA, had been spit in the eye. So much for foreign aid.

On the other side of the world, Vietnam invaded Cambodia. Refugees fled that country; then China attacked four Vietnamese border provinces. Washington watched anxiously to see if the Soviets would join the Vietnamese and fight both Cambodia and China. Meanwhile, the relentless Soviet ICBM buildup — which had begun back in the 1960s thanks to the McNamara-Kennedy increases and the U.S. entry into Vietnam — was now advertised to be capable of a devastating nuclear first strike on the United States. The SALT II accord, another symbol of American strength and confidence, was now shelved. It became a dead letter when the Soviets invaded Afghanistan in December.

Besides the wreckage to the Third World economies caused by oil prices, McNamara had the problem of China looming ahead. Peking was ending three decades of international isolation, even while making war on Vietnam. In February 1979 its leaders announced it wished to be admitted as a member nation of the World Bank, a step the Bank had expected once Jimmy Carter formally recognized the Peking regime.[13]

McNamara welcomed the prospect of fashioning an aid program for China's multitudes. He had come a long way since 1965, when his obsessive focus had been on Chinese Communist expansionism. Now he was just as intent on fighting his new enemy, poverty, in its many guises — malnutrition, illness, overpopulation, low economic growth. There were plenty of these to fight in China.

One obstacle was Taiwan's long-standing Bank membership. But the main hurdle was lack of money. China's per capita income was so low that it would make an enormous new claim on IDA funds, every dollar of which was already needed by India, Bangladesh, and other impoverished nations. McNamara also would have a hard time winning his Ward-inspired argument for moral compassion for the Chinese, when Peking was making Southeast Asia boil with blood.[14] Although McNamara had an odd ability to drop the past from his field of view as though it had not existed, Congress and American voters did not.

McNamara's great strength, and tragedy, was to look on the huge institutions below him as *too small* in relation to his always growing sense of what human will can achieve. When he circulated in international meetings, swinging out the right arm in a power handshake, the bass voice gruffly greeting his fellow lords of the planet, it was as though he saw himself on a commanding height like that 18,000-foot Himalayan spur he and Willard Goodwin had trekked up in 1973. Whereas many chief executives are intimidated by the bureaucracy below them, McNamara looked down on the United Nations Development Program, the Food and Agriculture Organization, the IMF, and the Bank from his great imaginary height as mere hillocks, minor compared to the limitless work he had in mind.

Now that oil-price hikes were tearing up the world economy, McNamara fixated on a new danger: The poor countries, unable to pay for oil, would limit their spending on fuel and move into a severe economic downturn, "a deflationary spiral and collapse."[15] McNamara's logic, according to one who worked with him, was that "avoiding all new debt" was not the answer; most developing nations, especially the neediest, now required more income to pay for fuel and keep going at their present economic pace, at the least. On the other hand, "just to borrow to cover increased repayment of oil bills" was also a bad idea, because the new higher debt levels "couldn't be sustained indefinitely" unless the countries experienced real economic growth.

McNamara had another fear shared by the aid community. With oil at $20 a barrel instead of $10, the cost of fertilizer, made from oil products, would rise beyond many countries' ability to pay. The agriculture revolution, by which he set such store, could grind to a halt.

Thus McNamara's answer, which sounded Pirandellian: Because poor nations were incurring greater debt, they should borrow more. His solution derived from the faith he had held since coming to the Bank that debt wasn't debt, but a creator of wealth; that his projects were working; that he was not "throwing money at problems," as his critics, such as the *Wall Street Journal*, charged. Now he believed that more lending was needed, not as something that was nice to have, but to stave off disaster.[16]

As always, McNamara was literal about getting results. The Bank's general capital increase, then being finalized, would double its subscribed capital to $85 billion, of which wealthy member nations, including the United States, would pay in $7.5 billion. McNamara now wanted to "grow" the Bank more. Yet another general capital increase was politically impossible.

He and the senior staff concocted other ways in which to make it grow. Papers circulating in the Bank in 1979 and 1980 discussed a possible 45 percent increase in lending through two schemes. The first was a version of the OPEC-funded Bank affiliate that McNamara and the shah had proposed back in February 1974. This time, the loans made by the affiliate would be to help non-oil-producing developing countries generate more of their own energy supplies. A second scheme was for a "bank" within the Bank. Since the Bank borrowed at long-term, fixed interest rates and made its loans on similar terms as well, it was threatened by worldwide rising interest rates at which it would have to borrow. The proposed "Bank's bank" would borrow and lend at shorter terms and perhaps adjustable interest rates. Not only would it expand the Bank's scale, but the shorter-term market could create profits to hedge against problems with longer-term loans.[17]

The irony of McNamara's impulse to expand the Bank was that he had warned in the past that the developing nations were carrying too much debt. In his 1972 address to the UNCTAD meeting in Santiago, McNamara predicted that the $60 billion in debt that Third World governments had guaranteed could be hard for them to service. Each year since, he plotted the mounting debt obligations of each country and region as annexes to the Bank's annual report. By 1977, for example, debt had reached $285 billion.[18]

He did not see this growing debt as the threat to the soundness of borrowing governments in the sense it later became. His quantitative mind fixed on the gap between rising bills and inability to pay based on current income. So he told the Bank's governors in his 1979 fall speech that "private capital flows [should] increase in the 1980s at rates close to those of the 1970s." He lamented that private banks, "already heavily committed" in several developing countries, might be reluctant to expand further.

McNamara had an alternative, of letting the rapid growth of Bank lending in the 1970s taper off, to allow the Bank and borrowing nations to consolidate their efforts. From private life, former treasury secretary George Shultz advised, "It's impossible really to conceive that the World Bank could keep on growing that fast. Anytime you have an organization that grows very rapidly, it doesn't do it any harm to have a period of pausing and consolidation and getting itself settled in a little bit."[19]

But McNamara dismissed inaction or slowing down. He stuck with resources as the solution — properly managed resources, of course. In his 1979 speech he told the governors that the Bank's job was not just to drum up resources but to "promote in individual countries strategies of development which are realistic and sustainable."[20]

In hindsight, a slowdown in the program's growth might have been wiser, and kinder to certain developing countries, especially some African ones. Consolidation might have helped some faltering rural development projects succeed. But to McNamara, retrenchment was defeatism.

He revealed one motive in a speech at the University of Chicago in May 1979. Chicago had been one of the great liberal campuses of the 1930s, like his alma mater, Berkeley. McNamara stressed his liberal values to this audience — ironically, while an antiwar, down-with-McNamara demonstration reminiscent of the 1960s went on outside. McNamara said,

> As I look back over my own generation — a generation that in its university years thought of itself as liberal — I am astonished at the insensitivity that all of us had during those years to the injustice of racial discrimination in our own society.
>
> Will it now take another 50 years before we fully recognize the injustice of massive poverty in the international community?[21]

Says Munir Benjenk, his vice president for external relations at the time, "McNamara had become a prophet."[22]

McNamara's new talk of expanding the Bank's program by another 45 percent plunged staff morale to an all-time low.[23] Many of the governments the staff dealt with had been borrowing at record levels from the Bank, other aid agencies, and commercial banks in the late 1970s. "There weren't any defaults at that period," says a staffer who was a project officer then. "But people understood it was just a matter of time. We were lending so much ourselves, and the commercial banks were lending so much. There just weren't that many good projects out there."

Already, project officers were pulling forward projects still in the planning stage to meet the quantitative lending goals set by Mount Olympus. They felt forced to do less careful planning and expend less effort on the critical matter of getting the borrowing country's national and local authorities committed to a proposed project's success. The staff knew that when a project was started without this painstaking preparation, it ran a higher risk of failure. There was also the danger that projects would be overfinanced — that is, more money given to local authorities than they could manage. Staffers who made too-hasty loans (and computed rosy rates of return to present to McNamara and the board to win approval) would pay the price later, when the projects didn't work; then their programs and promotion prospects would be damaged. Growing too fast hurt everybody.

Thus McNamara's mania for growth increased the chances his projects would fall short. Staff anxieties became intense; McNamara was told he should meet with employees more often.

But when he did so, he was censorious. "A lot of people got their careers ruined by standing up and arguing that [rapid growth] was not something you could do," says a senior budget official.[24] McNamara was "impatient" and "intolerant" of these arguments. During a meeting in which they discussed the projected flows of loans to different regions, one official raised the issue of how much more they should lend to sub-Saharan Africa; those governments weren't doing very well with the loans they had, and they seemed unlikely to be able to administer, or pay back, more loans.

When the man voiced this doubt, "McNamara shot out of his seat" in the back of the room. "He could not let the point pass. He kept repeating that absorptive capacity was not the issue."

At another meeting with some staff, the story went, a young man, thinking they were meant to *really* discuss the issues, brought up the problem of absorptive capacity. McNamara rebutted him. Afterward the word went around that McNamara also asked for the young man's name — not only to set him straight on the party line about debt, but so he would know that if he stepped out of line, his career could suffer.

"McNamara rode roughshod over those who accused him of being a growth maniac," says one of his protégés.[25] The budget officer says McNamara's attitude came from deep within him. "McNamara was unwilling to admit these institutional constraints. Since he's an impatient person, he couldn't accept advice to go slow. There is a deep-rooted denial there."

"He had become the big banyan tree under which the little banyan trees can't grow," recalls a member of the old guard about McNamara in his later years.[26]

"I felt an evolution in McNamara's personality," says another official. McNamara had become "impatient with . . . the boring things with which a chief executive officer has to deal. Instead, he behaved as if he were the holder of the truth. He became increasingly intolerant of internal criticism."

He did not hear much of it from his aides in those years. By 1979 J. Burke Knapp, the knowledgeable executive vice president who had been with the Bank since its founding, had retired. Succeeding Knapp was Peter Cargill, one of the few whose criticism McNamara tolerated in earlier years. Others had watched in amazement as McNamara would stop and listen, and change his mind, based on Cargill's advice. But by the end of the decade Cargill took longer and longer lunch hours, often at Sans Souci, a well-known French restaurant in Georgetown. He would come back at three in the afternoon "embarrassingly drunk," which was completely against the Bank's institutional style. Cargill was less useful, therefore, although McNamara tolerated his behavior the way he tolerated the eccentricities of others in his inner group. He had changed from his days at the Pentagon, when any odd behavior would be grounds to have a man banished.[27]

The phalanx of favored advisers formed a wall around him. Within their own circle they became a court. Ernest Stern, a Dutch Jew who had escaped the Holocaust and was almost the only one who matched McNamara's skill with numbers, was increasingly the keeper of the gate. "Ernie had a lot to do with the isolation of McNamara in his later years," says another aide.

There even had been a period when William Clark, still employed at the Bank, had refused to come into the office because, according to rumor, someone on the staff was having him investigated.[28] Jealousy and rivalries were rampant. The twelfth floor of the Bank's new headquarters building, a gleaming glass-and-white-stone tribute to technocratic rationalism, seemed, in contrast, like a Renaissance palace, full of rumor and intrigue.

In this environment, the numbers flowing to McNamara from the staff became a game. Everything stemmed from his seven master statistical tables that he had used so well in his first term to redirect the institution and get his program going. What frightened some staff who watched him now was that McNamara believed the numbers they handed him *more* than the written briefing materials. One budget officer had watched him go into meetings with both kinds of data and rely only on the numbers, "disregarding" the written report.[29]

Even when he went on vacation to Aspen he played with his tables to relax, the way other people do crossword puzzles. The budget officer remembers McNamara coming back from Colorado with new refinements for them. The officer thought to himself, No one else uses these tables in such detail; why change them just to please him? In fact they were serving a religious need for faith rather than a search for truth, which might be ambiguous.

"There was a lack of statistical sophistication about him, despite all of his numeracy," the budget officer says. "His numeracy struck one as that of an accountant, rather than a statistician's. When one talks about management information systems, the assumption generally is that as information moves up to the apex . . . you improve the quality of the information." Since successive layers check out data from below, "the credibility of the information at the top is assured."

But McNamara used numbers to suppress uncertainties. He did not say in his speeches, "We think the numbers of absolute poor could be as low as 551 million or as high as 950 million." This is how mathematicians or statisticians would express the range, in order to be responsible and show that they did *not* know how many absolute poor there were, that they had not counted every head, and that their figures were based on different universes of data collected differently in hundreds of places.

Staff who reported to McNamara, including this budget officer, would often pencil in the ranges for a number to indicate the extent of their uncertainty and to avoid pretending to know a fact they did not have. But McNamara would scrub out the ranges and pick one figure — or he would command the staff to pick one number for him. At each level, as individuals were compelled to simplify, the data lost robustness and stood an ever-greater chance of being plain wrong.

Among McNamara's manias was the requirement that staff state a figure for those supposed to be the "beneficiaries" of each project. This way McNamara could keep counting the numbers of poor he had helped. Recalls the budget officer, "By this means we got into the professionally questionable business of body counts."[30]

Why did McNamara insist on plain numbers, without variances or qualifications? He was searching for certainty, based on his roots in a household of simple ideas and absolute truths. This need is also reflected in his speech: He repeats "absolutely" and "never," even in casual conversation, often while banging his hand down on a table, while his face reddens in an outburst of passion. *"Absolutely"* and "never" — like "800 million absolute poor" — are not the words of a skeptic cautiously probing the world. McNamara sought religion based on numbers and made the staff supply him with these articles of faith, even when they weren't "true" as people in the field understood the term. Was McNamara fibbing?

"We didn't regard it as fibbing," says a former project officer. "We regarded it as a disregard of actual facts. He was very good at manipulating statistics."

Yet McNamara "did it not with ill intent, but in an excess of advocacy." He was trying to be "productive," not "destructive," the staffer says. "McNamara is so secure in his ideas and in running with what he wants to do, that it is a matter of building [his] case."

So the institution sailed on, outwardly sleek, steely with authority, and radiating facts and figures. Ostensibly it was ready to advance human progress by the next big leap of scale for which McNamara lobbied. But on the inside, "this place was wound up like a spring," says one official.

Then Vietnam reappeared in McNamara's life. After the Communists overran Saigon in April 1975 and the last Americans fled by helicopter from the U.S. embassy roof, the regime gingerly approached the World Bank about possible loans. The first contact was with Bernard Bell in Amsterdam, who reported the probe to McNamara.[31]

McNamara seemed reasonable about it initially. Other Communist countries had won Bank loans, although the staff was sometimes suspicious about what happened to the funds. Just as McNamara tried to make the Bank influential in countries, like Indonesia and India, on the margin between east and west, he also tried to influence economies in the East Bloc. William Clark recalled an occasion when the former chief of the Ford Motor Company lectured the Communist bosses of Yugoslavia on how to manage automobile production. And China was on the horizon.

After the first feeler from Vietnam, when the staff next approached him on whether to agree to a second meeting, he became "very heated" and "very emotional," according to one who was present. McNamara "changed his position several times" and "obviously was very upset with the whole idea of a relationship with Vietnam." He cut the discussion short with an order: "Don't do it." The next day he called the staffer and said, "OK. Do it." Burke Knapp warned others that McNamara was irrational on the subject.

In subsequent, guarded conversations McNamara said the Bank should lend to Vietnam only if other contributors joined in. A mission was sent, which helped to identify an irrigation project that would be appropriate for IDA support. Three other donors — the Kuwaiti Fund, the OPEC Special Fund, and the government of the Netherlands — agreed to lend $10 million each. The Vietnamese would put in $20 million more. Very quietly in 1977 a $60 million IDA credit was approved by the Bank's executive directors on McNamara's recommendation.[32]

Some people at the Bank wanted additional dealings with Vietnam; $60 million was a very small effort for the Bank, given united Vietnam's size and population. But in fact, McNamara had discussed with Knapp putting a ceiling on Bank participation, another sign he mistrusted his former foe.

The argument for lending more to Vietnam was that the Bank was supposed to be politically neutral and to lend to improve the productivity and well-being of ordinary people, not to endorse a political system or regime. The argument against it was that the U.S. government would never send aid to a bunch of Communists who had defeated it and remained unrepentant, and tyrannous, and withheld information about American soldiers missing in action. In retaliation Congress could easily wreak havoc with the replenishment of IDA's funds and the general capital increase that McNamara was working on.

Clearly McNamara reacted against lending to Vietnam for personal reasons: from unwillingness to drag out painful memories, and hatred of the enemy who had humiliated him and his country. After fighting him for years, McNamara's onetime adversary was now bowing and smiling and asking him for loans. He tried to keep a lid on the issue, personally and for the Bank's sake.

Jimmy Carter's presidency should have been smooth sailing for Robert McNamara. Carter was personally sympathetic to the Bank; McNamara's protégé Cyrus Vance, whom he had trained and promoted in his years in the Pentagon, was now secretary of state. A strong foreign aid program had been a keystone of American world leadership for most of the American Century. Thus, as the first liberal Democratic president since Lyndon Johnson, Carter had an opening to rebuild support for aid and the Bank.

The $60 million loan to Vietnam fired up some members of the House. Also, for most of 1979 the Bank found itself at the center of another controversy, started by William Simon, which neither the Carter men nor McNamara could dampen.[33] This was the issue of whether McNamara's Bank was too big and too rich. Simon had charged that staff salaries were too high, tossing up a handy target for critics of foreign aid.

During 1979, the shah's fall, the skyrocketing price of oil, and, after November 4, the imprisonment of U.S. hostages in Iran caused Americans' opinions of foreign aid to plunge to an all-time low. Whereas 43 percent of those polled in 1972 favored cutting foreign aid, by 1979 the figure had risen to 69 percent. As the salaries issue unleashed previously hidden resentment of the Bank around Washington, the Americans polled put the Bank at the bottom of a list of organizations — below the Red Cross, below U.S. corporations — in terms of effectiveness.[34]

Congressman C. W. Young of Florida was using the issues of fat-cat salaries and lending to Vietnam to whip up votes against the $3.6 billion U.S. share of the general capital increase and money for IDA. McNamara charged into the limelight to defend the tax-free pay and first-class travel of the Bank staff, their perquisites, lifetime employment, and benefits. They are *bankers,* he argued. To recruit good people he had to compete with Morgan Stanley, Citibank, and the big European banks.[35]

The fracas put McNamara back on the front pages of the *Washington Post,* but his prominence was a mixed blessing, since he was still not a credible figure in U.S. politics. Jimmy Carter meant to help, but his forte was not political spin control.

"McNamara brought the salaries issue on himself, because by then he had advertised the Bank as an aid agency," says D. Joseph Wood, who worked with him on the budget at that time. By continually speaking of the Bank as a development agency and calling attention to its war on poverty, McNamara "demeaned the public perception of it as a bank."

By late 1979, the Bank had become a political football: Congress was not acting on the capital increase, and the House had slashed the planned amount for IDA. An outside commission was studying the salaries matter. Congressman Young had attached a rider to Bank legislation requiring the Bank not to lend to Vietnam, Cambodia, Cuba, Laos, Angola, or the Central African Republic. The rider spelled death for the Bank's acceptance of any U.S. funds, for it was forbidden from accepting funds that carried restrictions. As the impasse dragged on, McNamara went hat in hand to other donor nations — including Great Britain and the Netherlands — to try to have them pay in their shares early to make up for U.S. paralysis and his and Jimmy Carter's inability to contain the issue.[36]

Edward J. Fried, the American executive director of the Bank; C. Fred Bergsten of the U.S. Treasury; and Ernest Stern, the Bank's vice president for operations, met McNamara at National Airport, outside Washington, when he returned from one of his trips.

The three presented him with a letter to Young, which stated that the Bank would not lend to Vietnam. McNamara was told that if he signed it, Young would spring the full funding for IDA and the capital increase. In the airport, McNamara signed the letter.[37]

But the letter made the uproar worse; by signing it McNamara had violated the Bank's rules that required him to deal with member governments — i.e., the U.S. Congress — exclusively through the secretary of the treasury. Moreover, a written commitment not to lend to Vietnam and other countries de facto compromised the Bank's integrity.

Then in January 1980, McNamara cut a deal on the salaries issue. He agreed to forgo some expected salary increases to get Congress to restore the funds it planned to slash from the U.S. contribution to IDA.[38]

The letter about Vietnam, although retracted, ultimately may have helped the bills pass. As for the compromise on salaries, says Wood, "in the long run it was a good deal. It bought us years of peace" on IDA, until the next replenishment fight, and quieted the negative vibes about the Bank around town.

But the symbolism of McNamara's paying his own people less to get more money for the poor was not lost on the Bank staff. One vice president made the mistake of reporting to McNamara that a loan

officer complained that he was trading part of their livelihood to help
the poor. The loan officer had said:

"Well, McNamara's rich, he can afford it."

"Who said that?" McNamara snapped.

"I won't say his name," came the reply.

"Well, he's going to stay a loan officer," McNamara said.[39] His
retort was irrational, since he didn't know the name of the man he
had just vowed to punish for such insolence.

The clearest signs that the political winds were turning against Mc-
Namara came in Britain. British Labor governments had cooperated
with McNamara's program, in general. Many of the Bank's senior
staff carried British passports. Denis Healey, McNamara's debating
partner from the Nuclear Planning Group in the late 1960s, was
chancellor of the exchequer under Prime Minister James Callaghan.
The winter of 1978–79 was a disaster for Callaghan's Labor government. Strikes, layoffs, and closings sank the country into crisis: even
gravediggers went on strike. "CRISIS? WHAT CRISIS?" said a headline,
mimicking Callaghan.[40]

In May, Conservative Margaret Thatcher swept into office, replac-
ing Callaghan, and immediately slashed the budget of the Labor-built
welfare state. British overseas aid had been a point of pride during the
long postcolonial period of Fabian-inspired Labor dominance. (The
British spent about 0.4 percent of their GNP on overseas aid during
the 1970s, even as the U.S. share of its GNP devoted to aid declined,
from almost 0.5 percent in 1965 to 0.22 percent in 1979.)[41]

Prime Minister Thatcher stated that she was a monetarist and fiscal
conservative — and she meant it. A month after taking office, she
lowered taxes and announced spending cuts, including decreases in
foreign aid. Laborites and liberals yowled that the Iron Lady was
steering the nation toward disaster. "You have had your chance," she
retorted, sticking to her philosophy; "now it's our turn."[42]

McNamara first met Geoffrey Howe, Thatcher's chancellor of the
exchequer, at the Bank's annual meeting in Belgrade, Yugoslavia, in
October 1979. He apparently repeated his case that more aid was
urgently needed to respond to the oil-price hike.

Howe was not impressed. By all accounts, he took an immediate
dislike to McNamara.[43] Thatcher had committed once-powerful
Great Britain to a bigger role in NATO and higher defense spending.
Her closest minister, Howe, did not need a lecture about British

responsibilities — least of all from McNamara, a walking symbol of the failure of American foreign policy. When someone asked McNamara how the meeting had gone, he said, "Terribly. Howe doesn't understand the issues."

"McNamara thought he was speaking to a Labor chancellor," says a close aide who was at the Belgrade meeting. If so, McNamara had been incredibly deaf to the clear signs of fiscal retrenchment emanating from 10 Downing Street since June.

During the following year, the Thatcher government did not invite McNamara to visit Britain, even though London had been one of his regular stops for a decade.

McNamara would not give up. He quarreled with Howe over the figures projecting future British overseas aid, which McNamara published in a table accompanying each annual address. He had made these figures public since 1972, in part to embarrass governments, such as America and Great Britain, that were near the bottom of the list and to reward with praise the Swedes, the Dutch, and others who spent 0.9 percent of their respective GNPs on overseas aid. Combative as ever, McNamara usually berated publicly those governments that fell short of the 0.7 percent target set by the United Nations.[44] But the laggard governments, including the one in Washington, ignored his rebukes.

The new high price of oil meant big business for the world's bankers who gathered in Belgrade. Billions in petrodollars were about to recycle through the world's banking system; they would generate fat commissions for bankers, no matter where they lent the new wealth out. Brazil and Mexico had an unhealthy load of debt before the OPEC rise. But both countries still were considered good prospects by many large banks. They assumed that whereas a business could default, sovereign governments wouldn't.[45]

The government of Colombia, by contrast, declined to add to its debt levels — although the treasury phoned R. S. McNamara to demand that the Bank threaten to cut off lending to Colombia to pressure that government into borrowing from commercial banks. McNamara refused. The Colombians were being prudent, and he was not about to push them into buckets of red ink.[46]

From the podium in Belgrade on October 2, McNamara reminded the finance ministers of their duty to fight poverty.[47] He spoke in messianic terms. Despite bad economic conditions, there had been some improvements: In the poorest countries, life expectancy had risen to age fifty, and one person in three was literate; in middle-income developing countries, nine of ten children went to primary school. More could be done, he insisted. For the next decade, the world community should set subtargets for improvement in nutrition, health, and other basic human needs, and to measure to what extent they were being met.

McNamara's lifetime habit of central control and quantitative plans, in which his personality and system fused, echoed through the speech. He deplored the fact that the international community "really has no adequate means to implement agreed-upon development policy." The target figures, such as 4 percent per year in agricultural growth, were "little more than hopes or aspirations." Population growth was hard to slow because the decision to have children "is ultimately in the hands not of governments or institutions or organizations" but of "literally hundreds of millions of individual parents" and thus was "diffuse and intractable."

He announced that the number of absolute poor still to be uplifted — even after nearly twelve years of his ministrations — was 800 million, the same figure he had given years earlier when he coined the term. If the Third World's growth in the next ten years matched that of the past decade, there would still be 600 million absolute poor in the year 2000. But if economic growth slowed, he warned, there would be 710 million. Thus after some thirty years of additional effort, they would have reduced the number in poverty by only 90 million. It was not in Robert McNamara to give up and let nature take its course and the poor suffer because of horrible inequities forced on them, often by their own leaders. Intervention and action were his religion in 1979 as much as in 1965.

For it was faith, at bottom, not facts and statistics, that underlay this crusade. In fact, the statistics showed that the war on poverty could not be won, just as his statistics had told him the war in Vietnam could not be won. Yet in both cases, McNamara instinctively urged that they fight on.

His solutions were lower trade barriers, to improve terms of trade for Third World nations, and a new kind of loan called a structural adjustment loan. This was a device to lend general revenues into national treasuries on the firm condition that the government would undertake specific economic reforms. Structural adjustment lending would become the Bank's answer to the macroeconomic problems that hit the Third World in the 1980s. But in 1979, although McNamara was preachy and out of step with the new mood, his invention of the structural adjustment loan illustrated that he had not run out of useful ideas.[48]

Except for a few remarks, McNamara's 1979 speech to the governors was blind to a possible Third World debt crisis. He even dwelt on his concern that commercial banks might not lend *enough* in coming years. "There is considerable uncertainty about the ability of the commercial banks to supply the necessary funds," he said.

In fact, the lending train was gathering steam; McNamara's emphasis on moral obligations and help for the poorest was out of touch. "He was giving the wrong speech to the wrong audience," says one of his aides. A conservative London paper had quipped, "Mr. McNamara should remember that he is president of the World Bank and not president of the world."[49]

In *Moby Dick*, Herman Melville wrote that life is made up of "chance, free will and necessity — all interweavingly working together as one" in which "chance has the last, featuring blow."[50]

Chance now struck another blow, although McNamara characteristically refused to accept that anything but his will could rule events.

In February 1980, Bob and Margy were in Aspen when she developed severe chest pains and her doctors told her to come back to Washington for tests. Ruth Graves, the executive director of RIF, was visiting Margy in the hospital when the doctor entered to tell Margy the result. Graves stood up and offered to leave, but Margy waved her to sit down.

"The doctor gave her a technical term," says Graves. "He didn't use the word 'cancer.' " But Margy knew right away that he meant she had cancer and that the prospects were not good. She turned to her friend and said: "It has to happen to us all sometime."

Graves thought she was being needlessly pessimistic. She reminded Margy that the doctor hadn't said anything about her condition's being fatal. But Margy showed tremendous calm in response to the idea that her days were now numbered.

"I think Margy accepted it instantly. She was accepting it long before anyone else that I know did," says Graves.[51]

Bob did not accept it. He did not hear the doctor say the cancer would be fatal. He thought they were saying she could live and therefore chemotherapy had some chance of putting the disease in remission. He recalls being told that progress was being made. In fact, Margy began growing weaker. Around the Bank the word was that "Mrs. Mac" was very, very ill.

The wife of a Malaysian diplomat offered to come and read to Margy at the McNamara's home. The visitor was dismayed that frail Margy should be in the house without a full-time nurse, given her condition. She was shocked at McNamara's conduct toward his wife: What kind of man — a rich man — would leave his wife without nurses? She thought McNamara must be very hard on her.

What the woman realized, as she came back several times and saw Margy stand up, move about, bring them tea, was that Margy wanted to be self-reliant.[52]

Margy and Bob had planned that he would leave the Bank on June 30, 1981, and would announce it a year ahead of time. That would give them more time together once he left the Bank. Meanwhile, he went on traveling. Those close to the couple wondered why Bob didn't just let up and stay home, especially when her possible loss seemed to be taking a large emotional toll on him. Perhaps business as usual was easier for them both.

Just as McNamara believed his wife could live, he believed still in his antipoverty projects. In Brasília the military generals who ruled Brazil faced discontent from displaced farmers in the south, driven off land by wealthy ranchers who expanded and consolidated their livestock farms, some with aid from the World Bank. The generals now asked the Bank if it would consider a loan to build a road plunging deep into the Amazon, to the western province of Rondônia.[53]

It was McNamara's policy not to lend for new roads; too many Third World governments built roads with foreign aid and then let them fall into disrepair. Roads were economically beneficial because they opened rural areas to settlement and made it possible for farmers to bring their crops to market; but a road's economic value vanished when it deteriorated into mud-filled ruts or was washed out by floods.

So his staff said no, it could not lend for a new road. But if the Brazilians applied to undertake an area development project in Rondônia, with plans to resettle and build new farms, then the Bank could consider funding the road as part of the package.

The Bank hired a consultant named David Price to investigate the project's feasibility, as well as charges by anthropologists that the government was in effect committing genocide by displacing native tribes of the rain forest by bringing in settlers. Price's report warned that Brazil's Indian agency was inimical to the tribes; it also cautioned that no one knew if the soils of the rain forest could support farming. But within the Bank, Price's report was rewritten to be more favorable; it was then cited to justify a green light to go ahead.[54]

In McNamara's final months, the plan for a project to build Brazil's later notorious Highway 364 moved forward within the Bank. Warnings and cautions were overriden, not from a wicked wish to chop down the rain forest, but because of the technocratic culture of McNamara's Bank. By 1981, large-scale area development loans were a standard way by which loan officers satisfied McNamara's drive to demonstrate that his money was helping large numbers of beneficiaries become productive.

The loan for Highway 364 was approved in December 1981, six months after McNamara left the Bank. The signature and final responsibility on the loans were that of his successor. But the preapproval work and classification of Amazon timber cutting as an antipoverty project occurred on McNamara's watch.

McNamara had promised at the Stockholm conference on the global environment back in 1972 that the Bank would lead in environmental protection worldwide.[55] And, during his later years, in his inimitable top-down manner, he had redirected Bank-sponsored activities to mitigate some ill effects of development — by 1981 Bank projects placed much more stress on soil conservation, replanting, and other measures, although the growing environmental movement hounded it on many matters and its actions often fell short of its environmental rhetoric.

Had McNamara stayed for his third full five-year term, he might finally have realized that the generals' Rondônia program continued to harm the native tribes. And as more soils became depleted after a season, settlers were forced to clear more forest and plant elsewhere. Thus the rate of forest cutting accelerated in Brazil, as well as in Indonesia, in the early 1980s. In the latter case, the Bank helped transmigration grow to a huge scale and denude large areas. Both Brazil's and Indonesia's deforestation hurt species diversity and the ozone layer.

To stop the juggernaut, McNamara might have attempted a redirection of the Bank programs in Brazil and Indonesia, just as he had tried to redirect the war machine during Vietnam. As it happened, this responsibility fell to his successor, who did not alter the Bank's course for years, despite ever-clearer warnings of disaster, despite the leak to *60 Minutes* of how David Price's report had been covered up and Price's open testimony to Congress in the mid-1980s.[56] Instead, the Bank piled loan upon loan; it stopped supporting the Rondônia program only in 1985, after thousands of square miles more of rain forest had been destroyed.

Even after Vietnam should have taught McNamara that his management system and numeracy could mislead him, even in his years at the Bank when he was depressed by pain and regret for past mistakes, his activism went unquenched. Thus through fear of inaction, the terror he inspired in the ranks, and his too-narrow focus on a single, overly heroic goal, the stage was set for another, large-scale institutional error.

The year 1980 had brought not only the election of Ronald Reagan, but new increases in the price of oil from OPEC. China acceded to membership in the Bank that year, and Robert McNamara, with relief and pride, sat down with his erstwhile enemy in Peking.

Experts predicted that oil prices would rise indefinitely. To McNamara this meant that the quantitative gap between what it would cost the poor countries to keep their economies running and the means they had to pay yawned wider. The oil-import bill of developing nations had been $7 billion in 1973; in 1980 it would be $67 billion. McNamara extrapolated out to 1990 and announced that the oil bill that year would be $124 billion. "He was fixated on this $67 billion gap, and how to fill it," says one of his senior vice presidents of the time. "Critical development tasks, never easy in the past, are now seriously threatened," McNamara said that September.[57]

Yet his ability to control the world's aid agenda was diminishing. Reagan appointed David Stockman, a thirty-four-year-old Whiz Kid of a different ideological stripe from McNamara's band, as director of the Office of Management and Budget. Stockman plotted deep cuts in what he considered useless, liberal, do-good welfare programs called foreign aid, and he proposed the biggest cuts ever to IDA and the World Bank. The new secretary of state, Alexander Haig, fought the cuts frontally; McNamara maneuvered to have them sidetracked and a study begun by the treasury of the "effectiveness" of multilateral lending institutions, including the Bank. During McNamara's final months, then, the fate of the Bank at the hands of the Reaganites hung in the balance.[58]

Yet even as he predicted a Reagan victory, McNamara outlined to the governors in his last address, that September, how the Bank needed to grow, because the condition of poor countries was worsening almost by the hour. His critics detected megalomania in his latest plans. On another front, friend and foe alike saw a debt crisis coming.

He stood before the governors a last time, looking as if he were eating too little and running around too much; he looked old, in fact. Prophetlike, McNamara hurled thunderbolts of moral judgment. Outside the huge World Bank meeting there were thousands more commercial bankers, doing business, ready to lend more.

From the podium, McNamara detailed the Bank's plans for structural adjustment loans. He urged governments to accept painful economic adjustments and conceded that sub-Saharan Africa was likely to go into crisis, while growth elsewhere in the Third World would be slower even than he predicted the year before. As with the sales of the Edsel and the odds of winning in Vietnam, African economic projections were sinking off the charts.

But the inextinguishable optimist ticked off actions that should be taken. McNamara formally proposed the energy affiliate and "Bank's bank" as means of expansion of loan volume. They were redesigning "social programs to reduce their per capita cost while expanding their coverage." Still sparring with Geoffrey Howe, McNamara singled out the British government's cuts in foreign aid in a passing remark.

McNamara worried aloud that commercial lending might not "expand" enough in coming years. Although he warned that several countries were in too much debt, he urged more lending: It just had to be managed according to a global strategy.

The Bank should reduce gastrointestinal disease and parasitic infection, so poor people would get more nutrition from food. More girls should go to primary school. It should deliver health care and education "synergistically," to allow more people to be helped at relatively less increase in cost.

Many in the room were aware that an important moment was coming. Once McNamara left the podium, an era would end. The *Wall Street Journal*, the severest media critic of his role at the Bank, would be overjoyed. His admirers, even those who thought his proposals were tired and his philosophy out of sync, were moved.

Margy was dying, many knew; by this time her cancer had advanced quite far. John Merriam, the Bank's information officer, for one, felt almost unable to hold back tears as McNamara came to the end.

"Bob has the greatest difficulty in keeping his coat on, even when he meets important foreign guests," Moeen A. Qureshi would say at one farewell reception by Bank staff for their prophet-president. "Since most people see him only in his shirtsleeves, the impression has gained ground that he is a flaming radical and is pushing the Bank and the developing countries into socialism.

"We thought that by dressing up in black tie we would provide convincing proof to the *Wall Street Journal* and others that we are . . . respectable . . . and are friends of both the establishment and capitalism."[59]

The establishment and capitalism were coming back into vogue — the eighties were on the way. And of course McNamara was a radical. He had become more so with the years, and with the mounting evidence that his dreams and plans were difficult, if not impossible, to realize.

At the end of the speech — and its list of unfinished business for the Bank and the world — McNamara picked up another paper. In farewell, he let the words of George Bernard Shaw speak for him:

"You see things; and you say 'Why?' But I dream things that never were; and I say, 'Why not?' "[60]

The McNamaras and Goodwins had planned a hiking trip to Nepal in 1980. A few weeks after her first operation, Margy decided she would still go as planned. She said to her friend Lydia Katzenbach, "Well, Lydia, if I have to go" — that is, to die — "I might just as well not miss this."

Willard and Mary Joe Goodwin remember vividly how differently each member of the party felt. Margy knew it was her last trip, Bob denied it, and Willard and Mary Joe and the others were unable to discuss it. It was an ironic distance among people who had been so close for so long.

Kathy now had a job at the World Bank and decided to buy a house. The real estate agent who showed them the town house Kathy chose remembers how frail Mrs. McNamara was as she walked around the empty rooms and fresh-smelling floors. "She wanted to get Kathy settled before she died."

The diagnosis was mesothelioma, a rare cancer. Willard Goodwin, a renowned urologist, wondered how Margy could have gotten it. He revisited the house Bob and Margy lived in before Bob's rising status and pay let them move to the big house on Highland Road. This smaller house had asbestos ceilings. This was the scientific cause for her tragedy.

But McNamara had a different theory. "I think she died because of" the Vietnam War, "or at least her deep trauma associated with it," he told journalist Carl Bernstein years later. There was something to this. Susan Mary Alsop, for example, remembers how in the mid-1960s, as Vietnam enveloped their lives, Margy had become tense, her gestures tight.

She had absorbed the pain of her husband's mistakes, and his failure to resolve the war as he had hoped. She suffered when protesters gathered outside the house on Martha's Vineyard and glared at them through the picture window, when people at the tennis club refused to play with them. Like the painting in Oscar Wilde's *Portrait of Dorian Gray*, Margy grew sick and visibly changed while Bob rushed about as usual.

On January 15, 1981, President Jimmy Carter awarded Margy the National Medal of Freedom for her work in battling illiteracy. Bob and the children had to bundle her up for the drive to the White House. She weighed eighty-five pounds and was heavily medicated, saying she saw camels as they rode downtown. She appeared skeletal when the president leaned over her and handed her the award, but she looked straight up at him, direct as ever.

McNamara's plan had been to spend time with Margy after he retired from the Bank in June, but on this too, his overoptimism tripped him up. Margy died in the wee morning hours of February 3.

A few hours later, Blanche Moore looked up from her desk outside the president's office at the World Bank to see her boss loping in past her into his office. The Jordanians were due to meet with him that morning, and he was not going to stand them up, although surely, his staff thought, they would understand if he had chosen to stay home that day. McNamara kept an appointment at the State Department, too, with apologies for being late.

There was a big memorial service at the Washington Cathedral at

which Lydia Katzenbach spoke of Margy's "quiet sense of destiny in
her life." She read a poem by Theodore Roethke that included the
lines

> *I wake to sleep, and take my waking slow.*
> *I feel my fate in what I cannot fear.*
> *I learn by going where I have to go.*
>
> *We think by feeling. What is there to know? . . .*
>
> *Great Nature has another thing to do*
> *to you and me; so take the lively air*
> *And, lovely, learn by going where to go.*

What Margy gave her friends, Katzenbach said, was "the greatest
gift of all, the strength to face our own mortality."[61] In the moments
just after Margy died, Craig tried to put his arms around his father,
but Bob McNamara shook him off, and sat there alone and sobbed.

Epilogue: An American Journey

HAD ROBERT MCNAMARA been a character in a novel, he would have retreated to a quiet retired life after he left the presidency of the World Bank on June 30, following his sixty-fifth birthday. On July 1, 1981, Mc-Namara awoke to the first day in more than twenty years that he was not running a major organization and without the stimulants of power: the people, phones, lockstep meetings, and keen activity that had been his daily diet.

Like other sixty-five-year-olds, McNamara could cultivate his garden now that the tumult and major contributions of life seemed over. The untended garden waiting for his attention, symbolically, was the thorny, sometimes poisonous bramble of his past — his neglect of his children; the problems in the management of the U.S. auto industry, which he helped to shape; the nuclear standoff between the United States and the Soviet Union, which had 17,115 nuclear warheads pointing at each other compared with the 7,316 he had inherited in 1961. There was not only his role in Vietnam, but his thirteen years of silence and lack of effort on behalf of the millions of military veterans of the Vietnam era. Through the 1970s, many of these veterans, confused about the war's validity and stung by their country's rejection, had been in flight from painful memory — as had McNamara.

He had a lot to contemplate. And to answer for, now that he had reached a stage in life when age and the march of time lead many men

of public affairs to look inward. Millions of Americans were safer
from the risks of nuclear war thanks to his work to stabilize the arms
race — although he had built up the American arsenal needlessly.
Millions more Europeans and even Soviets had stopped believing that
nuclear weapons were usable, partly due to McNamara's ceaseless
preaching. McNamara could look with pride to three needed, successful institutional makeovers — of the feudal postwar company of
old Henry Ford, of the Pentagon of 1960 with its myriad half-baked
programs and hollow Army, and of the small, clubby World Bank.
Each had been changed by him in radical, often beneficial ways that
would not have happened if he had not been there.

Yet he could wonder why his legacy was haunted by failure. By
1981, many U.S. manufacturing firms were being gutted by managers
who exploited his system of management controls to maximize short-
term profits at the expense of quality; the Japanese had exploited this
weakness to compete and win in shipbuilding, steel, electronics, and
in building cars. Ford Motor Company was in severe straits. The
Army he remade and equipped in the early 1960s was in a state of
crisis when he left it. And the World Bank in 1981 was "wound up
like a spring," as one observer notes, even as the mixed verdicts on
his antipoverty projects started to come in.

Overarching his institutional and intellectual achievements, in
moral terms, was the net balance to his country, the world, and his
soul. Had "McNamara's war" been necessary? Had its price been too
dear to America? Had American actions, as much as those of Hanoi,
undermined South Vietnam? Or, as rationalizers of the war argued,
had U.S. intervention bought time for other East Asian nations —
including Taiwan, Singapore, Malaysia, and Thailand — to Western-
ize their economies with less debilitating internal strife? As American
troops exited South Vietnam, the Communist-led Khmer Rouge
gained tyrannical control over Cambodia, which caused the slaughter
of a million people. Vietnam then invaded Cambodia and was attacked in turn by China.[1] The turmoil seemed to justify what U.S.
war critics had said: that the region's conflicts were local and Peking
did not call the shots. But it also bore out the judgment of the men
of Washington in the mid-1960s that Hanoi was a brutal, expansionary regime — although now, few Americans noticed or cared.

McNamara could wonder if his years of early management of the
war had set the United States on the wrong path, and whether the
bombing and troop deployments of 1965 were justified. He could

also ask whether, once he became disillusioned with the odds of military success, he was right to stay in power and become a party to Lyndon Johnson's schemes. Was he right to maneuver for a diplomatic solution while urging the troops to fight on and being publicly optimistic? If he had told Americans — and Hanoi — that the war would be much wider and more costly, would Congress and the public have voted to get out? Or would the hawks have won and widened the war? Did McNamara throw away a chance for quick victory — as many in uniform believe? Or did he astutely avoid a bigger, even more frustrating war?

He could ask whether he helped or hurt the nation's healing by his self-imposed silence on Vietnam after 1968. Was his silence during the Nixon years — which allowed him to stay at the Bank and spread the Green Revolution to small farmers and the poor — the right moral choice, in terms of helping "the largest number of people"?

Since he reads philosophy and ethics, McNamara in retirement might catch up on whether saving a soul in Samara offsets a crime in Jerusalem, to be ready for the day of reckoning for this self-critical elder of the Presbyterian Church. Using his quantitative approach, are the millions of Asian lives lost on both sides of the Vietnam War since 1961 and 57,000 Americans dead offset by the 300 million to 500 million people, most of them in Asia, fed through the organizations and financing he arranged to spread seeds and know-how throughout the developing world? Does his nourishing of new, young life in a more prosperous Asia relieve him of obligations to the middle-aged veterans in America who still suffer?

At a final press conference at the Bank, a reporter pumped him: Aren't you going to write your memoirs?

"Memoirs!" McNamara retorted. "Don't you fellows remember the Edsel? The TFX? Vietnam?"[2] He was being facetious — and too harsh. For the memoirs would tell not just of his creation of a World Bank big and powerful enough to be a major force in the tumultuous world of the 1970s and his feeding millions of poor, but also of his effort that began when he was mobbed and burned in effigy in Calcutta in 1968 to build support for foreign aid in the First World and among rich Arab nations that now contribute significantly. McNamara achieved much that is not well known in America. But he still refuses to write memoirs. Let the historians sort it out, he says impatiently. For which read: Let the historians sort *me* out.

٭   ٭   ٭

"He's lonesome. He's brilliant. If he were in Japan and sixty-five he'd be starting a new career," his former protégé, Chrysler president Lee Iacocca, said of McNamara as he left the Bank.[3]

He began a daily walk, coatless, hatless, and in sneakers, from his house on Tracy Place to a suite in a white and black office building at 18th and K streets in downtown Washington. The Corning Glass Corporation awarded him an office and a secretary as part of the arrangement by which he joined its board. The office had been planned by him and Margy after her diagnosis, so he could stay active while they spent more time together. Now there was no Margy. But, says a friend, he was thinking every minute: She's not here and I've got to *do* something.

More and more after Margy's death, he was subject to bouts of tearfulness. For some time at smaller meetings at the Bank, McNamara would interrupt his own, passionate talking to gulp, watery-eyed, stop, and then go on. Even before her death, when he would give his yearly address to the Board of Governors, he left the podium brushing away tears — whether caused by the tension of his major public performance of the year or by the plight of the poor and stunted children he pleaded for.

"I have always been a very emotional person, ever since I can remember having emotions," he told me in a rare moment of introspection one afternoon. It is a confession that never would have been made by the full-cheeked, square-faced young defense secretary of the early 1960s, who denounced emotion as any basis for policy or action. But that last year of running the war had almost broken him; then Bobby Kennedy died. And now Margy.

The tears had been understandable when McNamara had sat hunched over in Washington Cathedral, miserable and alone among two thousand people at Margy's memorial service. Nor were they out of place privately, for she left a vacuum he could not fill himself. But now, his tears flashed out in the midst of conversation, during interviews, at the mention of John Kennedy. Many who saw him were concerned; one hostess calls him "crawling around among the ruins of a life."

His instinct to keep on moving and fill the days with constructive action was healthier than the brooding or contemplative life. But McNamara, especially without Margy, could not, and perhaps refused to, examine what these roiling feelings were; so by running from the pain within — a speech here, a conference there, keeping the calendar full — he condemned himself to let it advance.[4]

So he slogged on unhappily. He was still convinced, however, that the problems of the world urgently needed solution and that he had a special moral duty to solve them.

Trying to live in the present, McNamara began to concoct a new career as public statesman in his own recognizance, which inevitably dragged his name and bitter memories into the American political scene after a thirteen-year absence.

The Reagan administration proved an unexpected help. Within weeks of taking office, Reagan began the largest peacetime defense buildup in U.S. history. His defense secretary, Caspar Weinberger, pandered to the military's claim, still believed twenty years later, that civilian overcontrol weakened the country horribly. Whereas McNamara had rearranged roles and missions in the name of the public interest, Weinberger stapled together the services' requests and blitzed them past startled budget officials and a dazzled Congress. The Reagan tax cut and defense increases raised the federal deficit first to $50 billion, then $100 billion, then $200 billion per year. The ease with which the conservatives conjured up billions for ill-defined defense purposes testified to the lingering memory of McNamara's cost controls and their association with a failed war. Whether or not the armed forces became stronger in proportion to the huge sums spent in the Reagan years, they got one thing they needed badly, which was respect.

The conservatives cast the liberals' reticence to use nuclear weapons as another sign of weakness: Weinberger and his aides began talking graphically about their willingness to fight a nuclear war. Societies had survived devastation before, they said; trains were running the day after the bomb fell on Hiroshima. T. K. Jones, a Weinberger appointee, sent chills up many spines when he told the *Los Angeles Times,* "Dig a hole, cover it with a couple of doors and then throw three feet of dirt on the top. . . . If there are enough shovels to go around everybody's going to make it."[5]

On nuclear matters, McNamara's credibility was high: He had stood on the brink in the Cuban missile crisis and invented Assured Destruction policy (now denounced by neoconservatives as immoral, since it proposed to target cities).[6] Robert McNamara drove himself back into the middle of public debate.

The somewhat forgotten Berlin and Cuba crises of 1961–62 were now dusted off and restudied by many. McNamara gave interviews mainly to stress that crises are dangerous, that misunderstandings lead to war, and that Reagan and his intransigent Soviet adversary were courting great danger. He built an odd symmetry between the growing public fears of nuclear war and the emotional, scary memory of crises he had lived through, which were racing around in his mind.

In interviews he was often objective and self-critical. But if interviewers asked about Vietnam, McNamara showed them out. He was controlling his media, seeking power again, this time through the press; he hadn't changed.

The Reaganites hammered on U.S. European allies to accept new medium-range nuclear weapons — the offspring of the five thousand nuclear arms McNamara shipped there in the 1960s.[7] But Reagan's nuclear-war-fighting talk alarmed the Europeans, too. Leonid Brezhnev foiled Reagan in the court of public opinion in June 1982 by declaring that the Soviets would never be the first to use nuclear weapons. Thus did the new men in Washington seem trigger-happy to growing grass-roots antinuclear movements on two continents.

McNamara joined with his friend and colleague from the 1960s, McGeorge Bundy; Gerard Smith, a former arms control negotiator and McNamara's neighbor on Tracy Place; and George F. Kennan, godfather of U.S. containment policy, to propose a no-first-use policy for the United States and NATO. In a 1982 joint article in *Foreign Affairs,* these major players in the cold war proposed to revoke the United States' guarantee that it would resort to the use of nuclear weapons first, if non-nuclear forces could not hold — and thereby risk drawing Soviet nuclear retaliation on New York and Chicago. "No first use" did not rule out using nuclear weapons second if the enemy used them first. But when coupled with the Soviet no-first-use pledge it would make the world safer — and calmer.[8]

So he positioned himself, with the other three, as a voice of reason in a dangerous world. He also sought out Reagan's arms control director, Kenneth Adelman, for regular breakfasts, imagining he could proselytize this card-carrying conservative. Even more curiously for a man positioning himself as tutor and spokesman for the reviving left, McNamara conspicuously praised Reagan personally. As always, he preferred dancing with those in the highest positions of power to joining the growing crowds in streets and the disorder of protest politics.

An underlying object of the no-first-use plan was for these former U.S. statesmen to show nervous governments in Europe and the Kremlin that the American establishment had not lost its mind, that there were sober people ready to follow a reasonable course to lower the escalating nuclear danger. Yet the reincarnation of these Vietnam hawks into spokesmen for liberals of the eighties, wrote a young journalist, David Talbot, in *Mother Jones,* is "one of the most astonishing twists in recent American history."[9]

Yet the establishment welcomed McNamara. Within fifteen months of launching his new career, he sat with Bundy and Smith at a formal lunch in New York, with tablecloths and flowers, whose subscribers paid two hundred dollars a plate to see them. The three were given the prestigious Einstein Peace Prize for their article. (Kennan had received it in 1981, the year before.)[10] The award was a bronze-colored plaque portraying Albert Einstein, which McNamara put on view in his Corning office suite, where it reminded visitors that the occupant was a man of peace.

Even as McNamara rose to receive the peace prize in October 1982, hundreds of Vietnam veterans were crossing the country. Some came by car, some on motorcycles; some made the pilgrimage on foot. Some stopped along the way to pick up buddies from their days together in "Nam" to take to the opening. One man drove with a sign in his rear window, "Nam Vet to DC," and people honked and waved. A loner with his backpack and his dog walked on foot all the way from Vermont. From Beaumont, Texas; Fergus Falls, Minnesota; Jesup, Iowa — they came as if they were all drawn by the same "ghostly bugle."[11]

As the cold, clear morning dawned on November 13, some 150,000 converged on the Mall in Washington, although held from their object by a fragile fence. Hundreds came in wheelchairs. The veterans were heavier and longer-haired than when they had served. Many had had a very hard time since their return. Would they be disappointed again?

"Let's just forget the whole thing," President Gerald Ford had remarked when the last helicopter lifted from the roof of the U.S. embassy in April 1975 as Saigon fell to the Communists. Ford expressed Americans' mood of exhaustion and flight. In his willingness to neglect the men who fought, he followed in the tracks of Lyndon Johnson, who had cut benefits offered in the GI Bill of the 1960s to less than those given to Korean War veterans (because the costs of waging Vietnam without price controls or a tax hike squeezed all other federal programs). Then Jimmy Carter took office and issued a blanket pardon for those draft evaders who had left the country (estimated at five thousand), earning the anger of many of the two million who served in Indochina between 1961 and 1975. Veterans Administration hospitals were found to give shockingly poor care to Vietnam vets; the VA also denied benefits for Agent Orange syndrome, a group of symptoms many vets felt sure was caused by the herbicides they sprayed in Vietnam. The veterans remained relatively less healthy, more problem-prone, and more likely to be unemployed than earlier veterans. And an influential study by Lawrence M. Baskir and William A. Strauss claimed that the low-aptitude recruits drawn in under McNamara's Project 100,000, from 1966 to 1970, had the worst time of all.[12]

It was fitting irony that a female architecture student of Chinese descent had won the competition for the Vietnam Veterans Memorial. Maya Ying Lin proposed a plain wall, a black slab of marble buried in the earth like a deep scar with the names of every American who died engraved on the surface. The proposed wall aroused controversy and rejection, aggravating the pain of the war the more.

On the morning of November 13, the leaders from the Vietnam era stood on a platform. General William Westmoreland was prominent, looking tall and ramrod straight as ever. The little fence had been removed.

The drums rolled, the ribbon was cut. Suddenly thousands of men, in hats and mufflers and vests, bounded across the open ground, whooping and shouting and crying. They scrambled to the wall, straining to touch the names of the dead engraved on its shining surface. As they reached it, they piled against it and climbed over each other to find the names of fallen friends, trying to touch the memory through cold stone.

Missing from the row of luminaries on the podium was R. S. McNamara. Jan Scruggs, the organizer of the memorial project, had telephoned McNamara when he was still at the World Bank.[13] Scruggs was put through right away when he told the secretary what he was calling about. McNamara came on the line, and Scruggs explained the project. We need big bucks, as much as ten million, he explained.

McNamara said he could put Scruggs in touch with people who

could help. The big bass voice of authority said, "Drop me a line and we'll talk again." Scruggs was thrilled to have as an ally this still powerful man, for many people, even some in Congress, had told him Vietnam was too shameful to justify commemoration.

Scruggs had written McNamara the next day. Then he waited. A week later he called and left a message. And again. Scruggs never heard back from McNamara.

The embattled veterans had had to fight this second war, to make people realize that even in the absence of a national reckoning that could heal the real scars, they needed that cold slab; the act of finding and feeling the names on the wall was like finding a missing piece of oneself.

Did McNamara go there? Says a friend: "He went once, very privately."

A few weeks after Margy died, McNamara telephoned Joan Braden. She and her husband, columnist Tom Braden, had known Bob and Margy since the early 1960s. Joan had lunched with McNamara in his private dining room at the World Bank occasionally since 1976, when she began a job as consumer adviser to the State Department. She told me, "I had a job that was totally economics and trade. I called Bob and said I want to know more. Could I see you and talk to you?"[14]

Bob had phoned to ask her if Tom would mind "if we had dinner together once in a while," she says. Tom replied, she says, "Fine. The guy's just lost his wife." Joan is petite, short-haired, tanned, with electric blue eyes and a Hollywood smile. And she rubs snuff onto her lower gum regularly, a habit that is as addictive as smoking.

Tom and Joan and Bob and Margy had long been part of a particular group of Washington influentials. In 1960 when candidate John Kennedy was trying to win California, Joan, working with Bobby Kennedy, had filled the Los Angeles Coliseum for the candidate. The Kennedys became friends; Jackie would have a lunch at the White House for Joan when she would come east; Joan, who free-lanced as a journalist, snagged an assignment to cover Jackie's trip to India.

Joan remembers first meeting Bob and Margy at Bobby and Ethel Kennedy's Hickory Hill "intellectual" evenings. In the 1960s the McNamaras and Bradens saw each other regularly, either at the home of columnist Stewart Alsop and his wife, Trisha, in Georgetown at Joseph and Susan Mary Alsop's, or elsewhere. Others they knew in common were the late Lorraine Cooper, wife of Kentucky senator John Sherman Cooper, and Polly and Frank Wisner, the latter a CIA official who, in a fit of depression, committed suicide in 1965. To these people McNamara was known as Bobby Mac.

Among these, however, the Bradens stood out for their open cultivation of people with glamour or power. In California, it had been actor Kirk Douglas who introduced them to the Kennedys; to this day a photo of Douglas sits amid the family photographs in the Bradens' sprawling yellow house in Chevy Chase, Maryland. Joan had been at one time a secretary and aide to Nelson Rockefeller, who put up $183,500 to help Tom buy the newspaper in California he published; when they moved to Washington, Rockefeller contributed $60,000 to help them buy the Chevy Chase house; as vice president in 1974, Rockefeller made a personal gift of $10,000 to Joan, according to public documents.[15]

The Bradens have entertained regularly, seeking out newsmakers. When Tom began writing a column with former Kennedy aide Frank Mankiewicz, they began giving Sunday night suppers for notables, to which Bob and Margy came.

For most of the past twenty-five years, the Bradens have led active professional and social lives; they have a certain cachet, because they are former members of Camelot and because they are informal and entertain a lot, with a good nose for those at the hub of each administration. They often complain of being short of funds yet have managed to raise eight children in their large home.

In the self-consciously respectable circles of Georgetown and Kalorama, Joan is famous for her close friendships with famous men. Criticism in the press of her appointment as consumer affairs adviser to the State Department cited her lack of credentials; the charge was that she got the job through another friend, Henry Kissinger, then secretary of state. She is also known for her on-the-record views on marriage. She told the *Washington Post:*

> "We're not Catholics, but Tom is Catholic about divorce. He just doesn't believe in it . . . I don't believe that anybody can be with the same person for 33 years and not be attracted to someone else . . . it's not necessary for a man and woman to be monogamous, but there's no sense in hurting or embarrassing [your husband] either. The prerequisites for a happy marriage are not monogamy but respect, trust and love."[16]

And so, she says, her husband, Tom, approved of her having dinner with Bob McNamara. In 1982, when he asked her to travel with him to South Africa, she asked Tom if she could go with Bob. Tom told her it was a great opportunity, she says.

Rumors grew of a McNamara–Joan Braden relationship. Lonely, miserable without Margy, McNamara turned to his other friends, who include a number of eligible women. The most royal match for him would be with Katharine Graham, publisher of the *Washington Post*. Graham, a widow since her husband Philip's death in 1963, has been devoted to McNamara, and he has served on the *Washington Post* board. There are rumors of a coolness in that friendship, however, since Joan Braden has figured in Bob McNamara's life, although it is not clear that a McNamara-Graham union was ever in the cards.

A younger woman whom McNamara occasionally asked to dinner in the early 1980s remembers hearing rumors that he was seeing Joan and sensing that he was "leaving room" in his life for someone else, without saying so.

In a book she has written (in which she denies having slept with Rockefeller or Kissinger or Bobby Kennedy), Joan says she hoped she was not preventing Bob McNamara from remarrying.

"In the beginning there was conversation" about marriage between them, Braden told me. "But I would never leave Tom for anybody." She indicated that at first some of her children did not approve because "they adore Tom." Now they enjoy talking about issues with Bob.

"It isn't an affair. That's what people don't understand," she said, drawing herself up with a steamy, outraged look. "This is a friendship. Like my friendship with Nelson Rockefeller." As for the fact that they use the same hotel room when they travel, her comeback is to say how mortified she was the first time Bob reserved one hotel room instead of two in their separate names. This was in Peking, when Winston Lord was U.S. ambassador. "I got really mad at Bob," said Braden. "I said to him, what will Win and Bette [Lord's wife] *think?*" Later she admitted their relationship was "ninety percent friendship."

She repeatedly praised Tom and said people misunderstand her "friendship" with McNamara. "What's wrong with loving two men?" she asked at one point.

What has driven Bob McNamara, in the aftermath of Margy's

death, not only to turn to Joan but pursue the "friendship" for more than a decade without resolving the triangle into some more normal, and respectable, duet, either by marrying her or breaking it off to leave Joan to Tom? McNamara only says, "Joan is terrific. We have shared values. She has had these jobs; she is interested in these things I work on. And," he adds, with clear appreciation, "she's a lot of fun."

He denies he will ever remarry, although he says Margy urged him to before she died. "I had forty years of marriage with one of God's loveliest creatures," he says, in the way he talks of Margy. "There's nothing more I can have from marriage than I already have had."

A male friend explains McNamara's ongoing interest in Braden as "need. Joan has an incredible talent for making any man feel like he's the only one on earth. She probably calls him up three times a day and tells him he's wonderful. Bob *needs* that."

A female friend also says she tried to tell Bobby Mac that this triangle was unworthy of his old straight-shooter self. "He will not tolerate *any* disloyalty," she adds with a sigh.

Little Margy and Kathleen McNamara's reaction to their mother's death was to realize how large was the gulf between them and their father. It occurred to them that they had to make the effort to reach out to him, because maybe he didn't know how to reach them. It was maturing to even think of filling their mother's role.

Craig, meanwhile, had lots of reason for contact. Having studied agriculture at the University of California at Davis, he persuaded his father to co-invest in a walnut farm near Winters, California, that is his livelihood. He married, and Bob McNamara became a grandfather.

Sometimes the crop succeeds and sometimes it doesn't; sometimes the market is undercut by foreign nut growers. Craig tries to explain farming to his father. [17] He feels he is more artful at getting him to open up than he used to be. But his success is mixed. "When I try to talk to him about something else, like politics, he just changes the subject and says: how many bushels are you getting this month." His father does the math better than he can but doesn't understand farming.

Jetting through northern California en route around the globe, McNamara rarely touches down on the walnut farm. "He doesn't like to spend the night here," says Craig.

But Craig keeps hoping. A large, formal Bachrach photograph of his father hangs by the doorway to the farm kitchen. In it McNamara leans forward across a desk, in a dark suit and compulsively combed hair. He looks directly at the viewer through his famous spectacles. One hand is in front of his chin, as if he is in contemplation. The other stretches out sideways along the desk, as if to control the encounter, as though he is closing a deal. Craig has slowly gained his father's respect ("He's constructive," McNamara says of Craig in a forced tone). But it is not clear which McNamara Craig will one day know, the man of overwhelming authority in his life or the bemused thinker.

Millions of Americans saw McNamara the thinker one night in October 1983, after the closing scenes of *The Day After*, the horrifying docudrama aired by ABC that showed how ordinary Americans would experience a nuclear war.

Fearing the show could cause public panic, the network followed it with a panel that included McNamara, Carl Sagan, and Henry Kissinger to discuss the issue dispassionately. McNamara looked younger than his sixty-seven years and was forceful and modulated, a balanced presence. He and Kissinger feared the show would start a stampede toward unilateral nuclear disarmament. McNamara made the establishment's case for why we have to have nuclear weapons, so long as the Soviets have them, why zero nuclear weapons by one superpower alone does not make a safer world.[18]

It was not an easy case to make, but the reborn McNamara did it. "I was sitting on the edge of my chair," watching his father, Craig says. "His persona on TV that night was a wonderful change from the Vietnam days. . . . He seemed compassionate and tempered by his experience."[19]

In the fall 1983 issue of *Foreign Affairs*, under his name alone, McNamara offered another glimpse of his "real" self.[20] "Nuclear weapons serve no military purpose whatsoever. They are totally useless, except to deter one's opponent from using them," he said — echoing his argument on *The Day After*. He went on:

"That is my view. It was my view in the early 1960s." He claimed he had *always* been a no-first-user. "At that time" — that is, in the 1960s — "in long private conversations with successive presidents — Kennedy and Johnson — I recommended, without qualification, that they never initiate, under any circumstances, the use of nuclear weapons. I believe they accepted my recommendation."

Thus McNamara seemed to repudiate his many public and private assertions that the United States would use "whatever weapons are necessary" — which the allies understood to mean nuclear weapons first, if needed. This promise was at the core of the alliance. Now McNamara seemed to be taking it back.

He had shown a draft of the *Foreign Affairs* article to a colleague, who, upon reading this passage, had objected. "You can't take it back now. If you believed in the alliance at all, you had to mean what you said back then about your readiness to exercise the nuclear guarantee. People in Europe will say you are untrustworthy."

McNamara was unconcerned about old loyalties and perceptions of his truthfulness, then or now. He was fixated on his new enemy: not China, as in the spring of 1965, and not world poverty, as when he rose to the podium at Nairobi in 1973. Now his enemy was the nuclear weapon itself. He brushed the colleague's objections aside. Oh no, he said, in effect — you don't understand how awful these weapons are. We have to get rid of them. The first step is to prove they are useless. They always were.

So he had charged ahead and was criticized. "No one is better at the selective disclosure of history than Bob McNamara," wrote Michael Gordon in the *National Journal*.[21]

I myself began by disbelieving that McNamara ever had the "long private conversations" with Kennedy and Johnson he claimed in 1983 or had consciously forsworn *ever* using nuclear weapons first during the 1960s. I told him I didn't believe it, several times, with no apparent effect. Then I put in writing for him a list of the times he said directly or by implication that he and the president were prepared to resort to nuclear weapons first if necessary.

My written charges seemed to open him up; he finally described his entirely plausible inner evolution, his private, literal fears — beginning as early as 1961 — of what could happen when nuclear weapons were used and his feeling that he had to publicly uphold alliance policy while pushing the allies, the president, and the military to consider the dangers and modify that policy.[22]

I found it plausible that McNamara *had* been a mole in the world of nuclear saber rattling that employed him. It fit with his secretiveness, his boundless ambition to do good, his habit of manipulative schemes built around simple, almost religiously held insights. With nuclear weapons, as with Vietnam, McNamara built a terrifying, destructive machine — almost from impulse — then fought it while defending it and being publicly identified with it. And I wondered at the effort he expended over thirty years concealing some of these positions, ducking and weaving about where he stood.

I also sensed the symmetry between McNamara's inner demons — the emotions that he spent a lifetime battening down — and the dark visions of uncontrolled terror that pervade his public statements. He paints not only the horrors of nuclear war, where the living envy the dead, but images of an overpopulated world in which children's minds are stunted, violence and amorality rule, and humankind declines because it did not have the wit to take charge of its destiny in the middle-to-late twentieth century.[23]

South Africa became one of his causes also. In a speech at the University of Witwatersrand in 1982 — his and Joan's first foreign trip together — McNamara warned there would be blood in the streets, turmoil, and chaos if the white-ruled government did not move toward accommodation with its vast black population. War could follow, which would not be short despite the government's advantage in technology and firepower. The Soviets would keep the black resisters supplied over South Africa's borders, so that "a relatively small number of guerrillas can tie up substantial military forces." He had some knowledge of this hazard of war.[24]

McNamara's reticence on Vietnam and revelations of his "real" positions on other issues earned him a mixed reputation with scholars. More than once at convocations I attended for this project, I heard snickers when his views or truthfulness was discussed. Some historians found him a scholarly, self-critical source, as often I did. But he still resists reflection on what he has done and who he is, thus staying in the comfort zone of present action, sailing on in his preferred role as manager of the future world.

Joan is picked up at the Braden home in the wee hours of the morning by the only former president of Ford Motor Company who drives a blue Escort (the company gives all onetime presidents a new Ford each year, and most of them choose Lincolns). She is whisked off to Honolulu and back, or to Peking, South Africa, Europe, or some combination of the above. She told me, "I asked Bob, when do you stop and *reflect*?"

"On airplanes. I reflect on airplanes," he answered.

But, she added, "He doesn't reflect on airplanes. He *sleeps* on airplanes."

The Flying Dutchman of legend is cursed to forever sail his ghost ship through the seas for this reason: Once, when he attempted to sail around the Cape of Good Hope and was driven back repeatedly by storms, he had cursed God and said he would sail through the storm if he had to sail on forever. God punished him for defying nature.

America's own Flying Dutchman touched down in courtroom number 3 in lower Manhattan on December 6, 1984, clutching a battered raincoat and TWA ticket envelope, just off a flight from Europe.

The courtroom of Pierre S. Leval of the U.S. District Court for the Southern District of New York, hearing the case of *General William C. Westmoreland* v. *CBS Inc.,* was packed, even though McNamara's appearance had been confirmed only days before.[25] People were standing three deep in the back, to hear the progenitor of "McNamara's war," under oath and in public, answer for his conduct of it, for the first time since he left office as defense secretary in 1968.

McNamara marched to the witness box and was sworn in. A Styrofoam cup sat on the wooden ledge next to him.

He had chosen to jump into the nation's most sensational media trial, which reopened the charge of official deceit as nothing had since the publication of the Pentagon Papers in 1971. CBS's 1982 broadcast of *The Uncounted Enemy: A Vietnam Deception,* charged that Westmoreland was part of a "conspiracy at the highest levels of government" to suppress larger enemy-strength figures and pretend the war was going better than it was. The show caused a sensation, which was heightened when *TV Guide* and an internal CBS investigation found bias in the reporting and filming. Westmoreland, backed by conservative foundations, sued the network and the producers, focusing the anger of many on the powerful, post-Vietnam, post-Watergate media.

McNamara had never been close to Westmoreland, but he agreed to give a deposition on behalf of the general's character. One motive was that McNamara did not believe that Westmoreland conspired to deceive him and the president. But another possible motive was that through his long years of public silence, McNamara was privately sick and tired of the press lambasting the leaders of the war for lying and deceit. "This is a disgrace, an absolute disgrace," he had blurted out furiously as CBS's lawyers took his testimony, or deposed him, in March 1984.

"I want it clear that you are extracting these answers against my wishes," he had also said. But he virtually invited the other side to depose and cross-examine him. For instead of submitting a simple statement attesting to Westmoreland's character, McNamara submitted an affidavit making ten points, many of which invited questions. In point seven, for example, he claimed that disputes about enemy strength in 1967 would not have made any difference to him because by that time, "I already felt there was no way to win the war militarily." David Boies, the lead lawyer for CBS, said that sentence alone waved a red flag, "as though he was asking us to depose him specifically on that."

Point seven went to the heart of the ethics of McNamara's choices on the war, issues that were only rumored while he held office and finally confirmed when the Pentagon Papers were leaked and revealed the depth of his pessimism. If McNamara saw the war was militarily unwinnable, was he not deceiving the country by his public optimism and his urging the men to fight on?

He had been cranky when the CBS lawyers took his deposition in March. McNamara claimed he couldn't remember the simplest facts about when he served as secretary of defense or the views of the president. He claimed the enemy-strength figures in 1967 could have been off by "as much as 50 percent" and that "the numbers never did add up." These were startling admissions from the man who had spewed statistics like a geyser in claiming success in the war's early years.[26]

But through several hours of questioning under oath, McNamara held fast to point seven. Those who had fought — for Westmoreland and his friends followed McNamara's strange revelations, too — wondered how the number-two man in the chain of command could have ethically gone on urging soldiers and pilots to fight and die. Was McNamara, the dove of the 1980s, trying to take back this part of his past, too?

In the courtroom, the graying figure in the witness box clutched a sheaf of scrawled notes to his chest. He sat hunched to one side, leaning away from the judge's rostrum. Westmoreland's lawyers planned to keep McNamara on the stand just long enough to vouch for their client and then whisk him off. But through a misstep they opened the door for CBS to question McNamara broadly.

David Boies believed he had a historic opportunity to show the
world that McNamara had deceived the public. In evidence was Mc-
Namara's pessimistic memo to the president of May 19, 1967, which
was declassified for the trial and of which the Pentagon Papers had
quoted only excerpts. Boies's grilling aimed to show, as Judge Leval
correctly interpreted the line of questioning, that "the witness is not
a truth-teller."[27]

The listing figure in the witness box said he did not believe in 1967
that they had reached the "cross-over point" and were winning, as
Westmoreland claimed. He said the tables attached to his May 19
memo showed this.

Boies protested: But you say in the memo's text that " 'we reached
the cross-over point.' " No, McNamara shot back, "the sentence
you have quoted . . . quotes General Westmoreland." He said he had
put the statement in quotation marks in the memorandum to show it
was Westmoreland's, not his own. McNamara had pulled up the
blind on his semantic game, the key to the riddle.

Boies put before McNamara the transcript of the August 1967
Senate hearing on the bombing. He read out a passage in which
McNamara sounded optimistic, because he told Senator Henry Jackson "from what you have heard from General Westmoreland and
General [Earle] Wheeler and the other Chiefs . . . each of them firmly
believes we are winning." Demanded Boies: You were saying Westmoreland and the chiefs thought this? That's right, McNamara said;
"that's not my judgment, that's theirs." Well, said Boies, summoning
up disdain, "did you tell Senator Jackson, in words or substance, that
you disagreed with the statements General Westmoreland and General Wheeler and the other chiefs were making?"

Well, said McNamara, I expressed so much skepticism during the
hearing that Senator Strom Thurmond accused me of "making a statement appeasing the communists" and a "no-win" statement.

Boies: When Thurmond accused you, you said, "I submit it is not
a 'no-win' program." McNamara came back: When I said "not a
'no-win' program," I was referring to not only the shooting war but
the "political track" as well. We had a "two-track approach," he
said, finally opening up his real position on the war in 1967, the
defense in *his* case.

Boies showed him an article from *Newsweek* from September
1967. In it McNamara was asked if "the war" was "stalemated"; he
had said, "Heavens, no." To Boies and the jury McNamara now

claimed he had been talking about the two tracks, not just the shooting war, he said. The courtroom was hushed; he was coming to life, assuming some of his old authority.

"I did say it's a no-win militarily . . . I said it cannot be won by military action. We had a two-track approach, one political and the other military, and the military was designed to move us along the political track."[28]

His subtext was: *Therefore I was being ethical. I was working for a resolution with probes to Hanoi as the carrot and military punishment as the stick. So the fighting was not in vain.* Yet it was hard to grasp, between his own digressions and the lawyer's verbal pounding. "I admit these seem like hairline distinctions," he said at one point, as Boies hung over him with body language that said, *Aren't you a damn liar, sir?*

McNamara was warming to why the political track justified his optimistic statements in the summer and fall of 1967. "We were in communication with Ho Chi Minh via a secret channel through two Frenchmen who were receiving messages . . . from me . . . through Henry Kissinger," he said. He was contacting Ho, trying to get some movement.

Just as McNamara started to explain, Judge Leval cut him off. Henry Kissinger and the chances of talks were not relevant, the judge said, trying to pull Boies and the witness back to the case at hand. Yet the defense in the United States versus Robert McNamara had just begun.

Of course, it was Boies's job to jump all over this hostile witness and make it as hard as possible for the jury to pick up McNamara's meaning. Yet writer Renata Adler declared in the *New Yorker* that McNamara's testimony had been "one of the few moments of real historic interest in all the testimony about the war."[29]

I happened to have a prearranged meeting with McNamara the next day. It was the only time I saw him relaxed. Apparently he thought he had won: Someone with him told him the jury had been spellbound; rarely had a witness been so precise. He seemed relieved.

"My father had been *so* worried about that appearance," says his daughter Margy Pastor.

"It was a huge price to pay for me to go up there. It was painful as hell. I cannot go before the American people and be forced to talk about Vietnam without a lot of pain and personal embarrassment. It's humiliating, frankly. But I did it and it's over and so the hell with it," he said when it was over.[30] Yet his halting statements in the West-moreland affair, the oral histories he released for this project, and his clarifications to me show the outlines both of his case and his private remorse. A historical process has begun.

The president, he, and Bundy were not "planning, in the sense of anticipating, embarking upon 'overt war' with North Vietnam" in 1964, he now says. There was no "*administration* plan," he stresses. Johnson's intention was "to continue as we were." In McNamara's mind, that is different from having a plan and deceiving by not re-vealing it to the public.

As to the strategic stakes, McNamara now says, "We misjudged Chinese geopolitical objectives." At the time, to him, China "sounded like a terrible threat" to the region. He says he now thinks that view was "either incorrect or only partially correct."[31] He questions it.

Any veteran who doubts McNamara believed in the cause need only read the tale of his impatience with Johnson's drifting policies of late 1964; of his collaboration with McGeorge Bundy urging the president to choose military intervention in January 1965; and fi-nally, of how, once he had a clear goal, he overrode dissent to get results.

Then came the insight by November 3, 1965, that the war was "unwinnable militarily." In his deposition, with memory made vague by buried and denied feeling, McNamara said he reached this con-clusion in "mid-1966 or sooner." At this point, the charge against him goes, he chose to deceive the American people by hiding the bad news while raising troop levels to 400,000, then 500,000, when he could have resigned, told the "truth," and stopped the American involvement.

That the war could not be won in the military sense was the administration's public position, in fact. From the start the United States did not seek military victory in the normal sense of the term and so stated. McNamara's trip report of July 20, 1965, on which the troop deployments were based, did not even mention "victory"; and his more detailed June 26 position paper said Westmoreland's goal was to reestablish "the military balance by the end of December" and then to get the enemy to "back off" over a longer period. So much for "winning" the shooting war.[32]

McNamara was stubborn, even when he saw how long and hard the war could be. He would not let the inevitable — the collapse of South Vietnam — take place. His persistence was shared by many others who also saw the U.S. strategy was badly flawed.[33] For example, Army general Bruce Palmer recalls: "We didn't understand the Vietnamese or the situation, or what kind of war it was. By the time we found out, it was too late. We were deeply committed. That old 'can do' syndrome got us. You know, Americans 'can do' anything!"

As White House aide John Roche said later, "What was he supposed to say to those fellows" — the soldiers — "get out there and die for a compromise?" McNamara's moral dilemma was no different from that of losing commanders through history: How much will continued sacrifice improve the terms of settlement? At what point is it futile?

Thus McNamara's passionate insistence on gradualism put him in square opposition to the American tradition of war that demands we lavish resources and technology and fight a violent, head-on-fashion war to shorten it and thus conserve U.S. lives.[34] McNamara was caught in a dilemma; he tried to limit the ground war and the bombing to hold down American casualties, yet in January 1966, he approved another 200,000 troops so Westmoreland could keep the pressure up and avoid defeat. He tried to lower the bombing with the thirty-seven-day bombing pause, yet its failure committed him to renewed, wider bombing that inevitably would lose more pilots. By 1967 Westmoreland saw victory coming; McNamara privately did not believe it, yet associated himself publicly with the general's optimism. He approved this clarification to me:

"The strategy of gradualism, which many officers blamed for prolonging the war, was critical to minimize loss of life."

As for critics who have argued that a heavier air campaign could have settled the war, McNamara says, "How do they *know*" the Soviets and Chinese wouldn't have come in? "By the way, how do they know that if we had gone all out, the North Vietnamese would have surrendered?"[35]

From the viewpoint of the early 1970s, when the antiwar movement was at its peak, people said that if McNamara had resigned in 1966–67 and spoken out, he could have stopped the war. Yet in 1966, a majority of Americans supported the war; even in the summer of 1967, a majority polled thought the war was a mistake but also favored going all out to win, now that we were there. Clearly McNamara feared that if he revealed all, he and the president would lose control to the hawks; his critics disagree.

Meanwhile, McNamara's inner torment grew daily. Habitually preoccupied with order, he saw himself failing to contain the chaos; each stroke and counterstroke he devised sucked the nation in deeper. To change the nation's course he needed credibility, but his years of arrogance left him with little. He was tormented; "sleeping pills help," he told the AP's Saul Pett in December 1967. From now on his thoughts and conversation would swing between the specters of tragedy and his reflex optimism, the side of him that jumps up and says, Stop, I have the answer.

The most interesting part of McNamara's emerging view is his belief at the time that he could wring a response from Hanoi and get Johnson to talk, too.

"If I didn't believe that we had a chance of progressing on the political track as a result of our military pressure . . . I should have strongly recommended withdrawing from Vietnam, and if the government wouldn't do it, I should have resigned. There's no question about that in my mind," he told me. But he hung on, believing he could fix it.

"So the fighting was not in vain," he now says, "even though I was pessimistic about how well we were doing in the field."[36]

Yet many have argued that there was no hope of negotiations in 1966 or 1967: Hanoi had no incentive to talk, because it was countering Westmoreland's military deployments. On the other hand, Johnson would not make the concessions Hanoi demanded, such as an unconditional bombing halt, so that it would talk.

McNamara's written record shows he consistently lobbied Johnson from the spring of 1965 on to push for a settlement "with continuing vigor and visible determination," as he urged in the July 20 report. It seems clear that Lyndon Johnson, whose other advisers argued that concessions would make him look weak, never pursued the "integrated" political and military tracks that McNamara deemed essential. He consistently bent to appease the right: In August and September, while the Kissinger probe McNamara described at the trial was contacting Hanoi, Johnson ordered bombing hits on new targets; Hanoi had grounds to think the probe was not sincere.[37]

Henry Kissinger confirms that McNamara was in a minority in his eagerness to probe Hanoi, that he was desperately sincere. "From the beginning," Kissinger writes, McNamara "urged — nay, pleaded for — a negotiated and not an imposed peace." McNamara "supported the search for diplomatic initiatives more vigorously and consistently than the agencies" charged with this job, meaning the State Department. He was "the principal impetus" in getting the rest of the administration to back Kissinger's 1967 probe and the San Antonio formula proposed publicly in September 1967, which contained fewer preconditions for talks. David Kraslow and Stuart H. Loory term this formula "a marked departure" from the president's earlier demands and "the most conciliatory Washington had made" until that time.[38]

McNamara incurred the opprobrium of the senior military for insisting on gradualism, as well as congressional and public mistrust, while maneuvering, he thought, for the greater good. He was doomed to fail. The climactic moment came in August 1967, when he testified before the Senate in an effort to build public support for a moderate course, with the result that the Joint Chiefs of Staff — led by General Wheeler, whom McNamara liked so much — secretly agreed to resign en masse. By early November, McNamara breached the bounds of accepted conduct in the president's inner circle by asserting in writing that a unilateral bombing halt, which he recommended, "would lead to talks." This brought protests from the other advisers and forced Johnson to remove him.

McNamara's pain and humiliation in thinking about Vietnam come from lingering faith that he, Bob McNamara, might just have brought off his scheme and ended it in 1967. He says now: "I do believe that the continuation [of bombing pauses] — and other political actions we might have undertaken — would have resulted in a reduction in the military action on both sides." He admits he has "no proof"; however, he says he thinks "that the tempo of the war would have been slowed and I [believe] that the ultimate peace settlement — the political settlement — would have been advanced." And then, with understatement, his sorrow: "I very much regret that we didn't carry it out." Thus he says:

"Our greatest failure of all was Vietnam. We failed in the sense that we did not foresee it would turn out as it did." It is the regret of someone who failed to control, to manage events. One friend even speculates that McNamara has declined to talk about the war to punish himself to the last.[39]

Finally, McNamara says here for the first time publicly that he and Kennedy planned to withdraw all U.S. advisers by the end of 1965, even if the South Vietnamese "were going to be 'defeated.' " He says, "I know for a fact that John Kennedy would have withdrawn from Vietnam."

Thus he adds his name to the list of former Kennedy advisers who have made this assertion, and like them, he has offered no proof.[40] He has not said what evidence he has: On this most sensitive issue of all, his habit of glimpse and concealment goes on.

Most of the lessons drawn from McNamara's life have been negative: that management by numbers ruined America's manufacturing know-how; that the Bank's lending left the poorest countries with crippling debt; that the deceits and subterfuges of Vietnam disillusioned a generation with government. David Halberstam has called McNamara a "dangerous figure" because it is his "special skill to fool people," to "seem better than his official acts," whereas "the real McNamara" is "someone who says one thing in public and always follows the mandate of his superiors in private."[41]

Purely negative judgments are too easy; in the end we are stuck with a more awkward and accurate truth — the same qualities that made McNamara sincerely work to help society and brought success led to failure as well. The paradox of his life cannot be resolved by ignoring the flaws or virtues. Thus the larger paradox of his legacy: He is a pivotal figure in the weakening and decline of America, despite the many virtues of the American Century he embodies.

McNamara can be gravely faulted for overoptimism, misjudgment, and deceit, for he is as manipulative and concealing in the service of fine ends as when he is carrying out the mandate of superiors. He tended to abuse the institutions he ran; he was too quantitative and too powerful. But to write him off for this is to ignore the hard fact that his judgment was often right — he saw the problems with nuclear weapons earlier than most; he saw that smallholder agriculture could multiply the Green Revolution and raise incomes of the poor. A final judgment is premature, but future historians will weigh his positive insights against his misjudgments, his many efforts to drive institutions in the right direction against the times he drove them off course.

His faith that he could resolve the war from within may have been delusional. Yet only someone who dreams "things that never were" and asks "Why not?" could have focused the World Bank on small-farmer agriculture. Only a manager demanding results, with five-year plans or other controls, could make that dream come true to the extent it did.

"I believe that there needs to be no conflict between the goals of a large institution and those of society," he told me in our first conversation, as a maxim of his life. Any judgment must consider his three major efforts to make giant institutions "serve society" and his successful managerial inventions on a smaller scale, like the Nuclear Planning Group; the Consultative Group on International Agricultural Research, which was the catalyst to feed 300 million; and structural adjustment lending.[42] If he made enemies, such as the Old Guard at the Bank, the very success of his Bank for the era it faced and his intellectual leadership there shows the truth of William James's words: "Institutions tremble when a new idea appears."

If McNamara the corporate man sparked a generation of youth to fight "the system" and be proud to hate government and big companies, perhaps today, as our problems become planetary, McNamara's attempts to make mainstream institutions serve larger social goals should be restudied. McNamara the reforming administrator may be more relevant now than McNamara the flawed leader.

Why did so many of his efforts backfire? One answer is trust, or rather the lack of it. Bob McNamara was not trusted, and he trusts few people; perhaps he trusted only Margy. He seems not to have realized he needed trust; he may not know what trust is. The lesson he took from his formative years was that he could transform his environment and invent the future by sheer willpower. He was raised with few close relationships and taught not to be bound by the world around him but to move on.

He made an extraordinary remark about "managing reality" in his February 1967 speech at Millsaps College. As he extolled management "as the most creative of all the arts, for its medium is human talent itself" and as the "gate" for spreading change through society, he said that the "real threat to democracy comes from undermanagement, not from over-management. To undermanage reality is not to keep it free. It is simply to let some force other than reason shape reality."[43] For "reason" shaping reality read: Bob McNamara, working alone.

Who knows you? Carl Bernstein asked him in 1991. "No one. My wife Margy did." Do your kids know you? Bernstein asked. "No,"

McNamara said, adding: "I realize that if people don't know you it means you haven't fully communicated." Then he yanked the blind down. "I'm not about to start now."[44]

Trust was not part of modern management as taught at the Harvard Business School in the 1930s. Alfred Sloan and Donaldson Brown's system of management controls and "scientific management," on which they were based, had been invented to run mass manufacturing at a time when legions of immigrants flooded the work force. Managers were taught to treat workers like cogs, who could perform only limited tasks. McNamara was taught that the most efficient organizations were those in which workers obeyed: Only men at the top had the right information to make decisions. The effect was to disempower foremen, engineers, craftsmen, and workers on assembly lines. Power flowed to those who spoke the new language of finance and used terms like "throughput," while knowledge at the bottom, held by those who did the work of the organization, was ignored. In Vietnam, of course, his need for throughput produced the body count.

McNamara managed and manipulated more than he led, although his intellectual leadership in nuclear strategy, arms control, and development is indisputable. He performed brilliantly in the closed meetings of a band of brothers that resolved the Cuban missile crisis, but in that case he needed no foot soldiers (although he did a good job of wrecking the trust of the Navy when he humiliated Admiral Anderson in the Navy's Flag Plot).[45] He could whip the World Bank to do his will and inspire its employees with his speeches, but he created so much fear that the problems with his projects, known to workers on the line, did not reach him.

It was his nature to be wedded to large organizations while mistrusting and fighting them. He made the same inner choice many times — at Ford, over Vietnam, and at the Bank — always at the center and alone, with secret insights and plans, maneuvering the machinery he had built, playing against his corporate self. Yet to redirect a faltering organization, a leader needs the trust of subordinates. So his past manipulations kept coming back to haunt him.

He said something startling in the Westmoreland deposition: "In the seven years" he served as secretary of defense, "I never had any feeling whatsoever that a uniformed person was seeking to mislead me or deceive me." He also said: "No responsible military officer would ever hold information from a superior that conceivably could bear on the superior's rightful decisionmaking power. . . . That is not the nature of a Government — when people understand that a wrong is being done, somebody talks about it."[46]

Why does he say this? The evidence that military subordinates did deceive him on certain occasions is very strong. Perhaps if he admits that he knew of such corruption in the system, he would not only insult former colleagues but undermine his authority as a *manager*.

When I pressed him on why he was so willing to alienate the Joint Chiefs and other subordinates, whether he didn't need the trust of those below in an organization to run it well, McNamara reacted with a wild-eyed, impatient glare. "What was I supposed to do? Wait for all those people to *die?*"

What became of the institutions he ran? When McNamara left the Bank in 1981, Ford Motor Company was fighting for its existence almost as hard as it had back in 1946.[47] Ford was losing market share to Japanese automakers, as were all the Big Three U.S. auto manufacturers, despite the fact that the Japanese challenge had been clear for a decade. The moment seemed a reckoning for U.S. auto managers, who had neglected engineering, quality control, and fuel efficiency over decades of emphasis on short-term financial results.

Then a curious thing happened at Ford. The heirs of Ernie Breech, Lewis Crusoe, and R. S. McNamara, along with union leaders, made a pilgrimage in 1980 to Mazda plants in Japan, in which Ford owned a substantial share. The result was a corporate overhaul at home. Ford's top-down management system was replaced by a Japanese-style system of teamwork, in which problems on the assembly line are prized information: Any worker can reach up to pull the cord and stop the line to correct flaws the moment they are found. But it took the severest crisis and creative managers to turn Ford around. As this is written, some Ford plants are as good as the best in Japan, and Ford is gaining market share.

The backlash against McNamara at the Pentagon set in right away. McNamara's successors bent over backward to heal the wounds he left. The Navy was quickly allowed to build the F-14 to perform the function of the hated TFX/F111-B, and Admiral Rickover got the new class of submarines McNamara had put off. The Army restructured its active-duty and reserve forces so that in future, even limited wars could not be waged without calling up the reserves. All the services went through a terrible period in the early 1970s, as the upheavals in society spread to the rank and file and they bore the blame for Vietnam. The sight of Navy men being heckled by a crowd as they stepped ashore from Vietnam duty convinced Caspar Weinberger, years later when he became defense secretary, that he would give them their respect.[48]

As for the biased and falsified reports that contributed to early military failures in Vietnam, the Army now gives required courses in situation ethics, to create a fighting organization that is honest from below — just as Ford's reborn managers now teach workers it is all right to pull the cord to stop the assembly line.

The reaction to McNamara's antipoverty program at the World Bank was more discreet but noticeable. McNamara's successor, A. W. Clausen, maintained the Bank's commitment to antipoverty lending officially. But the number of rural development projects of the sort McNamara had promoted decreased in the mid-1980s. The Bank now recognizes that unless the beneficiaries in local communities run projects themselves, sustainable development will not take place. Local agencies and nongovernment groups now have more power to adapt Bank programs on the scene, in contrast to the rigid blueprint approach of McNamara's Bank.[49]

It will take a long time for these big institutions to recover from the ills of the era of mass-production management, for the imperviousness of the old system is one of its most devastating traits. But basic insights are being applied about human fallibility, pride, and integrity. The next managerial age has arrived, which its own Bob McNamaras, still young and unknown, are carrying forward.

If the early eighties were difficult years for McNamara, reality began moving his way after 1986, when Soviet leader Mikhail Gorbachev responded to the Reagan administration's chutzpah by proposing that both sides cut their entire nuclear arsenals by half. McNamara had lectured Aleksey Kosygin about the evils of the ABM at Glassboro, New Jersey, in June 1967: Now, while Reagan and his men doggedly spent billions for Star Wars defense, the Soviets argued against this new incarnation of the ABM using the script McNamara had written.[50]

He trekked to Moscow to keep Gorbachev's momentum alive. McNamara the believer in self-wrought transformations evidently felt that if he reasoned with the Soviets — even if the Reagan men didn't — he could lower the dangers of the misunderstanding he warned of in his speeches. Says one professor who has watched him perform, "McNamara believes he is a force of history, and therefore that what he *says* will change events."

Blundering into Disaster is the title of a little book he wrote in 1986, which brushed past his memories of the great nuclear crises of Berlin and Cuba to prescribe what Reagan, the Soviets, and the allies should do to blunder back to safety.[51] McNamara's subtext was the same imagery of fear, chaos, uncontrolled emotion, and destruction that had run through his private imagination and public statements since his own internal crises in the 1960s.

But he could not revisit history without arousing controversy. He participated in several meetings to uncover the psychology of both sides in the Cuban missile crisis. During these sessions he claimed President Kennedy would not have attacked and invaded Cuba. But Pierre Salinger, Kennedy's former press secretary, and others confronted him with minutes of the meeting on Saturday, October 27, 1962, when the tension was at its peak, and McNamara said that invasion was "almost inevitable." Salinger assailed McNamara's truthfulness in the *New York Times*. McNamara's "insistence that the U.S. never intended to invade Cuba, either before or during the crisis, flies in the face of the facts," he wrote.[52]

But McNamara was impatient with history. "I came here under false pretenses," he said at the next session, held in Antigua, the West Indies, which some of Castro's men attended. "I'm not really interested in learning more about the Cuban missile crisis . . . I'm here for just one reason: I'm interested in the future, particularly the future of U.S.-Cuban relations." Says an associate, "I have the sense he wants to solve all the problems he left behind before his time comes."

It was almost radical for this former cold warrior to be drawing Cuba, the pariah, into dialogue. No less extreme was McNamara's response to George Bush's deployment of hundreds of thousands of U.S. troops to the Persian Gulf after Iraq's Saddam Hussein seized Kuwait in August 1990. Four months later, to the Senate Foreign Relations Committee, McNamara advised against military intervention to retake Kuwait, predicting large American casualties. The international sanctions against Iraq should be given twelve to eighteen months to work; "who can doubt that a year of blockade will be cheaper than a week of war," he said.[53]

But McNamara went further than even leading Democrats. He urged that the United States renounce, with other major powers, any "unilateral action in dealing with regional conflicts." McNamara, of all people, now wants the United States to forswear sending in U.S. forces on its own.

Yet he has not changed. To the senators and others describing the brave new world of "collective decision making" of the future, he also declares: "Such a world would need a leader" — echoing his lifelong preoccupation with centralized power.

Now that overpopulation, food availability, jobs, and the global environment have become international concerns, R. S. McNamara is stepping up as an activist for the planet.

I found him boyishly excited and flattered to be invited to give a lecture to the United Nations on population. He waved a paper at me merrily: "I've found a formula as important as Einstein's E equals mc squared. This will give ammunition to my critics who say I am nuts about numbers."

McNamara lectured his august audience of international civil servants in December 1991 as if they were wayward souls.[54] The world's population stood at 5.4 billion — well above the 3 billion it was passing when he started crusading on the topic in 1968. He cited a reputable estimate that population would not level off until it reached 14 billion. But with maximum human effort by governments and private groups, said the optimist, we might get it to level off sooner, at 11 billion. And what a difference this would make for humanity and the planet, he said.

Then he gave the audience his equation, which computes ED, or environmental damage, the burden to the planet of supporting a given level of population:

$$ED = p \times c \times d$$

This shows that environmental damage does not increase only in proportion to p, population growth. The environment is impacted as a *product* of population growth; c, which is consumption; and d, a factor for the rate at which people exploit resources, since per capita consumption of resources by richer people is much higher than per capita consumption by the poor. His arithmetic showed that a world of 14 billion would stress the environment twenty times as much as today's 5.4 billion. The planet could not sustain this.

McNamara was exploiting the same imagery of catastrophe and doom he has used before. But that is what managers of reality do:

After all, if he preaches long and hard enough that humankind can save itself, maybe it will.

And the solution proposed by this wealthy man is for the better-off people and nations to voluntarily consume less gas, less energy, less of the planet's phytoplankton and food. We should lower the *d* in his equation, the environmental damage done per unit of consumption, so damage to global resources will not be twenty times greater, but some lower number. His answers resemble his prescription for the auto industry in the 1950s: Buyers should stop wasting money on five-thousand-pound cars to do the same job that three-thousand-pound cars can do. Voluntary renunciation was the theme of McNamara's arguments against the supersonic transport, which he helped get America to forswear, and against building an ABM.

The man who has never lost the memory of having been poor, who wipes rings off his coffee table with care, who tells me his net worth isn't what it should be, who shops in discount bookstores, flies economy-class, and rides the subway, is the model for his prescriptions. Again, McNamara is at the center, virtuous and alone.

Robert McNamara and America have reached a point similar to the moment when he started his influential journey. Today the boom of the high-flying eighties has collapsed, just as another boom collapsed in 1929. Americans are feeling shaken and are reassessing their values, as they were then. John Kennedy's call to build a society where the strong are just and the weak secure has new relevance.

The 1990s, like the 1930s, are a time of unprecedented new conditions abroad; America remains the richest nation in a world fraught with new dangers and challenges. McNamara's vision to renew the United States is to redistribute 8 percent of the gross national product in the public and private sectors; his view that redirecting resources should be the cornerstone of policy opens him to the charge that he is too quantitative and another tax-and-spend liberal.[55] Nonetheless, as the mood shifts toward that of his formative years, McNamara's brand of activist liberalism at home and U.S.-centered leadership abroad is back in vogue.

His United Nations speech was well received; the Cuban missile crisis project resulted in McNamara's meeting Fidel Castro in Havana in early 1992, which got good press. McNamara seems happier. Says

Joan Braden, "I think now he no longer thinks every minute Margy's not here and I have to *do* something."

Yet I felt some frustration as our long and mainly fruitful relationship drew to a close, because McNamara was still bobbing and weaving on the surface of the truth. He angled for me to use a quote for this book that was the opposite of what he had just admitted privately (I used neither). When I suggested quoting some things he had said, he snapped that he would deny having said them.

I had often found him thoughtful, tactful, and careful not to criticize present and former colleagues. And very self-critical and honest. His lifelong habit of mental precision helped him explore the new frontier of history. But abruptly, the open and curious McNamara would vanish and the reality manager would march onstage, as if by habit.

As we finished our series of interviews, McNamara held a document I had compiled that included all his statements on Vietnam, in the Westmoreland deposition and trial, and in the oral histories. I knew he would react by seeing what a confusing record he left.

He repeated that he would not break his rule of public silence on Vietnam.

He had decided, however, to clarify. In a long, emotional interview to review his own words, McNamara was alternately excited and teary-eyed. As described in chapter 15, foremost in his memory was the recollection that he had doubts about the military intervention, that he had been unsure even in early 1965 when he pushed for action that success could be achieved.

We came to the fateful memo of January 27, 1965, when he and McGeorge Bundy recommended that the president choose a military course in Southeast Asia. McNamara agreed to comment and needed to look at the text, hoping it would confirm that he had had doubts.

He raced to the bookshelf to get the black binder with his Vietnam memos. He flipped through it as he moved to the desk to compose a sentence to explain his choice. He read aloud as he wrote with reddening features, in a low, rolling voice that almost wept:

"It was difficult to support any one of the three options considered, but a choice had to be made."[56]

That is the glory and tragedy of Robert Strange McNamara: He *feels* he must decide and then act, whether to save South Vietnam then or to save the planet today. Cooler heads may recognize the limits of their powers and decline to change the world. They may refrain from the constant manipulation McNamara engaged in and still does. Not he. For better and worse McNamara shaped much in today's world — and imprisoned himself. A little-known nineteenth-century writer, P. W. Bornum, offers a summation:

"We make our decisions. And then our decisions turn around and make us."

Acknowledgments

A WORD should be said about McNamara's relationship to this project. This book is unauthorized, and he had no review over any part of it with one exception: He granted a series of interviews with me on the condition that he could review the quotes attributed directly to him from our sessions. This he did. He did not agree to speak on the record about his role in the Vietnam War, about which he has maintained near-complete silence. But when several oral histories he had done, which he released to me, turned out to quote him on this matter, he added "clarifications" for the record, which appear here for the first time. He also clarified some statements made in 1984 when he was deposed and called as a witness in General William Westmoreland's libel suit against CBS, which was the only time before now that he broke his public silence. I want to thank him, his present and former staff, and his friends and family for being courteous and helpful.

I am grateful to my colleagues in the news business and academia and to my friends, who reminded me as I struggled that sometimes the most difficult labors are the most worthwhile. Particular thanks go to the Center for Strategic and International Studies, then of Georgetown University, and particularly to Amos A. Jordan, Jr., president, and William J. Taylor, Jr., executive vice president. The CSIS housed this project in its first phase with no strings attached, giving me wonderful freedom and stimulating company as I got under way. Subsequently, the Alfred P. Sloan Foundation and its vice president, Arthur L. Singer, offered financial and moral support. The John D. and Catherine T. MacArthur Foundation also supported the book with a grant from the program for Research and Writing in Peace, Security and International Cooperation. I am most grateful to that program's director, Ruth Adams, for encouraging me to cross academic disciplines and literary boundaries to get to the goal.

Thanks for research assistance, typing, and proofing go to Adela Bolet, Lisa Corpus, John Andrew Coy, Jessica Johnson, Robert Klyman, Nell Manning, Peter Marber, David Stievater, Veronica Sympson, Steven Talan, Laura Williamson, and Elsie Zapata.

The librarians and archivists at several collections were extremely helpful: the Ford Industrial Archives, in Dearborn, Michigan; the Bancroft Library of the University of California at Berkeley; the archives in the Baker Library of the Harvard School of Business Administration, in Allston, Massachusetts; the Lyndon Baines Johnson Library, in Austin, Texas; the John Fitzgerald Kennedy Library, in Boston; the Historian of the Office of the Secretary of Defense in the Pentagon, Arlington, Virginia; and the Current News Service of the Office of the Secretary of Defense. The history offices of the individual services were helpful: the Office of Air Force History, the Office of Naval History, the Center for Military History of the United States Army, and the Marine Corps Historical Center and Museum, all in Washington, D.C.

I also benefited regularly from the Library of the Paul H. Nitze School of Advanced International Studies and from the help of the World Bank History Project, both in Washington, D.C.

Fredrica S. Friedman, my editor at Little, Brown, deserves great credit for helping me realize the project's potential. My agent, Robert B. Barnett, was always helpful and enthusiastic. My copyeditor, Deborah Jacobs, worked on the manuscript with patience and professionalism.

My parents, Willis and Virginia Shapley, are owed the most thanks. The faith that my husband, Roger Cortesi, has shown cannot be measured. My children, Roger and Katharine Cortesi, and my stepdaughters, Elisabetta and Isabella Cortesi, are inspirations. Our extended family and many friends should be thanked for their support.

Notes

For details of books and journal articles cited, see the Bibliography. "Interview" refers to an interview conducted by the author.

Abbreviations used in the Notes:

FIA	Ford Industrial Archives
HBSA	Harvard Business School Archives
JFKL	John F. Kennedy Library
LBJL	Lyndon Baines Johnson Library
NA	National Archives
NSC	National Security Council
NSF	National Security Files
NYT	*New York Times*
NYTI	*New York Times Index*
OAFH	Office of Air Force History
OSDH	Office of the Secretary of Defense Historical Office
PP	Pentagon Papers
RSM	Robert S. McNamara
SGFL	Sherman Grindberg Film Library
Statements	Public Statements of Robert S. McNamara, OSDH
UCBA	University of California, Berkeley, Archives
WP	*Washington Post*

PROLOGUE

1. *Baltimore Sun*, March 1, 1968; *Aerospace Technology*, March 11, 1968; *Armed Forces Journal*, March 9, 1968; *Tampa Tribune*, March 2, 1968; interviews: Lawrence Levinson, Harry McPherson, Colonel Robert Pursley.
2. SGFL, February 29, 1968.
3. Trewhitt, *McNamara*, 278.
4. This was the term used by the administrator of the Federal Aviation Administration in the Johnson years, Najeeb Halaby, who fought McNamara bitterly over the SST.

5. Of many appearances, see SGFL, June 29, 1966.
6. Interview, Willard Goodwin.
7. Interview, RSM.
8. Interview, S. Shahid Husain.
9. Lippmann, *An Inquiry into the Principles of the Good Society*, 24.
10. Arthur Schlesinger diary, January 21, 1966, author communication.
11. Henry Luce, "The American Century," *Life*, February 14, 1941, pp. 61–65.
12. Interview, Vernon Goodin.

1. THE HELPER OF THE LARGEST NUMBER

1. Interviews: Vernon Goodin, RSM, others who lived in the region in the 1930s.
2. Interview, Peg McNamara Slaymaker; Trewhitt, *McNamara*, 26, 27.
3. Trewhitt, *McNamara*, 27, 28.
4. Ibid., 27.
5. Ibid., 26–28; interviews: Peg McNamara Slaymaker, RSM, Willard Goodwin, Marion Sproul Goodin.
6. Baby Book courtesy of Craig McNamara.
7. Trewhitt, *McNamara*, 28, 29; interview, Peg McNamara Slaymaker.
8. Trewhitt, *McNamara*, 28, 30.
9. Profile of Sproul and of Cal in the 1930s — interviews: Philip Farley, James Grant; material on file at UCBA; Stadtman, *The University of California*, passim.
10. Interview, Willard Goodwin; Trewhitt, *McNamara*, 31.
11. Trewhitt, *McNamara*, 32.
12. This and later discussions of RSM's quantitative talents are based on interviews with him and two unrelated people who have a similar mental makeup and were able to explain more clearly than he could the operation of his mind and its likely effect on personality. Curiously, RSM insists this talent is not hereditary but acquired.
13. Trewhitt, *McNamara*, 31. Although Phi Beta Kappa makes awards to juniors and seniors, according to society records the award was made to RSM in 1935, at the end of his sophomore year.
14. RSM to J. Arthur Harris, August 27, 1935, UCBA.
15. Stadtman, *University of California*, 283.
16. Sproul profile — ibid.; interview, Marion Sproul Goodin. Sproul was also trained in accounting.
17. The meeting and activities of this group are well recalled by all of those named.
18. RSM to Robert Sproul, October 13, 1937, president's file, 1937, UCBA.
19. Interview, Willard Goodwin.
20. Ibid.
21. Trewhitt, *McNamara*, 27.
22. Ibid., 34.

2. THE STUDENT OF CONTROL

1. Interview, Walter Haas.
2. RSM to Robert Sproul and Monroe Deutsch, October 16, 1937, and February 10, 1938, respectively, president's files, 1937, 1938, UCBA.

3. Trewhitt, *McNamara*, 35. HBSA files contain a case study titled "Harvard Athletic Association," which examines ticket pricing for football games in the upcoming season. Written by RSM in 1938, it shows the intense organization of his work and a stiff, formal writing style later to be familiar to many.

4. Profile of statistics teaching — Copeland, *And Mark an Era*, 166ff.; HBS course catalogues for 1936–37, 1938–39, 1939–40, HBSA.

5. The best discussions of the development of financial and management controls in U.S. industry are Chandler, *The Visible Hand*, and Sloan, *My Years with General Motors*.

6. Profile of HBS in the late 1930s — Copeland, *And Mark an Era*, passim; UCBA files generally; interviews: Edmund Learned, Eugene Zuckert, Charles Anderson, Robert Anthony, Myles Mace, Walter Haas, Paul Ignatius.

7. Interview, Eugene Zuckert. On the basis of competence and friendship, RSM appointed Zuckert secretary of the Air Force in 1961, a sensitive and difficult post.

8. Background interview.

9. Interviews: RSM, Edmund Learned, Peg McNamara Slaymaker.

10. Margaret Craig profile — Trewhitt, *McNamara*, 40; interviews: RSM, Myles Mace, Marion Sproul and Vernon Goodin, Mary Joe and Willard Goodwin, Margaret McNamara Pastor, Kathleen McNamara Spears; Trewhitt, *McNamara*, 35, 36.

11. Interviews: RSM, Eugene Zuckert. RSM also tells this story in Oral History, JFKL, April 4, 1964, pp. 11, 12.

12. Interviews: Crosby Kelly, Edmund Learned, Myles Mace.

13. Thornton profile — interviews: George Fenimore, Eugene Zuckert, Myles Mace, Beirne Lay; for Thornton generally, see Lay, *Someone Has to Make It Happen*, 50–53, 58–65.

14. Lay, *Someone*, 55, 56; interviews: Edmund Learned, Myles Mace; Zaleznik, *Managerial Mystique*, 100–102; "A New Start in Foreign Policy," *Fortune*, December 1947, pp. 81, 85, 217, profiled Robert Lovett and the work of Stat Control.

15. Learned wrote an informal memoir of the school in a loose-leaf binder, with letters pasted in, from which correspondence below is quoted. Edmund Learned Papers, vols. 4, 5 (AAF Statistical School, HBSA).

16. Edmund Learned Papers.

17. Acomb, "Statistical Control in the Army Air Forces"; J. F. Heflin, "Organization History," AAF Stat School, OAFH.

18. Edmund Learned Papers.

19. Trewhitt, *McNamara*, 37.

20. Ibid., 38. RSM's assignments, ranks, and promotion dates are from Trewhitt's account. He won geographic service ribbons, the Legion of Merit, and a personnel rating of "not less than superior."

21. Interview, David Hopper.

22. Tuchman, *Stilwell and the American Experience in China*, 387, 478, 582, 583, 618, 619.

23. Professor Learned later treasured a letter RSM wrote him praising LeMay. RSM often extols LeMay's air tactics against Japan, which is ironic in

view of his total disagreement with LeMay later. RSM's and Stat Control's role in the Pacific are in Kerr, *Flames Over Tokyo*, 114, 115.

24. Heflin, "Organization History."

25. Dan Throop Smith, "Putting Bombing on a Business Basis," Edmund Learned Papers, vol. 4; Lay, *Someone*, 73.

26. Lay, *Someone*, 70. Some of Stat Control's reports, most unsigned, are on microfilm at OAFH.

27. According to Learned, RSM told him he saw LeMay fudge figures. The "major" who called LeMay on the carpet is unnamed in Learned's memoir. The incident is interesting in view of the later hostility between RSM and LeMay, which ostensibly was grounded on high policy.

28. Interviews: RSM, Mary Joe Goodwin.

29. Record Group 107, Box 85, NA.

30. Interview, RSM.

31. Lacey, *Ford*, 421–422; Lay, *Someone*, 75–80; interview, RSM.

3. THE LEGEND OF CONTROL

1. Interview, Elizabeth Eisenstein.

2. Collier and Horowitz, *The Fords*, 212.

3. Courtesy of Michael Ciepley; Lacey, *Ford*, 422, 423.

4. Nevins and Hill, *Ford*, 309–311; Lacey, *Ford*, 423.

5. Interviews: Arjay Miller, Ben Mills; Collier and Horowitz, *Fords*, 217.

6. The "Quiz Kids" were on a radio show of the day; Collier and Horowitz, *Fords*, 218. As the Ford Quiz Kids' fame spread, "Whiz Kids" became the term used. See *Newsweek*, December 19, 1960; "The Whiz Kids and How They Grew," *Parade*, November 15, 1970; "Whatever Happened to the Whiz Kids?" *Forbes*, September 10, 1984. The ten Whiz Kids were Wilbur R. Andreson, Charles E. Bosworth, J. Edward Lundy, RSM, Arjay Miller, Ben Mills, George Moore, F. C. Reith, Charles Thornton, and James O. Wright.

7. Breech's and Crusoe's arrival — Nevins and Hill, *Ford*, 312–315; Collier and Horowitz, *Fords*, 219–221, 223–224.

8. Collier and Horowitz, *Fords*, 292.

9. Interview, Crosby Kelly.

10. The figure of $117 million is from interview, Arjay Miller.

11. Nevins and Hill, *Ford*, 327, 328.

12. Interview, Will Caldwell.

13. Collier and Horowitz, *Fords*, 239.

14. Everything they planned derived from the Sloan–Donaldson Brown system. For early Whiz Kid plans, see Nevins and Hill, *Ford*, 328, 330, 331; Collier and Horowitz, *Fords*, 239. For RSM's task-force plans, see Lacey, *Ford*, 281.

15. Interview, Fred Secrest. Iacocca gives a description of RSM's statistical abilities in *Iacocca*, 42.

16. Ford sales in 1949 are from Nevins and Hill, *Ford*, 342.

17. Collier and Horowitz, *Fords*, 237.

18. The social dimension of the Whiz Kids' advantages is described at length in Halberstam, *The Reckoning*, and elsewhere. The Whiz Kids were virtually the only people at Ford with college degrees, and after they were

hired, Henry Ford II ordered that the company hire fifty more college graduates. Lee Iacocca was the fifty-first.

19. Interview, David Lewis.

20. Lacey, *Ford*, 497, 498.

21. Interviews: RSM, Marion Sproul Goodin, Edmund Learned.

22. Halberstam makes much of RSM's opposition, between 1949 and 1953, to Crusoe's proposal to spend $1 billion to modernize Ford plants. As for the argument that failure to begin modernization when Crusoe wanted hurt the company's ability to "beat GM," a serious run against General Motors was not considered until after the Korean conflict ended, in 1953. Halberstam, *Reckoning*, 236–239.

23. Collier and Horowitz, *Fords*, 243, 241.

24. Ibid., 245; "Thunderbird — An American Classic," news release, Ford Motor Company, January 4, 1989.

25. The heart of the plan was not only a new car line but a restructuring of the company to have five divisions instead of three, like General Motors. Definitive accounts of how Crusoe and Whiz Kid Reith sold the company on the Edsel are in Nevins and Hill, *Ford*, 376–378, 384–387, and Collier and Horowitz, *Fords*, 251, 252, 259–263.

26. Nevins and Hill, *Ford*, 263.

27. RSM built a wall between himself over in the Ford Division and the Edsel–five division scheme, which also threatened his run at the top of the company. See Warnock, *The Edsel Affair*, 91; for the Ford Division's stretch Fairlane as a competing car, see Lacey, *Ford*, 492–493.

28. RSM "brought" the nation the Edsel — FIA, AR-65-115. His "phasing it out" remark is in Brooks, *The Fate of the Edsel*, 60, and Warnock, *Edsel Affair*, 207.

29. Trips are at Warnock, *Edsel Affair*, 208. RSM's November 27, 1957, memo is in FIA, AR-66-12:8, Edsel Box 2, Doc. 2.

30. December 4, 1957, memo — FIA, AR-66-12:8, Doc. 5.

31. Buyer survey, FIA, AR-66-12:8, Edsel Box 2, Doc. 3.

32. Warnock, *Edsel Affair*, 201.

33. Ibid., 202.

34. The $350 million loss is cited everywhere but was first published by Brooks, *Fate of the Edsel*, 67–68. RSM and Reith are in many accounts. The transfer is in FIA, AR-66-12:8, Edsel Box 2, Doc. 1A.

35. Indeed, modern management had saved the company after the war and gave RSM, Breech, and Henry Ford the control they needed to limit losses from the Edsel fiasco. Arguably, more new models flopped back in the days before Sloan and Donaldson Brown came to General Motors and the conservative, stabilizing forces of management control were in place.

In 1963 cartoonist Paul Conrad made the word "Edsel" synonymous with failure, with a cartoon showing Defense Secretary McNamara's ill-fated airplane, the TFX, sporting an Edsel grille and taking off from an aircraft carrier. In 1964 Conrad published another cartoon, which featured the Edsel as U.S. policy in Vietnam and made fun of RSM as the scapegoat for both. Warnock, *Edsel Affair*, v. (Warnock says the plane in the cartoon is an SST, but the SST was not a big issue in 1964, whereas the TFX was very controversial and identified with RSM.)

Barry Goldwater charged in 1964 that RSM brought the nation the Edsel. Breech denied the charge in writing and retracted Ford executives' contributions to the Goldwater campaign because of the falsehood (see chap. 14, "Test of a New Leader").

The other line of reasoning that makes RSM responsible for the Edsel disaster is that he undercut the quality of the Edsels being produced, in favor of Fords, Mercurys, and Lincolns coming off the line, and planned to break up the Edsel organization even before the car was introduced, in September. Warnock describes RSM's actions vividly, but the argument that the Edsel would have succeeded if only top management had pushed harder and spent more money is hard to support.

4. ORGANIZATION MAN AND MOLE

1. Collier and Horowitz, *The Fords*, 280, 281.
2. Interview, RSM. Regional Democratic leaders were aware that RSM sometimes supported their candidates and had taken political positions favorable to labor. In 1960, John F. Kennedy's talent scouts easily learned of RSM's independent voting record. See chap. 5, "Sons of the Morning."
3. More than 400,000 Falcons were sold the first year, a company record; Collier and Horowitz, *Fords*, 291.
4. Interview, RSM.
5. Collier and Horowitz, *Fords*, 249.
6. Ibid., 291.
7. Interview, Will Scott.
8. Ibid.
9. "He wears granny glasses and he puts out a granny car," someone said at the time; Lacey, *Ford*, 491. Although Ford's design staff did not like the Falcon, the automotive press gave it good reviews, while noting its resemblance to the Tin Lizzie.
10. FIA, AR-65-115:2, speeches file.
11. Asset control and revenue control are described in Nevins and Hill, *Ford*, 387, 388.
12. FIA, AR-65-115:2, speeches file.
13. Lacey, *Ford*, 492.
14. Iacocca, *Iacocca*, 43.
15. Interview, Will Scott.
16. RSM criticized dealer performance frequently in speeches to the company. In a September 3, 1958, speech, he reviewed his previous criticisms dating back to 1955. FIA, AR-65-115:2, speeches file.
17. Halberstam, *The Reckoning*, 243.
18. Interviews: Charles Ellis, Fred Secrest, Arjay Miller.
19. The displacement of engineers by finance men in positions of power at Ford is a theme of Halberstam's *Reckoning*.
20. Interview, Ben Mills.
21. There is a large diagnostic literature. See Zaleznik, *Managerial Mystique*, chap. 6; Johnson and Kaplan, *Relevance Lost*, chap. 6; and Clark et al., eds., *The Uneasy Alliance*, chaps. 2, 5, 6.
22. FIA, AR-66-12-10, "Automotive Industry Crash Research."
23. Courtesy of Michael Ciepley.
24. June 16, 1955, *Congressional Record*, 84th Cong., 1st sess., 54914.

25. FIA, AR-65-115:2, speeches file.
26. Ibid.
27. FIA, AR-65-112, speeches file.
28. FIA, AR-65-115:2, Greenbrier conference folder.
29. Iacocca, *Iacocca*, 61–63.
30. Lacey, *Ford*, 575; interviews: Arjay Miller, James Wright.

5. SONS OF THE MORNING

1. Collier and Horowitz, *The Fords*, 278, 281.
2. Glass House opened in 1957. Descriptions of it and the Schaeffer Avenue building are at Collier and Horowitz, *Fords*, 280, 281; Nevins and Hill's eulogy is in Nevins and Hill, *Ford*, 425–442.
3. Halberstam, *The Reckoning*, 212; interview, Will Scott; RSM with Henry Ford II—Collier and Horowitz, *Fords*, 281.
4. Interview, Ben Mills.
5. Collier and Horowitz, *Fords*, 291.
6. Nevins and Hill, *Ford*, 426.
7. Interview, John Kenneth Galbraith.
8. Interview, Crosby Kelly.
9. Collier and Horowitz, *Fords*, 282.
10. Nevins and Hill, *Ford*, 426, 438.
11. Ibid., 438.
12. Among many profiles of America in 1958–60 is Manchester, *The Glory and the Dream*, 818–853. The 1960 campaign is at 877–886. See White, *The Making of the President, 1960*.
13. Quoted in Fairlee, *The Kennedy Promise*. Fairlee (21, 24) shows that the Eisenhower administration knew and stated that there was no missile gap but was deliberately ignored by leading Democrats and others. As more information has become declassified since, the falsity of the missile-gap charge has been confirmed, although it was vociferously promoted by parts of the intelligence bureaucracy at the time. See chap. 6, "Power in the Pentagon."
14. Fairlee, *Kennedy Promise*.
15. Halberstam, *The Best and the Brightest*, 221.
16. Interview, Adam Yarmolinsky; Halberstam, *Best*, 222–223; Wofford, *Of Kennedys and Kings*, 70, 71.
17. Interview, RSM. "Mr. Shriber" is from FIA, AR-66-12:9, "McNamara Office Calendar, December 1960."
18. Interview, RSM. Shriver's account is in Wofford, *Of Kennedys*.
19. Interview, RSM; RSM, Oral History, JFKL, April 4, 1964, pp. 7–9. In only one account, RSM's description to the historian of the Office of the Secretary of Defense, did he say he decided to accept before his second trip to Washington to meet Kennedy; RSM, Oral History, OSDH, April 3, 1986, p. 4. In fact, the Ford Motor Company board of directors met on December 13 to discuss RSM's terms of severance, before RSM met with Kennedy the second time.
20. Interview, Roswell Gilpatric.
21. Robert F. Kennedy, Oral History, JFKL, February 29, 1964, pp. 5, 6.
22. RSM, Oral History, JFKL, April 3, 1986, pp. 4, 5.

23. SGFL, December 13, 1960; *WP*, December 11, 1960; *Wall Street Journal*, December 14, 1960.

24. *Oakland Star*, December 14, 1960.

25. Collier and Horowitz, *Fords*, 292.

26. See, for example, Lacey, *Ford*, 500.

27. *Detroit News*, December 26, 1960.

28. RSM, Oral History, JFKL, February 29, 1964, pp. 7, 8.

29. Kennedy quotes are from Fairlee, *Kennedy Promise*, 63–75.

30. The idea of an objective consensus described in Fairlee, *Kennedy Promise*, runs through the sociological and political literature of the time. Examples are Bell, *The End of Ideology*, and Neustadt, *Presidential Power*.

31. Interview, Adam Yarmolinsky; Wofford, *Of Kennedys*, 76, 77.

32. Borklund, *The Department of Defense;* Kinnard, *The Secretary of Defense.*

33. RSM, Oral History, OSDH, April 3, 1986, pp. 12, 13.

34. Senate Committee on Armed Services, *Nomination of Robert S. McNamara, Secretary of Defense Designate,* 87th Cong., 1st sess., January 17, 1961. RSM told people at Ford who tried to dissuade him from going to Washington that because he had made more money than anyone else named McNamara and because America was a great country where someone like him could rise, he owed it to America to go and serve. Collier and Horowitz, *Fords*, 292.

35. Interviews: Susan Mary Alsop, Ina Ginsberg, Elizabeth Eisenstein.

36. Sorensen, *Kennedy*, 244, 245; Wofford, *Of Kennedys*, 70.

37. Shriver's use of the hymn "Brightest and Best" is in Wofford, *Of Kennedys*, 68.

38. SGFL, September 7, 1968.

6. POWER IN THE PENTAGON

1. Kaufmann, *The McNamara Strategy*, 168; J. Wiesberg, *New Republic*, April 1, 1991.

2. The powers of the secretary are traced in Borklund, *The Department of Defense*, and Kinnard, *The Secretary of Defense.*

3. Andrew Goodpaster, "Memorandum of Meeting with Goodpaster, Lemnitzer and President Eisenhower, January 9," January 11, 1961, on file at OSDH.

4. Roswell Gilpatric, Oral History, JFKL, May 5, 1970, p. 4.

5. Interview, Lawrence Levinson.

6. Interviews: John Scali, Fred Hoffman, Warren Rogers. In 1972, Desmond Ball compared notes and recollections of several reporters who heard RSM speak. See Desmond Ball, *Politics and Force Levels*, 90, 91.

7. See *Denver Post*, February 9, 1961; *WP*, February 9, 1961; *Wall Street Journal*, February 9, 1961.

8. See chap. 5, "Sons of the Morning."
    In January and February 1961, the first SAMOS reconnaissance photographs were just being examined. Analysts looked for rail sidings, which were the only means for transporting Soviet missiles to launch sites. The first photos showed some tracks but so few missile sites that, in Kaplan's account, analysts were certain of only four operational Soviet ICBMs. Most classified estimates at the time pegged the number of operational

Soviet ICBMs at 35, compared with the 12 Atlas and Titan missiles then in the U.S. force. The expected Soviet advantage, or "missile gap," leaving America far behind was based on warnings of a crash Soviet program to build and deploy a force of 200 to 700 ICBMs by mid-1963. The Air Force was predicting the Soviets would have 1,200 by mid-1965. But in early 1961 U.S. analysts were having difficulty finding hard evidence of a crash program.

According to Ball's reconstruction, RSM told reporters at the briefing that the evidence was inconclusive and they were still looking. This statement was entirely accurate. Conclusive evidence of the unlikelihood of a missile gap only came after April, when Soviet double agent Colonel Oleg Penkovsky told the CIA that there was no crash program, that the Soviets had at most 50 to 100 missiles, and that the SS-6, the principal Soviet ICBM, was in such trouble that they were abandoning it. A good explanation is Garthoff, *Intelligence Assessment and Policymaking.* See also Kaplan, *The Wizards of Armageddon,* 295, and Desmond Ball, *Politics,* 90, 91.

 9. *NYT,* February 8, 1961.
10. John Kennedy quoted in *NYT,* February 9, 1961; interview, RSM.
11. For the trouble caused, see *New York Herald-Tribune,* February 10, 1961. RSM's denials in *WP,* February 17, 1961; statement to Mahon is in *Statements,* 1961, vol. 1, p. 298.
12. Interview, Warren Rogers.
13. Interview, Henry Glass.
14. Ibid.
15. Interview, Charles Hitch. Hitch and McKean, *The Economics of Defense in the Nuclear Age.* Accounts of Rand are at Smith, *The Rand Corporation,* and Kaplan, *Wizards,* chaps. 4, 6.
16. Interview, David Novick.
17. Ibid.
18. Stewart Alsop, "Master of the Pentagon," *Saturday Evening Post,* August 5, 1961.
19. *Newsweek,* March 12, 1962.
20. Ibid.
21. *Newsweek,* March 27, 1961.
22. One hundred and five "Trombones" were published in *Army-Navy–Air Force Journal,* April 15, 1961. The list reportedly grew from the original 76 questions to 131 in all.
23. T. H. White, "Revolution in the Pentagon," *Look,* April 23, 1963.
24. *Armed Forces Management,* November 1961.
25. *Newsweek,* March 12, 1962.
26. Beschloss, *The Crisis Years,* 402. *Armed Forces Management,* November 1961.
27. Beschloss, *Crisis Years,* 403.
28. *Business Week,* February 11, 1961.
29. *Journal American,* May 18, 1961; *WP,* March 3, 1961; *WP,* May 27, 1961; *New York Herald-Tribune,* May 5, 1961; interviews: Richard Fryklund, Fred Hoffman, Henry Trewhitt.
30. This conundrum is the starting point for several studies, notably Desmond Ball, *Politics.*

31. Ibid., 110–113.
32. WSEG-50 study contents are described by Kaplan, *Wizards*, 258–260, and Desmond Ball, *Politics*, 34–38.
33. Rand's arguments for the cost-ineffectiveness of bombers are summarized in Kaufmann, *McNamara Strategy*, 216, 217, 228, and Enthoven and Smith, *How Much Is Enough?*, 166–168.
34. The 900 B-47s did not have intercontinental range; SAC had them based mainly overseas to be in striking range of the Soviet Union. But Rand's studies had shown definitively that they were highly vulnerable to Soviet preemptive attack, as were bombers stationed on the ground within the United States. Rand had also shown that missiles would be much more cost-effective to maintain than a large bomber force. Details on the bomber force cutbacks can be found, among other places, at Desmond Ball, *Politics*, 114, 118, 137.
35. An Air Force proposal dated July 3, 1961, asked for 3,190 long-range missiles in addition to the 126 Atlas missiles already programmed, for a total of 3,316, not counting the Skybolt air-launched missile, which Kennedy had continued. The Air Force reduced its plans to a "more realistic" figure of between 1,700 and 1,900 Minutemen by the time it bargained with RSM in the fall. During a 1962 trip to Vandenberg Air Force Base, General Thomas Power, chief of SAC, told Kennedy and RSM that the Air Force planned to have 10,000 missiles eventually. RSM recalls that Kennedy was startled by this demand. See Desmond Ball, *Politics*, 244, 245. Interview, RSM.
36. See Desmond Ball, *Politics*, 215–217. Kennedy was also told by science adviser Jerome B. Wiesner, Herbert York, and David Bell, director of the Bureau of the Budget, to cut back the B-70 program.
37. Desmond Ball, *Politics*, 217–221.
38. Sorensen, *Kennedy*, 347, 348. A discussion of the issues from the Whiz Kids' point of view is in Kaufmann, *McNamara Strategy*, 220–228.
39. Seaborg, *Kennedy, Khrushchev and the Test Ban*, 77, 78, 85. An M.I.T. study in 1966 concluded that the main military reason for the Soviet resumption of tests was that the United States was producing far more nuclear delivery systems than the Soviet Union — i.e., the Kennedy-McNamara missile buildup ordered over the previous eight months. Ibid., 84.
40. See RSM, "Draft: Recommended Long Range Nuclear Delivery Forces, 1963–1967," September 23, 1961. This is the first of the top-secret draft presidential memoranda that RSM would send each fall to the president to justify his proposed decisions in the forthcoming budget for nuclear forces. This document summarizes the proposed bomber cutbacks and Polaris and Minuteman increases, as well as other decisions: the continuation of the Skybolt air-launched missile and the cut of the Nike-Zeus ABM, which he and Kennedy had made in eight months.
41. See note 8 above. Interview, Raymond Garthoff.
42. See RSM, "Draft: Recommended Long Range Nuclear Delivery Forces, 1963–1967," September 23, 1961. Here RSM chose to project "median" and "high" estimates of Soviet ICBMs by mid-1965 of 750 and 1,100, to justify a planned U.S. deployment of 1,200 Minutemen while retaining only a few old Atlas and Titan missiles. By September, the intelligence

community, baffled by its inability to find evidence of a Soviet crash program but with some members arguing one could be under way, failed to agree on projections for the future Soviet force. See Garthoff, *Intelligence Assessment and Policymaking*, 16, 17, and Desmond Ball, *Politics*, 156–181.

43. Desmond Ball, *Politics*, 22–31; Nitze, *From Hiroshima to Glasnost*, 248–250.

44. RSM habitually picked simple, round numbers to simplify issues and goals, as appears to have been the case with the figure of 1,000 Minuteman missiles, which he arrived at informally in 1961–62 and did not set into place as policy until three years later. At the World Bank, he argued that the world's population needed to level off closer to 10 billion than the higher figures that were more likely (see chap. 24, "The World Takes Its Price," and Epilogue). When he helped deploy U.S. troops to South Vietnam in 1965, he would say: "We moved 100,000 men 10,000 miles in 100 days" (see chap. 16, "Intervention and Promise"). His concerns with limiting the war became acute at the time U.S. deaths passed the 1,000 mark, in late 1965 (see chap. 17, "Two Enormous Miscalculations").

45. Interviews: RSM, Alain Enthoven, Herbert York. History and details of this SIOP, formally termed SIOP-62, are at Kaplan, *Wizards*, 263–272, and Martin, *Strategic Thought in the Nuclear Age*, 133, 139–141.

7. COLD WARRIOR STEPPING UP

1. Interview, Eugene Zuckert.
2. Interviews: William Bundy, Henry Glass.
3. RSM to John F. Kennedy, January 24, 1961, President's Office File 29A, File Folder "Eisenhower, Dwight D.," JFKL.
4. Hilsman, *To Move a Nation*, 127, 128.
5. Schlesinger, *A Thousand Days*, 338.
6. Wyden, *Bay of Pigs*, 121. The chiefs concluded at one point in their report that the invasion could not work without an internal uprising or U.S. support — but at another point said it would succeed, without naming conditions. See Schlesinger, *Thousand Days*, 238, 239, 269.
7. Wyden, *Bay of Pigs*, 215–221.
8. Interview, Elvis Stahr.
9. Krock, *Memoirs*, 369–371.
10. Roswell Gilpatric, Oral History, JFKL, May 5, 1970, pp. 13, 14. RSM, Oral History, JFKL, April 4, 1964, pp. 19, 20.
11. Schlesinger, *Thousand Days*, 339.
12. *NYT*, May 27, 1961. *Statements*, 1961, vol. 2, p. 558.
13. Slusser, *The Berlin Crisis of 1961*. These older accounts are largely premised on the assumption that Kennedy was reacting to Soviet belligerence in the spring and summer of 1961. More recently, Michael Beschloss has used newly available Soviet documents, as well as many primary U.S. sources, to show how much Khrushchev's belligerence was triggered by Kennedy's public rhetoric and immediate missile buildup.

   A case in point is a speech that Roswell Gilpatric, RSM's deputy, gave at Hot Springs, Virginia, on October 21. Kennedy, McGeorge Bundy, RSM, and Gilpatric collaborated on a text that would notify the Soviets publicly that the Americans knew the Soviets were behind in ICBMs. They realized that if they told the Soviets they knew, the Soviets might then speed up their ICBM program to remedy the gap, whereas to allow Khrushchev to go on bluffing, pretending he had superiority in missiles, was a safer situation. Gilpatric's speech had its intended effect: little publicity in the United States and much attention in the Kremlin. RSM followed up by specifying, in public, how strong the United States was relative to the Soviets. Past historical accounts have treated it as a logical move for the new administration; Beschloss shows that by puncturing the "illusion of Soviet nuclear might" on which Khrushchev's entire domestic and foreign strategy was based, Khrushchev could become fearful and so approve the detonation of a nuclear device, breaking the previous moratorium. Gilpatric's speech, RSM's statements, and other moves made Khrushchev more likely to keep pressure on Berlin and other points and to try to redress his inferiority in missiles fast. Beschloss, *The Crisis Years*, 328–332.

RSM, for his part, has made clear that at the time, he and the other Kennedy believed the Kremlin saw them as weak, and so acted as they did. See RSM, *Blundering into Disaster*, 6, 7.

14. Interviews: RSM, Paul Nitze, Seymour Weiss.
15. Kaplan, *The Wizards of Armageddon*, 296.
16. Interview, Elvis Stahr; *Statements*, 1961, vol. 3, p. 962.
17. Kennedy's statement was intended as a signal that he was prepared to go to war over Berlin, and Khrushchev took it as such. The civil defense campaign reinforced the message. Beschloss, *Crisis Years*, 262–264, and Kaplan, *Wizards*, 307–314. Interviews: Adam Yarmolinsky, Steuart Pittman.
18. *Times*, September 15, 1963.
19. A four-man team of four-star officers worked up scenarios on the basis of actual, very heavily classified war plans. Recent scholarship has shown the extent to which Eisenhower and even Secretary of State John Foster Dulles backed off from massive retaliation, although this was not understood at the time. See Rosenberg, "Reality and Responsibility," and Gaddis, *Strategies of Containment*.
20. RSM traveled with Assistant Secretary Nitze to a NATO meeting in Germany right before Kennedy's July 25 speech. Nitze, *From Hiroshima to Glasnost*, 200–202. Recently released documents concerning the military contingency plans are at National Security Archive, Berlin Crisis Collection.
21. Interviews: Roger Hilsman, Thomas Hughes, George Ball.
22. National Security Archive, Berlin Crisis Collection.
23. Stewart Alsop, *Saturday Evening Post*, December 1, 1962.
24. Interviews: Paul Nitze, David Alan Rosenberg; Kaplan, *Wizards*, 299–301.
25. Interview, Paul Nitze; Nitze, *From Hiroshima*, 202, 203.
26. The only place this text has been published is in Barnet, *The Alliance*, 231.
27. Interview, Paul Nitze; Nitze, *From Hiroshima*, 205. The incident took place in late November.
28. The leak about Rusk is in *Washington Evening Star*, February 27, 1961. For RSM's statements, see *New York Herald-Tribune*, September 24, 1961. Both General Lemnitzer and Bobby Kennedy said the president was willing to use nuclear weapons; see *Baltimore Sun*, September 25, 1961. RSM repeated his assurances the following January; see *New York Journal American*, January 20, 1962.

29. "Remarks by Secretary McNamara," JFKL, May 5, 1962, pp. 12, 13.

30. Department of Defense news release, November 18, 1963, pp. 14, 15.

31. RSM, "The Military Role of Nuclear Weapons," 79.

32. Interviews: Frederick Wyle, Kenneth Adelman.

33. Interview, RSM. He also tells this story in "The Military Role of Nuclear Weapons," 59–80, and in *Blundering into Disaster.*

34. Interview, William Kaufmann. The talk with RSM occurred in 1966 or 1967.

35. Trewhitt, *McNamara*, 31.

36. The best profile of Rusk is at Halberstam, *The Best and the Brightest*, 308–329.

37. Schlesinger, *Robert Kennedy and His Times*, 430, 432, 437, 438.

38. Beschloss, *Crisis Years*, 401.

39. Ibid., 402.

40. Trewhitt, *McNamara*, 83.

41. Interview, K. Wayne Smith.

42. Interview, Morton Halperin. The incident occurred in 1966.

43. Interview, Seymour Weiss.

44. Arthur Sylvester, Oral History, JFKL, August 2, 1977, pp. 26, 27.

45. Trewhitt, *McNamara*, 90–92.

46. Ibid. The confrontation took place on February 8, 1962.

47. Yarmolinsky was not involved in reviewing the speeches, although he sat on an informal Pentagon committee that reviewed Walker-type propaganda films. His participation in that group was public knowledge; Yarmolinsky even discussed the films with congressional staff. At one point, when the Stennis people threatened to make Yarmolinsky's file public in hopes of wounding the administration, RSM recalls he retorted — in prehearing exchanges with Congress — that he would release the file himself, first: Since there was so little in it, the administration would *not* be hurt.

   In that skirmish, RSM was bold; however, when Yarmolinsky had an opportunity to testify, RSM advised him not to, and he never appeared to discuss his file or clear his record in public. Interviews: RSM, Adam Yarmolinsky.

48. This is from RSM's leadoff statement on the Walker affair before the Senate Armed Services Committee, September 6, 1961. *Statements*, 1961, vol. 3, pp. 1174, 1175.

49. See, for example, Halberstam, *Best*, 169–179 passim.

50. PP 2, IV.B.1., pp. 122–123.

51. William Bundy, unpublished manuscript, chap. 4, pp. 20–29. Bundy writes (23) that RSM argued that "the gut issue was whether to make a 'Berlin-type' US commitment. By this phrase he and others meant a categorical pledge to use every US resource to prevent" South Vietnam's fall. The author is grateful to Mr. Bundy for making the manuscript available.

52. Interview, William Bundy. William Bundy, unpublished manuscript, chap. 4, pp. 26–32. PP 2, IV.B.1, pp. 122–123.

53. Henry Graff, "Decision in Viet-Nam: How Johnson Makes Foreign Policy," *New York Times Magazine*, July 4, 1965; PP 2, IV.B.1, pp. 125–133.

8. STATISTICIAN AGAINST COMMUNISM

1. Interviews: Craig McNamara, Margaret McNamara Pastor, Kathleen McNamara Spears, Mary Joe Goodwin.

2. Interview, William Kaufmann; profile of Kaufmann is at Kaplan, *The Wizards of Armageddon*, 191–203.

3. Many retrospective accounts of the war gamers of Rand during the 1950s stress the analysts' flip treatment of nuclear war fighting. However, some of those analysts, such as Kaufmann and Alain Enthoven, believed they were making the world safer by finding ways to lower the destruction in the next war, which they, like most people at the time, thought would be nuclear. The Rand men knew, at least generally, of SAC's plans to fight this war with an all-out, probably preemptive nuclear attack on the Soviet Union and China. They were devising rationales to move away from this dangerous scenario. From a vast literature, see Weigley, *The American Way of War*, chap. 17, and Freedman, *The Evolution of Nuclear Strategy*, chap. 14.

4. Interviews: William Kaufmann, Frank Trinkl; Kaplan, *Wizards*, 260–262.

5. The detailed information was a result of the intelligence community's effort to determine the size of the Soviet missile force in 1961–62.

6. The changes are described in Rosenberg, "The Origins of Overkill," 64–69. The details of the Sunday Punch war plans and their successor are still not public. See Kaplan, *Wizards*, 276–279.

7. RSM, "Draft: Recommended Long Range Delivery Forces, 1963–1967," September 23, 1961, p. 4.

8. Stromseth, *The Origins of Flexible Response*, 35–39.

9. Steinbruner, *The Cybernetic Theory of Decision*, lays out why the Eisenhower administration and Norstad saw "diffusion" of nuclear weapons to allied nations as a benefit and explains the Norstad MRBM plan.

10. The best of many accounts of French attitudes is Newhouse, *De Gaulle and the Anglo Saxons*.

11. Interview, William Kaufmann.

12. "Remarks by Secretary McNamara," JFKL, May 5, 1962, pp. 2, 3, 7, 10, 12, as declassified August 11, 1977.

13. Barnet, *The Alliance*, 219.

14. Bundy to JFK, June 1, 1962, Box 14, Nuclear History Collection, National Security Archive.

15. Ann Arbor speech, of June 16, 1962, is in *Statements*, 1962, vol. 3, pp. 1497–1510. Background materials for the press are on file, OAFH, Folder "McNamara — 1962"; Department of State telegram, no. 4702, June 19, 1962, Nuclear History Collection, National Security Archive; *WP*, June 21, 1962; Morton Halperin, *New Republic*, October 8, 1962; *Newsweek*, July 2, 1962.

16. RSM's clarification — *Statements*, 1962, vol. 4, p. 1511.

17. Roswell Gilpatric, Oral History, JFKL, May 5, 1970, p. 82.

18. Interview, Douglas Kinnard. RSM had other conflicts with Norstad, such as over the permission granted to producer Darryl Zanuck to use real U.S. troops for filming *The Longest Day*. Norstad appears to have disdained and distrusted RSM. Background interview; Arthur Sylvester, Oral History, JFKL, August 2, 1977, pp. 37, 38.

19. Bundy to JFK, January 30, 1963, Box 15, Nuclear History Collection, National Security Archive.
20. Background interviews.
21. Harkins profile — Sheehan, *A Bright Shining Lie*, 117.
22. Black Star Photo, May 1962.
23. Halberstam, *The Making of a Quagmire*, 183–187; Krepinevich, "The Army Concept and Vietnam," 226–228; Sheehan, *Lie*, 316.
24. A force of 170,000 versus 20,000 — *New York Herald-Tribune*, January 18, 1962; Galbraith is in PP 2, IV.B.1., p. 140.
25. Based on Sheehan, *Lie*, 44, 45.
26. *NYT*, May 12, May 13, 1962.
27. Interview, George Allen. The incident is documented in Newman, *JFK and Vietnam*, 248, 249.
28. Sheehan, *Lie*, 289, 290. RSM's quotes are in *Statements*, 1962, vol. 2, pp. 1166–1169.
29. Sheehan, *Lie*, 290.
30. The following history follows closely that in Sheehan, *Lie*. Other sources are Karnow, *Vietnam*, Buttinger, *Vietnam*, and FitzGerald, *Fire in the Lake*.
31. Ibid. Also consulted was Fall, *The Two Vietnams*. For the mood of the French-Indochina War, see Greene, *The Quiet American*.
32. Sheehan, *Lie*, 686.
33. Gelb and Betts, *The Irony of Vietnam*, 190, 231, 282.
34. Geneva terms and utility to Washington — PP 1, III. Diem installed — Sheehan, *Lie*, 132–139.
35. *NYT*, February 18, 1962; Hallin, *The "Uncensored War,"* 50–58.
36. RSM was praised at the time for applying modern management tools to war; see "McNamara Measures War," *St. Louis Post-Dispatch*, August 20, 1962. Later RSM was blamed for causing MACV to put forward false quantitative measures of success, particularly the body count, and for being overly optimistic. A number of the Army's most senior officers today say privately, however, that MACV under Harkins might have treated another secretary of defense to the same self-serving lore.
37. Roswell Gilpatric, Oral History, JFKL, May 5, 1970, pp. 99, 100.
38. A good analysis of the institutional Army's refusal to recognize the unusual nature of the war and respond is Krepinevich, "The Army Concept and Vietnam."
39. Halberstam, *The Best and the Brightest*; Hallin, *"Uncensored War,"* 40.
40. *Statements*, 1962, vol. 2, pp. 981, 988.
41. Interview, George Allen.
42. Sheehan, *Lie*, 290–291; PP 3, IV.B.4, pp. 3–5.
43. Sheehan, *Lie*, 291.

9. BATTLING CHAOS

1. Abel, *The Missile Crisis*, 43, 44–48; Robert Kennedy, *Thirteen Days*, 23, 24.
2. Maxwell Taylor, Oral History, JFKL, April 12, 1964, p. 8; Roswell Gilpatric, Oral History, JFKL, May 27, 1960, p. 48.
3. Presidential Recordings Transcripts, Cuban Missile Crisis Meetings, October 16, 1962, John F. Kennedy Presidential Papers, President's Office Files, JFKL (hereafter cited as Transcripts, morning or evening).
4. RSM, Preface to Robert Kennedy, *Thirteen Days*, 13.

5. For RSM's awareness of Operation Mongoose and 1975 testimony under oath, see chap. 22, "The Promise of Development." For the extent to which the Kennedy administration's effort to undermine Castro triggered the missile crisis, see Beschloss, *The Crisis Years.*

6. Hilsman, *To Move a Nation,* 181.

7. Tass's statement was on September 12, 1962.

8. Roswell Gilpatric, Oral History, JFKL, May 27, 1960, p. 48.

9. Robert Kennedy, *Thirteen Days,* 35, 36; Transcripts, morning, 13.

10. Garthoff, *Intelligence Assessment and Policymaking.* The intelligence community was reaching a consensus on the figure of seventy-five Soviet ICBMs — all on the Soviet landmass, of course — in the wake of the missile-gap controversy.

11. For RSM's arguments, see Abel, *Missile Crisis,* 50–53. Transcripts, evening, 40–47; Beschloss, *Crisis Years,* 438, 447, 451.

12. The president and Rusk were there but then left. Transcripts, evening, 9, 22, 39, 40, 42, 43, 45, 46, 47.

13. Ibid. Taylor first mentioned the possibility of a blockade in the morning meeting; Transcripts, morning, 12.

14. Roswell Gilpatric, Oral History, JFKL, May 27, 1960, pp. 51, 52.

15. The figure of eighty million is from Robert Kennedy, *Thirteen Days,* 35, 36, and based on what the attorney general and others were told at the time. Eighty million was therefore the potential U.S. casualty figure in RSM's mind during the crisis.

16. See Beschloss, *Crisis Years.*

17. Robert Kennedy, *Thirteen Days,* 34; Roswell Gilpatric, Oral History, JFKL, May 27, 1960, p. 51.

18. Abel, *Missile Crisis,* 72.

19. Ibid., 79, 80.

20. Arthur Sylvester, Oral History, JFKL, August 2, 1977, pp. 20, 21; Abel, *Missile Crisis,* 84.

21. Abel, *Missile Crisis,* 90–92.

22. Sorensen, *Kennedy,* 136.

23. *Baltimore Sun,* October 29, 1982; interview, Adam Yarmolinsky.

24. Blockade scene — Sorensen, *Kennedy,* 69–70.

25. Roswell Gilpatric, Oral History, JFKL, May 27, 1960, pp. 59ff.

26. Abel, *Missile Crisis,* 154–156; interviews: George Anderson, Roswell Gilpatric, RSM.

27. Interviews: George Anderson and senior naval officers.

28. Roswell Gilpatric, Oral History, JFKL, May 27, 1960, p. 61.

29. Events of Friday — Abel, *Missile Crisis,* 171–173, 177–184; Sorensen, *Kennedy,* 711, 712.

30. This came to light only in the 1980s. It was described in detail at Sagan, "Nuclear Alerts and Crisis Management." See also Blight and Welch, *On the Brink,* 75, 356. When RSM was told of General Power's unauthorized alert at a conference at Hawk's Cay, Florida, in 1987, his eyes "rolled toward the ceiling in mock exasperation at this military insubordination," according to J. Anthony Lukas. See Lukas, "Class Reunion," *New York Times Magazine,* December 20, 1990, p. 51. RSM's attitude was different from his tight control of the military during the crisis. At

the Hawk's Cay conference, former under secretary of state George Ball, also a member of Ex Comm, said: "We had one enormous advantage, and that was a secretary of defense who was more than just a spokesman for the military. I hate to think what would have happened if we'd had one like the present Secretary of Defense" — a reference to Caspar Weinberger. See Lukas, "Class Reunion," 51.

31. Quotes are from the letter as translated that night, which is published with the "official" translation in Department of State Bulletin, vol. 69, no. 1795, November 19, 1973, pp. 640–649.

32. Events of Saturday — Abel, *Missile Crisis*, 185–200; Sorensen, *Kennedy*, 712–716. The high emotion is also attested to by Roswell Gilpatric in his Oral History, JFKL, May 27, 1960, pp. 58, 59.

33. The declassified transcripts of Saturday's meetings were published in Trachtenberg, "White House Tapes and Minutes of the Cuban Missile Crisis," 170–203.

34. David Burchinal, Oral History Program, April 12, 1975, U.S. Air Force History Office, 112, 115.

35. All RSM's quotes from Saturday are from Trachtenberg, "White House Tapes."

36. Abel, *Missile Crisis*, 202–206.

37. Adam Yarmolinsky, Oral History, JFKL, November 11, 1964, p. 73.

38. Robert Kennedy, Oral History, JFKL, April 30, 1964, pp. 333, 334. RSM's full presentation, intended to convince Congress that the administration was monitoring the Cuban situation adequately, is in RSM, *Statements*, 1963, vol. 1, pp. 62–85.

39. Background interview.

40. Interview, Frank Gard Jamieson.

41. Abel, *Missile Crisis*, 90–92; Salinger, *With Kennedy*, 251, 252, 257, 258, 263.

42. The "right to lie" quote attributed to Sylvester is quoted in Salinger, *With Kennedy*, 287. Salinger said that Sylvester then denied making the statement, although an entire audience in Syracuse, New York, heard him speak.

43. Neustadt comment is at Blight and Welch, *On the Brink*, 23, 24; Lukas, "Class Reunion," *New York Times Magazine*, December 20, 1990, p. 24.

44. Blight and Welch, *On the Brink*, 54–55.

45. RSM, Oral History (with James Blight), OSDH, May 21, 1987, pp. 38, 23.

46. Salinger article is at *NYT*, February 5, 1989.

47. RSM quotes are RSM, Oral History (with James Blight), OSDH, May 21, 1987, pp. 15, 16, 38, 39.

48. Ibid., 15, 16, 19.

49. Interview, RSM.

10. UNTYING THE KNOT

1. Stewart Alsop, "Our New Strategy: Alternatives to Total War," *Saturday Evening Post*, December 1, 1962.

2. Kaplan, *The Wizards of Armageddon*, 213. Enthoven lists some problems with the doctrine in "1963 Nuclear Strategy Revisited," in Ford and Winters, *Ethics and Nuclear Strategy*, 75, 76. One reason he gives is that

"the goal of destroying enough of the Soviet strategic forces to make an appreciable difference in the number of Americans surviving a Soviet retaliatory attack generated an open-ended requirement for more strategic weapons" (75, 81).

3. The right came out of the missile crisis convinced that U.S. nuclear superiority was the reason Khrushchev backed down, and therefore it renewed the fight for more missiles and bombers. See Claude Witze, "Farewell to Counterforce," *Air Force,* February 1963, pp. 27–29. Air Force "requirements" are shown in RSM, "Memorandum for the President . . . DRAFT," November 21, 1962 (hereafter cited as DPM, November 21, 1962). The "first strike" report quoted in Kaplan, *Wizards,* 315, is dated October 1962, National Security Archive, Nuclear History Collection.

4. David Halberstam explains the public's change well: "The age was changing, and McNamara sensed the shifts," *The Best and the Brightest,* 245, 296. Alsop's December 1 *Saturday Evening Post* article shows the growing public doubts about nuclear war fighting. He quotes a "critic" of RSM's saying, "How can you rely on a weapon as your chief instrument of power when you know that using it will cost you *at least* twenty million dead?"

5. Of a large literature, the best description is still Kelleher, *Germany and the Politics of Nuclear Weapons.* European military attitudes are explored in Steinbruner, *The Cybernetic Theory of Decision,* and Schwartz, *NATO's Nuclear Dilemmas.*

6. Kahn profile — Kaplan, *Wizards,* 220–231.

7. Brodie was a teacher of the Rand nuclear theorists, but unlike most of them, he had started with the study of real wars. Brodie's work is reflective and detached, which sets it apart from most other Rand literature. The quote is from Weigley, *The American Way of War,* 434, 435, and appeared in Brodie, *Strategy in the Missile Age,* 307.

8. Kaplan, *Wizards,* 228; interview, Dennis Flanagan. The review appeared in *Scientific American,* March 1961.

9. Stewart Alsop, "Our New Strategy," *Saturday Evening Post,* December 1, 1962; interview, RSM. RSM relates that Alsop said he got the information from the CIA. See RSM, *Blundering into Disaster,* 46, 47.

10. *Washington News,* November 27, 1962; *WP,* November 26, 1962; *Los Angeles Times,* December 23, 1963; *War/Peace Report,* January 1963.

11. This review was declassified, published, and analyzed in Garthoff, *Intelligence Assessment and Policymaking.* He notes that hardly anyone considered *reducing* the planned size of the U.S. strategic forces, despite ever-lower estimates of the present and likely Soviet force in this period — "the fact of such superiority . . . was of little relevance at the time," Garthoff writes at 24. See also 1–5.

12. RSM, *Blundering into Disaster,* 52–57.

13. Brodie, *Strategy in the Missile Age;* Kaplan, *Wizards,* 235; Wohlstetter, "The Delicate Balance of Terror." Churchill is quoted in Schwartz, *Nuclear Dilemmas,* 47, and taken from *Hansard Parliamentary Debates* (Commons), 5th ser., vol. 537 (1955), cols. 1893–2012.

14. Interview, Alain Enthoven.

15. See Enthoven chapter in Hitch and McKean, *The Economics of Defense in the Nuclear Age.* RSM's 1961 DPM on Strategic Forces, which was drafted by

Enthoven, has the civilians' arguments against the B-70 and for shrinking the future bomber force.

16. Enthoven profile — Kaplan, *Wizards*, 253, 254. Enthoven, "Reason, Morality and Defense Policy," Appendix D, in Ford and Winters, *Ethics and Nuclear Strategy*.

17. DPM, November 21, 1962.

18. Kaplan, *Wizards*, 316ff.

19. RSM, "Draft Memorandum for the President," December 6, 1963, p. I-5.

20. The chart is sketched at Kaplan, *Wizards*, 318.

21. The yardstick of 400 megatons was not original with Enthoven in 1963. Before the ICBM was even built, one of its developers computed the likely future "sufficient" force. C. W. Sherwin, chief scientist of the Air Force, picked up on an analysis by Warren Amster of Convair Corporation, an Air Force contractor on the ICBM program, that 300 to 400 missiles could deter. Sherwin publicized this prescient conclusion in "Securing Peace Through Military Technology," *Bulletin of the Atomic Scientists* 12, no. 5 (May 1956): 159–165. Amster's view was published in the same issue of *Bulletin of the Atomic Scientists*, "Design for Deterrence," 164, 165. Discussed at Freedman, *The Evolution of Nuclear Strategy*, 191, 192. The WSEG-50 study, on which RSM was briefed in 1961, proposed that 200 to 300 survivable Polaris missiles would be sufficient. Therefore, Enthoven's conclusion that 400 delivered megatons, or 200 survivable missiles, was enough reflected a consensus.

22. Kaplan, *Wizards*, 318–319; RSM in DPM, December 6, 1963.

23. Interview, Glenn Kent. Kaplan, *Wizards*, 320–324.

24. Interviews: Glenn Kent, Frank Trinkl.

25. RSM, "Memorandum for the President . . . DRAFT," December 3, 1964.

26. *Statements*, 1965, vol. 1.

27. York and Wiesner, "National Security and the Nuclear Test Ban."

28. For example, RSM was very proud of the number of copies of his annual posture statements that were scooped up by the Soviet embassy in Washington. Freedman, *Evolution*, 248.

29. Background interview.

30. RSM speech to the American Society of Newspaper Editors, San Francisco, September 18, 1967.

31. *Statements*, 1965, vol. 2, pp. 402–416.

32. The best published account of SIOP is Henry Rowen, "The Evolution of Strategic Nuclear Doctrine," in Martin, *Strategic Thought in the Nuclear Age*.

33. For changes wrought by Secretary James Schlesinger, see ibid. as the most informative published source. RSM's failure to refine the options caused Henry Kissinger to criticize him later, when Kissinger began working in the White House and delved into the nuclear war plans. In fact, Kissinger says that when he asked RSM about it, RSM said he had "finally given up, in the face of bureaucratic opposition" to refining the war plans, "and decided to improvise." Kissinger, *White House Years*, 217.

11. CONTROLLER OF TECHNOLOGY

1. Interview, Herbert York; Art, *The TFX Decision*, 33, 34.

2. See note 22, chap. 6, "Power in the Pentagon," and Enthoven and Smith, *How Much Is Enough?*, chap. 2.

3. Interview, Thomas Morris; Haught, ed., *Giants in Management*, 44.

4. This was the MBT-70 program, which eventually collapsed. The U.S. Army could not reconcile itself to a tank narrow and light enough to move over German bridges, and the German army could not wait for the ponderous pace of U.S. armor development. See McNaugher, "Problems of Collaborative Weapons Development," 123–145. For why the F-4 succeeded as a "common" program, see McNaugher, *New Weapons, Old Politics*, 55, 65, 66.

5. Art, *TFX Decision*, 18–24.

6. Ibid., 15–18. The mystery of why these requirements — which proved ultimately incompatible with one another — were not reviewed critically by OSD is explored by Coulam in *Illusions of Choice*. He argues that Enthoven and the systems analysts in 1961–62 were reluctant to question the preferences of the more established DR&E. Thus analysis of roles and requirements was never done. Coulam maintains that civilians in DR&E were enthusiastic about Everest's proposed plane as a way to deploy an advanced avionics system and so did not closely question the requirements. Therefore Everest's Tac Air and DR&E were unopposed and quickly convinced RSM of the merits of the proposed plane.

7. The principal ordnance was to be nuclear bombs. The non-nuclear capability was added after Kennedy took office. Coulam, *Illusions*, 106.

8. Art, *TFX Decision*, 33, 34. Senate Committee on Government Operations, *TFX Contract Investigation*, 91st Cong., 2nd sess., 1970 (hereafter cited as TFX Report), 6.

9. Interview, George Spangenberg.

10. TFX Report, 7; Art, *TFX Decision*, 35, 36.

11. Senate Permanent Subcommittee on Investigations, Committee on Government Operations, *TFX Contract Investigation* (10 pts.), 88th Cong., 1st sess., 1963 (hereafter cited as Hearings), pt. 2, p. 377.

12. Interview, George Spangenberg.

13. TFX Report, 8, 9.

14. Blackburn confirmed how rough his calculation was in Hearings, pt. 5, pp. 1189–1191. *Aviation Week*, May 27, 1963.

15. Background interview.

16. Zuckert testified to this and produced a memo that RSM wrote notifying them he would tell the president. Hearings, pt. 8. *Aviation Week*, August 26, 1963.

17. Art, *TFX Decision*, 67–71.

18. Interview, George Spangenberg.

19. Blackburn in Hearings, pt. 5, p. 1204.

20. Brown's memo is in Hearings, pt. 5, p. 1194; Blackburn on low morale is at ibid., 1193; Navy tactic is at Art, *TFX Decision*, 58, 60.

21. Hearings, pt. 5, p. 1199.

22. Zuckert, RSM's old friend from their days as fellow closet liberals among the Harvard Business School junior faculty (see chap. 2, "The Student of Control"), had the hardest job of any of RSM's service secretaries; the Air Force had more direct conflicts with RSM than did the other ser-

vices. Zuckert wrote unusually candidly of his problems in "The Service Secretary," 458–479. His comment to the author was that the TFX controversy was "just like everything else in this damn town [Washington]. When something starts off bad, it only gets worse."

23. RSM statement, Hearings, pt. 2, p. 380.

24. Ibid., 385.

25. Hearings, pt. 8, pp. 1898–1920.

26. Interview, Eugene Zuckert; Hearings, pt. 8, p. 1908. McClellan concluded that the decision was effectively made as of November 13. RSM and Gilpatric met Kennedy at the White House that afternoon for forty minutes and told the president that General Dynamics was likely to win, according to Zuckert's testimony of August 26, although Zuckert has never confirmed this.

27. Interview, Eugene Zuckert.

28. Hearings, pt. 6, p. 1207.

29. Background interview.

30. Schlesinger, *Robert Kennedy and His Times*, 154, 155, 186, 187, 190, 191.

31. Interview, Eugene Zuckert.

32. Interview, David McGiffert.

33. Interviews: Eugene Zuckert, David McGiffert.

34. Hearings, pt. 1, p. 4, and testimony of February 26–28, March 5, March 6, 1963; *Wall Street Journal*, March 4, 1963; *Washington Star*, March 1, 1963; *Baltimore Sun*, March 15, 1963.

35. *Aviation Week*, April 29, 1963; Hearings, pt. 8, pp. 1209–1214.

36. *Baltimore Sun*, March 13, 1963. Sylvester's testimony, in which he angered the committee by refusing to apologize, is at Hearings, pt. 2, pp. 291–322.

37. *Washington Star*, March 21, 1963; TFX Report, 25, 26.

38. Department of Defense news release, March 12, 1963.

39. Hearings, pt. 2, pp. 374–389.

40. Blackburn testified about this in May — Hearings, pt. 8, pp. 1209–1214. Another member of the team, Colonel John Gregory, also testified that he regretted signing the statement. WP, March 30, 1963.

41. *Washington Star*, March 21, 1963. RSM's "indigestion" remark is at Hearings, pt. 2, p. 435. *Baltimore Sun*, March 22, 1963; *NYT*, March 22, 1963.

42. Hearings, pt. 2, p. 444.

43. Mary McGrory wrote that the tears were genuine, *Washington Star*, March 26, 1963. Military writer George Wilson reported that RSM had not cried, *Aviation Week*, April 1, 1963. Bradlee, *Conversations with Kennedy*.

44. However, *Fortune* did some excellent in-depth articles. See "McNamara's Expensive Economy Plane," June 6, 1967.

45. Robert F. Kennedy, Oral History, JFKL, April 30, 1964, pp. 399, 400. Kennedy's visit to McClellan, *NYT*, March 28, 1963.

46. Gilpatric's problems are summarized at TFX Report, 38–49. Robert F. Kennedy, Oral History, JFKL, April 30, 1964, pp. 399, 400.

47. Korth's situation is at TFX Report, 37, 38. Robert F. Kennedy, Oral His-

tory, JFKL, April 30, 1964, p. 401; Kerr, *A Journey Amongst the Good and the Great,* tells the story from Korth's viewpoint.

48. Hearings, pt. 3, pp. 902ff.; Trewhitt, *McNamara,* 148, 149. Campbell's discovery of RSM's informal decision process corroborates a remark Robert Kennedy made in 1964 about RSM's choice of General Dynamics: "I think he made the decision without going into it as deeply as he might have if he had known there was going to be so much fuss about it." Robert F. Kennedy, Oral History, JFKL, April 30, 1964, p. 398.

49. *NYTI,* 1963, p. 26.

50. Borklund, *The Department of Defense.*

51. TFX Report, 53–55.

52. Ibid., 56, 57.

53. Interview, RSM.

54. Coulam discusses how leaders of DR&E regarded missiles and advanced electronics as complex systems, while building aircraft was considered relatively simple; *Illusions,* 128, 130. He calls RSM's treatment of these highly complex engineering questions "simpleminded," 111.

55. TFX Report, 58, 59.

56. Ibid., 54, 55.

57. Ibid., 63–65.

58. When the F-14, the successor to the Navy TFX, was under development, the Navy decided to give up the requirement that the plane carry six Phoenix missiles, a criterion it had refused to drop for the TFX. The Navy let the F-14 carry 4,200 pounds less of missile, which would have been an important weight savings for the TFX. Coulam, *Illusions,* 271.

59. Report, 66.

60. Icarus was a code name used in correspondence and was not official.

61. The incompatibility of Air Force requirements was explained by Steinbruner and Carter in "Organizational and Political Dimensions," *Daedalus* 104, no. 3 (Summer 1975): 131–154.

62. Interview, Jacques Gansler. It is intriguing to speculate whether, had RSM given the lead role in producing the TFX to the Navy instead of the Air Force in the first place, the Navy would have bent various requirements and worked for the success of the plane, because it would have been a "Navy plane," or whether the TFX would have been obstructed, still, as RSM's airplane.

12. DAWN AND DARKNESS

1. See Robert F. Kennedy, Oral History, JFKL, February 29, 1964, pp. 28, 30. Fairlee, *The Kennedy Promise,* 244, 245.

2. Unemployment figures are from 1965 *World Almanac.* Kennedy tax cut is at Stevens, *Vain Hopes, Grim Realities,* 45, 46. Gold and payments balance are from Rolfe and Burtle, *The Great Wheel,* 79–81; Kaufmann, *The McNamara Strategy,* 277, 278; interview, Carl Kaysen.

3. He quickly reduced the net $2.6 billion deficit to $2 billion. See Kaufmann, *McNamara Strategy,* 278. Interview, Carl Kaysen. Kuss profile from Sampson, *The Arms Bazaar from Lebanon to Lockheed,* 115–118.

4. Two thirds of all arms sales is from SIPRI, *The Arms Trade with the Third World,* 5, 145, 146.

5. The $387 million is from ibid., 146. The decision to make Iran pay for weapons is 577. Interview, William Bundy.

6. Interview, William Gorham.

7. Kaufmann was quoting approvingly "a friend," who had first been quoted in *Newsweek*, February 11, 1961. See Kaufmann, *McNamara Strategy*, 43, 44, and Enthoven and Smith, *How Much Is Enough?*, 31. Like the new breed of finance men at Ford, RSM's Whiz Kids at Defense had contacts with universities. They made extensive contributions to academic literature describing their analytic methods and the resulting rational policy decisions made by RSM. Many in the military supported the use of analysis; each service set up its own systems analysis office and promoted officers who could work cost-benefit problems. Many senior officers who felt the brunt of this civilian-led revolution, however, did not articulate their case well, except to argue that "professional military judgment" was being downgraded. A good, brief discussion of why this tactic was futile is in Joseph Kraft, "McNamara and His Enemies," *Harper's*, August 1961. A blow-by-blow description of the three-way relationship between RSM and his reformers, each of the armed services, and key congressional committees is Fuller, "Congress and the Defense Budget."

8. RSM, press conference, February 17, 1961. See *Civil Service Journal*, April-June 1961, pp. 1–5. Halberstam, *The Making of a Quagmire*, 256.

9. *Washington Star*, August 4, 1963.

10. The analysis that went into measuring tactical air needs is summarized in Enthoven and Smith, *How Much Is Enough?*, 216–225. For the A-7, see 44, 109, 110; the C-5A is at 237, 240, 241.

11. The civilians' role in forcing the Army to consider seriously and then adopt the M-16 is told in McNaugher, *The M16 Controversies*, chaps. 1–5. For the gun's misfiring and congressional investigations, see ibid., chap. 6, and chap. 20, "The Modern Public Servant."

12. Enthoven and Smith, *How Much Is Enough?*, 100–104; Bergerson, *The Army Gets an Air Force*.

13. Enthoven and Smith, *How Much Is Enough?*, 325, 326.

14. Interview, Alain Enthoven. Rickover's opposition to RSM and the role of the Joint Committee on Atomic Energy is discussed in Fuller, "Congress and the Defense Budget," 84, 85, 102–104, 399–403. See also Trewhitt, *McNamara*, 154–156.

15. RSM speech to the American Economic Club, November 18, 1963; *Statements*, 1963, vol. 5, pp. 2548–2569.

16. The reexamination of the Warsaw Pact threat was one of Enthoven's major achievements. It was not an arithmetical exercise alone, however, for it required Defense civilians to wring new kinds of data from U.S. intelligence. RSM, Nitze, Enthoven, and others publicized their revised, lower estimates of the threat extensively in 1961–63, to help push NATO to adopt the policy of flexible response. Interviews: William Kaufmann, Alain Enthoven, others. The issues are summarized in Enthoven and Smith, *How Much Is Enough?*, chap. 4.

17. RSM makes clear in *Blundering into Disaster* that he and his colleagues were responding to perceived Soviet belligerence; see 43, 44, 53. For Khrushchev's alarm at the U.S. buildup, see Beschloss, *The Crisis Years*, 380, 381.

18. RSM briefing on Defense Department cost control — *NYT*, July 11, 1963. When the administration presented a record-high defense budget request of $51 billion in January 1963, RSM forecast defense budgets would level off without losing military strength, due to management efficiency. Some savings came from an ongoing program to close down military bases. See, for example, *NYT*, December 14, 1963.

19. Robert F. Kennedy, Oral History, JFKL, December 6, 1964, pp. 736–740.

20. Interview, RSM. *Statements*, 1964, vol. 1, pp. 262, 266.

21. *Saturday Evening Post*, March 9, 1963. See also Baldwin, "Slow-Down at the Pentagon."

22. RSM, Oral History, OSDH, April 3, 1986, p. 23.

23. *WP*, March 13, 1963.

24. Interview, Harold Brown.

25. *Armed Forces Journal*, November 1962; *New York Journal American*, July 21, 1963.

26. Interview, William Brehm; Enthoven and Smith, *How Much Is Enough?*, 267–274, describes how this analysis was applied to tracking force build-ups for Vietnam.

27. Interview, William Gorham.

28. Nitze, *From Hiroshima to Glasnost*, 228.

29. Background interview.

30. *NYT*, April 22, 1966.

31. Richard E. Neustadt, "Skybolt and Nassau," JFKL, NSF, Meetings and Memoranda, Staff Memoranda, Box 323 (hereafter referred to as Neustadt report), 4, 5, 8–11, 14–18. The fully declassified report is a far more complete account of these events than Neustadt, *Alliance Politics*. See also Schwartz, *NATO's Nuclear Dilemmas*, 96–100, and Schlesinger, *A Thousand Days*, 858, 859.

32. Neustadt report, 18–20.

33. Ibid., 33–43.

34. Ibid., 23–32. The effect of this instruction was to make the U.S. cancellation, once public, look like Washington wanted to terminate Great Britain's independent nuclear deterrent. To the Europeanists at State, this was a plus, although it was a drastic reversal of a long-standing U.S. policy.

35. Ibid., 62–67.

36. RSM was also mad at having been lectured by Thorneycroft in their meeting and at him for apparently permitting his ministry to leak the anti-American, anti-McNamara stories now all over London. Ibid., 68, 69.

37. Steinbruner, *The Cybernetic Theory of Decision*, 234–239.

38. RSM, Oral History, OSDH, April 3, 1986, p. 25.

39. Sorensen, *Kennedy*, 726–730.

40. The most detailed and accurate account of the dialogue between Kennedy, his advisers, the Joint Chiefs, and the atomic energy establishment is based on Glenn Seaborg's detailed diaries and published as *Kennedy, Khrushchev and the Test Ban*.

41. Ibid., 227, 240–242. Some of the consequences are discussed in Beschloss, *Crisis Years*, 618–619, 637, 638. In this author's view, the only way Kennedy could have achieved a comprehensive test-ban treaty would have been to make it a central goal of his presidency, have worked with

the Joint Chiefs and weapons community in a more organized fashion, and have better orchestrated the discussion with the Soviets over the critical issue of on-site inspection. A comprehensive test ban would have been so controversial in the context of 1962–63, however, that Kennedy would have had to sacrifice other goals, possibly his shot at reelection, to get both Soviet agreement and Senate ratification.

Kennedy and RSM — and the country — paid a high price for their haste and disorganization. Ultimately they were forced to give up on a comprehensive ban and to get a limited ban only with conditions imposed by the U.S. weapons community, which were very expensive. While the chances that Kennedy could have succeeded are debatable, it is clear that this juncture was a major missed chance to batten down the race in warhead technology and numbers.

42. Interview, Glenn Seaborg. See Seaborg's accounts of meetings of the Committee of Principals, June 14, 1963, and with the president, July 9, 1963, in Seaborg, *Kennedy, Khrushchev and the Test Ban*, 220–223, 228, 229.

43. Interview, RSM. RSM's statement is an exaggeration. A fresh account of Kennedy's other maneuvering to win Senate adoption, through Sherman Adams and former president Eisenhower, is in Beschloss, *Crisis Years*, 631–636. For Sorensen comment, see *Kennedy*, 738. RSM's full testimony is at *Statements*, 1963, vol. 5, pp. 2165–2178.

13. CRISIS MANAGER CHALLENGED

1. *NYT*, January 3, 1963. Also *NYT*, January 4, January 5, 1963.
2. Description based on Sheehan, *A Bright Shining Lie*, 203–264.
3. Ibid., 181, 198. Krepinevich, "The Army Concept and Vietnam."
4. Interview, George Allen.
5. Halberstam, *The Best and the Brightest*, 253, 254.
6. *St. Louis Post-Dispatch*, August 20, 1962. For new details on how MACV distorted the statistics flowing to RSM, see Newman, *JFK and Vietnam*.
7. Sheehan, *Lie*, 115.
8. "Deposition of Robert S. McNamara" in William C. Westmoreland v. CBS Inc., et al., U.S. District Court, Southern District of New York, taken March 26, 1984, p. 107; RSM, Oral History, OSDH, July 24, 1986, p. 29.
9. Sheehan, *Lie*, 100, 101, 308, 309.
10. Ibid.
11. PP 3, IV.B.4., p. iv, 2–6.
12. See also *Detroit News*, July 11, 1967.
13. Diem's massacre of 1955 was not well known outside of the country; U.S. officials conveniently ignored it, to paint a glowing picture of Diem as a benevolent ruler. Sheehan, *Lie*, 184–190.
14. Karnow, *Vietnam*, 279–281, 296; Halberstam, *The Making of a Quagmire*, 195–216; *NYT* articles for May-August.
15. Halberstam, *Quagmire*, p. 319; Sheehan describes Halberstam's faith in the U.S. role at *Lie*, 320–323.
16. Sheehan, *Lie*, 276, 283, 287.
17. For Madame Nhu, see, for example, Karnow, *Vietnam*, 265–267. The reporters' persecution is described at Sheehan, *Lie*, 351–352.

18. *Statements,* 1963, vol. 4, pp. 1863ff.
19. Figures are from PP 3, IV.B.3., pp. 32, 33, 34.
20. See note 18 above.
21. For positions of these players, see, for example, Gibbons, *The U.S. Government and the Vietnam War,* pt. 2 (hereafter cited as Gibbons, pt. 2), 139, 140. Interview, Roger Hilsman.
22. Interview, Roger Hilsman.
23. Kattenburg's story is told at Halberstam, *Best,* 369–371. The quote is from Gibbons, pt. 2, p. 161.
24. Roswell Gilpatric, Oral History, JFKL, May 5, 1970, p. 30; Gibbons, pt. 2, pp. 148–150; PP 3, IV.B.5., pp. 12–13.
25. Gibbons, pt. 2, p. 151.
26. *NYTI;* Halberstam, *Quagmire,* 254–258; Halberstam, *Best,* 283.
27. PP 3, IV.B.5., pp. 30–36; Taylor, *Swords and Plowshares,* 296.
28. Taylor, *Swords and Plowshares,* 297, 298.
29. Possibly handed to him by Kennedy. Halberstam, *Best,* 283, 284.
30. *WP,* October 7, 1963; Gibbons, pt. 2, pp. 183–184.
31. *WP,* September 30, 1963; *Washington News,* September 23, 1963.
32. Hilsman, *To Move a Nation,* 509, 510.
33. Gibbons, pt. 2, p. 192.
34. PP 3, IV.B.4., pp. 22, 23; Gibbons, pt. 2, pp. 185–187.
35. PP 3, IV.B.4., pp. 1–16; see also chap. 8, "Statistician Against Communism."
36. Gibbons, pt. 2., p. 186.
37. Roswell Gilpatric, Oral History, JFKL, August 12, 1970, p. 97.
38. RSM, Oral History, OSDH, July 24, 1986, p. 12.
39. Ibid.
40. This is the argument in Newman, *JFK and Vietnam.* The interesting theory that JFK was cautious about dumping Diem because he feared it could bring instability that would force the United States to stay is made in Schlesinger, *Robert Kennedy and His Times,* 768–780.
41. Interview, S. Shahid Husain.
42. *Statements,* 1963.
43. *Statements,* 1963, vol. 5, pp. 2289–2331; quote is at 2328.
44. RSM speech to the American Economic Club, *Statements,* 1963, vol. 5, p. 2569.

14. TEST OF A NEW LEADER

1. Robert F. Kennedy, Oral History, JFKL, February 29, 1964, pp. 28, 30; Trewhitt, *McNamara,* 238; interview, RSM.
2. RSM, Oral History, LBJL (with Walt Rostow), January 8, 1975, pp. 17, 18.
3. Drew Pearson in *WP,* January 9, 1963; interview, Willard Goodwin.
4. Files, OSDH. Following scene is from interviews: Willis Shapley, David Bell.
5. Taylor, *Swords and Plowshares,* 302, 303.
6. Ibid.
7. White, *The Making of the President, 1964,* 32.
8. Manchester, *The Death of a President,* 229–232, 234; White, *Making of the President, 1964,* 32, 33.

9. White, *Making of the President, 1964*, 33.

10. Interview, Margaret Stroud.

11. Interview, RSM. Taylor, *Swords and Plowshares.*

12. CBS film, November 22, 1963, JFKL; White, *Making of the President, 1964*, 11, 12.

13. Interview, RSM; Bradlee, *Conversations with Kennedy.*

14. CBS film, November 22, 1963, JFKL. Quote is from Manchester, *Death of a President*, 401.

15. Schlesinger, *Robert Kennedy and His Times*, 658.

16. Interview, Alfred Fitt.

17. Harry McPherson, Oral History, LBJL, December 5, 1968, p. 13. Interview, Harry McPherson.

18. Interview, Harry McPherson.

19. Interview, Mary Joe Goodwin.

20. Interview, Craig McNamara.

21. Interview, Jack Valenti.

22. Interview, Harry McPherson.

23. Background interviews. The Acheson incident was a well-known story around the State Department. See also White, *Making of the President, 1964*, 55–57.

24. Trewhitt, *McNamara*, 255.

25. Interview, Elie Abel; Robert F. Kennedy, Oral History, JFKL, May 14, 1964, p. 496.

26. Background interview. Robert F. Kennedy, Oral History, JFKL, December 6, 1964, pp. 649, 650, 651.

27. Interview, Najeeb Halaby.

28. Interview, Joseph Califano; RSM, Oral History (with Walt Rostow), LBJL, January 8, 1975, pp. 4, 5.

29. For Johnson's moods and techniques, see Geyelin, *Lyndon B. Johnson and the World*, 118–134.

30. A vivid profile of this side of Johnson is in Lemann, *The Promised Land*, 182–186.

31. *NYT*, February 12, 1964.

32. For the sudden shifts in mood, see Lemann, *Promised Land*, 141–143, 161, 170, 172; Manchester, *The Glory and the Dream*, 1058–1062, 1020–1023.

33. Interview, Margaret McNamara Pastor. RSM, Oral History, OSDH, August 27, 1986, p. 16.

34. The economic philosophy of the Great Society rejected the trickle-down theory that overall growth automatically raised up the poor. Trickle-down at this time was the accepted approach to economic development in the poor nations but was being criticized by some economists just when the Johnson administration rejected it at home. See "Economic Report of the President Transmitted to Congress January 1964 Together with the Annual Report of the Council of Economic Advisers," 14, 15. Also *NYT*, January 21, 1964.

35. Interview, Alain Enthoven. At the time Enthoven, although nationally known for his influence on defense policy, was not yet a deputy assistant secretary of defense.

36. Interview, Najeeb Halaby.

37. Interviews: William Gorham, Joseph Califano, Henry Rowen, Adam Yarmolinsky.

38. RSM, Oral History, LBJL, January 8, 1975, p. 22. The story of RSM as chief of PAC is told in Horwitz, *Clipped Wings;* interviews: Joseph Califano, Najeeb Halaby, Alain Enthoven.

39. Interview, Najeeb Halaby.

40. *New York Herald-Tribune*, January 10, 1964.

41. Quoted in *WP*, January 10, 1964.

42. Ernest R. Breech to Frank Middleton, finance coordinator, Goldwater campaign headquarters, April 5, 1964.

43. See, for example, *Statements*, 1964, vol. 3, pp. 1343–1345. Halberstam, *The Best and the Brightest.*

44. *NYT*, August 18, 1964.

45. Gates telegram, RSM reply — *Baltimore Sun*, August 24, 1964; *NYT*, September 20, 22, 1964; *Chicago Tribune*, October 20, 1964.

46. Dwight Eisenhower to Thomas Gates, September 22, 1964, LBJL.

47. See, for example, *New Republic*, October 10, 1964; Hanson Baldwin in *NYT*, October 18, 1964.

48. First published in Gaddis, *Strategies of Containment*, 210, based on September 25, 1964, memorandum of McGeorge Bundy on conversation with Rusk, RSM, and John McCone. NSF–National Security Council Staff Files, Box 2.

49. *NYT*, October 12, 1964. RSM's preparation of the public is shown in his repeated advance warnings that the Chinese capability would be "primitive" and unable to be directed at targets in the United States, Western Europe, or even much of Asia. See Department of Defense news release, October 22, 1964.

50. Interview, Roswell Gilpatric.

15. THE CHOICE OF WAR

1. Halberstam, *The Best and the Brightest*, 307.

2. Interview, Robert Ginsbergh.

3. Kaufmann, *The McNamara Strategy*, 48, 49; Stewart Alsop, "Our New Strategy," *Saturday Evening Post*, December 1, 1962.

4. RSM, Oral History (with Walt Rostow), LBJL, January 8, 1975, p. 35; Berman, *Planning a Tragedy*, xii.

5. See chap. 21, " 'McNamara Yanqui.' "

6. RSM, "Memorandum for the President," November 23, 1963, and meeting notes, "November 24, 1963," in NSF — Vietnam, Box 1, LBJL. See Gibbons, *The U.S. Government and the Vietnam War*, pt. 2 (hereafter cited as Gibbons, pt. 2), 209.

7. *NYT*, December 19, 1963; *Washington Star*, December 18, 1963; interview, William Bundy.

8. Sheehan, *A Bright Shining Lie*, 372; David Halberstam in *NYT*, November 24, 1963.

9. Halberstam, *Best*, 306.

10. *Washington Star*, December 19, 1963.

11. RSM, "Memorandum for the President," December 21, 1963, NSF Country

File, Vietnam, Box 1, File Folder "Vietnam — Memos & Misc., Vol. II," LBJL.

12. Sheehan, *Lie*, 374, 375.

13. Planning for "possible increased activity" is at Gibbons, pt. 2, p. 210.

14. RSM, Oral History, OSDH, July 24, 1986, p. 16. Colby story is in Sheehan, *Lie*, 420.

15. *Los Angeles Times*, December 21, 1963. *Statements*, 1964, vol. 1, p. 21.

16. Hedrick Smith in *NYT*, December 22, 1963. RSM's waffling included holding out the hope that "many of the other U.S. personnel" could return by the end of 1965. See, for example, *Detroit News*, July 11, 1967.

17. Dan Rather described the process on WTOP radio on October 17, 1967. See PP 6, IV.C.7.(b), 105–107.

18. *Statements*, 1964, vol. 1, pp. 22, 124.

19. Ibid., 83.

20. Robert Hotz, "The Credibility Gap," *Aviation Week*, June 15, 1964.

21. *Statements*, 1964, vol. 1, p. 264.

22. Taylor, *Swords and Plowshares*, 309.

23. Halberstam, *Best*, 352; SGFL, March 13, 1964.

24. RSM's demeanor toward Khanh is shown in meeting notes. See PP 3, IV.C.1., pp. 43–46. The trip report's statement of U.S. goals was an explicit commitment like that Kennedy had resisted adopting when RSM and Rusk proposed it in October 1961 (see chap. 7, "Cold Warrior Stepping Up"). Trip report is at PP (Gravel ed.), vol. 3, pp. 499–510. William Bundy, unpublished manuscript, chap. 12, p. 28.

25. *Statements*, 1964, vol. 2, pp. 1070, 1145. March 26 speech is ibid., 1130–1140.

26. Neil Sheehan in *New York Times Magazine*, October 6, 1966.

27. Trewhitt, *McNamara*, 212; Robert F. Kennedy, Oral History (with John Bartlow Martin), JFKL, April 30, 1964, p. 389.

28. Gibbons, pt. 2, p. 246.

29. May trip summary, briefings — PP (Gravel ed.), vol. 3, pp. 69–71; *Statements*, 1964, vol. 3, p. 1447. But privately to the NSC on May 15, RSM said that the situation was worse than when he visited in March. Gibbons, pt. 2, pp. 247, 248.

30. PP (Gravel ed.), vol. 3, p. 175.

31. *NYT*, June 3, 1964.

32. PP (Gravel ed.), vol. 3, p. 498; Gibbons, pt. 2, pp. 229, 234–235.

33. Momyer, *Air Power in Three Wars*, 15; Clodfelter, *The Limits of Air Power*, 76, 77; Sun Tzu, *The Art of War*, 63, 64.

34. PP (Gravel ed.), vol. 3, p. 556.

35. See Janes, "Rational Man, Irrational Policy." McNaughton's plan, quoted below, is from a May 23 response he drafted to a request Johnson made to his advisers for plans for U.S. action responding to the crisis in Laos and Vietnam. Gibbons, pt. 2, pp. 255, 256.

36. PP (Gravel ed.), vol. 3, pp. 556–559. William Bundy commented that McNaughton's paper "reads like the reductio ad absurdum of the planner's art." William Bundy, unpublished manuscript, chap. 9, pp. 18–19. The terms "Red and Blue Flash Points" and others appear in a McNaughton plan dated March 24, 1964; see PP (Gravel ed.), vol. 3, pp. 348–350.

37. Interview, William Sullivan.

38. Interview, Joseph Califano.

39. Senate Committee on Foreign Relations, *The Gulf of Tonkin, the 1964 Incidents,* 90th Cong., 2nd sess., February 20, 1968, pp. 21, 22, 24.

40. Interviews, RSM. McGeorge Bundy agrees. He adds of President Johnson: "He didn't want to take decisions on this issue [Vietnam] in an election year. He was extremely careful after he became president about timing and speeches. There was great frustration [among the advisers] because you couldn't get a decision out of him." Bundy recalls, "Bob became impatient with this as the year progressed. He was holding on for the president all year, but the president wouldn't decide." RSM later told Bundy that the year 1964 was a "lost year." Interview, McGeorge Bundy.

41. See, generally, Goulden, *Truth Is the First Casualty,* and "The Phantom Battle That Led to War," *U.S. News & World Report,* July 23, 1984, pp. 56–67.

42. RSM's receipt of information up the chain of command is in a "Chronology of Events, Tuesday August 4 and Wednesday August 5, 1964," issued by Department of Defense, Doc. 21 in NSF — Vietnam, Box 228, 229, File Folder "Vietnam, Gulf of Tonkin, '64."

43. Johnson's order was overheard by House majority leader Carl Albert, who was in his office while he talked to RSM on the phone. Gibbons, pt. 2, p. 289.

44. Goulden, *Truth Is the First Casualty,* and "The Phantom Battle That Led to War," *U.S. News & World Report,* July 23, 1984.

45. That both RSM and Admiral Sharp received and read this message is shown by another Department of Defense document, titled "Conversations," which is composed of transcripts of Sharp's dialogues with RSM and the chiefs throughout the day and evening. See "Transcript of Telephone Conversations 4–5 August," compiled by Department of Defense, Doc. 26a in NSF — Vietnam, Box 228, 229, File Folder "Vietnam, Gulf of Tonkin, '64."

46. Ibid.

47. This problem was examined most closely in Windchy, *Tonkin Gulf.*

48. Gibbons, pt. 2, p. 337. The full statement, from the report by William Bader, of the committee staff, is: "Secretary McNamara misled the Committee by not telling . . . how increasingly ambiguous the reports . . . became as the hours move[d] on" through the evening.

In fact, RSM may have satisfied himself an attack did take place before Admiral Sharp's callback. A "chronology" released by the Pentagon soon after shows that at 4:47, RSM met with Cyrus Vance and the chiefs "to marshal the evidence to overcome lack of a clear and convincing showing that an attack on the destroyers had in fact occurred. They conclude that an attack had taken place," says the official document. They have five reasons: "1. The TURNER JOY was illuminated when fired on by automatic weapons. 2. One of the destroyers observed cockpit lights. 3. A PGM142 shot at two U.S. aircraft (from COMINT) [communications intelligence]. 4. A North Vietnamese announcement that two of its boats were 'sacrificed.' (from COMINT) 5. Sharp's determination that there was indeed an attack." At this point, RSM may have banished further doubts and, in his own mind, told the truth to the president and the public. Crucially, he never even hinted that the matter had been in doubt or gave any indication of what the contrary evidence was. "Chronology of Events, Tuesday August 4 and Wednesday August 5, 1964," issued by Department of Defense, Doc. 21 in NSF — Vietnam, Box 228, 229, File Folder "Vietnam, Gulf of Tonkin, '64," 27.

49. Interview, RSM.
50. Bundy view — Gibbons, pt. 2, pp. 349, 350. Johnson quoted at *NYT*, September 26, 1964. The prescient analysis was done by Henry S. Rowen. See Gibbons, pt. 2, p. 345.
51. See Gibbons, pt. 2, pp. 355, 356. *New York Herald-Tribune*, September 20, 1964.
52. George Ball, *The Past Has Another Pattern*, 380–381. Text in full appeared as "A Light That Failed," *Atlantic*, July 1972, pp. 34–49.
53. George Ball, Oral History, LBJL, July 8, 1971, pp. 16, 17; interview, George Ball.
54. Alsop in *WP*, November 23, 1964; George Ball, *Another Pattern*, 383.
55. Gelb, *The Irony of Vietnam*, 110, 111.
56. George Ball, *Another Pattern*.
57. Interview, William Bundy.
58. Gibbons, pt. 2, pp. 364, 365.
59. Interviews: Joseph Califano, Victor Heyman.
60. Gibbons, pt. 2, p. 376.
61. McGeorge Bundy to Lyndon Johnson, January 27, 1965, NSF Country File, Vietnam, LBJL.
62. Interview, RSM. McGeorge Bundy agrees with RSM that the president did not cue them to write it. "It was generated by the clear sense that the time had come to get some action out of this guy. We say [in it]: If we keep on going the way we are going, we are going to get to where you don't want to be. It's motivated by the sense that we are in a declining situation, and by frustration, and by a feeling that the man really doesn't want it to come out that way." Interview, McGeorge Bundy.

16. INTERVENTION AND PROMISE

1. Gibbons, *The U.S. Government and the Vietnam War*, pt. 3 (hereafter cited as Gibbons, pt. 3), 50, 51. Bundy was also promoting McNaughton to go to Saigon as a "chief of staff" to coordinate the U.S. effort (191).
2. Ibid., 51.
3. PP (Gravel ed.), vol. 3, pp. 686, 687; Gibbons, pt. 3, p. 50.
4. Gibbons, pt. 3, pp. 57–63.
5. *NYT*, February 8, 1965.
6. Charles Mohr in *NYT*, February 8, 1965; Tom Wicker in *NYT*, February 11, 1965. NSC meeting is Gibbons, pt. 3, pp. 77, 78.
7. PP (Gravel ed.), vol. 3, pp. 688ff.
8. See chap. 9, "Battling Chaos."
9. Interview, RSM.
10. For Johnson's wavering, see VanDeMark, *Into the Quagmire*, 68–84. The irony of RSM's endorsement of a bargaining-chip war is that by 1965, he

was disillusioned with fine-tuned strategies as they applied to nuclear war. See chap. 10, "Untying the Knot."

11. VanDeMark, *Quagmire*.

12. Gibbons, pt. 3, p. 194. McGeorge Bundy makes this comment about whether RSM was pushing a "reluctant" Johnson in the spring of 1965: "Bob is executing Johnson's wishes rather than pushing Johnson into it. McNamara is not a man who persuades the president. He wants to do the thing that fits the situation. It never would have occurred to him that he should make the basic decision whether to stand and fight.

"We never saw this as a risk-free enterprise. Bob clearly believed in making an energetic try. But he would have been just as energetic if the president had said: 'Bob, I don't want to lose, but I don't want troops or a land war in Southeast Asia.' Bob is a man who did not think he was the president. He thought of himself as the president's defense secretary." Interview, McGeorge Bundy.

13. He was briefed on two plans, an eight-week interdiction bombing campaign and a twelve-week campaign. Middleton, *Air War — Vietnam*, 272; PP 4, IV.C.3., p. 44.

14. In addition, the reasons the civilians did not want to go "all out" were not transmitted clearly down the line, causing low morale. See Clodfelter, *The Limits of Air Power*, 118–123, 131, 134. Wheeler told an oral history interviewer in 1969 that "[w]e, in my judgment, misused our naval and air power with the result that the North Vietnamese were able to maintain themselves and continue the war. . . . [W]e never used, during the entire course of our military operations in Vietnam or Southeast Asia, even a fraction of the military power that is available to us. Now it happens to be my view that had we done so the war would have been over two years ago." Earle G. Wheeler, Oral History, LBJL, August 21, 1969, pp. 20, 30.

15. Interviews: Stephen Ailes, Bruce Palmer, Andrew Goodpaster. One profile of Wheeler is from Perry, *Four Stars*, 133–135, 140.

16. The best known is Palmer, *The Twenty-Five-Year War*, 46.

17. Clodfelter, *Limits of Air Power*, 118–123.

18. Interview, Stephen Ailes.

19. *Background Briefings of Secretary of Defense McNamara, 1965; Statements, 1965*, vol. 4, pp. 1505ff.

20. See Halberstam, *The Best and the Brightest*, 547–562.

21. William Bundy, unpublished manuscript, chap. 22, p. 31.

22. Westmoreland, *A Soldier Reports*, 149.

23. Interview, Chester Cooper.

24. VanDeMark, *Into the Quagmire*, 86. Halberstam in *Best* (496–499) writes that Ball almost persuaded the president in the fall of 1964, before Joseph Alsop's column appeared on November 23. "Bothered by the . . . attitudes he found around him in the . . . fall of 1964, and knowing that terrible decisions were coming up, Ball began . . . trusting his own instincts on Indochina. . . . He would, knowing there was a meeting the next day, stay up all night working on a paper . . . and then he would . . . have his staff play the part of the opposition as he went through the dry run. And he would go off to battle, taking genuine delight in it, and his aides could sense the excitement. . . . He would often return, not de-

pressed, but almost exhilarated, *Johnson was listening*. He was getting to him. We're getting through, he would say, and then he would start talking about the next paper. . . .

"He began, first by writing a memo to Rusk, McNamara and Bundy expressing his doubts, and expecting that Bundy would pass the memo on to the President. But to Ball's surprise the memo did not reach Johnson, so the next time Ball passed his memo to Bill Moyers. . . . Moyers passed the memo to the President, who encouraged it, and so, beginning in the early fall of 1964, Ball emerged as the voice of dissent." Here Halberstam summarizes the October memo, except that he omits Ball's scenarios involving U.S. first use of tactical nuclear weapons to counter the Chinese and Ball's discussion of allied, Third World, and Soviet reaction to U.S. first use. Halberstam continues:

"So Ball made his dissent, and he made it powerfully, and if he was not changing the men around him he was certainly affecting the President, touching those doubts which already existed. . . . Was the president waffling? Might he turn back? Sometime in the fall of 1964 Joe Alsop feared that he was."

25. Ball-Thompson plan quoted in Gibbons, pt. 3, pp. 87–91. Johnson's reaction is at George Ball, *The Past Has Another Pattern*, 390, 391.

26. George Ball, *Another Pattern*, 392. Interview, George Ball. Burke and Greenstein, *How Presidents Test Reality*, 172. According to the President's Office Calendar at LBJL, the meeting from 7:20 P.M. to 9:00 P.M. on February 26, which was when the decision on the Marines was reached, was the only one the president attended that day with Ball also present.

27. Background interview.

28. The most definitive discussion of the MLF's history is Steinbruner, *The Cybernetic Theory of Decision.*

29. December meetings are detailed at ibid., and Schwartz, *NATO's Nuclear Dilemmas*, 120–122. Background interview.

30. George Ball, Oral History, LBJL, July 8, 1970, p. 18.

31. These plans are described, among other places, at Gibbons, pt. 3, pp. 260, 261, 279–281, 320–324, 326–327.

32. The full meeting notes are in Berman, *Planning a Tragedy*. Quotes are at 107, 108.

33. Burke and Greenstein, *How Presidents Test Reality*, 234, 235.

34. This moment of doubt was not made public until Gibbons published it in 1988. Gibbons, pt. 3, pp. 153–157. Memos are from McGeorge Bundy, Memos to the President, Aides Files, LBJL. Johnson's remarks at Camp David are from Bundy's notes of that March 10 meeting, Bundy Papers, LBJL.

35. Berman, *Planning a Tragedy*, 54. The general's secret prediction of 500,000 troops was first published in Gibbons, pt. 3, p. 166.

36. Told in Halberstam, *Best*, 585–587, and Berman, *Tragedy*, 56.

37. Berman, *Tragedy*, 56, 60.

38. Enclave strategy is described at Krepinevich, "The Army Concept and Vietnam."

39. Bundy's comments here and below are from Gibbons, pt. 3, pp. 228–230; RSM's report is ibid., 231, 232. After this meeting, Admiral U. G. Sharp commented that "as with most conferences that Secretary McNamara at-

tended, the published results somehow tended to reflect his own views, not necessarily a consensus." Sharp, *Strategy for Defeat*, 80.

40. Berman, *Tragedy*, 67.
41. William Bundy, unpublished manuscript, chap. 26; Gibbons, pt. 3, p. 286.
42. Johnson profile and strategy are from Perry, *Four Stars*, 149–152. Gibbons, pt. 3, p. 358. Interview, Bruce Palmer. A description of other officers' doubts is at Gibbons, pt. 3, pp. 170–173.
43. Westmoreland, *Soldier Reports*, 169, 175–181; Krepinevich, "Army Concept," 437–439; DePuy is from Sheehan, *A Bright Shining Lie*, 568.
44. For details of this analysis, see Krepinevich, "Army Concept," 450–452. It was briefed to RSM on his arrival in Saigon.
45. June 24 draft and a discussion of it are at Gibbons, pt. 3, pp. 327–332.
46. Krepinevich, "Army Concept."
47. *NYTI*, 1965, pp. 1097, 1100, 1103, for controversy over unobserved strikes.
48. From David MacIsaac, writing of the expanding Allied air campaigns in the last six months of the air war in Europe. "If Parkinson is right in holding that 'work expands to fill the time available,' a corollary might be suggested to the effect that 'the degree of military force applied tends to expand to match the capacity available.' " *Strategic Bombing in World War II*, 79.
49. RSM, "Memorandum for the President," June 26, 1965 (revised July 1, 1965), File Folder "Deployment of US Forces, Vol. VI, Tabs 341–356." Reprinted in full in Berman, *Tragedy*, Appendix A, 179–186.
50. Berman, *Tragedy*, 77.
51. Ibid., 82, 83, Appendix B, 198–199.
52. RSM, Oral History, OSDH, July 24, 1986, p. 22. Interview, RSM.
53. RSM, "Memorandum for the President," July 20, 1985, NSF Country File — Vietnam, Box 74, 75, "Vietnam 2EE," 10.
54. *NYTI*, 1965, p. 1089; *Statements*, 1965, vol. 4, p. 1859.
55. Sheehan, *Lie*.
56. Bui Diem account quoted in Gibbons, pt. 3, pp. 371–376.
57. Interview, Chester Cooper.
58. Vance cable was declassified at the request of Gibbons. See Gibbons, pt. 3, pp. 380, 381.
59. Berman, *Tragedy*, 111–119.
60. Gibbons, pt. 3, pp. 414, 415.
61. Halberstam, *Best*, 593. Gibbons, pt. 3, p. 415.
62. Cost figures are from the Vance cable, in Gibbons, pt. 3, pp. 380, 381.
63. RSM, Oral History, OSDH, July 24, 1986, p. 19.
64. Interview, RSM. See also Gibbons, pt. 3, p. 389.
65. Excerpts of July 13 draft are in Gibbons, pt. 3, pp. 369–371.
66. Interview, RSM.
67. Clifford, *Counsel to the President*, 418–421.
68. *NYT*, August 5, 1965.

17. TWO ENORMOUS MISCALCULATIONS

1. Barrel Roll ordered — Gibbons, *The U.S. Government and the Vietnam War*, pt. 2 (hereafter cited as Gibbons, pt. 2), 375. *NYT*, January 15, 1965.

2. James Reston in *NYT*, September 5, 1965. For press reports of bombing, see *NYTI*, "Vietnam," August-September 1965.

3. Interview, Paul Ignatius.

4. *NYT*, August 10, August 12, 1965.

5. Lin Piao's article was deemed important enough to be excerpted at length in *NYT*, September 4, 1965. See also Stanley Karnow in *WP*, September 5, 1965.

6. Vance rebuttal, *NYT*, October 8, 1965.

7. Murray Marder in *WP*, January 27, 1966. Mao's keeping the Red Army home — Karnow, *Vietnam*, 329, 452, 453.

8. In 1964, intercepted enemy communications, as well as the movement of North Vietnamese regulars to the South, convinced U.S. leaders that a drive was imminent to dismember the South. But by the fall of 1965, U.S. officials were saying that the enemy was ordering its forces to prepare for a long struggle. See *NYT*, September 28, September 30, 1965.

9. September 11, 1965, meeting described in Gibbons, *The U.S. Government and the Vietnam War*, pt. 4, forthcoming (hereafter cited as Gibbons, pt. 4). Cable to Lodge is Department of State Central File, Pol. 27, Viet S, Washington to Saigon 753, September 14, 1965, LBJL. RSM, "Memorandum to the President," September Meeting Notes File, LBJL.

10. Quoted in Gibbons, pt. 4. Lodge cable is Department of State Central File, Pol. 27, Viet S, Saigon to Washington 953, September 18, 1965, LBJL.

11. The author wishes to thank William Gibbons for sharing this unclassified summary of the Thompson report. The summary will appear in Gibbons, pt. 4, and is based on Bundy Papers, Box 4, Drawer 2, LBJL. Some 11,000 enemy had infiltrated in the first nine months of 1965, but another 10,000 entered the South in September-October alone, according to U.S. officials in Saigon at the time, PP (Gravel ed.), vol. 4, p. 308.

12. Paul Hendrickson, "Daughter of the Flames," *WP*, December 2, 1985. Interviews: RSM, Adam Yarmolinsky. There had been a raft of antiwar and prowar demonstrations in October, triggering Justice Department investigations of who was behind them. Vice President Hubert Humphrey charged that Communists aided the demonstrators. See *NYT*, October 16–22, 1965.

13. When a group called the Nonviolent Action Committee demonstrated outside the Pentagon on June 16, 1965, RSM invited some of them up to speak with him in his office, *NYT*, June 17, 1965. Sheehan, *A Bright Shining Lie*, 687, 688.

14. "A personal tragedy" is RSM to Paul Hendrickson, "Daughter of the Flames," *WP*, December 2, 1985; "awful" is interview, RSM.

15. "Memorandum for the President," November 3, 1965, NSF Country File, Vietnam Box 74, 75, File Folder "Vietnam 2EE," Doc. 41a, LBJL. Although labeled "Rough Draft," the memo probably went to the president in this form, with charts and maps, because RSM opens his next memo on Vietnam to the president on November 30: "This is a supplement to my memorandum to you dated November 3." See note 21 below.

16. Battle of Ia Drang: Halberstam, *The Best and the Brightest*, 612; PP (Gravel ed.), vol. 4, pp. 303–308. The body count of 240 versus 2,262 is at *NYT*, November 25, 1965; HK Johnson quote is Krepinevich, "The

Army Concept and Vietnam," 485. After General Johnson visited Vietnam in December 1965, where he talked to General Harry Kinnard, commander of the First Air Cavalry, about the details of the battle of Ia Drang, Johnson concluded it had not been a victory at all and that Westmoreland's big-unit strategy was misconceived. But as with Johnson's earlier concurrence in the failure to call up the reserves, the chief of staff did not criticize Westmoreland, the field commander. Perry, *Four Stars*, 156, 157.

17. Interview, Henry Glass.

18. Westmoreland request is at PP (Gravel ed.), vol. 4, pp. 303–309. That Westmoreland's "Concept of Operations" of June barely mentions the possibility that his proposed attrition war could be neutralized by enemy infiltration is a striking, if irresponsible, omission on the part of a field commander seeking a limited commitment of troops.

19. Sheehan, *Lie*, 568; Halberstam, *Best*, 618, 619.

20. Interview, Chester Cooper.

21. RSM's November 30 memo is NSF Country File, Vietnam Box 74, 75, File Folder "Vietnam 2EE," Doc. 40, LBJL.

22. RSM's December 6 memo is ibid., Doc. 39a. The conclusion of the nearly identical December 7 version was quoted in PP 6, IV.C.7.(a), 46. The LBJL files contain another version, dated December 7, with a change in an unrelated passage. Thomas Wareham Janes collection of material on John T. McNaughton.

23. U.S. deaths reach 1,000 is *NYT*, November 12, 1965. RSM's disillusion has been credited to McNaughton's memos of January, based on the Pentagon Papers, which printed several McNaughton drafts of that month but not RSM's long November 3 memorandum. See, for example, Halberstam, *Best*, 617.

24. Casualty data are from "Southeast Asia Military Hostile Casualties, Summary, Friendly and Enemy," Table 52, October 18, 1972, courtesy U.S. Army, Office of Military History.

25. David Halberstam letter to the editor, *NYT*, June 10, 1979.

26. Interview, RSM. RSM's July 20 trip report made no claim on behalf of himself or Westmoreland that deployments would bring victory. He only defined a "favorable outcome" of nine "elements, including the Viet Cong reducing hostile activities, South Vietnam staying "independent (hopefully pro-US, but possibly genuinely neutral)," and U.S. forces withdrawing. At the report's end, all RSM promised the president was that by deploying troops, "if the military and political moves are properly integrated and executed with continuing vigor and visible determination — stands a good chance of achieving an acceptable outcome within a reasonable time in Vietnam." NSF Country File — Vietnam Box 74, 75, File Folder "Vietnam 2EE," 1, 10, LBJL.

27. *Statements*, 1966.

28. Arthur Schlesinger diary, January 21, 1966, courtesy of Arthur Schlesinger.

29. See, for example, Gelb, *The Irony of Vietnam*.

30. Arthur Schlesinger diary, January 21, 1966. RSM's long memo of November 3 addressed "whether we should be prepared ultimately to settle for a 'compromise outcome' for something less than the terms indicated above" but rejected this course as likely to put South Vietnam on the

skids toward communism. He therefore recommended that the United States press on with its original course. RSM's subsequent memos of November 30 and of December 6 and 7 do not deal with this point.

31. Arthur Schlesinger diary, January 21, 1966.

32. Interviews: Carl Kaysen, William Nierenberg.

33. The Fisher proposal and retyped version are both dated January 31 and are declassified in Thomas Wareham Janes collection of material on John T. McNaughton.

34. Memorandum of William Nierenberg, courtesy of William Nierenberg; Deborah Shapley, "Jason Division: Scientists Who Are Professors Attacked," *Science*, February 2, 1973, pp. 459ff.

35. RSM apparently still believed there was hope of changing enemy behavior by shifts in bombing levels, even though he knew of Hanoi's willingness to sacrifice any number of its own to outlast the Americans.

36. Karnow, *Vietnam*, 482.

37. Cooper, *The Lost Crusade*, 291, 295; "Daily Diary," December 27, December 28, 1965, LBJL.

38. *NYT*, December 30, 1965; Sheehan et al., *The Pentagon Papers as Published by the New York Times*, 481, 482.

39. Clark Clifford, Oral History, LBJL, July 2, 1969, pp. 19–21; Ball warning at PP 6, IV.C.7.(a), 47–50. The Pentagon Papers authors then comment, "There were, strikingly enough, no recommendations in Ball's memorandum" even though Ball knew the president placed avoidance of war with China and the Soviet Union high on his list of objectives. "Ball offered disturbing analysis but little in the way of helpful, practical advice." Ibid., 49, 50.

40. Herring, *America's Longest War*, 166, 167.

41. "We, by photographs" — *Statements*, 1966, vol. 1, pp. 21–24. Publicly, he said the bombing was justified, overall, in his view. On December 10 he said that bombing the North was "justified from a military standpoint." *Washington Star*, December 11, 1965.

42. Clark Clifford, Oral History, LBJL, July 29, 1969, pp. 19, 20.

43. There was little doubt in the Pentagon that McNaughton wanted to be secretary of defense himself one day. "Compromise outcome" is contemplated in "3rd Draft" memo of January 19.

44. January 19, 1966, Thomas Wareham Janes collection of material on John T. McNaughton.

45. January 18, 1966, ibid. This particular paper admitted that irregularities in the bombing pattern would *not* affect Hanoi so long as it thought it could win in the South — a startling shift from the premise McNaughton advanced in Rolling Thunder.

46. Requests and promises of effectiveness are at PP 6, IV.C.7., pp. 64, 67, 86, 87. Shift in views of intelligence and RSM's reasons for approving the strikes are at ibid., 68–87.

47. *NYT*, June 30, 1966; PP 6, IV.C.7.(a), 144, 145.

48. RSM told Congress in January that the strikes on fuel supplies had "very little effect on the importation level. . . . I would think it is about as high today as it would have been if we had never struck the Haiphong docks." PP 6, IV.C.7.(a), 86.

49. Johnson's full statement was that when RSM "told Congress that he was assuming the war would be over by June 30, 1967, it was not a lie; it was simply the most effective way to plan the military budget and enforce the requirement on the Joint Chiefs of Staff that they were not to receive one nickel without a plan." Kearns, *Lyndon Johnson and the American Dream*, 298.

50. Gibbons, *The U.S. Government and the Vietnam War*, pt. 3. Bundy also drafted a brief memo for Johnson at that time titled "Reasons for Avoiding a Billion Dollar Appropriation in Vietnam," Berman, *Planning a Tragedy*, 148.

51. Interview, Robert Anthony; Stevens, *Vain Hopes, Grim Realities*, 75.

52. Stevens, *Vain Hopes*, 75.

53. Bach, *Making Monetary and Fiscal Policy*, 123; Stevens, *Vain Hopes*, 73.

54. Halberstam, *Best*, 605; Ackley speech, *NYT*, September 10, 1965.

55. Background interviews.

56. The mention of this figure was unusual. RSM's memos on the war are devoid, for the most part, of cost data. These appear to have been kept in a second set of memos. Interview, Philip Odeen.

57. Interview, Walter Heller.

58. Halberstam, *Best*, 607. Interviews: Two high-ranking Treasury officials, Robert Anthony.

59. Interview, Walter Heller.

60. Background interviews.

61. Arthur Krock to Pat Munroe, July 11, 1972, author communication.

62. Gibbons, pt. 4.

63. *Statements*, 1966, vol. 1, p. 58.

64. This is Schultze's view and not based on Johnson's statements.

65. *Statements*, 1966, vol. 1, p. 58.

66. Ibid., vol. 1, p. 59.

67. Ford's charge is *NYT*, April 19, May 1, 1966; Baldwin's charges are *NYT*, April 24, 1966. Enthoven explained at the time that the services claimed to need 70,000 pilots by counting about 10,000 nonflying jobs as requiring fully trained pilots; they were ready to spend half a million dollars each to train pilots for such jobs while claiming there were not enough pilots for Vietnam. Enthoven and Smith, *How Much Is Enough?*, 278–290.

68. Interview, William Brehm.

69. Coverage, see *NYT*, December 1, December 7, December 8, December 11, 1966. No new funds for Great Society is at Stevens, *Vain Hopes*, 56–59. Stevens estimates that the war on poverty could have utilized $5 billion per year instead of the $1.6 billion or so it received. The conclusion seems inescapable that Johnson's social vision was stillborn, while the cost overrun on the Vietnam War was close to $10 billion.

70. Stevens, *Vain Hopes*, 80, 81; interview, Edwin Dale, Jr.

71. Quoted by K. Wayne Smith, Center for Naval Analyses talk, December 1988.

72. Interview, Edwin Dale, Jr.

73. Interviews: Margaret McNamara Pastor, Craig McNamara.

74. *Harvard Crimson*, November 8, 1966; Trewhitt, *McNamara*, 235; interview, RSM.

18. UTOPIA POSTPONED

1. Interview, Kenneth Bacon; *Washington Star*, June 4, 1966; background interview.
2. Interviews: Margaret McNamara Pastor, Kathleen McNamara Spears, Craig McNamara, family friends.
3. Interviews: Sam Brown, Kathleen McNamara Spears, RSM.
4. Interviews with friends and family members.
5. Interview, Craig McNamara.
6. Exchange with Passman is in *Statements*, 1966, vol. 6, p. 1958.
7. Montreal speech is Department of Defense news release, May 18, 1966.
8. Chatham speech is Department of Defense news release, May 22, 1966.
9. Mary McGrory in *Omaha World Herald*, May 25, 1966.
10. James Reston in *NYT*, May 25, 1966. Negative comments came from William Buckley, May 28, 1966, and editorial in (Phoenix) *Republic*, May 30, 1966. Hoopes's statements are from Hoopes to RSM, May 20, 1966, Yarmolinsky Files, JFKL.
11. Johnson fury — interview, RSM. Cancels Long Beach speech — Goldman, *The Tragedy of Lyndon Johnson*, 403–404.
12. Interview, Richard Neustadt.
13. RSM speech to Veterans of Foreign Wars, August 23, 1966.
14. Interviews: Thomas Morris, Irving Greenberg, Janice Laurence, Peter Riddleberger, Wayne Sellman, Charles Moskos, William Brehm. Moynihan, an assistant secretary of labor in 1963, argued consistently in those years that the military service should be used to help the one third who failed the test. The idea was taken up by the Cabinet-level Task Force on Manpower Conservation, of which RSM was an enthusiastic member. Moynihan, "One-Third of a Nation," *New Republic*, June 9, 1982.
15. Fitt to RSM, July 30, 1966, Yarmolinsky Files, JFKL.
16. *NYT*, March 10, 1966; Neil Sheehan in *NYT*, October 16, 1966.
17. Interview, Irving Greenberg; Nalty, *Strength for the Fight*.
18. An excellent discussion of the effect of King's antiwar stance on blacks' view of military service is Charles Moskos, "How Do They Do It?," *New Republic*, August 5, 1991, pp. 16–20.
19. MacPherson, *Long Time Passing*, 661, 662.
20. Interview, RSM. Also see RSM's interview with Sticht et al., "Cast-Off Youth," A1–A6.
21. Background interview.
22. Department of Defense news release, January 1967. RSM to Fulbright, *Statements*, 1963, vol. 5, pp. 2283–2285. RSM's civil rights programs in the 1960s are described in MacGregor, *Integration of the Armed Forces, 1940–1965*, 603, 604. Interview, Thomas Morris.
23. RSM speech to the National Association of Educational Broadcasters, Department of Defense news release, November 7, 1967.
24. Brock Brower, "McNamara Seen Now, Full Length," *Life*, May 10, 1968; MacGregor, *Integration*, 602.
25. *Statements*, 1967, vol. 3, pp. 1009–1020.

26. Enthoven's scenarios showed that a full-scale ABM system could not be expected to shield cities from an all-out Soviet missile attack, because some enemy warheads would not be intercepted and would "leak" through. But even leaky ABMs had a better chance of destroying one or two incoming warheads. Enthoven's analyses also demonstrated, therefore, that the ABM could be effective in defending the United States from nuclear attack by the "Nth" country, i.e., China. RSM's public presentations warned against ABM deployment but added that the ABM could be useful in this role, if there was sufficient evidence that China was building missiles capable of directing nuclear weapons at the United States. In this way, the issue of U.S. ABM deployment interacted with estimates of the Chinese threat. To take account of this problem, RSM hedged on his overall public anti-ABM stance in private memos in 1965. See Newhouse, *Cold Dawn*, 82, 83.

27. Halperin, *National Security Policy-making*.

28. Greenwood, *Making the MIRV*, 121. The independent targeting capability was developed for the Mark 12 warhead as part of the Minuteman program. In the fall of 1965 RSM approved the development of the Mark 12 warhead for the new Polaris B-3 missile, which was renamed the Poseidon C-3. Greenwood notes that although RSM's approval was only for Mark 12/Poseidon development, not deployment, the Navy considered the decision a de facto green light for later deployment. RSM subsequently approved development of the Mark 12 for the so-called improved Minuteman III.

29. Interview, RSM, by the author and David Alan Rosenberg. The quotes that follow are from ibid.

30. Greenwood, *Making the MIRV*.

31. Newhouse, *Cold Dawn*, 86, 87.

32. Interview, Morton Halperin.

33. Deborah Shapley, "Lessons of the Glassboro Summit," *WP*, October 9, 1986.

34. Accounts differ on the words Kosygin used but agree that he was totally negative about RSM's proposal. See Newhouse, *Cold Dawn*, 94, 95.

35. Interview, RSM.

36. *NYT*, August 1967.

37. Department of Defense news release, September 18, 1967. Reprinted in *NYT*, September 19, 1967.

38. The policy became most firmly established when it was repeated by the articulate band of scientists who led the anti-ABM crusade of 1969–71. Interview, Lawrence Freedman; Freedman, *The Evolution of Nuclear Strategy*, 335–340.

39. GET is described, for example, in Newhouse, *Cold Dawn*, 93. See Freedman, *U.S. Intelligence and the Soviet Strategic Threat*, 85–86, 125. "Is Russia Slowing Down in Arms Race?," *U.S. News & World Report*, April 17, 1965.

40. See Freedman, *U.S. Intelligence*, 111, 112, 113, and Prados, *The Soviet Estimate*, 190–192. The Soviets had reason to resent the condescending lectures from Americans of the period on how they should restrain their strategic forces, in the face of vast American superiority. See Freedman, *Evolution*, 246–249, 264–267.

41. See Freedman, *U.S. Intelligence*, 114, 115. RSM in his September 18, 1967,

speech gave this explanation of why they had overbuilt the U.S. force: "The blunt fact remains that if we had had more accurate information about planned [Soviet] strategic forces, we simply would not have needed to build as large a number as we have today." Department of Defense news release, September 18, 1967. In fact, as Desmond Ball has shown, the large McNamara-Kennedy missile buildup bore little or no relation to declining estimates of the Soviet missile force in 1961–62. See chap. 6, "Power in the Pentagon."

42. Interview, RSM, by the author and David Alan Rosenberg.

43. A former State Department official says that Johnson used to tease George Ball about his objection that the U.S. Vietnam commitment would distract the United States from its primary responsibility toward Europe. "You and your fat white European friends," Johnson would say in his unforgettable accent to Ball. "You don't want to protect brown people about to be overrun by communism." Hughes says this was a frequent, half-jocular conversation Ball and Johnson would have, which "enabled them to get along together." Background interview. Johnson's attitudes toward Europe are explored thoroughly in Geyelin, *Lyndon B. Johnson and the World.*

44. This episode and the following story of Johnson's treatment of Erhard are based on McGhee, *At the Creation of a New Germany*, 128–133.

45. Sampson, *The Arms Bazaar from Lebanon to Lockheed*, 131.

46. McGhee, *At the Creation*, 143–145.

47. Stromseth, *The Origins of Flexible Response*, 147, 148.

48. Ibid., 99–120.

49. Trewhitt, *McNamara*, 187, 188. Background interviews.

50. *Background Briefings of Secretary of Defense McNamara, 1966*, 271. Among many RSM assertions, see *Background Briefings of Secretary of Defense McNamara, 1967*, 52–65. Interviews. See Atkinson, *The Long Gray Line*, for the Seventh Army's later condition.

51. Interviews: RSM, Harlan Cleveland; Schwartz, *NATO's Nuclear Dilemmas*, 179–186.

52. Interview, RSM.

53. Stromseth, *Origins*, 120, 175. Procedurally, neither RSM nor the United States, nor any one power, could set the agenda for the meetings. But once the French were out of the room, RSM could influence the other defense allies to agree to set the agenda he wanted. A big part of this influence was not only force of personality, but the superior analytic expertise of RSM's NATO Whiz Kids, the young civilians who outgunned the European defense staffs. Schwartz, *Nuclear Dilemmas*, 191. Interview, Charles Rosotti.

54. Interview, RSM.

55. RSM, "Draft Memorandum for the President: NATO Strategy and Force Structure," revised January 16, 1968.

56. Interviews: Harlan Cleveland, Timothy Stanley.

57. The continuity of drive of two U.S. administrations, starting with Kennedy and Dean Acheson in April 1961 (see chap. 7, "Cold Warrior Stepping Up"), and of the State Department leaders was also responsible for the adoption of the doctrine.

58. See Denis Healey's introduction to Stromseth, *Origins*, viii–xi, and Schwartz,

Nuclear Dilemmas, for a clear discussion of the distinction between the original concept and that adopted in 1967. RSM to Johnson is in "Draft Memorandum for the President: NATO Strategy and Force Structure," revised January 16, 1968.

59. Interview, Harlan Cleveland. Kelleher, *Germany and the Politics of Nuclear Weapons,* 217.

60. RSM, "Memorandum to the President. Subject: Theater Nuclear Forces," October 1965. RSM interview with Greg Herken — courtesy Greg Herken. RSM to author, see chap. 7, "Cold Warrior Stepping Up."

61. An excellent description of this force buildup is in Stromseth, *Origins,* 88–95, 144. "We should have stopped" is RSM interview with Stromseth. "Let me . . . assure you" is RSM, Remarks, Defense Ministers' Meeting, Paris, May 31, 1965, NSF, LBJL.

62. Interview, Timothy Stanley.

19. HAWK AND DOVE

1. Interview, Craig McNamara.

2. Trewhitt, *McNamara,* 235; AP photograph, February 16, 1967.

3. Millsaps speech in *Statements,* 1967, vol. 3, pp. 1009–1020; AP photograph, SGFL, February 24, 1967.

4. See chap. 10, "Untying the Knot."

5. Schlesinger, *Robert Kennedy and His Times,* 828–836; Trewhitt, *McNamara,* 228, 234.

6. Background interview.

7. *Parade,* March 5, 1967.

8. See chap. 17, "Two Enormous Miscalculations." RSM's October 14, 1966, trip report outlined this approach in detail. See RSM, "Memorandum for the President," October 14, 1966, NSF, NSC Meeting File, Box 2, LBJL.

9. Harrison Salisbury in *NYT,* December 25, 1966, and following days, and in *Behind the Lines — Hanoi,* 68, 94–102.

10. Interview, Philip Goulding. Goulding, *Confirm or Deny,* 89, 90.

11. Interviews: Henry Glass, Admiral Ulysses Sharp, Admiral Thomas Moorer. For examples of the precision the civilians tried to impose, see two memoirs: Momyer, *Air Power in Three Wars,* and F-105 pilot Jack Broughton's *Thud Ridge.* Admiral Sharp was angry when the president and RSM ordered a letup in strikes close to Hanoi after the two in December; Sharp, *Strategy for Defeat,* 122–124.

12. Harrison Salisbury in *NYT,* December 25, 1966, and in *Behind the Lines,* 83–91.

13. RSM admitted there was a morale problem with the fliers. In his October 1966 trip report to the president he said, "Any limitation on the bombing of North Vietnam will cause serious psychological problems among the men who are risking their lives to help achieve our political objectives; among their commanders up to and including the JCS; and among those of our people who cannot understand why we should withhold punishment from the enemy." He added that Westmoreland reported that morale of Air Force personnel "may already be showing signs of erosion — an erosion resulting from current operational restrictions." See

RSM, "Memorandum for the President," October 14, 1966, NSF File, NSC Meeting File, Box 2, LBJL.

14. Westmoreland, *A Soldier Reports*, 241–243. The barrier is discussed in PP 6, IV.C.7.(a), 145–148, 155–160.

15. Interview, Alain Enthoven. For example, a "program budget" for the war Enthoven's office drew up in 1966 showed that for fiscal 1968, the United States would spend $850 million on pacification and beefing up South Vietnam's local defense forces, and $14 billion on offensive military operations. "Had even a modest part of these resources been used for activities which appeared to have a higher payoff . . . the course of U.S. involvement in the war might have been altered sooner." Enthoven and Smith, *How Much Is Enough?*, 294.

16. Enthoven and Smith, in *How Much Is Enough?*, 295–300, describe the study of mines (296) and the firefight study (297). The analysts continued to show how the enemy could control his losses indefinitely and therefore that "the notion of winning the war by wearing the enemy down was untenable." These memos influenced RSM's views and those of his successor, Clark Clifford. A penetrating account of the insights that the systems analysts gained from 1965 to 1972 is Thayer, *War Without Fronts*.

17. The explanation as to why pilot and aircraft "shortages" were nonexistent is made by Enthoven and Smith in *How Much Is Enough?*, 278–290. The useful statistical findings are described in Thayer, *War Without Fronts*.

18. RSM, Oral History, OSDH, July 24, 1986, p. 31.

19. Enthoven and Smith recognize this point in *How Much Is Enough?*, 291. Captain Timothy T. Lupfer, "The Dynamics of Doctrine: The Changes in German Tactical Doctrine During the First World War," Leavenworth Papers, no. 4, July 1981.

20. Interview, William Brehm.

21. PP 5, IV.C.6.(a), vol. 2, pp. 61–67; Westmoreland, *Soldier Reports*, 276.

22. RSM, "Draft Memorandum for the President," May 19, 1967, LBJL. See Epilogue.

23. Woods died in 1982. This account is based on interviews with Woods's biographer, Robert Oliver; RSM; and J. Burke Knapp. Trewhitt, in *McNamara*, 238, says that after the lunch with Woods, RSM and his wife talked until four in the morning. Margy then "spoke quietly with a friend" to say that her husband was torn and it was time to leave. This account is not corroborated. Even if it is true, it supports the idea that RSM kept some deniability by refusing to tell the president directly that he wanted out. Trewhitt also quotes RSM directly as saying that he and Johnson had another inconclusive exchange on the matter on October 16. Ibid., 273.

24. Westmoreland, *Soldier Reports*, 276, 277.

25. Ibid., 276, 277; PP 6, IV.C.7.(b), 23–29, 33, 37–41.

26. PP 5, IV.C.6.(b), 107.

27. Interviews. See Hoopes, *The Limits of Intervention*, and Janes, "Rational Man, Irrational Policy," 114. "Establishment" quote is at PP 5, IV.C.6.(b), vol. 2, p. 147.

28. RSM, "Draft Memorandum for the President," May 19, 1967, LBJL.

29. This careful phrasing of RSM's conclusion shows that he still wanted to play on Lyndon Johnson's team.

30. PP 6, IV.C.7.(b), vol. 2, p. 53.
31. Interview, George Allen.
32. SGFL, July 7, 1967.
33. Neil Sheehan comments that Johnson was at this point using RSM as a "foil," *A Bright Shining Lie,* 685.
34. Interview, Robert Komer; Sharp, *Strategy for Defeat.*
35. PP 5, IV.C.6.(b), 192–209. Briefings at *WP,* July 8, 1967.
36. *WP,* July 10, 1967; *Baltimore Sun,* July 6, 1967; *Chicago Tribune,* July 10, 1967.
37. Ibid.
38. *Statements,* 1967, vol. 7.
39. *WP,* July 10, 1967; *Baltimore Sun,* July 14, 1967; *St. Petersburg Times,* July 12, 1967.
40. *Newsweek,* September 12, 1967.
41. Minutes of White House meeting, July 11, 1967, NSF, Vietnam, Box 74, 75, LBJL.
42. But first RSM and Westmoreland had a public spat in Washington over whether he was using troops "effectively." See *Philadelphia Inquirer,* July 12, 1967; *Baltimore Sun,* July 13, 1967; *Washington News,* July 14, 1967.
43. Trewhitt, in *McNamara,* 271, quotes a former official as saying, "That was important to Bob. I think he read too much into it. Perhaps not."
44. *NYT,* July 20, 1967. Interview, Colonel Robert Pursley.
45. Janes, "Rational Man." *NYT,* July 20, 1967.
46. Interviews: Colonel Robert Pursley, John Roche; John Roche, Oral History, LBJL, July 18, 1970, p. 75.
47. Interview, George Christian.
48. Interview, John Roche. Clark Clifford also says that the Forrestal analogy was on Johnson's mind. See Clifford, *Counsel to the President,* 459, and Trewhitt, *McNamara,* 271.
49. Interview, Joseph Califano.
50. Background interview.
51. Interview, Jack Valenti.
52. *NYT,* August 24, 1967.
53. Kraslow and Loory, *The Secret Search for Peace in Vietnam,* 217–227; Clifford, *Counsel to the President,* 453, 454. See Epilogue.
54. *Statements,* 1967, vol. 6, pp. 2706–2440.
55. Paul Hendrickson, "Self-Inflicted Pain," *Washington Post Magazine,* June 12, 1988.
56. William C. Westmoreland v. CBS Inc. et al., U.S. District Court, Southern District of New York, taken December 6, 1984, pp. 4982–4994. See Epilogue for RSM's statements in the suit.
57. Interview, RSM.
58. SGFL, August 25, 1967.
59. Perry, *Four Stars,* 162–166. Background interview.
60. Interview, Thomas Hughes.
61. Interview, Joseph Califano.

62. RSM spoke to Paul Hendrickson about the march. See Hendrickson, "McNa-
    mara, Specters of Vietnam," *WP*, May 10, 1984.

63. RSM, "Memorandum for the President," November 1, 1967, NSF, Vietnam,
    Box 74, 75, LBJL.

64. Interview, George Christian.

65. John Roche, Oral History, LBJL, July 18, 1970, p. 52.

20. THE MODERN PUBLIC SERVANT

1. Schlesinger, *Robert Kennedy and His Times*, 885. Kennedy said publicly on
   March 16 that he was considering running for president — *NYT*, March
   17, 1968.

2. Sheehan, *A Bright Shining Lie*, 692.

3. President's Office Calendar, November 29, 1967; interview, Joseph Califano.

4. John Roche, Oral History, LBJL, July 18, 1970, p. 52.

5. Arthur Schlesinger diary, November 29, 1967, courtesy Arthur Schlesinger.

6. SGFL, November 29, 1967; *Statements*, 1967, vol. 7; Trewhitt, *McNamara*,
   275.

7. Interview, Joseph Califano.

8. Manchester, *The Glory and the Dream*; *NYTI*, January 1968.

9. Manchester, *Glory*, 1123, 1124. Headline is from the Fort Wayne, Indiana,
   News-Sentinel, February 7, 1968.
       At a meeting on January 24 at the State Department, RSM told
   Johnson's other advisers that the Koreans' aim was "to tie down the
   United States." Then he was silent while the others talked, until he said,
   "I would recommend a build up of forces, including authority from
   Congress to call up Reserves, and extend terms of service. We should call
   up Air Reserves." It seems that his suggestion was not taken up by the
   others, because it does not appear on the notetaker's list of ten possible
   "pressure actions" for further consideration. Meeting Notes File, January
   24, 1968, LBJL.

10. Fulbright's political odyssey is best seen in his remarkable speeches from the
    period. See *Old Myths and New Realities*, as well as *The Arrogance of
    Power, The Pentagon Propaganda Machine*, and a memoir, *The Price of
    Empire*. The steps he took to investigate the legal and political underpin-
    nings of the war, which effectively destroyed the administration's case,
    are told in Austin, *The President's War*, chaps. 7–10. See Gibbons, *The
    U.S. Government and the Vietnam War*, pt. 2, pp. 333–339.

11. Schandler, *The Unmaking of a President*, 74, 75; Braestrup, *Big Story*, 67–
    135. Braestrup (60) says that while RSM's posture statement did not pre-
    dict a massive enemy attack, it "was a far more candid view of the war's
    difficulties and of the strength of the . . . North Vietnamese Army than
    anything that came out of the White House or the Pentagon" at the
    time.

12. "Deposition of Robert S. McNamara" in William C. Westmoreland v. CBS
    Inc. et al., U.S. District Court, Southern District of New York, taken
    March 26, 1984, p. 103; *NYT*, May 16, 1984.

13. There were 525,000 troops already in South Vietnam at the end of 1967. By
    that time, 16,022 Americans had died in Vietnam since 1960. In the last
    quarter of 1967, U.S. deaths averaged 796 per month. In the first quarter

of 1968, which included Khe Sanh and Tet, the U.S. death rate leapt to 1,623 per month.

14. Interview, Alfred Fitt.

15. Interview, Harry McPherson. To another interviewer, McPherson added that "listening to the secretary of defense talk that way about a campaign for which he had ultimately been responsible" made him pretty "shocked." See Karnow, *Vietnam*, 512.

16. Background interview.

17. *Washington Star*, February 15, 1968.

18. Typescript, "Statement of Secretary of Defense Robert McNamara," given to the Senate Armed Services Committee, January 22, 1968 (fiscal year 1969 Posture Statement) (hereafter cited as FY 1969 Posture Statement), 7.

19. *Newsweek*, February 12, 1968; *Boston Globe*, February 5, 1968; *NYT*, March 1, 1968.

20. FY 1969 Posture Statement, 4; quoted in *Newsweek*, February 12, 1968.

21. FY 1969 Posture Statement, 15.

22. Henry Luce made a similar argument against isolationism in his February 1941 *Life* editorial defining the American Century. He wrote, "The fundamental trouble with America has been [that] whereas [it] became in the 20th Century the most powerful and the most vital nation in the world, nevertheless Americans were unable to accommodate themselves spiritually and practically to that fact . . . America cannot be responsible for the good behavior of the entire world. But America is responsible, to herself as well as to history, for the world-environment in which she lives." *Life*, February 14, 1941, p. 63.

23. Laurence Stern in *WP*, February 5, 1968; *New York Post*, February 6, 1968.

24. Ibid.

25. Interview, Roger Hilsman.

26. *Washington Star*, February 4, 1968; see also *Statements*, 1968, vol. 1, pp. 469–475. Pett interviewed RSM on December 9, 1967.

27. Quoted in *Washington Star*, February 29, 1968.

28. Joseph Kraft in *WP*, February 27, 1968.

29. The M-16 tragedy is told in Fallows, *National Defense*, 76–95, and McNaugher, *The M16 Controversies*. One of RSM's last official acts was to suspend manufacture and distribution of the IMR propellant believed to be a cause of the misfiring. Department of Defense news release, January 29, 1968; *NYT*, January 30, 1968.

30. The crash rate of early F-111s "did not compare unfavorably . . . with previous successful deployments," according to Enthoven and Smith in *How Much Is Enough?* RSM's denial that he was meeting weekly with the contractors on the troubled project is in Senate Permanent Subcommittee on Investigations, Committee on Government Operations, *TFX Contract Investigation*, 91st Cong., 2nd sess., December 18, 1970, p. 73. Different types of F-111 aircraft are at 75–77.

31. See chap. 11, "Controller of Technology."

32. Interview, RSM.

33. Joseph Kraft in *WP*, February 27, 1968.

34. S.L.A. Marshall, *Philadelphia Inquirer*, March 10, 1968; Ira Eaker in *Newport News Daily Press*, February 4, 1968.

35. *Wall Street Journal,* January 22, 1968. RSM told Walt Rostow in an oral history interview (LBJL, January 8, 1975, p. 9) that the F-111 program was
"sabotaged." Admiral Thomas Moorer, who was chief of naval operations at the time RSM left office, told the author, "I sabotaged it."

36. Neil Sheehan in *NYT,* March 3, 1968. While RSM did "accept parity" between U.S. and Soviet second-strike forces (see chap. 10, "Untying the
Knot"), he increasingly stressed that America would keep its safe lead in
warhead numbers, thanks to MIRV. See also *Wall Street Journal,* February 2, 1968; *Economist,* February 10, 1968.

37. The Democrats' vulnerability to charges of weakness in national security coincided with the weakening of the party center and capture of machinery
by special groups. See Edsall and Edsall, *Chain Reaction,* 69–72, 90–98.

38. Fuller, "Congress and the Defense Budget," 85, 86, 406–409. *Atlanta Constitution,* February 10, 1968.

39. Fuller, "Congress and the Defense Budget," 410–413. Enthoven's analysis
showed the mission of a new class of attack subs to be a sixth barrier (after minefields, air patrols, destroyers, et al.) to kill Soviet submarines
trying to enter the Atlantic and sink U.S. convoy ships in war. The issue
was whether this extra layer of attrition — i.e., the relatively few extra
Soviet submarines sunk and U.S. convoy ships saved — was worth the
$2 billion price of the new fleet. RSM thought it was not; Rickover, of
course, disagreed. See Enthoven and Smith, *How Much Is Enough?,*
225–232.

40. Fuller, "Congress and the Defense Budget," 412; U.S. Congress, House of
Representatives, Committee on Armed Services, Hearings to Authorize
Appropriations During the Fiscal Year 1969, 90th Cong., 2nd sess.,
1968.

41. Deborah Shapley, "Mac and Cap," *WP,* January 10, 1988.

42. Austin, *President's War,* 153–190; Gibbons, *U.S. Government and the Vietnam War,* pt. 2, pp. 335–338.

43. Senate Committee on Foreign Relations, *The Gulf of Tonkin, the 1964 Incidents,* 90th Cong., 2nd sess., February 20, 1968, pp. 1, 2.

44. Ibid., 8.

45. Ibid., 80. Because RSM failed to address openly the doubts of the senators,
they remained convinced he was lying, and the anger and controversy
festered ever after. See John Finney in *NYT,* March 3, 1968; *Washington
News,* March 1, 1968.

46. This fact was first discovered by the *Times*'s Anthony Austin and published
at the end of his book, *The President's War,* in 1971. Since then, two
former intelligence officials, Ray Cline of the CIA and George Allen,
have said that the messages on which Sharp and RSM based their certainty of a second attack referred to the attack of August 2. See "The
Phantom Battle That Led to War," *U.S. News & World Report,* July 23,
1984. Background interviews.

47. SGFL, February 28, 1968; Johnson text reprinted in *Armed Forces Journal,*
March 9, 1968; *WP,* March 29, 1968.

48. White House news release, February 29, 1968, 12:52 P.M. EST; *WP,* March 1,
1968; *Aerospace Technology,* March 11, 1968; *Washington News,* February 29, 1968.

49. *Washington Star,* February 4, 1968.

50. Trewhitt, *McNamara.*

21. "MCNAMARA YANQUI"

1. Maxine Cheshire, *WP*, January 7, 1968. Background interviews. President from Jim Jones, Meeting Notes File, Box 2, File Folder "September 15, 1967 — 7:27 P.M.," LBJL.

2. Interview, Brock Brower. The article appeared as "McNamara Seen Now, Full Length," in *Life*, May 10, 1968.

3. Interview, Rainer Steckhan.

4. Interview, John Lewis.

5. Schandler, *The Unmaking of a President*, passim. RSM's November 1, 1967, Draft Presidential Memorandum contained the pullback proposal. He repeated it in another Memorandum to the President, January 1968. For RSM's urging of a bombing halt and negotiations, see chap. 19, "Hawk and Dove," and Epilogue.

6. Clifford told his side first in "A Viet Nam Reappraisal," and recently in an autobiography with Richard Holbrooke, *Counsel to the President*.

7. Interview, Morton Halperin. Clifford was also handed another product of RSM's labors: a brief, dramatic memorandum from Alain Enthoven dated March 20, 1968, summarizing systems analysis studies of the enemy's attrition, which said, "If he so chooses, he can limit his casualties to a rate he can bear indefinitely. Therefore the notion we can 'win' this war by driving the VC/NVA [Viet Cong/North Vietnamese Army] from the country or inflicting an unacceptable rate of casualties on them is false." Enthoven and Smith, *How Much Is Enough?*, 298, 299.

8. Interview, Brock Brower. The Bank's Articles of Agreement, in Article IV, Section 10, say: "The Bank and its officers shall not interfere in the political affairs of any member." See Articles in Mason and Asher, *The World Bank Since Bretton Woods*, Appendix A. Please, *The Hobbled Giant*, 87–89.

9. *NYT*, April 14, 1968.

10. See chap. 20, "The Modern Public Servant." RSM to Fulbright, April 1968, is in President's File, World Bank Archives.

11. The following portrait is mainly taken from Mason and Asher, *World Bank*, 13, 20. A colorful portrait of the Bank's project lending in the 1950s is in Morris, *The Road to Huddersfield*. Background interviews also contributed to this and later descriptions of the old Bank.

12. Mason and Asher, *World Bank*, 23–31. Full text of Articles of Agreement is at ibid., Appendix A.

13. The International Finance Corporation was formed in 1956 as an affiliated body to borrow from and lend to the private sector; IFC has a different staff and structure from the World Bank, unlike IDA, described in the text, which is run by Bank staff. The three institutions are generally referred to as the World Bank Group. IDA is described in Mason and Asher, *World Bank*, 386–390, and chap. 12 generally. In addition to the terms noted, IDA borrowers must pay an 0.75 percent service charge.

14. The term "ward" comes from a background interview with a former high Treasury official.

15. Clark, "Robert McNamara at the World Bank," 168.

16. Clark profile is from interviews with William Clark, Hollis Chenery, and David Runnalls, among others. Another source is Clark's posthumous

memoir, *From Three Worlds,* completed by Julian Grenfell. Clark died in 1985.

17. William Clark's "diary" is actually a set of spiral ring binders numbered by year with undated, sometimes rambling entries. The author thanks Julian Grenfell for making them available. They are on file at the offices of the World Bank History Project, at the Bank's office, in Washington.

18. Background interview.

19. Clark diary.

20. Clark, "Robert McNamara," 168. Interview, J. Burke Knapp.

21. Clark, "Robert McNamara," 168.

22. Interviews: Benjamin King, William Clark.

23. Margaret Elliott, "Eugene Rotberg, Treasurer, World Bank," *Institutional Investor,* June 1987, p. 62.

24. Ibid.; *NYTI,* 1968.

25. Rolfe and Burtle, *The Great Wheel,* 94–96, and Stevens, *Vain Hopes, Grim Realities,* 112–113.

26. SGFL, June 5, 1968.

27. Interview, Alfred Fitt.

28. Interview, Walter Haas.

29. SGFL, September 7, 1968.

30. Interview, Paul Ignatius.

31. Mason and Asher, *World Bank,* 678; interviews: Bernard Bell, J. Burke Knapp.

32. Mason and Asher, *World Bank,* 224, 516, 517. The Netherlands chaired an aid consortium for Indonesia after the attempted coup, so that besides RSM's five-year plans, the Indonesians had to work through the consortium in order to continue to get aid. There was speculation that the CIA or other U.S. officials knew of, or even triggered, the countercoup. By making Indonesia a less vulnerable "domino," the countercoup greatly lowered the perceived stakes in South Vietnam as seen in Washington.

33. Interview, Bernard Bell.

34. Clark, "Robert McNamara," 172.

35. SGFL, November 21, 1968

36. *NYT,* November 22, November 23, December 1, 1968.

37. See note 11 above.

38. Clark, "Robert McNamara," 174. Interview, Munir Benjenk.

39. Background interview.

40. Clark diary.

41. RSM address to the Board of Governors, September 30, 1968, p. 1.

42. Ibid., 4–7. RSM also announced the formation of an international commission to be headed by Canada's prime minister, Lester Pearson, to study the needs of developing nations and what the international community could do. Ibid., 3, 4.

43. Interview, John Blaxall.

44. Background interviews.

45. Interview, John Blaxall.

46. Background interviews.

47. Ibid.

48. RSM address to the Board of Governors, September 30, 1968, p. 12.

49. Buenos Aires is described in Clark, "Robert McNamara," 2. RSM address to the University of Notre Dame, May 1, 1969, pp. 3–4. Interview, RSM.

50. Henry Trewhitt, "The Agony and Expiation of Robert McNamara," *Washingtonian*, November 1971, p. 38.

51. Interview, Perry Sellon.

52. The following is based on interviews with Craig McNamara, Margaret McNamara Pastor, Kathleen McNamara Spears, and friends of Bob and Margy's. See also David Talbot, "And Now They Are Doves," *Mother Jones*, May 1984, for Craig's story.

53. These were Rainer Steckhan (West Germany), Leif Christoffersen (Norway), Sven Burmeister (Denmark), Olivier Lafourcade (France), and Caio Koch-Weser (West Germany).

54. Interview, Craig McNamara.

55. "National disaster" is from RSM, "Draft Memorandum to the President," May 19, 1967.

56. For Nixon's policies and reaction to them, see Sheehan, *A Bright Shining Lie*, 741; Herring, *America's Longest War*, 219–237; and Karnow, *Vietnam*, chaps. 15, 16.

57. RSM met regularly with Kissinger in this period, although neither man has said much publicly about their relationship. See Kissinger, *White House Years*, 297.

58. Interview, Leslie Gelb.

59. Interviews: Leslie Gelb, Richard Holbrooke, Morton Halperin, Paul Warnke. Quote is from Gelb's letter of transmittal to Clark Clifford, secretary of defense, and appears at the beginning of each volume. See, for example, PP, vol. 1, pp. ix–x (hereafter cited as Gelb letter).

60. Gelb letter, x, ix.

61. Ibid., ix.

62. Ellsberg profile is from interview with Daniel Ellsberg. For his role in changing SIOP, see Kaplan, *The Wizards of Armageddon*, 275–279. For his hawkishness in Vietnam and conversion, see Sheehan, *Lie*, 739. See also Ungar, *The Papers and the Papers*, and "The Middle Age of Daniel Ellsberg," *California Magazine*, November 1985, pp. 95ff. "Zealotry" is at Sheehan, ibid.

63. The change in journalism is documented in Halberstam, *The Powers That Be*, and Hallin, *The "Uncensored War."*

64. Reston, *Deadline*, 329, 330. Interview, RSM.

65. Interview, Paul Warnke.

66. See *The Pentagon Papers as Published by the New York Times*, 166–169, 244–248.

67. Ibid., xiv, xvi, xvii.

68. Ibid., xvi, xvii.

69. Henry Trewhitt, "Agony and Expiation," 35.

70. Ibid., 35, 48; interview, Kathleen McNamara Spears.

71. Henry Trewhitt, "Agony and Expiation," 35; background interview.

72. Paul Warnke confirms that RSM appeared to think the study itself accused him and other officials and did not distinguish between what the study concluded and the interpretation in the *Times*. RSM, Oral History, OSDH, July 24, 1986, p. 24.

73. Interviews: Robert Komer, Leslie Gelb.
74. Interview, Len Ackland. By contrast, McGeorge Bundy did testify at the trial on Ellsberg's behalf, saying that publishing the study did not harm national security. See Ungar, *Papers.*
75. Kissinger, *White House Years,* 297.
76. See Halberstam, "The Programming of Robert McNamara," *Harper's,* February 1971, and "The Very Expensive Education of McGeorge Bundy," *Harper's,* July 1969, pp. 21ff.
77. Halberstam, *The Best and the Brightest.*
78. "A Light That Failed," *Atlantic,* July 1972. Editor Robert Manning referred to the "stream of written dissents and recommendations for alternative policies" that Ball "produced over nearly two years." Manning went on, "The full record shows, however, that the President devoted much attention to Ball's proposals and deferred some escalatory acts because of them. . . . The paper shows that the policymakers did have in fact before them, from the beginning of their deliberations, an argument that ran counter to their own assessments and cast a bright light on the inherent risks and the probable consequences of escalation."
79. Halberstam, *Best,* 655.
80. Victor Navasky, "How We Got Into the Messiest War in Our History," *New York Times Book Review,* November 17, 1972, pp. 1ff.
81. Letter to the editor, *NYT,* June 10, 1979.
82. Clark diary.
83. Account based on Paul Hendrickson, "On September 29, 1972 . . . ," *Washington Post Magazine,* September 6, 1987, pp. 16ff. Interview, RSM.
84. Background interview.
85. Interview, RSM. Ayres, *Banking on the Poor,* 57, 71, 72, summarizes the issue. In 1964, the Johnson administration apparently covertly aided Chilean presidential candidate Eduardo Frei to assure that Allende did not win election. See Geyelin, *Lyndon Johnson and the World,* 122.
86. Craig's return is from interview and David Talbot, "And Now They Are Doves," *Mother Jones,* May 1984.

22. THE PROMISE OF DEVELOPMENT

1. William Clark, "Robert McNamara at the World Bank," 169.
2. For RSM's early organizational moves, see Mason and Asher, *The World Bank Since Bretton Woods,* 101, 474, 475; Ayres, *Banking on the Poor,* 27, 28. Chenery's title was vice president for development policy. He played an important role in building up the Bank's research and economic studies. But his role was different from that of Charles Hitch, who, as controller of the Department of Defense for RSM, ran both the budget and Alain Enthoven's systems analysis group. At the World Bank, the budget was run by a separate office reporting to RSM. Chenery's role was more like that of Alain Enthoven, although Chenery's analyses were not integrated into the annual program budget cycle as Enthoven's were. Thus Chenery's office had relatively less influence on actual operations. See Ayres, *Banking on the Poor,* 29, 30.
3. RSM address to the Board of Governors, September 30, 1968, p. 1.
4. Background interview.

5. Data provided by Eugene Rotberg. RSM address to the Board of Governors, September 24, 1973, pp. 2–4.

6. *NYT*, July 6, September 30, 1969; *Institutional Investor*, July 1984, p. 19.

7. William Clark diary.

8. William Clark, Oral History, World Bank Archives, pp. 8, 9.

9. Rostow, *Stages of Economic Growth*. A discussion of the meaning of the term "economic development" is at Mason and Asher, *World Bank*, 481–487.

10. RSM address to the Board of Governors, September 30, 1968, pp. 8–10. John L. Maddux, RSM's speech writer, also compiled a summary of the evolution of his thought in "The Development Philosophy of Robert S. McNamara," June 1981, published by the World Bank. The author thanks Mr. Maddux for his assistance.

11. *NYT*, September 22, 1970; RSM address to the Board of Governors, September 27, 1971.

12. RSM address to the United Nations Conference on Trade and Development, April 14, 1972; Maddux, "Development Philosophy," 14–16; Mason and Asher, *World Bank*, 476, 477.

13. RSM address to the United Nations Conference on the Human Environment, June 1972; Maddux, "Development Philosophy" 16, 17.

14. RSM address to the Board of Governors, September 25, 1972.

15. Interviews: Hollis Chenery, William Clark, David Runnalls.

16. An excellent summary of Ward's life and thought is her obituary, "Barbara Ward," in *Economist*, vol. 279, no. 7188 (June 1981). The author is grateful to David Runnalls and Irene Hunter for their help in describing Ward's life and work. For a catty view of Ward, see Fairlee, *The Kennedy Promise*, 128, 129.

17. RSM, *WP*, June 3, 1981.

18. First-person quotes are from Mahbub ul Haq, Oral History, World Bank Archives. Interviews: Robert Ayres, Javed Burki.

19. Background interviews. For details, see note 42 below.

20. RSM address to the Board of Governors, September 24, 1973, pp. 7, 13, 14, 16, 8. *NYT*, September 30, 1973.

21. RSM in fact listed several goals as the tasks for "development" in different speeches at different times. This, of course, was a much looser use of the term "economic development," which economists have struggled to define. See note 9 above.

    The tension between the sweeping goals RSM announced for development as a field and the necessarily limited concrete results the Bank could deliver became a major problem. But in 1973, especially for the new, young staff members, many from the Third World, RSM's breadth of vision was an inspiration.

22. RSM address to the Board of Governors, September 24, 1973; Maddux, "Development Philosophy," 20.

23. David Talbot, "And Now They Are Doves," *Mother Jones*, May 1984, pp. 26ff. Jonathan Miller, "A House Built on Sand," *New Republic*, September 3, 1977, pp. 19–21.

24. Interviews: Joseph Califano, William Gorham. Background interviews.

25. Interview, Stanley Please.

26. Background interviews.

27. *NYTI*, 1973; William Clark diary.
28. William Clark diary.
29. Interview, Hollis Chenery. Chenery published a version of the paper as "Restructuring the World Economy" in *Foreign Affairs* 53, no. 2 (January 1985): 242ff.
30. The $20 billion and $300 billion figures are in 1974 dollars and from Chenery, "Restructuring the World Economy," 258, 254. RSM interview in *Der Volkskrant* of Amsterdam, March 23, 1974, for RSM's views at that moment (English typescript on file at World Bank–IMF Joint Library, *The Times* [London], July 25, 1974). *Meet the Press*, March 24, 1974.
31. RSM address to the Board of Governors, September 30, 1974, p. 18.
32. Interviews: Hollis Chenery, William Clark, Munir Benjenk.
33. *WP*, 1974. The IMF was part of the plan.
34. William Clark diary.
35. RSM address to the Board of Governors, September 30, 1974, p. 3.
36. Ibid., 20.
37. William Clark diary.
38. Interviews: Montague Yudelman, S. Shahid Husain, Leif Christoffersen.
39. Background interview.
40. This widely discussed issue is described succinctly in Ayres, *Banking on the Poor*, 79, 80.
41. Background interview.
42. Interviews: Warren Baum, Montague Yudelman, John Lewis, others. An authoritative discussion of the crisis in funding for the research institutes and its resolution through the founding of CGIAR is Baum, *Partners Against Hunger*, chap. 2.
43. Baum, *Partners*, 30.
44. Interview, M. S. Swaminathan.
45. See Baum, *Partners*, 164, 165, 236–238, 284, 285. China released high-yielding semidwarf rice varieties to its own people in 1959, before the International Rice Research Institute in the Philippines released IR8, its key high-yield rice strain. Peking's emphasis on food production helped increase the share of land planted with rice in China using the new types from 28 percent in 1965 to 77 percent in 1970. Since then, however, the IRRI-sponsored varieties have become a substantial share of China's rice crop, even though China was not a formal member of the CGIAR system. Thus indirectly, RSM assisted in improving the amount and quality of rice available to the Chinese.

    The figure of 500 million people is from Baum, *Partners*, 285, and based on an extensive "impact" study of the effect of the international centers on agriculture worldwide. An estimated half of those people are Chinese, who obtained new varieties partly through their own efforts and partly with IRRI strains. Thus the centers' — hence RSM's — contribution to food self-sufficiency is somewhat less than the 500 million, possibly closer to 300 million.

    While many effects of the Green Revolution can be criticized, "the key statistic," Baum writes, is that by 1983 "half the area devoted to wheat and rice in developing countries is now planted to the semidwarf varieties" (307). Baum also summarizes, "Modern varieties of rice and wheat have prevented mass starvation in much of Asia. But in Africa and semiarid Asia, increased production of these varieties has done much less for poor consumers who eat mainly sorghum, millet, maize, and cassava" (293).

46. Interview, M. S. Swaminathan.

47. Interview, David Bell. Facts about onchocerciasis are from the World Bank video "River Blindness" and information supplied by the West African Riverblindness Control Program of the World Bank.

48. Background interview.

49. See Andrew Kamark, letter to the editor, *Foreign Affairs* 60, no. 4 (April 1982): 943.

50. Background interviews. *NYT,* October 5, October 8, 1976; *Euromoney,* June 1976, p. 64. *WP,* September 1976. In 1976 it was widely assumed that RSM would not be reappointed if Gerald Ford won the fall presidential election. But if Jimmy Carter won, he stood a better chance of reappointment. RSM address to the Board of Governors, October 4, 1976.

51. The Japanese director was Taro Hori, who made a confidential speech to the board highly critical of RSM, which was then leaked to the press. The fact that Hori's criticisms of RSM closely echoed those of William Simon led to speculation that the Japanese were putting good relations with Simon and the U.S. administration ahead of the need for good relations with RSM. *Far Eastern Economic Review* (Hong Kong), December 10, 1976; *Barron's,* October 11, 1976; *Annual Report,* 1977, pp. 6, 7.

52. Background interview. *NYT,* October 9, 1976. Within a month, the White House announced the resignation of Charles A. Cooper, the U.S. executive director, who had represented Simon in the struggle with RSM.

23. MANAGEMENT IS THE GATE

1. In his 1973 speech at Nairobi, RSM had proposed to solve it in the lifetime of children born that day. He recognized that this goal was set back by shifts in the international economy after oil prices rose in 1973–74. Nonetheless, RSM continued to talk of significantly lessening absolute poverty in some unspecified, not-too-distant time frame.

2. Travel scenes are from two background interviews and an interview with Timothy Tahane, executive secretary of the World Bank.

3. William Clark diary.

4. RSM speech to the Board of Governors, September 25, 1978, p. 30.

5. Cary Reich, "The World's Greatest Borrower (as Told by Himself)," *Institutional Investor,* July 1984, pp. 57–69.

6. Background interview.

7. *Annual Report,* 1978. Over the period, the average rates of return on Bank loans were 1.2 percent for agriculture projects, 8 percent for water projects, 22 percent for transportation projects, for example. Of course, some projects earned nothing and had negative rates of return: 8 percent of all IDA projects were negative in this period, while another 11 percent of them did not attain the 10 percent positive rate of return. *IDA in Retrospect,* 53.

8. Interview, John Lewis.

9. Interview, Leif Christoffersen.

10. Of many sources, see Ungar, *Africa,* 397–404; "TP" is from Rosenblum and Williamson, *Squandering Eden,* 126. See also 126–135.

11. By 1981, the Bank's professional staff of 2,552 represented 101 different na-

tionalities; one third of them came from developing nations and 12.6 percent were women. *Annual Report*, 1981, p. 16. Interview, Benjamin King.

12. Among many sources, see *Encyclopedia Britannica*, 15th ed., vol. 3, "Brazil," passim. For conditions in the Nordeste, see "Rural Development, World Bank Experience, 1965–86," Operations Evaluation Department, April 1988, Report (hereafter cited as OED, Rural Development Report), 98.

13. OED, Rural Development Report, 63. Projects tended to be approved before much was learned about local conditions and constraints. Ibid., 82, 85.

14. RSM address to the Board of Governors, September 30, 1974, p. 5. He mentions the Mexican project at 6, 7. The PIDER project began in 1974 from the Mexican government's concern about unrest in the countryside; it had a strong political motive in expanding PIDER fast — with Bank aid. OED, Rural Development Report, 67, 68.

15. Mason and Asher, *The World Bank Since Bretton Woods*, 711, 712; OED, Rural Development Report, 23, 83. The Bank, through IDA, would lend Malawi 50 percent of its external aid from 1967–82. *IDA in Retrospect*, 57.

16. *IDA in Retrospect*, 67.

17. Statistics on Indian life expectancy and agriculture are from Baum, *Partners Against Hunger*. The Indian government role is summarized by S. Guhan in chap. 11 of Lewis et al., eds., *Strengthening the Poor*.

18. *IDA in Retrospect*, 41.

19. World Bank president Eugene Black organized the parting of the waters of the Indus and the construction of the irrigation and drainage systems, in almost biblical fashion, in 1960; ibid., 44. This was possibly the greatest single achievement of the old Bank. See Mason and Asher, *World Bank*, 610–627.

20. Of many sources, see *IDA in Retrospect*, 41, 42. There would be continuing controversy as to whether the Green Revolution was spreading adequately to the poorest farmers, as RSM's rhetoric claimed, or instead helped medium and large farmers. The ecological impacts of the Green Revolution also came under deserved scrutiny during the 1970s.

21. Wheeler in Lewis et al., eds., *Strengthening the Poor*, 213. See also ibid., chap. 12, generally. Interviews: S. Shahid Husain, Javed Burki, Chandra Hardy.

22. *IDA in Retrospect*, 58.

23. The Indonesian government resettled 90,000 families through the first ten years of transmigration through 1979, and the Bank's first loan concerning the program was made in 1976. In the next five years, 1979–84, the government helped resettle 366,000 families, while another 170,000 moved "spontaneously"; from 1984 to 1989 another 544,000 families moved in all. Thus the Bank was a party to transmigration's explosive growth. Data are from "Transmigration in Indonesia, December, 1989," courtesy World Bank Information Office.

24. RSM address to the Board of Governors, September 1, 1975, pp. 19, 20. In this same speech he said of the rural development program, launched two years before, "We have a long way to go, but the early evidence is clear: it works."

25. For RSM's urban programs, see Ayres, *Banking on the Poor*, chap. 7. The

Bank's involvement with the Marcos regime and Manila are vividly described in Bello et al., *Development Debacle*, 101, 106–117. The author's view is that by siding with the Marcos regime against local activists — and insisting on some form of "productivity" by beneficiaries of Bank projects — RSM and the Bank constituted a tool of oppression, engaging in "defensive modernization" to prevent social revolution in the Philippines. They were, in fact, perpetuating the political status quo.

The account is dramatic in showing how little the Bank's technocratic pose helps it when it faces a struggling people's revolution and when it is allied with top-down dictatorial regimes — in the name of expanding exports and growth and other capitalist values. The authors make a useful analogy with RSM's attempts to run pacification and guerrilla war topdown, in Vietnam, at least for the case of his intervention to "help" Manila slumdwellers.

26. A vivid examination of the growth of bureaucracy at the Bank is Oppenheimer, "Don't Bank on the World Bank." Oppenheimer's critique of RSM resembles that made by military writer Hanson Baldwin in "The McNamara Monarchy," *Saturday Evening Post*, March 9, 1963; see chap. 12, "Dawn and Darkness."

27. Background interviews.

28. Background interviews.

29. Interview, Joan Braden. In more than sixty interviews around the Bank, RSM's refusal to eat at or visit the cafeteria was frequently cited.

30. Background interviews.

31. William Clark diary.

32. Interview, David Runnalls; Guhan in Lewis et al., eds., *Strengthening the Poor*, 205, 206.

33. These problems are discussed in much Bank literature and writing since. See, for example, OED, Rural Development Report, 24, 29. The need to give to landed farmers to keep funds flowing is discussed in the Nordeste case at ibid., 64, 65. The rigidity of the "inflexible blueprint" approach to such projects is discussed at ibid., 51.

The difficulty in adapting to local constraints was shown in the gap between rhetoric and reality on population. RSM talked a lot about the important role the Bank could play on this issue, but the Bank's program, curiously, remained "small" and "fragmented." Background interviews. Quote from Ayres, *Banking on the Poor*, 27–30.

34. Joseph Lelyveld, *NYT*, November 30, 1975.

35. Crusoe's comment is in Nevins and Hill, *Ford*. Also see chap. 3, "The Legend of Control." Background interview.

36. Poem is unpublished, as far as can be determined. It was provided to the author by a member of the Bank staff.

37. Interview, S. Shahid Husain; Joseph Lelyveld, *NYT*, November 30, 1975.

38. *Annual Report*, 1978.

39. Ibid.

40. The 3.4 percent-a-year figure is the per capita growth rate; overall GDP growth for these countries would be 5.9 percent per year. These and the 1.5 percent growth in agriculture are from RSM speech to the Board of Governors, September 25, 1978, pp. 4, 28.

41. Covenants for the Brazilian Nordeste projects were allowed to slide, for ex-

ample. OED, *Rural Development Report*, 64. The Mexican authorities running the PIDER projects declined to perform monitoring and evaluation work required in agreements with the Bank, and thus were "unable to measure project impact." Ibid., 69.

42. Background interviews and documents.

43. Interview, Stanley Please. See Please, *The Hobbled Giant*, 87–89, and Shepherd, *The Politics of Starvation*.

44. In his major speech on population at M.I.T. in 1977, RSM only said, "No government really wants to resort to coercion in this matter. But neither can any government afford to let population pressures grow so dangerously large that social frustrations finally erupt into irrational violence and civil disintegration. That would be coercion of a very different order. In effect, it would be nature's response to our own indifference." Address to the Massachusetts Institute of Technology, April 28, 1977, p. 44.

45. This was an influential book that capped the Nairobi program, although published after RSM's 1973 speech. Chenery, *Redistribution with Growth*.

46. RSM address to the Board of Governors, September 25, 1978, pp. 25, 29.

47. *Europa*, March 1975, vol. 2, no. 6.

48. *IDA in Retrospect*, 63. Regional production figures from Baum and Tolbert, *Investing in Development*, 84.

49. There is a large literature on Africa's "failure." See, among many critiques, *NYT*, "African Famine: Is Aid a Villain?" November 29, 1984. The issue is how clear this was during the 1970s, when RSM's Bank projects for Africa were designed and approved. Many experts argue that it takes a decade for the results of project lending to be clearly understood.

50. How the Green Revolution bypassed African agriculture is described in Baum, *Partners Against Hunger*. The Bank officially acknowledged the shortcomings of past aid in "Accelerated Development in Sub-Saharan Africa: An Agenda for Action," 1981.

51. OED, *Rural Development Report*.

52. Tanzania's problems with external aid are summarized by Uma Lele in chap. 3 of Lewis et al., eds., *Strengthening the Poor*. OED, *Rural Development Report*, 60, says the institution "tended to downplay" conflicts between the government's and the Bank's objectives, "perhaps in eagerness to believe that the project would work in spite of the problems." See Rosenblum and Williamson, *Squandering Eden*, 128–131.

53. Inconsistent definitions are noted in OED, *Rural Development Report*, 4–6.

54. For Indian success, see, among other sources, Lewis et al., eds., *Strengthening the Poor*, 204–206. The lack of trained manpower is at ibid., 16, 90, 91.

55. OED, *Rural Development Report*, 31, 50, 56.

56. These criticisms were made frequently in staff interviews with the author. They are documented, among other places, in ibid., chap. 6.

57. Malawi — Rosenblum and Williamson, *Squandering Eden*, 208, 209; OED, *Rural Development Report*, 23, 83–87. See also Uma Lele's discussion in chap. 3 of Lewis et al., eds., *Strengthening the Poor*.

58. Overall, rural development projects made a 10.5 percent rate of return, according to this Operations Evaluation Department computation, which was barely ahead of the 10 percent cutoff point for approval by the Bank in the first place. OED, *Rural Development Report* hastens to point out

that in projects with low rates of return, and even "failed" projects, much good has been accomplished worthy of replicating in later efforts.

59. "Dynamics of Rural Development in Northeast Brazil: New Lessons from Old Projects," December 16, 1991, Report no. 10183.

60. This harder line is in keeping with the whole thrust of both the Bank and the International Monetary Fund since the debt crisis of the early 1980s.

61. Alto Turí project is in *Annual Report*, 1979. Interview, Bruce Rich.

62. William Clark diary. Interview, Sven Burmeister.

24. THE WORLD TAKES ITS PRICE

1. Interview, Sven Burmeister.

2. Interviews: William Clark, David Runnalls, Irene Hunter.

3. Background interview.

4. Interviews: Polly Wisner Fritchey, Craig McNamara.

5. Ibid.

6. Interview, Ruth Graves.

7. Mary Joe Goodwin, *A Mountain Reprieve*.

8. Ibid., 104. RSM made minor errors in quoting Eliot's poem.

9. Background interview.

10. Ann Hughey, "Is the World Bank Biting Off More Than It Can Chew?," *Forbes*, May 26, 1980.

11. RSM projected a world of 15 billion people growing to 60 billion in his address to the University of Notre Dame, May 1, 1969. The 11 billion and 8 billion projections are from his address to the Massachusetts Institute of Technology, April 28, 1977. Interview, Timothy Stanley.

12. See *NYTI*, 1979.

13. For the effects of the oil-price hike on poor countries, see, for example, *Business Week*, July 30, 1979, pp. 38, 39, and *Time*, December 24, 1979, p. 61. China's possible entry is based on interviews with S. Shahid Husain and D. Joseph Wood. China's formal announcement that it sought a role ended a long period of speculation. *NYT*, February 5, 1979.

14. *Annual Report*, 1978.

15. Interviews: D. Joseph Wood, John Lewis, others.

16. The thrust of many *Wall Street Journal* editorials opposing RSM is repeated, for example, in "McNamara's Ghost," October 3, 1984.

17. Background interview.

18. In his 1972 speech to UNCTAD (chap. 22, "The Promise of Development," note 12), RSM warned of a $60 billion debt. The $285 billion debt figure is actual external public debt. See *Annual Report*, 1979, p. 134.

19. Shultz was quoted in *Forbes;* see note 10 above.

20. RSM address to the Board of Governors, October 2, 1979.

21. RSM, "Development and the Arms Race," University of Chicago, May 22, 1979.

22. Interview, Munir Benjenk.

23. Background interview. Quote on staff morale is from *Forbes;* see note 10 above.

24. Background interviews. Those discussing the problem were adamant that they not be named, a sign of RSM's continuing influence over the field and the institution more than a decade after he left.

25. Background interview.
26. Background interview.
27. Peter Cargill died in 1981. This profile is based on several interviews with his close colleagues.
28. Background interviews.
29. Background interviews.
30. Joseph Lelyveld, *NYT*, November 30, 1975.
31. Interviews: J. Burke Knapp, Bernard Bell.
32. Details of the Vietnam loan are from the World Bank Information Office. One discussion of the pros and cons of lending to Vietnam is at Please, *The Hobbled Giant*, 86, 87.
33. For example, see *NYT*, March 19, 22, 28, May 21, 28, September 7, 1979.
34. Poll data are summarized in *IDA in Retrospect*, 15.
35. *NYT*, August 9, September 7, 1979.
36. *NYTI*, 1980.
37. Interview, Edward Fried; *NYT*, November 5, 1979.
38. *NYT*, December 10, 1979; January 15, 1980. Interview, D. Joseph Wood.
39. Background interview.
40. Chris Ogden, *Maggie*, 145.
41. Data from RSM address to the Board of Governors, October 2, 1979, Annex 1, p. 44.
42. Ogden, *Maggie*, 156–158.
43. Background interview.
44. Data from RSM address to the Board of Governors, October 2, 1979, Annex 1, p. 44.
45. From a large literature, see Kuczynski, *Latin American Debt*, chap. 2, for the onset of the debt crisis.
46. Background interview.
47. RSM address to the Board of Governors, October 2, 1979.
48. Ibid., 38, 39.
49. Background interview.
50. Quoted in Leslie H. Gelb's letter of transmittal of the Pentagon Papers to Clark Clifford, secretary of defense, PP, vol. 1, p. x.
51. Interview, Ruth Graves.
52. Background interview.
53. See, for example, "Bankrolling Disasters," 5, 7. Also *Ecologist* 15, no. 1/2, 1985. This is a special issue titled "The World Bank: Global Financing of Impoverishment and Famine." See articles by Bruce Rich, José Lutzenberger, and David Price on the Polonoroeste project.
54. Interview, Bruce Rich. Price's testimony is at Hearing of the House Subcommittee on International Development Institutions and Finance of the House Committee on Banking, Finance and Urban Affairs, *Environmental Impact of Multilateral Development Banks*, 98th Cong., 1st sess., 475–494.
55. RSM address to the United Nations Conference on the Human Environment, June 1972.
56. *60 Minutes* broadcast, 1987.
57. RSM address to the Board of Governors, September 30, 1980.

58. Stockman, *The Triumph of Politics.*
59. Moeen Qureschi, remarks on June 1981, to a dinner held at the Kennedy Center, Washington, D.C., courtesy of Moeen Qureschi.
60. RSM address to the Board of Governors, September 30, 1980; interview, John Merriam.
61. Background interviews. Theodore Roethke quote, from "The Waking," is from typescript of Katzenbach's eulogy, courtesy of Lydia Katzenbach.

EPILOGUE: AN AMERICAN JOURNEY

1. Washington encouraged the destruction of Cambodia through the secret bombing ordered by Henry Kissinger as U.S. forces left South Vietnam. American policy paid little heed to the needs of Cambodia as a nation and eventually starved the non-Communist Lon Nol government, which, ostensibly, it was backing in bloody fighting with the advancing Khmer Rouge. Thus Washington was partly responsible for Lon Nol's fall and the subsequent genocide by the notorious Khmer leader, Pol Pot.

   President Jimmy Carter's national security adviser, Zbigniew Brzezinski, announced that the Vietnam-Khmer struggle was a "proxy war" among Communist giants, with Moscow supporting Vietnam and China supporting Cambodia (Kampuchea), while most informed opinion concluded that the Khmer–Lon Nol, Khmer-Hanoi, and Hanoi-Peking conflict stemmed from ancient rivalries; in other words, Hanoi was expansionist in Indochina, but not across the whole of Southeast Asia, as U.S. leaders in the 1960s had claimed. See, generally, Shawcross, *Sideshow.*

2. Interview, Javed Burki.
3. Iacocca — *WP*, December 5, 1981.
4. See Paul Hendrickson, "McNamara: The Advancing Pain," *WP*, May 9, 1984.
5. Thomas K. Jones, deputy under secretary of defense for research and engineering, and for strategic and theater nuclear forces, said this to reporter Robert Scheer. See Scheer, *With Enough Shovels*, 18.
6. The acronym for the doctrine given it by critics in the early 1970s — MAD, for "mutual assured destruction" — could be taken to mean wanton bombing of civilians. For the critiques, see Gray, *The Soviet-American Arms Race*, chap. 3. See also chap. 10, "Untying the Knot."
7. The number of tactical nuclear weapons in Europe stood at approximately 2,000 when RSM took office and then increased to approximately 7,000. Larger increases, said to go as high as 20,000, were canceled. See chap. 18, "Utopia Postponed." The roots of the initiative to upgrade these older weapons are described at Schwartz, *NATO's Nuclear Dilemmas*, chap. 7.
8. McGeorge Bundy, George F. Kennan, Robert S. McNamara, Gerard Smith, "Nuclear Weapons and the Atlantic Alliance," 753–768.
9. David Talbot, "And Now They Are Doves," *Mother Jones*, May 1984, p. 26.
10. *WP*, October 8, 1982. When he accepted the prize, RSM proposed that the United States with NATO and the Soviet Union with the Warsaw Pact adopt policies of "no second use until," that is, to agree never to order a retaliatory nuclear blow until "it has been determined, beyond any possible doubt," through the hot line and/or aerial inspection, that the other

side has dropped a nuclear weapon on purpose. See RSM, "No Second Use — Until," *NYT*, February 2, 1983.

11. Interview, Joel Swerdlow. Scruggs and Swerdlow, *To Heal a Nation*, 139–140. See also Vietnam Memorial issue of *National Geographic* 167, no. 5 (May 1985).

12. Johnson action on GI Bill — Coleman McCarthy in *WP*, May 30, 1977. President Nixon in July 1974 threatened to veto any bill that increased benefits for Vietnam-era veterans as excessive and inflationary. See editorial, *WP*, July 25, 1977. Jimmy Carter's failure to support these veterans adequately is described in many *WP* articles in 1977; see, for example, October 24 and October 30. For the VA hospitals scandal, see *National Journal*, December 10, 1977, and *WP*, June 18, 1977. For leaders' silence, see Stuart Feldman, "America's Leaders' Values Matter," *Future Choices* 2, no. 1 (Spring 1990): 1–3.

For the relative problems of Vietnam-era veterans, see Frank Greve, "A Legacy of 'Lost Veterans,' " *WP*, November 18, 1977; Jan Scruggs, "Forgotten Veterans of 'That Peculiar War,' " *WP*, May 25, 1977. See also MacPherson, *Long Time Passing*, and Gloria Emerson, *Winners and Losers*.

The Baskir-Strauss book grew out of the work of the presidentially appointed Clemency Board. The book was sponsored by the Ford Foundation under the aegis of its president, McGeorge Bundy. However, the evidence Baskir and Strauss adduced for the condition of Project 100,000 veterans was anecdotal. See Baskir and Strauss, *Chance and Circumstance*, 122–131. Max Cleland, the Vietnam veteran and triple amputee who headed the Veterans Administration in the Carter years, wrote (*WP*, August 7, 1977): "Because of the war, and because of the outcome, a few years later the veteran becomes the guy in society responsible for terrorist activities, for crime and other bad things. And not just any veteran — the Vietnam veteran. Somehow the combination of losing the war and with Mylai and the drug scene, the Vietnam veteran has come to personify that which is wrong with the culture. He's got the character flaw. And the funny thing about it is, he's the guy that initially kept the faith. But he's the guy who ends up paying the price."

The author thanks Stuart Feldman and Joel Swerdlow for advice and information.

13. Scruggs and Swerdlow, *To Heal a Nation*, 153, 45.

14. Based on interviews with Joan Braden and several friends of the Bradens' and RSM's. Braden profile is based on *WP*, February 26, 1976; *WP*, January 25, 1982; *WP*, September 8, 1987. See Braden, *Just Enough Rope*, and Paul Hendrickson, "The Advancing Pain," *WP*, May 9, 1984.

15. The $10,000 is from *WP*, October 12, 1974; the $183,500 is from *WP*, February 29, 1976.

16. As told to Sally Quinn of *WP*, February 26, 1976.

17. Interviews: Craig McNamara, family members, family friends.

18. *WP*, October 23, 1983.

19. Quoted in David Talbot, "And Now They Are Doves," *Mother Jones*, May 1984, p. 47.

20. RSM, "The Military Role of Nuclear Weapons." See chap. 7, "Cold Warrior Stepping Up."

21. Michael Gordon in *National Journal*, September 24, 1983.

22. See chap. 7, "Cold Warrior Stepping Up."

23. For example, he said, "Humanity must step up and take charge of its destiny."

24. The Witwatersrand speech was taken as a gory prediction: "SOUTH AFRICA FACES BLOODY FUTURE" was one local headline about the speech. See *The Crisis* 90, no. 4 (April 1983). RSM, "The Road Ahead," address to the University of Witwatersrand, Johannesburg, South Africa, October 21, 1982, privately printed.

      In a lecture honoring the late Sir John Crawford in 1985, as sub-Saharan Africa's misfortunes compounded, RSM said: "The destruction of Africa's ability to feed itself need not have occurred. The fact is that agriculture [there] has been discriminated against for decades." He criticized the "politicizing of economic life," which "has proceeded further in Africa than in any other region of the developing world" and the elites' practice of "accumulating wealth through access to state power rather than . . . productive enterprise." These were systemic problems RSM knew of and condoned — however privately critical he may have been — by continuing to lend to many such regimes while he was World Bank president.

      RSM also said that sub-Saharan Africa's debt crisis took root in "the turmoil of the 1970s" with "the sharp increases in foreign borrowing, and the reluctance of governments to cut back on spending," trends that worsened in the 1980s. Many commercial banks had followed the World Bank's lead in deeming these governments credit worthy: By 1983, of the region's $60.3 billion government-guaranteed debt, $8 billion was owed to the World Bank Group and another $5.1 billion to the International Monetary Fund. RSM, "The Challenges for Sub-Saharan Africa," Sir John Crawford Memorial Lecture, Washington, D.C., November 1, 1985.

25. A good description of the origins and course of the $120 million libel suit is Connie Bruch, "The Mea Culpa Defense: How CBS Brought On the Westmoreland Suit and Sacrificed One of Its Own," *American Lawyer*, September 1983, pp. 82–90. Trial scene based on transcript of deposition, testimony, and interviews. Some details from this scene are from Paul Hendrickson, "Self-Inflicted Pain," *Washington Post Magazine*, June 12, 1988.

26. "Deposition of Robert S. McNamara" in William C. Westmoreland v. CBS Inc. et al., U.S. District Court, Southern District of New York, taken March 26, 1984, pp. 96, 111, 113. See Charles Mohr's analysis of his statements in *NYT*, May 16, 1984.

27. William C. Westmoreland v. CBS Inc. et al., U.S. District Court, Southern District of New York, transcript for December 6, 1984. Quotes are from 4919, 4943, 4955–4957, 4963, 4968, 4971, 4978, 4994, 4979, 4984. See chap. 19, "Hawk and Dove."

28. *Newsweek*, September 1967. RSM's statements did imply he thought the military side of the war was working. When Thurmond accused him of making a "no-win" statement, RSM had said, "I submit it is not a 'no win' program. Ask the field commanders and the joint chiefs." The *Newsweek* article said "McNamara was asked if he considered the war stalemated. He replied, 'Heavens, no.' "

29. Renata Adler, *New Yorker*, June 16, 1986, p. 73, and *Reckless Disregard*.
    M. A. Farber of *NYT* got the message, writing that RSM "said the opti-
    mism about the war he appeared to convey [publicly] reflected the think-
    ing of senior military leaders and his own belief at the time that 'the
    political track' toward negotiations with Hanoi was still open." Eleanor
    Randolph wrote in *WP*, December 7, 1984, that RSM said his public op-
    timism was based on his belief "that the war could be ended diplomati-
    cally." An analysis of the problems with RSM's statements in the
    deposition is Jonathan Alter in *Newsweek*, March 28, 1984.

30. RSM's statement that "I cannot go before the American people" and his view
    that he had "won" in his court appearance were said to Paul Hendrick-
    son, "Self-Inflicted Pain," *Washington Post Magazine*, June 12, 1988.

31. See chap. 15, "The Choice of War."

32. RSM's trip reports consistently avoid promising the president a military win.
    Each trip report urges a stronger diplomatic effort than that being pursued.
      When he recommended the deployments of July, RSM said that "an ac-
    ceptable outcome" could be obtained "in a reasonable time" only *if* "the mil-
    itary and political moves are properly integrated" and pushed "vigorously."
    Returning from Vietnam in October 1966, RSM advised Johnson to "take
    steps to increase the credibility of our peace gestures in the minds of the en-
    emy." Hanoi's public charges of U.S. "bad faith are not solely propagan-
    distic," RSM added, gamely criticizing the president. He urged the
    administration to "develop a realistic plan" for "a role for the VC in nego-
    tiations, postwar life and government of the nation," a position that was
    anathema to most other Johnson advisers at the time. By November 1967 he
    was privately urging the president to unilaterally halt the bombing of North
    Vietnam — sparing 115,000 sorties likely to be run and accompanying loss of
    pilot lives — and claimed that one "consequence" was that "it is probable
    that Hanoi would move to 'talks,' perhaps within a few weeks after the
    bombing stopped." The president himself apparently wrote on his copy of
    the memorandum, "Why believe this?" November memo is NSF Country
    File — Vietnam, Box 74, 75, "Vietnam 2EE," LBJL. See chap. 17, "Two
    Enormous Miscalculations," and chap. 19, "Hawk and Dove."

33. Many senior commanders did not believe Westmoreland's attrition strategy
    would bring military success, but did not oppose them and pressed on
    with them. General William DePuy, Westmoreland's deputy and a be-
    liever in search and destroy, did not believe the war could be won mili-
    tarily with the constraints on resources the civilian leaders imposed. One
    of the most striking failures was of the Army to either protest or adapt, a
    failing not entirely attributable to RSM. Palmer and DePuy statements
    are from Gibbons, *The U.S. Government and the Vietnam War*, pt. III,
    pp. 455, 456.
      Roche was speaking of the president's exhortation to the fighting men
    to "nail those coonskins to the wall." John Roche, Oral History, LBJL,
    July 16, 1970.

34. A historical description of how American war-fighting traditions evolved
    from the campaigns of General Ulysses S. Grant through World War II
    and Korea is at Weigley, *The American Way of War*.

35. "The strategy of gradualism" — interview, RSM. "How do they know" is
    from an oral history interview with James G. Blight on the Cuban mis-
    sile crisis and reprinted in Blight and Welch, *On the Brink*, 194.

36. Interview, RSM.

37. Kraslow and Loory, *The Secret Search for Peace in Vietnam*, and Cooper, *The Lost Crusade*, document the point widely noted at the time, that while Johnson claimed publicly he was doing everything possible for peace (and privately approved several peace probes to Hanoi), he often intensified the bombing of North Vietnam at the same time — which sent a contradictory signal to Hanoi.

38. Kraslow and Loory, *Secret Search*, 226. For details of the probe, see 219–229.

39. November 1967 "would lead to talks" quote — scribbled in the margin of the LBJL copy, probably by Walt Rostow, was "what is the basis for believing this?"

    "I do believe" is from oral history interview, ironically, with Rostow, LBJL, January 8, 1975, p. 37.

    "Our greatest failure of all" is from ibid, and interview, RSM.

40. Interview, S. Shahid Husain. He expresses this view to the author and in an oral history quoted in chap. 13, "Crisis Manager Challenged."

41. David Halberstam letter to *NYT*, June 10, 1979. See chap. 21, " 'McNamara Yanqui.' "

42. For the story of the Nuclear Planning Group, see chap. 18, "Utopia Postponed." The story of CGIAR is in chap. 22, "The Promise of Development." The innovation of structural adjustment lending is in chap. 24, "The World Takes Its Price."

43. *Statements*, 1967, vol. 3, pp. 1009–1020.

44. RSM interview with Carl Bernstein is in *Time*, February 11, 1991.

45. See chap. 9, "Battling Chaos."

46. "Deposition of Robert S. McNamara" in William C. Westmoreland v. CBS Inc. et al., U.S. District Court, Southern District of New York, March 26, 1984, pp. 175, 176. See *NYT*, May 16, 1984.

    In a similar way, RSM defended the CIA when Senate investigators confronted him with evidence that agents of the CIA were involved in plots to assassinate Fidel Castro. In 1975, under oath to the investigating committee chaired by Senator Frank Church, RSM said, "I believe that the CIA was a highly disciplined organization fully under the control of senior officials of the government." He admitted the investigators could have established the "fact" of agency people being involved but said, "I find that impossible to reconcile" with his view of the agency as well run. "I frankly can't reconcile it," he said. Quoted in "Alleged Assassination Plots Involving Foreign Leaders — Interim Report of the Select Committee to Study Governmental Operations with Respect to Intelligence Activities," U.S. Senate, 94th Cong., 1st sess., November 20, 1975, p. 158.

47. Womack et al., *The Machine That Changed the World*, 237, 238, 244, 87 and passim. Beverly Geber, "The Resurrection of Ford," *Training*, April 1989.

48. Among many sources, a summary of the Army's self-examination is at Stubbings, *The Defense Game*, 128–132. The kid-gloved treatment of the services by RSM's successors as defense secretary are well described in Stubbings' profiles of Melvin Laird (defense secretary January 1969–January 1973) and James Schlesinger (July 1973–November 1975).

49. For example, see *WP*, January 23, 1983. Also World Bank *Annual Reports*, 1982 and 1983, and "The World Bank Experience with Rural Develop-

ment, 1965–86," 13–15. Well-explained examples of how the Bank's rural development goals have changed since are found in "Dynamics of Rural Development in Northeast Brazil."

50. RSM was forceful in outlining the dangers of deployment of the MX land-based missile, which Reagan announced November 22, 1982, after years of debate over this first possible change in the strategic forces RSM left behind. RSM warned that during the many years it would take to construct even a partial Star Wars shield against nuclear attack, if these lethally accurate, ten-warhead MIRVed MX missiles were deployed in silos admitted to be vulnerable, the Kremlin could well conclude the United States planned to use them first, and therefore in a crisis feel tempted to preempt and launch first. See, for example, RSM, *Blundering into Disaster*, 199, 100. McGeorge Bundy, George F. Kennan, Robert S. McNamara, Gerard Smith, "The President's Choice: Star Wars or Arms Control," 264–278. *WP*, November 27, 1984.

51. For example, in *Blundering into Disaster*, RSM writes, "Although four decades have passed without the use of nuclear weapons in combat . . . it is equally true that for thousands of years the human race has engaged in war. There is no sign this is about to change. And history is replete with examples of occasions in such wars when emotions have taken hold and replaced reason" (6).

52. RSM said at the Moscow conference, in his own later summation, "If I had been a Cuban, I would have held many of the same views they held then," but these were based on "misperceptions. . . . We had no intention whatsoever of invading Cuba before the missiles were there. The fact that we didn't . . . is the best indication that we had no intention of doing it before [the missiles were discovered]." He also claimed that Kennedy would not have struck and invaded on Monday or Tuesday, October 30 and October 31, assuming Khrushchev had not backed down on Sunday. Salinger's charges are in *NYT*, February 5, 1989. See transcript of meeting "Cuba Between the Superpowers: Antigua, 3–7 January 1991," James G. Blight, David Lewis, David A. Welch, eds., 1991. Available from Center for Foreign Policy Development, Brown University.

53. RSM testimony in "U.S. Policy in the Persian Gulf," pt. 1, December 4, December 5, 1990, Senate Foreign Relations Committee, 101st Cong., 2nd sess.

54. RSM, "A Global Population Policy to Advance Human Development in the Twenty-first Century," Rafael M. Salas Memorial Lecture, United Nations, New York, December 10, 1991. The equation derives from work by Anne Erlich and others.

55. RSM, "A Vision for Our Nation and the World in the 21st Century." Program for the Study of Sustainable Change and Development, Center for Environmental Management, Tufts University, 1991.

56. See chap. 15, "The Choice of War."

Bibliography

BOOKS, THESES, AND DISSERTATIONS

Abel, Elie. *The Missile Crisis.* Philadelphia: Lippincott, 1966.

Abernathy, William J. *The Productivity Dilemma.* Baltimore: Johns Hopkins University Press, 1978.

Abernathy, William J., Kim B. Clark, and Alan Kantrow. *Industrial Renaissance.* New York: Basic Books, 1983.

Adler, Renata. *Reckless Disregard: Westmoreland v. CBS et al.; Sharon v. Time.* New York: Alfred A. Knopf, 1986.

Albion, Robert, and Robert Connery. *Forrestal and the Navy.* New York: Columbia University Press, 1962.

Allen, Tom. *War Games.* New York: McGraw-Hill, 1987.

Allison, Graham T. *Essence of Decision.* Boston: Little, Brown, 1971.

Alsop, Stewart. *The Centre: The Anatomy of Power in Washington.* London: Hodder and Stoughton, 1968.

Anthony, Robert N. *Management Accounting.* Homewood, Ill.: Richard D. Irwin, 1956.

Anthony, Robert N., John Dearden, and Richard F. Vancil. *Management Control Systems.* Homewood, Ill.: Richard D. Irwin, 1965.

Anthony, Robert N., and James S. Reece. *Accounting Principles.* Homewood, Ill.: Richard D. Irwin, 1983.

Anthony, Robert N., and Glenn A. Welsch. *Fundamentals of Management Accounting.* Homewood, Ill.: Richard D. Irwin, 1974.

Arendt, Hannah. *Eichmann in Jerusalem: A Report on the Banality of Evil.* New York: Viking Press, 1964.

Art, Robert. *The TFX Decision: McNamara and the Military.* Boston: Little, Brown, 1968.

Asprey, Robert B. *War in the Shadows: The Guerrilla in History.* Garden City, N.Y.: Doubleday, 1975.

Atkinson, Rick. *The Long Gray Line: The American Journey of West Point's Class of 1966.* Boston: Houghton Mifflin, 1989.

Austin, Anthony. *The President's War: The Story of the Tonkin Gulf Resolution and How the Nation Was Trapped in Vietnam.* Philadelphia: Lippincott, 1971.

Ayres, Robert L. *Banking on the Poor: The World Bank and World Poverty.* Cambridge: M.I.T. Press, 1983.

Bach, George L. *Making Monetary and Fiscal Policy.* Washington, D.C.: Brookings Institution, 1971.

Ball, Desmond. *Politics and Force Levels: The Strategic Missile Program of the Kennedy Administration.* Berkeley: University of California Press, 1980.

Ball, George. *The Past Has Another Pattern: Memoirs.* New York: W. W. Norton, 1982.

Barker, Randolph, and Robert W. Herdt with Beth Rose. *The Rice Economy of Asia.* Washington, D.C.: Resources for the Future, 1985.

Barnard, Chester. *The Functions of the Executive.* Cambridge: Harvard University Press, 1968.

Barnet, Richard J. *The Alliance — America, Europe, Japan: Makers of the Postwar World.* New York: Simon and Schuster, 1983.

Baskir, Lawrence M., and William A. Strauss. *Chance and Circumstance: The Draft, the War, and the Vietnam Generation.* New York: Alfred A. Knopf, 1978.

Baum, Warren C. *Partners Against Hunger: The Consultative Group on International Agricultural Research.* Washington, D.C.: World Bank, 1986.

Baum, Warren C., and Stokes M. Tolbert. *Investing in Development: Lessons of World Bank Experience.* New York: Oxford University Press for the World Bank, 1985.

Beard, Edmund. *Developing the ICBM: A Study in Bureaucratic Politics.* New York: Columbia University Press, 1976.

Bell, Daniel. *The End of Ideology: On the Exhaustion of Political Ideas in the Fifties.* New York: Free Press, 1962.

Bello, Walden, David Kinley, and Elaine Elinson. *Development Debacle: The World Bank in the Philippines.* San Francisco: Institute for Food and Development Policy, Philippine Solidarity Network, 1982.

Bergerson, Frederic A. *The Army Gets an Air Force: Tactics of Insurgent Bureaucratic Politics.* Baltimore: Johns Hopkins University Press, 1980.

Berman, Larry. *Lyndon Johnson's War: The Road to Stalemate in Vietnam.* New York: W. W. Norton, 1989.

———. *Planning a Tragedy: The Americanization of the War in Vietnam.* New York: W. W. Norton, 1982.

Beschloss, Michael. *The Crisis Years: Kennedy and Khrushchev, 1960–63.* New York: Harper and Row, 1991.

Betts, Richard K. *Soldiers, Statesmen and Cold War Crises.* Cambridge: Harvard University Press, 1977.

Blaufarb, Douglas. *The Counterinsurgency Era: U.S. Doctrine and Performance, 1950 to the Present.* New York: Free Press, 1977.

Blechman, Barry M., and Stephen S. Kaplan, with David K. Hall et al. *Force Without War.* Washington, D.C.: Brookings Institution, 1978.

Blight, James G., and David A. Welch. *On the Brink: Americans and Soviets Reexamine the Cuban Missile Crisis.* New York: Farrar, Straus, Giroux, 1989.

Borklund, Carl W. *The Department of Defense.* New York: Praeger, 1968.

———. *The Men of the Pentagon: From Forrestal to McNamara.* New York: Praeger, 1966.

Bottome, Edgar M. *The Missile Gap: A Study of the Formulation of Military and Political Policy.* Rutherford, N.J.: Fairleigh Dickinson Press, 1971.

Braden, Joan R. *Just Enough Rope: An Intimate Memoir.* New York: Villard Books, 1989.

Bradlee, Benjamin. *Conversations with Kennedy.* New York: W. W. Norton, 1975.

Brandt, Willy, et al. *Common Crisis: North-South Cooperation for World Recovery.* London: Pan Books, 1983.

Brennan, Donald G. *Arms Control, Disarmament, and National Security.* New York: George Braziller, 1961.

———. "The Case for Population Defense." In *Why ABM?*, edited by Johan Holst and William Schneider. New York: Pergamon Press, 1969.

Brodie, Bernard. *Escalation and the Nuclear Option.* Princeton, N.J.: Princeton University Press, 1966.

———. *Strategy in the Missile Age.* Princeton, N.J.: Princeton University Press, 1959.

Brooks, John. *The Fate of the Edsel and Other Business Adventures.* New York: Harper and Row, 1963.

Bundy, McGeorge. *The Strength of Government.* Cambridge: Harvard University Press, 1968.

Burke, John P., and Fred I. Greenstein. *How Presidents Test Reality: Decisions in Vietnam, 1954 and 1965.* New York: Russell Sage Foundation, 1989.

Burns, Richard D., and Milton Leitenberg. *The Wars in Vietnam, Cambodia and Laos: A Bibliographic Guide.* Santa Barbara, Calif.: ABC-Clio Information Services, 1983.

Buttinger, Joseph. *The Smaller Dragon: A Political History of Vietnam.* New York: Praeger, 1958.

———. *Vietnam: A Dragon Embattled.* 2 vols. New York: Praeger, 1967.

———. *Vietnam: The Unforgettable Tragedy.* New York: Horizon Press, 1977.

Byres, T. J., ed. *Foreign Resources and Economic Development.* London: Cass, 1972.

Califano, Joseph A. *The Student Revolution: A Global Confrontation.* New York: W. W. Norton, 1970.

Caro, Robert A. *The Power Broker: Robert Moses and the Fall of New York.* New York: Alfred A. Knopf, 1974.

Catudal, Honore M. *Kennedy and the Berlin Wall Crisis: A Case Study in US Decision Making.* Berlin: Verlay, 1980.

Chaliand, Gerard. *Guerrilla Strategies: An Historical Anthology from the Long March to Afghanistan.* Berkeley: University of California Press, 1982.

Chambers, Robert. *Rural Development: Putting the Last First.* Harlow, Essex, England: Longman Scientific and Technical, 1983.

Chandler, Alfred D. *The Visible Hand: The Managerial Revolution in American Business.* Cambridge: Harvard University Press, 1977.

Charlton, Michael, and Anthony Moncrieff. *Many Reasons Why: The American Involvement in Vietnam.* New York: Hill and Wang, 1978.

Chenery, Hollis, et al. *Redistribution with Growth: Policies to Improve Income Distribution in Developing Countries in the Context of Economic Growth: A Joint Study [Commissioned] by the World Bank's Development Research Center and the Institute of Development Studies, University of Sussex.* London: Published for the World Bank and the Institute of Development Studies, University of Sussex, [by] Oxford University Press, 1974.

Chenery, Hollis, and Moises Syrquin. *Patterns of Development, 1950–1970.* London: Oxford University Press for the World Bank, 1975.

Clark, Gerald. *Impatient Giant: Red China Today.* New York: D. McKay, 1959.

Clark, Kim B., Robert H. Hayes, and Christopher Lorenz. *The Uneasy Alliance: Managing the Productivity-Technology Dilemma.* Boston: Harvard Business School Press, 1985.

Clark, Paul G. *American Aid for Development.* New York: Published for the Council on Foreign Relations [by] Praeger, 1972.

Clark, William. *From Three Worlds: Memoirs.* London: Sidgwick and Jackson, 1986.

Clay, Lucius D. *Decisions in Germany.* Garden City, N.Y.: Doubleday, 1950.

Cleveland, Harlan. *The Knowledge Executive: Leadership in an Information Society.* New York: Dutton, 1985.

——. *The Transatlantic Bargain.* New York: Harper and Row, 1970.

Clifford, Clark. *Counsel to the President.* New York: Random House, 1991.

Clodfelter, Mark. *The Limits of Air Power: The American Bombing of North Vietnam.* New York: Free Press, 1989.

Cochran, Thomas B., William M. Arkin, and Milton M. Hoenig. *Nuclear Weapons Databook.* Cambridge: Ballinger Publishing, 1984.

Coffey, Thomas M. *Iron Eagle: The Turbulent Life of General Curtis LeMay.* New York: Crown Publishers, 1986.

Cohen, Warren I. *Dean Rusk.* Totowa, N.J.: Cooper Square Publishers, 1980.

Colby, William. *Honorable Men.* New York: Simon and Schuster, 1978.

Collier, Peter, and David Horowitz. *The Fords: An American Epic.* New York: Simon and Schuster, 1987.

Conrad, Joseph. *Heart of Darkness.* New York: Bantam Books, 1987.

Cooper, Chester. *The Lost Crusade: America In Vietnam.* New York: Dodd, Mead, 1970.

Copeland, Melvin T. *And Mark an Era.* Boston: Little, Brown, 1958.

Coulam, Robert F. *Illusions of Choice: The F-111 and the Problem of Weapons Acquisition Reform.* Princeton, N.J.: Princeton University Press, 1977.

Crankshaw, Edward. *Khrushchev: A Career.* New York: Viking Press, 1966.

Cray, Ed. *Chrome Colossus: General Motors and Its Times.* New York: McGraw-Hill, 1980.

Crozier, Michael. *The Bureaucratic Phenomenon.* Chicago: University of Chicago Press, 1964.

Damore, Leo. *Senatorial Privilege: The Chappaquiddick Cover-Up.* Washington, D.C.: Regnery Gateway, 1988.

Davis, Vincent. *The Admirals' Lobby.* Chapel Hill: University of North Carolina Press, 1967.

DeLorean, John Z. *On a Clear Day You Can See General Motors.* Grosse Pointe, Mich.: Wright Enterprises, 1979.

Dickenson, G. Lowes. *The Greek View of Life.* Ann Arbor: University of Michigan Press, 1958.

Donovan, Robert Frank. *Bridge in the Sky.* New York: D. McKay, 1968.

Douhet, Giulio. *The Command of the Air.* New York: Coward McCann, 1942.

Downs, Frederick, Jr. *Aftermath: A True Story.* New York: Berkeley Books, 1985.

——. *The Killing Zone: My Life in the Vietnam War.* New York: Berkeley Books, 1983.

Drucker, Peter F. *The Concept of the Corporation*. New York: John Day, 1946.
———. *The Effective Executive*. New York: Harper and Row, 1967.
———. *The Future of Industrial Man: A Conservative Approach*. Westport, Conn.: Greenwood Press, 1942.
———. *The New Society: The Anatomy of the Industrial Order*. New York: Harper, 1950.
Edel, Leon. *Writing Lives: Principia Biographica*. New York: W. W. Norton, 1984.
Edsall, Thomas Byrne and Mary Edsall. *Chain Reaction*. New York: W. W. Norton, 1991.
Ellsberg, Dan. *Papers on the War*. New York: Simon and Schuster, 1972.
Emerson, Gloria. *Winners and Losers: Battles, Retreats, Gains, Losses and Ruins from the Vietnam War*. New York: Harcourt Brace Jovanovich, 1976.
Enke, Stephen, ed. *Defense Management*. Englewood Cliffs, N.J.: Prentice-Hall, 1967.
Enthoven, Alain, and K. Wayne Smith. *How Much Is Enough? Shaping the Defense Program, 1961–69*. New York: Harper and Row, 1971.
Epstein, Edward Jay. *Between Fact and Fiction*. New York: Vintage Books, 1975.
Esposito, Colonel Vincent J., chief ed. *West Point Atlas of American Wars*. New York: Praeger, 1959.
Fairlee, Henry. *The Kennedy Promise: The Politics of Expectation*. Garden City, N.Y.: Doubleday, 1973.
Fall, Bernard B. *Anatomy of a Crisis: The Laotian Crisis of 1960–61*. Garden City, N.Y.: Doubleday, 1969.
———. *Street Without Joy: Insurgency in Indochina 1946–63*. New York: Schocken Books, 1972.
———. *The Two Viet-Nams: A Political and Military Analysis*. New York: Praeger, 1964.
Fallows, James. *National Defense*. New York: Vintage Books, 1982.
FitzGerald, Frances. *Fire in the Lake: The Vietnamese and the Americans in Vietnam*. Boston: Little, Brown, 1972.
Ford, Harold P., and Frances X. Winters. *Ethics and Nuclear Strategy?* MaryKnoll, N.Y.: Orbis Books, 1977.
Ford, Henry II. *The Human Environment and Business*. New York: Weybright and Talley, 1970.
Freedman, Lawrence. *Britain and Nuclear Weapons*. London: Published for the Royal Institute of International Affairs [by] Macmillan, 1980.
———. *The Evolution of Nuclear Strategy*. London: Macmillan, 1982.
———. *The Evolution of Nuclear Strategy*. New York: St. Martin's Press, 1981, 1983.
———. *U.S. Intelligence and the Soviet Strategic Threat*. Basingstoke, England: Macmillan, 1977.
Fulbright, J. William. *The Arrogance of Power*. New York: Random House, 1966.
———. *Old Myths and New Realities: And Other Commentaries*. New York: Random House, 1964.
Fulbright, J. William, and Seth P. Tillman. *The Price of Empire*. New York: Pantheon Books, 1989.
Fuller, Jon Wayne. "Congress and the Defense Budget: A Study of the McNamara Years." Ph.D. diss., Princeton University, 1972.

Gaddis, John Lewis. *The Long Peace: Inquiries into the History of the Cold War.* New York: Oxford University Press, 1987.

———. *Strategies of Containment: A Critical Appraisal of American National Security Policy.* New York: Oxford University Press, 1982.

Galbraith, John Kenneth. *The Affluent Society.* Boston: Houghton Mifflin, 1958.

———. *The New Industrial State.* Boston: Houghton Mifflin, 1967.

Garthoff, Raymond L. *Intelligence Assessment and Policymaking: A Decision Point in the Kennedy Administration.* Washington, D.C.: Brookings Institution, 1984.

Gavin, James. *War and Peace in the Space Age.* New York: Harper and Row, 1958.

Gavin, James, with Arthur Hadley. *Crisis Now.* New York: Random House, 1968.

Gelb, Leslie H., with Richard K. Betts. *The Irony of Vietnam: The System Worked.* Washington, D.C.: Brookings Institution, 1979.

George, Alexander, Philip J. Farley, and Alexander Dallin. *U.S.-Soviet Security Cooperation: Achievements, Lessons, Failures.* New York: Oxford University Press, 1988.

George, Alexander, David K. Hall, and William E. Simons. *The Limits of Coercive Diplomacy: Laos, Cuba, Vietnam.* Boston: Little, Brown, 1971.

Geyelin, Philip. *Lyndon B. Johnson and the World.* New York: Praeger, 1966.

Gibbons, William Conrad. *The U.S. Government and the Vietnam War: Executive and Legislative Roles and Relationships.* Washington, D.C.: U.S. Government Printing Office, pt. 2, 1984; pt. 3, 1988.

Goodman, Allen E. *The Lost Peace: America's Search for a Negotiated Settlement of the Vietnam War.* Stanford, Calif.: Hoover Institution Press, 1978.

Goodwin, Mary P. *A Mountain Reprieve: Trekking in Nepal.* Los Angeles: Natural History Museum Alliance, 1975.

Goulden, Joseph C. *Truth Is the First Casualty.* Chicago, Ill.: Rand McNally, 1969.

Goulding, Phil G. *Confirm or Deny: Informing the People on National Security.* New York: Harper and Row, 1970.

Graff, Henry. *The Tuesday Cabinet: Deliberation and Decision on Peace and War Under Lyndon B. Johnson.* Englewood Cliffs, N.J.: Prentice Hall, 1970.

Grant, Zalin. *Over the Beach.* New York: W. W. Norton, 1987.

Gravel, Mike, ed. *Pentagon Papers: The Defense Department History of United States Decision Making in Vietnam. The Senator Gravel Edition.* Boston: Beacon Press, 1971, 1972.

Graves, Ruth, ed. *The RIF Guide to Encouraging Young Readers.* Garden City, N.Y.: Doubleday, 1987.

Gray, Colin S. *The Soviet-American Arms Race.* Lexington, Mass.: Lexington Books, 1976.

Greene, Graham. *The Quiet American.* New York: Viking Press, 1956.

Greenstein, Fred I. *Leadership in the Modern Presidency.* Cambridge: Harvard University Press, 1988.

Greenwood, Ted. *Making the MIRV: A Study of Defense Decision-Making.* Cambridge, Mass.: Ballinger Publishing, 1975.

Hackworth, David H., and Julie Sherman. *About Face.* New York: Simon and Schuster, 1989.

Halberstam, David H. *The Best and the Brightest.* New York: Random House, 1969.

———. *The Making of a Quagmire.* New York: Random House, 1965.

————. *The Making of a Quagmire: America and Vietnam During the Kennedy Era.* New York: Alfred A. Knopf, 1988.

————. *The Next Century.* New York: William Morrow, 1991.

————. *One Very Hot Day.* Boston: Houghton Mifflin, 1967.

————. *The Powers That Be.* New York: Dell, 1979.

————. *The Reckoning.* New York: William Morrow, 1986.

Hallin, Daniel C. *The "Uncensored War": The Media and Vietnam.* New York: Oxford University Press, 1986.

Halperin, Morton H. *Contemporary Military Strategy.* Boston: Little, Brown, 1967.

————. *Defense Strategies for the Seventies.* Boston: Little, Brown, 1971.

————. *Limited War in the Nuclear Age.* New York: John Wiley and Sons, 1963.

————. *National Security Policy-Making: Analyses, Cases and Proposals.* Lexington, Mass.: Lexington Books, 1975.

Hammond, Paul Y. *Organizing for Defense.* Princeton, N.J.: Princeton University Press, 1961.

Harberger, Arnold C. *World Economic Growth.* San Francisco: ICS Press, 1984.

Hastings, Max. *The Korean War.* New York: Simon and Schuster, 1987.

Haught, Robert L., ed. *Giants in Management.* Washington, D.C.: National Academy of Public Administration, 1985.

Hayter, Teresa. *Aid as Imperialism.* Hamondsworth, England: Penguin Books, 1971.

————. *The Creation of World Poverty.* London: Pluto Press in association with Third World First, 1981.

Head, Richard G., and Ervin J. Rokke, eds. *American Defense Policy.* Baltimore: Johns Hopkins University Press, 1973.

Heller, Walter. *The Economy: Old Myths and New Realities.* New York: W. W. Norton, 1976.

————. *New Dimensions in Political Economy.* Cambridge: Harvard University Press, 1966.

Herken, Gregg. *Counsels of War.* New York: Alfred A. Knopf, 1985.

Herring, George. *America's Longest War.* New York: Alfred A. Knopf, 1979.

————, ed. *Pentagon Papers: United States–Vietnam Relations 1945–1967.* Austin: University of Texas Press, 1984.

————. *The Secret Diplomacy of the Vietnam War: The Negotiating Volume of the Pentagon Papers.* Austin: University of Texas Press, 1983.

Hersh, Seymour M. *The Price of Power: Kissinger in the Nixon White House.* New York: Summit Books, 1983.

Hickerson, J. Mel. *Ernie Breech: The Story of His Remarkable Career at General Motors, Ford, and TWA.* New York: Meredith Press, 1968.

Higgins, Trumbull. *The Perfect Failure: Kennedy, Eisenhower, and the CIA at the Bay of Pigs.* New York: W. W. Norton, 1987.

Hilsman, Roger. *The Politics of Policy Making in Defense and Foreign Affairs.* New York: Harper and Row, 1971.

————. *To Move a Nation.* New York: Harper and Row, 1967.

Hilsman, Roger, and Robert C. Good, eds. *Foreign Policy in the Sixties: The Issues and the Instruments; Essays in Honor of Arnold Wolfers.* Baltimore: Johns Hopkins University Press, 1965.

Hirschman, Albert O. *A Bias for Hope: Essays on Development and Latin America.* New Haven, Conn.: Yale University Press, 1971.

———. *Development Projects Observed.* Washington, D.C.: Brookings Institution, 1967.

———. *Exit, Voice and Loyalty: Responses to Decline in Firms, Organizations, and States.* Cambridge: Harvard University Press, 1970.

Hitch, Charles J. *Decision Making for Defense.* Berkeley: University of California Press, 1965.

Hitch, Charles J., and Roland N. McKean. *The Economics of Defense in the Nuclear Age.* Cambridge: Harvard University Press, 1960.

Holland, Max. *When the Machine Stopped: A Cautionary Tale from Industrial America.* Boston: Harvard Business School Press, 1989.

Hoopes, Townsend. *The Devil and John Foster Dulles.* Boston: Little, Brown, 1973.

———. *Driven Patriot: The Life and Times of James Forrestal.* New York: Alfred A. Knopf, 1992.

———. *The Limits of Intervention: An Inside Account of How the Johnson Policy of Escalation in Vietnam Was Reversed.* New York: D. McKay, 1969.

Horwitch, Mel. *Clipped Wings: The American SST Conflict.* Cambridge: M.I.T. Press, 1982.

Huntington, Samuel P. *The Common Defense.* New York: Columbia University Press, 1961.

———. *The Soldier and the State: The Theory and Politics of Civil-Military Relations.* Cambridge: Harvard University Press, 1959.

Iacocca, Lee. *Iacocca: An Autobiography.* New York: Bantam Books, 1984.

Ions, Edmund S. *The Politics of John Kennedy.* New York: Barnes and Noble, 1968.

Janes, Thomas Wareham. "Rational Man, Irrational Policy: A Political Biography of John McNaughton's Role in the Vietnam War." M.A. thesis, Harvard University, 1977.

Johnson, H. Thomas, and Robert S. Kaplan. *Relevance Lost: The Rise and Fall of Management Accounting.* Boston: Harvard Business School Press, 1987.

Johnson, Haynes. *The Bay of Pigs: The Leaders' Story of Brigade 2506.* New York: W. W. Norton, 1964.

Johnson, Lyndon B. *The Vantage Point — Perspectives of the Presidency 1963–69.* New York: Holt, Rinehart and Winston, 1971.

Johnson, Paul. *Intellectuals.* London: Weidenfeld and Nicolson, 1988.

Kahn, Herman. *On Escalation: Metaphors and Scenarios.* New York: Praeger, 1965.

———. *On Thermonuclear War.* Princeton, N.J.: Princeton University Press, 1960.

———. *Thinking About the Unthinkable.* New York: Horizon Press, 1962.

Kaplan, Fred. *The Wizards of Armageddon.* New York: Simon and Schuster, 1983.

Karnow, Stanley. *Vietnam: A History.* New York: Viking Press, 1983.

Kattenburg, Paul M. *The Vietnam Trauma in American Foreign Policy 1945–1975.* New Brunswick, N.J.: Transaction Books, 1980.

Kaufman, Richard F. *The War Profiteers.* Indianapolis: Bobbs-Merrill, 1970.

Kaufmann, William W. *The McNamara Strategy.* New York: Harper and Row, 1964.

———. *Planning Conventional Forces 1950–80.* Washington, D.C.: Brookings Institution, 1982.

Kearns, Doris. *Lyndon Johnson and the American Dream.* New York: Harper and Row, 1976.

Kelleher, Catherine. *Germany and the Politics of Nuclear Weapons.* New York: Columbia University Press, 1975.

Kennedy, Paul. *The Rise and Fall of the Great Powers*. New York: Random House, 1987.

Kennedy, Robert F. *The Enemy Within*. New York: Harper, 1960.

——. *Thirteen Days: A Memoir of the Cuban Missile Crisis*. New York: W. W. Norton, 1969.

Kerr, Andy. *A Journey Amongst the Good and the Great*. Annapolis, Md.: Naval Institute Press, 1987.

Kerr, E. Bartlett. *Flames Over Tokyo: The U.S. Army Air Forces' Incendiary Campaign Against Japan, 1944–45*. New York: Donald I. Fine, 1991.

Kinnard, Douglas. *The Secretary of Defense*. Lexington: University Press of Kentucky, 1980.

——. *The War Managers*. Hanover, N.H.: Published for the University of Vermont [by] the University Press of New England, 1977.

Kissinger, Henry. *Necessity for Choice: Prospects of American Foreign Policy*. New York: Harper and Row, 1971.

——. *The Troubled Partnership: Re-appraisal of the Atlantic Alliance*. New York: Published for the Council on Foreign Relations [by] McGraw-Hill, 1965.

——. *White House Years*. Boston: Little, Brown, 1979.

Kistiakowsky, George B. *A Scientist at the White House: The Private Diary of President Eisenhower's Special Assistant for Science and Technology*. Cambridge: Harvard University Press, 1976.

Knaack, Marcelle Size. *Encyclopedia of U.S. Air Force Aircraft and Missile Systems*. Vol. 2, *Post–World War II Bombers 1945–1973*. Washington, D.C.: Office of Air Force History, U.S. Government Printing Office, 1978.

Kolb, Lawrence. *The Joint Chiefs of Staff: The First Twenty-five Years*. Bloomington: Indiana University Press, 1976.

Kolkowicz, Roman, ed. *The Logic of Nuclear Terror*. Winchester, Mass: Allen and Unwin, 1987.

Kolodziej, Edward A. *Uncommon Defense and Congress, 1945–1963*. Columbus: Ohio State University Press, 1966.

Komer, Robert W. *Bureaucracy at War: U.S. Performance in the Vietnam War*. Boulder, Colo.: Westview Special Studies in National Security and Defense Policy, 1986.

Kraslow, David, and Stuart H. Loory. *The Secret Search for Peace in Vietnam*. New York: Random House, 1968.

Krepinevich, Andrew F., Jr. "The Army Concept and Vietnam: A Case Study in Organization and Failure," Ph.D. diss., Harvard University, 1983.

Krock, Arthur. *The Consent of the Governed, and Other Deceits*. Boston: Little, Brown, 1971.

——. *Memoirs: Sixty Years on the Firing Line*. New York: Funk and Wagnalls, 1968.

Krulak, Victor H. *First in Fight: An Inside View of the U.S. Marine Corps*. Annapolis, Md.: Naval Institute Press, 1984.

——. *Organizing for National Security: A Study*. Washington, D.C.: U.S. Strategic Institute, 1983.

Kuczynski, Pedro-Pablo. *Latin American Debt*. New York: Twentieth Century Fund, 1988.

Lake, Anthony, ed. *The Vietnam Legacy: The War, American Society and the Future of American Foreign Policy*. New York: New York University Press, 1976.

Lansdale, Edward. *In the Midst of Wars*. New York: Harper and Row, 1972.

Lapp, Ralph E. *The Weapons Culture*. Baltimore: Penguin Books, 1969.

Laqueur, Walter. *A World of Secrets: The Uses and Limits of Intelligence*. New York: Basic Books, 1985.

Lay, Beirne, Jr. *Someone Has to Make It Happen: The Inside Story of Tex Thornton*. Englewood Cliffs, N.J.: Prentice-Hall, 1969.

Lele, Uma J. *The Design of Rural Development: Lessons from Africa*. Baltimore: Published for the World Bank [by] Johns Hopkins University Press, 1975.

Lemann, Nicholas. *The Promised Land: The Great Black Migration and How It Changed America*. New York: Alfred A. Knopf, 1991.

LeMay, Curtis E., with MacKinlay Kantor. *Mission with LeMay: My Story*. Garden City, N.Y.: Doubleday, 1965.

LeMay, Curtis E., with Major General Dale O. Smith. *America Is In Danger*. New York: Funk and Wagnalls, 1968.

Lester, Tanzer, ed. *The Kennedy Circle*. Washington, D.C.: Luce, 1961.

Levine, Arnold. *Managing NASA in the Apollo Era*. Washington, D.C.: Scientific and Technological Information Branch, National Aeronautics and Space Administration, 1982.

Lewis, John P., Richard E. Feinberg, and Valeriana Kallab, eds. *Strengthening the Poor: What Have We Learned?* New Brunswick, N.J.: Transaction Publishers, 1988.

Lewis, John P., and Kaper Isham. *The World Bank Group, Multilateral Aid and the 1970's*. Lexington, Mass.: Lexington Books, 1973.

Lewis, John P., and Valeriana Kallab, eds. *U.S. Foreign Policy and the Third World: Agenda, 1983*. New York: Praeger, 1983.

Lewy, Guenter, *America in Vietnam*. New York: Oxford University Press, 1978, 1980.

Lippmann, Walter. *An Inquiry into the Principles of the Good Society*. Boston: Little, Brown, 1937.

Lipset, Seymour M. *Political Man, the Social Basis of Politics*. Garden City, N.Y.: Doubleday, 1960.

Lodge, Henry Cabot. *The Storm Has Many Eyes: A Personal Narrative*. New York: W. W. Norton, 1973.

Logsden, John M. *The Decision to Go to the Moon: Project Apollo and the National Interest*. Cambridge: M.I.T. Press, 1970.

McDougall, Walter A. *The Heavens and the Earth: A Political History of the Space Age*. New York: Basic Books, 1985.

McGhee, George. *At the Creation of a New Germany: From Adenauer to Brandt: An Ambassador's Account*. New Haven, Conn.: Yale University Press, 1989.

MacGregor, Morris J. *Integration of the Armed Forces, 1940–1965*. Washington, D.C.: Center for Military History, U.S. Army, 1981.

MacIsaac, David. *Strategic Bombing in World War II: The Story of the United States Strategic Bombing Survey*. New York: Garland Publishing, 1976.

McNamara, Robert S. *Addresses to the Board of Governors of the World Bank, 1968–1980*. Washington, D.C.: World Bank, 1979.

———. *Blundering into Disaster: Surviving the First Century of the Nuclear Age*. New York: Pantheon, 1986.

———. *The Essence of Security: Reflections in Office*. New York: Harper and Row, 1968.

———. *The McNamara Years at the World Bank: Major Policy Addresses of Robert*

S. McNamara 1968–1981. Baltimore: Published for the World Bank [by] Johns Hopkins University Press, 1981.

———. *One Hundred Countries, Two Billion People: The Dimensions of Development*. New York: Praeger, 1973.

———. *Out of the Cold*. New York: Simon and Schuster, 1989.

McNaugher, Thomas L. *The M16 Controversies: Military Organizations and Weapons Acquisition*. New York: Praeger, 1984.

———. *New Weapons, Old Politics: America's Military Procurement Muddle*. Washington, D.C.: Brookings Institution, 1989.

MacPherson, Myra. *Long Time Passing: Vietnam and the Haunted Generation*. Garden City, N.Y.: Doubleday, 1984.

McPherson, James M. *Battle Cry of Freedom: The Civil War Era*. New York: Oxford University Press, 1988.

Mailer, Norman. *The Armies of the Night: History as a Novel, the Novel as History*. New York: New American Library, 1968.

Manchester, William R. *The Death of a President*. New York: Harper and Row, 1967.

———. *The Glory and the Dream*. Boston: Little, Brown, 1973.

Mangold, Tom, and Penycate, John. *The Tunnels of Cu Chi*. London: Hodder and Stoughton, 1985.

Martin, Lawrence. *Strategic Thought in the Nuclear Age*. Baltimore: Johns Hopkins University Press, 1979, 1981.

Mason, Edward S., and Robert E. Asher. *The World Bank Since Bretton Woods: The Origins, Policies, Operations, and Impact of the International Bank for Reconstruction and Development and the Other Members of the World Bank Group: The International Finance Corporation, the International Development Association [and] the International Center for Settlement of Investment Disputes*. Washington, D.C.: Brookings Institution, 1973.

May, Ernest R. *"Lessons" of the Past: The Use and Misuse of History in American Foreign Policy*. New York: Oxford University Press, 1973.

Mecklin, John. *Mission in Torment: An Intimate Account of the U.S. Role in Vietnam*. Garden City, N.Y.: Doubleday, 1968.

Middleton, Drew. *Air War — Vietnam*. Indianapolis: Bobbs-Merrill, 1978.

Momyer, William W. *Air Power in Three Wars: World War II, Korea and Vietnam*. New York: Arno Press, 1980.

Morganstern, Oskar. *The Question of National Defense*. New York: Random House, 1959.

Moritz, Michael, and Barrett Seaman. *Going for Broke: Lee Iacocca's Battle to Save Chrysler*. Garden City, N.Y.: Doubleday, 1984.

Morris, James. *The Road to Huddersfield: A Journey to Five Continents*. New York: Pantheon Books, 1963.

Moulton, Harland B. *From Superiority to Parity*. Westport, Conn.: Greenwood Press, 1973.

Nalty, Bernard C. *Strength for the Fight: A History of Black Americans in the Military*. New York: Free Press, 1986.

Neustadt, Richard. *Alliance Politics*. New York: Columbia University Press, 1970.

———. *Presidential Power: The Politics of Leadership from FDR to Carter*. New York: John Wiley and Sons, 1980.

Neustadt, Richard, and Ernest R. May. *Thinking in Time: The Uses of History for Decision Makers*. New York: Free Press, 1986.

Nevins, Allan, and Frank Ernest Hill. *Ford: Decline and Rebirth, 1933–1962.* New York: Scribner, 1963.

Newhouse, John. *Cold Dawn: The Story of SALT.* New York: Holt, Rinehart and Winston, 1973.

———. *De Gaulle and the Anglo Saxons.* New York: Viking Press, 1970.

Newman, John M. *JFK and Vietnam.* New York: Warner Books, 1992.

Nitze, Paul H., with Ann M. Smith and Steven L. Rearden. *From Hiroshima to Glasnost: At the Center of the Decision, a Memoir.* New York: Grove Weidenfeld, 1989.

Norman, Colin. *The God That Limps.* New York: W. W. Norton, 1981.

Oakeshott, Michael. *Rationalism in Politics, and Other Essays.* London: Methuen, 1962.

Ogden, Chris. *Maggie: An Intimate Portrait of a Woman in Power.* New York: Simon and Schuster, 1990.

Oliver, R. W. *Early Plans for a World Bank.* Princeton, N.J.: Princeton University Press, 1971.

Palmer, Bruce. *The Twenty-Five-Year War: America's Military Role in Vietnam.* Lexington: University Press of Kentucky, 1984.

Palmer, Gregory. *The McNamara Strategy and the Vietnam War: Program Budgeting in the Pentagon 1960–68.* Westport, Conn.: Greenwood Press, 1978.

Pearson, Lester B., et al. *Partners in Development: Report of the Commission on International Development.* New York: Praeger, 1969.

Perl, Lila. *East Africa — Kenya, Tanzania, Uganda.* New York: Morrow Junior Books, 1978.

Perry, Mark. *Four Stars: The Inside Story of the Forty-year Battle Between the Joint Chiefs of Staff and America's Civilian Leaders.* Boston: Houghton Mifflin, 1986.

Pierre, Andres J. *Nuclear Politics: The British Experience with an Independent Strategic Force, 1939–1970.* London: Oxford University Press, 1972.

Pike, Douglas. *Viet Cong: The Organization and Techniques of the National Liberation Front of South Vietnam.* Cambridge: M.I.T. Press, 1966.

———. *Vietnam and the Soviet Union: Anatomy of an Alliance.* Boulder, Colo.: Westview Press, 1987.

Please, Stanley. *The Hobbled Giant: Essays on the World Bank.* Boulder, Colo.: Westview Press, 1984.

Polmar, Norman, and Thomas B. Allen. *Rickover.* New York: Simon and Schuster, 1982.

Porter, Gareth, ed. *Vietnam: The Definitive Documentation of Human Decisions.* Stanfordville, N.Y.: Earl Coleman Enterprises, 1979.

Powers, Richard. *Secrecy and Power: The Life of J. Edgar Hoover.* New York: Free Press, 1987.

Prados, John. *The Soviet Estimate: U.S. Intelligence Analysis and Russian Military Strength.* New York: Dial Press, 1982.

Price, David. *Before the Bulldozer: The Nambiquara Indians and the World Bank.* Cabin John, Md.: Seven Locks Press, 1989.

Public Papers of the Presidents of the United States. Washington, D.C.: Federal Register Division, National Archives and Records Service, General Services Administration.

Quade, E. S., and W. T. Boucher, eds. *Systems Analysis and Policy Planning: Applications in Defense.* New York: American Elsevier Publishing, 1968.

Quester, George H. *Nuclear Diplomacy: The First Twenty-five Years.* New York: Dunellen, 1970.

Rainwater, Lee, and William L. Yancy. *The Moynihan Report and the Politics of Controversy.* Cambridge: M.I.T. Press, 1969.

Ramos-Horta, Jose. *Funu, the Unfinished Saga of East Timor.* Trenton, N.J.: Red Sea Press, 1987.

Raymond, Jack. *Power at the Pentagon.* New York: Harper and Row, 1964.

Reston, James. *Deadline: A Memoir.* New York: Random House, 1991.

Rhodes, Richard. *The Making of the Atomic Bomb.* New York: Simon and Schuster, 1986.

Ridgway, Matthew B. *Soldier: The Memoirs of Matthew B. Ridgway as Told to Harold H. Martin.* New York: Harper, 1956.

Ries, John C. *The Management of Defense: Organization and Control of U.S. Armed Services.* Baltimore: Johns Hopkins University Press, 1964.

Roherty, James M. *Decisions of Robert S. McNamara: A Study of the Role of the Secretary of Defense.* Coral Gables, Fla.: University of Miami Press, 1970.

Rolfe, Sidney E. *Gold and World Power, the Dollar, the Pound, and the Plans for Reform.* New York: Harper and Row, 1966.

Rolfe, Sidney E., and James L. Burtle. *The Great Wheel: The World Monetary System, a Reinterpretation.* New York: Quadrangle Books, 1973.

Romanus, Charles F. *Stilwell's Command Problems: The United States Army in World War II, China, Burma, India Theatre.* Washington, D.C.: Office of Chief of Military History, Department of the Army, 1956.

Rosenblum, Mort, and Doug Williamson. *Squandering Eden: Africa at the Edge.* San Diego: Harcourt Brace Jovanovich, 1987.

Rostow, Walt W. *The Diffusion of Power: An Essay in Recent History.* New York: Macmillan, 1972.

Rotberg, Eugene H. *The World Bank: A Financial Appraisal.* Washington, D.C.: World Bank, 1981.

Rubin, Barry. *Paved with Good Intentions: The American Experience and Iran.* New York: Penguin Books, 1980, 1981.

Salinger, Pierre. *With Kennedy.* Garden City, N.Y.: Doubleday, 1966.

Salisbury, Harrison E. *Behind the Lines — Hanoi: December 23, 1966–January 7, 1967.* New York: Harper and Row, 1967.

Sampson, Anthony. *The Arms Bazaar from Lebanon to Lockheed.* New York: Viking Press, 1977.

———. *The Money Lenders: Bankers and a World in Turmoil.* New York: Viking Press, 1981, 1982.

Sanders, T. H. *My Japanese Years.* London: Mills and Boonis, 1915.

Schandler, Herbert Y. *The Unmaking of a President: Lyndon Johnson and Vietnam.* Princeton, N.J.: Princeton University Press, 1977.

Scheer, Robert. *With Enough Shovels: Reagan, Bush and Nuclear War.* New York: Random House, 1982.

Schell, Jonathan. *The Village of Ben Suc.* New York: Alfred A. Knopf, 1967.

Schelling, Thomas C. *The Strategy of Conflict.* New York: Oxford University Press, 1960.

Schelling, Thomas C., and Morton H. Halperin, with the assistance of Donald G. Brennan. *Strategy and Arms Control.* New York: Twentieth Century Fund, 1961.

Schlesinger, Arthur M., Jr. *The Bitter Heritage: Vietnam and American Democracy, 1941–1966.* Boston: Houghton Mifflin, 1967.

———. *The Crisis of Confidence: Ideas, Power, and Violence in America.* Boston: Houghton Mifflin, 1969.

———. *Robert Kennedy and His Times.* Boston: Houghton Mifflin, 1978.

———. *A Thousand Days: John F. Kennedy in the White House.* Boston: Houghton Mifflin, 1965.

Schwartz, David N. *NATO's Nuclear Dilemmas.* Washington, D.C.: Brookings Institution, 1983.

Scruggs, Jan C., and Joel L. Swerdlow. *To Heal a Nation: The Vietnam Vet Memorial.* New York: Harper and Row, 1985.

Seaborg, Glenn T. *Kennedy, Khrushchev and the Test Ban.* Berkeley: University of California Press, 1981.

———. *Stemming the Tide: Arms Control in the Johnson Years.* Lexington, Mass.: Lexington Books, 1987.

Shames, Lawrence. *The Big Time: The Harvard Business School's Most Successful Class and How It Shaped America.* New York: Harper and Row, 1986.

Shaplen, Robert. *The Lost Revolution: The U.S. in Vietnam.* New York: Harper and Row, 1965.

———. *The Road from War: Vietnam 1965–1970.* New York: Harper and Row, 1970.

———. *Time Out of Hand: Revolution and Reaction in Southeast Asia.* New York: Harper and Row, 1969.

Sharp, Ulysses S. G. *Strategy for Defeat: Vietnam in Retrospect.* San Rafael, Calif.: Presidio Press, 1978.

Sharp, Ulysses S. G., and W. C. Westmoreland. *Report on the War in Vietnam, 1964–1968.* Washington, D.C.: U.S. Government Printing Office, 1968.

Shawcross, William. *Sideshow: Kissinger, Nixon and the Destruction of Cambodia.* New York: Simon and Schuster, 1979.

Sheehan, Neil. *A Bright Shining Lie: John Paul Vann and America in Vietnam.* New York: Random House, 1988.

Sheehan, Neil, Hedrick Smith, E. W. Kenworthy, and Fox Butterfield. *The Pentagon Papers as Published by the New York Times.* New York: Quadrangle Books, 1971.

Shepherd, Jack. *The Politics of Starvation.* New York: Carnegie Endowment for International Peace, 1975.

Sigal, Leon V. *Nuclear Forces in Europe: Enduring Dilemmas, Present Prospects.* Washington, D.C.: Brookings Institution, 1984.

SIPRI [Stockholm International Peace Research Institute]. *The Arms Trade with the Third World.* Stockholm-Almqvist and Wiksell, 1971.

Sloan, Alfred P. *My Years with General Motors.* Garden City, N.Y.: Doubleday, 1964.

Sloan, Alfred P., with Boyden Sparkes. *Adventures of a White Collar Man.* Garden City, N.Y.: Doubleday, 1941.

Slusser, Robert M. *The Berlin Crisis of 1961: Soviet-American Relations and the Struggle for Power in the Kremlin; June-November 1961.* Baltimore: Johns Hopkins University Press, 1973.

Smith, Bruce L. R. *The Rand Corporation: Case Study of a Nonprofit Advisory Corporation.* Cambridge: Harvard University Press, 1966.

Snow, Charles P. *Science and Government.* Cambridge: Harvard University Press, 1961.

Sobel, Robert. *The Rise and Fall of the Conglomerate Kings.* New York: Stein and Day, 1984.

Sorenson, Theodore C. *Kennedy.* New York: Harper and Row, 1965.

Spector, Ronald. *The Early Years 1941–1960 — The U.S. Army in Vietnam.* Washington, D.C.: Center for Military History, U.S. Army, 1983.

Stadtman, Verne. *The University of California.* New York: McGraw-Hill, 1970.

Stanley, David. *Changing Administrations: The 1961 and 1964 Transitions in Six Departments.* Washington, D.C.: Brookings Institution, 1965.

Stanley, Timothy W. *NATO in Transition: The Future of the Atlantic Alliance.* New York: Published for the Council on Foreign Relations [by] Praeger, 1965.

Starr, Paul. *The Discarded Army Veteran After Vietnam: The Nader Report on Vietnam Veterans and the Veterans Administration.* New York: Charter House Press, 1973.

———. *Inventing the Dream: California Through the Progressive Era.* New York: Oxford University Press, 1985.

Steinbruner, John D. *The Cybernetic Theory of Decision: New Dimensions of Political Analysis.* Princeton, N.J.: Princeton University Press, 1974.

Stevens, Robert Warren. *Vain Hopes, Grim Realities: The Economic Consequences of the Vietnam War.* New York: New Viewpoints, 1976.

Stevenson, Charles A. *The End of Nowhere: American Policy Towards Laos Since 1954.* Boston: Beacon Press, 1972.

Stimson, Henry L., and McGeorge Bundy. *On Active Service in Peace and War.* New York: Harper, 1948.

Stockdale, James B. *In Love and War: The Story of a Family's Ordeal and Sacrifice During the Vietnam Years.* New York: Harper and Row, 1984.

Stockfisch, Jack A. *Plowshares into Swords: Managing the American Defense Establishment.* New York: Mason and Lipscomb, 1973.

Stockman, David A. *The Triumph of Politics: How the Reagan Revolution Failed.* New York: Harper and Row, 1988.

Streeter and Nigam, eds. *Basic Needs in Danger: A Basic Needs Oriented Strategy for Tanzania: A Report on the Government of Tanzania Commissioned by the JASPA Basic Needs Mission.* Addis Ababa, Ethiopia: International Labor Office Jobs and Skills Program for Africa, 1982.

Stromseth, Jane E. *The Origins of Flexible Response: NATO's Debate over Strategy in the 1960's.* New York: St. Martin's Press, 1988.

Stubbing, Richard A., and Richard A. Mendel. *The Defense Game: An Insider Explores the Astonishing Realities of America's Defense Establishment.* New York: Harper and Row, 1986.

Summers, Harry G., Jr. *On Strategy: The Vietnam War in Context.* Carlisle Barracks, Penn.: Strategic Studies Institute, U.S. Army War College, 1981.

Talbott, Strobe, ed. and trans. *Khrushchev Remembers.* Boston: Little, Brown, 1970.

Taylor, Maxwell D. *Swords and Plowshares.* New York: W. W. Norton, 1972.

———. *Uncertain Trumpet.* New York: Harper, 1960.

Taylor, William J., Jr. *The Future of Conflict: U.S. Interests.* New York: Praeger, 1983.

Thayer, Thomas C. *War Without Fronts: The American Experience in Vietnam.* Boulder, Colo.: Westview Special Studies in Military Affairs, 1985.

Thies, Wallace J. *When Governments Collide: Coercion and Diplomacy in the Vietnam Conflict 1964–1968.* Berkeley: University of California Press, 1980.

Thompson, James C. *Rolling Thunder: Understanding Policy and Program Failure.* Chapel Hill: University of North Carolina Press, 1980.

Thompson, R. G. K. *Defeating Communist Insurgency: The Lessons of Malaya and Vietnam.* New York: Praeger, 1966.

Thompson, Robert. *No Exit from Vietnam.* New York: D. McKay, 1969.

Tinbergen, Jan, coord. *Reshaping the International Order: A Report to the Club of Rome.* New York: Dutton, 1976.

Trask, Roger T. *The Secretaries of Defense: A Brief History 1947–1985.* Washington, D.C.: Published by Historical Office, Office of Secretary of Defense, 1985.

Tregaskis, John. *Vietnam Diary.* New York: Holt, Rinehart and Winston, 1963.

Treverton, Gregory. *Covert Action: The Limits of Intervention in the Postwar World.* New York: Basic Books, 1987.

———. *The Dollar Drain and American Forces in Germany: Managing the Political Economics of Alliance.* Athens: Ohio University Press, 1978.

Trewhitt, Henry L. *McNamara.* New York: Harper and Row, 1971.

Trilling, Lionel. *Sincerity and Authenticity.* Cambridge: Harvard University Press, 1972.

Tuchman, Barbara W. *Stilwell and the American Experience in China, 1911–1945.* New York: Bantam Books, 1972.

Tucker, Samuel A., ed. *A Modern Design for Defense Decisions: A McNamara-Hitch-Enthoven Anthology.* Washington, D.C.: U.S. Government Printing Office, 1966.

ul Haq, Mahbub. *The Third World and the International Economic Order.* Washington, D.C.: Overseas Development Council, 1976.

Ungar, Sanford J. *The Papers and the Papers: An Account of the Legal and Political Battle over the Pentagon Papers.* New York: Columbia University Press, 1989.

———. *Africa: The People and Politics of an Emerging Continent.* New York: Simon and Schuster, 1985.

United States. Congress. Joint Economic Committee. *An Analysis and Evaluation of Public Expenditures: The PPB System: A Compendium of Papers Submitted to the Subcommittee of Economy in Government of the Joint Economic Committee, Congress of the United States.* Washington, D.C.: U.S. Government Printing Office, 1969.

United States. Congress. Senate. Committee on Foreign Relations. *Background Information Relating to Southeast Asia and Vietnam.* Washington, D.C.: U.S. Government Printing Office, 1975.

United States. Congress. Senate. Committee on Foreign Relations. *Nuclear Test Ban Treaty. Hearings Before the Committee on Foreign Relations, United States Senate, 88th Congress, 1st Session, on Executive M, 88th Congress, 1st Session, The Treaty Banning Nuclear Weapon Tests in the Atmosphere, in Outer Space, and Underwater, Signed at Moscow on August 5, 1963, on Behalf of the United States of America, the United Kingdom of Great Britain and Northern Ireland, and the Union of Soviet Socialist Republics.* Washington, D.C.: U.S. Government Printing Office, 1963.

Valenti, Jack. *A Very Human President.* New York: W. W. Norton, 1975.

Van Creveld, Martin. *Fighting Power: German and U.S. Army Performance 1939–1945.* Westport, Conn.: Greenwood Press, 1982.

VanDeMark, Brian. *Into the Quagmire: Lyndon Johnson and the Escalation of the Vietnam War.* New York: Oxford University Press, 1991.

Van Dyke, Jon N. *North Vietnam's Strategy for Survival.* Palo Alto, Calif.: Pacific Books, 1972.

Walton, Mary. *The Deming Management Method.* New York: Perigee, 1986.

Walton, Richard. *Cold War and Counterrevolution.* New York: Viking Press, 1972.

Ward, Barbara, and Rene Dubos. *Only One Earth: The Care and Maintenance of a Small Planet.* New York: W. W. Norton, 1972.

Warnock, C. Gayle. *The Edsel Affair.* Paradise Valley, Ariz.: Pro West, 1980.

Watanabe, Takeshi, Jacques Lesourne, and Robert S. McNamara. *Facilitating Development in a Changing Third World: Trade, Finance, Aid — Report on the Trilateral Task Force on Strategies for Assistance to Developing Countries to the Trilateral Commission.* New York: Trilateral Commission, 1983.

Weidenbaum, Murray. *Economic Impact of the Vietnam War.* New York: Renaissance Editions, 1967.

Weigley, Russell F. *The American Way of War: A History of United States Military Strategy and Policy.* Bloomington: Indiana University Press, 1973, 1977.

———. *History of the United States Army.* New York: Macmillan, 1967.

Wells, H. G. *The War in the Air and Particularly How Mr. Bert Smallways Fared While It Lasted.* New York: Macmillan, 1908.

Westmoreland, William C. *A Soldier Reports.* New York: Dell, 1980.

Wheeler-Bennett, John Wheeler. *Wooden Titan: Hindenburg in Twenty Years of German History, 1914–1934.* New York: William Morrow, 1936.

White, John A. *The Politics of Foreign Aid.* New York: St. Martin's Press, 1974.

White, Lawrence J. *The Automobile Industry Since 1945.* Cambridge: Harvard University Press, 1971.

White, Theodore H. *The Making of the President, 1960.* New York: Atheneum, 1961.

———. *The Making of the President, 1964.* New York: Atheneum, 1965.

Whiting, Alan S. *The Chinese Calculus of Deterrence: India and Indochina.* Ann Arbor: University of Michigan Press, 1975.

Whyte, William. *The Organization Man.* New York: Simon and Schuster, 1956.

Wieseltier, Leon. *Nuclear War, Nuclear Peace: The Sensible Argument About the Greatest Peril of Our Age.* New York: Holt, Rinehart and Winston, 1983.

Windchy, Eugene G. *Tonkin Gulf.* Garden City, N.Y.: Doubleday, 1971.

Wise, David. *The Politics of Lying: Government Deception, Secrecy, and Power.* New York: Random House, 1973.

Wofford, Harris. *Of Kennedys and Kings: Making Sense of the Sixties.* New York: Farrar, Straus, Giroux, 1980.

Womack, James P., Daniel T. Jones, and Daniel Roos. *The Machine That Changed the World: The Story of Lean Production.* New York: HarperCollins, 1991.

Woodward, Bob, *Veil: The Secret Wars of the CIA.* New York: Simon and Schuster, 1987.

———. *The Commanders.* New York: Simon and Schuster, 1991.

World Bank. *Annual Reports,* 1968–1981, and selected later years.

———. *World Development Report,* 1978–1981.

Wyden, Peter. *Bay of Pigs.* New York: Simon and Schuster, 1979.

Yarmolinsky, Adam. *The Military Establishment.* New York: Harper and Row, 1971.

Yates, Brock. *The Decline and Fall of the American Automobile Industry.* New York: Empire Books, 1983.

Zaleznik, Abraham. *Managerial Mystique: Restoring Leadership in Business.* New York: Harper and Row, 1989.

Zumwalt, Elmo R., Jr. *On Watch: A Memoir.* New York: Quadrangle Books, 1976.

SELECTED ARTICLES AND MONOGRAPHS

In the course of my research, I have delved into a wide range of articles and am indebted to many for information and ideas. Citing all the journal literature pertaining to Robert McNamara's relationship to management, defense budgets and policy, Vietnam, strategic arms and arms control, development economics, population, and international finance would be impossible. This list comprises only those articles in peer-reviewed journals and monographs that have been most immediately useful. It does not include articles from the popular media (such as newsmagazines), whose citations appear in the end notes.

Acomb, Dr. Frances. "Statistical Control in the Army Air Forces." *Air Historical Studies* 57 (1952): 101–157, Office of Air Force History.

Amster, Warren. "Design for Deterrence." *Bulletin of the Atomic Scientists* 12, no. 5 (May 1956): 164–165.

Anthony, Robert N. "Reminiscences About Management Accounting." *Journal of Management Accounting Research* 1 (Fall 1989).

Baldwin, Hanson. "Slow-Down at the Pentagon." *Foreign Affairs* 43, no. 2 (January 1965): 262–280.

Ball, Desmond. "Targeting for Strategic Deterrence." London: Adelphi Papers, no. 185, International Institute for Strategic Studies, 1983.

Ball, George. "Slogans and Realities." *Foreign Affairs* 47, no. 4 (July 1969): 623–641.

Bovard, James. "The World Bank vs. the World's Poor." Washington, D.C.: CATO Institute Policy Analysis, no. 92, September 18, 1987.

Brodie, Bernard. "The McNamara Phenomenon." *World Politics* 17, no. 4 (July 1965): 672–686.

———. "Why Were We So (Strategically) Wrong?" *Foreign Policy*, no. 5 (Winter 1971/72): 159–162.

Bundy, McGeorge, George F. Kennan, Robert S. McNamara, and Gerard Smith. "Nuclear Weapons and the Atlantic Alliance." *Foreign Affairs* 60, no. 4 (April 1982): 753–768.

———. "The President's Choice: Star Wars or Arms Control." *Foreign Affairs* 63, no. 2 (Winter 1984/85): 264–278.

Caldwell, Dan. "A Research Note on the Quarantine of Cuba, October 1962." *International Studies Quarterly* 22, no. 4 (December 1978): 625–633.

Carver, George A., Jr. "The Faceless Viet Cong." *Foreign Affairs* 44, no. 3 (April 1966): 348–372.

———. "The Real Revolution in South Viet Nam." *Foreign Affairs* 43, no. 3 (April 1965): 387–408.

Chenery, Hollis B. "Restructuring the World Economy." *Foreign Affairs* 53, no. 2 (January 1975): 242–263.

Clark, William. "Robert McNamara at the World Bank." *Foreign Affairs* 60, no. 1 (October 1981).

Clifford, Clark. "A Viet Nam Reappraisal: The Personal History of One Man's View and How It Evolved." *Foreign Affairs* 47, no. 4 (July 1969): 601–622.

Cline, William R. "International Debt and the Stability of the World Economy." Washington, D.C.: Institute for International Economics, September 1983.

Consultative Group on International Agricultural Research, CGIR Secretariat, Washington, D.C.: 1984 Annual Report.

Daedalus. "Arms, Defense Policy and Arms Control." *Daedalus* 104, no. 3 (Summer 1975).

Drew, Elizabeth. "PPBS, Its Scope and Limits." *Public Interest* (Summer 1967): 9–29.

Ecologist: Journal of the Post Industrial Age 14, no. 5/6 (1984); 15, nos. 1/2 (special issue — "The World Bank: Global Financing of Impoverishment and Famine), 3, 4, 5/6 (1985); 16, nos. 1, 2/3 (1986).

Elson, Robert T. "The New Strategy in Foreign Policy." *Fortune*, December 1947, pp. 81ff.

Emmerson, Donald K. "Indonesia: No Miracle, No Mirage." *Wilson Quarterly* 4, no. 2 (Spring 1981): 125–137.

Geyelin, Philip. Interview with Robert McNamara, *SAIS Review*, no. 3 (Winter 1981–82).

Goldberg, Alfred, ed., with Ernest R. May, John D. Steinbruner, and Thomas Wolfe. "The History of the Strategic Arms Competition, 1945–1972." Pt. 1. Office of the Secretary of Defense Historical Office, on file National Security Archive, Washington, D.C.

Grant, James P. "Development: The End of Trickle-Down?" *Foreign Policy*, no. 12 (Fall 1973): 43–65.

————. "Disparity Reduction Rates in Social Indicators." Washington, D.C.: Overseas Development Council, monograph no. 11, September 1978.

Hardy, Chandra S. "Rescheduling Developing Country Debts, 1956–1981, Lessons and Recommendations." Washington, D.C.: Overseas Development Council, monograph no. 15, June 1982.

Hayes, Robert H., and William J. Abernathy. "Managing Our Way to Economic Decline." *Harvard Business Review* 58, no. 4 (July-August 1980): 67–77.

Heflin, Lt. Col. John F. "Organization History." Army Air Forces Statistical School, Harvard Business School, Office of Air Force History.

Ikle, Fred C. "Can Nuclear Deterrence Last Out the Century? *Foreign Affairs* 51, no. 2 (January 1973).

Kaufmann, William W. "Planning Conventional Forces, 1950–1980." Washington, D.C.: Brookings Institution Studies in Defense Policy, 1982.

Kelly, Brian J., and Mark London. "The New Frontier." *Wilson Quarterly* 7, no. 3 (Summer 1983): 62–79.

Komer, Robert W. "Bureaucracy Does Its Thing: Institutional Constraints on U.S.-GVN Performance in Vietnam." Santa Monica, Calif.: Rand Corporation, no. R-967-ARPA, August 1972.

Kushnerick, John P. "The Motives and Methods of McNamara." *Aerospace Management* (October 1962): 13–18.

Lauder, John A. "Lessons of the Strategic Bombing Survey for Contemporary Defense Policy." *Orbis* 18, no. 3 (Fall 1974): 770–790.

Lupfer, Capt. Timothy T. "The Dynamics of Doctrine: The Changes in German Tactical Doctrine During the First World War." Leavenworth Papers, no. 4, July 1981.

McNamara, Robert S. "Managing the Department of Defense." *Civil Service Journal* (April-June 1964): 1–5.
———. "The Military Role of Nuclear Weapons: Perceptions and Misperceptions." *Foreign Affairs* 62, no. 1 (October 1983): 59–80.
McNaugher, Thomas L. "Collaborative Development of Main Battle Tanks: Lessons from the U.S.-German Experience, 1963–1978." Santa Monica, Calif.: Rand Corporation, no. N-1680-RC, August 1981.
———. "Problems of Collaborative Weapons Development: The MBT-70." *Armed Forces and Society* 10, no. 1 (Fall 1983): 123–145.
Maddux, John L. "The Development Philosophy of Robert S. McNamara." Washington, D.C.: World Bank, June 1981.
O'Neill, Edward A. "India: Unreal Expectations." *Wilson Quarterly* 2, no. 4 (Autumn 1978): 115–121.
Oppenheimer, Franz. "Don't Bank on the World Bank." *American Spectator*, October 1987.
Posvar, Wesley W. "The Impact of Strategy Expertise on the National Security Policy of the United States." *Public Policy*, 13 (1964): 36–38.
Presidential Recordings Transcripts, Cuban Missile Crisis Meetings, October 16, 1962. John F. Kennedy Presidential Papers, President's Office Files, JFKL.
Rosenberg, David Alan. "The Origins of Overkill: Nuclear Weapons and American Strategy, 1945–1960." *International Security* 7, no. 4 (Spring 1983): 3–71.
———. "Reality and Responsibility: Power and Process in the Making of United States Nuclear Strategy, 1945–1968." *Journal of Strategic Studies* 9, no. 1 (March 1986): 35–52.
Sagan, Scott. "Nuclear Alerts and Crisis Management." *International Security* 9, no. 4 (Spring 1985).
Schelling, Thomas C. "Controlled Response and Strategic Warfare." London: Adelphi Papers, no. 19, Institute for Strategic Studies, June 1965.
Sherwin, C. W. "Securing Peace Through Military Technology." *Bulletin of the Atomic Scientists* 12, no. 5 (May 1956): 159–165.
Sierra Club. "Bankrolling Disasters: International Development Banks and the Global Environment," 1986.
Smith, Steve. "Allison and the Cuban Missile Crisis: A Review of the Bureaucratic Politics Model of Foreign Policy Decision-Making." *Millennium: Journal of International Studies* 9, no. 1 (1981): 21–40.
Sticht, Thomas G., William B. Armstrong, Daniel T. Hickey, and John S. Caylor. "Cast-Off Youth: Policy and Training." San Diego: Applied Behavioral and Cognitive Sciences, February 1986.
Tannen, Melanie S. "International Bank for Ruination and Destruction." *Conservative Digest* (March-April 1989): 45–52.
Trachtenberg, Marc. "White House Tapes and Minutes of the Cuban Missile Crisis." *International Security* 10, no. 1 (Summer 1985): 164–203.
Wohlstetter, Albert. "The Delicate Balance of Terror." *Foreign Affairs* 39, no. 3 (April 1961).
———. "Is There a Strategic Arms Race?" *Foreign Policy*, no. 15 (Summer 1974).
———. "Optimal Ways to Confuse Ourselves." *Foreign Policy*, no. 20 (Fall 1975).
———. "Rivals But No Race." *Foreign Policy*, no. 16 (Fall 1974).
Wohlstetter, Albert, and Roberta Wohlstetter. "Controlling the Risks in Cuba." London: Adelphi Papers, no. 17, Institute for Strategic Studies, April 1965.

World Bank. "Annual Report on Operations Evaluation, 1986." Washington, D.C.: October 10, 1986.

———. "Dynamics of Rural Development in Northeast Brazil: New Lessons from Old Projects." Washington, D.C.: Report no. 10183 of the Operations Evaluation Department, December 16, 1991.

———. "Sub-Saharan Africa: Progress Report on Development Prospects and Programs." Washington, D.C.: 1983.

———. "Rural Development, World Bank Experience, 1965–86." Washington, D.C.: Operations Evaluation Department Report, April 1988.

Walton, Lt. Col. F. H. "How to Get Facts and Influence People." *Military Review* (December 1944): 53–55.

York, Herbert, and Jerome B. Wiesner. "National Security and the Nuclear Test Ban." *Scientific American,* October 1964.

Zuckert, Eugene. "The Service Secretary: Has He a Useful Role?" *Foreign Affairs* 44, no. 3 (April 1966): 458–479.

Index

A-7 close-air-support craft, 205, 228
ABC (network), 474, 595
Abel, Elie, 173, 178
ABMs (antiballistic missiles), 196–200
    Kent's analysis of, 196–198
    RSM's opposition to deployment of,
        192–193, 199, 200, 389–397, 610,
        613
    RSM's San Francisco speech on, 200,
        394–395, 396, 429, 512
Absolute Weapon (Brodie), 192
Acheson, Dean, 127, 157, 297, 331
    Cuban missile crisis and, 171, 173
    on Johnson's public humiliation of
        RSM, 278
    nuclear strategy and, 117, 118, 141–142
Ackley, Gardner, 369–370, 371, 372
Adelman, Kenneth, 124, 588
Adenauer, Konrad, 398, 399
Adler, John, 479
Adler, Renata, 601
Adlerman, Jerome S., 210, 212, 217
Advertising Council, 159
Afghanistan, 561
Africa, 468, 527. *See also specific countries*
    backfiring of foreign aid to, 547–548
    Communist threat and, 88, 298, 351
    river blindness, 523–524
    ruinous economic policies, 545–546
    sub-Saharan, 547–548, 549, 565, 579
    World Bank and, 469, 478, 481, 510,

511, 514, 519, 522, 528, 531–532,
    534–535, 547–548, 550, 564
Agency for International Development,
    U.S. (AID), 381–382, 536
Agent Orange syndrome, 590
Ailes, Stephen, 325
Air Cavalry, 229
Air Force, U.S., 46, 89, 90, 102, 181,
    188, 196, 231, 273, 287, 386. *See also*
    Strategic Air Command
    B-70 bomber and, 106–107, 109, 188,
        193, 211, 242, 286
    common fighter-bomber for Navy and.
        See TFX
    interservice rivalries and, 106, 229
    Minuteman force and, 106, 109
    Rand studies sponsored by, 99, 100,
        101, 140, 228
    Skybolt program and, 241–243
    strains in RSM's relations with, 106–
        107, 228, 241–243
    Vietnam and, 251, 357, 407, 444
Air Force intelligence, 108, 109
Air Force One, 273–275
Alaotra, Lake, 534, 548
Allen, George W., 159–161, 250, 422
Allende, Salvador, 483–484, 496, 497, 503
Alsop, Joseph, 91, 313, 591
Alsop, Stewart, 121, 187, 189, 191, 199–
    200, 591
Alsop, Susan Mary, 91, 581, 591

Alsop, Trisha, 591
Amazon, area development projects in,
    552, 576–578
American Century, xvii, 472, 473, 547,
    570, 606
American Civil Liberties Union (ACLU),
    82
American Economic Club, 123
American Society of Newspaper Editors,
    381–384
American University, 244
Amherst College, 378
Anderson, Charles, 28
Anderson, George W., 182–183, 207,
    211, 264
    Cuban missile crisis and, 176–178, 239,
        240, 608
Anderson, Rudolph, 180
Ansara, Michael, 377
Anthis, Rollen "Buck," 251
Anthony, Robert N., 368, 371
anticolonialism, 155–156
antiwar movement, vii, ix, 12, 336, 378,
    444, 487, 556, 603
    at Columbia, 507
    draft card burning and, 353
    at Harvard, 377
    Kent State shootings and, 484–485
    Morrison's self-immolation and, 353–355
    and personal attacks on RSM, 463,
        513, 581
    RSM's children and, xiii, 379–381, 408,
        483, 485
    RSM's disdain for disorderliness of,
        435–436
Ap Bac, battle of (1963), 247–250, 251,
    252, 255
Ap Bac Emulation Drive, 293
Apollo program, 283
area development projects, 537, 550
    in Brazil, 552, 576–578
Argentina, 478
Arlington National Cemetery, 95, 276,
    473
Armed Forces Management, 103, 236
Armed Forces Qualification Test
    (AFQT), 384–386
arms control, 81, 128, 192–193, 312, 389,
    392, 409, 608
    nuclear test-ban treaty and, 88, 243–
        246, 264, 269
    SALT and, 193, 389, 392, 395, 561

Arms Control and Disarmament Agency
    (ACDA), 392
arms race, 199, 378, 397, 584. See also
    nuclear weapons and strategy
    continued despite nuclear test-ban
        treaty, 245, 246
    RSM's San Francisco speech on (1967),
        200, 394–395, 396, 429, 512
arms sales, 449
    balance of payments and, 225–226,
        371, 374, 398, 399
    to NATO nations, 226, 398, 399–400,
        529–530
Army, U.S., 89, 90, 100, 102, 108,
    181, 205, 231, 287, 315, 584, 609,
    610
    analysis of requirements, 237
    bureaucratization, 240–241
    expansion, 118, 121
    interservice rivalries and, 229
    low-aptitude recruits, 386, 387
    rifles issued by, 229, 449
    RSM as commissioned officer, 30–37
    Vietnam and, 133, 150, 158, 248, 251,
        252–253, 300, 316, 327, 334–338,
        339, 341, 345, 357, 414, 415
Army Air Forces (AAF), Harvard's sta-
    tistical control system and, 29–37
Army Corps of Engineers, 276
Army of the Republic of Vietnam
    (ARVN), 151, 419
Arnett, Peter, 255
Arnold, H. H., 29, 30, 35, 36
Asia, 298, 351, 468. See also specific coun-
    tries
    agricultural growth, 547
    expansionary nature of communism,
        88, 360–361
    Green Revolution, 520, 522
    World Bank projects, 535–537
asset control, 63
Associated Press (AP), 97, 254, 255, 442,
    447
Association of Southeast Asian Nations
    (ASEAN), 445
Assured Destruction policy, 194–201,
    291, 389, 395, 512, 587
    SAC war plans never revised for, 200–
        201
AT-6 training plane, 113
Atlantic, 493
Atlantic Fleet, 175

Atlas missile, 108
atomic bomb, 99. *See also* nuclear weapons and strategy
Atomic Energy Commission (AEC), 244
Austin, Anthony, 456n
Austin, Cristina Vettore, 80, 87
Aviation Week, 296
Ayres, Robert L., 509
Ayub Khan, 345

B-17 bomber, 36
B-24 bomber, 36
B-29 Superfortress, 33–34, 36
B-52 bomber, 106, 221, 441
  in Vietnam, 340, 350, 357
B-58 bomber, 106
B-70 bomber, 106–107, 109, 188, 193, 211, 242, 286
balance of payments, 472–473
  arms sales and, 225–226, 371, 374, 398, 399
  Vietnam and, 444
Baldwin, Hanson, 232–234, 374
Ball, George, 275
  Cuban missile crisis and, 171, 180, 181, 183
  joint European nuclear force and, 243, 330–331, 401
  "tiger's back" memo (1964), 309–315, 328, 329, 493
  Vietnam and, 257, 309–315, 316, 320, 328–333, 334, 347, 352, 364–365, 370, 493
Baltimore Sun, 424
Banda, Hastings Kamuzu, 551
Bangladesh (formerly East Pakistan), 508, 536–537, 545, 561
Barron's, 525–526
Baskir, Lawrence M., 590
Batista, Fulgencio, 114
Baum, Warren, 521
Bay of Pigs invasion (1961), 114–117, 167, 446
Beacham, Charles, 64
Beaverbrook, Lord, 145
Bell, Bernard, 475, 476, 537, 568
Bell, David, 523
Bellino, Carmine, 217
Benjenk, Munir, 517, 518, 564, 566
Bennett, Harry, 41, 42
Bergsten, C. Fred, 571
Bergstrom, George Edwin, 95

Berkeley. *See* University of California at Berkeley
Berlin, Cuban missile crisis and, 172, 176, 181
Berlin crisis (1961), x, xvi, 116–126, 128, 131, 141, 144, 168, 224, 225, 236, 270, 342, 368, 400, 588, 611
  building of wall in, 120–121
  potential use of nuclear weapons in, 117–126, 188–189
Bernstein, Carl, 581, 607–608
Berry, Sidney, 271
Best and the Brightest, The (Halberstam), 492–494, 495–496, 497, 513
Bien Hoa, attack on (1964), 315–316
Bisplinghoff, Raymond, 220
Black, Eugene R., 464–465
Blackburn, Albert W., 206, 207, 208, 209, 210, 214
Black Panthers, 487
Black Power, 487
Blaxall, John, 478
Blight, James G., 184
Blundering into Disaster (RSM), 611
body counts, 30, 251–252, 337, 350–351, 356, 414, 431, 443, 608
Boeing, TFX contract and, 207–214, 217, 218, 222
Boies, David, 599, 600–601
Bokassa, Jean-Bédel, 501
Booth, Hattie, 15, 26
Borlaug, Norman, 520
Bornum, P. W., 615
Bosworth, Charles, 37, 41
Bowles, Chester, 114, 465
Braden, Joan, xiii, 540, 591–594, 597–598, 614
Braden, Tom, xiii, 591–594
Bradlee, Benjamin, 216, 439
Braithwaite, B. S., 543
Brandon, Henry, 115
Brandt, Willy, 472
Brazil, 478, 509, 514, 516, 519, 550, 573
  clearing of Amazon rain forest, 552, 576–578
  World Bank projects in Nordeste, 533, 542, 548, 549, 552
Breech, Ernest R., 46, 51, 52, 53, 59, 60, 61, 72, 285, 609
  appointment of, 43–44
  Crusoe's rivalry with, 48–49
  eased out by Ford, 58, 71, 77, 78, 80

Edsel and, 54, 58, 77
Ford restructured by, 47, 48, 66, 68
Brehm, William K., 237, 415
Bretton Woods agreements (1944), 467–
   468, 472, 473
Brezhnev, Leonid, 288, 588
Brodie, Bernard, 139, 190, 192, 409
Brower, Brock, 463–464, 466
Brown, F. Donaldson, 22–23, 24, 529,
   608
Brown, Harold, 196, 197, 198, 236, 242
   TFX contract and, 205–206, 207–208,
      210, 214, 219–220, 221
Brown, Sam, 379–380
Browne, Malcolm W., 254, 255
Bruce, David K. E., 433–434
Bucharest, 178
Buddhist revolt (1963), 254–255, 256
Bugas, John, 42
Bundy, McGeorge, 92, 121, 144, 493
   Cuban missile crisis and, 165, 172, 173,
      183
   Kennedy assassination and, 271, 272,
      275
   multilateral force (MLF) proposal and,
      331
   Reagan's nuclear strategy and, 588–589
   RSM's Ann Arbor speech and, 144,
      145–146
   Vietnam and, 305, 309, 310, 313, 314,
      317–321, 323–326, 328, 329, 331,
      333–337, 341, 345, 352, 368, 370,
      602, 614
Bundy, William P., x, 131, 226
   Vietnam and, 132, 292, 298, 308–309,
      315, 327, 365, 421, 493
Bunker, Ellsworth, 423
Burchinal, David, 180
Bureau of the Budget (BOB), 90, 238,
   271–272, 372
Burke, Arleigh, 129
Burki, Javed, 544
Burma, 313, 345
Burmeister, Sven, 482–483
Busby, Horace, 346
Bush, George, 611
Business Week, 104
"Buy American" policies, 225

C-5A cargo plane, 228
Cadillac, 51
Caldwell, Will, 46

Califano, Joseph, 283, 284, 304
   on changes in RSM, 434–435
   on RSM's admiration for Johnson's
      social programs, 280, 282
   RSM's appointment to World Bank
      and, 427, 439, 441
   Vietnam and, 286, 316, 432
Callaghan, James, 572
Cambodia, 157, 159, 313, 345, 349, 571
   in aftermath of Vietnam War, 561, 584
   enemy sanctuaries, 335, 337, 352
   mapping of border, 293, 301
   secret bombing of, 298, 484, 487, 491
   U.S. incursions into, 416, 420, 423,
      425
Cameroon, 535
Camm, Frank, 405
Campbell, Joseph, 218
Camp David, 277, 346, 347
Canada, 381, 507
Cannon, Howard, 428
Car and Truck Division (Ford), 53, 54,
   58
Cargill, Peter, 509, 566
Carmichael, Stokely, vii
Carnesale, Albert, 184
car radios, 63
Carriker, Marie, 9
Carter, Barry (son-in-law), 379, 483
Carter, Jimmy, 526, 554, 556, 560, 561,
   570, 571, 581, 590
Carter, Margaret McNamara (daughter).
   See McNamara, Margaret
Carver, George, 422
Castro, Fidel, 131, 483, 611, 613
   Bay of Pigs invasion and, 114, 115
   Cuban missile crisis and, 167, 172–173,
      182
   U.S.-backed covert actions against,
      167, 172
Catholic World, 88
Cavanaugh, Robert W., 471
CBS, 251, 274–275
   Westmoreland's libel suit against, 251,
      342, 420, 430–431, 443, 598–602,
      608–609, 614
CBS Reports, 264–265
Central African Empire (later Republic),
   501, 571
Central Intelligence Agency (CIA), 108,
   128, 256, 273, 392, 497, 592
   Bay of Pigs invasion and, 114–115

Central Intelligence Agency (*continued*)
  Cuban missile crisis and, 165, 171,
    179–180, 182
  Vietnam and, 157, 260, 291, 294, 299,
    367, 422
Ceylon, 478
chain of command, 90, 175, 273
Champa, 153
Chandler, A. D., 22
Chatham College, 378, 382, 383
Chenery, Hollis, 498, 505, 506, 510, 516,
  517, 546
Cheney, Richard, 201
Chennault, Claire, 34
Chevrolet, 44, 46, 48, 63, 68, 69
Chevrolet Division, 69
Chevrolet Monza, 74
Chiang Kai-shek, 34, 156
Chile
  Craig McNamara in, 483–484, 496–497
  World Bank and, 496
China, imperial, 152–153
China, Nationalist, 154–155, 156, 494.
    See also Taiwan
  Hump operation and, 34–35
  Japanese aggression against, 18–19, 147
  "loss" of, 296–297
China, People's Republic of, 113, 382,
    531, 596
  Ball's "tiger's back" memo and, 311–
    315
  Cultural Revolution in, 352, 445
  first nuclear device detonated by, 288,
    296
  geopolitical objectives of, 157–158,
    297, 318, 345, 442, 476, 561, 602
  Korean War and, 302, 311
  Soviet split with, 288, 296, 311, 445
  U.S. nuclear strategy against, 110, 394,
    486
  Vietnam and, 156, 296–297, 300, 302,
    303, 306, 308, 311–315, 318, 322,
    323, 325, 329, 332, 340, 341, 343,
    345, 347, 349, 351–352, 355, 358–
    359, 365, 366, 382, 409, 412, 418,
    424, 428, 434, 561, 584, 602, 603
  World Bank and, 522, 561–562, 569,
    578
Christian, George, 416, 427, 436, 439
Christoffersen, Leif, 498, 499, 531
Church, Frank, 172, 261
Churchill, Winston, 192

Citation model (Edsel), 55
civil defense, 133–134, 188, 192, 196,
    197–198
  shelters, 118, 120, 134
civil rights, ix, 224, 232, 280–281, 282,
    289, 487
  housing discrimination against black
    servicemen and, 388–389
Clark, William, 477, 495, 498, 500, 501,
    507–508, 516, 518, 519, 521, 525,
    528, 529, 539, 540, 553, 555, 566,
    568–569
  background, 469
  departs World Bank, 555
  on RSM's impersonality, 541
  RSM's relationship with, 469–470, 555
Clausen, A. W., 610
Clay, Lucius, 120
Cleveland, Harlan, 402, 405
Clifford, Clark, 113, 347, 364, 365, 424,
    436, 452, 492
  as RSM's successor, 443–444, 450, 466
Clifton, Ted, 272–273
Cline, Ray, 456*n*
Cling, Marie, 38
Colby, William, 294
cold war, viii, 81, 157–158, 244, 355,
    442. *See also* Berlin crisis; Cuban
    missile crisis; nuclear weapons and
    strategy; Vietnam War
  Bay of Pigs invasion and, 114–117,
    167, 446
  Laotian insurgency and, 113–114, 116,
    117, 131, 157
  willingness to use nuclear weapons in,
    122–125
Cole, Ed, 69
Colombia, 573
  agricultural research institute in, 520–
    521, 522
Columbia University, 507–508
Columbus Dispatch, 358
Commerce Department, U.S., 284
commonality principle, 63, 202, 203, 214,
    218, 222, 232–233, 449–450
Common Market, 145–146
communism, Communists, viii, 71, 81, 88,
    107, 131, 155, 156, 167, 288, 319,
    382, 445, 536, 538. *See also* cold war
  expansionary nature of, 157–158, 345,
    360–361
  in Indonesia, 475, 476

Laotian insurgency and, 113–114, 116, 117, 131, 157
Southeast Asia's vulnerability to, 296–297
in South Vietnam, 131–133
Walker affair and, 128–131
World Bank and, 535, 568, 569, 571
Concept of the Corporation, The (Drucker), 47
Congress, U.S., 89, 90, 97, 103, 130, 199, 224, 226, 238, 244, 269, 271, 283, 321, 370, 383, 407, 417, 451, 479, 562, 578, 591. *See also* House of Representatives, U.S.; Senate, U.S.
defense budget and, 102, 107, 108, 211, 219, 297, 587
domestic legislation and, 232, 281–282, 289, 336, 344, 367–368, 372, 373, 375–376
draft and, 385
IDA appropriations and, 467, 481, 525, 536, 560, 569, 570, 571
Joint Committee on Atomic Energy, 229, 230, 241, 452
legal powers of defense secretary expanded by, 96
multilateral force (MLF) proposal and, 330
RSM's testimony before, 234–235
tax hikes and, 367–368, 371, 372, 373
Vietnam and, 302, 304, 307, 308–309, 324, 344, 345, 346, 347, 348, 374, 375, 420, 442, 585
World Bank and, 469
Connally, John, 208, 211
Conservative party (Great Britain), 241, 242
Constitution, U.S., 130, 442
Consultative Group on International Agricultural Research (CGIAR), 522–523, 524, 529, 607
Continental Bank of Illinois, 90
Continental Division, 53
control (control accounting; management control; statistics-based management), ix-x, 62–64, 584, 608. *See also* systems analysis
applicable to any type of business, 515
applied to Vietnam, 251–252
concentration of power in, 67, 459–460

curtailment of weapons programs and, 233
at Defense Department, 233
development of, 21–24
as end in itself, 236–237
fatal flaws, 65–68
at Ford, 44–49, 56–57, 61–62, 63, 65–68
Johnson's interest in, 283–284
Rand PPB system compared with, 100
revenue control and, 63–64
short-term profits and, 67–68
at World Bank, 527, 529, 606
in World War II, 29–37. *See also* Statistical Control
Conway, Jack, 82
Cooper, Chester, 319, 328, 358
Cooper, John Sherman, 592
Cooper, Lorraine, 592
Copp, Harley, 61
Corddry, Charles, 116
Cornell University Medical College, 69
Corning Glass Corporation, 586
Corsair model (Edsel), 55
Coulton, A. G., 41
Council of Economic Advisers (CEA), 369–370, 371
counterforce–no cities policy, 125, 139–146, 185, 187–193, 196, 197, 199, 200, 323
problems with, 187–189, 190
counterinsurgency war doctrine, 146, 338
Craig, Margaret (wife). *See* McNamara, Margaret Craig
crash of 1929, 13
Cravath, Swaine and Moore, 217
Crawford, Sir John, 509, 522
"Credibility Gap, The" (Hotz), 296
Crown family (Chicago), 211
Crusoe, Lewis D., 52–54, 58, 60, 66, 68, 77, 542, 609
Breech's rivalry with, 48–49
Edsel and, 53–54, 56, 57
in makeover of Ford, 43, 44–45, 47, 48
RSM's conflicts with, 52–53
Cuba, 131, 279, 571
Bay of Pigs invasion and, 114–117, 167, 446
U.S.-backed covert actions in, 167, 172

Cuban missile crisis, x, xvi, 165–189,
    191, 192, 193, 195, 211, 213, 224,
    231, 233, 238, 264, 270, 307, 323,
    342, 395, 466, 587, 588, 608
  domestic U.S. politics and, 167
  Kennedy's televised address on, 174–175
  Khrushchev's Friday night letter in,
    179, 185–186
  military options considered in, 166,
    169–170, 172, 173–174, 181, 184–185
  naval blockade or quarantine in, 170–
    180, 183, 184, 239–240
  Navy operations, 175–178, 239–240
  nuclear test-ban treaty in aftermath of,
    243–246
  participants' recollections of, 183–186,
    611
  press coverage of, 171, 172, 174, 178,
    179, 183
  RSM's thinking during, 169–171
  Soviet capitulation, 181–182
  strategic nuclear balance and, 168–169
  U.S. intelligence, 165–168, 171, 179–
    180
Cudlipp, Charles, 86–87
Cultural Revolution, 352, 445

Dale, Edwin, Jr., 500
Daley, Richard, 211
Damage Limitation policy, 196, 197–198
Da Nang, landing of Marines at (1965),
    327, 329
David, Donald, 33
Davisson, Malcolm, 16
Day After, The, 595
de Bose, Herb, 387
defense budget, 90, 118, 188, 198, 219,
    236, 242, 271, 297, 414
  backlash against RSM and, 451–452
  bureaucratization and, 233
  cost-effectiveness and, 231–232
  defense secretary's powers and, 96, 107
  plan with Soviets for reciprocal lower-
    ing of, 232
  under Reagan, 587
  RSM's overhaul of, xv, 97, 99–102,
    103, 109, 202, 229, 233, 239, 269
  Vietnam and, 344–348, 367–376, 416,
    419, 473
Defense Department, U.S., xiv-xv, 95–
    460, 465, 541, 550, 556, 584. See also
    specific topics

backlash against RSM at, 609–610
bright and dark sides of RSM's rule at,
    227–246
civilian-military split at, 104, 195–196,
    230, 232–233, 237–241, 246, 407,
    413–414, 428, 432–433, 453
commonality principle at, 202, 203,
    214, 218, 222, 232–233
cost-control efforts at, 46, 231–232,
    233
crackdown on press leaks at, 104, 232
delegation of responsibility at, 128,
    235–236
drafting of papers at, 127–128
entrusted to civilian experts, 103–104
failures of, during RSM's last days as
    secretary, 448–452
history of, 89, 90, 96
interservice rivalries and, 103, 229
rivalries among staff at, 195–196
RSM's growing power at, 126–131, 144
RSM's last posture statement at, 444–
    446
RSM's loyalty to his subordinates at,
    234–235, 452
senior officers' speeches edited by,
    129–130
staff recruited by RSM for, 96–97, 99–
    100, 130
strategic planning. See nuclear weapons
    and strategy
Defense Intelligence Agency (DIA), 202,
    250, 273
Defense Research and Engineering, 222
defense secretary
  Clifford's takeover of post, 443–444,
    450
  Pentagon office of, 96
  powers of, 89–90, 96, 104, 107, 219
  RSM's appointment to, 82–89
  RSM's departure as, 437, 438–441, 448,
    458–460
Defense Supply Agency, 202
de Gaulle, Charles, 141, 145–146, 400,
    401
Democratic National Committee, 286–
    287
Democratic party, 59, 82, 224, 269, 409,
    451, 497
  social spending and, 231–232
  Vietnam as disaster for, viii-ix
Denison, Robert, 175

Depression, Great, 3–4, 12, 13, 24, 68,
     281, 448
DePuy, William, 338, 340
DeSoto missions, 305, 309, 319
détente, viii, 244, 269
deterrence, 105–106, 124, 125
     Assured Destruction policy and, 196,
          197, 198–201
     as prime purpose of nuclear weapons,
          198
     second-strike ability and, 192, 194
Deutsch, Monroe, 15, 16, 20–21, 70
Diem, Bui, 343–344
Diem, Ngo Dinh, 133, 247, 251, 252,
     292
     abandonment of, considered by U.S.,
          256, 257, 258–261
     civil strife and, 253–256, 257, 259, 260,
          262
     distortions in RSM's depiction of, 298–
          299
     limited partnership with, 131–132, 146,
          147, 149, 157–161
     officer corps chosen by, 248, 249–250
     overthrow and assassination, 264, 291,
          299, 314
     reforms resisted by, 146, 147, 295
     RSM's first meeting with, 148
     strategic hamlets and, 147–148
Dien Bien Phu, battle of (1954), 156, 441
Dillon, C. Douglas, 173
Dirksen, Everett M., 98
disarmament. See arms control
Dobrynin, Anatoly
     Cuban missile crisis and, 168, 178, 181,
          184
     nuclear arsenals and, 200, 392, 393
Dr. Strangelove, 189–190, 382, 383
dollar, U.S., 472, 473
Dollar Line, 18
Dominican Republic, U.S. intervention in
     (1965), 336, 397
domino theory, 313, 434, 445
Dong, Pham Van, 351
Dong Xoai, attack on (1965), 336
Donham, Wallace, 26, 29
Doolittle, Jimmy, 32–33
Doomsday Machine, 189
Douglas, Kirk, 592
Douglas, Paul, 470
Dow Chemical Company, 435
Doxiadis, Constantinos, 505

draft, 227
     and Carter's pardon of evaders, 590
     draft card burning and, 353
     Johnson's reform of, 384
     low-aptitude recruits and, 384–388, 590
     universal national service proposal and,
          382, 384
Dresden, bombing of, 140
Drucker, Peter, 47
Dulles, John Foster, 140, 157, 296
du Pont, Alfred, 21–22, 23, 24, 36, 51,
     63, 515
du Pont, Coleman, 21–22, 23, 24, 36, 51,
     63, 515
du Pont, Pierre, 21–22, 23, 24, 36, 43,
     51, 63, 515
Durant, Will C., 23, 233
Dyna Soar, 228

Eagle long-range missile, 205
Eaker, Ira C., 31, 33
E Car Division (later Edsel Division),
     53–54, 56. See also Edsel
economic growth, stage theory of, 502
Economics of Defense in the Nuclear Age,
     The (Hitch and McKean), 100
Economist, 506
economy, 224–226, 227, 336
     balance of payments and, 225–226,
          371, 374, 398, 399, 472–473
     damaged by Vietnam War, 367–368,
          369, 374, 375–376, 399, 400, 444,
          471
Eden, Anthony, 469
Edsel, 53–57, 58, 60, 68, 77, 87, 585
     RSM's name linked to, 285–286, 362,
          481
Egypt, 469, 478
E. I. du Pont de Nemours Powder Com-
     pany, 21–24, 529
Eighteenth Air Force, 34
Eighth Air Force, 31, 32
Einstein, Albert, 13
Einstein Peace Prize, 589
Eisenhower, Dwight D., 90, 96, 99, 114,
     157, 241, 271, 273
     Army neglected by, 118, 150
     defense budget under, 231, 232
     honest battle reports demanded by,
          293–294
     Indochina and, 113, 156, 327
     McCarthyism and, 81

Eisenhower, Dwight D. (*continued*)
  nuclear weapons and strategy under,
    81, 88, 102, 105, 106, 108, 109, 118,
    119, 140, 141, 405
  RSM's attacks on defense record of,
    286–287
Eisenhower, Mamie, 271
Eisenstein, Betty, 91–92
elections
  1940, 27
  1960, 81–82, 88–89, 113, 114, 211,
    269, 591
  1962, 167, 172
  1964, 269, 270, 271, 285–288, 290, 321
  1968, 270, 409, 417, 418, 438, 441,
    457, 465, 466–467
  1976, 526
Eliot, T. S., 446, 454, 460, 558
ELITE–Ex Comm group, 171–174, 175,
    178, 179–181, 183–185
Ellis, Charles, 52
Ellsberg, Daniel, 262, 286, 485, 486–488,
    490–491
enclave strategy, 335
Enthoven, Alain, 192, 195–196, 227, 237,
    239, 283, 316
  conventional forces in Europe and,
    230–231
  new weapons systems and, 228, 229–
    230
  nuclear strategy and, 110, 140, 192,
    193–196, 197, 199, 390, 394, 486
  nuclear submarines and, 229–230, 451,
    452
  as sacrificial lamb for RSM's judg-
    ments, 452
  Vietnam and, 413–414, 417–418, 425
environmental concerns, 504
  area development projects and, 552, 577
  population growth and, 612–613
Erhard, Ludwig, 398, 399, 400
Ervin, Sam, 218
Essex, U.S.S., 175
Ethiopia, 545–546, 547
Europa, 547
Evening Standard (London), 145
Everest, Frank, 204, 222, 228
Everest, Mount, 558

F-4 Phantom, 203, 222, 449
F-14 fighter, 221, 609
F-104 Starfighter jet, 398, 399

F-105 fighter, 203
F-111 fighter-bomber. *See* TFX
Fabians, 505, 516, 572
Face the Nation, 137
Fairlee, Henry, 89
fascism, 12, 126
Federal Aviation Authority (FAA), 284
Federal Bureau of Investigation (FBI),
    130, 393–394
  secret files of, 279–280
Felt, Harry, 158, 159–160
financial control. *See* control
Financial Times (London), 437
first-strike policy, 188, 192, 242
  no-first-use plan and, 588–589, 595–
    596
Fisher, Roger, 363
Fitt, Alfred, 276, 385, 443, 473
Flag Plot episode (1962), 176–178, 239,
    240, 608
Flanagan, Dennis, 190
Flax, Alexander, 220
flexible response, 88, 117, 118, 141, 144,
    145, 230–231, 269, 397, 400, 401–406
Food and Agriculture Organization, 562
Forbes, 559
"force ratio" analysis, 338–339, 341, 355,
    357
Ford (car), 44, 48, 49, 51, 60, 69
Ford, Benson, 53
Ford, Cristina, 80, 87
Ford, Edsel, 41, 57
Ford, Gerald R., 374, 524, 554
  Vietnam and, 589
  World Bank and, 525
Ford, Henry, 23, 41, 42, 44, 45, 62, 80,
    226, 509–510
Ford, Henry II, 17, 38, 43, 48, 49, 52,
    54, 57, 58, 59, 64, 69–73, 77, 79, 82,
    271
  Ford Motor Company taken over by,
    41–42
  RSM's Cabinet appointment and, 83,
    86–87
  RSM's obedience to, 78
Ford, William Clay, 53
Ford Cardinal, 71–72, 73–74
Ford Division, 48, 52–53, 60, 63, 68, 71, 72
  RSM's managerial strengths and weak-
    nesses at, 62, 64–66
Ford Fairlane, 54, 62
  stretch version of, 63

Ford Falcon, 60–62, 66, 69, 71, 72, 74, 203
Ford Foundation, 380, 509, 520–521, 522
Ford Motor Company, viii, ix, x, xiv-xv, 24, 39, 40–81, 100, 101, 103, 109, 126, 202, 203, 233, 234, 237, 238, 239, 269, 315, 350, 427, 542, 556, 584, 597, 608
  competition among divisions at, 228–229
  conformist corporate culture, 49–51, 70
  desire for speed and, 68–69
  in disarray at end of war, 44–46
  dividends to public shareholders of, 67, 80
  Edsel debacle, 53–57, 58, 60, 68, 77, 87, 285–286, 362, 481, 585
  fatal flaws in control apparent, 56–57, 65–68
  finance department, 66
  growing demand for quality, 66–67, 68, 71
  Henry II's takeover of, 41–42
  meetings at, 47–48, 65–66
  new language of finance at, 64, 65
  in 1980s, 609
  orientation program for Whiz Kids, 43, 44
  performance of, during Kennedy administration, 224–225
  reorganization, 45–46, 48
  RSM's departure from, 73–74, 77, 82–89, 90–91
  RSM's description of problems facing, 72–73
  RSM's divergence from values of, 50–51, 58–59, 70–71, 82
  RSM's long-term plan for redirection of, 72–73, 80, 87, 88
  RSM made controller of, 48–49
  RSM's relations with dealers at, 64–65, 72
  safety issue and, 69–70
  sales aspect and, 64, 72–73
  secret meetings and plots at, 77, 80
  senior auto men brought in, 43–44, 49
  Thornton team hired by, 38, 40–41, 42
  three-volume history of, 80
  Whiz Kid legend at, 49
Ford Mustang, 60, 74, 87
Ford Thunderbird, 49
Ford World Headquarters (Glass House), 77, 80

Foreign Affairs, 123, 131, 192, 492, 588, 595–596
foreign aid, 381–382, 441, 570. See also International Development Association; World Bank
  Americans' opinions of, 570
  British cuts in, 572–573, 579
  critiques of aid establishment and, 503, 505–509
  GNP growth and trickle-down as basis of, 502, 503, 508, 509, 510–511
  military, 225, 226
  moral foundation for, 547
  Reagan's cuts in, 578–579
Forrestal, James V., 90, 96, 415, 426–427
Forrestal, Michael V., 257, 258
Fortune, 79
Foster, William, 392
Fourteen Points, 154
Fourth World, 516
Fowler, Henry, 371, 372, 373, 437
France, 122, 245, 403
  Indochina and, 154, 155, 156, 252, 253, 311, 312, 315, 339
  nuclear arsenal, 244, 401
  nuclear strategy and, 141, 143, 144, 145–146, 187
  withdrawal, from NATO's military command, 397, 402
Franklin, Bruce, 483
Freedman, Lawrence, 396–397
Fried, Edward J., 571
Friedman, Irving, 471
Fritchey, Polly Wisner, 556, 592
Frost, Robert, 92
Fryklund, Richard, 104, 147, 214–215, 228, 233
Fulbright, J. William, 304, 388, 442, 453–455, 456, 457, 467, 492

Galbraith, John Kenneth, 79, 148, 361, 506
Gandhi, Indira, 531, 535–536, 546
Gandhi, Mohandas K., 535, 549
Gandhi, Sanjay, 546
Gansler, Jacques, 222–223
Gardner, John, 283
Gates, Thomas, 81, 83–84, 85, 91, 98, 99, 287
Gavin, Leon, 102
Gayle, Charles, 208–209, 212

Gelb, Leslie H., 485–486, 488, 490, 491, 494, 495
General Accounting Office (GAO), 96, 218
General Dynamics, 230
  TFX contract and, 207–214, 217–220
General Electric (GE), 207
General Motors (GM), x, 44, 48, 49, 52, 57, 68–69, 79, 233, 529
  control legend and, 23–24, 51–52
  Ford reorganization modeled on, 43, 45–47
  Ford's challenge to, in midprice market, 53–54, 56
General William C. Westmoreland v. CBS Inc., 251, 342, 420, 430–431, 443, 598–602, 608–609, 614
Geneva accords (1954), 156–157, 299
Genghis Khan, 153
Germany, Democratic Republic of (East Germany), 399
  Berlin crisis and, 117, 120, 122
Germany, Federal Republic of (West Germany), 122, 141, 203, 272, 403, 404, 449
  arms sales to, 398, 399–400
  nuclear weapons wanted by, 330, 401
  strains in U.S. relations with, 398–400
  World Bank and, 472
Germany, imperial, 355, 415
Germany, Nazi, 355
  Allied air bombardment of, 36, 140
Ghana, 477, 506
Giap, Vo Nguyen, 155, 156
GI Bill, 589–590
Gilpatric, Roswell L., 85, 115, 145, 245, 288
  Anderson's removal and, 182–183
  Cuban missile crisis and, 165–166, 168, 171, 176–178
  John Kennedy assassination and, 271–272
  TFX contract and, 208, 211–214, 217, 218
  Vietnam and, 132, 158, 258, 262
  Walker affair and, 130
Ginsbergh, Robert, 290, 437
Giscard d'Estaing, Valéry, 530
Glass, Henry, 99, 101, 356, 412
Glassboro summit (1967), 392–393, 394, 610

gold, currencies and, 225, 472, 473
Goldman, Eric, 384
Goldwater, Barry, 102, 285–286, 287, 411, 428
Goodin, Marion, 11
Goodin, Vernon, 3–4, 8, 10, 11–12, 15, 16, 25, 26, 137
Goodwin, Mary Joe, 136, 558, 580
Goodwin, Richard, 361
Goodwin, Willard, 20, 26, 58, 271, 376, 463
  Asia trip of (1937), 18–19, 147, 492, 501
  as Berkeley student, 15, 16–17
  Margy's death and, 580, 581
  RSM's hiking and camping trips with, 376, 558, 562, 580
Gorbachev, Mikhail, 610
Gordon, Michael, 596
Gore, Albert, 116, 456n
Gorham, William, 237–238, 283
Gorman, Paul, 485
Goulding, Philip, 412
Graff, Henry, 133
Graham, Katharine, 439, 497, 593
Graham, Philip, 593
Grant, Ulysses S., 252
Graves, Ruth, 557, 575
Graznyy, 180
Great Britain, 140, 433, 449, 505
  Berlin crisis and, 122, 124
  nuclear arsenal of, 145, 241–243, 245, 401, 402
  nuclear strategy and, 124, 187, 192, 403, 404
  refused entry into Common Market, 145–146
  Skybolt affair and, 241–243
  World Bank and, 468, 554, 571, 572–573, 579
greater-than-expected threat (GET), 395–396
Great Society, ix, 281–283, 314, 336, 367–368, 369, 372, 373, 375–376, 386, 513, 552
Greece, 142, 345
Green Berets (U.S. Special Forces), 158, 316, 336
Greenberg, Irving, 385
Greenbrier Hotel, RSM's speech at (1960), 72–73, 80, 88
Greenfield Village, 510

Green Revolution, xv, 492, 509, 520–
    523, 534
  extended to smallholders, 509–515,
    585, 606–607. *See also* rural develop-
    ment
  in India, 509, 521, 522, 536, 547
  oil prices and, 562
  research institutes and, 520–521, 522
  sub-Saharan agriculture and, 547–548
  World Bank's lead in dissemination of,
    521–523, 524, 529
Grumman Corporation, 208, 222
Guam, 340
Guatemala, coup in (1954), 115
Guhan, S., 541–542
Guinea, 528

Haas, Walter (Wally), 15, 17, 20, 21, 41,
    474
Haig, Alexander, 286, 578
Halaby, Najeeb, 283, 284–285
Halberstam, David, 228, 247, 250, 255,
    259, 360, 492–495, 606
Halperin, Morton, 125, 128, 390, 394,
    466
Hamburg, bombing of, 140
Hannah, John, 521
Harder, Delmar S., 61
Hardy, Porter, 235
Harkins, Paul D., 256–262, 300, 327, 340
  appointed MACV commander, 158
  misleading reports of, 149–150, 160–
    161, 250–251, 255, 256–257, 260,
    262, 293–294, 337
  press relations of, 148, 151, 255
  RSM's first trip to Vietnam and, 146–
    151, 159–160
  self-aggrandizement, 252
  withdrawal schedule, 160–161, 261–
    262, 357
Harper's, 493
Harriman, Averell, 257, 258
Harris, J. Arthur, 14
Hart, Philip, 59
Harvard Business School, 44, 71, 100,
    126, 142, 208, 233, 237, 376, 515,
    527, 608
  control accounting revolution and,
    21–24
  RSM as student at, 17–18, 20–25
  RSM's teaching position at, 26–29, 38,
    45

in war effort, 29–37. *See also* Statistical
    Control
Harvard Institute of Policy Studies, 384
Harvard University, 376–377
Hassel, Kai-Uwe von, 399, 403
Healey, Denis, 402, 553–554, 572
Health, Education, and Welfare Depart-
    ment, U.S. (HEW), 283
helicopters, 229, 248–249, 356
Heller, Walter, 232, 371–372
Helms, Richard, 422
herbicides, 158, 258, 350, 590
Herken, Greg, 405
Herrick, John J., 306, 307, 442, 453, 454
Heyman, Victor, 340
Highway 364, 576–578
Hill, Forrest ("Frosty"), 520, 521, 522
Hill, Frank Ernest, 80
Hilsman, Roger, 120, 257–258, 260, 446–
    447
Hiroshima, atomic bomb dropped on
    (1945), 587
Hitch, Charles J., 103, 193
  in overhaul of defense budget, 99–100,
    101, 202
  Skybolt program and, 242, 243
Hitler, Adolf, 126, 351, 438, 482
Ho Chi Minh, 154–156, 157, 297, 322–
    323, 339, 365, 408, 429, 431, 601
Ho Chi Minh Trail, 300, 301
Hoffman, Fred, 104
Hoffman, Paul, 507
Holbrooke, Richard, 485
Hoopes, Townsend, 383
Hoover, Herbert, 4
Hoover, J. Edgar, 279–280, 393–394
Hoover, Joseph, 370
Hoover Commission, 96
Hopper, David, 510
Horwitz, Solis, 213, 214
Hotz, Robert, 296
House of Representatives, U.S., 525, 571
  Appropriations Committee's Subcom-
    mittee on Defense, 374
  Armed Services Committee, 295, 449,
    451, 452, 458
Howe, Geoffrey, 572–573, 579
Hughes, Thomas L., 434
Huk insurgency, 257
Hump route, 34–35
Hunter, Irene, 556
Husain, S. Shahid, 514, 543

Hussein, Saddam, 611
"Hymn to the President" (Braithwaite), 543

Iacocca, Lee, 60, 64, 71, 73, 74, 80, 87, 586
Ia Drang, battle of (1965), 356, 358, 370
Icarus Project, 222
ICBMs (intercontinental ballistic missiles), 105–106, 108, 140, 195, 395, 451, 561. *See also* Minuteman missile
"hardened" by Soviets, 191–192
IDA. *See* International Development Association
Ignatius, Paul, 350, 475
IMR ball propellant, 449
India, 345, 465, 475, 502, 505, 510, 527
antipoverty loans to, 549
Communist threat in, 345, 535
Green Revolution in, 509, 521, 522, 536, 547
population control in, 546
RSM assigned to Statistical Control in, 33–35
RSM's trip to (1968), 476–477, 528, 531
World Bank and, 467, 469, 476–477, 535–536, 549, 561, 568
Indochina, history of, 152–157. *See also* Vietnam War; *specific countries*
Indonesia, 445, 527
Communist threat in, 313, 318, 475–476
World Bank and, 469, 475–476, 478, 537, 542, 547, 552, 568, 577–578
Industrial Revolution, 502
inflation, 467, 472
Vietnam War and, 368, 369, 371, 374, 375–376, 444
Institute for Defense Analyses, 363
International Bank for Reconstruction and Development. *See* World Bank
International Control Commission, 377
International Development Association (IDA), 478, 479, 517, 545, 561, 569
creation, 469
credits offered by, 528–529, 530, 534, 535–537
funding, 467, 469, 476, 481, 525, 536, 560, 569, 570, 571, 578
International Institute for Environment and Development (IIED), 555

International Monetary Fund (IMF), 467, 496, 500, 503, 507, 559, 562
International Security Affairs (ISA), 127, 128, 225, 230, 390, 418, 466, 488
Iran, 554
revolution in, 560–561, 570
World Bank and, 517–518
Iraq, 611
Irony of Vietnam, The (Gelb), 495
irrigation projects, 549, 569
in sub-Saharan Africa, 547–548
ITT Corporation, 497

Jackson, Barbara Ward, Lady, 505–507, 510, 512, 555–556
Jackson, Henry M., 210, 211, 212, 600
Jackson, Robert, 506
Jakarta, 538
James, William, 407, 607
Japan, 345, 355, 473, 586
agriculture in, 509, 511, 514
China occupied by, 18–19, 147
Indochina occupied by, 155
industry and manufacturing in, 67, 71, 236, 584, 609
World Bank and, 472, 525, 529
in World War II, 34, 36
Jason Division, 363
John Birch Society, 128–129
John F. Kennedy, 94, 474–475
Johnson, Harold K., 334, 337–338, 345, 433
Johnson, Lady Bird, 274, 275, 277, 364
Johnson, Lyndon B., 81, 115, 121, 211, 265, 270, 297, 379, 382, 388, 441, 450, 463, 502, 506, 570
balance of payments and, 472–473
control management attractive to, 283–284
domestic agenda, ix, 278, 280–283, 289, 314, 321, 336, 344, 367–368, 369, 372, 373, 375–376
draft and, 383–384, 387
election of 1964 and, 285–288, 290
election of 1968 and, 417, 438, 441, 465, 466
FBI files and, 279, 280
multilateral force (MLF) proposal and, 330, 331
NATO and, 330, 331, 398, 400
nuclear strategy and, 124, 125, 390, 391–393, 404, 405, 595–596

presidency assumed by, 273–277
Robert Kennedy as rival of, 409–410,
  438
RSM appointed World Bank president
  by, 416–417, 427–428, 437, 439–441,
  465, 481
RSM awarded National Medal of Freedom by, 458
RSM's mental state as concern of, 426,
  427, 436
RSM's relationship with, xi, 17,
  275–281, 283, 284, 285, 328, 345–
  346, 365, 425, 436–437, 439, 458,
  460
strains in West German relations with,
  398–400
Vietnam and, x, 289, 290–294, 297,
  298, 300, 301, 304–309, 313–329,
  331–341, 343–349, 352, 353, 355–
  356, 358–362, 364, 365, 367–373,
  375–376, 398, 400, 406, 409–410,
  412, 416–421, 428, 432, 433, 435,
  436–437, 442, 443, 446, 453, 457,
  465–466, 484, 487, 490, 493–494,
  585, 589–590, 598, 599, 602–605,
  614. See also Vietnam War
Johnson, Stanley, 15, 126
Joint Chiefs of Staff, U.S., 96, 104, 234,
  240, 244, 272, 285, 452
Bay of Pigs invasion and, 114–115,
  116
Berlin crisis and, 119
chain of command and, 90
Cuban missile crisis and, 169, 170, 172,
  175
defense budget and, 99
mass resignation considered by, 432–
  433, 605
nuclear strategy and, 391
nuclear test-ban treaty and, 245, 246
RSM's intolerance of dissent at, 233
RSM's memos on behalf of, 132
Vietnam and, 132, 156, 290, 301–306,
  316, 325–326, 327, 336, 337, 341,
  356, 359, 360, 366–367, 368, 421,
  428, 432–433, 605, 609
Wheeler's chairmanship of, 325–326
Jones, B. K., 587
Jordan, 581
Jupiter missiles, in Turkey, 168, 172,
  178–181
Justice Department, U.S., 217, 488

Kahn, Herman, 189–190
Kaplan, Fred, 121
Karnow, Stanley, 367
Kattenburg, Paul, 258
Katzenbach, Lydia, 280, 580, 582
Katzenbach, Nicholas, 280, 421, 444
Kaufmann, William Weed, 227, 290
nuclear strategy and, 125, 139–140,
  142, 144, 193, 197
Kaunda, Kenneth, 545
Kaysen, Carl, 108, 361, 362–363
Kearns, Doris, 368
Keating, Kenneth, 167
Kelleher, Catherine, 405
Kelly, Crosby, 39–40, 44, 52, 79
Kennan, George F., 588–589
Kennedy, Caroline, 474
Kennedy, Edward M., xi, 384, 458,
  474
Kennedy, Ethel, 458, 506, 591
Kennedy, Jacqueline, xi, 84, 94, 136,
  274–275, 276, 288, 305, 474, 591
Kennedy, Joan, 458, 474
Kennedy, John F., viii, xi, 5, 17, 101,
  102, 127, 137, 140, 227, 234, 237,
  278, 330, 361, 362, 385, 388, 407,
  448, 506, 586, 591, 592
aircraft carrier dedicated to, 94, 474–
  475
arms transfers to Third World and, 226
assassination of, ix, 216, 271–276, 280,
  291, 314, 473–474
Bay of Pigs invasion and, 113–117,
  167, 446
Berlin crisis and, x, 116–118, 120–123,
  126, 131, 188–189
buildup of nuclear arsenal under, 104–
  109, 210, 228, 231–232, 394, 396,
  405, 561
Cuban missile crisis and, x, 165–169,
  171–176, 178–185, 191, 342, 611
Defense Department entrusted to civilian experts by, 103–104
domestic agenda, 231–232, 281–282
economic policy, 224–225
election, 81–82, 88–89, 113, 114, 211,
  269, 591
FBI files on, 279
higher ideals espoused by, ix, 88–89,
  97, 613
inauguration of, 92–94
Johnson's relationship with, 280

Kennedy, John F. (*continued*)
  Laotian insurgency and, 114, 116, 117,
    131, 157
  missile gap and, 81–82, 88, 97, 98, 99,
    104–109, 113, 117
  NATO and, 141, 143–146, 397–398
  nuclear strategy and, 141, 143–146,
    174–175, 188, 191, 195, 196, 405,
    595–596
  nuclear test-ban treaty and, 243–246
  nuclear weapons, willingness to use,
    122–125
  public confidence in, 224
  reelection campaign planned by, 269,
    270
  RSM appointed to Cabinet by, 82–89,
    90–91
  RSM's crying episode and, 216
  RSM esteemed by, 270
  RSM's first meeting with, 84, 87–88
  RSM's reverence for, 263
  Skybolt affair and, 241–243
  TFX contract and, 207, 211, 212, 213,
    218
  at Vienna summit, 113, 116–117
  Vietnam and, 131–133, 146, 147, 157,
    158, 159, 236, 247, 250, 252–264,
    269, 292, 294, 295, 296, 299, 327,
    409
  Walker affair and, 129, 130
Kennedy, John F., Jr., 474
Kennedy, Paul, 398
Kennedy, Robert, 81, 84, 91, 92, 123,
    127, 210, 270, 346, 379, 458, 501,
    506, 591, 593
  assassination of, xi, 473–474, 476, 586
  brother's assassination and, 274, 276
  Cuban missile crisis and, 165, 168, 173,
    176, 181, 182, 184, 466
  election of 1968 and, 441, 466–467
  FBI files on, 279, 280
  on Johnson, 279
  McClellan hearings and, 217
  RSM's Cabinet appointment and, 83,
    85–86
  RSM's commercial for, 466–467
  RSM's World Bank appointment and,
    437, 438–440
  Vietnam and, 299, 380, 409–410, 437,
    438–439, 457, 460
Kent, Glenn, 196–198, 199
Kent State University, 484–485

Kenya, 534, 550
Keynes, John Maynard, 467–468
Khanh, Nguyen, 297, 298, 300, 301, 302,
    324
Khe Sanh, siege at, ix, 441, 451
Khmer, 153
Khmer Rouge, 584
Khomeini, Ayatollah Ruhollah, 560
Khrushchev, Nikita, 81, 107, 114, 125,
    191, 195
  Berlin crisis and, x, 116–117, 118, 120–
    123, 126, 144, 342
  Cuban missile crisis and, x, 166–169,
    171–174, 176, 178–179, 182, 184,
    185–186, 187, 231, 322–323, 342, 395
  ouster, 288
  at Vienna summit, 113, 116–117
  wars of liberation encouraged by, 146
Killed By Air (KBA), 251
King, Benjamin, 471
King, Martin Luther, Jr., 386, 441, 470,
    478, 487
Kissinger, Henry, 428, 431, 485, 487,
    491, 492, 518, 592, 593, 595, 601,
    604–605
Knapp, J. Burke, 566, 569
Kohler, Foy, 127
Komer, Robert, 423, 490
Korea, Democratic People's Republic of
    (North Korea), *Pueblo* seized by, ix,
    441, 524
Korea, Republic of (South Korea), 157,
    533, 547
Korean War, 51, 53, 150, 156, 240, 302,
    310, 311, 312, 315, 337, 341–342,
    369, 436, 444, 445, 487, 494, 590
Korth, Fred, 182, 208, 209, 211, 217, 219
Kosygin, Aleksey, 392–393, 394, 396,
    610
Kraft, Joseph, 107, 448, 450, 453, 459
Kraslow, David, 605
Krock, Arthur, 115, 372
Krulak, Victor, 258
Kuss, Henry, 225, 226
Kuwait, 472, 518, 529, 611
Kuwaiti Fund, 569
Ky, Nguyen Cao, 336, 343–344, 355,
    357

Laird, Melvin, 300
land reform, 504, 512, 546
Lanman, Maurice, 370

Lansdale, Edward, 158, 256
Laos, 157, 300, 313, 345, 362, 413, 571
  air attacks on border of, 298, 316, 328,
    349
  Communist insurgency in, 113–114,
    116, 117, 131, 157
  enemy sanctuaries and supply routes
    in, 301, 316, 328, 349, 363
  expansion of Vietnam War into, 159–
    160
  mapping of border, 293, 301
  U.S. incursions into, 356–357, 416,
    420, 484
Latin America, 468, 478. *See also specific*
  countries
  Communist threat in, 88, 298, 351
  Green Revolution in, 511, 520, 522,
    547
Lawrence, Ernest O., 12
Lawrence Livermore Laboratory, 244
Learned, Edmund P., 25, 29–31, 33–35
Legion of Merit, 34
Lelyveld, Joseph, 543
LeMay, Curtis E., 116, 193, 208, 264,
  285, 286
  Cuban missile crisis and, 182
  in World War II, 35, 36–37
Lemnitzer, Lyman, 96, 99, 145, 147,
  159–160
Lenin, V. I., 154
Leval, Pierre S., 598, 600, 601
Levinson, Lawrence, vii, ix
Levitt, Theodore, 72–73
Lewis, John, 544
Library of Congress, 264
Life, 120, 188, 463–464, 466
Lilongwe project, 534
Lima (Peru), 538
limited nuclear war, 139–146, 231. *See*
  also counterforce–no cities policy
  Kahn's theorizing on, 189–190
Lin, Maya Ying, 590
Lincoln (car), 63
Lincoln Continental, 66–67
Lincoln-Mercury Division, 56, 72
Lin Piao, 318, 351–352, 355, 359
Lippmann, Walter, xvii, 178
Lisagor, Peter, 446–447
"Little Gidding" (Eliot), 446, 454
Litton Industries, 29, 46–47
Lodge, Henry Cabot, Jr., 259, 260, 264,
  291, 306, 352–353

Long, Russell, 295
Longworth, Alice Roosevelt, 458
Loory, Stuart H., 605
Lord, Bette Bao, 593
Lord, Winston, 593
Lorenz, Paul, 70
Los Alamos, 244
Los Angeles Times, 587
Lossberg, Fritz von, 415
Lovett, Robert A., 29, 30, 35, 36, 82–83
Luce, Henry, xvii, 547
Lukas, J. Anthony, 183
Lundy, J. Edward, 42, 44, 66, 72

M-14 rifle, 229
M-16 rifle, 229, 449
MacArthur, Douglas, 177, 311
McCarthy, Eugene, 441, 457
McCarthy, Joseph, 81, 494
McClellan, John L., 210–221, 224, 230,
  449, 450
McCloy, John J., 464–465
McCone, John
  Cuban missile crisis and, 167–168, 179–
    180, 182
  Vietnam and, 291, 292, 293
McConnell, John P., 433
McDonald, David L., 321, 345
Mace, Myles, 28–33
McGhee, George, 399
McGiffert, David, 212
McGrory, Mary, 383
McKean, Roland, 100
McLucas, John, 214
Macmillan, Harold, 144, 145, 241, 242,
  243
McNamara, Anne (aunt), 5
McNamara, Claranell Strange (mother),
  6–10, 11, 12, 16, 25, 26, 38, 86, 137
McNamara, Kathleen (daughter), xiii, 33,
  35, 38, 39, 86, 135–136, 137, 425,
  458, 482, 490, 556, 580–581, 594
  Vietnam and, 378, 379
McNamara, Margaret (Little Margy)
  (later Mrs. Barry Carter) (daughter),
  xiii, 28, 33, 35, 38, 39, 85, 135, 376,
  379, 383, 425, 458, 556, 557, 594, 601
  as civil rights activist, 282
McNamara, Margaret Craig (Margy)
  (wife), xii-xiii, 15, 31, 32, 33, 35, 50–
  51, 59, 68, 91–92, 135, 136, 137, 264,
  271, 277, 354, 409, 416, 427, 447–448,

McNamara, Margaret Craig (*continued*)
    453, 458, 460, 463, 464, 474, 475,
    480, 482, 488, 497, 506, 556, 557,
    591–592, 607, 614
  childbearing, 28, 33, 50
  courtship and wedding, 25–27
  illness and death, xii–xiii, 575–576,
    580–582, 586, 593–594
  literacy program (Reading Is Funda-
    mental), 380, 425, 505, 557–558, 581
  marriage, xv, 40, 379, 380
  National Medal of Freedom awarded
    to, 581
  personal disorganization, 137
  phone taps and, 280, 393–394
  physical appearance, 25, 26
  polio, 37–38, 39–40, 50
  RSM's Cabinet appointment and, 85,
    86, 91
  ulcers, 380, 406, 425–426
  vacations, 40, 558, 580
  World Bank spouses' group run by,
    540, 557
  on World Bank trips, 470, 476, 501,
    523, 528, 531, 557–558
McNamara, Peg (sister). *See* Slaymaker,
    Peg McNamara
McNamara, Robert Craig (Craig) (son),
    50, 135, 136, 137, 277, 425, 458,
    460, 464, 482–484, 509, 582
  RSM's relationship with, xiii, 464, 482,
    497, 556–557, 594–595
  in South America, 483–484, 496–497
  Vietnam and, 376, 380–381, 408, 483,
    485
McNamara, Robert James (father), 5–6,
    7–8, 10, 11, 18, 26, 28, 137
  death, 25
  RSM's relationship with, 16–17
McNamara, Robert Strange. *See also* spe-
    cific topics
  affinity for logic and statistics, 13, 17,
    24, 44, 47, 277–278
  aloofness and emotional coldness, 10,
    11, 25, 539–541
  ambitiousness, 14, 88, 270
  Ann Arbor speech (1962), 144–145,
    168, 199, 231, 400, 402, 404
  appearance of conflict of interest
    avoided by, 90–91
  appointed to Cabinet, 82–89, 90–91
  appointed World Bank president, 416–

    417, 427–428, 437, 438–441, 458,
    465, 481
  approval of authority figures sought
    by, 15–16, 17, 78, 284, 285, 347,
    368, 372, 460
  Athens speech (1962), 142–144, 199,
    400, 401, 402, 404
  attacked on ferry to Martha's Vine-
    yard, 496
  attracted to power, 52, 112–113, 235–
    236, 270–274
  author's interviews with, xiii–xvi, 614
  birth, 6
  bruxism, 59, 427, 434
  certainties sought by, 568
  Chatham speech (1966), 378, 382, 383
  childhood, 6–11
  combativeness, xv–xvi, 21, 234, 235
  as commissioned officer, 30–37
  congressional testimony, 234–235,
    452
  courtship and wedding, 25–27
  crying bouts, 216, 444, 586
  Defense Department farewell ceremony
    for, vii–viii, x, 458
  dishonesty ascribed to, xi, 230, 294–
    295, 359–360, 470, 489, 490, 495
  economic mission, 21, 24
  education, 3–4, 8, 9–18, 20–25, 281
  as embodiment of rational policy-
    making, ix–x, 80, 227, 231, 233–234,
    236–237, 290, 448
  as enigma, x–xii
  ethical and moral preoccupations, 20–
    21, 70, 78, 79, 88
  family background, 4–6
  as father, xiii, 137, 380, 482, 556–557,
    583, 594–595
  finances, viii, 28, 31, 38, 79, 85, 90–91,
    142
  Greenbrier speech (1960), 72–73, 80,
    88
  historians' views on, as source, 597
  homes, 7–8, 28, 50–51, 91, 135, 136–
    137, 460, 463–464, 513, 581
  legacy, 584–585, 606–607, 609
  as lonely crusader, 234–238, 241
  managerial strengths and weaknesses,
    xiv–xv, 31, 33, 64–66, 227, 236–
    238, 457, 539–543, 550, 565–568,
    577–578
  memoir writing refused by, 585

military institutions and culture disdained by, 232–233, 237–241, 246
Millsaps speech (1967), 408, 435, 527, 541, 607
mistakes admitted, 434, 446–447, 459, 605
Montreal speech (1966), 381–384, 465, 469
Nairobi speech (1973), 510–514, 516, 520, 528, 544, 545
National Medal of Freedom awarded to, 458
party affiliation, 59
physical fitness, 8, 12
as potential presidential candidate, 270–271
poverty experienced by, 3–4, 10, 513–514
in precarious mental state, 426–427, 436
preference for any action over no action, 103, 104, 108, 314
as public moralist, 381–389, 394
public service as aspiration, 79
public stiffness, 271, 297
religious practices, 6, 8, 354
San Francisco speech (1967), 200, 394–395, 396, 429, 512
technology as viewed by, 203–204, 205, 222, 520
trust issue and, 607–609
vacations, 40, 50, 137–138, 376, 558, 567, 580
work and home life separated by, 137
McNamara, Timothy (uncle), 5
"McNamara Monarchy, The" (Baldwin), 232–234
McNaughton, John T., 175, 213, 374, 402
death, 426
as student of bargaining and escalation theories, 302–303, 316, 327
Vietnam and, 262, 291, 300, 302–303, 310, 314, 315, 316, 319–322, 327, 332, 333, 363, 365–366, 418, 489, 490
McPherson, Harry, 276, 277, 278, 427, 444
Madagascar, 534, 548
Maddox, 306–307, 441, 453–455, 456n
Magsaysay, Ramon, 257
Mahon, George, 98, 99, 374

Mailer, Norman, 435
Malawi, 534, 550–551
Malaysia, 313, 345, 445, 584
Mali, 523
management control. *See* control
Manila (Philippines), 538
Mankiewicz, Frank, 592
Mao Tse-tung, 156, 296–297, 352
Marcos, Ferdinand, 538
Marcula, 178
Marder, Murray, 351–352
Marines, U.S., 205
  in Vietnam, ix, 309, 316, 327, 329, 339, 363, 413, 441
Marshall, S.L.A., 450
Marshall Plan, 506
Martin, John Bartlow, 270, 279
Massachusetts Institute of Technology (M.I.T.), 559
massive retaliation doctrine, 106, 110–111, 119, 140, 145, 174–175, 322
Mazda, 609
"MBA syndrome," 68
Meet the Press, 446
Mein Kampf (Hitler), 351
Mellon, Bunny, 276
Mellon, Paul, 276
Melville, Herman, 575
Mercury cars, 54, 63
Mercury Division, 53
Meredith, James, 224, 232
Merriam, John, 580
Mesta, Perle, 276
Mexico, 509, 510, 516, 534, 550, 573
  agricultural research institute in, 520–521, 522
Mexico City, 538
Meyer, Eugene, 464–465
Miami Herald, 174, 183
Middle East, 392, 393, 445
military aid, 225, 226
Military Assistance Command, Vietnam (MACV), 425
  Army's institutional goals and, 253
  commanders appointed to, 158, 327
  misleading reports from, 149–150, 160–161, 250–251, 255, 256–257, 259, 260, 262, 293–294, 337, 339, 418
  press relations with, 148, 151, 255
  RSM's trips to, 146–152, 159–160, 259–260, 422–423
  upgrading of, 133, 146

military pay study, 237–238
military personnel. *See also* Defense Department, U.S.; Joint Chiefs of Staff, U.S.; *specific services*
    race discrimination against, 388–389
Miller, Arjay, 42–47, 52, 73
Miller, David, 353
Mills, Ben, 45
Mills, Wilbur D., 372, 375
Millsaps College, RSM's speech at (1967), 408, 435, 527, 541, 607
Minh, Duong Van (Big), 259–260, 264, 293, 297
Minshall, William, 256
Minuteman missile, 106–109, 121, 188, 196, 198, 230
MIRVs (multiple independently targetable reentry vehicles), 390–391, 396, 397, 451
Missileer, 204–205, 207
missile gap, 81–82, 88, 97–99, 104–109, 113, 117, 141, 287, 356, 395, 457, 460
Moby Dick (Melville), 575
Mohammed Reza Pahlavi, 226, 517–518, 560, 563, 570
Monroe, Marilyn, 279
Monroe Doctrine, 167
Montgomery, Ala., civil rights march from Selma to, 282
Moody's, 471
Moore, Blanche, 581
Moorer, Thomas H., 433
Morgenthau, Henry, Jr., 467–468
Morris, Thomas D., 203, 234, 235, 385, 386, 387, 388
Morrison, Norman, 354–355
Morse, Wayne, 299
Mother Jones, 589
Mountbatten, Lord Louis, 41, 124, 505
Moyers, Bill, 329
Moynihan, Daniel Patrick, 385
MRBMs (medium-range ballistic missiles), 141, 145
multilateral force (MLF), 242–243, 330–331, 401
Mustin, Lloyd, 316
MX missile, 556–557

Nader, Ralph, 59, 69, 240
Nam Dinh, bombing of (1966), 411

napalm, 158, 258, 340, 350, 435
Nash, 60
National Academy of Sciences, 285
National Aeronautics and Space Administration (NASA), 219, 220, 221
National Guard, 233, 282, 373, 484
National Journal, 596
National Medal of Freedom, 458, 581
National Military Command Center, 175
National Military Establishment, 89
National Security Act (1947), 89, 90, 100, 208, 219
National Security Council (NSC), 171, 179, 487
    Berlin crisis and, 117–118
    Vietnam and, 299–300, 320, 321
National Security Industrial Association, 298
Nation's Business, 225
NATO. *See* North Atlantic Treaty Organization
Navasky, Victor S., 494, 495
Navy, U.S., 41, 89, 90, 94, 96, 100, 102, 103, 231, 386, 407, 608, 609, 610
    carrier modernization and, 229–230, 241
    common fighter-bomber for Air Force and. *See* TFX
    Cuban missile crisis and, 175–178, 239–240
    nuclear submarine program, 229–230, 241, 451–452, 609
    Polaris missile and, 105–106, 108
    strains in RSM's relationship with, 176–178, 183, 230
NBC, 298
Nehru, Jawaharlal, 531, 535, 549
neoconservatives, 587
Nepal, 478, 558, 580
Netherlands, 532, 569, 571, 573
Neustadt, Richard, 183, 242
Nevins, Allan, 77, 80
New Deal, 12, 281
New Economics, 224
"New Journalism," 493
Newport News, 175
New Standards men, 384–388, 590
Newsweek, 216, 218, 424, 431, 445, 600–601
New Yorker, 601

New York Herald-Tribune, 99, 123
New York Times, 115, 149, 151, 157–158, 159, 184, 241, 247, 256, 290, 294, 320–321, 351, 358, 372, 375, 383, 411–413, 428, 440, 466–467, 477, 487–489, 490, 494, 500, 543, 611
  Pentagon Papers and, 488–489, 491
Nhu, Madame, 253, 254, 255, 256
Nhu, Ngo Dinh, 253, 255, 256, 257, 259, 260, 264
Nigeria, 535
  agricultural research institute in, 520–521, 522
Nike-X ABM system, 196
Nitze, Paul, x, 127, 220, 231
  Berlin crisis and, 119–122, 128
  Cuban missile crisis and, 173, 185
  Vietnam and, 457
Nixon, Richard M., 81–82, 497, 524
  OPEC and, 517, 518
  Vietnam and, 290, 428, 436, 444, 484, 485, 487, 488, 491, 492, 495
Nkrumah, Kwame, 506
no-first-use plan, 588–589, 595–596
Nolting, Frederick, 146, 150, 159–160
nonproliferation talks, 399
Norris, John, 98
Norstad, Lauris S., 121, 141, 143, 145
North Atlantic Treaty Organization (NATO), 236, 292, 357, 378, 397–406, 441, 472, 572
  balance-of-payments issue and, 226, 371
  conventional forces of, 230–231
  costs of U.S. commitment to, 397–398
  multilateral force (MLF) proposal and, 242–243, 330–331, 401
  Nuclear Planning Group of, 402–404, 405, 459, 479, 553, 559, 572, 607
  nuclear strategy and, xv, 117, 123–126, 138, 141–146, 397, 400, 401–406, 459, 460, 588, 596
  proliferation of nuclear weapons in, 141–146, 242–243, 401
  Turkish missiles and, 172, 178–181
  U.S. arms sales to, 226, 398, 399–400, 529–530
  Vietnam War's effects on, 400–401
Norway, 546
Nosavan, Phoumi, 113
Notre Dame University, 480–481
Novick, David, 100, 101

NSAM 109, 122, 126
Nuclear Planning Group (NPG), 402–404, 405, 459, 479, 553, 559, 572, 607
nuclear-powered aircraft carriers, 229–230, 241
nuclear submarines, 229–230, 241, 451–452, 609
  Polaris, 99, 105, 230, 242
nuclear test-ban treaty (1963), 88, 244–246, 264, 269
nuclear weapons and strategy, xv, xvi, 81, 88, 138–146, 150, 187–201, 236, 265, 287, 296, 299, 340, 351, 389–397, 460, 480, 583, 584, 606, 608. *See also* arms control; arms race; *specific weapons*
  ABMs and, 192–193, 196–200, 389–397, 610, 613
  Americans fearful of, 133–134, 188, 189–190
  Assured Destruction policy and, 194–201, 291, 389, 395, 512, 587
  Berlin crisis and, 117–126, 188–189
  China's first detonation of, 288, 296
  computer programs enacting use of, 194–195
  counterforce–no cities policy and, 125, 139–146, 185, 187–193, 196, 197, 199, 200, 323
  Cuban missile crisis and, 165–186
  Damage Limitation and, 196, 197–198
  deterrence and, 105–106, 124, 125, 192, 194, 196, 197, 198–201
  first-strike policy and, 188, 192, 242
  flexible response and, 88, 117, 118, 141, 144, 145, 230–231, 269, 397, 400, 401–406
  Goldwater's supposed readiness to use, 286
  greater-than-expected threat (GET) and, 395–396
  ICBMs and, 105–106, 108, 140, 191–192, 195, 395, 451, 561. *See also* Minuteman missile
  Kahn's theorizing on, 189–190
  Kent's analyses of, 196–198, 200
  Laotian insurgency and, 114
  limited nuclear war and, 139–146, 189–190, 231. *See also* counterforce–no cities policy

nuclear weapons and strategy (*continued*)
  massive retaliation doctrine and, 106,
    110–111, 119, 140, 145, 174–175,
    322
  MIRVs and, 390–391, 396, 397, 451
  missile gap and, 81–82, 88, 97–99, 104–
    109, 113, 117, 141, 287, 356, 395,
    457, 460
  multilateral force (MLF) proposal and,
    242–243, 330–331, 401
  NATO policy on, xv, 117, 123–126,
    138, 141–146, 397, 400, 401–406,
    459, 460, 588, 596
  no-first-use plan and, 588–589, 595–
    596
  overemphasis on, 102–103
  overhaul of budget arrangements for,
    101
  Polaris missile, 105–106, 108, 140, 143,
    168, 169, 178, 195, 230, 242–243,
    330, 395
  proliferation of, in NATO, 141–146,
    242–243, 401
  rapid buildup of, 104–109, 188, 195,
    210, 228, 230, 231–232, 269, 286,
    389, 394, 396, 405–406, 561
  under Reagan, 587–589, 610–611
  RSM's attitudes on, 119–120, 122–126,
    238–239, 397, 405, 595–597
  SAC war plans and (SIOP), 109–111,
    139, 140, 189, 190–191, 194, 200,
    486
  second-strike ability and, 191–192,
    193–194
  signaling and bargaining theories and,
    189, 190, 302, 322–323
  Soviets' drive for parity in, 396–397,
    451, 561
  strategic balance and, 168–169
  testing of, 88, 107, 121, 243–246, 264,
    269
  U.S. willingness to use, 122–123, 124,
    125, 405
  Vietnam and, 300, 305, 312, 315, 329
  yardsticks of sufficiency for, 193–196,
    198, 199
nuclear weapons laboratories, 244, 246
Nyerere, Julius, 531–532, 534, 548–549

O'Donnell, Ken, 272, 273
Office of Economic Opportunity
  (OEO), 281, 284

Office of Management and Budget
  (OMB), 578
Office of Strategic Services (OSS), 155
oil prices, 515–517, 524, 537, 554, 560,
  561, 562, 570, 572, 573, 578
Okamoto, Okie, viii
O'Keeffe, Georgia, 181
Okinawa, U.S. occupation of, 128
onchocerciasis (river blindness), 523–524
173rd Airborne, 327
On Escalation (Kahn), 190
One-Third of a Nation (Moynihan), 385
On Thermonuclear War (Kahn), 189
OPEC. *See* Organization of Petroleum
  Exporting Countries
Operation Barrel Roll, 316, 349
Operation Explosion, 161, 261
Operation Flaming Dart, 320, 321, 328
Operation Mongoose, 167, 172
Operation Plan 34A, 294, 304, 305
Operation Ranch Hand, 350
Operation Rolling Thunder (bombing of
  North Vietnam), 190, 290, 298, 316,
  320–329, 331, 333, 336, 340, 341,
  349, 351, 355, 410, 411, 416, 419,
  420, 421, 425, 438, 444, 457, 460,
  488, 502, 512
  Ball's criticism of, 310–311
  Bundy's trip report and, 321–323
  Flaming Dart and, 320, 321, 328
  gradualism in, 324–326, 411, 428, 429–
    430, 432, 451, 603, 605
  initiation of, 300–309, 315, 316, 320–
    324
  Johnson's approval of, 323–324
  Johnson's curtailment of, 465–466
  pauses in, 356, 363–365, 366, 372, 410,
    412, 421, 428, 432, 436, 491, 603,
    604, 605
  POL targets in, 366–367
  questions about usefulness of, 352–353,
    362, 365, 367, 412–413, 429–430,
    432
  rationale for, 321–323, 362
  Salisbury's Hanoi dispatches on, 411–
    413
  Senate hearings on, 428–432, 600, 605
  success claims in, 326–327
  target selection in, 324–325, 326, 412,
    413, 443
operations research, 99
Oppenheimer, Robert, 12

Order of the Golden Bear, 14, 15, 26
Organization of American States (OAS), 174
Organization of Petroleum Exporting Countries (OPEC), 515–519, 524, 527, 544, 554, 560, 573, 578
special fund established by, 517–518, 563, 569
Ostpolitik, 400
Oswald, Lee Harvey, 274
Overseas Weekly, 129
Oxford-Cambridge Society, 477
Oxford University, 17

Paar, Jack, 226–227
Pacer model (Edsel), 55
pacification, 353, 359, 419, 423–424, 445
strategic hamlet program and, 147–148, 151, 257, 264, 292
Pakistan, 345, 502, 505, 508, 510
Green Revolution in, 509, 547
World Bank and, 469, 477, 547
Pakistan, East (now Bangladesh), 508, 536–537, 545, 561
Pakistan, West, 528, 536
Palmer, Bruce, 603
Panama Canal, 18
Parade, 410
participatory management, 236
Passman, Otto, 381
Pathet Lao, 113
payments balance. *See* balance of payments
Peace Corps, 382
Penkovsky, Oleg, 108
Pentagon (the Building), 95–96. *See also* Defense Department, U.S.
antiwar protests at, vii, 353–355, 435–436
Pentagon Papers, xii, 156, 290–291, 304, 355, 364, 420, 421, 434, 444, 460, 485–491, 493, 494, 497, 498, 499, 513, 598, 599, 600
compilation of, 485–486, 490
leaked by Ellsberg, 487, 488, 490–491
RSM's reaction to publication of, 488, 489–490
Persian Gulf War, 611
Pett, Saul, 447, 448, 458–459, 604
Phi Beta Kappa, 14, 65
Phi Gamma Delta, 12–13
Philippines, 257, 445, 509, 538

agricultural research institute in, 520–521, 522
Phillips, Rufus, 260
PIDER projects, 534, 550
Piedmont High School, 8, 10–11, 12, 26
Plain of Reeds, battle on (1962), 248–249, 250
planning, programming, and budgeting system (PPB), 100
defense budget converted to, 100–102, 103
"Planning and Control" (RSM), 71
Please, Stanley, xi, 514
Pleiku, attack on (1965), 320–321, 328
Polaris missile, 105–106, 108, 140, 143, 168, 169, 178, 195, 230, 242–243, 330, 395
Polaris nuclear submarine, 99, 105, 230, 242
pollution, global, 504
popgun (M-16 rifle), 229, 449
population growth, 465, 480–481, 502–503, 511, 522, 545, 546, 559–560, 574, 612
Porterfield, Dusty, 32
Potter, Clifford, vii
poverty programs, 232, 280, 281, 282–283, 321, 367, 470–471. *See also* Great Society; International Development Association; World Bank
Project 1,000 and, 384–388, 590
Power, Thomas, 109, 110, 178
Pratt and Whitney, 207
President Hoover, 18–19, 147, 501
President's Advisory Committee on the Supersonic Transport, 284–285
President's Council, 470
Price, David, 576–577
Price Waterhouse, 25
Project 34, 205, 206
Project 100,000, 384–388, 590
Pueblo incident (1967), ix, 441, 524
Punjab (India), 509, 527, 536
Purple Heart, 159
Pursley, Robert, 426

Quang Duc, 254
Qui Nhon, attack on (1965), 321
Qureschi, Moeen A., 580

race discrimination. *See also* civil rights
against military personnel, 388–389

Radford, Arthur, 156
radios, in cars, 63
rain forests, damaged by World Bank
    programs, 552, 576–578
Rand Corporation, 99–103, 109, 142
    missile gap and, 104, 105, 106
    new weapons systems and, 228, 229
    nuclear strategy and, 139–141, 189–
        190, 192, 193, 486
    planning, programming, and budgeting
        system of (PPB), 100–102, 103
    Vietnam and, 351–352, 487
Ranger model (Edsel), 55
Rangers, 316
Raskin, Marcus, 121
rationalism, 13, 17
Raymond, Jack, 351
Read, Benjamin, 309
Reading Is Fundamental (RIF), 380, 425,
    505, 557–558
Reagan, Ronald, 578–579
    nuclear weapons and strategy under,
        123, 124, 587–589, 610–611
Reasoner, Harry, 264–265
Red Army, 352
Reith, F. C., 44, 49, 53–54, 56, 57, 58
Republican party, 27, 59, 167, 232, 271,
    283, 451
    RSM's attacks on defense record of,
        286–287
reserves, 118, 609
    call-up of, avoided in Vietnam War,
        337, 338, 340, 341, 344–348, 358,
        368, 369, 419, 425, 433, 443
Reston, James, 241, 350, 383, 439, 487,
    488, 494
Reston, Sarah, 488
revenue control, 63–64
Rhodes scholarships, 17, 18, 196
Rickover, Hyman G., 229–230, 241, 451–
    452, 609
Ridgway, Matthew, 156
rifles, 229, 449
river blindness (onchocerciasis), 523–
    524
Rivers, L. Mendel, 451, 452
Roche, John, 426–427, 439, 603
Rockefeller, Nelson, 592, 593
Rockefeller Foundation, 509, 520–521,
    522
Roethke, Theodore, 582
Rogers, Warren, 99

Rolling Thunder. *See* Operation Rolling
    Thunder
Romney, George, 59
Roosevelt, Eleanor, 129
Roosevelt, Franklin D., 12, 27–28, 29,
    30, 34, 41, 83, 95, 231, 239, 281, 494
Roosevelt, Theodore, 459
Rostow, Walt Whitman, 114, 270, 326
    economic-growth theory of, 502
    Vietnam and, 131–132, 420, 421, 444,
        490, 493, 494
Rotberg, Eugene, 471–472, 500, 518,
    521, 529
Rowen, Henry, 121, 142
Royal Air Force, 140, 241
RS-70 reconnaissance plane, 107, 188,
    242
Rubel, John, 242
Runnalls, David, 507–508, 541
rural development, 509–515, 532–537,
    564, 610
    global economic stagnation and, 518–519
    goals set for, 511, 545
    landless and, 520
    local administration of, 549–550
    projects in, 533–537
    results of, 547–552
    RSM's Nairobi speech (1973), 510–
        514, 516, 520, 528, 544, 545
    use of term, 549
    and World Bank's lead in dissemination
        of Green Revolution, 521–523, 524,
        529
    World Bank staff resistant to, 514–515
Rusk, Dean, 92, 126–127, 273, 277, 286,
    297, 330, 332, 436
    China's nuclear capability and, 288
    Cuban missile crisis and, 165, 169, 173,
        179, 180
    Kennedy's frustration with, 126, 270,
        361
    Laotian insurgency and, 114
    nuclear strategy and, 117, 122, 145,
        245, 392
    personality and demeanor of, 113, 126
    RSM's relationship with, 126, 127
    Vietnam and, 133, 157, 257, 258, 291,
        305, 306, 310, 313, 328, 329, 333–
        334, 336, 352, 353, 355, 364, 370,
        420, 444, 446, 494
Russell, Bertrand, 179
Russell, Richard, 397, 428, 450

Sagan, Carl, 595
Sahel, 523
St. Petersburg Times, 424
Salinger, Pierre, 440, 611
   Cuban missile crisis and, 174, 183, 184, 611
   missile gap and, 98
   Vietnam and, 261, 264
Salisbury, Harrison, 411–413, 432
Saturday Evening Post, 187, 232–234
Saudi Arabia, 518
Scali, John, 97
Schlesinger, Arthur M., Jr., xv, 87–88, 115–116, 243, 276, 279, 361–362, 439–440
Schlesinger, James, 201
Schultze, Charles L., 372, 373
Schweitzer, Robert, 485
Scientific American, 190, 198
Scott, Will, 52, 60–61, 62, 65–66, 78
Scott Paper Company, 83
Scruggs, Jan, 590–591
Seaborg, Glenn T., 245
seat belts, 69
Second Fleet, 175
Secrest, Fred, 52
Secret Service, 273, 346, 473
Securities and Exchange Commission (SEC), 471, 472
Selective Service laws, 353
Sellon, Perry, 481–482
Selma, Ala., civil rights march to Montgomery from, 282
Senate, U.S., 398, 497
   domestic programs and, 321
   Foreign Relations Committee, 453–455, 456, 611
   hearings on bombing of North Vietnam, 428–432, 600, 605
   nuclear test-ban treaty and, 245–246
   RSM's confirmation hearings in, 90–91
   Select Intelligence Committee, 172
   TFX contract and, 202, 210–218, 219, 224, 230, 294, 296, 449, 450
   Tonkin Gulf affair investigated by, 442, 453–455, 456, 457
   Walker affair and, 129–130, 131
separation of powers, 130
Sequoia, 217
Seven Days in May, 233
Seventh Army, 398, 400–401

Seventh Fleet, 321
Shanghai, Japanese bombing of (1937), 18–19, 147
Shaplen, Robert, 343
Sharp, Ulysses Grant, 423
   bombing of North Vietnam and, 308, 309, 413
   Tonkin Gulf incidents and, 306, 307, 454, 456, 457
Shaw, George Bernard, 580
Shearer, Lloyd, 410
Sheehan, Neil, 151–152, 159, 161, 249–250, 299, 386, 424, 438, 451, 487, 488–489
Sherman Antitrust Act, 471
Shriver, Eunice, 475
Shriver, Sargent, 81, 82, 83, 92
Shultz, George, 564
Sidwell Friends, 135–136
Sigma Delta Chi, 183
Sigma II war games, 310
signaling and bargaining theories
   nuclear warfare and, 189, 190, 302, 322–323
   Rolling Thunder and, 190, 322–323, 351, 363
Simon, William E., 517–518, 524, 525, 526, 570
Singapore, 445, 584
Single Integrated Operating Plan (SIOP), 109–111, 139, 140, 189, 486
   never revised for Assured Destruction policy, 200–201
   revision of (SIOP-63), 190–191, 194, 200
Six-Day War (1967), 392
60 Minutes, 578
Skybolt missile, 188, 241–243
Slaymaker, Peg McNamara (sister), 7–12, 17, 26
Sloan, Alfred P., Jr., 23, 24, 36, 43, 49, 63, 67, 68, 233, 235, 515, 608
Smith, Bromley, 179, 180, 184
Smith, Gerard, 588–589
Smith, Hedrick, 294–295
Smith, K. Wayne, 227
Smith, Margaret Chase, 122–123
Snowmass, Colo., RSM's home in, 460, 463–464
Sorensen, Theodore, 92, 246
South Africa, 556, 593, 597
Southeast Asia Report, 414

Soviet Union, 93–94, 131, 158, 224, 226, 232, 238, 312, 318, 340, 355, 382, 444–445, 535, 560, 597
  Berlin crisis and, 116–126, 128, 131
  Chinese split with, 288, 296, 311, 445
  Cuban missile crisis and, 165–186
  Laotian insurgency and, 113
  liberalization in, 264, 265
  nuclear arsenal of, 191–192, 230, 231, 396–397, 451, 561, 583, 584. See also missile gap
  nuclear test-ban treaty with, 88, 243–246, 264, 269
  space program, 71, 81, 90
  U.S. strategic planning against. See nuclear weapons and strategy
  Vietnam and, 156, 308, 322, 323, 341, 345, 397, 409, 418, 430, 561, 603
Space Council, 276
Spangenberg, George, 207
Special Forces, U.S., 158, 316, 336
Speer, Albert, 482
Spock, Benjamin, 81
Sproul, Marion, 16
Sproul, Robert Gordon, 12, 14, 15, 20, 70
Sputnik, 71, 81, 88, 102
SS-9 missile, 396
Stack, John, 204, 205, 212
Staebler, Neil, 82
Stahr, Elvis, 115, 118
Stalin, Joseph, 116, 131, 155
Stanley, Timothy, 406, 559–560
Star Wars, 610
State Department, U.S., xi, 121, 128, 145, 179, 297, 392, 581
  Braden's job at, 591, 592
  Bureau of Intelligence and Research, 108
  Laotian insurgency and, 113–114
  multilateral force (MLF) proposal and, 242–243, 330
  and offering of Polaris missile to Great Britain, 242–243
  Rusk's administration of, 126–127
  Vietnam and, 258, 444, 486, 493, 605
station wagons, 63
Statistical Control, 29–37, 38, 44, 83, 236, 250–251, 302, 550
  assessment of, 35–37
  authority issues in, 31–33, 36–37
  goals, 29–30

statistics-based management. See control
Steckhan, Rainer, 464
Stempler, Jack, 213
Stennis, John, 129, 130, 344, 425, 428–432
STEP, 385
Stern, Ernest, 566, 571
Stevenson, Adlai, 506
stock car racing, 68–69
Stockdale, James, 376
Stockman, David, 578
Stoner, Eugene, 229, 449
Strange, Bess (aunt), 4, 9
Strange, Claranell (mother). See McNamara, Claranell Strange
Strange, Gideon (grandfather), 4, 5, 6
Strange, Mary May (Mayme) (aunt), 7, 10, 26
Strange, Shelby (uncle), 4, 9
Strategic Air Command (SAC), 102, 106, 178, 204, 228, 232
  war plans of (SIOP), 109–111, 139, 140, 189, 190–191, 194, 200–201, 486
Strategic Arms Limitation Treaty (SALT) (1972), 193, 389, 392, 395
  SALT II and, 561
Strategic Bombing Survey, 352
strategic hamlet program, 147–148, 151, 257, 264, 292
Strategy in the Missile Age (Brodie), 190
Strauss, William A., 590
Strong, Maurice, 507
Stroud, Peg, 175, 274
structural adjustment loans, 574–575, 579, 607
Student Affairs Committee (Berkeley), 14
Students for a Democratic Society (SDS), 377, 487
sub-Saharan Africa, 547–548, 549, 565, 579
Sudan, 547
Suez crisis (1956), 241, 469
Suharto, 475–476, 537, 552
Sukarno, 475
Sullivan, Leonard, 221
Sullivan, William, 261, 303
Sully, François, 148
Sun Tzu, 301
supersonic transport (SST), 284–285, 613
Supreme Allied Commander, Europe (SACEUR), 143, 145, 403

Supreme Court, U.S., 488
Sutton, Meredith, 292
Swaminathan, M. S., 522–523
Sweden, 532, 546, 573
Sylvester, Arthur, 97, 104, 412
    Cuban missile crisis and, 174, 183, 213
    and political content of senior officers' speeches, 129
    Saigon trip of, 260
    TFX affair and, 210, 213, 296
Symington, Stuart, 81, 89, 428, 431–432
systems analysis
    of Army requirements, 237
    Johnson's fascination with, 283–284
    of new weapons systems, 228–230
    of U.S. troop deployments in Vietnam, 413–414, 417–418, 425
    of Warsaw Pact vs. NATO conventional forces, 230–231
    at World Bank, 519, 520

Tactical Air Command (Tac Air), 204, 222
Tahane, Timothy, 528
Taiwan, 547, 561, 584
Talbot, David, 589
Tanganyika, 531, 532
Tan Zam railway project, 531
Tanzania, 528, 531–532, 534, 545, 548–549, 553
Tass, 168
taxes, 224
    Vietnam War and, 346, 347, 358, 367, 369, 371–373, 375–376, 406, 590
Taylor, F. W., 13
Taylor, Maxwell, 233, 240, 327, 458
    Cuban missile crisis and, 165, 166, 173, 175, 185
    flexible response and, 88, 118
    Kennedy assassination and, 272, 273, 274, 275
    Vietnam and, 131–132, 158, 257–262, 264, 293, 297, 301, 306, 315, 316, 335–336, 338
Taylor, Mrs. Maxwell, 458
Teilhard de Chardin, Pierre, 82
Teller, Edward, 244
Tet offensive (1968), ix, 442–444, 524
TFX (Tactical Fighter Experimental; now known as F-111), 46, 204–223, 228, 233, 234, 265, 269, 285, 299, 362, 389, 458, 471, 481, 585, 609

choice of contractor for, 202, 207–210, 217–218
commonality principle and, 202, 214, 218, 222, 449, 450
demise, 449–450
ironies, 222
physical problems in building, 219–221
resignations resulting from, 217
RSM's true purpose for, 222–223
Senate hearings on, 210–216, 218, 219, 224, 230, 294, 296, 449, 450
specifications for, 204, 205, 206, 222
Thailand, 113, 313, 316, 345, 349, 445, 516, 584
Thatcher, Margaret, 572, 573
Thieu, Nguyen Van, 343–344
Thinking About the Unthinkable (Kahn), 189
Third Stage war, 339
Third World, 296, 445, 477, 492, 500
    angry at affluent nations, 503–504
    arms transfers to, 226
    cities and slums in, 537–538
    commercial bank loans to, 544, 564–565, 573, 575, 579
    development, 502. See also World Bank
    fear of imminent Communist takeovers, 345
    Fourth World and, 516
    overindebtedness in, 563, 564–565, 573, 575, 579
    population growth in, 465, 480–481, 502–503, 511, 522, 545, 546, 559–560, 574, 612
    power of, ix, 524
    RSM's Montreal speech on, 381–382, 465, 469
    terms of trade for, 544–545, 574
Thomas, Tommy, 56
Thompson, Llewellyn, 171, 173, 328–329, 353
Thorneycroft, Peter, 242, 243
Thornton, Charles Bates (Tex), 49
    at Ford, 38, 40–46
    at Litton, 46–47
    in war effort, 29–33, 35, 36, 37, 236
Thousand Days, A (Schlesinger), 361
303 Committee, 294
throughput concept, 23, 24, 529
Thunderbird, 53, 60, 62
Thurmond, Strom, 129, 430, 431, 600

Time, 148
Tito (Josip Broz), 155, 156
To Huu, 354
To Move a Nation (Hilsman), 446–447
Tonkin Gulf incidents (1964), 286, 304–308, 453–457
    Senate hearings on (1968), 442, 453–455, 456, 467
Tonkin Gulf resolution (1964), 302, 304, 307, 308–309, 442, 455
Toynbee, Arnold, 506
Toyota, 71
Trachtenberg, Marc, 184
Tran Hung Dao, 153
transmigration, 537, 552, 576–578
Treasury, U.S., 225, 370
    World Bank and, 465, 467, 468, 469, 524, 525, 536
Trewhitt, Henry, 218, 409, 432, 481
trickle-down theory, 502, 508, 509
Trinkl, Frank, 194–195, 197
Triune, 15
"Trombones," 103
Truman, Harry S, 112, 155, 156, 157, 177, 297, 311, 314
Trumbull, Robert, 157–158
Trung sisters, 153
Turkey, 345
    Jupiter missiles in, 168, 172, 178–181
Turner Joy, 455*n*
TV Guide, 598
Twentieth Bomber Command, 33–35

U-2 spy planes, 140, 165, 180, 181, 279, 303
ul Haq, Mahbub, 508–509
Uncertain Trumpet (Taylor), 118
Uncounted Enemy, The, 598
United Auto Workers (UAW), 82, 384
United Nations (U.N.), 81, 107, 174, 270, 348, 499, 503, 521, 573, 612
    Conference on the Human Environment (1972), 504
    Conference on Trade and Development (UNCTAD), 503–504, 563
    Development Program (UNDP), 507, 562
United Press International (UPI), 116, 151
"United States–Vietnam Relations, 1945–1967." *See* Pentagon Papers
universal national service, 382, 384

University of Alabama, 70
University of California at Berkeley, 3–4, 11–17, 21, 26, 281, 377, 382, 476
University of Chicago, 564
University of Michigan, RSM's speech at (1962), 144–145, 199, 231, 400, 402, 404
University of Mississippi, 224
University of Witwatersrand, 597
Unsafe at Any Speed (Nader), 59
U.S. News & World Report, 225, 395–396

Valenti, Jack, 277–278, 427–428
Vance, Cyrus, 344, 346, 351, 368, 388, 391, 570
Vann, John Paul, 251
VAX, 205
Venezuela, 516, 518
Versailles conference (1919), 154
Versailles Treaty (1919), 12
Veterans Administration (VA), 590
Veterans of Foreign Wars (VFW), 384–385
Vienna summit (1961), 113, 116–117, 167
Viet Cong (VC), 132, 148, 149, 151, 161, 251, 253, 254, 255, 261, 264, 292–293, 309, 313, 315–316, 321, 322, 327, 339, 341, 348, 350, 352, 357, 358, 362, 419, 420
    at Ap Bac, 247, 248–249
Viet Minh, 155, 156
Vietnam, Democratic Republic of (DRV) (North Vietnam), 132, 157, 262, 263, 288
    air defenses, 325
    China's move away from, 351–352
    covert U.S. actions against, 290, 294
    fuel supplies, 366–367
    Laotian insurgency and, 113
    military inadequacies, 289–290
    mining of sea approaches to, 301, 302, 316, 341
    U.S. bombing of. *See* Operation Rolling Thunder
Vietnam, Republic of (South Vietnam), 113, 114, 131–133, 138, 146–161, 226, 236
    civil strife, 253–256, 257, 259, 260, 262
    corruption, 343
    devastation, 340, 349–350, 357

enemy infiltration, 327, 328, 336, 349, 353, 358, 361, 362–363, 365, 432, 443
geography, 152
history, 152–157, 298–299
leadership changes, 264, 293, 297, 324, 328, 336
pacification, 258, 353, 419, 423–424, 445. *See also* strategic hamlet program
RSM's trips to, 146–162, 259–260, 343–344, 346–347, 357–358, 368, 421, 422–424, 528
strategic importance, 296–299, 310, 313, 314, 445, 475, 602
U.S. advisers, 146, 149, 159, 229, 247, 248, 249, 252, 253, 255, 261, 289, 292–296, 314, 320, 321, 605–606
U.S. limited partnership with, 131–132, 146, 147, 149, 157–161, 247, 252–253
weaponry sent to, 158
Vietnam, Socialist Republic of, 500, 561
World Bank and, 568–569, 570, 571
Vietnam Veterans Memorial, 589–591
Vietnam War, viii, ix, x, xii, xiv, xv, xvi, 35, 55, 118, 177, 200, 237, 240–241, 247–264, 269, 288, 289–377, 382, 389, 391, 395–399, 407–448, 450, 465, 484–496, 498, 499, 500, 506, 507, 509, 524, 527, 542, 561, 578, 584–585, 588, 597, 610
appropriations for, 344–348, 367–376, 416, 419, 473
Army strategy, 337–338, 339, 357, 415
B-52s, 340, 350, 357
Ball's dissent, 309–315, 328–333, 334, 493
body counts, 30, 251–252, 337, 350–351, 356, 414, 431, 443, 608
bombing of Laotian trails, 298, 316, 328, 349
bombing of North. *See* Operation Rolling Thunder
buildup of enemy forces, 353, 355, 357, 358, 361, 370
civilian-military split and, 407, 413–414, 428, 432–433
"crossover point," 417, 419, 420, 423, 600

difficulty of finding enemy, 339–340
election of 1964 and, 286
enclave strategy proposed for, 335
escalation, 311, 329, 331–332, 334–347, 348, 352, 355–363, 366–367, 369–371, 373, 447
"force ratio" analysis, 338–339, 341, 355, 357
gradualism, 324–326, 411, 428, 429–430, 432, 451, 603, 605
growing unpopularity, 418–419
herbicides, 158, 258, 350, 590
high black death rate, 386, 387
high-technology barrier, 362–363, 410, 412, 413, 415, 432
Johnson's decision to widen, 319–320, 323–324
Johnson's domestic agenda and, 344, 367–368, 372, 373, 375–376
Johnson's stealthy approach to, 345–348, 367–376, 487
Joint Chiefs' resignation plan in, 432–433, 605
justification for air war, 321–323
Kennedy camp consulted by RSM on, 361–362
low-aptitude recruits, 386–387, 590
M-16 rifle, 229, 449
McNamara family affected by, 379–381, 581
as "McNamara's war," 299
major-unit action avoided by enemy in, 352, 353
as militarily unwinnable, 323, 342–343, 358–361, 364, 410, 430–431, 490, 574, 599, 600–603, 614
misleading battle reports in, 149, 150, 160–161, 250–251, 255, 256–257, 259, 260, 262, 293–294, 302, 337, 339, 418, 608–609, 610
model counterinsurgency war fought in, 146
napalm, 158, 258, 340, 350, 435
NATO affected by, 400–401
1964 as "lost" year of, 289–290
Nixon's conduct of, 484, 487, 491, 492, 495
official justification for U.S. military intervention in, 299
plan for withdrawal from, by 1965, 253, 261–264, 265, 292–296, 303, 314, 605–606

Vietnam War (*continued*)
  political track in, 322–323, 342–343,
    348, 356, 360, 363–365, 410–411,
    418, 419, 428, 431, 432, 445, 465,
    491, 600–601, 604–605
  possible use of nuclear weapons in,
    300, 305, 312, 315, 329
  press coverage of, 146, 148, 149,
    150–152, 157–158, 159, 247, 249–
    250, 251, 253, 255, 257, 260,
    294–296, 316, 320–321, 350, 358,
    375, 411–413, 424, 444, 487–488,
    493
  protests against. *See* antiwar movement
  public deceived about, 290, 295–296,
    298–299, 347–348, 369, 373–374,
    442, 443, 488, 489, 599, 600–601,
    602
  reluctance of South Vietnamese to
    fight, 248–250, 251, 252
  reserve call-up avoided, 337, 338, 340,
    341, 344–348, 358, 368, 369, 419,
    425, 433, 443
  RSM's Dec. 6, 1965, memo on, 358–
    359
  RSM's decision to go to war in, 289,
    290–318, 319, 320, 602, 614
  RSM's development work as expiation
    for, 481
  RSM's final posture statement on, 445–
    446
  RSM's gloom over, xi–xii, 420–421,
    443–460, 489
  RSM's inner tension during, xi–xii, 59,
    378–379, 380, 406, 408–409, 410,
    415, 434–435, 443–444, 489–490, 604
  RSM's May 19, 1967, memo on, 418–
    420, 421, 423–424, 489, 600
  RSM's Nov. 2, 1967, memo on, 491
  RSM's Nov. 3, 1965, memo on, 355–
    356, 358, 363
  RSM's press briefings on, 320, 408
  RSM's quantitative approach to, 158–
    159, 251–252, 260, 293, 338–339,
    350–351, 431, 434–435
  RSM's rationale for continued fighting
    in, 359–361, 410–411, 415, 445
  RSM's reflections on, 318, 342–343,
    598–606, 608–609, 614
  RSM's refusal to enter public debate
    on, 359–360, 437, 438–441, 491–492,
    494–495, 497, 583, 584, 614

  statistical analyses of troop deploy-
    ments, 413–414, 417–418, 425
  study on, commissioned by RSM, 485–
    491. *See also* Pentagon Papers
  supposed shortages, 374–375, 414
  Tet offensive, ix, 442–444, 524
  Tonkin Gulf incidents and, 286, 304–
    308, 442, 453–457
  U.S. casualties, 358, 359, 360, 410,
    411, 414, 418, 430, 436, 443, 444,
    447, 484, 495, 603
  U.S. economy hurt by, 367–368, 369,
    374, 375–376, 399, 400, 444, 471
  U.S. ground forces committed to, 309,
    310, 311, 314–315, 316, 327, 329,
    331–332, 334–348, 360, 368, 369,
    400
  U.S. public opinion on, 418–419, 603
  veterans, 485, 556, 583, 585, 589–591
  Vietnamization, 436, 484, 487
  Westmoreland-CBS suit and, 251, 342,
    420, 430–431, 443, 598–602, 608–
    609, 614
  Westmoreland's requests for additional
    troops, 327, 334, 336, 352, 357, 358,
    359, 368, 371, 411, 414, 416, 417–
    420, 422–425, 603
  withdrawal with honor as RSM's goal,
    361–362
Viets, 152–154
Vinson, Carl, 102, 107, 295
Volkswagen, 60, 71, 73, 79–80
Volkswagen Beetle, 59, 60

Wakelin, James H., 205, 220
Walker, Edwin A., 128–131
Walker, Ross Graham, 24, 35
Wall Street Journal, 562, 579, 580
Ward, Alfred G., 175, 178, 179, 180
Ward, Barbara, Lady Jackson, 505–507,
    510, 512, 516, 555–556
Warnke, Paul, 466, 485, 488
Warnock, Gayle, 55–56
Warren, Chief Justice and Mrs. Earl, 458
War Resisters League, 487
Warsaw Pact, 460
  conventional forces of, 230–231
wars of national liberation, 107, 146, 351
Washington, D.C., riot in (1968), 470–
    471, 478
Washington Post, 84, 98, 351–352, 424,
    439, 446, 517, 570, 592, 593

Washington Star, 104, 214–215, 228, 233
Watergate, 492
Waud, Neil, 65
Weathermen, 487
Webb, Beatrice and Sidney, 505
Weber, Bruce, 17
Weinberger, Caspar, 587, 610
Weiss, Seymour, 128
West, Mr. (driver), x, 137
West Africa, 528, 535. *See also specific
    countries*
    river blindness in, 523–524
Westlake Junior High, 8, 9
Westmoreland, William C., 413, 431,
    441, 446, 590, 604
    appointed MACV commander, 327
    B-52s requested by, 340
    CBS sued by, 251, 342, 420, 430–431,
        443, 598–602, 608–609, 614
    "force analysis" ratios, 338–339, 355
    military tactics, 339–340, 344, 350,
        356–357
    misleading reports, 443
    RSM's disagreement with assessments
        of, 355, 359–360
    RSM's Saigon meetings with, 422–423
    three-year war predicted by, 341–342
    troops requested by, 327, 334, 336,
        352, 357, 358, 359, 368, 371, 411,
        414, 416, 417–420, 422–425, 603
Wheeler, Earle "Bus," 240, 339, 364,
    412, 420, 423, 600
    chairmanship of, 325–326
    resignation considered by, 432–433,
        605
    Senate testimony of, 304, 430, 453, 455
Wheeler, Joseph C., 536
Whittmore, Annalee, 11, 12, 26
Wicker, Tom, 375
Wiesner, Jerome B., 108, 198
Willkie, Wendell, 27
"Will the Real Robert McNamara Please
    Stand Up?" (Shearer), 410
Willys, 60
Wilson, Woodrow, xvii, 154
Wisner, Frank, 592
Wisner, Graham, 556
Wisner, Polly, 556, 592
Wittveen, Johannes, 507
Wofford, Harris, 82, 84, 92
Wohlstetter, Albert, 192
Wood, D. Joseph, 570–571

Woods, George, 416, 427, 464–465, 469,
    470, 475, 479, 481, 531
World Bank (International Bank for Re-
    construction and Development), xv,
    xvii, 8, 10, 234, 368, 381, 387, 459,
    464–473, 475–483, 485, 489–554,
    555, 556, 559–580, 584, 585, 591,
    608, 609. *See also* International De-
    velopment Association; *specific client
    countries*
    absorptive capacity issue and, 542, 551,
        565
    antipoverty loans, 541–542
    area development projects, 537, 550,
        552, 576–578
    Articles of Agreement, 468, 525
    assessment of RSM's programs at, 551,
        552–553
    backlash against RSM at, 610
    The Best and the Brightest read widely
        at, 495–496
    Board of Governors, 468, 478, 480,
        503, 504–505, 510, 518, 534, 538,
        546–547, 564, 573–575, 579, 586
    bureaucratization, 538–539, 550
    capital-to-loans ratio, 530
    commonality principle applied at, 450
    control system applied at, 527, 529,
        606
    covenants in loan documents, 545–546
    decision making, before RSM, 477
    difficult or brutal regimes as clients,
        545–546, 551
    direct attack on poverty as focus of,
        503, 504–505, 508, 510–515, 519
    dissemination of Green Revolution led
        by, 521–523, 524, 529
    enlargement, 471–472, 478, 480,
        498, 508, 516–519, 525–526, 532–
        533, 538–539, 549, 550, 562–566,
        579
    environmental concerns and, 552, 577
    executive directors (EDs), 468, 479–
        480, 482–483, 521, 522, 525–526
    failed projects, 547–551, 552
    flaws in RSM's management, 539–543,
        550, 565–568, 577–578
    founding, 467–468
    funding, 467, 468, 529–530, 578
    Great Society as precursor of RSM's
        programs at, 281, 282–283
    influences on RSM at, 505–509

World Bank (*continued*)
  insufficient preparations for projects,
    565
  intellectual foundation, sought by
    RSM, 499, 500, 501–515
  internal criticism not tolerated at, 566
  Iranian revolution and, 560–561
  liquid assets traded by, 529
  local administration problems, 549–550
  meetings, 565–566
  mistrust of American power and, 496
  Nairobi speech (1973) and, 510–514,
    516, 520, 528, 544, 545
  new world economy and, 544–545
  oil prices and, 515–517, 560, 561, 562,
    572, 573, 578
  old hands at, 477, 539
  OPEC Special Fund and, 517–518,
    563, 569
  Operations Evaluation Department
    (OED), 551, 552
  persistence of poverty and, 543, 544,
    545, 574
  power acquired by RSM at, 479–480
  present-day projects of, 551–552
  rates of return and, 530, 539, 542
  river blindness and, 523–524
  road projects and, 542, 576–578
  and RSM's refusal to enter public de-
    bate over Vietnam, 492
  RSM appointed president of, 416–417,
    427–428, 437, 438–441, 458, 465,
    481
  RSM's departure from, 576, 581, 583,
    586
  RSM's firsthand experience of poverty
    and, 513–514
  RSM's isolation and aloofness at, 539–
    541, 566
  RSM's legacy at, 606–607
  RSM's missionary zeal at, 499, 500,
    512, 532–533, 573–574
  RSM's overhaul, 477–480, 498
  RSM's quantitative approach at, 478,
    519, 520, 542–543, 567–568
  RSM's staff at, 469–470, 471–472, 477

  RSM's tight financial control at, 542–
    543
  RSM's travels to client countries, 476–
    477, 498, 501, 523, 527–528, 531–
    532, 537, 540, 557–558, 576
  salaries issue, 570–572
  stages-of-growth philosophy and, 502
  striking successes, 547
  structural adjustment loans, 574–575,
    579, 607
  third term sought by RSM at, 553–554
  urban development projects, 537–538
  Vietnam's dealings with, 568–569, 570,
    571
World Development Report, 544
World Health Organization (WHO), 523
World War I, xvii, 415, 467
World War II, 28–37, 99, 103, 126, 140,
    150, 179, 240, 241, 294, 337, 341,
    352, 387, 428, 429, 444, 472, 487,
    502
  Ford Motor Company in, 41, 44
  Harvard's statistical control system in,
    29–37. See also Statistical Control
Wright, James O., 73
WSEG-50, 105, 193
Wyle, Frederick, 124

Yale University, 172
Yarmolinsky, Adam, 59, 82, 129, 130,
    283–284, 383
  Cuban missile crisis and, 175, 180, 181
Yevtushenko, Yevgeny, 264, 265
York, Herbert F., Jr., 109, 198, 205,
    206, 219–220
Young, C. W., 570, 571
Yudelman, Montague, 509, 519, 520
Yugoslavia, 155, 569

Zambia, 545
Zanzibar, 532
Zenger, John Peter, 488
Zuckert, Eugene M., 27, 39, 112
  TFX contract and, 208, 209, 211, 212–
    213, 217–218, 219
Zumwalt, Elmo, 239–240